Unwo[rthy,] Chosen, *and* Forgiven

A Life and Love

That Was Meant to Be

Marshell,
That's love... and
keeping it real!!
Stay Blessed
Mike Gilcreast

Michael Gilcreast

ISBN 978-1-63874-662-1 (paperback)
ISBN 978-1-63874-664-5 (hardcover)
ISBN 978-1-63874-663-8 (digital)

Copyright © 2022 by Michael Gilcreast

All rights reserved. No part of this publication may be reproduced, distributed, or transmitted in any form or by any means, including photocopying, recording, or other electronic or mechanical methods without the prior written permission of the publisher. For permission requests, solicit the publisher via the address below.

Christian Faith Publishing
832 Park Avenue
Meadville, PA 16335
www.christianfaithpublishing.com

Printed in the United States of America

I dedicate this book to my lovely wife, Melody,
the lifesaver by the grace of God, and in
memory of my mother, Emily!

Honorable mention to

—Elect-Lady Lillian Wallace (Holy Truth Church). She was
the first person to encourage me to write a book after I had
preached at their church in DC.
—Pastor Timothy Criss (Faith Kingdom Builders Outreaching
Ministries, South Carolina). He was the second person to
encourage me to write a book at a breakfast after preaching
one of the services while attending the National Apostolic
Fellowship Association Conference in North Carolina.
—Elect-Lady Grace Rogers (House of the Lord of the Apostolic
Faith Church, Maryland). She was the third person to encourage me to write a book after I told the story at the church
conference in Leesburg, Virginia, on how Melody and I met.

Preface

———— ∽ ————

I am writing this much-needed book of my life to hopefully touch and help the lives of many people from all walks of life. To say the least, relationships, marriages, and families are in trouble. I have discovered through my life and ministry that people are hungry for any direction to find real happiness and true love. The ongoing search of love through seminars, romance novels, how-to books, and big screen movies of our pasts have not provided us a solid point of view that will open your eyes to the fulfillment and happiness that God have intended for us. I will invite you to take this journey of my life as you read this book, to find out what you have been missing or can identify with for so long and so many years. If I am right, this book will not only be one of the best but a made for television movie or one better—the big screens. Furthermore, while my story remains true, I have only changed some names, dates, and locations to respect the privacy of others. Nevertheless, I am inspired that your life will be nothing less than changed!

End: My Present Life to the Past

Wow, it is now the summer of 2009, and I can say, "My life has evolved!" I began to think of how many times my life could have ended and on so many occasions by making stupid decisions, having multiple stupid and bad relationships. Maybe I can go as far to say terrible (as in bad) relationships, and yes, my first marriage was at the top of my list. As I look back over my life to realize that for one reason or another, God has given me a stream of second chances, I kept noticing that my life turned out totally different, better than I could have ever imagined. Frankly, I have become someone different. Not only that, I have become or made a difference in the lives of so many people. In so many ways, I have become you, or you can become me. I believe that's why so many people have requested me to write this book when I would preach from city to city and state to state. Noticing that our lives are so similar, and the solutions are from one source, God—whether you will admit it or not.

God has truly blessed me! Every day, it is something different because helping people is what I do, and fulfilling as it is, at times, I just don't know what to expect next. As a government employee trying to sell real estate, real estate meetings, meeting the clients, house-hunting, church services, numerous marriage feedback sessions, church planning, church events, weekly sermons and Bible studies, work and church traveling, school, community service, the numerous phone calls, my family, personal traveling, personal time with my wife, and not to mention my chores around the house, I have a full life. Still, I always say, "I love it!" It is better than death. In order to live, I have to continually push myself and keep my faith.

Currently, for the past five years, I have been retired from the US Air Force stationed at the Pentagon, Washington DC, and in my seventeenth year there. Even though part of my multiple lifestyles have ended, such as, serving our country as military by day (retiring in 2004), still I am a preacher also by day and night, and now I am back in the government as a government contractor. Eventually, I became a government civilian employee. I must continue this working lifestyle, which enables me to keep my life's standards until the hope of full-time ministry is obtainable. Yet while I continued to grow the ministry, a year or so after retiring from the Air Force, I had to embrace another career in the real estate industry as a real estate sales agent. Our church is now in its eighth year, with a steady but unpredictable growth. This is really hard work. The real estate market has become "soft," but with the favor of God, I will remain available to sell real estate whenever possible. In the real estate world in Virginia, I am known as Pastor Mike. The integrity of my position offers my clients the promise of faith and hope in their potential blessed new home. I do love what I do because my careers are so interchangeable. You can only imagine my calendar and many times I am going as long as twenty hours in a day. I am really active in the community—helping families in need. As the chaplain for the American Legion (from Post 181 to now Post 34), I always find ways to give back to the community. During the holiday season, I simultaneously work with the American Legion and our church we provided numerous Thanksgiving and Christmas baskets. Many times as I drive through the roads of Washington DC, Maryland, and Virginia, I begin to think and remember where I once was, yet my life keeps evolving. As the thoughts pass through my mind, I know I am not finished, and there will be more lives I can touch. I keep a positive thought in my mind of hope of new and better beginnings for everyone, myself included.

Anyway, in my busy life, one day during a hot summer day in July 2006, my wife and I were in attendance to a national church. The National Apostolic Fellowship Association (NAFA) held a meeting at the Holiday Inn historic hotel in Leesburg, Virginia. The meetings were just at completion. Everyone had dispersed indoors and outdoors. Somehow as we were leaving, I struck up another conversation with a friend and associates of mine from one of the other churches. We ended up back in the hotel with a group of people from various churches, sitting in the lobby area, as they waited for a bishop from one of the churches to return. There must have been fifteen to twenty people gathered around sitting, standing, and in deep conversations. Church folks really know how to talk—amen to that! One thing led to another, and I heard someone mentioned something about relationships and their experiences. Nevertheless, I interjected my thoughts on relationships and noted that all relationships are not so bad. It is really what you make of it. Definitely, yes! I began to say, "Why, relationships are not so bad" that time, and again we (Melody and I) have told our story often over the years as to how we met. I find that people always seemed to be fascinated or to have a valid interest in our life's story of finding true love, which is always a showstopper, and this case was also holding true of this. All the eyes in the place were fastened upon me with my beautiful wife by my side and commenting as necessary. I began to tell our story on how I found my soul mate. The people were on the edge of their seats and were paralyzed as I looked at their faces of suspense. The words of our life on how we met dropped from my lips. All of a sudden, someone stopped the people as they were entering the room, so that one word would not be missed. I said, "Wow" as a sigh of amazement. I really could not believe my own eyes. Our life our story is so, so romantic, and people wanted to know our love story. We are just too blessed! I now know that people overall wanted what we have—true love! Now I wanted to tell my whole story from the bird's-eye view.

So here it is…

The Beginning of My Present

How can I go from one spectrum of life to the other; one can only imagine. Nevertheless, it's true. It happened for me. My life started back in 1962 when I was born in the lovely state of Ohio (the Buckeye State). Somehow, I really did not have a choice in the matter as to where I would be born or to whom my parents were. With no choice about it, it was my destiny to be born, to face every challenge or achievement reaching my final destination. The same holds true for everyone!

I was definitely a product of where I came from in my environment or culture. So let me tell you how I remember my life's story. My father, Cleo, after serving in the military, was in jail for one reason or another and still found time to own his businesses. Back to the other stuff, I somehow remember the one time that I visited him in jail. I was only a child, and after that, I never felt the need to do it again. I did not appreciate seeing my father in the Akron county jail. My motivation really needed a boost of sorts. My father was one of the few businessmen to open up an electronics repair shop on East Market Street (the corner building is now gone). My father was one of the few black men to accomplish this task, and I did remember visiting a few times when I was a child. He was smart, but from my eyes, he was a not-so-successful business man working in two different career fields, which were automotive and television repair. The thing was, he was very good at it, but he was never around long enough to go anywhere fast or to become the franchise business-owner. Who knows… If he was the normal father, I may have followed in his footsteps. I really enjoyed electronics, and at fewer times than expected, just hanging out with Dad was good too. My father was definitely a ladies' man and a bad man (kind of hoodish) too.

My mother, Emily, would tell us, my brothers and sisters, her memoirs. My mother was relating to us of my father. Like most families back then, they were busy having babies and in record numbers. I was told by my mother, two of my siblings, had died at birth, and I would never know them. Henceforth, I was number five out of ten children. Boy, did we ever manage to find ways to get into trouble. But during the course of my mother and father's life of making babies, my father always seems to have lived what seemed to be a double or triple life. He was never home, and boy, did I miss my father. Sometimes, as my mother would put it, my father would come home with other women and would have arguments of sorts with my mother, and if my mother would intervene or he would come home drunk, they would go at it again. My mother never mentioned calling the police. Actually, things were really different back then. Family lives were private and secretive. In my early years of age, I only remember seeing my father a few times, and one of those times was when he was in jail. Now, moving ahead in during my first year in school, kindergarten, and in kindergarten is where I believe I started the physical aspects of having physically intimate encounters with the opposite sex. I was in kindergarten and remember sitting at the round table with other classmates, girls and boys. I then fastened my eyes upon this cute little light-skinned black girl. We smile at one another, and before I knew it, my hand was up her dress. Wow, we were still smiling at each other. The older I grew, the more mannish I became. I was looking under dresses, from under the table, as girls and women walked up the stairs. I even looked through keyholes to see what I could see. This got old because I was not able to see much of nothing. I moved on to other methods of trying to get to the girls.

Once, I remember seeing my father when my mother gave me an old pacifier at age two or three, and my father tried to take it from me. So I ran to my mother for protection. I really did not know him, like I wished to have known my father time and again. Another time, I remember my father was in the state institution for several years, and at this point, my mother had finally had enough. So she filed for a divorce, and I was about age seven, and I remembered seeing the divorce papers at some point in a drawer or box. That divorce was one of the happiness days of my childhood. I really didn't know my father and forgot how to miss him, yearning for his love. But the older I got, the less I yearned for my father's love but would only know the true love and commitment of my mother. I really felt safe with my mother. I'm not sure what my mother was feeling at that time, but I thought she seemed happy as well, but maybe in a strange way. She missed my father—I think it's normal. Anyway, my mother never showed us (my brothers and sisters) that she missed or hated my father. My mother's mental state from the abuse kept her focus to keep going and moving forward, raising her children, church, and serving God would be the center of hers and our lives. Every time she learned something about God or got a revelation, she shared it with us. Sometimes, just her stories made us fear God. God knows that we needed every bit of it. And some more than others! Even more, my mother was gifted. She truly had gifts from God for as long as I could remember.

In a period of time, there were accounts I remembered of being a firebug. Yes, I was very into fires. I had probably just turned six or seven years old and could have and should have been dead out of stupidity. This is what I did: My mother was washing the clothes and hung them on the clotheslines outside or in the basement. I remembered playing with matches in the basement; we did not have many toys of such to keep our attention or my attention. So I played with matches in the basement, and I held the match to a drying sheet on the basement clothesline, and then I ran upstairs through all of the smoke and hid behind the sofa in the living forgion. It was miraculous; smoke was quickly and was massively rising through the dark wooded floors. I was on the floor and my mother. My mother moved the sofa and picked me up. She was my *hero*! My mother! It is weird to speak on this matter. As I tell the story, even now, I get this weird feeling. But my mother, even now, I know without a doubt, it was through the grace of God that enabled me to know the fear of God, and at some point in my life, this fear of God would eventually save me again from burning up and a burning hell to come! I just did not know it! My mother made sure my other brothers and sister were out of the burning house and safe. I do not know how she really accomplished this panic of a task. She did. God. God must have charged His angels for my safety and our family's safety! Wow!

At this time, I guess our family was on low-income housing and moving from place to place all over Akron, Ohio. I remember in April 1968, when Martin Luther King was assassinated (shot dead), there were, in the black neighborhoods, race riots in Akron, on the west side, and we were living on Thornton Street, across from the Lawson food store (similar to the now 7-Eleven stores). When we were not on the floor keeping our heads down because of the riots, broken glass, fires, violence, etc. Yes, I lived through this…this ordeal! History!

Thereafter, moving forward, and things were getting back to normal or as "normal" could be living in the hood. The money was not growing on trees, so I became a thief and liar without any training. Some would call it hereditary, just like my father. I went into the Lawson's corner store and stole snacks and candy. At the same time, I would even talk to the cashier and steal before her eyes. I was unstoppable, or so I thought, but for years, I was unstoppable and very good at stealing. Getting caught was not something that I could not afford to do nor could my mother. One day, as we live on 315 West Thornton Street, I remember my mother was out, maybe trying to get some items for the house. I did not burn up everything this time, but we had to start over. Somehow or someone called the police, and my family (brothers and sisters) were turned over to the authorities by one of the neighbors, and I remember going to the Akron Children's Home. My brothers and sisters were there for a short time, and I just knew my mother loved us so much. As bad as we all were, she, being a single parent, fought the system and obtained approval for us all to get back together. My brothers and sisters were released from the Akron Children's Home. Wow! I just did not know how she (my mother) had the strength to continue on, day after day, turning into months, and the years too. I know she told us in many of the stories on her struggles as to how the people were against us all. They said she would never make it. They were wrong! My mother was more than tough and had plenty of love for us and the other people in the hood. My mother would help or feed anyone. I mean *anyone*! People teased her, saying, "The lady in the shoe had so many children—which are Cleottis, Robert, Annie, Teresa [Terri], myself [Mikey or Hog Guy because I ate with two plates], Ernest [Ernie], Marsha, David, Kelvin, and Shawn—she did not know what to do." My mother loved us beyond taking persecution and beat the odds to become successful at keeping our family together.

Over the years, people kept talking about us, and she kept struggling to keep us all together! She definitely had a God-fearing love for us in spite of all of our wrongdoing! Well, we somehow lost the house on West Thornton Street. Elder Page was our pastor at that time, and I remember that we did not have a place to live, and we lived with them for a short while. We both had big families, and I did not remember any arguments. Elder Page had his own private trailer and hauled trash for a living. I remember his wife. She was kind of heavy. The daughters, Sharon, Pamela, and I believe the other one was Faye, and one son David. That was nice of them to have had taken us in because we had nowhere to go and live. There was not much to do back doing those times, so we would be creative.

I know that I was young, but I remember doing a bad thing. The older kids played house, and Pamela and I, well, I guess we were the parents or something like that. But back then, we called it "to play house," and I still remember, being on the table with Pamela, playing house. Our reward for playing house and not to tell what we were doing was a pack of Kool-Aid. I had never forgotten that time with Pamela. To say the least, it was not an experience that I remembered or enjoyed, but I do remember the laughter. Moving on, I also remember that they lived on a little dead-end side street (right-hand side) off of West Thornton Street. Stuart and Calhoun Funeral Home was close by and across the street. Then I remember the little grocery store called Roush's Market. We did go to church as well. Even though my memory was vague, there was one incident that I would never forget. It was weird. It was getting late, and the sun was going down, and I remembered that it was very foggy outside on the corner of our street and West Thornton, and I could barely see my way back to the house. But before going back, I remember seeing this big tall creature coming toward me. I was scared out of my mind and got out of there. I had never told anyone, and I don't know why. Somehow, I still remember seeing this creature.

Somehow between moving from 315 West Thornton Street to 10 Manila Place, the unthinkable happened to me. I was about nine years old, smart, poor, and full of life. Yes, again that very life of mine almost left my lifeless body, and I almost died—literally died! My oldest brother Cleottis and I was hanging out with our then pastor (Elder Page) and his son (David), and the pastor hauled and picked up stuff of sorts, even junk/trash. We were over Akron, Ohio, working moving and lifting, loading and unloading. Anyway, on our way to the trash dump, the (I believe it was an) U-Haul trailer attached to the back of the grayish blue color station wagon. The rear window was down, and my brother went from the back of the station wagon to the trailer, and he landed on top the trash/junk. I then, like a younger brother would, followed him. Somehow, as I can still remember, I tripped and slipped under the trailer. I was in the Children's Hospital for approximately three months. I think on my left side I had a few broken ribs (or such), a split in the back of my head on the right side (the scar is still there), and my right ankle was fractured. I was in a bad kind of way, just because the trailer totally ran over my lifeless body. The last thing I remember vaguely was my oldest brother jumping off the trailer to my rescue and carrying me back to the car for safety. The next thing I remembered was waking up in the hospital. I guess I have to learn how to follow my older brother more carefully, yes, indeed. This was my second God moment. This accident happened to me and was etched in my mind forever. I could never forget it. I know that this second event could have been my death before my life really got started! Yet I was to live!

After my release from the hospital, and out of my brothers and sisters, I was still getting most of the attention and mainly from my mother. Over the years, I learned to stay active, mixed with a little shyness, and the attention was very much afforded to me.

One day, my family and neighborhood friend were outside playing kickball, hide-and-seek, and other games of sorts. And after that was over, we hung out on our front porch, talking, laughing, teasing each other, playing the dozens, and dreaming of what-if for our lives to come. I wanted to be a doctor. So I was labeled the "smart one"—more attention! Now, I am healed completely and just having fun. Time is not stopping, but moving on. So I was about ten years old. One of my older sisters and I were on a little mission to see what we can get into. So we ventured out into a neighbor's backyard adjacent to the right side of our house. We knew of the crabapple tree and decided to climb it. My sister went first, and I climbed the tree next. We gathered the apples, and as I was coming down the tree, I felt something sharp on the bottom of my foot. I stepped on a rusted nail attached to a piece of a wood. The pain was crazy. I was just a mere child and what did I see next, blood and a lot of blood. We were only less than a block away from home. Seemed like forever, but we finally reached home, and my sister made me to stand by the side door so I did not drip blood throughout out the house. The longer I stood there, the more I bled, and after a few minutes, seemed like five or six minutes, my mother came to the door, and I was standing over a huge puddle of blood. It clotted like jelly. Then my mother had them wrap a towel around my foot and got a neighbor take us back to the Children's Hospital. I do remember many trips to the hospitals—not forgetting the severe nosebleeds, packed nose, breathing through my mouth and back and forth to the hospital or doctor offices. Anyway, after the stitches, I healed, and life was back to normal.

Now I returned to our new home (it was actually an older home) located on 10 Manila Place, in Akron, Ohio, after doing some time at the Children's Home. We had four bedrooms, I think, and a completed attic (hot in the summer and cold in the winter). There were nine people in our home at first, and two more came later on, Kelvin and Shawn. Never a dull-moment with my family, including the capturing of many mice—one even ran across my foot—and killing the roaches. We had our share of suspense, excitement, fighting with neighbors and family, sharing beds, wetting beds—and yes, we went through some mattresses (it's funny now), and we ate in shifts due to lack of table space. The oldest children ate and then the three little ones, or the three little ones were first and then the older ones. I was number five and was considered one of the older children. Oh, I did have another brother born in the same year, but he was considered one of the little ones. Being the middle child had it benefits. Let put it like this. I was not so fond of spaghetti, but obtained my mother's favor and was then allowed to eat my favorites, such as french fries or bread mixed in with pork and beans. One of the best meals ever or at least I thought so! Plus, my nickname was Hog Guy because when possible, or on cookouts, I would eat my food using two plates.

It was not long after getting settled in our new neighborhood, some people, a young family, moved in next door. I guess the house was vacant for a while. Anyway, I befriended their little precious Drew Barrymore (as in the movie *Firestarter*) lookalike daughter. She was gorgeous and a real looker, and my eyes, as a young boy, could not believe it. Even though interracial relationship was really frowned upon, but we were kids, and I was working on my second girlfriend. A few months passed us by. Dawn's father was kind of mean. That son of a gun was also a policeman or something in the field of security. I was really too young to care or know the difference, but I managed to hook up with his daughter anyway. We were standing up behind our house in the corner. I was so glad no one had seen us. All my mother had to do was to look out the back window, and we were right there. We were kissing and trying to do the nasty. If the truth were to be told, neither of us knew what we were doing, but we kept doing it or something as we stood up. After one or two times of hanging out, I did not see Dawn as much, or I would see her a few times at school, but nothing came of it. Dawn's father kept her away from us. From a child's perspective, like myself, if I were in his shoes, I would have done the same thing. Most definitely, he was on the right track of thinking.

Anyway, I was up to no good and decided to play with fire once again. It was a summer hot day and very dry, so I took the matches, and from behind the bushes, I set his backyard on fire. I never realized that the fire would spread across the grass so quickly. Boy, was that a stupid idea. The fire department came and put the fire out before any real damage could be done to their house. Now, as I am looking back, I was so glad no one was injured, you know. Playing with fire was so amazing, I did not give a real thought to the possible outcome or any outcome. Now, I really thank God no one was hurt. Over time the grass eventually grew back. However, after about a year had passed, Dawn and her family moved away. I never heard from them again. By this time, we had a few bikes around the house, and I remember my sister Annie was going to the store and that she would ride one of our brothers' bike. Anyway, I was younger and wanted to ride too. I wanted to go! So she let me get on the top bar between the seat and the handle bars, with my hands on the inside of the handle bars. We went down our street on Manila to turn right on West South Street onto a right turn on South Main Street. However, we did not get that far! We were headed down the hill on West South Street pretty fast, and a car was behind us. Annie had got scared because of the cars that were behind us, and she moved quickly to the sidewalk, just past Yale Street, one block down from my street. Anyway, the second concrete block was not flat like the other blocks. It was angled up from right to left, and the more left, the higher it got. The bike's front tire that we were on came off at the impact. I came off the bike head first at the left highest end of the concrete block, and the bike or something hard like the sidewalk cut my chin. Now, I had a busted head and chin; blood was everywhere. I remember the blood on the front of my white shirt, but I did not remember how I even made it to the hospital. I was unconscious, but when I had awakened, my faithful mother was in the hospital room with me, again. I had stitches in my chin and in my forehead. I was kinda disoriented too. With all of the visit I made to the hospital, my mother would be there, especially with the nosebleeds I had going on. There were many. Yet more God moments with me. I had always remembered the prayers of my mother for her children.

As the years passed by, my mother, she became a stronger woman, and as dedicated churchgoers, including all of the children, going to church is what we did. And I mean, it seemed like that was all we did. It was now another Sunday, meaning church time and other days as well. Once again, the family was packed in the station wagon (deep green Dodge) like sardines with at least fifteen to eighteen people at a time. This was no television commercial. Sardines in the can would have definitely been more comfortable. It was crowded, and I mean crowded! We were at church most times, twice for Sundays. Like America's baseball, going to church became our favorite pastime and all the time. Now years later, like we used to ride in the station wagon going to church with Elder Page; once again, my family are in a station wagon going to church, in another station wagon is Elder Pope and his family. We attended church together on Sundays, Wednesdays, Fridays, and Saturdays. We were selling dinners, cakes; and having clothing drives for giveaways.

We attended church revivals, shut-ins, and Bible studies. The Bible games were a lot of fun (I actually learned a lot about the Bible that was never forgotten). We went on conventions and traveling between churches. Year after year, we were at church. There were times as my brothers and sisters were preparing to go to church on Sunday mornings, if we could not find our shoes or were half-dressed, we were going to church as we were. Seriously! I really did not know why church was so important. In my early days, or to say those days, parents did not explain many things to us children. It was "Do what I say," "Don't ask questions," and "Respect your elders." Or else, you were smacked or whipped with switches, belts, extension cords, pop bottles, brooms for whatever her hand could picked up. I do recall plenty of the previous types of discipline. I had a taste (to my flesh) of them all. The Bible resembles this note: "Spare the rod or spoil the child." For me, I think it worked, and I believe I am alive today because my mother loved beatdowns and had prayers for me in the only way and the best way she knew how. Too bad being a parent does not come with instructions. From a feeling that I sometimes get, I think I reminded my mother the most, between my brothers, of my father. What a shame because I did and currently do not really know him, my father, the way a son or children should be, but I only know of him. Our relationship is still very shadowy. I will keep searching myself for what I know of love. I still love my father. I really did not know much of my father's family history either. I only met one of my uncles (my father's brothers) in passing on their visits to Akron, Ohio, and that was it for some of my younger days.

My childhood days in school was a little mystic. We all (my brothers and sisters) went to school and did as we were told but not really. The thing that was missing was the direction of why school was important. I guess this was normal because as I got older, I kind of figured it out. Things were going to get better (I did not know how or when), as I would be more in control of my life decisions. Being in school gave me the sense of belongingness, and when our lives finally settled down, getting used to the house we lived in, things were looking okay. Being poor, "okay" would always be okay for me. I remember being in the third grade and having my first so-called real love. We passed notes, this girl and me. It was between us to decide if we were going to become boyfriend and girlfriend, and that test was passed with the block checked "Yes." From then on, I did not mind traveling to school in all the seasons. The summers were hot, and winters were cold and snow passed the knees. We all walked to school and not having the opportunity to be bused. I did not mind. I found my one true love—Denise Young. She was so, so beautiful, and shortly afterward, Denise and her family had to move away. Boy, oh boy, oh boy, did the pain of love strike me in my heart. My heart was truly broken. I felt that adult pain. Love hurts, and (don't laugh) it was worse than my beatings. I had walked home with my head down, and shortly thereafter, I found myself on the living room chair. Then it felt as if my heart stopped. The tears begun to roll down my face, and the next thing I knew, I was crying. Being a little boy and out of concern, my family members asked me what's wrong. I couldn't tell a soul, afraid of being laughed at, but anyway, I kept crying, and for hours, I cried. Denise was gone and now a memory of my very own first love. As life moved on and as I grew older, I still searched for my Denise but to no avail. This encounter would bother me for years to come, and somehow, this memorable experience changed me forever. The thought of her (Denise) would never perish, but I managed to keep pushing by. The thought of what-if would fade!

As the days and years went on and my mother being divorced and single, I guess she was beginning to feel lonely that time. I just knew something in her was missing and feeling the need for companionship in life's moments. In 1968 and 1972, I ended up with two more brothers. For one of my brothers, his father met and knew her (my mother) through church, and he was married. I guess not all

21

church folks are really committed to God. Yes, the difference between a saint and sinner is the sin, including adultery. While I could not stop sin, I could acknowledge sin. We met my other younger brother's siblings, and nothing really came of it. How can families come together when it is built on betrayal? I really watched my younger brother as he tried, they all tried to bond with his other family members, but the wounds, I believe on their part, were deeper. They never really got to know their fathers, but at least they would know of them over time. As for one of my other little brothers, his father died. I vaguely remember him getting shot or something like that after getting in an argument at a bank. This was a very hard experience for my brother, and to add the dreams, nightmares in the depth of winter, and about four times, he broken his hip. I even chased him once, and he bumped the blue car in the next-door neighbor's drive and reinjured that hip. Back to the hospital, my little brother was on his way. I felt very bad! Yet he pressed to live and eventually had his own family. To this day, my little brother is way bigger than I. But still, I know he's my little brother.

I am about ten years old, and to sum things up thus far, my heart has been broken, spent time in the children's home on Arlington Street, messed around with a little girl (sort of), fought in the hood, and my parents divorced. I did figure out that being at a disadvantage in life created the next opportunity. So I became one of the school's bully, taking other children's money, things, books, but mostly money. I did not believe it was so easy to take other kids' money. But Pam Rucker. I do remember her. She still thinks I took her books because I like her and reminds me that I had got in trouble for it. However, I do remember Bobby Burns. He was a little boy that became big, just like my younger brother. By the time we reached the sixth grade and twelve years old, not only did I get or stay in the hallway, taking the paddle (swats) to the rear end (I do recall the one paddle by Mr. Richards) for talking, throwing spitballs, or whatever. This positive reinforcement pushed me to focus and try to do well. Also for the fifth and sixth grades, I stayed on the honor roll and sometimes on the merit roll. I placed once in the science fair for making a clay model of the heart or something like that. It was pretty close. I sure wish I could have stayed focus in my academics, which was very good for me, and I was good at it. I did remember placing in the spelling bee and receiving several certificates for GPA, passing the 3.5 range. Wow!

One way or another, the attractions to the opposite sex just kept getting in the way of my success. At some point in my life, I would have to think rationally on the facts of life, when it pertains to girls and staying on the path to success because I was very book smart in school. It will have to be one or the other, but not both. Another important fact, while attending school, I was selected to serve as a patrol boy. In the sixth grade, I made sergeant (my mother did not get too involved with me because I was basically a good kid). So making sergeant was the main thing for me. This was such a proud accomplishment for myself! On the other hand, just two years later, guess who was the lieutenant. It was Bobby Burns, the boy whom I used to beat up and take his lunch money. This dude was bigger than me. I was so glad he had no hard feelings as he reminded me on how I used to take his money. So I became friends with Bobby, and we stayed cool throughout the year and some years afterward. The captain was this small, thin-built, and short and nerdy type white dude Steve Sergeant, not a brother, but he was cool. And the captain!

Back on Manila place and going home after leaving the corner store, there was this lady Ms. James. This single, elderly black lady always liked to feed the neighborhood children cornbread. This buttermilk, dried, and stale cornbread... In a way, she was being nice, but by this time, I have had enough of that nasty cornbread. My niceness was done, just finished, so I did a no-no. I lifted up my hand and gave her, Ms. James, the offensive middle finger. What was I thinking and what did I do that for? In those days, the neighborhoods were old-fashioned, in the village kind of way (like the old saying goes, it takes a village to raise a family), friendly for the most part. The neighbors that really knew your parents, and in my case one parent, could chastise the children. That would include me. By the time I got into the house, my mother called me into the living room from the kitchen to beat my behind. And after the tears, I have to go back outside a few doors down and apologize to Ms. James. This was a hard thing for me to do. Ms. James, an elderly old lady, was no longer my good neighbor, but I did have respect for her because respect can be forced upon a child, like me, or I knew otherwise that was not a good idea. Anyway, I did not want any more of her cornbread, none for me! I did learn my lesson, but no more cornbread for me, which was a good thing.

Afterward, I also recall going to the corner store, right around the corner from the Lincoln Elementary School, 175 West Crosier Street, in Akron, Ohio, the school that I attended. The excitement and the fearful moment had my unexpected attention. I was only going to pick up some penny and five cent candy. As I approached the store at the corner of Princeton Street and W. South Street, right before the bridge to Russell Avenue, brazen guns were flashing. Policemen, detectives, cars, guns, some dark and some shiny silver-plated guns were everywhere. How much money can one get from a little candy store, as we called it, but it was actually a corner store with all kinds of stuff—cigarettes and alcohol too. The (candy store) robbers thought otherwise. I just hope these robbers learned their lesson. With the time in jail that they could only learn that. The reality of it all, the robbers did, in fact, only robbed themselves of time in life. I knew one of the guys because I had a crush on his little sister from school, but nothing would never come of it. However, I still remember them hazel-like eyes that most of them had. Tawanna Veal, as I will remember, the crush and the beautiful eyes of hers that never went anywhere with me. However, one day at school, still to this day, I do not remember if I was being bullied for something or because of this girl Tawanna, but word had got back to me that after school, I was going to get my butt kicked. In those days, those were the fighting words: *butt kicked*. So after school had ended for the day, I could not wait for the bell. The school bell rung, and normally all of the kids chase after you. It would seem like one versus many. This would not be the case for me. The bell rung, I was at the door, I quickly had exited the school, and I ran. I was moving about what seemed to be 50 mph—not a brother or sister in sight. So the next best thing was to really run! This day, I could have made the world-wide Olympics. I was so fast, really fast. I saw nothing but a blur, and in less than three minutes (probably two minutes, to be exact), I was home, less than the normal eight or nine minutes. Safe and sound! The funny thing was on the next day, I went back to school, and nothing, I mean nothing, happened. Boy, was I so blessed (that's me) or was an angel watching over me. I really cannot explain it, the feelings that I was having. Unbeknownst to me, there must have been an angel watching over me!

As I was getting older, I have always found a way to develop my own pastimes, such as pulling the fire alarms (pull, run, and hide, or hide again in the bushes right by the alarm on W. South Street). By the way, it was good exercise with sweat in a bad way! Then as I hid in the bushes, trees, or whatever could hide me, I would watch the fire department trucks come and go. There was no fire and no rescues; however, I did this for years. Finally, the City of Akron had gotten smart and removed the fire alarm box! How ironic. I used to set fires and graduated to pulling fire alarms. At every chance and anywhere, I would set off fire alarm boxes. Now, looking back, I come to realize that a new thrill would soon come to pass, and just like that, it did. I did have an unfortunate experience with my curiosity running away with me: what would happen if I would jump off the second-story roof from our house. Not only did I let the thought rest within my mind, I actually did it. I went up to the second floor of the house, raised the window, and climbed onto the roof. It was a little slanted, but once I reached the edge of the roof, I decided to hang down. This little guy (me) did it… I jumped off the roof and painfully got up, then shook it off. Now, I know I am not crazy because I know that I would never do this crazy event again, and to consider this a type of science project, I think not! Again, crazy I am not because I did learn from it. I still remember it, and if I had to teach it to others, it was on the not to do list!

Now, boredom I was not, and this is what I did next. Throwing rocks at cars on the highway was short-lived because there was just too many police that stayed the block. It was too dangerous, and I just did not want to be the cause of anyone getting hurt, injured, or even death. Another childhood venture was to throw eggs for the egging of homes. This was fun for a while. Mostly my brothers and sisters and a few friends, we engaged to egg homes or cars and never was caught for this misdemeanor of our neighborhood fun. I guess it was in me to do devilish things. Besides, mostly what I did was to go to church. My body was in church or at the church, but my mind was on girls, sports, or others things… Anyway, throwing eggs was the mischievous thing to do, if you wanted to learn from it. To learn what? Once you have to clean up the eggs from your doors or windows, I got delivered. I did not like cleaning eggs from our home, so we all stop throwing them. Lessons learned!

Again, to get into something foolish or to find something to do other than homework was forced upon me in a strange way. Stuff just happened, or we or I just made it happen. Timing was just everything, good or bad! Oh, I did hang out with a few of the guys in the neighborhood, George Shook. He lived at the first ugly brown house on West South Street and on the right corner side was Manila Place, my home street. He was one crazy dude with massive plaque on his teeth. We overlooked it because he was cool. Normally, he would have definitely been one of the guys to get teased. Sometimes, I hung out with Jeff Tyler and Tyrell McGuire (the karate man). These guys were cool and very athletic, and we played basketball, pickup football, and definitely played the dozens. But overall, they were cool. We also hung out with Jeff two sister's Terri and Tina. The mother Dorothy was cool too, but when their father called for Bodean (Jeff's nickname), that was our cue to leave. We did not mess with that man. He never bothered anyone anyway. He also was cool to be around and talked briefly sometimes with us… Hey, I was never invited or never asked to go inside their home! My family was a little on the bad side. Mr. T was correct because I would have probably stolen something or some money. Jeff's dad was a smart man to keep me out! By the way, I did have much respect for the whole family. The family was solid!

Back at the house, after playing kickball on our one-way street (not really a lot of traffic) with some of my family and friends. Now, kickball was eventually over, and it was time to get something to eat. Weeks earlier, a few of my brothers and sisters stumbled across a garden really close to our house in the neighborhood. With the thought of eating for free, they decided to eat from the neighbor's garden. They came home with the news, and wow—the next thing you know, we were frying some green tomatoes, with yellowish corn mill, salt and pepper, with a touch of hot sauce or more like drenched in hot sauce for some. Growing up poor and not having a lot of funds, I think the price was just right! Those tomatoes were delicious, I still have the thought of that fried tomato taste, timestamped to my mind! I was not sure if they were so delicious because they were stolen, or we just were great cooks. All of my brothers and sisters were taught by my mother to cook and know their way around the kitchen and to clean up the house. This was one thing that was good about the summer and fall season in the neighborhood. We somehow found us some green tomatoes to be cooked and fried—oh, can't forget the hot sauce—at my house. Not only that, nevertheless, life goes on. I even remember doing this too sometime one evening, and Halloween was a something to do kind of fun. I remember this particular year I dressed up as a girl. There was not a lot of costumes to buy. Besides, we could not afford them anyway. However fun it was, I really just could not believe that I would ever do something like this, dressed like a girl of all things! Just more great times to remember!

Summer was passing, and now, I was back in school and going through another girl crush after girl crush. The love notes were flowing. "I like you. Do you like me? Please check the appropriate box and return to me." It is amazing how we really had to get permission to date each other in the earlier years. Now, we do not have that much respect in dating. Back then, carrying books for the girls you liked and the small talks on the phone were the highlights that could last for months. Still at times, I reminisce on the females I wished it could have been. Let's call it, the secrets of my heart. Even though I know I am a bit old-fashioned, but it is who I became based on where I am from. My memories drifted back in my life's path and wish or hope for what could never be. So many females and so little time, I could not have them all. Something happened to my psyche; these females affected me, and that affected my life and life's choices. I was becoming something, someone. It was happening so fast. I was changing so fast. Something was developing in me. It was life's nature. This is so surreal, but not. I was evolving in the girl arena, and I wanted it (young male hormones) to happen to me. To be honest, I was allowing the fantasy to keep happening. The older I got, the more the fantasy became the reality. Life at times guides you through life, without instructions or books and other folk's memoirs. I had learned the hard way that what works for some will not work for the whole, as in me.

As my life continued, getting older and hanging out at home or on the porch as a teenager, just chilling on Manila place in the great Akron, Ohio, the smell of burnt rubber (in the rubber capital) on most nights and the most horrible smell of rubber on the hotter nights. Again, I had great hopes of leaving Akron, Ohio, when I was older. Akron could just keep what it was mainly known for, the huge rubber factories and the Soap Box Derby. I wanted to get out of there, and for me to work in the factories was not an option. The massive and numerous layoffs was not for me. I needed a way out. Sometimes to pass time, I just fixated my attention on this half-breed little boy (half black and half white). Not sure if it was the boredom, adolescence, or just plain hate. I did not like this little boy. It's strange! I was not brought up to be prejudiced. My mother would, as poor as we were, would provide food for everyone in the neighborhood, black and white. We were not used to seeing, Hispanic, Asians, and out of towners, you know, foreigners. In my early teens was the first time some Mexicans moved to the neighborhood. We all were so amazed to see them, touch them, and hear them talk. I thought this is why I hated this half-breed boy and wanted to kill him. Why was I so focused on this boy? Truly I did not know. I think I was with a touch of bigotry, but it did not add up. Besides, I sort of dated my neighbor's daughter. I mixed some stuff together (lotion, poison ivy, water, and pills). I just kept it and was never alone with the little boy to give it to him. For what I know now, I would have only made him possibly sick and not dead. Thank you, Jesus! Some good came out of it. I took Spanish as a second language in my fifth and sixth grades. I whole-heartedly believe that I was truly trying to find a reason from past history (slavery) that did not exist to hate whites or half-and-half children. Not my thing to hate any person regardless of where they were from. My mother had a lot to do with it on how she raised me up. Thank God that it (hatred) was and is not in me! From that day on, I have had friends from all walks of life!

This little boy I hated so much, he had a black father, a white mother, a little sister (half-breed), a little brother, and an older white sister by the name of Denise Streisand. My older brothers dated, or so-called was dating, her, and then I tried to get with her too, but I did not go all the way with her. Never! My brother and I would frequent their home because my mother worked there part-time as a secretary for the mini construction company. The more we went over their house when the parents were not home, the more we got into things with the kids who lived there. The more my brothers had gotten with her, the more I wanted to get with her too. All I ended up with was some porn books we all shared together. I never knew why Denise (the older sister) sprayed deodorant on her private parts after my brothers fooled around with her. All I know is I wanted to be with her. Yes, another fantasy. I think we kissed once or twice, but in reality, Denise S. was too old for me. Yes, she would have been too much for me. My crush on Denise was as good as it would get between the two of us, forever!

Moving on. Since money was tight in our family, I pieced together some found bikes for immediate transportation since my mother was fearful of driving, and having a car or license was not in the equation. Taxis, buses, family members, the pastor, and other people were our mode of transportation. My mother and I had an unique bond of trust, so I was privy to her adult secrets as a child. I ran errands to pick up money from my younger brother's father or my father's mother for food to feed our family. Welfare was not enough. Generally, once a month, I went and did the grocery shopping with the governmental stamps and very little cash. Who also would watch the other children, my younger brothers and sister, from time to time. Yes, I became one of the responsible ones within my family. Also part of being one of the responsible ones, I took the grocery list, walked to the store, did the grocery shopping having two to three shopping carts full of food, and prayed that no classmates would see me as I paid for the groceries with food stamps. What an embarrassment, or so I thought, but we had to eat! I was still called Hog Guy. By chance, I got noticed and was teased by my other classmates! This part of my childhood was definitely not one of the highlights. It's a good thing we get to grow up and leave this part behind us. Yes!

Not only did we use the ADC program (aid for dependent children), food stamps, limited cash, and the health care card, for our family, we were one of many families in the early 1970s that qualified for the state government-wide welfare programs receiving free governmental cheese, butter, and powder milk. What unique taste, but we ate it because we were hungry and hated that food at the same time. God does have a sense of humor!

Being poor doing those days were not an option. I was just like some others in the neighborhood. Poor and not a lot of jobs going around, but it was not a big deal but to be nice about it. We just had a lot less than others. Nevertheless, we were blessed but did not see it. After a while, you sort of get used to not having the nicer things or just doing without, so I had gotten more creative in managing the "art" of stealing. Once I had my selection in mind, if I could touch it or carry it (mainly cash), it was mine! Not to toot my own horn, but over the years, I became good! At least for a while, I did not get caught.

It was a hot summer day in the mid to late-1970s. You know, we played the real fun games, like kickball, hide-and-seek, tag, and hanging out. Our dog, our family dog Misty, the small off-white Alaskan husky, just totally beautiful brown-eyed lady dog and smart too. Not sure how we came across Misty. Wow, this was a dog! Anyway, there were no dog leash laws back then, unless the dog was a viscous one—but not our Misty! Misty was everywhere in the neighborhood, yards and in the street. One day, while we (friends and family members) were playing in the street, Misty ran into our next-door neighbor's yard, and the lady's boyfriend (it's a long story, but the short version was that the husband that became my nephew's father) changed our lives in more than one way. So we, the two houses, the next-door neighbors, our families were feuding for quite some time. Also their son and I were best friends, and I had a crush on his sister. One day, I was hanging out with my buddy Charlie McCormick or Charlie. We went into his kitchen where his mother was cooking, and his mother was still married at the time. Somehow, I laid my left forearm on the silver toaster over that was on the little table, and before I can say "Ouch!" I was burnt. Boy, was it painful. I had a scar that I would never forget. Life was moving along on this hot day, which was the last day my (our) dog would run into the next-door neighbor's yard to the left of our house. Then one of the most unfortunate, mean, and nasty mishaps struck. Evil in its purest form. The lady's boyfriend ran out of the house with a machete and swung it across Misty's head. In that moment, the joy that was brought to our family was slowly fading in the wind. I still get this weird feeling as I describe what happened. There was a major gash on the top of Misty's head, and the ear was loosely hanging from her head. Misty ran back into our house as she bleeds out from the wound on the floor, down the stairs, and into the basement. Misty was wounded for life, and yes, as she was dying, my mother or someone called the dog pound patrol to pick her up. I remembered some of my brothers and sisters crying, wailing, and some were just quiet as we watched our Misty slowly drift away from us. A whole lot can happen in a moment, and in our case, it was sadness. It was a very slow death and pitifully painful. We did not actually see her die, but we did see the fear, hear her whining sounds, and see trembling in her eyes. Other than my older brothers, there was not man in the house, and the guy next door was too big for us to retaliate. Time does heal wounds! My family and I were sad for weeks, and to this day, I have never owned another dog... The sight of watching our dog Misty dying would affect me, and this one event has always affected me in such a way that I have pretty much planned to never own another dog. Misty's beauty—yes, my dog, the only dog that I would ever love—could never be replaced! The thing that happens in time is really just that. Things by the choices we make in that split second are gone. I do know that just before all the bad blood (figure of speech) had come about between the two families, our family and the neighbor next door's three kids used to hang out with us, and we all played together for years. To this day, I still miss those guys. This scar on my arm enables me often to remember some of my great childhood days! The scar now reminds me of the pain once suffered. Charlie and I had never found a way to become friends again.

At this point in time, my family and I have to share the loss of a bird and a dog. In a healing effort, my brother and I got the great idea to become paperboys and have us a paper route. This was cool for a while, and it did get old fast. Anyone doing a paper route is not easy task. Actually, it is hard work, manual labor, and too much for me, but I hung in there for as long as I could while I got smarter and worked slower. My brother did most of the work; he was older and stronger. Why not let him earn us some money! Besides, my plan worked, and I got paid in more ways than one. Like I said, this was a lot of work and very much labor intensive. I thought I was too young for this, and as my brain was developing, the male hormones were beginning to come about. I just had to keep living and definitely to do something else. All right, I got it! Onto my next growing up venture: I was a wannabe con artist in the making, without being a con (convict). However, as I graduate with life, I was well on my way of becoming a convict. It was a great thing that the technological advances evolved at a very slow place. Just think about it, I would have been caught, but that's not the case. So I did the paper route and carry grocery bags for people to their cars from their shopping carts at the Kroger grocery store, just on East Miller Road and before South Main Street. After doing it for a while, this got old too. I just had to find a way to bring in more cash, dough, better known as that "mean green." Bonnie and Clyde did not have a thing on me, minus the guns, of course. They did their thing, and I was trying to do mine. I was carrying grocery bags at Kroger, and delivering newspapers was beginning to fade in the near distance. But not before we started to collect funds from other people's paper routes. I hate to admit this, but this was fun and funny. My older brother and I knocked on the doors, and people opened the doors, and we collected funds from a paper route that did not belong to us. What! The funny thing was that on many occasions, people scratched their heads, sighed, questioned us about if they had paid already. We just told them we were filling in or collecting the paper route fees in advance. They just did not know how grateful we were when people gave us the fees for the entire month. My brother and I could not believe this ourselves, but the plan worked, and the dough was coming in. We were moving on up, just like George Jefferson on the television show. We did this paper route scheme for approximate three to six months, maybe longer. The paper route thing was very cool and very short-lived. Not long after, me, one of my brothers and a sister came up with the idea to take up donations, you know, like the church deacons, and offerings in the church.

So in the area on the south side of Akron, Ohio, by the Kroger, off of East Miller, we had several of the coin book-like holders from five cents to twenty-five cents that we picked up from the bank. Believe it or not, we did it, and it worked! We were walking around the area approaching anyone, strangers, black, white, foreign, old, or young (just not the classmates, no one could know we did this and attend the same school). We were approaching these people, and just guess what we said. We said, "Hello, would you like to make a donation to our church?" It worked. These people were giving us money. We were filling up those little coin booklets and on both sides. It seemed like a lot of money, but back then, $20 or $30 was a lot of money. On different days, we were collecting money, lying on God and the church. We did not even put those funds in the offering basket. This only went on for a few weeks, and the giving became less and less. Then we changed the plan to on and off. Sometimes, I collected the money by myself. After all the work, just so we could buy some more junk foods, such as, the orange Chilly Willy drink (my favorite), OK Potato Chips, Hostess cakes, Sugar Babies, banana taffy, Chick-O-Sticks, and more candies—more junk foods. Actually, I did learn from this experience that taking up fake donations was definitely not the business for me. This area of my life, this event, was a value added as I got older. I know that I can take from wrongdoers, but I really have an issue of taking or deceiving people that had something to do with the church. In a weird kind of way, I am glad I did it, so I would know not to ever do it again. For some reason, my heart will not allow me to move into that direction or to do anything negative when it involves the church. Believe you me, in general, I would cheat, steal, or lie to others, but that God stuff was never comfortable for me. So I would just leave the God things alone… My mom's put the fear of God in us all time and again with all of her stories. Plus, she was a dreamer. I mean, she had dreams. She would always tell us what God would do to us time and again. We (my family) knew not to play with God nor mess with those church folks. Still, we played church and would take turns being the preacher. I really did not think that I did God justice on my turn of being the preacher.

These two places were very cool to hang out at—Tastee Market on South Main Street and Kroger on West Miller Avenue (around the corner). My brothers and sisters and I did not steal from these two stores as much as we would have wanted to. But we did our share, and once I almost was caught by a moonlighting Akron Police detective named Frank. He had dark hair and walked sort of pigeon toed. Each time, I have always gotten rid of the evidence. There were a few close calls, and once, my older sister, Annie, barely saved me from being caught by Policeman Frank. Wow! I have seen Policeman Frank run on other occasions, chasing after dudes from Kroger for stealing. Policeman Frank was fast! The dude was fast! However, on other occasions, we would hang out in front of Kroger and talk to Policemen Frank. He had small crooked teeth. I did remember that! I really wanted to stay on Frank's good side. I could see it in his eyes that he probably done some things through his career that he was not so proud of. At the Tastee Market across the parking lot from Kroger's, I remember that my sister and I, through two M-80 firecrackers in the back of the store that had brick walls on both sides. Boy, was that loud and we got out of there. No way, were we going to look back! That was some kind of scary fun!

Anyway, I did not understand how stores—the Krogers, Lawsons, corner stores, K-Mart, Miracle Mart, and the five and dime stores—stayed in business, but in the grand scheme of things, we really did not steal that much, even though to me, the things we stole were not of the big-dollar value. The thing was, if it was on the shelves and within our reach, it was ours. Most times, I was with a brother or sister, but I did not recall who was with me at the time of the occurrence. We were very similar to gypsies and how they

34

operated, smoothly! We made our rounds, and the same thing, it had gotten old. We were in the planning stages to move. Actually, we had to move. That house that we lived in on 10 Manila Place was, in the nicest term, ruined! Looking back at this thing my family had done and if at some point in time, I really did not believe that I could ever rent a home that I may own within the Section 8 program, especially if there were a lot of children involved. If so, it would have been a miracle! I still remember that house—we totally destroyed it. But my mother would always, in spite of what it looked like, try to make it our home. However, I did recall one blizzard in the mid-1970s that we survived, and one Christmas that was very special to me. At most, Christmas was just that Christmas, and that I was not ungrateful. It was one of my best Christmas. I did not believe in Santa Claus because as my mother take items off lay-away (sometimes I ran errands, and I would make the lay-away payment for my mother) and bring them home and lock the gifts in the closet. We would sneak to see what was packed away in the closet. Whatever my mother did not work for or handed over to us, we would receive the items from the Salvation Army or a place similar to it. That year, I did receive most of what I wanted—the Rock 'Em, Sock 'Em Robots, a record player that folded up, and a few odds and ends. We had family games like Trouble, Sorry, Old Maid, Operations, and Twister. Also in the 1970s, I recall it was around Thanksgiving, just before turning ten years old, right before Christmas. Over the years, I was used to walking in the snow up to about fifteen or more inches to school, stores, or wherever I decided to go. This year, in 1971, this winter was quite different, speaking about it mildly—it was bad, very bad! I remember seeing the lightning flashes across the dark skies. I must've jumped a few times, and the winds were just raging fiercely from house to house and should have blown some houses over. I was by the upstairs window, and *scared* was not the word. I was definitely terrified. It was lightning in the winter, definitely new for me, imagine that! God must have seen me in the window and had mercy on me, and our home was safe. Wow!

Moving along, my school attendance at Lincoln Elementary was fast approaching the end of the school. School was out, and it is summer once again. We were sneaking to smoke cigarettes, outside and behind the garage, and my younger brother breaking his hip and the death of our dog. These we some of my best and worst days I remember growing up. There were many, many more memories... Hopefully, I may reflect upon the memories more in detail as my life's story goes on. But this Manila Place was the fondest times that I would ever know of and shared with my family, not to forget the few friends I had on our street, like the families of the Andersons, Tylers, and LeFevres. Oh, I cannot forget the songs in that period, like the Jacksons, Osmonds, Diana Ross, Minnie Riperton ("Back Down Memory Lane"), The Manhattan's ("Let's Just Kiss and Say Goodbye"), and Betty Wright ("The Clean-up Woman"). We sang that song while holding the broom for the mic and most songs alike. Much of what we all heard was country and western, like Johnny Cash, Charlie Pride, Charlie Rich, James Cleveland, Shirley Caesar, and the Mighty Clouds of Joy. These were some of my mom's favorites (mine too).

Over the years, it seemed to be a very strange blessing. This was another weird moment for me, but the word of all these things we (I) did never had gotten back to my mother or maybe she did not tell us. To this day, I do not know. Nevertheless, I would have been a poster boy for child abuse. I think by me not getting caught, I had a false sense of hope that I was beginning to build up within my mind, and eventually, I did believe I was good...and still my mom's favorite! The good son!

In the eighth and ninth grades at Thornton Junior High School, my life was not very eventful, but yes, going to church was something to do, so I was there. I was kind of growing up; school was cool and I was doing quite well. By that, I was not close to failing, so I kept using the brain God gave me. The ninth-grade things became a little different for me. For one reason or another, I was selected to make some honest money. Through the Akron Board of Education, there was a program that existed to help students with low income or something like that. My life was about to change! I was making an honest living by working at McDonalds on East Exchange Street part-time. My first assigned duty was to learn how to fry the french fry or french fries, if you will. Not to toot my own horn, but I was the young handsome black man on fries, and I was quick, quicker, and became the quickest. I was so happy for my achievements. I believe that my quickness would pay off later on. I had taken first place on the fries and do not remember what was won. From time to time, I had to go to the basement of McDonald's to watch the McDonald's history, featuring the business agent Ray Kroc. At that time, we were part of history, too, wearing the pointed paper hats with the screens on top, the white shirt with the golden *M* arches on the pocket, and a black clip-on tie. I was playing it cool for a while. The money was cool back in 1975. I started making about $1.35 an hour for the probation period within the Occupational Work Adjustment (OWA) middle school program at Thornton Junior High School. I attended both school and work part-time. For about a year, I was making about $1.60 and later $1.90. Boy, was I getting paid *legally*! Now, with the training under my belt, I was on to cleaning bathrooms, taking out trash, cleaning the lobby area, unloading the delivery trucks. It was cold to do the trucks, not cool, but cold and worst in the winter months. Now, I was the newest or the first ever french fry trainer. I trained everyone and really tried to impress the girl hires. I just kept looking forward to working and school. What a life, and I went to work one day, and just like that, I was working on the grill. I was making those world-famous hamburgers, cheeseburgers, big Macs, and later on, quarter-pounders. This was one dirty, sticky, sweating, working, and smelling job. I too became very good at flipping burgers. I was so good that McDonald's had another contest to see who was the fastest. I believe I took first or second place. I won my first Polaroid instant camera. *Click, click.* I was off and running with my new camera.

My sights were evolving as I took notice of the store manager, Mr. Jim Rice, and one of the assistant store managers, George Clark, which was also his cousin, nephew, or some kin. The ladies were always around them, and I wanted to be like those guys. I do remember two of the ladies in that time were Sharon (I think Italian) and Lois (light-skinned with dyed tan-gold hair). This woman was nice to see. Even though Sharon was one of the assistant store managers, she was pretty cool to be around. If only her brown eyes and her short brown-haired self was not too old for me. Sharon never gave me notice or maybe she did. Nevertheless, I still don't know. I somehow did not mind riding the bus to work just to see these women. I didn't mind picking up trash or whatever she asked of me. I was at her service! Then Mr. Rice hired this nineteen- or twenty-year-old dark-haired Italian woman—small medium built and all together. I was about sixteen years old or close to that. My rap game was too weak for her. All I remember was her name was Toni Pecora. All she did was work and smile. I would know that smile anywhere. Toni was really a happy person who loved her job. Toni must have told me no a good hundred times, and she smiled as if she would have loved to say yes but could not. We (Toni and I) could have had a future, but I already knew the outcome—*no!* My dream of wanting to become a manager at McDonald's was gone as fast as I thought of it. This McDonald's scene was just not the job for me. The girls were not working for me, and I was beginning to get bored. I simply just wanted more, but I just did not know what that "more" was. I was becoming good at working at McDonald's and onto the next station since I had become the "grill trainer"—nametag and all. I was now learning how to work the cash register. Oh, I did not mention that McDonald's fed my family for a while. We were still poor and on welfare. This was not enough! I had created and devised a way to retrieve food (such as, Ronald McDonald's birthday chocolate cakes, much fries, and much 100 percent beef patties) from the freezer area to my car (yup, my cheap $200 1964 beige Plymouth Belvedere, but it did run). I thought it was my job to help out my mother, so our family—my brother and sister—would be able to eat as often as possible. For about a year or so, I fed my family. This was not counting the leftovers that I took home at the end of the day. On the weekends, I assisted in closing the store at night and sometimes after school for the store inspections, especially in the grill area. I do not regret what I did. In essence, I believed it was my duty to step up in helping to feed my family.

Working at McDonald's overtime allowed me to save up a few hundred dollars and buy me a light-blue 1969 Chevy Caprice, with a 350 engine. This car was sweet and smooth riding mobile! I drove it for a few months or so and shared with one of my older brothers from time to time, and shortly thereafter, the engine or transmission went out. Then back into the 1964 Belvedere. When I was going to church, I was still paying my tithes to the church, just like my mother had taught me. By this time, I was a regular employee at McDonald's and no more OWA work study program.

I was working at McDonald's and attending school and church. Money, yes, I needed more. Gas was cheap, going for about 70 cents a gallon. I was making about $2.35 an hour, giving my mother money time and again to help out the family. Plain and simple, I just needed more money, or I just wanted to have more money. So I started to take money out of the cash registers with every order—a little here and there. This scheme was pretty easy since we were using the paper tablets to take orders, mostly for my friends, classmates, and of course, different family members (brothers, sisters, cousins, aunts, etc.). I would ring up a dollar or two, and they would leave the store with $20 to $30 worth of food. Or sometimes people would kick me a few bills on the side. Since I was very, very good with numbers, I would take $20 from the register and make up the difference from the orders that I had received. Then one day, I was home with my mother, and she had told me that she had a dream. I did believe in God. Really, I did. It was sort of mandatory without options that I would get it in my mind, and at one time, I had a close relationship with Him. Besides, I stayed on the honor roll at Thornton, but at Central Hower High, my grades were not the same case as junior high. Anyway, my mother told me that God have given her a vision or dream that the people at McDonald's were watching me. I listened and decided to blow it off, so I thought no more of it and kept doing my thing. It was sometime on a Saturday morning. I just started the dayshift, and the cash register drawers were sitting on the meat freezer and was too tempting for me. Just as cool and collected as I was, I snatched a $20 bill and thought that no one had seen what I had done. Was this a setup? My mother's dream? I could not have been totally far from the truth. I knew I was wrong! I was totally wrong as I did not listen to the warning from my God-fearing mother. But as I was very good with numbers, I was also quick with my hands. I was approached by one of the assistant managers. I followed him to meet up with the other managers and Mr. Rice in the basement. We walked through the store, and I followed and noticed the bread buns on the counter. I was in the perfect position behind the manager before meeting the other managers in the basement. So we moved one foot in front of the other, down the narrow path, bread buns stacked high and between the high stainless-steel freezers. We walked and the opportunity presented itself. I quickly slid the $20 that was in my hand between the stainless-steel countertop and under the McDonald's fish fillet bread bun rack with the bread in it. Just in the nick of time, just before heading downstairs to empty my pockets, shoes, and socks. I did not get caught. I kept my job and went back to work to be paid for the job that I was doing. I just don't believe that I was not caught! I was not caught, and yet I didn't know how to really pray. It was for sure that my mother was praying for me—no doubt! I was glad that that shift was over!

So I was still attending Central Hower High. I made the baseball (softball) team, did the practices, and played the games. I do believe we had lost every game that season 1976–1977. I did not stay on the team. I guess I did not have the heart for the defeats, time and again. But I was beginning to catch this girl's eye. I was a sophomore and dating a senior—Tracy Mashore. Yes, I thought and acted like I was grown. Most of the time, we were all over each other, and I thought I was doing something. At sixteen, almost grown and out of the house but not yet, I decided to spend the night out at Tracy's house. And there lived her gay uncle who was always complaining and taking hormones so he could have a chest like a woman. This was strange for me to know that such a thing could ever happen, but true, I was never exposed to anything as such. But the uncle was cool and I did not judge him. However, I was only trying to score with Tracy. So after one night spent out, going against all my mother's rules, I only got several kisses, a few grinds that ended up in a situation not being too comfortable for me, to say the least, and no score, only fooling around—just like my softball days. I totally struck out! My mother thought I was missing, and being worried about me, one of the ten children, my mother called the police and gave them notice that I was missing. That next morning, when I had finally reached home, my mother, my hardworking mother was, in the backyard, hanging up the clothes, sheets, and linen. The washer was very old-fashioned with the separate ringer that each piece had to be individually fed through the rollers. Yes, I do remember my days of using that thing too. One day, I even used bleach on the colors, and everything turned pink. On a fast tip, I had to get it together and had to learn how to wash properly by my mother because she made us wash our own clothes, clean, and cook. After the worry in my mother's face was gone after seeing me again and I was all right, I had told her that I was at a friend's house. Of course, I did not want to upset my mother any more than what I had done by not returning home on time the day before. So she calls the police station back again and informed them that I was home. Nothing more came of it, and I would never do that again. However, my mother did take my car keys, and I had got very mad. I, for the one time, told my mother that I hated her, but I said this under my breath (I just know she would have back-handed my face, if I had stated this aloud). This was a Saturday, and I had no keys. I would not be going out that evening. I just wanted to die. In a fierce moment of anger, I tried unsuccessfully to kill myself by the method of pills or whatever. I thought my life was over by not being able to hang out with Tracy, Jackie, Doris, Kim, Phil, and the other school friends. My attempt to kill myself was very unsuccessful by way of taking multiple pills. This only made me very, very sick. I was vomiting time and again and cramping, but I lived to tell the story, and believe you me, I told myself I would never to do it again or at least that what I thought. Getting back to the more show-and-tell relationship with Tracy that did not last long. Being a senior, she would move on after graduation or back home because she was only visiting her uncle from somewhere in Pennsylvania. We did sleep together, but nothing happened. But the way we stayed all over each other, one would definitely think the obvious. Wishful thinking but nothing happened.

I was hanging out with my sister Terri and her husband Robert. We were all drinking that Irish Rose drink, and I got drunk rather quickly. We were all talking and laughing. I was laughing so hard that I broke her kitchen chair. I must have stayed at her house that evening. The first strike that was against me. I was too drunk to drive. The second strike was my mother could not see me like that, so I slept it off at my sister's house. Everything else was definitely a blur! This was my first time being drunk and could not remember most all of it! Meanwhile, I was trying to catch the attention of many other girls, trying to get the phone number of any girl that caught my eyes. As the days and nights moved along, I got a number here and there, a date here and there, girls from the hood, from school, but the church girls, they were really taught to pay attention very well and to be careful. My respect for the church girls was automatic. They did not play with the boys. No fooling around, at least for the saved ones. This I know for a fact. We liked each other in church here and there, but not much of nothing was happening, and nothing was going on but to continue to hang out at church for time was moving on. Under the direction or pastorship of Bishop JE Pope, with his sons too, we started going to church there. Then we had our little church group called The Sons of God (James, Mike, Anthony "Red Bone," Robert Brown, and myself) and the choir, teaching, and of course, preaching what I would know and how it would affect me later in life. But at sixteen, I did not have too much to do with church, becoming distant, and I did not have the patience to hang out with the guys and talk sports and girls. Deep inside my mind, I wanted more. I just did not know what that "more" was, and the girls were in the headlines of my mind. In church, the girls were not happening for me fast enough. In those days, one could get a fast car, but in church, the girls were not what you would consider fast. Because they were definitely "saved." I did have my eye on one girl by the name of Denise Robinson. We were both cousins to the Clay family, but not cousins to each other. We worked hard to figure that out. She was definitely a church girl, no touching whatsoever! It would have never worked; we were cousins to the same cousin on my mother side of the family. Oh my god! OMG! At my age, marriage was what other people did. My other brothers and sisters and I were getting older, and my mother, being the only parent, she pretty much had her little hands full. Therefore, I did respect my mother and had a great relationship with her, but I was being pulled into the world, and that sin was the thing I did as I continued to stray away and stay away from church. I really was not that strong in the Lord! Nevertheless and over the years, my mother stayed a praying woman; she prayed for God's protection over her children. She was a praying woman! My mother stayed in church and kept her children, my brothers and sisters and other family members and friends, in prayer. There were days and nights I would hear my mother praying in her bedroom. And I would be smelling the rubber from the rubber factories in the nights of Akron, Ohio, and yet I would hear my mother singing or praying. This praying, the long talks, the values she taught me, and her love would always be the glue that binds our relationship to each other, the church, and most importantly to me, being the guide to a personal relationship with God.

Yet I knew that my separation from the church and God could only mean one thing, more trouble, better known as sin. So one day, it was not long after that the greed of life was right in front of me. I did not understand that thrive to do whatever and still not know what I was missing. But I wanted more. I just did not know what that "more" was. For one reason or another, I still wanted the more. My heart and desires thrived and thrived. So I had got together with a few people, my brother-in-law Robert McGowan and a young lady-to-be, which was my sister Terri. I was still working for McDonald's and would become the man, the one on the inside. We were plotting to rob this famous restaurant, McDonald's. We had it all plan out. We went over it a few times, step by step, and after that, you would not believe what had happened next. The perfect plan to get the daily bank money drops as the manager would leave the McDonald's restaurant was halted. The robbery plan was stopped as cold as ice. What happened? It would be my praying mother just happened to mention this upcoming event to me by the grace of God. I cannot explain it. I just know that God was not going to let it happen! One would have thought that I was lying or it's a science fiction movie or maybe a dream. No, it is true! My mother, once again, saved me from the errors of my sinful and lustful life. This is what had happened: I have gone home, actually, to our new (at least, it was new to us) home at 537 Talbot Avenue on the east side of Akron, Ohio. We lived there overall about a year or so, and there was a little park and basketball court across the street. This was okay for us and a close place at home to hang out. Joy Park Recreation Center, Church's Chicken, and a few other places with the mall a short bus ride away. Also there was a Golden Gloves boxing gym around the corner, which was also in walking distance to our home. A lot of my cousins, aunts, and uncles lived there on the east side, as well. So we felt right at home. I even started training to box for the Golden Gloves. Wow, after all of that training, I even boxed with my brother-in-law Robert, but my nosebleeds kept coming back. My boxing career was over rather quickly, but I kept training, and the training would always stay with me. I really enjoyed the boxing and especially the six-inch exercises with the heavy ball be bounced off my stomach. I had a really tough and durable midsection. I still miss that training. But this was the end of my Golden Gloves boxing career.

At this point, on the east side of Akron, working, going school, and trying to find myself, along with playing a lot of pickup basketball games, and some street football. Other than walking or riding the bus, taxis, and borrowing my older brother's car, my life on the east side was very boring. I did meet this girl, young lady, if you will. She lived around Joy Park, and we became friends. I did not run around much with the fellas. I just wanted to get to know Robin. She was about five feet and five inches, mild to light-brown skin and a good grade of hair, but Robin kept it medium-short to long. She was a pretty little thing. Yes, Robin did get my attention. I was all into getting to know her and wanted to make her my girlfriend. I didn't know to think anything different, but I should have been more focused versus my thoughts all in one place, her anatomy. By this time, we discussed going somewhere for Robin. I went too. I had no car and no way to impress her on or to drive her to school. Besides, she went to East High School. The more I got to know her, the more the disappointment. The disappointment would not only shock me but hurt me as well. Then one evening, we were hanging out, and Robin told me about the most unthinkable thing that I could have imagined. I was really green with the facts of life and had plenty of room to grow. Robin dropped this bombshell on me, as we were walking in the middle of the street, the red brick road. Okay, my ears were open, and my eyes to her eyes. She then Robin stated she was gay. "*What?*" I said. Back then, girls just didn't say things like that. I was in the state of shock and disbelief. How could this beautiful young lady of my interest be gay? I was done! Through! Then I left in a hurry and left her alone…only to see her a few times in passing. This one affected me and woke me up a little concerning women and the facts of life. She was definitely all of that, but I had to shake that experience off and find myself in life. I was so glad that girls like Robin stayed away from my direct path of life. But I was thinking, what if she only told me of this thing being gay just to get rid of me. I guess I will never know!

Getting back to the McDonald's on East Exchange Street by my high school Central Hower and the University of Akron. Now again, while at home, my mother and I were talking. She was sitting down with a very patient demeanor. She looked at me and said, as big as day, "Don't do it." "Oh my god," I stated under my breath. "How in the world does she know this?" What was she, my mother, talking about. I just did not know how to respond. How did she know? Who told her? Then my mother said it again, "Don't rob McDonald's!" I have told this story many times as my life went on. The only way my mother would have known this thing about me is that God had to have revealed it to her. I believed! Not sure if people who heard me tell them this part of my life believed it or not. I do not care because I still tell this story. God knows that I would have robbed McDonald's, but instead, I am thankful to God for giving my mother sight in His realm to do His will. My mother, with this experience for the robbery that I did not commit, placed the fear of God in me, but still I was searching for other things in my life and running from the very one who could save me. I just did not know it at the time that I would one day really know God!

I was glad our next move for our family was just in time. I really did not catch the attention of too many honeys on the East Side of Akron, from the hood, school, or work, but the north side of Akron was another story. I had just transferred my McDonald's for the east side of Akron to the north side and on a main strip, Tallmadge Avenue. Also very close to Chapel Hill Mall, a place where I and the boys hung out, or most times, I was by myself. The old saying goes, as I was on the prowl for finding the girls, three's a crowd! There I was. I had obtained a waiver, or maybe I just did not tell the school system, so I could stay at Central Hower High School versus going to the high school in my district, which was North High School. Regardless to the reason, my path of life remained at Central Hower High School.

Unknowingly, my soon-to-be baby's mother and, if only I could have known, my future ex-wife attended North High School. Since I was still working, my mother loaned me $200 to get my car fixed. My mother would always come up with money if her children needed it, and she did it for me. This I did find out. My mother either saved the money, made a personal sacrifice, or borrowed the funds, but she was never without money. I just know the welfare and ADC did not give her that much money and food stamps. I did realize it from time to time God did show up for her when there was a need. My mother was very much a praying woman. I always paid my mother back with interest because she was my mother. This was my way and my thoughtful obligation to her. I had always had a close relationship with her. I also felt that I owed her something because she was my mother. I just love to hear my mother tell me of our family history or her relationship with or how it was with my father. The stories were long but worthwhile. I remember her saying over and over, "Always be sure to have your wife sleep in a bed." She would also tell us of how she used to sleep on a mattress but on stacks of wood/plywood that was stolen by my father and her brothers. I do remember this story, and I planned to keep it close to my heart and apply it to my life.

Get this, I'm in high school at Central Hower High, in the tenth grade, soon turning seventeen years old, working at McDonald's, and driving a 1964 light beige and with chrome all over it Belvedere with a push button gear shift and with no headrest. In my mind, I was the man, and pushing this load. Yes, *my load* the cool term used back then, which meant my car.

Another humongous snowfall came, and the winter season was ending, Akron is known as a snow belt, and we got plenty of snow in the winter. While I was chauffeuring my brother Robert and his girlfriend Dorita around town and just hanging out, another venture came into my mind on how to receive some quick cash. The snow was right, and this same night, I was playing in the snow with my car in which I also learned how to drive in the snow. This empty ACME grocery store parking lot on the west side of Akron was great place to learn how driving in the snow would affect my everyday driving, such as, fish-tailing, spin-outs, swerving, and the whole nine yards. I caught on pretty quickly. Then my brother tried it and gave it back to me. We did not help the tires any, but I was glad winter was ending. Anyway, back to my venture. All of a sudden, like a flash, I decided to back up my rear bumper to the concrete wall and then make an insurance claim. What a silly idea? My brother and his girlfriend, Dorita McDaniel, were shocked after being shook from their cozy moment in the back seat. He had no idea for what I was doing. My brother shouted to me, "Are you crazy?" He said some other things too, but anyway! He also stated that I could have blown everyone up. From that point of view, it was a bad idea, and also it was a good thing that we did not have much gas in the car. I did have a little damage to the rear bumper. Nothing came of the insurance claim. For one, the car was too old to pursue a claim, and I did not have that type of coverage. I realize at that moment I did not have a career in insurance fraud!

I believe it was the summer before I was to start the tenth grade at Central Hower High. We moved from 537 Talbot Avenue to 117 Tallmadge Avenue on the north side of Akron. That summer I started working at Cotter Moving and Storage, and one of my older brothers worked there as well. I was with my older brother on most times and even on the distance moving locations. We did not go too far on the local runs, driving twenty-two to thirty-two-foot trucks or something close to these sizes. Anyway, getting to my '64 Belvedere. On occasion, I would allow my older brother to drive my car to work or to go a date with his girl Dorita. Well, one cool morning, we had got up, and the car was not working. By this time, I was wearing a splint (arm sling) from the doctor's office to ease the pain because I had bursitis in my left shoulder. I needed my brother help to fix my car. We found out that we needed an alternator, but we had no funds. Well, as we are aware of my earlier days, I could steal but an alternator? It was on. We had gotten a ride to the Giant Auto Salvage yard on Tallmadge Avenue. As soon as you would walk in the door, there were shelves of alternators, starters, batteries, etc. So the plan was for my older brother to point out the alternator that we needed and then to distract the clerk, and I would steal the alternator. Finally, I figured how to get the alternator out of the junk yard store. I then placed the alternator under my jacket (one sleeve not used) and between my arm sling and grip it to my body. Not only was my shoulder being sore, but I placed myself in more pain because of the stolen alternator. I then eyed my brother to signal, "Let's get out of here." If was funny afterward, but I was successful again that time. Awesome!

It was 1978, and the summer was over, and the eleventh grade was unwinding. The school thing at Central Hower was on. I still wanted to become that doctor. I had the premed course on my daily schedule and taking for math elementary functions for the eleventh grade. I did geometry in the tenth grade. Most folks did consider me as a smart person. Get this, I was really trying to become that doctor, and at that point, I was not sure of the field of study. I barely got through the math, so why? Because of the girls, girls, and more girls. I normally drove or rode the city bus to school. And then, sometimes I would just hang out downtown Akron, around the Peanut Shoppe, Hamburger Station, or O'Neil's Department store. While downtown, from the bus, or the library, I met this one honey, this fourteen-year-old light-brown-skinned young lady. Wow! We met and her name was Deanna Sinclair. I was seventeen, and she was a little younger than me. It did not take long. Deanna was my girl. End of story! We begin to hang out, and school was becoming out of focus, and my grades were continuously falling. Let's just say I made it through but did not give it my best at all! Deanna was a bad girl, or let's just say, she and her mother did not see eye to eye. So Deanna was staying at the YWCA in downtown Akron with other girls. I guess for the same domestic stuff. Anyway, Deanna and some of her friends sneaked me in the women's YWCA, and let just say for the sake of details, I was so glad she did not conceive on my behalf. I was way over my head as for an additional responsibility to care for a child. Even though I did not have a child, still I continued on being reckless to myself and many girls to come. At the rate that I was going, I was definitely a candidate of becoming a young father. Weeks later, it was time for Deanna to return home. Sometimes, Deanna's mother would talk with me, trying to determine how to make things better between the two of them. I did listen out of respect. Besides, I think Deanna's mother loved and cared for her. Even after the talks, Deanna and I still skipped school by signing myself out with fake parent's permission slips, just so Deanna and I could hang out, going swimming at Turkey Foot or to the malls like Chapel Hill Mall or Rolling Acres Mall (normally the cool black folks' mall). We had had a great time together. The relationship between Deanna and myself was just that—a relationship without much in common, other than the obvious, but we did have this closeness, like I knew her pain. I did understand her in that way, and I had her heart. I still remember our favorite song, "Reunited" by Peaches and Herb. But also, our favorite makeup song was "Baby, I'm for Real" by the Originals. I did sing that song at times to her.

By this time, I did not get too much play (girl action) at school. The ones I wanted to get to know did not go over to well, such as Monique Crooks, Frankie Bell, Doris Bushner, Phoebe Cheatham, Jackie Melton, Shawna Carey, Francine Batie, Tamarah Beckley, Sylvia Wilson, Annette Williams, Tracy Johnson, Lori Wallace, and a few others. We had some very attractive young ladies in high school. There was this other student by the name of Tina Turner, like the singer, but not the same. I could not touch her because she was in a class all by herself. In a way, I was kind of shy, and my game (rap to girls) was still in the developmental stages. I went on a triple hanging out on the night with Jackie and Doris, with my lane rap. I tried to run a game on both of them, and the plan definitely backfired. My advice to everyone else is to never try to date or like two best friends. It does not work. So with my lane rap, and even though they were nice-looking females, I had to be on the pressed and continued to

49

find myself. But I was getting "play" from everywhere else. My fellow classmates (my boys Philip Anderson, Kim White, and sometimes, Victor Milan) that I hung out with would not believe the play from the girls that I was getting. Fact is, I too was in disbelief. But I stayed in the game. Therefore, I began to be on the prowl for the next one. My cousin Regina and I hung out for a while since we both were attending Central Hower. We went to a few basement house parties with the strobe lights, which was the thing. To me, house partying was boring. I was just looking and wanted multiple females. Yes, I wanted to become a player (from time to time, my life reminded me of what I knew of my Dad) after this first real occurrence of a relationship with Deanne. I just wanted more. Besides, my cousin always thought Deanna was this crazy, wild, weird person. There were times I went to pick up Regina, and Deanna would not get out of the car. I did not care! Now that I was secure in this relationship Deanne, I pursued this other girl named Kelly, a beautiful mixed (half black and white) girl, just beautiful, with long hair, and greenish gray eyes. Both of her parents lived at home. We dated, sort of. I was at her house many times and spent some time talking with her father, but nothing was going to happen, not even a kiss. Maybe we did kiss once or twice. Kelly was definitely a nice girl that attended North High School, and we were very short-lived. No groove there, so I had to go!

Also I was getting tired of the McDonald's scene, and as the job was ending per my lack of interest, I did meet this nice and attractive young lady by the name of Diane Robinson (no relationship to Denise Robinson, from church). She attended Buchtel High School on the west side of Akron. This light-skinned brick house that was too much for me. I was going through a stage of life, beginning to become more and more attracted to older females. For days, even months, I was back and forth at her house and to no avail. A relationship in the near future was out of the question, but no one told me. I eventually figured it out. That's life! Diane was an all-time tease, and I was caught for the moment in her web, her web of deception and a waste of my time. I could have just dated one girl at a time, but not me. Finally, I had enough and gave Diane a piece of my mind, showing my frustrations and disappointments. This one was over, or

I just received the memo later on. Besides, I still had Deanna, and she was still, sort of, cool to be around. My age of seventeen was busy one for me. I even got my wisdom teeth pulled, all of them! I was out of commission for a while and stayed home. After a few days of lounging around the house being miserable and swooshing with salt water, I was beginning to feel better. I was back at school and normal it was. The teeth thing was a painful experience and a memorable one at that!

Now, I was just hanging out in the neighborhood and meeting some of the people in the neighborhood. The people were hanging out doing their thing. The elementary school was about forty-five seconds from my house front door, and we shot basketball hoops there from time to time. I even tried to teach the almost seven-footer Grady Mateen the basics of basketball and a few of my moves, in which I was not that good, but each year, I was getting better. Enough of Grady. Besides, I did not see him much, so we were never close, but he was cool, and I would never forget that seven-footer. I had always hoped that he would get better. However, I did wish I had that height. Then basketball would have become my new passion of life—the girls too!

I was a very busy young man at the rightful age of seventeen and had much to accomplish with the opposite sex. Yes, I looked at all of the porn books—actually, before I was seventeen. I do believe that I was definitely a realist. One may ask why, and the truth of the matter was this: looking at the books did teach me a few things. For one, what not to do, what I never wanted to do, and even though I learned a thing or two, the porn books and movies deal (the thing young men went through while trying to pass through puberty) did not do much for me. It had gotten old very fast. In my heart of hearts, I wanted my life experiences to be natural and as real as possible. And not to share my best possible moments of my life's sexual experience in a book or on a television screen. I wanted to live, really live my life and not by imitating scenes in a book or something! That has never become my style. I... Let's say my confidence was maturing. *Fast!* Just like the motto of Coke Cola—"I wanted the real thing." I do think that guys begin to smell themselves (think highly of themselves) because of having girl relations. I was guilty of that air for myself too!

Life goes on. I really did not spend my time at home, and so I kept meeting the girls! Believe you me, what was happening to me was not a blessing from God. But I did know that something in my life was different, but I could not explain it. So I kept it (being me) moving. Looking back, I should have been known as the lover on Tallmadge Avenue. I first met this young lady by the name of Cynthia, and I believed she was living with her grandfather who hauled trash, junk, and rubbish, like the dude on TV—Fred Sanford and son. I think her grandfather's name was Zek. Anyway, this girl was tall and thinly built. For the time we spent together, hanging out, and overall, it was totally cool to be around each other. My rap (game) was getting better because I know and believe that Cynthia was tempted to be with me. We had a few moments of being face-to-face staring at each other with our eyes locked, eye to eye, and even though nothing happened between us, I was very close! Of course, Cynthia was a little older than I, and the Marine Corps—Uncle Sam—had their hooks into her. Now, the school year was closing fast, and I was still trying to make my moves—any move. Again nothing was going to happen. Life goes on, and for me, it did just that! The times between Deanna and I just faded away. There was no breakup and no broken hearts. We talked from time to time, but I was about three years older, and I believe that made the difference, as most of me desired the lust of older women. Don't get me wrong. I do mean that my attraction to older women would have definitely been less than ten years older. That's it!

Anyway, my older brother and I were hanging out in our back-yard on Tallmadge Avenue, talking and shooting the breeze. He was giving me some big brother advice to join the military. We did not have many of these talks. Normally, I would want to borrow his car for weekend dating, but this one conversation was good. He was sharing his experiences of the military with and what to expect if I did decide to go in the military. In the 1970s, the military was different and a little more violent to the Marines. Including beatdowns by the training instructors, suicides committed from the receipt of a

Dear John letters, in which, I think was the line of the military that my brother did not want me to cross. I believe that my brother Junior was exposed to more than enough for the both of us. Therefore, my brother trained with me on the next several months to prepare me for basic training. Because after a few talks, I wanted to follow in my big brother footsteps. Mind you, I had no father to grow up with nor look up to. I had decided to join the military. My older brother specifically instructed me to join the Air Force. I listened to that military type of order that my brother gave to me! Actually, in my heart, I wanted to follow in my older brother's footsteps and into the Marine Corps. But I remember the talks with my brother and the Marine training that I participated in with him, before joining for the Air Force. One day, in the early fall of 1979. the leaves on the trees were beginning to change their color, so beautiful. I was at the recruiting office in downtown Akron. Surprisingly, I passed the Armed Services Vocational Aptitude Battery Test (ASVAB) and was sworn into the delay entry program for the US Air Force as an enlisted young man, recruiter SSgt. Jim Buchanan, sold me a bill of goods. I was set to leave the following year on July 1, 1980, after my high school graduation.

Anyway, another hot day and another hot conversation with my brother Junior in the backyard of our house. Girl talk never seem to get old, especially about the conversations of life. We asked the what-if question: "What would I do if it was me?" We were just chilling, dealing with the issues of life of being poor, being some folks that fell into the category of the "have nots," and of course, with more girl talk. This young lady appeared out of the car—her dad's Cadillac. This car was dark blue and just plain cool. But Maxine Jones—aka Lynn because she was not fond of her first name, so Lynn it is—was there on the driveway. For my brother and myself, it was on, and the prize was Lynn. We both wanted her. Or was he proud of me and testing my game. I just don't know and never thought to ask. Not to mention that she was only seventeen, and my brother was in his twenties. Not only did I meet her, the brother and sisters, mother and father, uncle, cousins, and close friends. I was in there because of Lynn's brother Jeffrey and I hung out, and the family just loved me, especially her mother Gertrude and her father Saul. Anyway, I was able to know of Lynn and her family firsthand before my brother. Therefore, from my standpoint, I had won already. Next or shortly thereafter, Lynn was my girl or, by definition, as close to my girl as one could be. I don't believe we ever made a notion about the boyfriend-girlfriend thing. Besides, we never went out on a date or anything that resembled one. We sort of hang out a lot and became an item. I was still out of order, and so were my male testosterone levels. Case and point, I was in it for the game, fun, and sex—not a commitment or, at least, not a commitment from me. I would never tell. I believe that she already knew there would be others. I was too young, and it just was not going to happen! Besides, in my young life, I had developed a double standard that went something like this one: I could do it, but you could not. This standard—the chauvinistic point—was not about control, but a choice. If you wanted to be with me... Anyway, it worked! I was learning the game of life, learning the responsibilities of relationship, the female value systems, and morals. You know, if I did want you, I dogged you, or if I wanted you and you did not want me, then I would dog you first. The game of life at its best! The female's emotions represented weakness, weakness represented failure, or the next candidate to be dogged. It was most definitely on—the game of life, aka the dog-eat-dog world!

Lynn and I were moving forward. I sometimes drove her dad's caddy with her mother, with her sister's (Renee) two kids, and Lynn who were often at Lynn's house. Deanna became my ex and definitely was out of the picture by then. I was at school, and I found out that one of my classmates was also my neighbor. I tried for a while with Sharon and nothing. This shorty was attractive, but her goods would definitely pass me by. She would not be tainted by my charm or looks. I somehow seen it in her eyes, the glean was there, but so was the doubt. By now, I was eager to move ahead. I did meet Sharon's cousin, Tammy—brown skinned, beautiful eyes, and let's say big-boned. She was my well-kept secret. But her weakness was that she was too into me, and yes, I did take advantage of this situation. I was getting it all, including her money and time. I was a senior in high school, and this honey was keeping green in my pockets.

While Tammy was not my type, we did not date or go out. Her parents liked me, and they were cool. So I kept coming back to pretend that Tammy and I had this thing going on. It was all materialistic relationship, nothing less and nothing more! I was still interested in her cousin Sharon until I met Charlene Williams. We met somewhere in downtown Akron (or Rolling Acres mall or on the bus). I truly do not remember where we met, but I had to have another girlfriend, and Charlene was it. She was a down-to-earth young lady, a little older than me. A healthy five feet and nine inches, this girl was a total brick house. She too was crazy about me. The family was cool with me, and Charlene's dad treated me like a son. This man was taken to me; the mother and the other two sisters were all right too. To be truthful, Charlene's sister, Tamela, was in my sights. You know even though Charlene knew karate, still she was so gentle and kind to me. Though I was feeling the hots for the sister, I just stayed with Charlene because by this time, the money had stopped with Tammy, and Tammy had to go on, and we were very distant. Another time I went over Charlene's house, her dad gave me the grand tour of the house. In the basement of the house was a room filled with dirt and full of bullets. Get this, he used that area for target practice, and I did not want to become one of his targets. Anyway, this man had guns all over the house, under chairs, behind the sofa, by the windows, etc. This man had guns for days! I was not ready for marriage, but he could call me son! Charlene attended Buchtel High School on the west side of Akron. I would make my way over there, especially, when her parents were gone. I did feel protected and was the man when Charlene's dad was gone. At least I thought so! There were times when I was over to Charlene's house, and the sisters play the lookout part for us, just in case the parents would come home early. We spent as much quality time together in her room as possible. It wasn't the Holiday Inn, but their home worked for the occasions. This was a very cool setup. I had it going on as I must say so myself.

Now it was about nine months had passed and toward the end of 1979. What a year it was. By the end of the nine months, high school would had been a thing of the past, and I would be off to the Air Force and leaving in July of 1980. What a feeling! Anyway, one night, I was over Lynn's house. I was normally over there, late into the evening, and I was friends with her brother too. Anyway, her dad had gone to work. Everyone was tired and headed to bed. Something was a little different that evening in the years that I have lived in that neighborhood, this thing had never happened before. I would have never imagined this happening to me of all people. I was a little fast for my age or let's say a fast learner. Remind you that I was only seventeen years old, and everybody was in bed, and the house was quiet. I was thinking that this is not real, but it was. We were watching the television, Lynn's sister and I. Leanna Jones had a boyfriend named Daniel, but they had their issues. I would see some disagreements between them every now and then. Then I would see Leanna around the house being quiet or upset. She was a pretty healthy and tall for a woman, about 5'9" but thick and well put together. I was always cool with her. One was never to expect anything, not even I. But going back to the late night and the TV was on, I decided to tease with her a little and play around, just being friendly. That's it! However, it was beyond me. The timing must have been right. Anyway, Leanna turned off the big console TV in the carpeted living room with some plastic-type rugs to protect the carpet. Anyway, right before the lights are out, Leanna was messing with her pants and said, "Come on." The tone of her voice was not forceful, but it was not sexy either. Leanna had some type of power over me, or was I too young to understand what was really happening. This was different, and I could not understand this reality. After a short time together, it was all over, so I left her house in amazement, beyond my thoughts, beyond my dreams. So I was home in less than fifteen seconds. What just happened? What did I do? I looked in the mirror, and my eyebrows were raised up in amazement. What did I do? Wow, I was excited but did not feel like I won anything. This was... beyond words.

For real, this experience forever changed me. This was definitely a catalyst to me and the center of my manhood. It was only one-time, but it forever changed me. I think I was in shock. I kept saying that she was twenty-four years old, and I was seventeen years old. It was definitely our little secret and Leanna's family secret. It was her sister

Lynn that I was seeing, and she could have never, never known or to be the wiser. By this time, we had found out that Lynn was pregnant. I just do not understand it. Nevertheless, it happened and happened to me! My mother used to love watching *General Hospital* and *Peyton Place*, the soap operas. My situation was not a soap opera. It was for real! I even made mistakes and sometimes called Lynn "Deanna" or "Charlene." I did have some careless moments!

The one thing that I truly miss when I was growing up and coming into manhood was my father and a father's wisdom (but my father was not that type of father, but somehow, I was a lot like my father). I truly learned things about growing up as a young man the hard way. These girls had me going, and I had thought that I was really doing something. The reality of it, I think not!

My hanging out with Charlene was cool, and I thought I could grow to like her, but Lynn got pregnant, with my help, of course! This really sent me into a tailspin. What in the world was I to do? To think that one could play the game, sleep around, and not get caught. That way of thinking was truly asinine. I was slowly finding out the consequences. The fact remains I really was not thinking. Lynn's mother Gertrude and her father handled that situation for their seventeen-year-old daughter. So my first child was aborted. Just believe you me, abortions on anyone's part are a hard thing to do. Doing this time, I was going through as well as Lynn and her parents. I really did not have anyone to talk to nor did I want my mother to find out. So I suppressed it and coped a little with Lynn. I must say that it brought us a little closer together. Now, I was in the middle of two women and living a double life. Going to school was pretty decent, sort of involved with some of the sporting activities, and of course, we had a school blood drive, and I wanted to give. Being eighteen years old, I had to register to vote. My boys Kim and Philip were all over it. Then I met Lynn's best friend Adrian Garrett. Garrett was her adopted last name, but everyone called her Renee, and that is what I called her, Adrian or Renee. Adrian Renee! Wow! As JJ would say it, "Dyn-o-mite." Adrian was all of that, plus a well put together 120-pound brick house, in some tight, tight, short, short pants. She definitely got my attention. When it was time for Adrian to go home,

I volunteered to walk her home! All I can say is I knew her and we definitely got together. Period. I met Adrian a month earlier. Then later on, around March or April 1980, Lynn was pregnant again. Her father had paid for her to lose the first one. Boy was I sad, but I did not know the impact of my immature decisions and actions of lust. I had only tried to comfort Lynn for the loss of our first child. I guess I had gotten too close. An abortion was not going to happen this time. Plus I was not going to pay for one. Besides, I did not make that kind of money. My hustle was lame, working part-time after school or weekends at McDonalds or borrowing funds from Mom. Also the girls help me here and there. Also joining the Air Force was not coming fast enough, but I knew things or just believe that it would get better. I was too much for my own self. Especially, in the beginning of our getting to know each other, I used to call Adrian "Lynn." This was something that I had to truly work on and get it right to know the right names.

As the school year was moving toward graduation, I had to get through the planning of my prom at Central Hower High School. Now, Adrian was the other woman that had a plan for me to become hers. A best friend's betrayal! I was even trying to get the attention of other family members of Lynn, like that cousin. It was not happening because she was so in love with her cool husband and was unsuccessful and still too young for the most part. My timing was a little off, but I do know the story of betrayal all too well. I was in it (the game) for all that I could achieve. Back with Charlene. We were also planning to attend the prom for Buchtel High School. I somehow manage to keep what I was doing from my family, nor did I want to get busted! For one reason or another, I just did not want them to know or to think shamefully of me. Boy, was I busy. I was living a triple life with a baby on the way and searching for more. I do thank God that it was only one baby. Adrian gave me a scare for being pregnant, but it was a false alarm. Even though I had these other girls, Adrian was the one for me. Since Adrian seemed okay for being the other woman, on the secret, I did not have to rush things along. My part-time job was at the Spaghetti Depot Restaurant at the Quaker Square in Akron. It was jobs like this I did to keep money in my pocket busing tables and stealing tips. Cool! I had women to see, places to be, and a baby on the way. I was looking to join the military. What a pleasant way to escape. That is what I did. I attended the prom with Charlene for Buchtel High School. Things between us were good, so we stayed in touch from time to time. Then I attended the North High School prom with Lynn and our unborn child. Get this, neither of us own a car, and I could not borrow my brother's car, so my other woman Adrian, Lynn's friend, borrows her father's red Plymouth Fury, and we all attended their prom. At times, Lynn had to come to get me for pictures because I was spending too much time with Adrian. I really thought that she knew something was up with Adrian and I, but Lynn never said a word. Neither did I! So at the very end of the prom, we all said our goodbyes to fellow classmates. Afterward my night would get very awkward, for Adrian would have to return her father's car. Therefore, Lynn and I was to be dropped off at our respective homes and at the same time since we were neighbors. So I reached home, called Lynn to say I was tired and was going to bed—yes, I lied. Then I could not wait to call Adrian and talk for the remainder of the night before falling to sleep on and off again while on the phone. This phone thing went on for months. Adrian had my attention. I mean, all of it! I do think often women can just open up a guy's nose. I mean, women, of course, one must be interested, but they do know how to get and keep a guy's attention. I was such the guy, and I was cool about it and all, but I could not wait until I would see her again. Adrian was everything that I was missing from all the others. She was very interesting, and she always asked a question that you would want to impress her upon your answering it. Again, I was very interested, hook, line, and sinker. When she was talking, I would be listening, no matter what I was doing. My nose was wide opened. There were several times I just had to see her to spend time with her. I just had to get to Adrian or over to her house. It did not matter if I had to walk, catch a ride, ride the bus, or ride my bike. I just had to see her! I didn't even have time to think about what was happening to me and all my emotions. Adrian, even on occasion, drove her father's car to pick me up, just so we could be together or just hang out. I did not mind! I wanted everybody to see us together. Or just for the guys to see me with her! I really thought I was the man. I was! Adrian was also going to church. In fact, her mother was one of the church mothers at Shelton's Temple on North Howard Street, and Bruce Hoodah was the pastor. Adrian may have not served God the way she should have based on her knowledge of the Bible and the fear she has of God. In fact, Adrian—no matter what—did not play with God, in no way, shape, or form. She was not ever close to a hypocrite. Even to this day, I can definitely be a witness to that! Just maybe, that would be the bond for us to become tighter and closer to each other. We really connected at all levels in our relationship. As our relationship grew stronger, I do not remember Adrian forcing me to leave her best friend, Lynn. Adrian was not the type of woman to make such a choice for me. She left it all up to me. I don't believe most people would have behaved with such character, but Adrian did just that. She was the type of woman where I had to make that choice and to choose Adrian, and Adrian would not deny me that chance. To me, and because of her commitment to what we had, I had to choose to leave Lynn alone, and no force could have been a part of my decision. Again, it truly had to be my choice because I wanted to push myself to do the right thing, and this was a chance in the right direction to having any type of real relationship with Adrian. So I thought, yes, I also had that doubt of settling down, creeping and sleeping around would still be on the edge of my mind!

Meanwhile, when driving my 1971 Ford LTD (formerly a real police car, with a speedometer of 200 mph and only had front brakes), I typically drove that car very dangerously. On another note, I played cards from time and again with my family and sometimes for money. Boy, did I hate to lose, so I was in line to become an up-and-coming gambler. I did have that feeling because I would not stop nor would I call myself a gambler. For me to always have money, I think not! I had to figure something else out. So I remember back on that day around, October to November 1979, I had got caught for stealing at a Target Department Store—yes, petty theft. For the first time in my young, girls-playing day of my life, I was arrested for petty theft and on my way to the juvenile detention center on Dan Street in Akron,

Ohio. I did not like getting caught. My sister Terri and her friend Robert did not get caught. I had thought that over the years, I had never been caught, so in my own deception, I really thought that I was that good—wrong! Dead wrong! The store detective caught me dead in my tracks. This was bad. He had my pants jacked up from the back, underwear, and all. I was very uncomfortable. Anyway, I had gotten caught, to my disbelief! The store detective only had caught me because I had gone through the wrong doors. Who in the world would steal something, in my case, a portable clock radio, and go through the wrong doors for an escape? Get this, I went through the Fire Escape doors, and the alarm sounded! Yes, I did it and was caught stealing a portable brown clock radio, only to return it for cash! This was a great idea with poor execution! Now, I was at the juvenile detention center on Dan Street, in Akron, Ohio. My older sister Terri and Robert tried to get my mother to get me out of the juvenile detention center, and get this, I would have never guessed this, me being her favorite. She, my mother, said, no. I was stuck. Finally, my family and all finally convince my mother to get me out of that place. My mother told me I ought to be glad that I had good grades. Or should I say that the grades were good enough to get out of that place. Being seventeen does have its advantages, but my lesson was truly learned. I was to never be caught, and I never got caught again for anything. Being good at stealing only made me to get better overall. I even learned how to steal hearts. I did learn that the principle of stealing can apply to more than materialistic things!

Okay, time was winding up and the countdown was happening for me—the Central Hower High school graduation and my leaving to the Air Force. I just had to keep my nose clean and stay on path. I have a pregnant baby momma but no children at that time. Lynn and I have since broken up (the official version), but we stayed cool with each other—just in case. One day, in the March to April time-frame, I was hanging around Lynn's house. We were in the kitchen. Sitting around, they ate a lot of fish and white rice. None for me as I always turned it down. Most of the time, I only ate soul food. My mom was the best cook. Anyway, while we are sitting in the kitchen, even though I was too young to be a father, I was glad that only Lynn was pregnant. What! I thought for a moment. So I said something like "Both of you could have been pregnant at the same time." I stood up, Leanna was leaving, but she turned around, and before I knew it, Leanna, with all the power of her hand, smacked—I mean, *smacked*—me! Why? My mind was blank! Just like that! The right side of my face. It stunned me at first, but in reality and in my reality, it had hurt me, so I was in pain! I was done. Fact is, I had already forgotten our secret—the one-night stand! Not to be funny, but Leanna had smacked our secret right out of my head. My pride was hurt a bit, so I did the next best thing with two women that lived in the house and sisters at that! What was going on? I had not a clue because I did not know. Afterward, every time, I consider to think or thought to imagine that I may have two children on the way or the possibility of it, as fast as that thought came to me in my mind, it never held any water on my brain. That thought was gone but not forgotten. The residue would show up to me on and off. Then I would keep living and moving. Really, it was not the best conversation to have with no one, so it stayed our secret! But why did she smack me? I never figured that piece out.

On the other hand, if I was a single parent in joining the military, it would have definitely caused some obstacles for me. But definitely not the case. Who knows, I may have gotten married to Lynn just to join the military. It was not so and therefore not meant to happen. Now, before leaving Akron, Ohio, I was running all over the town, trying to graduate high school and leave for the military, the United States Air Force. I was thinking I was very grateful that I had only one child on the way; things could have easily gone out of control. I could have easily had three or more children on the way. Boy, was I fortunate. I did escape that multiple baby momma drama. I escaped!

Now, it is June 1980, and to this point enough of hanging out at the malls, eating at Akron's finest restaurants, such as, drive-in movie theatre, Swenson's burgers, Mama Roses Pizza, Parasson's Italian Restaurant, and Churches Chicken; borrowing my brothers' cars; riding the bus; and most importantly, walking all over Akron, Ohio—north side, east side, and west side of town. I had visited my family, cousins, friends, and my ladies. They did not know this from an individual's perspective, but they were, Adrian, Lynn, and Charlene. Even though I had attended a total of two proms, one for Buchtel High School and the other was for North High School. Now, the thought of leaving Akron, Ohio, was very near and dear to me. Of course trouble was not my friend. My graduation was on time and did not come too soon. Now, I have just graduated from EJ Thomas performing arts hall at the University of Akron. No graduation parties for me, so I continued my usual hangouts, but I guess deep down inside me, I was ready to go. I was ready to leave this smelly rubber capital city. I have never flown before, so I was getting excited. Now that I was all trained up with my older brother and was expecting so much of life outside of Akron, Ohio, I was ready for life's challenges and to make my mark. I was ready to face the world but did not know exactly what to expect. I was beginning to realize that some things about life cannot be taught at home, in school, by someone, or at church. I must keep going regardless of the ups and downs in life and taking things from my past and past experiences. I just thought I had to make my own mark and contributions to society from my own viewpoint! That's just cool!

I can say that I did spent a lot of my time on the west side with Charlene and a baby on the way with Lynn, coupled with Adrian on the north side of Akron. Just to admit the truth, I was on the wild side. To say again, I was humbly wild, and for the most part, if a door had opened, then I was there, always keeping my options open! A few times, we even broke up, Adrian and I, over Lynn, but songs like The Floaters' "Float On" or the Shalamar song "Second Time Around" or Marvin Gaye's "Let's Get it On," or "Never Too Much" by Luther Vandross or the Commodores or The O'Jays' "Use Ta Be My Girl." Cool! If you could hold any type of note, the rest was on! I did just that!

Even after graduation, the place to be was in the vicinity or at Buchtel High School, whether it was going to some function or another or knowing someone from there. Buchtel High was still, in fact, the place to be. Not to mention, it was the ideal place to be if you were able to get a girl hookup from Buchtel. The thing was you were doing something cool, even just to say, "I was hanging out at Buchtel," you were doing something. I may have struck out at Buchtel and not to mention, wasting my time, but I too still I had it going on. I was there for a time or two but was only marking time. My time was getting short and shorter. I was getting prepared to leave Akron for the military. The days was coming fast and faster. I was running all over town to see, visit, and be with my ladies. I wanted to spend as much time as possible with them. I did not see my family much and was only home for the most part to get some sleep, bathing, sometimes eat, wash clothes, and set up the next day. I was moving, and the last day in Akron was June 30, 1980. Wow, exciting! My emotions were all over me! I was with Adrian at the Easter's corner store on Glenwood Street and North Howard Street. The last thing I still remember Adrian buying for me was a snickers candy bar that I had promised to payback. Then she had gone with me to the Greyhound Bus Station on the city bus. I was a little excited and disappointed at the same time—yes, full of mixed feelings. The bus ride was good until the bus arrived to downtown Akron. Well, we had just a few more blocks to walk onto the bus terminal located at 631 Broadway Street. We were there with my government bus ticket in hand that I received from the Air Force for my start in the military. So we chilled at the bus terminal for a while, and that short time disappeared as the clock was ticking. An hour felt like only minutes. That is how it goes when you're waiting to leave someone that you care for. Adrian was strong for me and not really expressing her feelings for me, but I knew—I just knew—that she was missing me already and also holding back a tear. She was tough and not expressing much emotions. Well, this was something I just had to do. Grow up! Yup, I had to go and to grow up! I would not have wanted to wonder the infamous "what if." The fact was, I did have an obligation to the United States Air Force and to serve my country. Cool!

Leaving Home

The Greyhound bus driver was making the call to get on board the bus heading toward Cleveland, Ohio. No family, no females. It was just me, and I was a little overtaken emotionally by this by my growing up experience. I was feeling the home blues. What a journey, I was on my way to spend the night, one night in Cleveland, Ohio. I believe I stayed at the Holiday Inn. I sort of thought I was doing something important with my life and have never experience anything of such, but as the time was moving forward, that was a terribly long night in the hotel. So I decided to call Adrian, and we talked for a few hours through the night! You know, I have fallen asleep on the phone a many nights, but this one was different. This time on the next day, I would not get to see Adrian (my girl) or Lynn who was carrying my child. No, not likely, but yes, the Air Force would show me something totally different and a more different approach for growing up!

The next morning, I got up, showered, and got dressed to meet some of the Air Force recruiters and other military personnel to receive our governmental airplane tickets that would take me to San Antonio, Texas, by way of St. Louis, Missouri, that included a layover for a several hours. This was my first time being away from home like this, first time flying, and I did not know a soul. I believe I have received a food voucher to eat at the airport, as well with the airline ticket. Okay, I have arrived at St. Louis airport and did as instructed—to locate the USO office, a place at the airport serving military and veterans. So I hung out, talked with a few people, and played a little pool until the time was over. It's on, and I was searching to find the boarding gate. I could not miss this plane, and at the same time, I was too scared to miss the plane. But I was getting it, pacing myself down the hallways of the airport and looking for every gate number. Here I am, at the gate boarding the plane for the second time and San Antonio, Texas was my next destination. I must admit again I really thought that I was doing something special with my life. Well, that lasted for the moment. From twenty-five to thirty thousand feet in the air, the view was spectacular. It was beautiful! Beautiful! Then we landed! Off the plane and onto baggage claim and again up and down the airport terminal hallways to seek out the USO office the meet the Air Force personnel. People were there from everywhere. I mean, all walks of life, and I was not used to seeing people of sorts. From the early morning of flying, it felt like I had been flying all day long. Now that we were all there, these nice Air Force people escorted us to one of several buses that would take us all to Lackland Air Force Base, San Antonio, Texas. I made it, and by this point, the buses were approaching to enter the gates. Now, it was approximately 9:00 p.m., and I was tired and ready to go to bed. Yeah, right, or so I thought! What had happened to the nice Air Force personnel that I was expecting to show us to our sleeping quarters. Things were supposed to be in order, right, or I was not thinking far enough ahead!

Now, we are off the bus, with luggage in hands, and some of us had bags on our shoulders. The Air Force people that was with us from the airport were gone, and some other guys and gals showed up with their round Smokey-the-Bear type of hats on their head. They were yelling and screaming at us. I do declare I went from being tired to shocked! Shocked! And totally shocked! Now I was confused. Totally! What in the world is going on? These people were screaming, yelling, screaming, and shocking our mind, time and again! They were telling us to put down the bags and luggage, and as soon as we put them down, someone yelled and screamed, "Pick up your luggage and bags." And then back to "Put down your luggage and bags." Then the opposite, the opposite again. This went on for about six to eight, maybe even fifteen minutes, and no, as tempted as I was, I was not going to look at my watch. I was absolutely scared! We were all called *rainbows* because of our civilian clothing. That I had learned later on. And our new names were Slick or Rainbow. Get this, we could only give one response of "Yes, sir" or "Yes, Sergeant" or "Sir, yes, sir." That was it. Or we would get screamed at again! I totally thanked God that I was not in the Army or Marines. Then I would have been doing running or pushups. Maybe even doing kitchen patrol. No way would I take that chance to say anything differently. I was scared in my pants. When I had realized what was going on, all I kept thinking was, "What did I do?" or "What did I get myself into?" My mind was in total disbelief! I was in the military. My mom or dad could not help me out. However, my mind was made up. Do or die. I was in it to win! I was not going back to Akron, Ohio, as a loser or failure. My mind was made up! I just had to make the best of this experience in my life if I wanted to grow up and, more importantly, become a man! Period. And period. If there was ever a time in my life that I was determined, this military experience that I was serving in this Air Force was it. Yes, this was it—do or die! Okay, we were in for the night, and we stayed in the non-air-conditioned MOB (mobile dorms with open bay) or barracks. I believe that we were one of the last flights for the Air Force to utilize these MOB dorms. We had our assigned bunk bed, with white sheets, pillow, and an army green wool blanket and an army green footlocker. That was it! Home! Well, it was home for a short time!

The next day were the haircuts, and on our way, we all rushed to get breakfast (normally called chow or mess), and the military way was to hurry up and wait. Yes, standard procedure. Next, we were on our way to get the clean shave, so we rushed to the barbershop to see the shear heads and all the hair on the floor and in all colors. What an ugly mess. Now, I am eighteen years old in San Antonio, Texas, with a bald head and soon-to-be wearing some homely-looking green uniforms. I had never expected this, yet surprisingly, I got used to it. Quickly! Actually, this experience was not too bad, after all. We marched everywhere and onto this boring-looking warehouse to get fitted for uniforms, issued uniforms that we carried in our issued duffel bag that I was planning to keep forever. Mostly every day, we did the same thing with very little deviation: jumped out of bed at five o'clock in the morning; did physical training (PT); ate breakfast, lunch, and dinner; did training throughout the day; had personnel processing, did mail call, and learned military customs and courtesy, and of course, cleaned up the barracks. By the way, I was one of the squad leaders and responsible for some of the guys. Also I was responsible to march the squad of airmen around the base, overseeing details to completion (duties around the base) for picking up trash, cutting grass, marching exercises, or marching to class and marching back to the barracks.

One day, several squadrons were outside waiting for chow or to get medical shots. Anyway, I was called out of the lineup by my training instructor (TI) Team Chief SSgt. Chad Johnson. This guy was sharp all the way down to his shoes, and he meant business, not a smile in sight. SSgt. Johnson had me to quote the code of ethics that we were forced to learn. I was so on it from the first one down to the last, and I did not miss a beat. I know SSgt. Johnson was so proud of me, even though he would not show it. Even now, I just know he was well pleased. Another day, I think it was right before parade practice, he called me again from the squadron 3723, flight 004, and also known as (get this) the Little Marines. We were bad (as in good) and even in our marching. We had the march and the razzle dazzle march down to a science. We were all of that, yes, Little Marines. But again, I was in front of SSgt. Johnson. I believed that I was either talking or flirting with one of the girls from another squadron on that hot July day in 1980, standing in formation at the command of Parade Rest or At Ease—either way, I had gotten caught. While in his presence, I believed he almost pulled an AF Form 341 from me, also known as a demerit, and too many demerits spelled trouble. So we are all back at the barracks. I had to visit SSgt. Johnson in his office. While I was sure that I was one of the sharp ones, I also had to be disciplined for my actions while in formation. I was demoted and no longer a squad leader. I was now a "latrine queen." Not bad! One might ask, what in the world is a latrine queen. It is a person that is in charge of ensuring that the bathroom is cleaned on a daily basis. Yes, I, yet in charge of a group of guys, to ensure that the bathroom was clean. I really think SSgt. Johnson favored me. Even in the presence of SSgt.

Martinez, the assistant TI, I still did not do any real work. This was a cool experience that was happening to me, and I was enjoying every moment of it.

Get this, on another note, I was the flight (within a squadron) clown and very cool with most of the guys. Besides, I had a lot of power with the guys, being in charge of cleaning toilets, messy sinks, and dirty floors that was dusted, swept, and mop up. Who would want to mess with me? I think the ball was in my court. There is about ten days left before graduation. One night all was well, and we were just about to go to bed. Anyway, I am already smelling myself, from writing letters to and from girls that I have meet at Lackland AFB, Texas, while doing a few of the details. So that night, we all got together. Most of us had decided to sneak out to try to go and visit some of the girls that stayed in the RH&T dormitories (more modern dorms). There was not much action. So back to our barracks, the guy on the lookout saw someone coming. Everyone made a mad dash to take off our clothes and neatly hang them in the dark and play sleep. Everything had to be in order. We all just made it back and into our beds. While I was pretending to sleep, I felt a slight heat from the light that was shining in my face. I did not move a muscle. My eyes did not twitch nor was I sure that I was breathing! Close call for all of us. Oh boy, by the grace of God, we did not get caught. Now, this mental note would be with me during the rest of my basic military training: "No late rendezvous with the fellows to find the girls during my training." Yes, I definitely learned something here. Never again!

After many days of getting up early, yes, five o'clock in the morning before the sunrise, we were running (no stretching), ate breakfast, and had classroom training. After weeks in the basic training, this day was different. It was the day for the obstacle course or field training, and on the same day, we had M-16 training. The obstacle course was a great disappointment. I was expecting the most exhausting time of my life. Especially, after training with my Marine brother who served with the Marines. Definitely, no comparison. I was truly disappointed. But to everyone else, I was in the military and serving with the Air Force. Now, it was (the basic training) almost over, and things seemed to be as normal as could be. I was shining boots, getting uniforms in tiptop condition, sharing stories with the guys, and going over our training notes. The guys were bonding a little, and from time to time, we received base liberty to make calls home. Well, in my time of liberty, I stopped by the mini-base exchange (aka BX or commissary) to pick up a few items and postcards. Then I would call home collect or third-party billing by charging the phone call to some unknown person or business. The telephone companies like Bell South or AT&T did not have all of the security features in the 1980s. The payphones and phone booths were the preferred method of choice. Often times, I remember being in basic training and calling home—that's Akron, Ohio. It was the place I still really called home, and then, I remember speaking to my mother, and from time to time, I would say hello to my brothers and sisters. These calls were actually very short. But most of my real time was spent on the phone speaking to Lynn (my unborn baby's momma) and Adrian, my main girl. I really could not wait to see either one. Yes, I was two, three, and four timing everyone. Girls everywhere and more to come. Whatever! Yet at most times, everyone thought that they were the main one for me. Lynn was pregnant with my child, and Adrian was my main squeeze, and both were waiting on me, and either did not care for the other because of me. I was the man in the middle for both of them. Not sure how I had so much power, being so far away in Texas. Therefore, I was still in the best position. Adrian and Lynn were not talking to each other. They hated each other, but both of them were talking to me and waiting to see me. I was still the man!

Onto the next phase of my life. Basic training for the Air Force had just ended. I made it. Zero demerits. I had never received a writeup. Let's just say, I had never gotten caught but once, with no write-up. And I received a certificate to prove it. I had graduated with everyone else, except for the few guys that were setback, which meant certain portions of the training had to be repeated prior to graduation. And I almost lost it all, and for what? Chasing after some young girls I never found. The next day, we boarded this Greyhound-looking bus, and I was looking for a cute female recruit to sit next to. Not this seat, not this one, nor that seat, the seats were filling up, and wow, suddenly, I looked up, and there she was. This long twelve-hour ride just got better. I don't remember her being a fox (cute and sexy), but she was this little white girl from I believe, Omaha, Nebraska, with a small nice body and medium black hair, which was good enough to get my attention. Still, I cannot remember her name, but maybe something like Jamie, and she was a girl that I would definitely try to know and to be my next conquest. Well, that girl and I just talked. We slept while riding the bus. The road was long and never ending, and of course, in August of 1980, it was definitely hot, very hot! This sun was working and shining our way. What else was I to do on the long bus ride to Kessler AFB, Biloxi, Mississippi? Okay, we were on our first scheduled, this much-needed bus stop in Louisiana. I was not familiar with this place (other than from school the Louisiana purchase taught from my history class), but we all received Air Force's food vouchers for this specific restaurant. Boy, was this the place! The young lady and I were hanging out, then decided to get something to eat, and to this day, I still remember the sweet-smelling biscuits rolls. They were the bomb. Those rolls were just awesome! How can I still remember those rolls, but not that girl's name? I did remember where she was from. I guess it is what it is. I am not saying this to be cold-blooded, but to be truthful. I did enjoy her company on that long ride, and much better to hang out with a young lady versus another dude. Well, we became friends and would see her at the technical school at Keesler AFB where the classroom was co-ed.

Well, the first week of classes were over and being in the military, certain rules had to be followed, such as each dormitory had to clean and inspected. This was weird, but I looked at the duty roster, and there I was, the dorm chief. What in the world was going on? How did I get that position? I did not know, and at the same time, I was not about to complain. I was dorm chief for the next six to seven weeks. I made friends fast. My friends received the easy jobs, such as dusting or washing windows. Then I had this tall fellow to tell me what he was not going to do. I was supposed to be scared stiff because of his reputation. He was from New York. I was from Akron, Ohio, and sort of hoodish myself. So what! I was not scared!

This dude disobeys an order, so I wrote him up and turned it in to the Student Command Post. From that point on, he apologized. We became cool, too cool, and friends it was. The following week, it was time to get ready for inspection, and I wanted to pass. Therefore, I called for a GI Party on a Friday night. The fellow Air Force technical students had no thought of anything to mess up the weekend liberty. Not so! The dude from New York, my buddy, was in-charge of dusting duty, and we cleaned up for about four hours. The command post inspected our dorm and every area. Nevertheless, we passed the first, second, and third one! The fellows had it together, and they did not want another Friday night GI Party. I was good from that point on. What had surprised me was I was leading these guys without having a TI to overshadow me. The guys were really, following my leadership. And for the most part, I kept it about business when I was around the guys. Base liberty is something to enjoy when it happens, taking a break from the dorms, classes, and studying, just to get off base to experience something new and know the areas that were off-limits, some places the military prohibited us from patronizing, end of story. Well, anyway, I was thinking about my girl Adrian in Akron, and I thought or was trying to think that I was getting serious in stepping up our relationship once I see her again. It is definitely true that absence makes the heart grow fonder. So I made it to one of the local jewelry stores. I still somehow thought that I wanted to get married to Adrian. In a very weird way, I was feeling I was falling for her and decided to buy the rings for marriage and to start planning a proposal. So in that moment, Shalamar, the music group, must had been playing the song "For the Lover in You" (aka "This Ring"). It had touched me. I got the rings, and if I did not do it, then I would have never had continued my relationship with Adrian. Wow!

I too really enjoyed my base liberty that time and some of the weekend passes to go off the base. Yes, after the thing, it was not really a relationship that I had shared with the girl from Nebraska. On our first date, we hung out on the town in Biloxi, Mississippi. It was hot, humid, and misty and muggy, and it smelled funny. The air was kind of strange smelling. One Saturday afternoon, we were walking down the street, and a white man was washing his bluish car and noticed us walking hugged up and holding hands. Hey, this was the 1980s, in the Deep South, and let's just say, I am from the North. I was not used to this either, the real South! Well, I just stayed hugged up, and then, the white man spat on the ground. But I stayed hugged up with Jamie. Not a good sign! Okay, I kept going and was not smart enough to go back to the base. Besides, I was in the Air Force. I thought that I was somebody, not to mention a little hotheaded. So then, we were kissing on the beach and playing around. It was getting dark. The air was very misty and smoggy, and then, we heard some people coming. We were quiet, could not see anything, and the fog did not help. That fog reminded me of the time when I was a child and my family lived with the Pages off of West Thornton Street. I had that feeling again, that same feeling when I was a child and thought it to be another creature-like being, but I was too scared to find out. I knew also that I was in the South with a white female, and make no doubt about it, I was black. This was not a good situation to be in, not in the year of 1980. We have come a long way but still not that far in reality! I just knew better! I believed that by being in the Air Force allowed me to get away with dating white women. Still, I had to be extra careful! Not in Mississippi! Anyway, I felt that it was time to go! I had this weird feeling come over me that I cannot explain. It could have been an angel from God. I got out of there. The many times I have looked back over this event in my life, I would now have done it differently! Then, we decided to check into this motel a few blocks away and was not that expensive for that time. One motel night, and it was over. I was alive! I realized that she was not really my type. For some reason, I had remembered her yellow teeth, and yes, I was done! One night together, and this relationship was done! Yes, truly done to the point of avoiding any contact with her! Another weekend pass, and there she was, Miss Kentucky. This girl reminded me of Pam Grier, the actress, with a gold front tooth. She looked good and was cool to be around. Regina from Louisville, Kentucky, was a little older than I, but I was in there. Plus, I had the hookup by knowing a motel close by the base. Regina was my girl for tech school, and I was making plans with Adrian and Lynn when I reached home. I cannot recall how I accomplished so much, being a dorm chief marching formation, inspections, homework from my military technical training, a beer here and there, constantly on the payphone (illegally, that is), and finally, the ladies. I was busy and was learning about the facts of life, without really knowing what was going on, and most importantly, I really did not know what I was doing. However, I was doing something, and in a strange way, I was learning and being molded by these events the more times I kept reflecting back. These stupid mistakes and situations I kept involving myself in was teaching me, but I just did not know it at the time. I cannot explain it, but somehow, I knew God was with me, or at best, I knew that His hand was on me. My mother was a praying mighty woman of God. Having ten children would have that effect on anyone! Yet I remember that I had a young lady, pregnant with my child, and another young lady that I was in lust/love with waiting for me in Akron, Ohio. No one person can have this may coincidences in one's life and yet still live (I kept having flashbacks of my cousin being killed by a woman, how ironic). Still, life goes on. As tech school comes to an end, and yes again, I graduated military technical school for enlisted personnel. Also at this place, I received my first ever college credits. Now, we are all at the command post for our next assignments, and the next day, we were off to the airports and bus stations. Our last night to say our goodbyes in Keesler Air Force Base, Mississippi!

It's now toward the middle of September 1980. I was leaving the sticky, nasty, muggy, smelly, and prejudice poor, poor state of Mississippi. I must admit I had made it a good time. While I would visit there with the hope that it would change, it would never be a place that I would want to live—not because of the people and their mindset, but because of the weather. It was not for me. Get this, you could go outside dry on a sunny hot and humid day, and in less than ten minutes, you are soaking wet from the heated hot sweat of humidity (and not from a sauna or steaming sex). It was not the most comfortable feeling that I experience over and over. I will not miss the weather!

Well, my next assignment from my "dream sheet"—a wishful eight choices of assignments and with the hope to get one—would be my first choice, Wright-Patterson Air Force Base (AFB), Dayton,

Ohio, Area B, Building 640, Air Force Institute of Technology (AFIT), School of Engineering. I was an administration clerk (AFSC: 70210), administration specialist. First order of business was to check in and meet the folks that I would be working with. Donna, Bessie, Capt. Sylvester, TSgt. Steve Norton, and an old Amish guy who worked the video room. I met a host of other people, the dean, and other professors within the School of Engineering. This was looking good. I did not know them, and they did not know me. In their eyes, I was a good guy. But I must admit, I had my own agenda: to go home as much as possible, basketball, girls, and college, and yes, in that order! As I remember my days of living at Wright-Patt, there were three areas: A, B, and C. I worked in Area B, lived in the dormitory, with a cool white roommate named Bill from Peoria, Illinois. A beer here and there, but he was kind of boring, so we did not have much in common, and he already had his own car. Around September 1980 was when I got there in Area C. Next to the Commissary and Base Exchange (BX) were the cleaners, movie theaters, the bowling alley, clubs, recreations centers, and a few places to eat on the base that were owned by the BX. There were even places to give blood, and I continued my giving from high school. I tried always to give my blood to help someone. Also, I played basketball in Areas B and C, and the base hospital and personnel offices were located in Area C, next to the airplanes and military jets. The city called Fairborn, Ohio, was there as soon as you would leave the gates. With all this to do, I often wondered if this was the Air Force military. It was too good to be true. The male dorms and female dorms were separated by the chow hall (for daily meals). I could not believe it. The girl's dorms were right here. What! I learned rather quickly that the uniform was like a magnet, yes, magnet to pick up girls, chicks, women! What! And I thought that I was doing something as a player with girls before joining the military. This was one crazy ride! I was... Girls... Words from my mouth were lost quite often! And I was in the military, serving my country. This was too good to be true. I learned how to rap (talk to women quite smoothly). My game was on, and I should have not been trusted by anyone who wanted a real relationship. By the way, I was nowhere close to faithful to my ladies in Akron, Ohio, or to anyone! My brain was not wired to think like that! Really, I did not know what the word *faithful* meant, and no time to look it up in the dictionary. Again, my brain was not wired to think like that! This place at the base was a man's playground—*my playground*—and no car necessary. However, I started to get to know Bill (my roommate), and he did have a car. I rode the military base transportation to get around and to go to work. This was an awesome setup!

Yes, Wright-Patterson AFB was my first choice for a duty station, so I could be close to home, family, and of course, my ladies. With a baby on the way, I was beginning to become more excited at the date, as Lynn's delivery date came closer. It was also home of the Wright Brothers and music groups featuring Midnight Star, Ohio Players, Zapp with Roger Troutman, and many other local groups that played or performed at the NCO club. I was not there one month before I was practicing some martial arts in my dorm room, something I picked up here and there for just in case situations. Anyway, I had this stick (nice and solid and about two inches in diameter) and that I was using to do my usual routine. As I was twirling it in the air, I blinked, and before I could change the motion or stop it, the end of the stick connected to my top left front tooth. And that was all she wrote. My front tooth snapped and popped, and the damage was done. The pain shot in my mouth like never before. I called the dental clinic, and no one would be available until Monday. It was only Saturday. I could not believe it. I just broke my front tooth. I was in terrible pain. It was awful, just awful! I could not sleep well. I kept looking in the mirror, but it was sensitive to the touch. I was eating very gingerly and only light, soft food. By Sunday morning, it was difficult, but I managed to brush most of my teeth and got dressed. I made it to the chow hall and pretty much stayed in my room. I was waiting for Monday to get here. By Sunday night, I was good as long as nothing touched my tooth, but when something touched it, like food or my tongue, it hurt me very badly. Just bad! On Monday morning, I got dressed and took a base taxi to the Air Force dental clinic. I could not wait to get there and called off work due to sick call. I would be there all day; the Air Force dentist did an emergency surgery on me. I was the first one there in the chair, and they went to work. After that tooth got out, they were able to make me a temporary bridge, so it would not be so noticeable. These guys were good! I remember one of the dentist's name. It was Dr. Benedetti. He was young and enthusiastic. I was glad to have him work on my teeth. That dentist told me, after it was said and done, that many procedures would have to take place, and it would take almost two years to complete everything. I just know at that time that I would be in good hands. I had a problem staying numb and had to get fifteen to eighteen dental carpule shots of Novocain per visit and was noted in my charts. My mouth would not stay numb. The dentists kept talking amongst themselves about me and then told me that I would be in some medical journals for teaching. I was a first and a special case. I was definitely appreciative, wowed too!

Time was moving on, back and forth, on most weekends at the club or the movies and meeting new friends. Now, going to the gyms was another highlight. Get this, there were three base gyms on the base, one in each area (area B and two in area C). During the week and most weekends, I was at the gym playing my favorite sport—basketball. Even though I played a little baseball in high school, the dream took off, but my interest in baseball faded fast because in the 1978 season, it stayed on my mind that we had never won a game. On the dream side of things, I would have probably had been a really good baseball player. Basketball was my game, and I was totally inspiring to get better... So one day at work, I met this airman at Building 641. He was in the mailroom sorting the mail. We were both admin clerks in different buildings. Anyway, he was cool, and we were talking, and the common thing to ask people in the military was "Where are you from?" It was on. Steve said Cleveland, Ohio, in a little town called Oberlin, Ohio. I then told him that I was from Akron, Ohio. We started to hang out and had most things in common, work, girls, basketball, and Ohio. In a short time, we became friends and eventually best friends. Steve was a bit bigger. We were about the same height, but he was a little thicker with fat cheeks. From playing basketball every day for lunch, while at work, we were together. It was the perfect setup. We were very competitive. We played a lot of one-on-one basketball. Steve had some very good handles; he could really dribble that basketball. I dribble the basketball okay, but Steve was good, and I had a better shot. Hanging out, going out, chasing girls, and of course, playing basketball all of the time drew us closer together. From time to time, I was able to use Bill's car. Boy did this come in handy.

Now, while doing all these things at the base, room and board, three meals at the chow hall, plus midnight chow were all included. This gave me the opportunity to send money home to my mother from time to time. Plus, we both were saving money. With months being away from home, we both were really feeling that we missed home. Yes, we both were homesick! It was around December 1980. I did not know at the time, but Steve showed up with a 1985 white Cordoba. I don't remember what he paid for it. But, Ohio, here we come, and this was a smooth-riding car on the luxury side. We were on our way to Ohio, just in time for Christmas and New Year's, and my nineteenth birthday was right around the corner on the fourth of January. This was a great experience. I was a man! Steve could see his family, and I could see my family, along with my girlfriends, and one had a baby on the way. It was good to be back home for my two weeks of leave from the Air Force. By the time we made to Akron, and Steve went on to Oberlin and also a college town to visit his family, I was excited. My baby was here born on December 10. This was my baby boy, and he was definitely beautiful to me, with all this fine straight hair and light skinned. This was my first and only baby boy, and I would never forget what he looked like at my first sight of him! I was hovering all over him (Michael Jones, aka Big Mike) and would not let him out of my sight. I was at Lynn's house, right behind my mother's house at 117 W. Tallmadge Avenue. It was great to visit the family and seeing my mom with that proud look on her face. I could not get all of her attention because she had ten children in all, but I felt that day that I made her proud. Or I reminded her of my father. I was always teased about that. Mom and I were very close (and if she had a favorite child…).

I had to see my baby! I was over the fence and there all the time to see my baby boy! This was so exciting for me. I told everyone that I had a baby boy. It was lucky for me that I did not mention this to my recruiter that I had a child on the way. It may have prevented me from joining the Air Force. Believe you me, I did not say a word, and I had planned to add him to my personal records. If and when the question did arise, my ready answer would have been "I did not know." I did not have a problem to add my son to my records. My son was my baby! Sometimes, I felt like my little baby was that chess piece to get me back with Lynn. I was beginning to feel sort of trapped, and I knew that I would not respond well under that type of pressure that was presented before me. And right before I left for the military, Lynn's mother has put out there that we were going to get married. What? Married? Faithful? One woman? One wife? Really, I did not know what words I could say to make any of that make sense. Really, I did not have a clue. Being a father was more than I could bear, but I really tried to be a good father. So I brought Big Mike everything, the best of everything. For a time, it made me feel good or made me feel like a father. I wanted to be a good father! I was definitely an absent father, most of the time. This part hurts. I truly loved my son, but that was it! I did not know how to let go of where I was to do the right thing. The days were approaching fast, and my time was getting short, and before long, I was to be back on the military base in Dayton, Ohio. I had to still make my rounds, on the city bus, in Akron. Whether downtown on South Main Street, Chapel Hill Mall, or Rolling Acres Mall, I found the time to hang out. Plus just in case someone or anyone new may come along, I would be there to get those digits and start another long-distance relationship and doing those illegal long-distance phone calls and charge it to someone else. I did this for a really long while, while staying in the military. Get this, many people in the service did the same thing.

I must not forget that my time was short in Akron as I was on a two-week leave from the Air Force, and I remembered I had no car. It was always the city bus, walk, borrow my brother's car (plus I had to add gas to it), or I would ride with Adrian in her dad's red 1979 Plymouth Fury. Red was not my color, but eventually, I got used to it. I had to get around and most definitely spend quality time with my main squeeze. She was kind of excitedly hot, wearing those hot, hot short shorts in the summertime and from time to time! I must admit, she had my attention and all for the wrong reasons. My mind was not in the right place when I was around her or in her presence. Let say, there was always chemistry in our midst! She would be the last to admit it, but Adrian was moonstruck and was falling in love with me. Her adopted parents (uncle and aunt) were elderly, but her mother was the sweetest churchgoing lady I knew. She never talked much but always would know what was going on. That lady could cook some greens and peach cobbler. Those were some of my favorite dishes. Anyway, I was back and forth between home, Lynn's house, or I would sometimes walk to Adrian's house. It was only ten to twelve minutes away to get to 380 Bailey Court, just off of North Howard Avenue, one of the steepest roads in Akron and a real bear in the wintertime, and this was that time, but the big snow did not arrive yet. North Howard Avenue was very popular at that time for hookers and pimps and the Tropicana Club at the other end. I had been there a time or two, but it was not my kind of place. The crowd was older, and I did not want more than I could handle. This area brings back memories of those days.

About halfway down from St. Thomas Hospital, there was the little corner store called Easter's in the middle of the street, right next the little white-bricked church and pastored by Mother Story that my mother and us used to attend. I guess I was starting to reminisce and did not want to forget these things that I had experienced from home. I did not want to forget where I came from. No one told me. However, I was realizing that my life would eventually be somewhere else. All of these thoughts were in my head while I was walking to Adrian's house on Bailey Court to see my girl. I noticed that I was not the same. My true innocents of high school were gone, and I was on my own to make my own choices, my own decisions. I had a brand-new baby, and I am with another woman. I loved my son at first sight, but I did not have an example. I did not know how to be a real father, so I ran and did not know that I was running! Who am I? Who was I? Who? What was I doing? The right thing for me to do was not in the plan or my plans. My raging hormones of testosterone chose my bodily desires to dictate my life and my paths. I cannot explain this because I was in it to win. Right? No. I was only winning and desiring the things to please my flesh. Every thought was to please my flesh. I did not know how I got here. The truth of the matter was I did not know how to get out! Girls, women, or just them were like a drug, and I was really addicted. Now I have arrived to Adrian's house. I had just thought about it. Seeing her could not have helped me, but it made me more of being out of my mind. I was not crazy, nor was it an imagination, but I was truly addicted, and it was not for love! From time to time, we would hear the songs on the radio, "You and Me (Just Us Two)" by Rockie Robbins or "Sitting in the Park" by Billy Stewart and not to mention "Reunited" by Peaches and Herb. To be honest, I would often sing that song, but my mind wandered off to Deanna back when I was seventeen years old. I just could not help myself! I was really trying to see Deanna on this trip too but could not get that opportunity available to me! I was really trying to get in touch with her. Somehow, I was missing her, Deanna, too. Now, my head got bigger and was beginning to become more conceited. It's true. I thought that I was somebody, at least in my mind. Well, being handsome, my brown skin, and bowlegs were also making me more attractive. I had a tooth being repaired and replaced, and it was working and barely noticeable. At least that was what the ladies were telling me all the time! People always complimented me on my bowlegs. I did show them off every chance I got! Or at times, I just had that walk! I was happening! It was happening! My conceited self in some weird way gave me confidence. I thought that I was all that, or I deserved the best. Not only could I get girls, I could have girls and take my pick. I had such a confidence and boldness, I thought that my game was on, so I went from average ladies to beautiful ones. In all honesty, it took me a minute to get there. So average to nice, I was doing good, and the Air Force uniform that I was in was an enabler. The uniform helped my confidence, my game, and my rap became better polished. The words just flowed from my lips to their ears!

Now, my leave was closing fast. My birthday happened that day. Then I celebrated my nineteenth birthday between my new baby boy, Lynn, and Adrian. Steve was on his way to pick me up to be headed back to the base at Wright-Patterson AFB, in Fairborn,

Ohio. Back to the barracks it was. I said my goodbyes, and it became touching. I really didn't want to leave. But I knew that I or we had to get back to the base. I was too early in my Air Force military career to go absent without leave (AWOL). That was not about to happen. Anyway, Steve and I were sharing stories about spending time at home with our family and friends. It was an exciting conversation all the way back to Dayton (that was the major city) for the next two hundred miles we share and shared. These conversations were drawing us closer on the way to become best friends. The fact was we were just up to no good with the ladies. All of them!

Shortly, after returning to the base from Ohio, we heard that it was time for the recruitment of the 2750th Air Base Wing, WPAFB, Basketball Teams. Our team name (the one we tried out for) was Air Force Institute of Technology (aka AFIT Basketball Team), and yes, both of us made the team in 1981. And by the end of the base basketball season—I don't believe it, I just can't believe it—we took first place with the score of 43–41. Our team had all the right pieces: David Means (awesome guard), Eddie Wright (center), Claude Jones (forward), Steve (guard), the other guys, and myself (guard). We took first place with trophies. I did manage to get a copy of the base newspaper with our team picture, which will always be my keepsake! Boy, oh boy, did we get noticed. We had girls, and they were coming for the both of us. Since I arrived to the base before Steve, I had a roommate from Peoria, Illinois, and Bill was still cool. He even answered the hallway payphone for me, lies included. Now, I had roommate and loyalty. He gave me plenty of privacy. He left the room as needed and for longer periods of time. Bill became my first and best roommate! I enjoyed every moment while they were lasting, sneaking in the ladies and not getting caught. I did not intend to get a court-martial, all bases covered. We were definitely the boys from Ohio. Things were moving faster and faster! Life was happening! We were own our own, and there were no parents to get permission from. We were grown men! Wow! Something else happened that was exciting and terribly bad at the same time. Our President Ronald Reagan... Since I was in the military, he was the commander-in-chief. It was all over the news. Supposedly, John Hinckley had shot him to impress actress

Jodie Foster. I had thought that Jodie Foster was cute as a button, but to murder to get her attention was not how I would operate to pick up a lady. Not my style, but it was a highlight in my life that was worth remembering! I was glad that he lived and kept his saying, "Win one for the Gipper," the old football story. I still remember that saying!

After the championship game was over, things were getting back too normal—work schedules, lunch, basketball, appointments, attending some military classes, commander's call, where all the units would meet in a large space to listen to what that commander would say. Then after about an hour, we were back at work from Building 125 (Civil Engineering School or CE). This was also the headquarters building for AFIT Airman Steve Witherspoon, who was at the School of Systems and Logistics, and I was at the School of Engineering Building 640. The three buildings made up AFIT to train young officers toward graduate degrees to work for the Air Force (owe the Air Force time, in lieu of the training received) all over the world. Now I was there at AFIT. I was truly amazed in my mind, where there were new, bright, and smart world leaders. There were even some foreign exchange officers there as well. Some days for duty, we wore our blue uniforms with or without a tie and the blue (McDonald's-type hat) flight cap, and on other days, we wore our fatigues uniform, the ones of cotton and plain green and a green base-ball cap. At times, these young officers from ROTC or army schools would call me the "sir" word. That was not allowed, so I would have to teach them that they were no longer in ROTC and that they were the "sirs" in the military. Sometimes, it was quite humorous! There was a daily mail run or two, and the weather did not stop the mail to be made at Building 125 to pick up the mail and bring it back to my building. We had always figured it out regardless of the weather. The same held true for Amn. Steve or Steve. We distributed the mail to the offices and the several hundreds of officer's mailboxes (referred to as students). We had several PhD professors and, of course, the dean Dr. J. Przemieniecki. He was a cool dude and always sharp as a tack!

I was in the main admin shop for Building 640. We did every-thing for the students. In the office was Ms. Bessie Lark (secretary, and later changed last name to Farley), Donna Perdue, Pam Blalock, and another lady Christy that handled the course registration for classes, and they worked with the professors. There was Capt. Sylvester. He was an older Air Force captain with all white hair, not much for arguments, easygoing, and a dirty old man. I had no respect for him. Then there was the NCO Steve Norton. He was a nerdy, cool white guy and down to earth. We had an Amish-like guy, Willie, with a long salt-and-pepper beard, suspenders, and steel-toed shoes who ran the audio vision room, and I was the administration specialist 70230B, also known as the admin clerk. I did everything else to include the day-to-day admin business and interaction with the students. I only went to the NCO or the captain if I had an issue that I could not resolve. I remember doing this time in 1981. We only have typewriters, Selectric IIs. I also got to drive the Air Force's new 1981 twelve-to-fifteen passenger van. Once I pass the military driver's exam, I would receive my military driver's license. I could not believe that I was driving a new vehicle. I was from the hood in so many ways and was able to get the keys to a new vehicle. It was a little moving for me, and I did think in my mind that I was moving up in the world. However, I was not getting any chicks in that vehicle. Also I used it on many occasions to go to my dental appointments. As soon as I healed, I was onto the next surgery and partial. That military van was right on time. It was new, good to drive, and that was it. I had a license but no car. Boy, did I have a few plans up my sleeves. The days seemed to go pretty fast, by being active at work, playing basketball at noontime, and lunch. Then I was back home or back to the barracks. Once there, sometimes I would stop by the base exchange (BX) to pick up a few items, personal, electronics, clothes, shoes, or whatever, and a few snacks. Then I rushed to change clothes, hanging up my uniform, and threw on some cool clothes. I sped through the barracks to the mess hall (or chow hall or just chow), trying to be first in line for the fresher food. We had good cooks and folks to clean up after us. It was three meals a day, plus midnight chow up until 1:00 a.m., strictly carryout. Tips were not allowed; however, it was not free either. The funds were deducted right from our checks every two weeks, the first and fifteenth, which were our monthly military pay dates. This was a good deal, and I was able to keep saving like this. Plus, I had to go to the stores, and sometimes the malls to pick up some clothes for going out on the base on Fridays, Saturdays, and sometimes on Sundays. Most of the time, I would bring some things from home, or I did some shopping while at home and brought the new clothes with me. Often times, I would check in with my mother before going out since we remained close since my childhood. Yes, I was still a momma's boy. Then I would call Lynn to check on my son and see how things were going. Last but not least, this would be my third or fourth time throughout the day. Mostly definitely, I would talk with Adrian again and even late at night. In the barracks, we all had to share the hallway phone. Yup, when the phone rung, the closest person would pick up the phone and knock on the room door, sometimes waking you or interrupting you, whatever the case. If you had company, then it would always be a friend or my mother on the line, not actually, but that is the excuse we used. Or you were not here! This worked most of the time.

Steve would show up, and we would hang out to see what we would do or get into. In Fairborn, Ohio, there was not much to do. If it did not happen on the base, then it was not going to happen. If we didn't walk, then Steve would drive us over to the dance at the recreation (rec center) or the NCO club. We were not allowed at the Officer's Club (O-Club) unless you were invited, and that was a slim chance. It really didn't matter. The O-Club talk of the town was boring, and most of the officer's wives were too… I am not trying to be mean, but they were "through." Let's say that they were ugly and not pleasant to be around. Snotty, they were, and nose in the air! All of the happenings, fun, better music, and yes, the pretty young things (PYT) were definitely on the enlisted side of things. I always tried to be right there at the club until closing. Now, folks were getting to know us, and we started to get to know the other guys. Things were going well!

Months have gone by. We are hanging out, drinks here and there, and Steve sometimes smoked a cigar every now and again. We are just doing the same things, calling home, working, clubbing, and riding around. Some weekends we would ride to Dayton to see what was up.

Even at the mall in Dayton at the Salem Mall, Dayton, did have some beautiful ladies but a little stuck-up. Then one weekend at the NCO Club, we got word of the parties at Wright State University (WSU), so Steve and I went there to the parties to see what was happening. They were partying, and we went a few times, but I guess because they were a little older, Steve and I didn't fit in. So back to the base we go! Work was cool, but that weekend itch always gave us that spark to look forward to the night at the club. I don't know what it was, except for summertime! But we finally met some new arriving female (military type) that were on the base and at the club. I was not supposed to be looking anyway because my main girl Adrian was in Ohio, waiting for me. I had her ring for marriage, and I was trying (well, not really but to have a stronger love), but I did care for her. To be truthful, this 5'9" slender honey caught my eye. She was really pleasant to look at, with her medium-short hair and brown eyes. And wow! I had her attention. Miss New York was in the house! Emila! Slim goody! We hung out for a while. Then Steve met this other shorty, Crystal or something like that. Steve was smitten, and so was I! We were just being men trying to find some honeys. This is where we really started to learn about adulthood relationships. Now we are working, calling each other across the base, smiling, grins, movies, fun, bowling, riding around, or should I say cruising… Get this, Emila and Crystal are roommates. I could not plan something like this. However, this was cool and convenient. At this time, Steve was the only one with the car, but we were jamming all the time, playing the hits for the ladies! I was always trying to sing my whole life and would catch a few good notes at times! We had to bring something to hang around these ladies. In those days, you had to have game or rap to speak for myself. I was getting better and better. I was pretty good as selling false dreams about becoming a doctor. That worked every time! Eventually, I would get started at some point in my life and strive to become a doctor for real. Nevertheless, we were on our way to the girls to sort of hang out or something like that. In less than two months, we were staying most of the night in the same room with the roommates that we met at the club. We have to leave before morning, just in case there was a surprise dorm inspection or an unannounced fire drill (not many of those).

With nights like this or that, many times, if I had missed Adrian's call, I needed some good explanations. Boy, was I creative with stories of oversleeping, too much to drink (that was the furthest from the truth, I was not a big drinker, anyway), didn't hear the phone, or they never knocked on my door, or my roommate would stand up for me (like he forgot to tell me), or something along those lines. This excuse kept everything honest—making multiple trips to the hospital on different occasions for nosebleeds. Then once my nosebleed would slow down, they would pack my nose with gauze and send me back to the barracks. This truth made my other lies seem true. I never ran out of excuses. I thought that I was just that good. I still was a smooth talker. My mother always told me that I could talk the ginger out of the gingerbread man. Well, I took that as encouragement that I was good. Well!

While Steve and I were never roommates, we did share another room a few times in the girl's dormitory. At first, there were the visits in the day room. It was a common area for mainly the guys to watch TV, talk, or play games (i.e., ping-pong, shoot pool, board games, or darts). But the boys and girls meet there or outside, and we sort of followed the curfew rules for the girl's dormitory for the most part. We met some of the other military girls at the dorms and hung out until the night came. Maybe the girls were showing us off a little I don't really know. Then we snuck into their room, and the only privacy were the sheets and covers. It was working, the time that we all were spending together seeming becoming relationships, at least for a while, and we would leave in the early morning hours to go to work or to do something for that weekend, like movies or a plan for going to the club. Normally, playing basketball was it or washing Steve's car or running errands, following up on other females. Now, time seems to be going in the right direction. Things were good for Steve, the ladies, and myself! We were definitely in the grove of things. We had our routine down and cool with everyone around the base. Definitely had it going on! My head was getting bigger, my confidence getting stronger, and I was on that road of conceit. I really thought a lot of myself as I got older.

So many moving parts to life. It was always interesting. Did I say interesting? Really, it was just that! Summer came so fast, and school was out. It was here before I knew it. Work was good and getting better. Well, one day at work, this young captain had an issue with his mailbox, and he did not like my response and called me "son," but all I heard was "boy." It kind of had that tone, and I was offended. So I had reported it to Capt. Sylvester, the officer in charge. By the end of it, he, the young captain, had apologized, and from that point on, I did not see him much but did not trust him and was careful in all my dealings with him. It was all good after that little incident. On the other hand, a day or two later, we had some summer hires come in to work at the three buildings. They were high school, juniors, and seniors! They were nice. About four summer hires worked at the main building 125, one female summer hire that worked at Steve's building 641, and one at my building 640. I remember her name being Nadine. She was thin and average looking and with braces. She was about sixteen or seventeen. I tried several times with no success. Nadine was a good girl. One fact for sure, I was already thinking of my marriage to Adrian and was most indeed not going to wait until she would be eighteen years old. We were just friends. I was so glad that Nadine was quiet and stayed to herself. I could not afford getting in trouble for trying to mess around with her. The ones that caught our eyes were working at the main headquarters building 125. We made extra trips over there for the mail pickups. Steve introduced himself to one of them as being interested, and of course, I was interested in two of them. So we made our acquaintances and talked a little. I was able to get the number for the thin one, just as fine as her brown-skinned completion could be. They all were from Dayton, Ohio, and commuted to the base to work. They were impressed that we were in the military, and we were impressed that they were females. It so happened that one day at my office… I remember Smitty or, like most folks, they called him Mr. Smith. He was a serious older gentleman but cool. He was black, tall, and big and heavy, but not fat. He probably played some sports too. Well, he would stop by our office to make military deliveries, paper, books, etc. Anyway, the conversation came up that I was getting married. Smitty uttered these words that I would keep with me for the rest of my life. It went like this: "Why buy the cow when you can get the milk for free." At that time, I must admit I did not know the true meaning of that saying. That was one of those live and learn kind of things. Those words uttered by Mr. Smith, I would always remember it! It was during this time we were introduced to the computers and the dot matrix printers and the DOS operating system, with the big (huge) floppy disks. This is when I first started to use computers. This was pretty neat. I learned how to type a little in school and gotten better to build up my speed in technical training school with the Air Force, and then I was on my way. I took a liking to computers and wanted to know everything possible about them. I even managed to go to the computer room in my building. They were using key-punched cards to talk with the big computer machines. The floors were high on a platform, with a lot of cables underneath, and I do remember the room was always cool. So that the machines would not overheat and stop working. I was definitely in the beginning of the computer ages. I vaguely remember the startup of the e-mails discovered by some MIT guy name Ray Tomlinson. I was part of some awesome times, and I do remember it and to never be forgotten!

Anyway, back to Evette. I must say that she was cool and confident. I must also admit that she thought that she was it. The way she walked, being bowlegged and all did get my attention. In less than two weeks, things were beginning to take shape. Steve was working it out with his honey, and Evette was my other girl to be. One day after work, Steve worked it out to take the two girls' home. They were both seniors and in high school. I stopped by Steve's office, so we could all leave, and when Evette and I walked in his office, the lights were off, and they were behind the copier. Well, I can say that we probably stopped something, in the middle of it, because their clothes were still on, but almost off. So we took them home! It became more exciting to go to work. Again, that summer hire in my office named Nadine. She was okay and kind of plain, too plain. Really did not give me the time of day, just general conversation. I guess that my reputation was getting ahead of me.

One Friday night in probably early July, I borrowed Bill's (my roommate) car to pick up Evette for a date. I would take her to the club and stop by my dorm. Of course, my roommate Bill knew that he had to not be there. Bill gave me much respect, and we got along just fine. No issues with Bill whatsoever. He didn't even really care. Plus I gave him beer every so often or put gas in the tank! This was a good setup! After a few hours, Evette had to be home. She was doing her last year of school. We were together for maybe three weeks, maybe four weeks, because I did meet her sister LuAnn. She was nice too but quiet. We, Evette and I, had a few weekends like this, and that was it. I ran into Emila outside my dorm, as we were leaving and said our hellos. She was still my girl. So Emila was with Crystal, and all seemed to go well, or so I thought. After they were gone and out of sight, things begun to fall apart as fast as it started. I had learned very quickly that Evette was jealous. Jealous with a capital *J*. It was over. Us, it was over, and Evette had nothing else to say to me, except "Take me home!" The night was quiet. The ride from WPAFB in Fairborn to Dayton seemed like it took forever. We were doing good and hitting it off just fine, but I only had one chance to mess this up, and I did!

Anyway, during that same time while back at work, I did the mail run to Building 125 and decided to meet the other summer hire, Lorraine Huntsman. By meeting her, I meant to get her number if possible and to find out more about her. She was also cool and like The Commodores's declaration in the song "She's a Brick House." Lorraine was every version of that song. However, Lorraine was respectable and very decent in how she carried herself. Most of these females were respectable, which was a part of who I was and part of my attraction. If my memory serves me right, she was a young lady, working her last summer job and doing the last year of high school. Evette's jealousy did not last with me here. She was totally done with me. So I went ahead and decided to get to know Lorraine better and to meet Lorraine's parents. They fell in love with me at first glance. Maybe because I was in the military. Wow! I could do no wrong. I was in just like that. I ate with them, did some type of cookout, and played with the siblings. She was really taken by me; her mindset was just perfect and smart too. If I was not so caught up with trying to be somebody with the ladies, we could have gotten very serious. I was glad that they all really accepted me. They were a really nice family and fun-loving. I had a really good time with Lorraine. However, I was about to get engaged to my girl in Akron. I was still trying to figure that part out, plus a new baby boy. I had to find a way to let that come out. Anyway, I was in no rush to tell my whole history. So I decide to roll with the good times. I decided not to say anything, and it worked!

With my roommate's car, one night, while leaving Lorraine's house, it was around midnight in Dayton, Ohio, on Salem Avenue. It so happened that Evette did not live too far from Lorraine, and other than the work at the base for the summer, they did not know each other. Also good for me!

So I tried once again to see if I can patch things up with Evette. I called Evette's home number from the gas station. It was late, parents were asleep, she did not want to talk with me at all, and she had nothing to say to me. She was done with me. So I managed to get LuAnn's attention to see if she would speak to her sister on my behalf. I was trying everything to win her back, even with her jealousy. It was nice being with her. LuAnn and I talked for a while and asked me to stop by the house so she can see what she could do so I could see Evette. So I drove over and had to keep very quiet. The parents and everyone else was sleeping, even Evette. In that house, no one was awake, except LuAnn and myself. We were really trying to figure something out. She was helping me or trying to help me before I had to leave. Nothing, absolutely nothing, was working. I could not come up with anything. Now, this situation became a bad ideal. It got later, and LuAnn was in her long cotton night gown. I started to come on to her out of nowhere, kissing this and that, on the dining room floor… How could this be? She kept telling me to be quiet and not to wake up her father because he was mean or something like that. So I kept as quiet as possible! This was not my original plan or intention. I could not had planned this any other way, except I was there… The house was dark and quiet. Then it happened. Afterward, LuAnn rushed me out of the house before her mean father would wake up. I was gone and on my way back to the base. What was I to do? Sisters and I, intimate again…in Akron and now Dayton? Twice! I thought that I should have went straight home after I had left Lorraine's house, but I had to be greedy to get back with Evette. Neither time did I plan this! Confused, and really confused—yes, I was at a loss! But I was there! Now, no way could I have a chance with Evette ever. It was officially over for the three of us. More secrets sisters cannot tell their sister about me. And there was a potential bigger problem right before me, in my thoughts after the fact. Was she pregnant? It was one time, but did LuAnn get pregnant? What was I doing? My plan was to be a future doctor. This episode in my life threw me a curve ball! I was truly off-balance with my life and the decisions that I made, with the right intentions at the wrong time and place. I should have went back to the dorms at the base. Possibly another baby on the way and a fiancée?

Now, I have to plan time and phone time with all of these women. I was just one man!

With Emila fading into the background, Steve and I decided to get to the NCO club at the base, and we went without our girlfriends that were roommates. It was good to have a little breather. Things were going really well, and it was good for Steve and I to be hanging out again with drinks in our hands. I was a fan of the Singapore Sling drink. It was kind of sweet and just right for me. So we decided to split up and make our rounds around the club to get a feel of what was happening or to see if there were any new honeys. This girl was at the bar to get a drink. I noticed her, and she noticed me. I had caught her eye. I could not take my eyes off her. She was one of the most beautiful women that I have ever seen in person, at the base, in Dayton, that I have had the pleasure of meeting. She could have passed for the lookalike of Beverly Ann Johnson of the 1974 *Vogue Magazine*. And I caught her eye. I was not dreaming. What was I going to do? I could no way in God's green earth say no. I was not going to do that. She was beautiful, nice, soft, kind, pleasant, and mysterious. There was something very mysterious about her. However, I was not going to take me eyes off her. After she got her drink from the bar, she went back to her table, and yes, I followed her. Plus I wanted to dance with her. She told me her name and introduced me to her light-skinned sister Jo, who was also in the Air Force, but she did not stay in the dorms. Also not my type, cool. She lived with her mom in Middletown, Ohio, and drove back and forth to the base for duty. Jo Jackson was with this other guy named Eddie Kearse, also in the Air Force. I believe that they worked together too. Now, getting back to Lynette Jackson. This slender-build and just over and above skinny, nicely built, and long hair, with a pretty light-brown complexion was just my style! I was able to get one slow dance with her and off the "Just to Be Close to You" song by The Commadores." Plus, I sang a few parts of it to impress her, but I really just wanted to touch her. I was glad that Steve and I went out without the roommate girls. I struck it big, may even be my best. The more we talked, the more I was infatuated. I liked her at our first meet! She was a little quiet, so I kept talking and did manage to get her home number. It was that time, and the club was closing. So I introduced them to Steve and walked them and talked to Lynette on the way to the car. Steve and I left and made it to the girl's dorm. This was a strange evening. All seemed to go well after the club, but something was off. The dorms were in walking distance to the club. Was this too close to home? Was I busted by Emila? I really did not pay close attention to what my head was telling me. I should have followed my first thought. But no! So we were there at the girls dorm room until the early hours of the next morning, and Steve would sometimes just stay the entire night until 8:00 a.m. or 9:00 a.m. He was a little bolder than I. It was too risky for my blood. So I left but not without feeling pain. I thought, was I that good? Yes or no? I don't know! I do know that I was in pain, real pain. I could barely put my shirt back on. My back was so scratched up, raw, and bleeding a little too. Was she, Emila, really enjoying my company and our time in the night together, or was it something else? Looking and thinking back over everything, I guess I got over easy. She could have killed me or if I had a car, flatten the tires. Well, I probably got over easy since we both were on the young side. Regardless, I was done with her and cut my loss. Deep in my heart, I truly believe that I got secretly busted from hanging out with Lynette at the NCO club. Emila had to go! Me thinking that I was a ladies' man by this time, I picked up the nickname at the base of Don Juan. My life was like a mini-version of the *Playboy* mansion. Somehow, I never got into the *Playboy* style, emblem or jewelry. Then I would feel like my game was cheap. Cold turkey I just left Emila alone. Her being from New York, I probably got off easy, thinking about my back. I will never know! When we would see each other, thereafter, it was only a hello in passing. I was totally done, and she or the thought of another try was just out of the question. I was soon to be in Ohio. I had another meet at the club with Lynette on the following weekend, and I was still seeing Lorraine when possible. How would I explain my back to the ladies or to Lynette? Steve gave me no good stories to tell. So I was on my own for my own story to tell. I was racking my brain and found it was very difficult to concentrate. I had to come up with something! The next morning, as I was getting dressed and putting my T-shirt on, I had the perfect excuse (or perfect lie). I told everyone how I wore this sweater and found out that I was allergic to it and scratched up my back, like it was. I told the ladies about my allergic reaction with the sweater that I never had. I told them that I scratched my back up, and they believed me! They not only believed me but had sympathy for me and treated me with tender loving care (TLC). By the following weekend, I was getting better and still experienced a little discomfort, but no more bleeding. The scars were definitely there for a longer time to really heal. So I was back and no more Emila for me! I think I learned my lesson. Let's just say, I got smarter.

I had a new thing going on and everything else too. My calendar, dates for dating, was no longer dull like when I first arrived at the base back in September 1980. With everything that I had going on, I managed to get a date with Lynette at the club and no Jo. Her sister did not come with her. We talked, dance a few songs, and hung out at the club. She was the only one that mattered to me. Everything else was blank in my mind except Lynette. My God was she beautiful! Then I found out that she was a little older than I. It was happening to me again! I am currently just infatuated with older women. Let just say that I needed a touch up on my rap game. I was good but had to step it up on the game. And no room for error. She was twenty-four! My second twenty-four-year-old woman in less than two years was in my presence. What was I to do? I did not have my own car. Lynette had her own place, made her own money, I guess, still mysterious, and somehow, I impressed myself that I caught her eye. Really, I did not know what I was doing. I was just doing it. Whatever it was, I really did not know how life worked outside of Akron, other than church travels to other churches. I have not been outside of that Akron area most of my life until I joined the Air Force. One thing for sure, I could tell that her mind was on me. I had those beautiful eyes on me. Her eyes! I did not care at all! I didn't know why! The more we spent time together, the less time I had to hang around Steve, except to work and basketball. For the time being, it was cool, or I thought so. That Steve and I was cool. I really thought that we were boys and friends. After all that we had done and the trouble or court-martials that could have happened to us! Really, both of us could have got kicked out of the Air Force. I thank God that we never got caught! Both of our military careers would had been ruined, to say the least! Again, I do thank God, as I am remembering these events of my life! At the same time, I was back at the hospital and in the emergency room with another nosebleed. I remember this one forever. It would not stop; my nose was bleeding for hours. If I was lying back, I would then spit up thick blood clots. Nothing still was working. One of the Air Force doctors got this great idea to put cocaine—yup, cocaine—to my nose to constrict my nose blood vessel, and it started to work. Then the doctors packed my nose once again and sent me on my way. That was one day I was feeling good. I had that cocaine high, and the fact was that it was totally legal. I really did not get involved with drugs, but I would never forget that day! Not ever!

Now back to Steve and me. We broke the base in together, participated in talents shows, and really had fun. Days were passing and weekends too. Lynette, would pick me up at the base, and as long as she had a base sticker, she could get on base (thank her sister Jo for that). Back and forth to Middletown, Ohio, we were doing all the fun things possible. One time after work, we went roller-skating. I used to skate when I was younger but forgot the basics. Lynette had her own roller skates and drove a manual stick shift. She could really drive that foreign car. Lynette held me most of the time until I could skate a little on my own. I had forgotten most of it. So after the roller-skating, she took me for pizza and ice cream. This date was like something that would be in the movies. I was in school, and yes, she was teaching me on how to become a gentleman. Lynette was not the normal type of woman that I have met, ever. She was a lady and totally in control. I was intrigue, infatuated, and I was, for the first time, not in lust. She was different! In a class all by herself! Life with her and being with her was like a breath of fresh air, early in the morning and looking at the sky. It was just beautiful being with her. Our second date, roller-staking, pizza, and ice cream. It was cool! From that night forward, she let me drive the stick shift to her apartment in Middletown. This was a little scary for me, but she kept me calm, and we got there safely. Now, onto her apartment, nothing was rushed. We sat around in the living room drinking pop and juice. Lynette did not drink, and I wasn't a big drinker either. We were good to go. The entire weekend was over, and I now have a new (older) girlfriend. She would take me back to the base, and then I would borrow Bill's car and go to see Lorraine. No one knew each other. They were in different cities, and they had no family relationships. I was glad that they were not kin, not really my style. I now currently only had about four or five women to keep up with. And I had to make time for each of them. Still, I did not know if I had a baby on the way with LuAnn.

Lynette kept me on my toes some weekends. She was not able to pick me up, and I could not contact her. Somehow, the other 90 percent of her time, she was with me. Now, that was mysterious! I did not want to make demands of her and mess up a good thing that we both had going. So I always accepted her as she was. At least, I was trying! Anyway, I had to put a little distance between Lynette and I to plan some time to see my family in Akron. And to get back together once I had returned from Akron. It was partly true even though I did not go straight to Akron.

Then I would see Lorraine some evenings and weekends since the government summer hire program was done and over. I spent phone time with her as much as possible, my family, and my baby momma, and then my soon-to-be fiancée. With all of this going on, I had somehow still made up my mind to get married to Adrian. My time with Emila was totally gone, and I saw her less and less and except for a few nights here and there. I did not see Steve much because that young high school girl faded rather quickly, and he seems to be falling in love with Crystal. Lynette was my main girl off the base. But we were still boys! I blamed it on work as an excuse, so I had the perfect excuse not to see Lorraine that much. I used to borrow Bill's car and drove to LuAnn's job at the grocery/retail store. I would check on her from time to time. For one, to see if we could date and the answer was no because it was too close for comfort with her sister and also quite obvious and understandable. But the main reason for me to see her (LuAnn) was to see if she was pregnant. It was the end of summer, and Steve and I would make another trip to Ohio to see the family, and so I could do my wedding proposal to Adrian. I also would introduce Steve to Adrian's cousin Melody. Melody was looking forward to meeting Steve. Steve drove back and forth from Oberlin to see Melody, and that weekend before we left to go back to the base, we double-dated.

It was obviously noticeable that Melody did catch Steve's eye. I borrowed my brother's car, so that Saturday night, Adrian and I spent the night at the Knights Inn at Kent State University right outside the college campus. I had a lot going on. Girls were everywhere in Akron too. What was I thinking? We were just lying around the hotel room, and I popped the marriage question, with this questionable statement in front of it, "I know God is probably going to get me." I proposed that Saturday night, and Adrian's reply was yes! She was happy, but I did not really know what to think. I remember Stevie Wonder's song playing on the radio, "Signed, Sealed, Delivered, I'm Yours" and more songs on the Forever Lovers Only Radio Station. And I did not know how to fix my life. I was just letting it all happen, not thinking of who will get the bad end of things. Well, I did not care. I was a lady's man. I was too selfish, to say the least. It was all about me! Now a with a few months to plan the wedding on October 17, 1981. I have a crazy busy summer and now this! Plus,

I still did not know if there was another baby on the way. Anyway, I wanted it all, and I was going to get it by lying, stealing, and cheating! This was who I had become. I did not try, but it happened. It was like being in a curse. Women kept coming my way, staying, and sharing themselves. I did not know if they were addicted to me, or I was addicted to them. That's why I called it a curse! Unexplainable at best! I spent a little time with the family and cousins, giving my mom some money, making my rounds (normally, it was about seeing the other girls), and to see my son, bearing gifts… I did share to all that I was engaged to Adrian. My mother liked her as well. Once, we (Adrian and I) took my mother to the doctor's office, and my mother asked Adrian to keep her purse. Like back in the day, the older ladies kept everything in envelopes in this or that place. Anyway, the bonding happened, and the trust was on. Adrian was my mom's girl. My mom would say, "That's my girl," just like that! I must admit that many times my mom would be upset with me on how I treated the girls. I caught a lot of slack from her, my mother, especially with Deanna. That was her girl too the first one that I had brought around the family. They really like her, and she really fitted in with my family. Lynn was just around the corner. I did have some tight corners to maneuver. Lynn used to pull knives on me. I still remembered those times, even after our son was born. I have learned to keep the girls at a distance, for the most part. Especially, the younger ones. The closer that they got with you in a relationship, the more that they want to hurt you. I am remembering what had happened to my back in Dayton, Ohio, not too long ago with my back getting scratched up!

Anyway, Steve and I made it back safely with the speed limit of 55 mph, not that he went over the speed limit at times. On the way back from Akron, I mentioned to Steve that I was engaged and had asked him to be my best man at the wedding. I did this based on a prior conversation that I had had earlier with Adrian and to see which of my brothers would also be in the wedding as the groomsmen. My two oldest brothers were in the wedding, Cleottis, Robert, and Valerie's boyfriend. On the drive back to Dayton, we sometimes went faster following the truckers, and the brakes were on once we saw the Ohio State Highway Patrol cars. They really had some good hiding places to catch speeding cars or trucks.

As time moved on, September it was, and school was back in session. We were back at the base, and I was about to get married with the baby mama drama. Now, more confusion to see my son was beginning to take place, a little here and there. Making plans to get back there and again in December 1981.

I was back in touch with Lynette and Lorraine, and things were back in order. My time off and weekends were full. I had to maintain separate lives, and be the best Air Force airman that I could be at the job. All was well! My job had no idea of everything that I was doing. Other than the good news that I was getting married. Folks were excited for me! I had congratulations coming from everywhere. I mean everywhere! I was having a really good time in my life, and it was all about me and girls everywhere! I stayed off-base quite a bit and ate at the chow hall even less. But I did eat there. I never have to worry of surprise visits from anyone, especially Adrian. She did not have her own car, and I was still in the dorms. I made as many calls to Adrian in Akron and Lorraine in Dayton to keep them at ease. It was working. Adrian's hands were full with the wedding planning. Then most of my time was well spent with Lynette. This was where I really wanted to be. She had no idea that I was getting married but knew that I had a child and not with the baby's mother. Lynette and Lorraine knew the same story, which made it easier for me not to tell a lie. I had to keep everything consistent, and no one expected anything different. I gave everyone my undivided attention. I took Lorraine to a Roger Troutman and Zapp concert. It was fun, and no one knew me. See Lynette was more a little more secretive. We went to the Midnight Star concert at the base. In the time that we spent together, somehow, I thought that she had someone else. She was kind of well-to-do, if you will. Sometimes, I thought from the information that I had gathered for our time spent together that she was married. But I could not prove it. For some reason and because of her last name, I thought that she was married to a professional baseball player in Toronto, but I could not prove it. That was the mysterious feelings I got but could not prove it. That feeling made it impossible for me to leave my fiancée Adrian in Akron. Lynette and I had a great thing going, and truly I was falling in love with her and had a dozen of mixed emotions. She was it and different for me, and she loved eating that cornstarch by Arco in the blue box. I could not stop her from eating that stuff. Still, we spent a lot of quality time together, and she really kept her place clean, even showered in the middle of the night. I really enjoyed her and missed her every moment that we were apart. This was that kind of relationship that I would never imagine. Lynette had me hooked, line, and sinker... I was almost all in! I would have even left Adrian, wedding and all. We kept growing together, and then I would meet the rest of her family and even her mother. I met her mother. Did I read the signals wrong? Did I get bad information? I did say that I met her mother. Now I was confused again! Really confused! So I could only enjoy it (her) while it would last.

October 1981 was here, and Steve decided to be my best man from our drive back. Capt. Sylvester and my office gave me gifts for the wedding that I had brought back with me. What a nice gesture. I did make a good impression, and they thought that I was a good guy. And now the fifteenth of October was here. Steve dropped me off and went to Oberlin, and he would be at the wedding that Saturday morning to get fitted for the tuxedo for him and me, and it was a good thing that went to coordinate our sizes at first. Our tuxedos were a fit for us both. We took them with us, and we were well on our way. We were hanging out and Akron. I took him to meet my son Big Mike and then around the corner to my mom's house to change into the tux. Yes, we looked good! Anyway, Steve was looking forward to seeing Melody again. Even though he was trying to date a new lady at his building that was half Hawaiian (her father was prior military). She was beautiful as well! Therefore, the show must go on. Adrian always had mixed emotions about her father, Ben Thurman (brother of Nate Thurmond the former NBA player; Nate did not seem to believe it) who was from Akron, Ohio. They went to Central High that later became Central Hower High from that which I had graduated (Central Hower Eagles). Ben would give her away in the wedding. They look just alike with the high cheek bones. To me, and after we all met the parents of Ben and Nate Thurmond that lived on Lovers Lane in Akron, denied or not (she was never accepted into their family), but I believed that they were definitely family. The only thing that was missing was the blood test! Ben, Adrian's father, was definitely a ladies' man! I liked and accepted him as my father-in-law-to-be. Plus, we had a lot in common, but I never told him of the things that I was doing behind his daughter's back. Well, we met with the pastor that Friday evening, and Pastor Hoodah agreed that it was okay for him to perform the wedding at Shelton's Temple (COGIC), 527 North Howard, in Akron. It was an old church at that and in pretty good shape, with nice wood furniture on the inside, and a sound to be heard all over the church building!

The wedding was on. My first wedding and not many of my family showed up for one reason or another. My little brother was in it, and that was good, and my mother was there and a few others. That was it! However, there was plenty of people there mainly from Adrian's side of family and friends. By living out of town, I had lost touch of many folks. And my home was not to be there. That was not my plan! The wedding was on, and everyone was in place. Adrian's best friend could sing her face off. She could go! Elaine Williams (Kalembo) sang a duet with Roderick Henning (pastor), to the song "Endless Love" by Lionel Richie and Diane Ross. It was just beautiful. I was surprised to see Valerie Dawson as one of the bridesmaids. She was one of my high school classmates. It so happened that she went to Kent State with my new wife. What a small world. Paul, her cousin, played "Here Comes the Bride" on the organ. It was a nice touch. Then we took our vows to each other. Pastor Hoodah did the ring presentation to Adrian. I kissed the bride Adrian, and we were introduced as Mr. and Mrs. Michael Gilcreast. Applauses were everywhere. Then a funny thing happened. The wedding was officially over with no rehearsals. I was married. It hit me! I was married! The photographer snapped the photo of us walking down the church aisle. My eyebrows raised up as they normally do. The photographer caught my emotion, but this picture was talking. There's an old saying that says, "A picture is worth a thousand words." Well, this one was a thousand and one words. I was thinking the total truth: "What did I just do?" I had many questions in my mind. These were my last thoughts, with questions, on my wedding day: "I was not ready for marriage." Not at all! Nor was Adrian! The pressure was too high, and I think that we both got caught in that moment that we could not undo in our immature state of mind—protect our image—which was not so easy to do! I was truly disappointed with myself nor was I or would be ready for a real commitment to her. To be fair, at some point, I would have to give it a try somehow! We shall see! There was no honeymoon. I was saving for a car and to get an apartment off base. Adrian understood, so we stayed the night at her parents' (that raised her) house in the brother's room (in reality, her cousin), this old bedroom furniture. I was disappointed again, but it was their best, and her parents really loved Adrian. Besides I was leaving on that Monday, going back to the base as a married man. Still, I was not fazed, nor did my ways change. But now I am a newly married adulterer from the Bible side of things for what little that I knew of the Bible or going to church, and everyone that was or would be connected to me would have that sin follow them. I knew it was wrong for what I was doing, but my conscience was not bothered. I still had Lynn in Akron (it was on and off), Lorraine in Dayton, and Lynette in Middletown, where I still spent most of my time. Yet now, I had a wife. I did think of that from time to time. Now, I was trying to get some things right, and my first priority was to see if LuAnn was pregnant. Finally, I went to her job, and she was trying to avoid me at first, thinking that I still wanted to pursue a relationship with her, not telling her that I was now married—and no more games. I was well beyond another relationship, but I had to know if she was pregnant, and she said that there was no pregnancy. Boy, was I relieved. We both agreed to go our separate ways. That was the end of that. And for me, no more sisters! Well, maybe one more, still in question, if or maybe! I did keep reminding myself of the Don Juan mentality.

Really, I would have married Lynette instead if I could have just shook off that feeling I had! But that feeling did not leave me. The only missing link that we shared, and I could not confront her nor find comfort in my thoughts. That same doubt allowed me to marry Adrian instead. My heart was still beating to be with Lynette.

I did not know how to heal or help that side of me. At some point, soon, I must face my heart to be broken and yet find a way to move on. Frankly, I was stuck between a rock and a hard place, playing songs like "Love TKO" by Teddy or Harold Melvin and the Blue Notes. My heart was sad, and I held it in and playing more sad songs, including Smokey Robinson & The Miracles. That was great music back then. I said to myself, "There's never a dull moment with me." One evening, at Lynette's apartment, probably around November 1981, we were sitting around the living room, and I decided to tell her. I believe my conscience was still there. I was trying to change because being married really does something to the mind. We were sitting on the sofa together, and I told her that I had gotten married in the previous month. Wow! The tears, her tears were falling on me, and it touched my heart again. I did not understand her pain or the pain it caused by my words to her. This was not easy for me in that I had never meant for this to happen. Nothing even close to this. We had something good, something special. We had in every sense of the word, *love*! This was the best relationship I had ever known. I was trying to be married together with Adrian in some kind of way! There are no instructions for matters of the heart. In that moment and in those moments, I was wounded. Lynette was wounded! I felt our pain, every single drop of it! I too was hurting and did not know my healing or how to heal my broken heart! I was trying to move on! But really, I did not want to move on from Lynette! The next morning, Lynette took me back to my dorm at the base. We were done! Over! No arguments. It was one of the best peaceful breakups I ever experienced. No scratches, no argument, no attitudes! My Lynette was truly a class act. I was thinking about that feeling that concerned me. Was it true? If so, why did Lynette cry the way she did? It did not add up for me. Was I wrong about Lynette? Was she not holding back on me? Was she truly into me? Now, I had questions to ask of her. I have experience more in less than six months than my entire time with anyone else. We had something special. I single-handedly messed that up. I was cussing myself or just cussing out loud. Lynette, she was everything to me! Why? My questions could not be answered because Lynette had nothing else to say to me. Any contact she had with me was gone! Water, bathtub, and all was gone. She would not talk to or see me again because the phone calls went unanswered. It was over! Still, I had another dental surgery to do with Dr. Benedetti, and I would be good until Adrian, my new bride would arrive. Then she could go with me.

Now, work was good, and my schedule was back to normal. I was still reaching out to Lorraine as we continued to stay in touch because she kept a special place for me in her heart. We were back on, Lorraine and me. I was glad about it. It was good. She was a little older and getting ready for her upcoming homecoming and graduation in 1982. It was good seeing her. It also gave me room to heal from Lynette. The borrowing of Bill's car would be also coming to an end in March of 1982. I would have to have a car by then because Bill was getting a permanent change of assignment (PCS), and I would no longer have a roommate. Then more privacy for Lorraine and me at the dorm. Lorraine was glad to be with me, and that made me feel good. Her innocence of life was allowing her to begin to fall in love with me. Like it or not, it was happening. She was at my every beck and call. I did not want to hurt her too, so I tried to take it easy. At the same time, while I am at the dorm in the hallway, hugging the phone, making plans for Adrian to move here to Dayton and more talk for getting a car. Adrian and I were doing good; my son and my family are good as well. Then I would have more talks with my mother to explain what was going on with me. Believe you me, my mother really understood me. She always knew what was going on with me or what I would be going through. Mom's was good, and we were close as always! One evening, I was out in Dayton with Lorraine. I guess Steve came by my room, and I was not there. Then while Steve came to visit me as he was leaving because I was not there, the hallway payphone was ringing. It was located closer to my end of the second floor in the dorm about five rooms down on the right side in the middle of the brick wall. My room was the closest to the door by the outside brown stairs, really convenient. Get this, Steve, my best man at my wedding, we had secrets together and my partner in crime. I thought that we were cool! Steve answered the payphone after many rings. I was not there.

What did Steve just do to me? Adrian told me all and everything that Steve told her. Now, get this, Adrian loved me, just married me, and whole-heartedly trust me. My game was tight, and my rap was on. Adrian told me what Steve had said. She said Steve told her that I was out with other women in Dayton and Middletown. Then she said Steve told her that I was cheating on her and that she should be with him. I was undone! Now, this situation was a first for me, and my words were not so kind for Steve. He was no longer my friend. While it was partially true, I had to lie in order to keep my marriage and new wife. For the time being, she believes me. I told her not to worry because Steve was jealous, and we had already had a fallen out. He proved my case for me by trying to talk to her to start their own relationship. His game was not that good. Not at all. Steve and I became more distant and had not much in common. We were no longer friends or brothers. Other than basketball and gearing up for practice for the next season, we were on our own. These few events of my life and what Steve did in betraying my business, my personal business, has taught me to never trust another guy, ever, with my wife and to keep my secrets to myself. I had learned a valuable lesson on friends or boys. For me, it does not exist! Now, in growing up, the affairs, and marriage, I too was focusing on trust. I did not trust no one, girls, guys, and the wife. Something was happening to me. I did not even trust myself! I kept asking myself, can people really be trusted?

Back at work, and now TSgt. Steve Norton was leaving for a PCS or his next assignment. We had a going-away party, and we looked for our next and new NCO to arrive. At the beginning of December, Sgt. Fred Clark arrived, and he was a white dude with shaggy-type hair and wrinkled clothing/uniforms from Canton, Ohio, and his wife and child was there, and he would go up to Canton. And around Christmas, he was going to pick them up. The job is still good. Sgt. Clark offered me a ride to Akron after knowing that I did not have a car. He dropped me off and brought me back to the base with his family, Sue, and the kids. It was cool to have Sgt. Clark as an immediate supervisor. I am just about to pick up my second stripe to become an airman first class. I was moving up and planning my future in the Air Force.

While in Akron, the drama was beginning to unfold. I am married now, and Lynn wants to do things a bit differently. I could come over to see my son, but my wife Adrian was not allowed over. This became a real mess because Lynn and I still had a thing going on, like the song by Billy Paul, "Me and Mrs. Jones." So true, especially when I needed some bad (good) lyrics! The closer we were, Lynn and I, the more the trouble for Adrian and me. But Adrian calmed down and allowed me to see my son. I played the game and acted like I was hurting, and when the time was right for each of them. I would sing some slow jams, like the one I did often with the other ladies: "Baby, I'm For Real" or "Let's Just Kiss and Say Goodbye" (another favorite by The Manhattans) or "Ooh Child" (by the Five Stairsteps). I would sing and pretend to not see them watching. Those were great makeup songs. I did rock with the ladies for romance or when I was in trouble with them! For real! I would also tighten up things with my new wife. We only had a short time from Christmas to the January 2 and then back to work.

We arrived back safely from the holidays in Akron and just did beat the snow. Basketball season was on. We added some new players because of some new assignments due to the PCS of service members. We still had a decent team, and we just played ball, even Steve and myself. After all was said and done, we brought home another trophy for second place. It was exciting once again. We placed two years in a row. But I still had a lot on my mind and things to work out on the personal side of things. Then I had a few things to figure out. After getting back from Akron and with the basketball games going on, I ran into Jo (Sgt. Jo, Lynette's sister) at one of the Air Force personnel buildings. We spoke and then I asked about Lynette and how she was doing. I was genuinely concerned as we have not spoken for about two months. I had mentioned to her for Lynette to call me or something. For some reason, I did not want to let go and still wanted more. I truly wanted to be with Lynette. A few days or so passed by, Lynette and I made contact! Unbelievable, but true! We made arrangements to start seeing each other again. I got a second chance! Just like that we picked up a few pieces and moved on as she was about to turn twenty-five years old, and I had just turned twenty years old. I was quickly growing into manhood, with a wealth of experience and well beyond my young years. I was still not sure why she changed her mind. Maybe I was not ready to know, but maybe she wanted me to undo Adrian and I and start over again with her. I was just enjoying all of our time together. How would I pursue a divorce? Then, she did not say any more about my marriage. I just did not know why!

Yet Lynette was still so sweet to me! Yes, I finally learned how to drive a manual transmission car. Lynette patiently taught me that too! Since I had some money saved, Lynette took me out to find a car around the base, here and there. Then I would be able to find Adrian and I an apartment in Dayton. Allowing me to only be about thirty minutes to Middletown, just in case I needed to see Lynette. And I was minutes from Lorraine. Deep down inside of me, I knew Adrian would not have any parts of that the other woman thing. It was not going to happen without somebody going to jail. It's now March 1982. I heard that Steve got an assignment, and I was glad, and not so glad but not so happy for my roommate Bill. He was one of my enablers to help me to visit other girls. Bill was to be leaving soon. He was cool. An awesome roommate, and I will truly miss him! The following weekend, Lynette took me out again to look for a car. I even looked at a stick shift, but it was not for me. I was for strictly automatic. After several searches, I found a 1978 blue Dodge Monaco, with the 8-track to play my soulful music. This was my car, so I took out a loan for about $5,000 from the bank and took the check to the car dealer. Then I drove it off the lot. Lynette had to go home, so I would catch up to her later. So I rode around the base so the fellas would see me profiling, and then, I was off to Dayton to see Lorraine. Right after that, the first time driving my care to Fairborn, Ohio, it happened! I could not believe it! The first time driving my car off base, I received my first, my very first ticket for speeding. How could this be? I just left the gate, and there the police were at, the light, and across from that light was Fairborn. I did have a little nosebleed that day and also received my first ticket. I forever watched my way in Fairborn. Bottom line, and truthfully, I was not speeding. But best believe that it was a "black and white" thing!

Now, with no roommate, it got easier to see and spend some time with Lorraine. I would drop her off the next day and onto Middletown. That night in Middletown, being married, the new car, and all was too much for me. I made up an excuse about all the excitement because there was no chemistry happening with me. I was finally getting tired, and my body needed much rest and some real rest. After the rest, I was back in the groove of things. I was back! A month later, being April, I finally broke up with Lorraine. I flat-out lied and told her that I had gotten into trouble and had to stay on the base. Then I told her that we had to stop seeing each other. It was over! Wow! The tears again. She was about to graduate high school. We were good, felt good to be around her and her presence and innocence. And I liked her. She was so down to earth, and that was it! More tears from the disappointing news I presented her in my new car. I could not stop her crying. Still, she did not want me to leave. I really felt bad. Again! Those tears of hers did touch me! I ruined her innocence of life and love. In that moment, I knew that I had a heart. My heart was just a little broken, and I never gotten it fixed! Still, I kept trying to cleanup my life and do better for my wife! Adrian had a little college and no job. I had to spend most of my time with her. My former excuses and lies would not work once she was here and we would live together. Because of what Steve had done, or tried to do, I had no room for error.

In Akron, Adrian was finishing up some college courses for pre-med at Kent State University before moving to Dayton to be with me, and we would celebrate being married together. So while I was waiting, Lynette and I made the best of every moment. We spent a lot of quality time together. We were doing everything together. I felt free being with her, though my life's baggage was piling up. We were going to the movies, parks, walks, some restaurants, and her cooking was not bad either. The food was good too. Our lives were simple but fulfilled. It was good being together. In the back of my mind, I had to figure out my next move. May, June, and July was gone so fast. However, I did manage to find us (Adrian and I) a place in Dayton. I had to do this part by myself. It was located at the Grandview Apartments, 633 W. Grand Ave, Apartment 11 (on the lower level, with utilities included), Dayton, Ohio, 45406. This would be our first apartment together. I was beginning to get a little excited for being married and the marriage. August was here. I have to take some leave to make the trip to Akron and pick up Adrian and bring her back to Dayton. Once the leave was approved, I was good to go! Now, I had to say goodbye again. I can hear the song in my ear by The Manhattans "Let's Just Kiss and Say Goodbye." Of course, I would be singing it too. It was songs like this that helped me in my escapades of women. But I did not want to let her go. Deep down inside me, I knew that once Adrian arrived, Lynette would in no way be second or on the side for me. I guess the 30 miles of distance made it a little easier for her to digest or to live with herself. I am doing it again, like a few months ago. And again to the same person. This was really and probably my second chance to make Lynette my main lady and possibly my wife (after the divorce), but I had plenty of mixed feelings to go around. My head was spinning with confusion. She really made herself available to me, commitment and all. I believe that Lynette was all in. Again! I thought hard about! It felt right! It was built wrong! I also had in my mind, since I was a cheater, I knew how to be a cheater firsthand. The saying goes, "If you cheat with me, then you would cheat on me." That resonated with me for every person I have been with. Lynette came back to me, and I was married. As painful as it was that thought would be with me. Still! And I was living by that. Plus, Adrian used to say that all the time. So now the time was here to say goodbye for good and on my terms. I was trying to do right and really I cannot tell anyone why because I was at a loss myself.

This time, I drove myself to Lynette's apartment and stayed through the weekend. She was not a churchgoer at all, nor did the topic ever came up. I had grown up in church, and so did Adrian. We did have that in common and probably our real true connection. We had plenty of Bible conversations or arguments, and that was cool. I slowly mentioned that my wife would be coming down from Akron, but I did not want to dampen the weekend, so as the weekend ended and I was about to leave, I brought it up again, the whole thing, so we talked. As my mind was trying to gather the right words, I was thinking, if Lynette, would have gotten pregnant, this alone would have definitely changed the course of all my actions. My wedding would have abruptly ended, just like that. This would not have applied to anyone but Lynette because, as much as I knew about love, I was still in love with her and really did not want to let her go. Was my mind playing tricks on me? I don't know. I stayed busy so I was not able to give it much thought. Regardless, she would not be so easy to let go of in the most of the year that we spent together without a hole being left in my heart. I said this was it, and I have to move on. What did I say that for? This time, it had hurt me more, so it seemed! How can I hold back my tears? And her tears too. I was feeling that feeling in my chest. The pain of hurt. It was awful, and it hurts! Love can hurt. Really hurts! I thought that I was doing the right thing! Just to let go! Was this truly right? I don't know! It does not feel like it is right! When I was seventeen years old and dating Deanna, she used to always say, "It is better to love and lost than to have never loved at all (by Alfred Lord Tennyson)." I kept this with me as well! It would remind me to keep chasing love or that I knew that love really exists! Really, these few words helped me to keep believing and searching for love, even though I was already married. Really, I wanted love too. I just tried to find it in all the wrong places and lost myself with the distractions of life and chasing women. When I would hear the song "She Used To Be My Girl," I would think of so many women, and yet Lynette would become my main focus. "Cruisin'" would be another song by Smokey Robinson that Lynette and I would play together, and it would become one of our songs. Plus sometimes, I would sing along at times! The time we shared together seemed to have been longer than it really was. I guess I was a little lost in her! Or shall I say that we were lost in each other! Other times, if I knew that we had to go our separate ways. I would somehow play the song "Let's Just Kiss and Say Goodbye." That was a true sign that I would be planning my next move or a new song would come along to fit my purpose in planning my next move.

I just had to keep it moving. I had found the place, and I was on my way home to Akron, Ohio, even though I was away with the military and left home. The City of Akron will always be my home. My roots started there. Never, did I ever want to forget where I came from being born and raised. My military career started there, as well as school, sports, girls, my church foundation, and my first family. Then of course, my mom's. So I was on my way to pick up my wife Adrian in my new car! Also before leaving, I had to make sure that any and all belongings of any kind was removed from my car. I had to make sure there was not one single bit of information or evidence in my car! Period! I was on leave for a few days and on my way to drive two hundred miles and go to my wife Adrian. After arriving, I went to see my son and his mother. And to say our good-byes to family and friends. It was a little sad but it went okay! So we packed up my car, and the next day, I made more rounds to see my family. I was not leaving Akron without taking me a Boston Sub from Mama Rosa's and some Church's Chicken, my favorite chicken wing place, and a pepper. We had not time to get Rasicci's (pizza and chicken) or Swenson's too (Adrian turned me on to this place). Plus, I was trying to do the right thing, and I could not spoil it, no way, no how. My job had part of my conscience in check. There was an image to uphold while serving in the military I was a part of. This military code of ethics did have an effect on me and some parts of the Uniform Code of Military Justice (UCMJ). Even for credit worthiness, I had to keep my bills paid or face a court martial. Plus, the folks at my job were inquiring about meeting my new wife. They wanted to see her, and of course, I wanted to show her off. She did look good to me. Everything went well as we made it back to Dayton safely. Adrian was a little quiet and reserved, especially arriving to a new home, county, and city. This was it for me until my next assignment came up. It was nice to have a furnished apartment, and the utilities were included. We were off to start our new life! There were a few things to do in the area as we would leave the apartment and make a right on West Grand Avenue, then a right on Salem Avenue, just up the street was Church's Chicken, and on the next block was Roger Troutman and Zapp Recording Studio. On up the street was the Salem Mall. In the other direction as you leave the apartment, make a left on Salem Avenue, on down was the grocery store, restaurants, Sinclair Community College, and to keep going, you would run into downtown Dayton, Ohio. This was a pretty good area and not too busy and low crime. As we made it back to the apartment, we located our parking spot and then took some stuff into the apartment. I put the stuff down at the door and carried Adrian across our door threshold. This was all right. I was feeling some excitement too! We were getting settled in, washing and wiping down everything, especially in the kitchen and bathroom, to make it our own. This one-bedroom apartment was just right and kind of private. And no way in Dayton would I be able to bring up my past. This was the perfect fantasy as perfect could be! Because I did not know what I was doing, and somehow, I was not concerned about getting caught for all of these things that I done. At times, our relationship did not seem real. I was all over the place. Well, my mind was all over the place, plus my wandering eyes did not help. My aim as most of the guys was not to get caught. I was really getting the hang of it, so I would look and dislike or like something about those women, avoiding any suspicions. I would even ask my wife, do you like or dislike something about a girl or a guy? I even did it with the TV, just to keep throwing her off. Adrian kept her feelings protected, even if she would lie about her true feelings. I always knew the real her. I kept trying to be a married man, going home right after work. Adrian did go to the dentist with me as we were moving towards the last final stages and make the permanent bridge for my front teeth, but in order to connect the bridge for my front teeth, the other front tooth would have to be shaved down, as on the other side. Dr. Benedetti wanted to know if I wanted to keep my natural gap in the front of my mouth or not. I stated no that it did not matter. By this time, Adrian came back into the room, and I had told her what had happened, and she disagreed with me, and she wanted me to keep my natural gap. I agreed and wanted to look as natural as possible. The dentist let us know that it would be difficult and was never done before. But he would give it his best shot. That was over for the time being!

Every now and again, we would go to the NCO Club for a night out for some dancing. Winter was here and gone and now quickly approaching spring. New Year's was pretty awesome. We did take in a Frankie Beverly and Maze concert, and folks were getting high in the upper stands, smoking weed. I did stay away, just in case Operation Golden Flow (military surprise pee test for drugs). I did not want to take any chances. I gotten high a few times with my brothers back in the day. Somehow, that was not my thing. We had made weekends plans for a movie and back to the NCO Club for dancing. Adrian would always catch me checking out the women, and then, I believe that she was a little suspicious regardless. But sometimes she would just act funny and say that nothing was wrong. This would be the same place in my life, my hangout, where I was playing the field. I have been off the scene for a while. I was beginning to get focused from the marriage perspective. A family man of sorts! By this time, my brothers Shawn and Kelvin. They were the baby brothers in the family, about eleven years old and fifteen years old. At that time, I was twenty years old. Anyway, Shawn and Kelvin came down for visit for about a week or two and decided to go back to Akron. I could tell that they were a little homesick and wanted to get back with their friends and the family. I know that they were a little bored, and all I did was work and school. I too would have been bored as well. Somehow, I could tell that they were still excited to be with me in Dayton. We all had such an age difference I did not know how to spend quality time with them, having the schedule that I had. I believe that the only thing that I had going for me was that I was one of their big brothers in the military and that they were excited to come down to see and spend a little time with Adrian and me. I must admit, it was fun in my mind having my little brothers to come down from Akron to see me. I did not show it much, but I was glad that they were in Dayton. While I wanted them to stay, I knew that they had to be leaving. It would have been nice to be close to family versus all of the friends. Well, it was too good to be true, so we drove them back to Ohio. Again, points to Adrian for allowing them to come down to visit as well. This time, Adrian and I had a little fun.

We watched a little TV. I was definitely into sports and westerns, so they would normally watch what I wanted to watch.

It was not working; my marriage was in trouble. Again, Steve did not help my innocence. Somehow, Adrian and I have gotten into a big argument for her trust issues with me, and again with Lynn and the baby mama drama. We were trying to be husband and wife. It, my marriage, was not working. I was totally upset at this point. I did deny it, but I was only looking for a way out! No crime. I was tired of this stuff and nonsense, but we were really cussing each other out, in the car, and on the way home. And then, we would make up—but not this time. I was used to having many women but was really trying to do right. Not so! I told Adrian to pack her stuff and that I was taking her back to Akron. We had loaded up the car and were on our way to Akron. This really screwed up my weekend. We argued all the way there! We stayed in the car and talked, but our conversations were just raw! So then, I dropped her off and went to see my family, and then, I had to see my son. Well, I spent some time with Lynn too. One thing that I knew for sure that I could not get in trouble more for seeing my son, and Adrian could not just show up. So Lynn was there for me anyway, and whenever, it was rumored by her family that we were going to get married. Well, I just used that to my advantage, even though I was already married. I quickly found out that when I spent time with her, Lynn and Adrian became bigger enemies. They used to be best friends until I had got into the middle of them. The next day, I left and went back to Dayton. After about a week, I was missing Adrian and decided to call and make up. Plus I was kind of lonely and trying to be married. The folks at the job were asking about my wife, and I had just told them that she was checking on her family. Actually, that placed some pressure on me. I was definitely about image, and so was she. Now, I was anxious to pick her up and bring her back to Dayton for all of the wrong reasons. But now, every time that I had seen my son, it was a hassle and especially since I did not make an honest effort to get back with Lynn. Plus, by this point, Lynn was not taking care of Big Mike the way that she was supposed to. I noticed that all of the expensive things and gifts that I had brought him was damaged or something.

Well, to change the focus of things, I decided to share my thoughts with Adrian. Especially since it was getting harder and harder to see my son. So I shared with Adrian that I had decided to go for child custody and take my son. I figured that I was in the military and married so that it would be easier for me to gain custody. Not so! I did not know the law, and at the same time on how the normal favor would go to mother and not the father. We had talked all the way back to Dayton. Now, we had a common interest, and it would give me some space. Adrian had found us a local attorney in a two-week period. I had to file to the court in Akron for visitation rights just to see my son. And another basketball season was starting up. This time we did not win. Life has been good, for as long as this would last.

My wife Adrian was being a good wife when things were going good and no alarms of female threats, and this pretty much surprised me on how she treated me. I would come in from work, and after dinner, she would run my bath water. I can still remember the song playing in my head, "It's a Thin Line, between Love and Hate." This happened on many occasions, the bath water thing, along with having my dinner ready, but sometimes, she would be singing that song. Adrian was motivated to get custody of Big Mike from Lynn. She wanted nothing more than to take him from her. Especially after he was born, Lynn told Adrian, "Now you cannot name your son Michael Anthony because I did it first." Inside Adrian, silently, this angered her even more, but I really found out that this really motivated Adrian after the fact. The arguments had settled down, and I was amazed and surprised. We would talk about things at dinner, and one day, it came up that I should go to college and pursue my dream to become a doctor. This was my childhood dream. To become a doctor. I have had this dream even before I graduated high school. I wanted to become a doctor for ER or OB/GYN, so I could deliver babies and maintain women's health. I have always thought that the woman's anatomy to be very interesting and not boring. So I would pursue my dream to become an OB/GYN or ER doctor! This was my lifelong dream. I wanted to pursue this; and then, I was on my way! This was another inspiring reason for me to donate blood every chance made available to me. I always had natural instinct and wanted to help people. It was truly another burning desire that I had inside me.

My first attempt of school was the local community college at Sinclair Community College, located down the street from our apartment. I took one course since I have not been to a formal college or university. My Air Force Military Basic Training in San Antonio, Texas, and thereafter Technical School at Keesler AFB, Mississippi, was accredited for college. Then by joining the Air Force, I was automatically enrolled in the community college of the Air Force, and it was also an accredited military college and transferrable for college credits. As I got the hang of it, I was more and more excited. I took one class, Accounting I, very basic, and I thought that I was smart. Not so! My first grade was an F. So the first thing I did was to run to my professor. As disappointed as I was, I wanted to bring up my grade. Then my schedule was after work, I ate dinner and studied. I had to get serious. The class was on a quarter system and not semester credit hours, which means, I had a short time to get this right and bring my grade up. I have to convince myself that I can do it. Then I got baths already ran every now and again. The kitchen table was getting most of my time with ledgers all over the table. It was accounts receivable and account payable and the balance. It was a whole list of things that kept me up and some nights very late. Plus I had to go to work. Adrian sometimes left me up studying because she went to bed. I did not understand how she passed the time. I do know that some of the time was passed by arguing. Adrian was very, very, very jealous! All the time! I knew that I could not even look at another woman, let alone smile at one. She would swear up and down that I had something going on. The more time we spent together, the more we would argue. It was a good thing that I was the only income and did believe in taking care of my wife or family. Those type of values were ingrained in me from the many talks that I used to have with my mother. She had always told me to take care of my wife and to ensure that she would always have a bed to sleep in. So real family values were definitely becoming a part of my life. I was really trying to do it right. But the arguing had to go! I had to also push and remind myself of that too. Let's say that I kept encouraging myself, and it was working between the arguments. If I had complimented someone on TV, we did have cable and a phone, then I had to say something nice about her. It had gotten to the point where I would just find any excuse to get out of the house. I was glad to go to work, even though I went from ten minutes to get to work from the dorm to twenty-five minutes from Dayton, Ohio, the time it took from my apartment. This became an adjustment that I had to get used to.

We had a morning appointment for my final dental appointment to install the final bridge and to get rid of the temporary one. I was so excited, and they were working and working and had to give me a few more shots to get numb but not as many shots as the last time. Okay, I can now see it in the mirror. For the first time since the accident, I had my natural teeth look back, and not without thanking my wife who helped me make the right choice. I was so pleased with my new teeth, and they were stronger and attached to the roof of my mouth. Everyone wanted to see it, starting at the dental office, and then they took plenty of pictures. I was so amazed. I only had one more checkup to go. Now, afternoon work, I was getting used to have a wife. After the arguments, it was the making up did the job for a while. But that was it. Our furnished apartment was beginning to look like home, with most of the unpacking almost done. So to say the least, we were broken. I can't really explain it. Deep inside me, I wanted to better myself, with the military, schooling to become a doctor, and at the same time, I tricked myself to believe that we were going to get better. I had gotten used to Adrian, and I called it a relationship, better yet, a marriage, especially when people at the basketball court, work, or even hanging out. We pretended to be happy, especially after the arguments we got into. Maybe she was more into us and yet pretending like she didn't care for me, but I was there and really trying to see if we could be more. One thing for sure, Adrian always would have my back no matter what. That's the thing. I did not know how to deal with that. She gives me a hard time, she's jealous, and yet, if I needed her, she was there. On another note, she was glad or happier than normal that she had helped me to decide on the proper bridge to select as my permanent bridge in my mouth. I had gotten major marriage points for that. Still, maybe, I just had a lot to learn about women and certain other things in particular. The harder the marriage got, the more that I stayed busy and stayed away from much temptation, with the women that were there in the immediate college area. I would tell myself that I had a wife at home. Temptation is not a laughing matter; it was a total burden to me and my flesh.

Sometimes, Adrian would get up to see me off to work, and I would take our only car with me, the 1978 blue Dodge Monaco, with the 8-track to play my soulful music. It ran pretty well. I was always one that would keep the maintenance up on my car. It came naturally since my brother and father worked on cars anyway. They both were pretty good. My father was better, and for a while, he owned a car repair shop. Well, the day has started, I got my morning goodbye kiss, and I was on my way for another day of work. Work was good. Sgt. Clark was still good, and my work was good! Not anything to complain about, except to get my grade up for my college course. I did focus on work a lot easier because the summer hires were gone. I do remember Steve's replacement showing up, this young female airman. She was just cool and average and built kind of nice too. I believe she was from New Jersey and found out that she played a little ball too. The more we played ball together, the more I had to fight myself to be married and stay positive. I really enjoyed guarding her when we played opposite teams for the lunchtime crowd. Or we would just play one-on-one. I must admit, this honey could really play ball and not a joke. She, Carmen, was just a good ball player and worked hard for every point. This girl played defense too. This was a great replacement for Steve, especially after he sold me out or at least tried too! Steve and I never touched base ever again. This used to be my boy! To be truthful, he was my boy! Now, the days were gone, and back and forth at school and work at a faster pace. School was about to come to an end, and yes, I have been working hard and focused to bring the grades up, something that I had to do. Also basketball was about to start. So in December 1982, I finished my first quarter at Sinclair Community College, and I did not believe it, but somehow, I made it. I finished the accounting course with an unexpected C and was as happy as I could be. I had a C that caused me to pass my first official college course outside my military training. I felt pretty good! Wow! That was my test for college and next challenge would be to attend a four-year school, also on quarter hours that would be Wright State University (WSU) to study nursing.

Adrian would be attending too. We applied for Pell Grants and student loans to be in college for the spring quarter 1983 at WSU. What did we do that for? I was a little nervous that we would get in to it and have another silly argument. But we both did the school thing, at least for this our first spring quarter together. The grades were okay, not much to brag about. I believe that I received a B in chemistry, and Adrian got a C. The sociology and psychology grades were average for us both. Then her English grade was just above mine with a B. She had help me with my studies. Well, let say my English course. I assisted her with chemistry. Adrian would quiz me at times for the exams, and I would cram the materials prior to each quiz, test, or midterms. The summer times were not really the best because we did not do the barbeques, not enough space for it. So we made do by finding us some barbecue restaurant place that was close by. We could not buy too much because the bills were piling up, credit card after credit card. Other than the part-time restaurant job I had from working at Burger Chef, in Dayton, on Salem Road, up the street from our apartment as a cook, I still had some skills from my work experience in my earlier years at McDonald's. Except this time, I didn't bother the ladies, and I wasn't stealing. The other cooks and team really liked working with me, and it helped me by being in the Air Force. The recognition was great, but my paycheck needed some help. Being a lower rank in the military was tough at times. Plus, my wife was not working. I was okay with that. It was who I was. I wanted to take care of her. In many ways, she was taking care of me too. I was changing and had to take care of my Adrian. I was really liking that fact that I was a husband. Well, since the court stuff was over, after going back and forth to Akron, I even did my paternity blood test at the base. Of course, no charge for me, and I knew that he was mine. I thought that I had a strong case against Lynn. Plus, being married and also in the military, I really thought that I had a strong child abuse case at that. Not so. The judge told me that I was a good father and to keep doing the things that I was doing, However, I had to pay something like $80 per month in child support. I did not get custody of my son, but I got weekends and four weeks in the summer and alternate holidays. Then my case was over. To say the least, I really loved my son, my firstborn. I was bonded to him and broken inside at the same time. Every time that I would think or discuss it with Adrian of how the court custody turned out, it was not an easy feeling. While I wanted to cuss someone out, I did hold my peace because of my son! Disappointed, I would say she won. I still did not miss the fact that Lynn and I did not get married. My mother always told me to do it (get married) for love and not for the kids. Still, my mom's words stayed with me.

Well, anyway, the summer was here, and we drove once again to pick up Big Mike from Akron. I was excited, and Big Mike took my mind off things. He had my undivided attention. And that was a fun time! Adrian was watching my son as usually, and now, he's almost three years old. I remember the time that he was still in diapers, and I would come home, and he just had boo-boo everywhere, and even eating it, I could not believe the mess he made. So one of us gave him a bath, and the other cleaned up the mess. That boy *stank* really bad. But for some reason or another, he did not like her. Well, Adrian did not, let's say *never*, treat him like her own child while she watched him, but she did not abuse him, and she did the best she could when he visited us. The good that he got was because of me. Another, I remembered, he was quiet and did not talk much, so when he ate, especially chicken, Big Mike would eat the bone too. He was always greedy, so we had to watch him closely. I still loved my son! Other than those few times mentioned before, we had so much fun that I did not want to take him back home to Akron. I purposely missed the custody cutoff time to take him back to her. Lynn did have permanent custody. Her lady lawyer did good and later became a judge. Nevertheless, I went to work and then, onto play ball, after work. That was my routine, which worked for me and us. Anyway, while I was playing basketball, Adrian was going through some things. I just did not know! Lynn showed up to our apartment on Grand Avenue in Dayton with her mother and the Dayton Police Department to regain custody of Big Mike. Adrian tried her best to fight and fought with Lynn to keep him, not wanting to disappoint me. My baby herself almost went to jail. One thing for sure, if it was not for me—I looked good with them fighting over me (my son was just there)—so to this day, I take that credit for the disturbance! Get this, Adrian told me that the policeman stated that if I was there, then I would have gotten arrested! Therefore, we both almost went to jail. I was sure that was one of the times that I was glad that my mother was praying for me.

So going forward, it was a little difficult for me to take Big Mike out of town without going to court to adjust the custody papers. So I just kept the peace. I would then see Big Mike when I was in Akron and would take him shopping. No longer did I buy him expensive clothing or toys because the clothes or items would get messed up by the next time that I saw him. So I did learn my lessons and shopped for the bargain. I was not one to think that he would grow out of it. I just wanted him to have the best that I could afford at the time because he was my son! Boy, did I have me some baby mama drama! I did get more out of it from time to time. Lynn did pretty good with me because I respected her family. If it was not for her family, especially her mother, I would had had been a lot meaner to her. Just because! Plus she only lived around the corner from my mother and family! Plus, my older brother had liked her too. I just beat him to the chase. And I got the drama. The irony of my youth, emotions, and flesh over wisdom. I did not have much wisdom! True wisdom is to not get caught and pay the child support. I never liked paying child support. It was not because of the child but because she would or could spend my money on another dude. That was a big issue for me! Now, we are back in Dayton, Ohio, and living the married life with Adrian. Things are different for us now. Something changed with us even more, especially from the loss of custody. Incidentally, this affected us and our relationship. Now we were arguing a bit more. I did not blame Adrian, but in little ways, I did. I know that she had my back, at least for the custody, even though her reasons may have been self-serving. Maybe us having a child would answer the call or bring us closer together. That answer kept being no because I was not ready for another child. Plus, I wanted to become a doctor. I have several dilemmas facing me and avoiding certain family conversations with her. So we would argue more! I guess marriage was confusing me too. Or did I not know what I want! I don't know.

Now, Adrian was becoming even more jealous and insecure. At this point, Adrian had her first miscarriage, and there was nothing she could do to stop it. The little baby (fetus) came out in the toilet. After going to the hospital, the doctor informed us that these things happen, and there was nothing that could be done. I tried to forget the argument and get closer to her. I did want to be a good husband, even with my faults, and I did have plenty. Somehow, the arguments made it a little easier to get over the loss with the miscarriage. Truthfully, there was not much to say. We just dealt with it and accepted it for what it was. Well, I was sort of messed up too. My life got off to a very unique start, not to mention the ladies that I kept crossing paths with, but something in me wanted to be married. I wanted to really love Adrian. I did not know what I was doing, but I wanted to keep trying. I would look at her, then her eyes, and try to get closer. I wanted to get closer! Then we would somehow get on the subject of church and God, which reminded me of the times we talked about religion. We would talk about it all the time. I don't know, but I was placing the cards on the table. Now, Adrian had met somebody at the hair salon, and her name was Jillian, and her boyfriend was Jacob. Long before you knew it, they set it up to play cards. Well, it was spades. Well, I started playing cards with my brothers and sisters, and we would be up all night sometimes. Plus, my dad had his own reputation. He was a bad dude and could gamble too. Anyway, we would go to their house all the time, just to play spades, bid whist, and drink a beer or two. I was not much for drinking, especially beer. This card playing went on for a few months or so. Adrian and I were pretty good, and we had our signals together, and they would not know that we were cheating. Signals such as touching your watch means to play diamonds or scratching your arm means I got it, and so on and so forth! We got really good, and then we started playing for money. Well, I kind of had to since I had the part-time job, and every little bit helped our situation. It was cool for everyone, and we all respected each other. It was good times especially when we won! Jacob even had his gun on the counter. We did not pay much attention to that, and we were not intimidated. Adrian and I were doing well, and our minds were at ease. Well, I thought it was a good time to bring up the church subject again. Believe you me, church was dealing with me, or let's say God was dealing with me. Every time I think I want to go to church, something would come up. Every time! But my mind was pulling me in the opposite direction. I could not get God off my mind! Adrian loved playing cards more than I.

Nevertheless, we were pretty, pretty close in our relationship and now inseparable! One day, after playing cards we are in the front of our building at the apartment. I will never forget it. I had told Adrian of a pastor that I knew of in Dayton, Ohio, by the name of Bishop Eugene Ringer. During the same time, Bishop JE Pope (he was my pastor when I was in Akron, and the church was on the south side on Getz Street, a nice big church) was to visit us for a church convention with Bishop Ringer. The other pastor was Bishop AD Porter in Cleveland, Ohio. They all travel and fellowship doing conventions together. They all had nice-size churches too. Anyway, Bishop Pope stopped by our house and had dinner with us. Anthony was his son, and we sometimes stayed in touch. We knew each other since age ten. I spent the night over his house and had become like brothers. Anyway, we had dinner talked and Bishop Pope, and he was on his way. This timing was a little strange for me, even with Bishop Pope showing up. I had to call my mother and tell her about it because she used to be the church secretary when our family was under Bishop Pope. I was not in church, but Bishop Pope was still my pastor, and I had much respect for him, the god-fearing kind. I truly believe that Bishop Pope was a man of God! Anyway, I had started the conversation with Adrian as we arrived to our apartment, and at this point, I do not know what came over me!

All of a sudden, I was serious about my wife, and having a relationship with God at the same time. I knew that I wanted my family to be in church. Since Bishop Eugene Ringer was the pastor of Faith Temple Pentecostal Church of God located in Dayton, Ohio,

I thought that we would be on our way. Well, it did not go as I had expected. Actually, Adrian did a 180 on me! Yes, she did! What in the world was going on! I was doing a good thing! I was ready to serve Jesus! I was ready! However, I wanted to put everything on the table and let her know the things that I was doing. I really wanted Adrian, and at this point, I wanted our relationship. I wanted to be married to her. I did not want anybody else. I was ready! As I begin to confess my past to the present, she surprised me. Adrian wanted to know every detail and every fact. She wanted nothing to be left untold. Now this is the point, I had wished for marriage counseling. Bishop Pope was there, and I wished that I had talk with him first. My lips were sealed. Besides, I had too much respect for him and to tell him all the things that I had done. Nevertheless, Adrian wanted to know everything. Everything! She was furious, but she held it in! This was like sometime approximately in September. So I decided to tell her everything, starting with Steve answering the hallway phone at the dormitory. I told her that it was true! I told her from the times in Akron, Ohio, to Dayton, Ohio. You should have seen her face—disappointed, betrayed, confused, madness, hatred of the other women, perplexed. She didn't like any of it as she was turning a little red too, yet she wanted more and more!

So here I was as I begin to tell on myself for as much as I could remember. Really, my reality was just that, so I told her. Let's start with Akron.

"You see, Charlene and I was still a thing until I left for the military, and maybe once or twice when I was home on leave with the Air Force, we saw each other. I really did not have any feelings. I just wanted to be busy all the time. I sort of felt important by having all of the ladies. I heard that she even got caught for stealing, trying to get some money for me. We just lost touch, and I stopped calling her. Plus, I did not have much time between you and Lynn. At one point, I was still trying to find Deanna but to no avail. So I kept it moving! I will save Lynn for last. So I leave for basic training, and you took me to the bus stop. Yes, I was missing you and was believing that we had something special. But my mind did not know how to handle the missing part. You really had a special place in my heart, but I did not know how to ignore what was in front of me. I could not control my desires! So while at BMTS in San Antonio, Texas, I was flirting with everybody. Well, the only other females there were the female training instructors (TIs), and that was not happening. Or the other females dressed just like me. I made time to get their addresses at the base. We began to write each other across the base. I had about four military females writing to me from across the base. We even had to add postage stamps, all of 15 cents per letter. It helped us to pass time and something else to look forward too. Plus, I was calling you by third-party calling and did not get caught. In our letters, we have planned to sneak out of the barracks and meet up with each other. That never happened because it did not work. The night we, about half of us waited until the lights were out. Then we snuck out, and one of the guys were on watch to look out for us. We were out for about twenty minutes, dressed and all, and they spotted someone coming. You should have seen us, rushing to undress and put our clothes neatly up in the dark, without getting caught by our team leader. We got in the bed, just seconds before some of the dorm lights came on. My heart was racing, but I played sleep. I did not move a muscle as the flashlight hit my face with the light. I was in the bed, nice and tight. We all were as quiet as a mouse and breathed a sigh of relief. I could not believe that we did not get caught. But for some reason, my bed was wet that next morning, the only night being there that happened to me. I knew what it was, but I did not tell anyone. Then I could not wait until it was time to change the linens. I needed and wanted fresh linen.

"Now, moving on to technical school onto Keesler AFB, Mississippi. First of all, I picked up the wedding ring because I thought that we would get married eventually. I really was digging on you. However, I met this white girl, and I believe that her name was Jamie or something like that. We hangout and dated briefly. Then still while in Mississippi, I met this met this young lady at the base club. This was a normal weekend after all week in technical training for our specialty that we signed up for. My field was between an administration and information technology in short admin specialist. The weekends were for unwinding, and that's when I met Regina.

We hung out, walked sometimes, and went shopping; it was cool being around her. Even though she was a single parent, I made an exception, I just had to because my thing that I stood by was to never date a woman with a child. Seems like from the things that I have seen, there always seems to be a connection with the baby's daddy. I really did not like that type of drama. I was a perfect example of what I was talking about. But at the same time, I had to believe that people will change. Myself included! Anyway, I was still chasing the women, even though my time was getting short at Keesler AFB, Mississippi. Still, I made time to call you, Adrian. Now, I was at Wright Patt AFB, Ohio. First, it was Emila from New York. We were a couple for a while until my back got badly scratched. You remember that when Steve and I visited you all in Akron? Yes, I lied about that too. Then I sort of dated Evette. She was very jealous, like yourself. I just looked a little too hard at the women and especially when one of them were my ex-girl, Emila. Evette told me to take her home, and that was it. I thought I would try and get her back. It was cool for someone to be jealous, and then, I thought that I was the man! By trying to get her back one evening, I met up at her house and met LuAnn, her sister. The talking turned to something else, and I found out after we got married that LuAnn did not get pregnant.

"Now, Lorraine and Lynette were the last two. Lorraine and was a senior and getting ready to graduate from high school. I met her and Evette as summer hires who worked at the base. And right before we got married, I broke it off with Lorraine. I remember seeing her still, even after we got married. But Lynette is the other one that by meeting her, I did not think that I would get married to you. I was contemplating everything over and over again. She even taught me how to drive a stick shift car, her car. I was the most serious with her, but I guess I was really into you more because I told her that I was getting married, and I just know I had hurt her a lot. More than I can say because of the tears, there were just too many. So we went our ways just before you moved down here. To tell you the truth, I did not know why we were together, Adrian. You hated Lynn, we argued all the time, but I did not know why I was still attracted to you. I let go of everyone to get with you, and now, I was in the Air Force.

I did not get caught with my supervisor, Sgt. Clark. Let me tell you what we did. One day, just after lunch time, I went back to the office. Then Fred, that's Sgt. Clark, took me to the roof, and he pulled out a joint and wanted to share it with me. He looked like he did this type of thing all the time, but I only smoked it with him once. We got high on the roof of the building and on a military base. It was just once, and we were just cool, and both of us were from Ohio. That was it. I never gave him any type of issue nor would I had never told on him. He definitely could have been a pothead, and I was just glad that we did not get caught. My military career would have been gone. I never told you, Adrian, that story until later on. I just was not totally faithful! Last but not least, as for Lynn, the affairs had never stopped until just before we went to get custody of Big Mike.

"Now I want to change and my family to be on God's side. I have done enough! I am ready to serve God, but I want my family in church. In my heart, I thought that you would forgive me. I truly thought that you and I would be together! But what was going on in my mind. I spent a little time with my childhood pastor and had this come to Jesus moment. Well, to put it truthfully, my guilt, and the guiltiness of all that I have done—the lies, infidelity, sex—were all in front of me. Yes, this is the only reason that I came clean. Also Adrian, I wanted you to know that I wanted a clean slate with you! My mind was twisted. I was confused and guilty all at the same time."

You know, the truth has a funny way in showing up or, should I say, people like my wife, Adrian, have a funny way of reacting to truth. At that moment, my life, my guilty conscience, and my reality had me for the first time in my life to be off-balance. I did not know what else to do! As I remember, my marriage to Adrian was over. She looked at me crying and why was she crying? She was mad. Really mad! She was not mad because I cheated, but she was mad because she was saving herself for me and had plenty of opportunities to have cheated with other people, or men to be exact. But she chose to believe that I was faithful to her, so she waited for me. Now get this, she wanted to be with me still. However, it was only after she would pay me back! Other than packing her clothes to go back to Akron, Ohio, we were pretty much quiet. Deep down inside her, she did not want me to go back to Lynn and probably regrets helping me to get custody of Big Mike. I kept thinking to myself, "Why, would I take you back after you paid me back for my affairs with the ladies?" Being in the military, leave was still important to me and didn't want to really use it unless necessary. So since the weekend was near, I took Adrian to Ohio. Something inside me really wanted to be married, but we were pretty much done. So I decided to play tough like and man up. And then I acted like I did not care. After the silent drive, we were there on Bailey Court. I tried talking even though we made it to Akron, but my game was off. The right words I could not find. My sentences, even to me, did not make sense. But I had to play strong. So we put the stuff, her things, on the front porch, and I backed out from across the street, the empty lot, and I was on my way to my mother's house. By this time, my mother had moved to 98 Vesper Street in Akron. It was good to see my mother as always, but I was always on the move. Her (my mother) new house was around the corner, on West Tallmadge Ave and Lynn's house! So I decided to go see my son, Big Mike. Lynn and I were over. No relationship was there, or so I thought, especially after the child support case we lost, and I did not do anything. Lynn and I were over. The good thing was that I was still cool with the family. Lynn's family was not the type to get into someone else's relationship.

Later that evening, while I was there, Lynn's sister Renee was going out to the night club Harry O's on the east side off Waterloo Road and Arlington Road. So I decided to go with Renee. She used to be married and had two kids but moved and had a boyfriend that I knew. So we hung out that night and the only night ever. I was cool and unsuspecting as a threat since I was her sister's baby daddy. However, my mind was in a different place. She was well put together—thin, light-skinned, short-styled hair, and well-put together. I was automatically attracted to her. She was older, and yes, she had it like that. I would have messed everything up for her, but I was already messed up and separated from Adrian. Anyway, after Harry O's clubbing, we went to see her boyfriend. He was cool and definitely not worried about me. He was gangster-type cool, not one to mess with. Hey, I was with his lady and just cool with that. I was just glad that she did not tell him that I was trying to get with her. To be honest, I did not think that she took me all that serious. Plus, she knew my wife Adrian, and she was the auntie to my baby. Well, my little game was not much, flattery at best. I received a little kiss on the cheek, and that was it. I can honestly say nothing happened! I was just separated with Adrian, and that night helped me to ease my mind, but overall, I did not go forward with my life, only backward. I went back to my old self. After we left from seeing her boyfriend, we went back to her house to get my car, where her sister Lynn watched her two kids, so I spent the night there with Lynn, and this was our last time together like this. I know it sounds a little crazy. I just talked to Adrian and ended up being with Lynn. How ironic, but that was how my life rolled together. I managed to get into some crazy type of situations with the ladies.

Well, I got cleaned up and was back at my mother's house to say goodbye and see my brother, sisters, nieces, nephews that were there. I would normally give the children money, or if someone had a newborn, I would give money to buy an outfit. I had started doing this for everyone in my family. Then I was off to see my other cousins Mary, Regina, and Rocky, and of course, my favorite, Aunt Beck (Barbara Ann). She used to threaten me and all of my brothers and sisters with the gun. We were definitely scared of her. What she did actually kept me out of jail. I have much respect for my Aunt Beck. Then I would be on my way after picking up some Church's Chicken and then on to I-76 West to I-71 South, to I-270 West, to Route 4 South, to I-75 South, onto Dayton, Ohio, and was careful not to get a speeding ticket. Being in traffic staying up with the other cars and truckers was a good thing. Plus I stayed on my CB radio, talking to everyone, and sometimes I would be rude and nasty, calling the truckers "Good buddy," which means to be gay or homosexual and really offensive to the real straight guys. I did not care! They did not like that nor did they know who I was, but it was sure enough fun for me. Boy, that was a lonely ride but interesting. I was all by myself. Seems like the first time and much to think about. Like what lie would I tell everyone that my wife left me. What about church? All of a sudden, I… Well, I believed in God, church, and everything. I didn't know how to get in church without my wife because we were supposed to be one, together, and a family. That time, I was lost. Sincerely lost! Adrian and I did not talk much on the phone. I was working in the Air Force, the basketball season was soon to start, and I was getting ready to go to Wright State for my medical classes. My mind was even more confused, especially since I was missing Adrian. I decided not to think about her, so I stayed busy with everything going on. Carmen and I picked up where we left off with the playing basketball at lunchtime, and that was it. Carmen and I always played tough basketball. If she did not like men, I could not tell, or maybe, I was not her type. I could not tell that either. There were not a relationship signal in my sights. So the closest that I could ever gotten to her was on the basketball court. I was almost tired of trying but stayed tired from playing basketball with her.

Still, I was now working at Arby's. I am married and single. What was I to do? One night, when I got home, I decided to go up to a Church's Chicken that Adrian and I used to go to. From home on Grand Avenue and a right turn on Salem Avenue and I was on my way. I got to the parking lot to go inside to get some food. Wow! This beautiful girl, light-skinned, and long, long curly hair, jet-black. I saw all her teeth, her beautiful white smile. Then she blushed at me! No way! Adrian has always told me that girls would be my downfall. I just did not believe her. It was on for Teresa and me. She was eighteen and single! Sexy, as I don't know what! I talked to her. She was definitely a tease, and I did not get that number. And I was going to keep trying. She was a gorgeous and silly young girl, but I did not mind, nor would I tell her that I was married.

Then I would go back to work and about a week later at my military job. I delivered some mail to the math department. What was going on? I met this cute young lady, and she looked at me with the cutest little smile only exposing a few of her teeth. It was quite amazing, and she introduced herself as Nancy Buck. Just brown-skinned she was, and again in less than two weeks, I am interested again. But I had to hold my horses. Nancy had a live-in boyfriend. Somehow, I could tell from her smile that she was the nice and sneaky kind. She would definitely cheat on her man! I believe Nancy and Teresa wanted that chase, or should I say, they wanted me to chase them. So I thought about it. For Teresa, most definitely, and for Nancy, not really because we worked together, and I would see her anyway. I just had to let Nancy know that I was married before someone like Bessie, Donna, Pam, or Sgt. Clark would tell her that I was married. It took me about a week or so, and I told her that I was married and that my wife went home to visit her mother because she was missing Akron, Ohio. My little lie worked, and the more I said it, the more it sounded true! So that was my new story on my absent wife. Still, I could not figure it out, but Nancy did not care. She was interested in me, so we started talking. I would eventually sneak her in the mailroom away from the mailboxes, so when the officers would get their mail, they would not see us, and I was in her face, with the kissing and stuff, but nothing serious. This was really a big chance of getting caught for not doing nothing. Plus, everyone knew that I was married. The military held strong to marriage and family values at that time. Nancy and Teresa wanted the chase, but Nancy was definitely the woman of opportunity and convenience.

My timing for Teresa was a little bit difficult because my schedule was so hectic. I did not get her phone number for a while, so I saw her when possible at the Church's Chicken on Salem Avenue. I believe if Teresa was a little more serious or mature. We could have been an item or something more or even had an awesome relationship. But I was attracted to her and kept trying. Nancy gave me more motivation to go to work for the work-play thing. We did not talk on the phone much at work because of the push button lines and anyone could pick up the phone, so I stopped by her office quite often, so we could talk or walk outside as coworkers or make our rendezvous in the mailroom as often as possible. This would be most of our relationship until I got her phone number. Then we would talk around her boyfriend work schedule. I could have never had a serious relationship with her, just a plaything. I believe that most of the ladies gave me time. Because, they being genuinely interested was for the fact that I was studying to become a doctor. I used this line quite often, and it kept working time and again. After I mentioned that to Teresa, I was able to get her number too. Now, the hard part was to figure out the real reason that they wanted to be with me. This was not an easy task! Nevertheless, I got plenty of play or girls, I should say! So I always used that doctor line, and it always worked! The O'Jays or Smokie Robinson, LTD or the Commodores would normally be in my background. I have always played music, especially when I was touched in some fashion by a woman.

Music was definitely a part of my life, and I played or sang music, all of the time. I must admit, even though I played that music, and certain songs made me think of Lynette, down in Middletown, somehow as I was missing her, I found the time to take the forty-minute drive there for a rekindling of what we had that I had messed up. I went to her apartment, and to my surprise, no answer. So I knocked again. Nothing! Then I drove to her mother's house, and they did not tell me where she was. Then I started to think as my mind was leading me again. Just maybe, she was married! At that point of my loneliness for her to be in my presence, I decided to leave it alone! Leave her alone! Just maybe, she was done with me! I didn't know for sure. So I drove home and chilled listening to music for some type of comfort. At that moment, I was all by myself and married, but separated. I did not like that feeling at all. The girls of my past down in Dayton were just that my past. I had got rid of all the numbers when I got married. I did not like being alone and feeling the loneliness and emptiness. It was not a good feeling! Not at all! I just know that if I would have hooked up with Lynette again, I would have stayed and filed for my divorce. No doubt! Somehow, it was not meant to be, but my mind was made up to be with Lynette. Maybe I just had too much baggage! I thought to go back to Middletown to try to see Lynette, but I just could not bring myself to do it. I don't think I could handle the disappointment just in case she was not there again. Now, I was trying to find someone else, so I could forget Lynette. She was the closest thing to true love than anyone I have known, including my wife. I would not forget her, ever! I just started to focus on filling that void in my heart. Adrian was not here to go play cards with Jacob and Jillian, and there was not much to do but to go to work, gym, and school, and no card playing. It was actually stopped.

For the very first time, since becoming a man, I was lonely, and hurt. I actually felt like that of what I was doing to others, the other females. I was hurting, and the tears were in my eyes. I had to get rid of this feeling, but I did not know how. I have never felt like this with Adrian or Lynn. Never! Just Lynette! Again, I remembered what Deanna had told me, even though I could have fallen in love with her. Deanna told me more than once: "It's better to have love and lost than to have never loved at all." These words were forever with me. And it would not come to my mind unless something serious was going on in a relationship. Those words were special to me from Deanna, a keepsake, if you will. Those words definitely applied to Lynette. Now, I am figuring out that I had left Lynette and that special kind of love we had shared. For an obligation that I had shared with Adrian. I had asked myself over and over why did I marry Adrian. My answer were obligation and convenience, and of course, lust! It was not for love, but somehow, call it crazy, I thought that I wanted to be in love with Adrian. But... But I could never and never be committed to her. Not ever! I had a fight, a constant battle going on in my mind, all of the time, even when we were together! Then, I thought that her jealousy and misery drove me to cheat or stay unfaithful. Because that was exactly what was happening! Then I started to miss my crazy jealous wife, but I would not call her either. I got to keep moving on with living my life. I went to work with the Air Force, working part-time at Arby's in Dayton, off Salem Avenue, and I was separated from my wife. Busy is what I had to be. Also I was in school at Wright-State, finishing up the fall quarter.

In one of my classes, I met this young lady by the name of Vicky Stokes. She was nice and had a very nice personality. She had a nice figure, short hair, and sort of light-brown, but not a dark complexion, like me. For some reason, I have always noticed that I notice the color of the female. But I did not know why, and somehow, it was part of my taste, my selection. Hmm! Somehow, Vicky and I were in a conversation, and I was able to get her number, and before I knew it, she was at my apartment. I wanted to really get over Lynette! Vicky and I started hanging out after school or work for the both of us. I had a tight schedule, plus I had to study. She did not mind. It seemed like she was glad that I paid attention to her. It was sort of weird in a way, but I appreciated her being with me. I was starting to enjoy being with her, and we were getting to know each other. Sometime doing the time that I was seeing and spending time with her, I thought something was wrong with me and decided to get checked out. I could not go to the military base doctors at Wright Patt because it would get reported to the commander. That was not happening on my account, so I decided to go to the health department in Dayton, Ohio. They did offer free testing for STDs, and I was so glad. I took the test and to say the least. It was so uncomfortable for me. They hurt me and my manhood. Anyway, I did it to find out if I had any diseases. I could not afford that to be the case for me. Now, I just had to await the STD test results. So Vicky knew that I was married but separated, and Vicky seemed to be into me a bit more. I was not thinking about Lynette or Adrian as much. The test results were the biggest thing on my mind. I was busy and busy with Vicky. We were cool being together, seeing her on certain nights at the college was good. I finally got the call from the health department but missed the call, and once I had a free moment at the payphone, I called them back to get the STD test results. The nurse stated that I was free and clear, and there was no evidence of any STDs in my system. I was ecstatic and overboard with joy. My first test ever like this, and I was surprised to had passed. But for Vicky, the one thing that kept bothering me more, since I was free and clear and did not want to catch nothing close to anything, was the eczema of her skin that made me a little paranoid. She had eczema in certain areas of the skin—her hair, face, arms, and legs. I was nice, and we were good for the few months of our part-time relationship. Somehow, I knew this one would not last long. She was nice and not demanding, but I must be getting my grove back, and my body was good to go.

Well, let's just say that on another note, I was healing and my brain was not hurting so bad from missing Lynette. Yes, after the fact, Lynette did a number on me. I did try to fake it, but she would find her way back to my mind! From time and again, I would think of her. I remember going to Salem Mall on Salem Avenue in Dayton, and I stopped by this little pretzel or hot dog place to get a quick bite to eat. I was thinking about I was just with Vicky the night before, and I could feel that that little thing we had was about to be over. I was getting a little bored, and my old self was trying to show up. Then I would be chasing the ladies again. Anyway, I do not know why I stopped in this place. The mall was just after you get to Roger Troutman and Zapp studio, on the left side, about two miles on Salem Avenue. As I go to this little place, this girl or, should I say, young lady was on the cash register, and I was next in line. She was light brown with thick, shiny, wavy black hair. She was beautiful and with the whitest teeth showing her smile. Wow. I had made my order and asked for her name. She also looked a little familiar, but I could not place her, so I had asked Pam for her last name. Boy, did that do it. Pam stated that her last name was Ringer, and everything came together. Yes, her dad was Bishop Eugene Ringer, a pastor. When Bishop JE Pope came to visit me and Adrian for dinner, he was in church convention with Bishop Ringer's church. Now, this was truly a small world. Pam and I instantly connected. When I saw her, I had a quick thought. If I had gotten myself together and turned myself around to get in church for my soul to be saved with my wife, I guarantee you that I would have had an affair with this woman. Not a doubt in my mind, and God did not allow this to happen. I was not ready to serve God. When I saw Pam, all I could say is "Wow!" She was just as beautiful and in church! This girl, if she had only known it, would have been a game changer for me and definitely she would have changed the course of my life. And I would have gone to church with her.

Anyway, Pam gave me her number right away. She was automatically comfortable with me because I used to go to Bishop Pope's church (Zion Pentecostal Temple). I got my food, did my quick shopping, and was on my way home. I was so excited and on cloud nine, thinking about Pam. I remembered her whole family—little Kevin, Karen, Alford, Lady Ringer. They were a really attractive family. Karen was so beautiful too, no joke, but she was a little older. Bishop Ringer was almost my pastor, but I had never attended his church. I had called Pam a few times, and finally, we talked and arranged for her to meet me at my apartment. So I had stopped calling Vicky, and she got the message. It was over for Vicky and me just like that! I had all my attention on Pam. So we started to hang out. I know her dad was a pastor, but Pam was not the churchgoing type, not from our time together. We just talked over the phone, and when she found time, she came to meet me at my apartment. We had this attraction instantly! I cannot explain it, so we were in the living room and talking, and I kept trying to get close to her. Something about the young ladies from Dayton, they sure did believe in the chase. This was one lady that could have had my baby. No doubt! But because of the chase, we played a little, talked, and she was gone. I was still chasing Teresa, and between both of them, nothing was happening. But I was after both of them at the same time. Pam had the advantage because she had been to my apartment. I was not much for watching TV at that time. I was chasing women as much as possible, just like Pam. She would come over to talk, or we hangout. She was the tease, with only little kisses, and then, leave. Maybe God was giving her a guilty conscience or something. Because what we had or what we were doing, or should I say not doing, was pretty strange. This thing we had was totally out of character for me. I was used to getting more and not in it for the chase. Somehow, not to fool or make a fool of myself, I thought that Pam would really be worthwhile. Maybe that is my truest feelings because I wanted so much more with Adrian. Pam, she was really cautious with me and not to make her dad, the preacher, look bad. Still, we kept seeing each other, from time, and again, Nancy and I still had that work thing going on. There was not much on the romance side. But we did pastime in the moments at work.

I had to get my registration information together to go back again to Wright State for the winter quarter, but I still had a few months to go and follow my dream of becoming a doctor. I truly enjoyed all aspects of medicine. I was busy with life, work, and the ladies. But definitely on the dry side of things. My romance side of things were on the dry side, to mention it again, which was okay. I had too little time to do much. I had received a call from Pam, and she wanted to see me, and I just had to make it happen, and a few days later, we were together again. She seemed different this time and a little friendlier. I was liking this. Right when everything was just right between us, we were just like Adam and Eve in the Bible. We ran around the apartment chasing each other. By the time we got to the bedroom and in the bed, the strangest thing happened. Maybe, it was a God moment, or divine intervention. I was ready, in every sense of the word, but what she did threw me for a curve. It totally shocked me! I would have never imagined something like this. Pam got up, put her clothes back on, and ran out the door. What in the world was going on? Truly, I believe it was God! That was another God moment for me! Plus, her dad, Bishop Ringer, was a pastor. I believe that Pam was under God's protection. I had never seen Pam again. We were almost totally in adultery, a sin against God! Pam was definitely an *almost*, but in reality, in God's eye, *a definitely not*, no doubt about it. It was stuff like this that kept making me realize that something was different about me, and I deemed or called it weird, which meant from my definition, the mysterious ways of God! Weird is what I had started to say for my personal expression of the mysterious ways of God. While my time with Pam was, to say the least, memorable, it will not be forgotten.

So now it was Monday, and I was back in uniform and working at the base. Sometimes I had to drive the fifteen-passenger van to pick up other military personnel or supplies or equipment. This one day, Sgt. Clark said that he had gotten an assignment to leave I was so glad. Glad to say the least. He probably would had gotten me a court martial and a dishonorable discharge. Not in a mean way, but I was glad that he was leaving. You see, I really didn't get into drugs or the getting high thing. I was truly an into the girls and definitely a want-to-be ladies' man! I was definitely into the ladies! Not a doubt in my mind! Sgt. Clark would be leaving, and his replacement was this little short brother that worked in my office who would be promoted from Senior Airman (E-4, SrA) to Sergeant (E-4), aka Buck Sergeant. I had just made senior airman (E-4). The money helped with the promotion, and I was soon to cut back my hours, so I could play basketball. It was right on time! Now I would have to work for Sgt. Eddie Johnson from Cleveland, Ohio, and old school (old music, old clothes, etc.). Eddie, as I called him, and Sgt. Johnson when I was in front of other people. Eddie had this thing for Ms. Bessie Lark. He would flirt with her all the time. Eddie was really into Bessie. And I was liking her oldest daughter, but Bessie did everything she could to keep her daughter from me. And she did. Anyway, Eddie played a little ball, too, but Eddie had a weird shot, and he was not that good, I never wanted him to be on my basketball team.

Okay, getting back to the fifteen-passenger van, I worked I area B and had to pick up supplies and Air Force and military or DOD forms from the other side of the base in area C, the logistic side. While there, of course I was flirting with the ladies and trying to get those phone numbers. Nothing happened and no numbers, but I had been gone too long and had to get back to the job. On the way back, I believe that I took Kauffman Road to Springfield Street and onto the gate. I remember that I made a hard-and-fast left turn from Kauffman Road to Springfield Street, and I am not kidding, that blue military fifteen-passenger AM radio van was on two wheels on the driver side. I had that joker on two wheels. I could not believe it… I was saying every curse word that I could think of. And believe you me, I was so scared. I could not tell anyone! That two-wheeled driving deal was my secret, just like the ladies! Never would I do that again, nor did I want to get a court martial, if I had of been caught! Never to do that again! Never! This was my most dangerous and most exciting thing that had ever happened to me at this job, except for meeting Nancy, my coworker that kept things with me very interesting. What an experience to remember, both of them!

It was now January 1984. Going back and forth to work, it was bound to happen. I had to try to talking to her, but my intent was to be with her. Carmen was not having it, not one single drop of my mess. She probably saw right through me. Carmen and I were still friends too. Yeah, on the real. We were just coworkers and friends. She was about twenty and very mature for her age. Sometimes, she would come and support me at the basketball games that I had played for the base league for my third straight year. While at Wright State in school, I did meet another tall-like light-skinned young lady, also beautiful, maybe between an 8 and 9 on a ten-point scale. She was no doubt beautiful. I got her name and number, and thankfully, I did not run into Vicky anymore. Or maybe it's because a new school quarter just started. Well, I was again glad. I was trying to get to know this young honey. I like her right off. Lisa gave me her number, and within two days, I was at her house in Dayton, and she lived by the Salem Mall. I never made it into her house. I could only spend time outside, at the mall, or inside my car. Lisa was kind of protected and moved with me pretty slow. I presumed it was another Dayton thing. The chase was on! I was getting tired of playing these games, and they were not my real style. Don't get it wrong, Dayton, Ohio, had beautiful women all the way around. A lot of time in the *Jet* magazine around the society page, you can always see someone on the model centerfold from Dayton, Ohio. This dry spell was not really working for me; the chase for romance was not working for me either.

I decided again that I wanted to be married. I needed to be with someone on a full-time basis. I was beginning to start missing being married to Adrian. So I decided to call her to see what was she doing. So I decided to chase after my wife. I could have pursued true romance and happiness with Pam, and then again, probably not Pam. But there was Teresa. She was a little silly and still working at Church's Chicken and probably not truly ready for me. Nancy at work was definitely not to be on the serious side. Therefore, the only real chase would have been Lisa or to take a chance on finding something new. Really, I was too busy and tired and tired of being dry, with no steady lady by my side. So if Adrian comes back, I would have a wife again. The other part concerning Adrian is I did not know at what cost. I did not know if I could trust Adrian, or if I did not care and I want her to be my wife again. I was confused for real! I knew that I needed structure if I wanted to be successful. Adrian and I did not come from much, and it was in the back of my mind that I wanted to build something together with her. Still I did not know why. So I have a part-time job, school, work, and on a basketball team, but I have to figure out how to go to Akron and have a real conversation with Adrian, so she would come back home. I knew that I could not tell the truth about what I had done. Again, I would have to live a lie. I was terribly busy, and that helped. Now, I just found two days in my schedule to get to Akron and return to Dayton. I had a short window to see my family and cousin Mary and everyone else. This was hard but fair! I was definitely not going to tell Adrian that I had other women in the apartment and in the bed. I was not going to do that. I do know and learned the hard way that like the old saying, "Absence make the heart grow fonder." So true! Yes! Adrian did miss me for real. Somehow, I knew there would be a catch to it. If I wanted to have her back, I had to accept her for her payback to me from my previous cheating days. She told me every detail. What else was it to do so I played my part. I acted or pretended that I cared and was shocked that she had paid me back. My mind was blank again, just like on my wedding day to her. What was I doing? Again? It was not about love, but for me, it was convenience and structure. I needed structure in my life. On my part, it almost felt like I had to have her come back to me. And I had to win, whereas she would not have the last say against me. Especially, if she was calling herself to pay me back. My mind was a little different at this point. I want to pay her back even more this time with some ladies that I could not name, but they did not count. I wanted to have the last say. She told me that she was hanging out with this Joey dude and some other fellas too that I have never met and that they had a short-term affair. If it was even true, I decided to accept her back anyway. I was not an angel, but I felt like Adrian belonged to me. She was my wife! Plus, I did not have to see him or them, the other guys. If I had of done something crazy, things may have gone down a bit differently. For the first time in my life, I believe I became a little jealous. For real! I had thought for a brief moment that Adrian's jealousy was wearing off on me. No, I was not really the jealous type, no reason to be that way. Because I could already get or have had a whole lot of ladies. So we made up. I went to pick her up, and Adrian came back to Dayton with me!

For some strange reason, I really wanted to try again, and pay her back even more at the same time! I was not sure if I was a little crazy myself about Adrian. Now, I was on another mission or tangent of sorts. I somehow had this double standard. I could do it, but you could not. This payback from her bothered me! I knew one day that I would get her back! We said our goodbyes, and I saw my son while Adrian sat in the car with the heat on. Well, it was wintertime. We did manage to see Adrian's real mother (Betty Spears) and stepfather (Chris and a preacher at that) at her mother's restaurant on North Howard Road. Betty had a restaurant and sold clothes and things on consignment. She served us a free meal, and we tried these Glory Dogs. They were just awesome and good hot dogs, buns, ketchup, mustard, chili, and coleslaw on top. They were good! Adrian and Betty (her mother) did not get along that well. It was fairly okay, this visit. Adrian wanted to know why she gave her up for adoption and if Ben Thurman was really the father (Nate Thurman, former NBA player, his brother). Adrian had a brother Arvis, and truly, they both looked like Ben, high-cheeks and all. Only a DNA test would tell the truth and the whole truth. We used to visit with Ben, his parents that lived on Lovers Lane in Akron. Anyway, time there was spent short. We were off and on our way home to Dayton. Sometimes, I would have these five to ten minutes nosebleeds, and then, it would go away for a while and even months. Sometimes, the nosebleeds were shorter, but they seemed to come mostly unexpectedly and place a damper to any plans I may have had.

Other than the nosebleeds, it was nice sometimes to be in public with my wife Adrian. We would show up only to show off. Adrian was not totally happy at this point. Somehow, we were pretty good in the public. Of course, I really did not want to tell my wife about her (my lunchtime basketball friend) to prevent another argument or making a scene because I was already a suspect for being too friendly with the ladies, and there would not be any problems, and it worked for a while to keep my mouth shut. So I did not tell her at first that we play basketball together at lunch. Well, Adrian was back, I needed and wanted to have structure, but it was not happening. We were on a roll, arguing, kissing, fussing, and fighting. When things would calm down, it was good for those moments. It surprised me that no one called the police ever because we were often loud at times. One day, I went to work and decided to start looking for an attorney, so I could file for a divorce. I was getting tired! I no longer wanted this thing called marriage with her. I was done in so many ways with her. I kept thinking about what was to be my last basketball season at Wright Patt. I thought that my time to move to another base was approaching, I just did not know the date. Carmen and Adrian visited my games here and there, and at those games, I had to be sure to play a little harder and get me some points. I would score here and there at times. It was definitely fun while the basketball games lasted. On the way home, all I could think about was that dude smacked you on the butt. So I would start an argument. I was getting pretty good at it. Actually, I learned how to become an expert at arguing. The more we argued, the better I got, and the better I got at lying. I was getting so good at arguing that I cussed, lied, and cheated without a smile, nor blinking my eye. I would say to her as she would say back to me—hurtful things, but it felt like we both did not have a conscience. I believe the respect was gone! Totally! We both did not really do much apologizing either.

Well, I could just feel or it felt like I would be leaving, based on updating my military dream sheet with bases and to places that I wanted to transfer to. Generally, around two to four years on station would be a good estimated judgement, in which I would be leaving Ohio soon. But on that last game, I remember one of the players, a big stocky dude, smacked Adrian on the butt. Truthfully, I saw it but pretended not to see it. I was waiting for Adrian to tell me that it happened. I would have confronted it then at that time with him, but she did nothing! I knew that I had doubled standards, but more importantly, I needed trust! I needed to trust her, and at that moment, she did not say a word. That trust was not seen from her. The basketball season was over. We did not take a place in the game that time either, and still she never told me a thing. Truthfully again, she had to prove herself to me, especially after I took her back from cheating on me or paying me back. I wanted to take her home to Akron, but then again, I was getting very tired of her and for what we did not have between us—love! We were definitely missing the love in the relationship.

One day while at work again, I had to find an attorney. I wanted a divorce! No doubt about it! I was working like a dog to support her, even though she was not working. I was taking care of her and also made matters worse between us. And more to argue about, the word *lazy* came up more than a few times. I also found out in my search for a lawyer that I had to divorce her cheaply. We did not have a whole lot of money with the child support to Big Mike and Lynn managed the support anyway that she wanted to. I definitely did not like that either. While I was looking and searching in the phone book, I saw an advertisement on how to obtain a dissolution and a lawyer's name and number. It was much cheaper than getting and paying for a regular lawyer. Besides, we had nothing to fight over. I mean nothing and no money too! She didn't have a job, and I had two jobs. To top it off, the car was mine. The only thing is that once it was paid for and set with the court system and everything was submitted correctly, the dissolution would be granted. It could be done. Again, the big kicker was neither one of us could contest the divorce or the dissolution, or it would be voided and my money could not be refunded. I wanted this thing to happen, the divorce, so I decided to take the chance. It took me almost a month to get together the $250 needed to file the dissolution paperwork. It would have been money well spent for my stupid mistakes to freedom. I now had the money, and as soon as I received the dissolution papers in the mail and as it was discussed with Adrian, so we could agree that it would be best for the both of us. It was done, and we would be on our way in different directions. I had had enough, the arguments and her jealousy too. I would only had missed the meals and her warm body. I knew that those things could and would be replaced.

Really, I did not know if I truly wanted the divorce, but somehow, I knew that the truth of my past for the second time would come to the surface. It was always on my mind, and if I decided to get serious with God and to want my family in church, I just had to tell the truth. Also if I had gotten a divorce, the truth would never have to come out. For some reason or another that every time I thought about the church or getting back in church or getting my life together with God, it meant that my conscience would bother me. That was not going to happen. I needed for my mind to be free! I knew that God, church, Adrian and I could never mixed together. No not never! Based on how she wanted to know everything, nope, I was not doing that again. Deep down inside me, my image was important to me. Because of how we were at the time, always wanting to impress other people. I did not know why, but I cared about what other people thought about me. That was an underlying reason why I went back to Akron and got her to come back to me. Plus, I was confused. I was only lying to myself, but I didn't really care. I was satisfied for the moment. I really did not see. Or now I would set myself up to see that it would not work. Eventually, I still got tired of it and wanted a divorce. I would have been divorced by the age of twenty-two. I was busy as ever and dealing with a side chick at work. Nancy was a good outlet. I could talk to her. It was very easy to do. But still, Nancy had a boyfriend and live in at that. I was reminded of that whether I wanted to think about it or not. To this point, there was no sex involved. But we were doing everything else. This, however, kept me interested in Nancy, and I kept coming back to her and trying to no success. During this same time, we also were installing the sound-proof cases on the job for the noisy printers. They were often loud when we would print something from the office computer that we shared. We were so glad when the cases arrived.

By the time I arrived home from work, I was a little tired but decided to look at the mail that I picked up from our lobby mailbox, and there it was, the documents to file for the dissolution. I immediately open it up and got a pen. I was filling in the blanks as best I could. I did not want Adrian to help me at all. Once it was all filled out, I had to return it with the check. Then to wait for the court date for the dissolution to be approved by the judge. This was good, and Adrian and I did not have any children to dispute over as well. Besides, it would not have made a difference. My mind was made up to get my divorce. End of story! At least I thought so! Now, we were on the way to the courthouse. Adrian did not say a word. I wish that I was smart enough to have figured out that she was up to something. Anyway, we were in at the courthouse in downtown Dayton, Ohio. It was a nice room, nice wood everywhere and the table and chairs also. But the lawyer that was doing the dissolution had to discuss with us the procedure and how the process worked—also what would be expected from us. The lawyer kept saying, "If you are not sure or you contest it, either one of you, then you will not be able to see the judge." The lawyer said this three or four times. Somehow, on the last time, Adrian stood up and said that she changed her mind and did not want a divorce. I too tried to talk some sense into her, and the lawyer tried again. The lawyer saw me out the door. I was furious, mad, and upset, all at the same time. I was just done with Adrian's refusal to divorce me, and to top it off, I lost my $250 at the same time. I went home, pacing the floor, and locked the door. I was absolutely mad! I left her at the courthouse, and at that point, I did not care what would happen to her. I did not want to see Adrian again! I was done with her! For real! I had never in my life been like that. I did not want her anymore, not ever!

A few hours later, I had not heard anything from Adrian. I had thought that maybe she caught the bus and went back to Akron. No, not so. The strangest thing happened and to my surprise and disappointment, Adrian was knocking at my door. For the longest while, I would not let her in. I did not want her at all. I was done! But Adrian would not leave my door. So eventually, I was tired of the knocking (maybe my neighbors were tired too), so I decided to let her in. Then my mind was made up to take her home back to Akron. So she knows that I was done with her. I did not even want her to touch me. I did not even want to look at her. I wanted absolutely nothing. So I decided to prove to Adrian that I wanted to be free. I was lying in bed and called Nancy, and we started to talking about things and stuff at work. I was glad that her boyfriend was not home. The first time we talked, it was only for a few, and I hung up the phone. I decided to test the waters…so to speak, to see how far I could go with her. What could my limits be? Which was a good question to myself. Anyway, she had felt comfortable enough to talk with me because she knew how much I wanted to divorce her. Not much time had passed, and I was sure that she was intrigued. So out of curiosity, Adrian had asked me who that was on the phone, and I told her Nancy from work, and we were friends. Really, I just wanted to rub it in her face that I was truly upset and make her more and more jealous. Just because!

Something clicked in my brain that I may have been pushing my luck without realizing what she could be capable of. She had told me of a time that she was into another guy at Kent State when she attended. I did not know or remember the whole story, but she said something to the fact that she almost killed him, but he awakens in time because she had set the room on fire while he was sleeping. I did recall that story from her and decided to chill out a little, just in case Adrian had got fed up with me and decided to get a little crazy on me too. I did not want to take any chances. Anyway, I made it through the night with a woman that I had almost divorced. Nope, I was still legally married and only by paper. "Minor stipulation" is what we used to say. "Only by paper" is another thing that we used to say when referring to the marriage license! Nevertheless, I was going back and forth to work, busy as ever and working more in the summer, to go to Akron to see my son and family, and yes, I was still taking care of the wife that I did not truly want to be with. Yet it was in me to do so because that was who I was. I couldn't explain it or even tried to explain it. It is what it was! Now, I was beginning to understand the saying, "Don't buy the cow, if you can get the milk free." It was beginning to make sense. So I kept working, trying to talk to every woman possible. I was not getting much action from the ladies, like before. It was always better at Wright State University when my wife was not attending school with me. Only wishful thinking! I did remember a conversation on the basketball court with the guys hanging out after we have played the games. We were just talking about the military, supervisors, old times, and of course, girls...this and that. But I remember one guy saying to someone else who had wife issues. I could relate too, so I was listening, and these words would stay with me because you would hear it many, many more times: "It cheaper to keep her!" I hear that for the first time because it applied to me. But on the real, I had heard that saying "it's cheaper to keep her" many times before. That was amazing but true! So I thought about it even though I did not have much to lose. I had a wife for one reason or another and a side chick. Nancy and I was still living life at a very different pace. Not much was happening with me.

That summer, it was not that much fun, and then slowly but surely, the arguments seemed to slowly start happening again. I was trying to deal with her, but this time, I did not take her home. I was in a not-so-happy place. I started to mistreat her and push her around. I had brought a few six-packs of beer and placed them in the fridge. A twelve-pack of beer would last me about a year. I wasn't much of a drinker. I wanted to mellow out and stay to myself. Then one day, while I was at work, Adrian called me, and I had saw Nancy earlier that day as I was making my mail runs throughout the building. Of course, I made a point to see Nancy that day. I remember what she was wearing, blue pants and a brown blouse, and I was trying to get them off her in the mailroom. Nancy dressed pretty nice and had good style. What a joy to see her. It was good for the moments we shared. Short and sweet times together. That was truly it with many tries! When I arrived back to my desk to continue my work there, Adrian had called me. She did not bother me or called me often. This was good, but she would call me from time to time. This day, I was baffled and confused. She had told me the she had a dream and that I was with a girl with blue pants and a brown top. I denied doing anything wrong. But I admitted to knowing Nancy, and that was what she was wearing that particular day, the same as Adrian's dream, and then, I remembered that my mother dreamed too. At that moment, it, this reality, became so real to me. I had the only car in the family. Adrian did not have a car. It was impossible for her to know. So after I hung up the phone, I was suspecting her to be lying and went outside to see if she was there. I looked and looked. There was nothing that I could see and no other vehicles or taxis, except for military vehicles for the Air Force. Really, I did not want to believe that she had dreamed something like that and about me, but it was as real as it could be. This was one dream that I was in, and it was true. I was done, to say the least. How could this be? I called my mother to see if she had told Adrian of a dream, such like what Adrian revealed to me. And my mother did not have such a dream. That truly scare me for real! This would be another wake-up call to me from God. Another God moment. I wanted to deny the dreams, the source of it being my wife. We both were sinners. How could this be? How did Adrian know what Nancy was wearing?

Now, after that, Nancy and I had to back away from each other. I had told Nancy that we had to stop what we were doing. Then Nancy mentioned that her and her boyfriend were having issues. This was strange how all of this happened at that time. Regardless to what, God scared me enough to leave her alone. Somehow, I think that her boyfriend found out about me. My life was sort of weird that way and on that day. Our apartment was really small, and at times, I would want to distant myself and sometimes get lost in watching the television. I remember watching one of the best movies ever. Actually, I did watch it by myself. We did not watch the television that much together, or Adrian would fall to sleep. Anyway, this movie was just awesome from the beginning to the end, and I watched every moment of it. I was just captivated by this movie and the very attracted lady actress by the name of Rachel Ward (played Jessie) in the movie. There was also Jeff Bridges (played Terry), and of course, the bad guy was James Woods (played Jake). All three of them were just fantastic in their roles. Just to be candid Rachel Ward stole my heart in that movie. She was just everything that I was looking for and reminded me of my former girlfriend Lynette. While I was a fan of all three of the actors and actress, I would just watch her on anything. Rachel Ward was just simply put gorgeous! Also the song by Phil Collins was my song too, and a hit song at that. It was titled like the movie "Against All Odds." That movie and the song really meant a lot to me, especially for what I was going though! It was right on time because for Adrian and me to really make it, it was really against all odds, I thought!

Anyway, from Adrian's dream onward, I had always denied that anything had happened between Nancy and me. It would be another lie added to the lies that I was already telling Adrian about girls that I had messed around with, even the ones that I no longer remembered their names. No way I would tell her the truth. I agreed to let her stay, and she was in school and the marriage was rocky to say the least. Anyway, I just wanted to play this out to see what would happen. The dreams could have been worst for me, but this alone was too much for me. I knew it was stupid and still too young to know the difference. The car would not work well from time to time, and I had to get it fixed at Montgomery Auto Repair Shop or Sears Automotive, or wherever I could charge to get it fixed. Plus our debt that was building up was mostly on my mind. Then we had to buy some new clothes because we had to look nice. Plus, I had to get Adrian's hair done because I wanted her to look nice because she was with me. I kept wondering to figure out how was I going to get these credit cards paid off and some of the cards Adrian was the authorized signer. Better yet, I had to keep paying the monthly minimum, which was the real challenge. We were in the last quarter of college in 1984, and so much had happened and beginning to quickly approached 1985. Adrian was talking to her cousin Melody in Alabama who had gotten married with an older dude in Atlanta and moved to Talladega, Alabama. Then we decided to rent a car and of course charge it, then drive down to see her. We could not drive any car. It had to be a nice car, so we rented a Lincoln Town Car, nice and luxurious.

The one thing that we, Adrian and I, had in common was that we always wanted folks, especially family, to believe that we were doing better than we actually was, and I was stupid enough since I was the only one working, with two jobs and partially paying for college. The Pell Grants and Air Force paid the rest, so I just went along with it. Besides that, I did most of the driving. I did not mind it much because the car was new and nice to drive. I had never driven anything like that car, nor could I afford to own it, but I did take out the rental car insurance, just in case. Yet my credit card was on the way to getting maxed out. I had just got into an argument with Adrian because she would buy things and hide it in the closet and not inform me of how much money she spent. I was so disappointed and thought to pursue the divorce again. Still I did nothing! So instead, we went on down there at a moment notice. All I had to do was take some leave from the Air Force and take off from my part-time job. We had a good time down in Talladega. It was different and country. It was really country. Some of the homes were still on bricks, and some with outhouses (outside bathrooms). Melody was cool. We met her husband, and he seemed nice. All was well. We were with some of the other cousins and family down there on her side. We hung out, talked, and ate. Oh my, it was so different. Let's just say that I was a little culture shock from being away from the city. I did not know these Southern-type places existed. Even when I was in Mississippi, it was not like a thought in my mind. I must admit, the folks did not have much, nor was there much to do. All in all, they were happy. When that day was over, we went back to our little hotel. It was Days Inn or Holiday Inn, and I must give credit, the people were always nice.

Two things that stood out for me while being there was that we were close to the Tuskegee Airman that I had learned about and Talladega National Racetrack (I had watched racing from time to time). Regardless, I was surprised to see that style of living since I was from the city and now in the country. Now, admitting that I was a little sheltered, even though I did not have much, as I was growing up, I was not used to seeing homes on bricks or the outhouses. Wow! Well, time does fly while having fun. It was now Saturday, and we would be leaving on Sunday. Then back to work for me on Monday. Driving back was cool. We were feeling good about the car and had some positive things to talk about. Not an argument in sight. We did make it back to Dayton safely to pick up our car, so we could take the rental car back with a full tank of gas to Budget Rental Car. I believe it was at the mall. I dropped the keys in the slot on the door and left with Adrian to drive us home. It was over and just like that, and also just as September would begin. While at work, Capt. Sylvester called me into his office to notify me that I would be leaving and provided me with a set of orders that would pay for everything as well. I did not know whether to be happy or sad. So I just accepted it for what it was. I was so used to being at Wright Patt, and most importantly, I was close to home, to Akron. This was a great location while it lasted. I had received orders to my next assignment to PCS by the end of the year. I guess with everything that was happening in my life and all the damage that I had done, I believed that God saw fit for me to leave Dayton, Ohio. Plus, I had a praying mother who keep all her children in prayer before the Lord. This I knew for a fact! I remember the times I seen her pray and call out all my sibling's names before God. I was scared of her and her spirituality when it was her praying time.

There was not a delay in telling her that I would be moving on to my new assignment in Oklahoma and that I would still continue to send her some monies when possible. That was my mom's and I had always tried to give her money. Most of the time, I did it in secret.

I did not want the rest of my family to know that I gave her money. My mother had a big heart and would give to everyone, especially her children. Mom loved her children and did keep us in prayer. I just know that she was praying God to keep me in my mess and the mischief that I would get into. Somehow, my mother knew that I was doing something. And I did know that that was a God thing, too! Anyway, I had never been to Oklahoma City, Oklahoma, Tinker AFB. I told folks that I was moving to Tinker AFB, Oklahoma, and found out that the nickname for Tinker AFB from most Air Force folks was "Tinker Stinker." That was not a good sign for something to look forward to. Not at all! Now I had big decisions to get in order, plus military briefing to out process for the PCS to Oklahoma City, Oklahoma. I had to put in my notice for Arby's to quit my part-time gig. That job really helped me keep up the bills. I had Visas, Discover, Filenes, Sears, Montgomery Wards, D&L, JC Penney, Shell gas card, and a few more, not to mention that a few of them were almost to the point of being maxed out. The military briefers, including financial briefings on the move, gave me options to move. They could do it or I could do a do-it-yourself, or for short, we called it a Do-It-Yourself (DIY) move, same thing. However, if I did do it myself, I keep the remaining funds and claim the mileage for myself and the family. This was the method that I chose because I needed the money, and every little bit helped.

In a weird way, I enjoyed the advantage that I had over Adrian that she had to ask me for money. My value of family was all that I had known was the old chauvinistic way. The woman was to be barefoot and in the kitchen. I was changing because I allowed her to go to school, and we both wanted to be doctors. The student loans, Pell Grants, and the Air Force education office paid for some of my classes. I needed all the help possible. I did remember Adrian was pregnant, and in October–November, we rushed her to the base hospital, and she was in the process of a miscarriage (the medical term was a spontaneous abortion) that happened all by itself. Adrian had to stay in the hospital overnight for observations because of the minor procedure dilation and curettage (D&C), which is normally performed after a miscarriage. This incident grew us together a little closer, and even though she had to take it easy for a few days, we were nicer. I became nicer, as well. I kind of looked at her different. I was beginning to try to have feelings for her. Plus, she didn't really want to leave me. Of course, she had something internal going on, not to let Lynn win me back, if we had had a divorce. I am not quite sure, but I did know that I was having some type feelings again for Adrian. Just maybe, it was the baby we just miscarriage. I don't really know! This loss did something to us and leaving my past behind in Dayton helped us bond a little closer together. At the same time, we would never know what those twins could have been. We did bring it up the baby conversation from time to time but never to point fingers or argue about it. Even though we were a little shaken up about our babies not making it to be born, we both did handle it well. We talked about the amazement on how she was able to get pregnant in Alabama, Talladega, while visiting her cousin, Melody. It was very memorable for the both of us and that we had to be careful going forward. I am sure it was just talk between us both about being careful about having a baby because no one knows when the next one would happen. However, this time was the second miscarriage, so we just lived not knowing what to expect. Shortly after we left Talladega, maybe a month later, we received the news that Melody, Adrian's cousin, was shot by her husband in the stomach. What in the world was going on? We just could not believe it. We were talking amongst ourselves, trying to figure out what had just went wrong but did not find any answers. And what makes this story worse was Melody was also pregnant and in serious condition. This was some of the worst family news that we received since being married. The good news was after a long fight and Melody was holding on, they both pulled through, and a daughter was born, and she was my first godchild. Her name is Veeta. The miracle was that they both lived. We were not able to make it back to Alabama but stayed in touch. We were definitely glad that Melody had pulled through. This I knew even at my young age. You cannot have a miracle unless God is in it.

Therefore, while at Wright State during this same year, we did pretty well. Regardless to all events, it was time to pack and leave. We packed up the entire apartment, and I loaded most of the U-Haul truck, headed one-way to Tinker AFB, Oklahoma City, Oklahoma. We would be on are way via Akron, Ohio. See, the more weight that you had on the moving truck, the more the money we would get back from the Air Force. Well, I really did not have a whole lot of stuff. Besides, the apartment was already furnished. Since we were going to Akron to get the rest of Adrian's things that she left at her (adopted) mother's house, we just added that to what I had. Finally, we were acting like husband and wife for the first time in a long time. Also it seemed like we were moving up in the world and onto Oklahoma City. Well, all was packed, and once again, we said good-bye. First I spent a little time with my family and did let my mother know that Adrian had a miscarriage and lost the baby. My mom was so encouraging and told me that what was meant to be will be and that God is in control. I was encouraged. My mother was always the best at giving me a good way ahead for the future. I was not one to broadcast things like another miscarriage to the family. Sometimes, I just like to be private, especially in relationships. I don't know if that would ever change about me. Anyway, saying goodbye again. I know I have done this many times before and yet again. Then before leaving again, I went to see my son, Big Mike. I did not stay long at all because Adrian was not allowed in Lynn's mother's house. Gertrude, Lynn's mother, and family got along with me pretty good. I was in a good place with Adrian, and I did not want to mess that up. Now, we have to go back to 380 Bailey Court to say goodbye to Adrian's family. Then we attached the car to the U-Haul moving truck. Then we would be on our way. The street was one-way, and I was glad that Lynette had taught me how to drive a stick shift or we would have had major problems getting that truck to Oklahoma City.

That was a long trip there and my longest ever. Plus I had my car hitch on the back. What an introduction to manhood and family man at the same time. I was not scared to take a chance to drive that truck. This was a great experience for us both to drive over a thousand miles to get there. We had mapped out our world travel Atlas map passing through from Ohio to Indiana to Illinois to Missouri, then to Oklahoma. We were flattered to see the signs to the Ozarks and the animal wildlife parks. I remembered getting called a nigger in

Peoria, Illinois, as I passed through there to get some gas for the truck on the backroads. I did have a knife and tire iron, just in case. But we made it through all right. Those backroads there were no joke. I was glad to get out of there and had to remember to only stay on the main roads and highways, no exceptions. I never reported this incident. I just made sure that I would be ready, just in case. This was so different again; this was another different part of the country to see and experience. It was definitely a lot to see. I was beginning to get tired. I really did not want to pull over to sleep unless it was well lit up for safety. The lights had to be in place and in public with traffic. I was not taking any chances after what happened to us back in Peoria. I also remember that my roommate was from there, but he was cool. And I used his car all the time. Plus, I had never seen the confederate flag around him. Anyway, this drive took us almost nineteen hours versus the fifteen to seventeen normal time to drive it, depending on how much sleep we had got, which was not a whole lot. I had gotten smart to get me some sleep while we were driving, so I decided to give Adrian a quick lesson on driving a stick shift with a straight shot while driving on the interstate highway. Adrian was a little nervous at first, but somehow, we figured it out. So we had got back on the highway, and she was doing it. Each time she needed me to shift the gear shaft, she would wake me up to shift the gears for the truck. This time, we made a fantastic team for the drive to Oklahoma. Once we got to Oklahoma City and at Tinker AFB, I checked into the base and remained on permissive TDY (free leave time) for about two weeks and get checked in, to locate a place to live. Plus I had to find a part-time job, to pay the other bills. My rank was not high enough at that time to really support my family, so I had to find a part-time job. If needed, then I would add on another week to get us settled in. The timing was good. We found these brand-new apartments just built in Midwest City, Oklahoma, and about six miles from the base. Our new address was 1517 North Midwest City Boulevard, in Midwest City, Oklahoma. It was flat and beautiful. We signed a year lease, and we were ready to move in. It took about one week to find that place, and we were lucky enough to find it brand-new. We were the first occupants but slept on the carpeted floor until we got some beds and furniture. We were looking and did find what was needed. The Levitz was the first place we could get furniture. I did not know what to do but, to do what I was doing. My credit was good enough to get some $4,000 worth of furniture, with a GE credit line, and that is exactly what we did. We added more credit to the mess that already existed concerning the credit cards. It was not a smart choice, but it was the only way out at the time. So we went furniture shopping and had it delivered—our brand-new versus already furnished, like the apartment that we had just left in Dayton, Ohio. The first night there on the floor. I heard some scratching noise in the bathroom. It was two bedrooms and two bathrooms—one bathroom for each bedroom and everything else in the middle of the one-level townhouse. The scratching continued, and I told townhouse manager to get maintenance to come to see what was going on in my bathroom. I truly thought that a mouse was trying to get in. It was not two pipes rubbing together from growing up. I definitely knew what mice sounds like in the wall. They took the bathroom cabinet under the sink apart and found nothing, and after a few days, the scratching noise stopped. We were so relieved! We also had a swimming pool out in the back of the apartment. It all was all nice. Now I had to find another part-time job, and Adrian had to find a job too. I did what I knew. Plus I would be able to get free food for us since the money was still tight to manage. We only had one car too, so our planning had to be carefully planned once Adrian got a job. Shortly, she found a temporary position at the Presbyterian Hospital in Oklahoma City. This job was right on time. I also signed up to work at the Kentucky Fried Chicken restaurant, only two blocks from our townhouse. This Kentucky Fried Chicken was conveniently close to our home. I could not have planned it better. I had to obtain the work release form from the Air Force first before I could start working part-time. So by the time three weeks of permissive TDY ended, it was actually twenty days total. I was at my new job with the Air Force and working for the Security Police as the NCO of administration (admin).

The base was responsible for hosting the E3A Sentry aircrafts, with big thirty-foot-wide radar for surveillance and early warning detection system. They were big dome-type radar mounted on top of the aircraft. Sometimes I had to track or monitor the special security police and working with law enforcement. First of all, I did not like working with these guys. The NCOIC of the Security Police was MSgt. Roscoe and the NCOIC of Law Enforcement was MSgt. Thomas and their NCO were SSgt. Schram. He was pretty cool and down to earth. They were in charge at the hangar and pulled all of the strings. But the other two I had to watch my back. I had no trust for them. They did not seem to like me from day one. Mostly everyone was white, and I had to work in this little office in the hangars where the E3As were housed or serviced. Nevertheless, they had to be protected in Oklahoma City at the base. I thought that I had to be protected to. I was able to work with computers to setup dental appointments, some schedules, ordering forms, get supplies, and do the airman performance reports (APRs). I was in charge of those duties and very seldom I would monitor a guard post without a gun. That did not make sense, but I knew that I had to watch my back. SSgt. Schram did show me the quick tour and the ropes. SSgt. Schram was very helpful. We had to do standup formation every morning and without question. I was not the police and had never fitted in with these guys. I managed to get by every day and kept my distance from MSgt. Roscoe and MSgt. Thomas. Those two were always together. Each time they gave me something to do. One would conflict the other, which was confusing to me and fun for them. Then SSgt. Schram would see right through it and point me in the right direction. SSgt. Schram was like their right-hand or go-between man. I always thought that those two master sergeants were prejudiced toward me, for the way they treated me, but I could not prove anything.

Sometimes, I was called over to the orderly room for the squadron to work there as well and be under TSgt. Haas (he was a tall, blond-haired and country). At the same time, we were waiting for the new second lieutenant to arrive to head up the security police squadron. There was no time to learn the jobs at both places where I was put to work. I was not used to that pace, but I was definitely keeping up. I would walk across the base to the orderly room and back to the hangar. I did manage to get my work release form approved at the orderly room by TSgt. Haas. I needed to make the extra money part-time. The weather did not matter. Then it was time to go home. I noticed that people did not bother you much, if you knew what you were doing. Believe you me, I was a fast learner. I was kept things moving but did not like it there and was quietly planning an exit. Oklahoma City was nice and had flat grounds. When it rained, it flooded and a lot of puddles to step over. Since, it was wintertime, it did not snow much, but when it rained, the rain froze, and there was a lot of sliding on the ice. I also did not like the winter. I even fell a few times. I would have rather had the snow. For real! There was a lot of cattle, oil, and steak house restaurants. There were not pro-basketball teams there and frankly not much to do. The big sports events were college football between Texas Longhorns and Oklahoma Sooners. That was a big, big deal there in Oklahoma City or the all-you-can-eat steak houses. We were new to the area, and the money was still very tight and getting the new furniture did not help our cause. My wife would drop me off at the base to the hangar most of the times since I was an NCO, and once I was out of the car, the security police would announce that I was there, to be logged in. That was standard. I felt a little important because doing that time rank had it privileges. One thing about the police, their hierarchy was in place. They had to give respect to authority and especially the rank structure. I did not have much of it, but it did. My rank came into play sometimes and made a difference for me. This year of 1985 was quickly moving along. I had turned twenty-three years old, and there was not much to do because we did not have much money to spend or waste. My hours at Kentucky Fried Chicken were paying off. We needed the money and ate the leftovers. Actually, I brought it home most times. We ate a lot of chicken, fries, and sometimes coleslaw. If we did not have groceries, then we had some seasoned, pressure-cooked chicken. Every penny counted, Adrian managed the money most of the times, and I did not know much of what was going on. I did not always have money for lunch. Sometimes I would eat at the mess hall close to the barracks. The meals were usually under $2.

It was now February, and we were settling in at our new town-house and on our jobs. I found out from some of the guys at the gym that the basketball tournament was about to begin and for me to get signed up if I wanted to play. So that is what I did. I joined up with the Security Police Team. We did have some ballers and some tall guys too. The police guys were pretty competitive anyway, so it was a good team to be on. SSgt. Schram also played on our team. In playing the games, I did hold my own. My wife came to a lot of the games, and of course, I showed off a time or two. It was pretty well organized. We played a few games a week and some weekends after work. Some of the guys could not play because police or security duty was for twenty-four hours a day. With no questions asked, it was always duty first. Well, I did administration as the NCO, and it was not the case for me. I was thankful for that. I went to work, and I was home for dinner. All was working well. Life with Adrian was getting better. I was always busy or never home. It was all good with my schedule. Except for the bills! Our debt as mounting, and still we were having car issues from time to time. But somehow, we had to keep the car running, so we both could get back and forth to work, the basketball games, shopping for groceries, amongst other things. Definitely we had to keep that car running. The mileage was getting up there to about 177,000 miles and rising. A lot of times the mechanics at Montgomery Ward's Automotive could not figure out what was wrong with the car, but my car was drinking oil like water. I was spending all kinds of money and credit to the mechanics to just keep adding oil to that car.

We had decided that we were going to try again to have baby. I just wanted a little girl, but that February, Adrian did a pregnancy test and found out that she was pregnant again. This was the third time, and we were a little nervous, and things were better for us with less arguing and stress for her. These months from December to March, we were getting by, and she was still holding that baby in her belly. It was wonderful, to say the least. Yes, I was getting excited and decided to announce it, as fathers do. This was a lot on our plates. We could not stop, even though the car was on it last leg. The bills, car, and pregnancy were our only topics to talk about. We had to really put our heads together to figure something out. We desperately needed help or a miracle. We saw a flyer or an advertisement on the

TV for a technical school called United Technical Institute (UTI) that provided financial aid. We both signed up to become Registered Medical Assistants (RMA) and ended up with a registered medical license. The program was for six months to start in April. We were to be done in November and the baby to be born in October. Plus, we needed a car! Working these things together would definitely be tough, close, and very doable. So we did it and signed up. We were able to get the financial aid and the excess funding we were able to keep. We both stayed busy. Plus I played on the basketball team. Still, it was not working. We could not keep up with the bills, but the baby in Adrian's belly was doing fine. I really wanted a girl, but the ultrasound proved to be a boy. I was still excited and hopeful because I/we did not want to lose another baby.

Somehow or another, Adrian got a ticket for speeding on the base while coming to pick me up, and if you get too many of them, she would lose her driving privileges. We did not need for that to happen. Once the security police would announce to the command center that the NCO wife was there waiting, she was not allowed to the hangar without an escort. You had to be careful how you would walk in the painted lines by the E3A Sentry aircrafts. So you would not get arrested or shot for suspicious behavior. This secure area of the base, you just had to be careful. Very careful! Once I left the job, I was going to my second job straight after work or home to change my clothes for the second job or school and to pick up Adrian. The other times I played basketball. Our basketball team were actually very challenging and tough to beat. This was my life with some big major changes and challenges on a personal level. The month of March was still busy for us, and we talked and shared our thoughts for our family and baby that was on the way. The money was not enough to stretch to pay all the bills, especially adding the furniture. From a military standpoint, we had to get our bills in order or face a court martial for financial irresponsibility. I really was doing everything in my power not to let the Air Force leadership know that I was in financial struggles. The new Second Lieutenant Watson had red hair and a short red mustache that resembled Hitler's mustache.

It did not look right at all. He was always serious looking. I did want to talk to him about my finances.

This was a big problem for me and Adrian. I wanted to keep my privacy too! So we decided to take a day off of work to go and see a bankruptcy lawyer. This is something that we had to do in order to get some relief financially. We were able to find this older attorney, and his name was Harold G. Pierce, and we met him at 3801 NW 46th Street, Oklahoma City, Oklahoma, 73112. This dude was on the ball and knew his stuff. It costs us about $350 to file bankruptcy on $18,300. We gave up about fourteen credit cards, telephone bills, Fingerhut, and a personal loan. Mr. Pierce was truly a gentleman and understood our hardship, which he then allowed us to pay it in two payments that was something we could managed, starting with the first $160 down payment. The remaining was due ten days before the court date at the United States Bankruptcy Court, Western District in Oklahoma City, Oklahoma. This was a chapter 7, Title 11 bankruptcy, which meant some creditors debts were canceled, and some we kept and was to pay it back at a lower monthly rate, but the creditors did not bother us, call us, or mail us until the discharge of the debts. Nevertheless, we still had some other credit cards about six or seven more that we did not file on.

We were now in a more manageable mess with our finances. Neither one of us were good with money, nor did we know how to save, but we knew how to spend. I was doing so much; we were doing too much. I felt like my life was just spinning out of control. Plus I did not like that place we were stationed at. I was over five years in the Air Force and did not have a plan nor did I have a plan for my future in the Air Force. Adrian and I never discussed a future. We only lived a fantasy to become doctors, yet we were in school in a technical program for becoming registered medical assistants, which in truth, we were on the wrong paths and just did not know it. I could not make sense of it at any time because we were only living to make the best of each day. I realized that the future was not for us, so I could not pursue it. I was waiting for my child to be born and trying to get ready for that same newborn. The second child on the way by two best friends, except for I married this one!

Somehow, I was rooted so that the value of family was important to me, and I did want children and a wife. I truly wanted that with no doubts in my mind or reservations. I did not know how to present my feelings or this conversation to Adrian, nor did she bring it up. I had these thoughts from time to time, but these thoughts would never be fulfilled. I had never looked at Adrian in her eyes and told her that I wanted to spend the rest of my life with her. I could never say that my heart skips a beat when I was missing her. The thing is I have never really missed her! When I was not in her presence, my eyes started to wander, and my mind sought that next woman to find happiness. I realized that I could never be my true self with Adrian, never that. Because I had to always hide my secret lies. My heart kept searching and desiring more than where I was at, so I stayed stuck and kept ignoring my heart. My true feelings kept hiding inside me. Most of the time, I was just miserable! I kept fighting within myself not to deny or give up. I met a lot of women and went through a lot of relationships, with my nosebleeds and all. Most of the time, these were the short nosebleeds. Still, I had hope to find true love.

Nothing has changed in my life to this point, except we had just filed for bankruptcy. The finances still needed some help. I was glad that I learned how to do my own taxes. While I was at Wright Patt, I attended the free VITA program course for filing taxes and did my own taxes. I started to think about how that will be a way to save money and not to pay someone to do our taxes. That was the thought I needed to give, me a sense of responsibility. I was thinking as to how I would get control of my finances, and that thought came to mind. I did not like being overworked like this. I was almost burnt out. I still was playing on the security police basketball team, and we were doing great, and the season was coming to a stance. We were in the top three teams for the best record and few games left in the season. I was able to meet some of the guys that I worked with. I remembered this one brother named SrA Donnie. I had forgot his last name, but we were cool. He was over six feet tall, and that boy could play ball. We talked a little and went home. I was keeping my schedule all the time. I went to work and home, then whatever. I went to school and home and the part-time job. Adrian was pregnant and all over the place with the car, or I was all over the place with the car. Still we went to class together. Adrian's stomach was getting bigger. I used to put my headphones music on her stomach for the baby to hear all the time with hope to feel the baby move. What a feeling of joy! It felt outstanding to do. I was excited for the little boy that was coming. Adrian was being seen at the Tinker AFB hospital, and Dr. Vinay Bhoplay was her doctor. I thought that he was from India and also a civilian doctor with the Air Force at Tinker AFB.

I have always been skeptical about military or VA hospital doctors from the stories that I had come across in my life. He seemed to be doing good, and the medical benefits of the military made him free for her. Since we did not have a lot of money or any savings, we could only say that he was a good doctor. And at the same time, we were not allowed to sue if something had gone wrong in any of the treatments, including delivery of our child. I knew this information from the many trips there for my nose bleeds. I was still having them, and really there was no cure. The doctors and nurses would just pack my nose with some lubricated strings of gauze and tape it up for a few days, and I would be fine for a while until my next nosebleed. I always kept hoping for the best. To keep my mind soothing, music would be my way out and to escape some of the realities of life. One thing about be in Oklahoma City was there was not much to do there, especially on our budget. I heard on the only black radio station would be off the air in a few months. Now that added to me wanting to leave even more. No black radio station. I could not believe what I was hearing in my ears. But it was true! To true to be real! Now we would have to listen more to the oldies on the 8-track. The track thing was getting old, and some of 8-track tapes would start getting stuck. Or they would break off inside the player. This was no fun, at all! I could not buy more 8-track tapes because I was in the Air Force and broke! The both of us working part-times jobs too. We just kept going day after day. That's what we call life or just the lie that I was living!

Now, back at work, there was a lot of moments on the base, and the security police were scrambling everywhere. It was so different being at work this time. We had a special formation called to order at the hangar and was briefed on what had transpired in the area. We were briefed news that an F-16 aircraft had went down, crashed, in Oklahoma City and two people in the house were killed. The F-16 were new to the Air Force at that time. Then one of them would have crashed by where I was stationed. Not good! The next part of the news I did not want to hear nor be a part of it. But I was selected to be a part of teams to set up sentry points for security to guard the parts (especially the classified records and systems of the F-16 until the recovery team arrived. I had a pregnant wife at home, but that did not matter to the Air Force. The mission was first. Especially I would know this after working with the Security Police. I kept saying to myself that I was not the police. My team was one of six teams on the third shift. I was thankful that I had realized my advantage after we arrived to perform our security point at the sentry. An hour or so had passed. It was dark too. While there, I discovered that I was the highest-ranking person at my sentry. I believe SSgt. Schram had set that up for me. I performed my first order while protecting the sentry point. I then found me a piece of some cardboards and made me a pad and as comfortable as possible. I called all the Air Force Security Police together within my supervision and told them to wake me when it was morning. It was a little tough at first, trying to get comfortable. Somehow, I managed. My mind was racing at first and also thinking about Adrian and the baby. Plus, I was thinking about the elderly couple that loss their life in the house that was totally destroyed. It actually looked like a bomb went off into the house. Nothing was left. Somehow the pilot survived by using the emergency ejection seat. That was all I knew to ponder upon, and sometimes, my mind would be racing with ideas of "what ifs?" It may as well had been a gravesite.

Thinking about this kept me going for bit until I fell asleep. This turned out better than I could have imagined, even though I did not want to be here. I was awakened in the morning, just in time for the food truck to arrive with hot a breakfast for everyone. An hour later, our shift was over, and it was time to go home. What a duty. I was so glad that was for only one night. The cardboard was not that comfortable at all, and it was a little chilly, but I believe that I would do it again, only if I had to. By this time, home was to good place to be with my family. I had moments when I would be thankful, especially after what happened with the jet plane crash. Truly, I was happy that we all were safe. Now, it was Sunday. I worked on the car, changed some light bulbs, and added some oil, including the much-needed chores around the house. Then we went to the Heritage Park Mall off of Reno Avenue, our favorite mall and the place to take our car, for repairs at the Montgomery Ward's Automotive. This time we would do some maternity shopping for Adrian. Her belly was getting bigger, and her clothes did not fit well. I did want the baby, my baby to be safe, and for the clothing not to be too tight. I did what I had to do, and a few hours later, we were at the mall. The budget was limited, but we had to get some maternity clothes. It was not an option. While at the mall and as soon as we arrived inside the mall building, we spotted a lady's wallet on the ground, and I picked it up. No one was around to see us, not a soul. I get it that we were supposed to turn it in to security, but security was the furthest thing from my mind. However, we thought about how much we needed the money that was in the wallet, and it was a few credit cards.

After we put the wallet back on the floor to go shopping, Adrian recognized this dude. I was hoping it was not one of her exes, and by God, it was not. It was her old classmate from North High School where they graduated from in Akron. Their names were James and Danetta King, and James was in the Air Force as I was stationed at Tinker AFB. We had got along just fine. James was a little shy but outranked me, and Danetta spoke her mind. Danetta would talk about it or you in front or behind your back. She would definitely be saying something. We exchanged numbers and planned to have dinner together at their house. I told Adrian I was glad that he was not your past boyfriend. Overall, James and Danetta were just nice people. I liked them both because they made a real good impression to me. Okay, they were gone, and it was time to shop. Well, it would seem strange for me to be using another woman's credit card, so we took the money out of the wallet, checked the wallet thoroughly, and then, pulled out a couple of credit cards and placed the wallet back on the ground. Those funds were right on time! So I told Adrian to go and use the credit cards to the limits, run them up, those credit cards, but we did not know the credit limits. So she kept spending money using the credit cards at Dillard's, Montgomery Wards, and Sears. I remember getting some of the baby clothes, a black and white Vectrex Electronic Video Game. She spent those credit cards until we could not spend anymore. No one was expecting any foul play at the cash registers from a pregnant woman. I had to keep making trips to the cars because the bags kept stacking up. Anyway, Adrian was still scared to do it, but her pregnancy was the perfect distraction, and the people were so nice to assist us. We did get some things that we really needed and stuff for the house. Now, it was time to load up the car and get it home. We must have spent overall at least a grand of credit easy or close to it, and I was too glad, we did not get caught. I did not know that my Air Force career would include all this stuff, and plus, I worked with the Air Force Security Police. Wow!

Our lives were never boring; it was just the opposite. Come to think of it, it has been just busy since I had left home to join the military. This upcoming next week would be the last week to playball to win the basketball championship. While back at work, I ran into SrA Donnie. We talked about the game big day, and he mentioned to me how his apartment complex was giving move-in discounts and referrals. I was definitely interested on every opportunity to save a buck. So I told him that I would look into it, and he would get referral, only if we could split it. The deal would be out of $500, he would get $300, and I would get $200 if I used Donnie's name as the referral. Donnie mentioned that there was a swimming pool there too. We made the deal and shook hands on it, as I was going to do it. That was all I needed, and it was on for us both. If we were to move in, we would get first month's rent free, with a security deposit. That was good and right up my alley. That deal was on point! He was a brother and a security police that I worked with. I figured that he would be on the up and up. Besides, it was not that many brothers there anyway! I thought that we would lookout for each other and stick together. Well, we shall see… I did not let my doubts cloud my judgement. I did like to give people a fair chance. Especially the police! I also asked Donnie, where could I get a traffic fixed or erased from the driving record, and he referred me to the Police headquarters building to the second floor and in the traffic division. Then I was on my way to the police headquarters building. The orderly room was downstairs, and the traffic section was upstairs to get the ticket fixed. This was my first time upstairs in the traffic section.

I saw this fine, tall, long and tinted-haired, light-brown-skinned, and beautiful young lady. I noticed her name was Cynthia which was stated on her name plate. I knew that I had a baby on the way, but this girl was something else. What was I doing again! Really, I could not resist the temptation. She was so, so sweet. Oklahoma was not known to have a whole lot of beautiful women. It was definitely not like Dayton, Ohio. I was shocked to see Cynthia working there, at all. Now, for the first and only time in Oklahoma City and at Tinker AFB, I had to find a way to be a gentleman. There was nothing fast about this girl, nor was she easy. Cynthia kept everything so professional, and I just had to respect that for what it was. Plus, I wanted her to do something to erase my ticket for my wife. At that moment, I knew that Cynthia and I would have to had gone very slow. She was always so sweet, and she did not seem like the cheating kind. At my first impression of her, all she had to do was say yes! I would have left my wife. Then I thought about it I had too many bills and a baby on the way. So I decided to take baby steps to keep trying to see where it would lead us as far as a future relationship. My schedule would not have allowed time for another relationship. Not at all! However, I was also the EEO monitor (who would think that I would have a duty like this) for the squadron and had to make sure I did things that was appropriate and not to get in trouble for sexual harassment. Boy, was this a right job for me? I think it was to keep me or prevent me from getting into trouble with the ladies.

That reminds me that out of all the things I was doing, part-time job, school, etc., the ladies were very normal and average looking, except for Cynthia. I think that if I would have lived in Oklahoma City, it would be a place that I would really become faithful to one person. Especially to Cynthia! On the other hand, whether or not I wanted to be faithful to Adrian, I was and totally faithful. I thought, well, let's just say that I was glad that I met Cynthia! Even if we only became real friends. After all, Cynthia was not the fix for my wife's speeding ticket. It was too late to reverse it; however, she had informed me that she could only get two more tickets in a year or our base driving privileges would be revoked for three to six months. Well, I looked at Cynthia again. I thanked her and headed back to work. I had to figure out a way to get to know Cynthia better, if not on a personal, then I would get to know her on a more professional level. That way, she could take care of any future tickets on the base from me or my wife. It was on my agenda to keep trying! If I did not have another baby on the way, sincerely things with Cynthia would have been totally different. I love a good challenge, and she would have been worth the chase to conquer. It was just a thought. Now I am back at the job doing what I do. My days were often filled with things to do, so time came and gone rather quickly. Then I would have the next thing on my mind. The fast-food industry was really not for me. I did it so I could have become a manager pretty much anywhere. If I were to truly be honest, it would have been too much temptation for me. When I was younger and working at McDonald's, I remembered watching how the managers treated their employees. With that manager's power and authority, I probably would had been worst with the females than like the managers of my past. That was something I just would not do. I could have never been a restaurant Casanova. Let's just say that was not my style. I know I would have figured out a way to steal the money too!

As I was daydreaming at my desk, I knew that this would be my last restaurant job. I was able to get free food, and nothing else really interested me. Truthfully, I would totally work at a restaurant, if I really, really needed to and if it involved taking care of my family. As I was leaving the Air Force job, often times, I would wonder in my mind, when will I get a day off. I would be tired a lot of days. I was going six or seven days straight, without really having a lot of time off. Now, I am waiting at the hangar post for Adrian to pick me up. She was running late as usual. This time, when she arrived, she told me that she had almost got another ticket. The security police followed her all the way to the gate where I was by the hangar. The police were at the car before I had gotten there, and she told them that I was the NCOIC of Security, and they let her go. No ticket this time! Wow! What in the world was she thinking? Actually, I was the NCO of Admin. I was so disappointed to see them and happy and the same time. Boy, that was so close! I expressed again to Adrian that she had to stop getting tickets. I did not want to lose my base driving privileges.

Cynthia told me from before that the car with the license plates would not be authorized to come onto the base, regardless of who was driving. So we still had two more chances or tickets to get. Now with that settled, we had to hurry over to the apartment complex to sign up for the special. We did not have to pay first and last month's rent but a security deposit. This was a good deal, plus they had a swimming pool. It was definitely older, but Donnie and his family lived there too, which helped me to move forward in this effort. We did the paperwork. It was approved, and we would pick up the keys in May to move in. That was good, but we had to figure out how to break the lease at the place in Midwest City. So Adrian and I came to with the plan that I was getting a PCS transfer, and they just took our word for it. It was better than the obvious to let them know that we would be saving about $400 a month because we cannot afford the current rent. It worked like a charm. We really did not know a whole lot of people in Oklahoma City and did not want to ask any-one to help us. I really enjoyed my privacy. Plus, we could go home to visit the family, and of course, I would be able to see Big Mike, my son. Adrian would not be happy about that at all, but she was okay because she was pregnant. Her family and my family would be glad to see her and that big belly.

That evening, I called my mother and brother to say hello and to see if my younger brother David would come to Oklahoma City to help me move if I came to pick him up. We were going to work and school and now had to plan a trip home and was hoping to add oil, so, the car could make it to Akron and back. I was going to take a chance anyway and do it. We were going to Akron and hope that we did not break down on the road. I scheduled a U-Haul truck and took a few days of leave each way around May 1, 1985. That was most certainly doable! My work day has come and gone, so has playing ball late in the evenings at the base. It was game time, now or never. We made it to the finals for the Tinker AFB base basketball championship. Yes, Adrian was there to watch and support me. Actually, we got closer and closer since the credit card and money incident at the mall. Adrian was a bad girl and wanted me to be a bad boy. I was really taking mental notes. We lied to change the apartment to get a lower rent and the credit cards we used that did not belong to us. I definitely was not going to mention Cynthia from the Security Police Traffic Section. We were there to play ball, and it was on. Donnie was a starter, and I came off the bench. So he and the other guys would play more than I would play, but I did get to play and scored a few points and free throws. The game was going well. At halftime, I mentioned to Donnie that I would be moving over to Elderberry Court in Oklahoma City. He was glad to hear that, and I mentioned that I was still looking for my $200 as part of the deal. Donnie did well in the point category. I was okay; however, we took second place or as the trophy states, we were "runner-up!" I had played four years of basketball between Wright Patt and Tinker AFB and placed three times. Awesome! Guys like Andrew Toney, Maurice Cheeks, Julius Erving, Dominique Wilkins, Magic Johnson, James Worthy, Byron Scott, Michael Cooper, Moses Malone, and Clyde Drexler were some of my favorite players and provided me the inspiration at that time. I used to watch those guys playball on TV all the time!

All I had going on and as we were busy, I still did not like being in Oklahoma City. There was something about that place having such a Western feel to it. All the excitement and having to soon go back to Ohio, we did that to get ready for that long drive and remember not to stop in Peoria, Illinois, not a chance. That was definitely in the front of my mind. Now we are off back to the hospital with another nosebleed. These things did get on my nerves, and even though, I wanted to be frustrated. I had to keep calm. Even though I have plenty of nosebleeds over the years and still found time to donate blood to the Red Cross, I would be close by because I never knew when it would happen. My nosebleeds were unpredictable at best. This was the last straw. The specialist (military doctor) at Tinker was feed up with not knowing how to diagnosis my medical condition, so I would be referred to Lackland AFB to see another specialist. This guy would be better and more specialized in the ENT field. Plus I have to be tested for allergies, including my sinuses. I had to get an appointment and make flight arrangements for my wife and I; if she was going to be there on a permissive TDY, the hospital would pay for the travel and hotel. I am all patched up again and have to move and then on my way to San Antonio, Texas, Lackland AFB, which is the same place that I went to basic military training school.

I was a little excited to get there to see what it would be like since I left the military training. First, we had to get my brother David here in Oklahoma City. I kept wondering how bad my nose-bleeds were. I have been dealing with this most of my life. Like forever! To include the packing of my nose with gauze dressing and tape. It was never a pretty sight to have your nose packed. I was sure hoping that the Texas doctors at Lackland would figure it out for me. The good thing about having my nose packed to stop the bleeding, I would get the doctors note to be off work for a few days until the I had visited the doctor to have it removed. Then on top of that, I had never had allergies, but now I may have it. Now I had something else to look forward to or not. The thing is, every time the packing from my nose was removed, I could breathe so much better, and my nose would not bleed for longer periods of time. I was always thankful each time that stuff was removed from my nose. Now, back at work, folks are giving me congratulations on the basketball runner-up trophy. It was not as good as first place, but I would respond thanks or thank you and keep it moving. If some responded "maybe next year," I would not say a word because I really knew that I did not want to be in Oklahoma City nor at the base. Again, I did not like it there. Anyway, while I was at the orderly room, SSgt. Haas would be leaving, and I met the replacement who just moved in on a PCS. His name was TSgt. Bobby Green. He just looked smart and rather nicer than SSgt. Haas. TSgt. Green seemed like he cared, and I did not feel like he disliked blacks. It was some of that going around, and I had never felt comfortable with MSgt. Roscoe or MSgt. Thomas. I tried to avoid them as much as possible. Maybe I felt that way because they were dedicated security policemen. I highly doubted that, but I could not prove anything, except my suspensions. Before leaving the orderly room, I put my leave in to go to Ohio and make a stop upstairs to give my hellos to Cynthia in the traffic division. This time, I made mention that we were making a trip to Akron just to draw up some conversation. Still not working. I did this as much as possible. It was all the same. She was nice and pleasant to be around. Nothing more and nothing less. After finishing my short visit upstairs, I stopped again at the orderly room to pick up the correspondence and mail. I was good, just to see her and be on my way back to my desk at the hangar. Under my breath, I would say quietly, "Bye, Cynthia," and that little thing made my day.

While at my desk, I was going through the mail to distribute it throughout the hangar and give the typed correspondence to NCOICs MSgt. Roscoe and MSgt. Thomas, if there were any for them. Today they both did. They would look at it and let me know if I had to do anything. Sometimes I had to prepare correspondence to return to the orderly room. While back at my desk going through the mail, I noticed a teletyped message notifying all airman for opportunities to the bootstrap program. It concerned college training and education at a college. I was interested but did not get the gist of it. I had to seek for additional insight and the first place that I would check was the orderly room. Everything we did had to pass through the orderly room. All our approvals came from there. No questions asked! This was my last day at work for a few days because I was in the process of moving but had to get to Akron first. I managed to get a U-Haul truck on reserve once we returned. Adrian picked me up again with no speeding and no tickets. She was finally figuring it out, and I was good with that and excited to go back to Ohio.

The car was drivable. I just had to keep checking the oil every few hundred miles or so, and I kept extra cans of oil in the trunk of the car with the spout. I would add a can of oil every five hundred miles, and that was it. At least I knew where we were not stopping. This was definitely a long drive! Adrian would drive in spurts, so I was able to get quick naps, or we would pull over to rest stops and sleep. The hotels were not even an option at all. We just could not afford them at whatever the cost. Adrian was very pregnant and was always uncomfortable for most of the whole trip. I gave her the pillow that we brought with us and blanket. If she was not comfortable, then she had to go to the bathroom. I just had to get some sleep, so we could keep moving. We stopped like this one other time. Then I would be good after that to keep going. Then it would be onto Akron to see everyone and bring my brother David back with us. David was twenty at the time, and I was so glad that he had the time and availability. We stayed at Adrian's mom's house on 380 Bailey Court in Akron, and that was as good as we could do with little money. We made our normal rounds, but this time was so different. Because Adrian was pregnant, everyone wanted to see her or touch her belly. I did not care a bit. I was excited as well. We went to see my Auntie Beck and cousins Mary and Regina, so they could see her (Adrian) too. I wanted everyone to see her. They would be a short visit each way and leaving on the next day to get back to complete the move. We ate out that evening, and David was planning to be packed and ready to go back with us on tomorrow. We were all set and ready to get out of there.

The morning came quickly, and it was time to go, and I was ready to hit the road to drive these nineteen to twenty-one hours, sleep included. We picked up some food, and then got David. Plus I had to see my mother and drop her off a few dollars because we had to be on our way and did not have much time to waste. I was on a mission! We had Ohio in April and May and then San Antonio in June. Plus Adrian's birthday in June. She would be turning twenty-four. I had always teased her about her age and how she was older than me by six months. Since its daylight on the way back, we stopped by the Ozark Exotic Wildlife Park, and it would impress and be a little fun for David. We were making good time, and that made me happy too because really, I did not want to lose time unnecessary. The animals would walk right up to the car. How different this was a first time for all of us from Ohio. After we left the exotic animal park, we had a lot of laughs playing with the giraffes and monkeys and a few others that walked up to the car, and we were able to feed them. Boy, did we have some laughs. David was naturally funny with all the jokes anyway. I remember as kids, he was about twelve, and he walked up to the white lady who was pushing her baby in the stroller. David said, "Aw, that's a pretty baby." The mother said thank you, and he said again, "That's a pretty baby." The lady smiled. I will never forget what happened next. David looked at that baby with no hair and as fat as it could be and said, "I'm lying. That's an ugly baby!" That lady looked at him, and words could not explain her facial expressions! My brother Ernie and I were laughing so hard, tears and all. We could not believe he said that. It was too funny and so unexpected. We talked about that for days. And now, I am remembering it again. David was always funny and kept us, especially me, entertained while driving back to Oklahoma City.

The car was doing fine, and I kept checking the oil. All was well. We talked about the animals at the park on how we even teased one or two of them and then rolled up the windows. They even drooled on my car windows. Yucky, it was messy, and now I was hoping for rain so it would be cleaned off the car windows. David was to stay with us for a week, and then, I would take another day of leave and take him back home. I was so glad that he answered to the call to assist us with the move. Adrian and I were doing good, and I was glad he was there. Early the next day, we now have to get the truck and get the move going, packing, and all the moving going. We got everything out of the old place, so we could get the security deposit returned to us. We were moving to an older place, but there was more to do, and you could see more people, even at the swimming pool. I was down for that. Back to the moving. Turning in keys, we were able to get all our security deposit back, and we pressed on to our new place in Oklahoma City. Time was also important to turn in the truck. David was solid and strong. He was getting down and not taking breaks or slacking. This dude worked, and he could eat! I was glad that he enjoyed the time with us, but he did not want to stay. There was no way I could feed him on our budget. He was impressed and proud of me. I was not going to tell him anything about our financial situation. We were just broke and filing for bankruptcy, and that's another reason for the move. We got a quick bite to eat and back to unpacking the truck and bringing in our furniture. The one thing that was good about this old townhouse was it was good and strong for the tornadoes. That area had plenty of bad storms, past and present. But we kept moving while Adrian was cleaning the kitchens and bathrooms so we could put our things away in the cabinets and refrigerator to keep the food cold and to put away the freezer stuff. We all were working so well together, pretty amazing, but that was my brother. We were not afraid of hard work or get our hands dirty. David was always there when I needed him. I love that boy!

The truck was unpacked, and we had just enough time to put gas in it and returned it. Then we would pick up something for dinner and get back to the house and start unpacking. We had our work ahead of us to cover up the windows and put up the beds. My pregnant wife was not having the floor as an option. We needed to get some sleep and comfortably once we were done for the evening. Getting the townhouse in order and together was our first priority with cleaning the bathrooms, kitchen, and mopping to be done. Everything was going smoothly. David would be here, and we are back at work in the next week for the telephone, gas, and cable guys to come and hook up things. The timing could not have been better, and I did not have to take time off work for each of the installations. Work and school for Adrian and me still kept us busy and the week was moving fast. David would go out and about while we were gone most of the day. I can say that he made the best of the time while there. He was truly a lifesaver and time saver. I was able to take him over to the base to let him check it out after work. We also did a little sightseeing while he was visiting, and we stopped by the Heritage Park Mall. We were having a great time, and he really worked hard for his big brother. The next day, he would be getting ready for us to take him back to Ohio. Adrian would be uncomfortable once again during the drive. We were packed and ready to go again. We had fun, and we did eat some Mexican fast-food at some Del Taco Restaurant for takeout on the way back. Again, this was a good trip and for David being with us. We had to make that long drive. By now, I was getting used to the drive and was starting to like the long-distance driving. I just wanted that car to keep holding up.

We kept pushing this car, even though it was on its last leg. It kept going, and we kept adding oil and driving it! This car was our only mode of transportation. We only had it altogether for about three years. We did the same thing going again. Everybody was sleepy and tired. The rest stops were the next best thing, as long as I could get a nap. Sometimes, I needed fifteen to twenty minutes more toward the end of the trip, and the other times, I would definitely require at least an hour and very seldom two hours. Then I would be good to drive for a while. Normally, I did most of the driving. It was a thing I had and really never enjoyed—women drivers. I did let my wife drive when it was absolutely necessary. I was one of those that always thought that men are better drivers than women. Of course, that is not something that can be proven. It's probably just an old wives' tale. When Adrian drove, it would only be at one speed. Fast! I was always telling her to slow down! Then, we would compare who really drives fast. Never an argument to win. Regardless, I always did most of the driving. It was no different in our drive back to Akron to take David home. Other than the sleep, we stopped when it was necessary, or we kept it moving. We had to get back for work and school, not to mention that we had to get more rest. We made it there, seen everyone, and the next day we were back on the road headed to Oklahoma City. We knew we would get additional rest on the road at the rest stops. It worked very well. I had gotten to a point where I no longer needed a map. I had the directions packed in my brain. Sometimes paper maps were no fun to deal with, and other times, they can distract you while driving and obstruct your view. Even if I had gotten lost, I would not ask for directions. It was very hard for me to ask for directions from anyone. So I would remember as much as possible while driving, just like the drive back-and-forth to Akron.

This time while going back to Oklahoma City, we had several things to think about, like the bootstrap program that I had to find out more information, the baby that would be here in five months, finances, bankruptcy, school and us. Also I made a mental note to see when Donnie would give me my portion of the referral fee. We were not letting those funds go. So we talked and talked, and the more we were talking, the more I was alert and not getting too sleepy. What a wonderful concept we discovered; it was working for us. We were actually bonding a little and building our relationship. Every now and again, we would bring up the church conversation and even have a debate or two for what was in the Bible. If we had gotten stuck in a heated argument, we would call our parents to help us resolved it. I must admit it that Adrian really knew more than I did about the Bible. We did have some interesting conversations. Especially the ones on how we grew up in church. Those were some of the best conversations we have had. Besides, the conversations we had nothing to deny because we both had grown up in the church and similar in the faith.

We were moving, and the time was moving, and before we knew it, we were almost home. Adrian was never lost for words. She could talk and had the brain of an elephant. She remembered everything. Absolutely everything, which made me to become a better liar. Or I just distorted her truth. It was a challenge for her catch me in a lie. We even talked about the times when I would be talking in my sleep. She told me that I kept talking to her in my sleep and she would be trying to find out in my conversation to see what I was talking about. This was truly an interesting drive home with so much insights to gain. I was actually intrigued that I had to get smarter, just in case. She was good at bringing up the past and to see if I would change or add something to my story. Adrian always wanted to catch me in a lie! Period! Anytime that I got stuck in the conversations, I would ask the question again or change the conversation effortlessly. Or change the direction of the conversation. But one thing for sure: I was a better liar by far. Actually, I had to be and know my stories like the back of my hand. Plus, I still had some relationship secrets from being in Dayton, Ohio. We are at our second townhouse in Oklahoma City and in less than six months. I was living some kind of life! One thing for sure: you do not grow up and plan a life like this. How did I get here? I can only say that I made selfishly bad and lustful choices. It was thoughts like this in my mind that made me realize that something was missing. I could never place genuine thoughts to go deeper in my mind because I would start to think on my current situation and just something that I really did not want to deal with. Anyway, it was good to be back on the highway. The CB radio was getting old and not much conversation with the truckers. Plus, it was always terrible, with hopes to find a good soulful radio music. The good radio stations only lasted until we drove out of the frequency listening area. We still had some stuff to unpack to be put up after we figured out where to place it in the house, and we had some other stuff that we had planned to leave it boxed up because we had nowhere to place it. All in all, our place was taking shape, and it was home for now while we would be there with the Air Force.

That Monday, I had gone back to work, and after my daily task were done. I made it over to the orderly room to watch some prisoners for a few hours while their paperwork was being processed for the federal prison, court martial, or discharged from the Air Force. Some of the charges were for sleeping while on duty at the guard post, caught with drugs, drunk driving, and some more serious stuff. I figured while I was there I would sign up for the medical TDY orders to go to Lackland AFB. I thought they would pay for my wife and I, but it was only for me. I was able to get a rental car, hotel, per diem for food, and the airline ticket, which meant we had to charge an airline ticket for Adrian to go with me. Well, we would be leaving in two weeks for the medical appointments. I was not looking forward to having surgery to get my nose cauterized to stop the bleeding. This was a crazy week for us because we had to study for test at the United Technical Institute for our medical training. Plus we had to know the materials to learn how to take x-rays and draw blood. I could not wait for the work day to be over so Adrian could pick me up. But while there at the orderly room, I did ask TSgt. Green about the bootstrap program, and he informed me that I could get out of the Air Force and join the Air Force Reserves to go to school, but the catch was that I had to pay for all of the college schooling on my own. Then once completed and I had obtained my bachelor's degree, I would then come back into the Air Force as an officer. I was very interested in that concept and very much thought that I could accomplished such a task with my family. I also thought that being close to home would be a great idea too and to be close to my family in Akron.

At that time, I was just relieved from my duty of guarding the few handcuffed and chained prisoners and pass onto the law enforcement police. I was smiling about the light at the end of my tunnel, and I would be able to leave Oklahoma City and Tinker AFB. I also thought that it would be a brighter path for me to become a doctor for both of us. The how part would definitely be the problem, which I truly ignored and only chased the carrot, figure of speech. On my way back to the hangar to finish up the day at work, I once again ran into Donnie and told him that I had moved in, and it was official. Yet he pretended that he did not get the $500 referral check. So I had Adrian to check with the office to see how long it takes to get a referral check, if we referred someone to the property. This time when I had asked him about the check, I did not believe that SrA Donnie was telling the truth. Plus, I needed the money regardless. Things were tight for us. I kept thinking about the court martial for my financial indebtedness, and I was not getting better. Plus the bankruptcy was looming over my head, and finally, if I would get an PCS for overseas and my family to stay in Oklahoma City. That would be terribly bad, and I would be ruined! I really had to keep pushing to get out of there. No questions about it! This stuff was heavy on my mind and all the time. We were back-and-forth with life, and it was moving at warp speed like one of my favorite TV shows *The Star Trek Enterprise* going from galaxy to galaxy. That was the life that I was living. I used to say all the time "Scotty, beam me up." Especially, when I was in a difficult situation. This was one of those times for me facing two opposites: on getting my finances together or going to college full-time to pursue the dream, my dream of becoming a doctor. I really knew that was what I really wanted to do.

Now, it was time to plan our departure to Lackland AFB in San Antonio, Texas, and there was no way we were going to be driving there for the distance of over 1,300. I was glad that the Air Force paid my portion. We drove to the Will Rogers International Airport and would be on our way to get a fix for my nosebleeds and allergies. This was Adrian's first flight and about my fifth flight, if you count layovers. She was a little nervous but got over it quickly because we were in the air. We both had been going a lot these last couple of months, including the two trips to Ohio by car. Once we got back, Adrian told me that she would have a doctor's appointment to see Dr. Bhoplay for a checkup. She was doing well to have lost two others with the miscarriages. I did not want to lose another baby, so I must admit that I sometimes got a little nervous. I would put my hand on her belly to feel the baby move while we were in the air. It was awesome, that feeling!

Once we arrived to the San Antonio Airport, we picked up the rental car and checked into the Marriott Hotel. It was nice. Downtown was nice, except for the big flying cockroaches. Those things were not afraid and made a crunch sound when you stepped on it. Nasty! Yucky! We do not want to see any more of those things. I was so glad that I did not live in Texas. I remember growing up in Akron, our roaches at our house were never that big, nor did they fly. We did not like seeing those roaches, ever. Period! So we walked around town a little for some quick sightseeing and then to the car to ride around to find some places to eat. There was a lot to see, and we noticed that San Antonio was also flat, like Oklahoma City. I had always made an observation that when it rained, it flooded. So, so true! We were not too familiar on the Mexican culture, but we knew about tacos, and that was fine. I kept thinking about the bills and had thoughts that we were doing a whole lot, not to have a lot of money, but enough to get by and then some overflow, every now and again. We used to get an advance payment for travel prior to going TDY. Anyway, going TDY would also bring in a little money after you file and settled the travel voucher, and if there was any money left over, it would come back to us.

Adrian and I were having a nice time and no arguing. I was glad not to be arguing for a change. It had gotten better since the shopping spree with the lost wallet that we found at the mall. Well, we hung out in downtown San Antonio and had rode by the Alamo but did not stop. We ate and back to the room to get ready for the next day visit at the Lackland AFB Hospital. The next day we got up, got dressed, and went to breakfast. After that, we were on our way to the hospital. That was a big place and bigger than the one at Tinker AFB Hospital. Maybe because it was the largest Air Force training base in the world. Anyway, we were there. My first stop was to get to the immunizations clinic to be tested for my allergies. After we arrived, the nurses prepped me for the tests to see what I was allergic to. Adrian went in the room with me. After I took off my shirt, I had to lay flat on my stomach, and after a few minutes, the nurse came in with these trays and little labeled bottles in them. Some labels read, moth, lice, roaches, fleas, grass, weeds, ragweed, dust, tobacco, mice, etc. The list did not stop. After she placed drops all over my back, she took a sharp object and pricked my skin, and that's where it all began. It was cruel and unusual punishment. Get this, I could not even touch or scratch. I was miserable for the entire time. Then it happened my back was welching up. It looks like mosquito bites everywhere, and I could not scratch it. I was so miserable, again and again. When the nurse left the room, I had Adrian to blow air from her breath onto my back to get me some relief. That process lasted for about an hour. I could not wait to wipe me back off. Even after that appointment was over and onto the next one in the ENT clinic to see the specialist for my nosebleeds. My back was better but still itching. I could not wait to take another shower. How much fun was I to expect with my outpatient surgery on my nose and on both sides. This would not be my first rodeo as far as getting my nose cauterized. I had got it done once or twice as a child. Well, I was to do it again, and this time for the first time, the doctors would put me to sleep.

When I had awakened on the table, my nose would be packed again. I was not expecting that because my breathing would be difficult. I would only be able to use my mouth to breathe. Now, I would have to look funny for a few days until I would get back to see the ENT doctor at Tinker AFB, Oklahoma. I was glad to be off work until after the patched for my nose was removed. Two more days would then be Friday. People will sure look at you funny with a patch on your face. They told me that my records would be transferred to my doctor at Tinker AFB, and I was done and to get the prescription to us an ointment in my nose after the patch and gauze were removed. I was looking forward to the flight home. They also gave me extra patches and gauze to use and show me how to do it, just in case I needed. I did get a little dizzy at times and managed to be okay. I just held onto Adrian as needed. By the time we reached the room, the dizziness had gone away. I still had to get used breathing through my mouth. However, it did not stop me from eating. By the next day after breakfast, I wanted to take the stuff out of my nose myself, but I didn't. I took it like a man. My back was getting better from the allergy tests, and my breathing was a little difficult at times from the patch on my nose. We were on the way to the airport and back to Tinker AFB. I had one more day to go to have this removed from my nose, and then I could play some basketball and work at my second job. First, we had to get back Oklahoma City and get in the grove again.

On the way back, while we were on the plane, I mentioned to Adrian that I have talked with TSgt. Green in the orderly about the bootstrap program if I was to apply for it. Then Lt. Watson would have to be the final approver. I explained that I really wanted to become a doctor and you too, if you elected, and I also had the desire to become an officer in the Air Force. I don't believe that I was smart enough to realize the what ifs and what if it does not happen like I had planned. So I just explained to her my plan, and she stated okay and that to go for it. I did not think twice about not doing it. Really, I thought it was the way to go. My mind was made up. I did have a little time to get it submitted, not to rush anything, and just maybe I could have changed my mind. Adrian did not really give me good advice on most things I talked about, but she would agree with my decisions. I guess that is one way not to be blamed if something was to go wrong. I am pretty sure that she was playing it safe, so she could blame me. Now that was smart, especially now I should have learned that from past arguments. I like to share anyway, just in case other insights may be gained by either party. I know that it was pretty plain to see that I really was not the family type from my past and partly my present. I have always loved family and wanted to be married. I just had to keep reminding myself to be good, and deep down inside me, I truly knew and could admit that I was not ready at all. I somehow kept running "to" Adrian and not "from" her. I would be totally satisfied for my next ENT appointment, and my nose can be totally healed in every sense of the hope. I just wanted to be healed.

So Adrian took me to the hospital to have this stuff removed from my nose. It was the very first thing that I noticed: I could breathe. I did not like nor never liked it when the doctor pulled the gauze string out. He was going very slow. This time, you could see the old dried-up blood on the gauze string. I was so relieved when he was finished. I could breathe very good! "Good job," he told me and also that he had the results from the specialist at Lackland AFB, Texas, and provided me a list of things that I was allergic to and that I had to start taking a few types of allergy medicines to control my seasonal or year-round allergies. He prescribed me all types of stuff and medicine for my eyes too. He informed me that I would be on this medicine long term, and if it didn't work, I would then have to take allergy shots on a weekly basis. The allergies in combination to the rubbing and irritation in my nose caused the membranes in my nose to keep thinning, causing it to bleed unless damage was further up my nostrils. I also had to keep using the medicated ointment, and I was instructed to use Vaseline every day in my nose thereafter to keep my nostrils moisten. It had seemed like we were on a good prognosis for recovery. I was just as happy as I could be. So we thanked the doctor, picked up the scripts, and went back home.

I was home and Adrian had gone back to work. For the first time in almost eighteen years, I was on the path to recovery. I had had nosebleeds since I was five years old. All was well, and we were back on schedule. On Monday, I would be back at the hangar to catch up and do my job. I was also looking for SrA Donnie to see what story I would get next. I was hoping that he would be on the up and up. I did not see him, but I knew that we would cross paths again. He did live in our apartment complex but in a different building. So I would be looking for him and had hoped for the best outcome for when I did see him. I know that he had two cars, but the one I remember was an older light blue VW bug. That was the car I always see him drive the most. So I would be looking for him. I walked around the apartment complex and by the pool, and I did not see him or his family. I would be nice or give that nice appearance, but truly I was not raised like that. One way or another I would get my $200, or he would not keep it. I was not trying to go that way.

Anyway, Adrian and I had to plan what we would do for her birthday. That $200 would have definitely came in handy for that, but I had to figure something out. So I called SSgt. King. We could do first names once you get to know someone on a personal level, especially if they outranked you. I had called James to see if he and his wife were available to go to dinner with us to celebrate Adrian's birthday. He knew her as Adrian, and he agreed that we could do something that following Friday. Her birthday was June 6 and on a Wednesday. I told him that I would let him know the name of the restaurant once I had found one. That was an excellent plan, and it was working. I guess that they were excited to meet people as we were, especially if you were at high school together, as James and Adrian were. Now, Adrian and I had to find a restaurant that she could eat at since she could not eat shellfish. Adrian was allergic to it regardless to how it would be prepared. It would be sad for her that she could not eat shellfish, in which I did not have a problem. I could eat it and most foods to taste. When Adrian got home, I had told her what was planned and had her to find a restaurant place that she wanted to eat at. She did find some little restaurant place by the Heritage Mall. It was our favorite mall anyway. So I called James again and confirmed the time and location. We had a plan to do something for her birthday. I really did not want to put a lot a stress on her or the baby. I wanted them both to be healthy. And I hoped for a healthy delivery.

I must admit, being in Oklahoma City was really good for our relationship. The arguments were down to none or something very seldom, if any. I do believe that our baby had a lot to do with our interaction, including the crazy busy schedules. No matter how I tried, I did not want to be in any part of Oklahoma City. I was probably looking at all the wrong factors. I was stuck and did not know how to be or have that inside creativity. I was still working part-time, but some of the school work was keeping us up in the late hours. We have to keep pushing to work and find some much-needed rest. We did take advantage of it every time we managed to find it, and we did sleep. For the most part, Sundays were the best day to get that real sleep. Really, our weeks felt like days. Time was moving, and time kept moving. We were just keeping up. It was now Friday after work. Adrian and I planned to do some homework after the dinner. I did find time to get her a card and gave it to her at dinner. We got dressed and were on our way to meet the Kings for dinner. Once we arrived and of course, we were a little late as always. They were at the table waiting for us. It was nice, and the restaurant was nice as well and within our price range. We started to talk and order and talk and order the entrees. Everything went well. The talks were good all around, except James and Adrian had more in common about North High school than Danetta and me. The conversations went well anyway. It felt like we had known them for a while. I remember talking about James's overseas assignments when they were stationed over there in Europe. I think if Adrian and I had been stationed overseas, instead of Oklahoma City at Tinker AFB, our outcome would have had been quite different as a family. Of course, I will never come to know the results of such thoughts. Not at all!

Anyway, life goes on! We made plans to meet again and to have dinner at their house. Then they would share pictures and stuff that they had when they were stationed overseas. That was something Adrian, and I looked forward to as well. We each received our dinner checks and would be on our way. That was truly a good birthday dinner for Adrian, and she did like the card I gave her. So I got up on Saturday to check out the Monaco and check the oil to get it ready to go to work and Kentucky Friday Chicken for my part-time job and hopefully to bring home some chicken home. That was not the case. Not at all! The car would not be having me to drive it again. It would not start. And when it did start, the engine sounded worse than a broken muffler. I knew at the moment that the engine was gone, being totally dysfunctional. Then it would not start at all. That car did way more than I ever thought that it would. I was really on pins and needles when we just went to Akron twice and back. The engine was gone, and I could not and did not think I was worth it, and the car was worth about $1,500. Now I have to find another car like yesterday. So I got the newspaper and started to look. I had less than $2,500 to get another car. I was looking and looking and calling everywhere. Nothing was working for us. I needed a car! Then,

I found one in the automotive section of the newspaper—a white Mercury Cougar XR7 for $1,800. I called the lady and her son to look and test drive the car that they were selling privately. I called a taxi, took off my Ohio plates from the car, and we were on our way to see if we would work this deal. I was hopeful that we could work out something doable. Wow, it was nice, and the motor looked good with no leaks visible. That car drove smoother than my car. I was impressed and just had to have it. They would not barter the price, but I had to try. All I had was a check. Of course, they did not want the check, and since it was Saturday, the banks would close early. I told the lady that I was in the Air Force, and they saw that my wife was pregnant, so she had some compassion for us and took the check, then signed over the title to me and a handwritten bill of sale. Now, that was truly a blessing and a God moment at that.

Throughout my life, I have always taken notice that something was different about me. Still moments like these types of blessings did not make me understand what was really going on. In saying that I would get so involved in the TV series *Ripley's Believe It or Not*, I would also stay up late at night to watch the *Twilight Zone* and the *Outer Limits*. I was hooked to the mysterious things that happened on these television shows. My life kept being weird like this car waiting for me, and it was very similar body style to the 1978 Dodge Monaco that had just died on me. These TV shows had always caught my attention. Call it a phenomenon, if you will. Even the word *phenomenon* has amazed me at times. This is a big reason why I started using the word *weird* early in my life; it was the things that I could not explain about God or life, but I knew it could be possible. Often, I would remember that my mother saved me from robbing McDonald's because of a dream she had. I just knew somehow that God had something to with these strange things that were going on in my life. Somehow, I always knew that my mother would be praying for me. When I talked with my mother on the phone, she would tell me to be careful. If my mother knew something that God had shown her, she did not tell me nothing but to be careful. We had to find sometime in the week to get the car registered and get the Oklahoma state license plates. We did and was driving illegal for a few days with my newly purchased car. I also reminded Adrian to be careful on the base in that we could not afford to get caught until we had the car registered in state of Oklahoma. She agreed. Boy, I could not wait to get that car registered. It was like that car was waiting on us and too good to be true. But it was true and right on time! I believed that God knew that we would have had problems trying to finance a newer car because our credit was not so good. This was our best shot.

On Monday, while I on my way back to work, I had to find out where the Oklahoma Department of Motor Vehicles was to get car registered. This time, we would put the car in both names Adrian and myself. We definitely had to go when Adrian would have time to take off for her job, and she would just pick me up. I was glad that her job gave her flexibility due to her being pregnant to attend appointments and other things in our life. We had to hurry up and get that money saved up again to pay on some other bills, like paying the lawyer the rest of his money for the final filing of the bankruptcy and then try to take a trip to Akron and rent a car to see the family. The time was moving, weeks went by, and the car was driving pretty good. I did keep up on the maintenance and the normal oil changes, and then I had to register it with Cynthia in order to drive it on base legally and show proof of insurance. At this point, I had giving up on Cynthia. We would be coworkers at best, and now, I would focus on being the expecting father and a husband, carrying a lie that I had to keep to myself. So I kept living with it. I thought that I would deal with it once I decided to get serious with God and church again. This was not that time!

The day was almost over, and I planned to go to the part-time job at Kentucky Fried Chicken. I would be there for a while. This job was helping us out tremendously on the finances. Our bills were getting paid, and of course, the free food helped. I did not have to steal anything. Everything was beginning to take shape again. I starting to think we could have actually made a pretty good life there if I could have possibly stayed there in Oklahoma City for four years, like it happened at my first assignment for four years at Wright Patt. In my true reality, I knew that we would eventually end. I wanted to stay focused on getting my baby born. I was not going to lie to myself. This was one thing that I knew for sure. If I had found that one girl for me, with all of the right qualities, and like Cynthia in the traffic division, I know, without a doubt, I would have been gone. I was not unhappy for the eight months. Adrian and I were in Oklahoma City and were about to have a baby. I just knew that this would end. It had to. I was twenty-three years old, and I just knew that I was missing something in my life. The life that I was living with Adrian and the baby on the way was not it. I had already had a son with Lynn, and we tried to get serious. I would remember that one time Lynn pulled a knife on me. I just could not commit some things I could never forget! Lynn also had asked me or made the assumption on many occasions that I was seeing someone else. Or she would make a statement anyway to say, "You are coming to see me after you have been screwing someone else." I would deny it or laugh it off and say, "Why would I do that?" I was thinking that the one thing that I had asked to Lynn to do, even before I had got with the sister Leanna, was to stop smoking. She had lied about it and pretended to quit. I personally have never liked any type of lies to me. So I played along and stayed in the picture, but I knew that I would never commit to her. I have these thoughts about how did I get here. I just love my son Big Mike and the one on the way that was who I am. I went from being in Akron, Ohio, and have multiple pregnancies with two best friends that now hate each other and they had a fight in Dayton. I believe that something in our relationship was off. I could not come close, nor could I proved that she was with me, so Lynn could not have me.

Adrian's love for me was off or at best, awkward. Many times, I had the same thoughts as before. Why did I marry her and why did I have to have her back, even after she got even for my previous affairs? That was another part of my own phenomenon. I did not know how to embrace her as a husband would do. I tried many, many times on several occasions to say "I love you," but she never seemed to believe me. Yet Adrian has to stay. It became...let's just say convenient. Yet she wanted me to still embrace her or provide her with confirmations. I could only think about the predicament that I was in with Adrian, with no resolve in sight. Still, to this day, I still wonder why

I married her. Now, back to reality. Sometimes Adrian would catch me in my deep thoughts and then asked me what was I thinking, just like she would try to catch me in something, as if I was talking in my sleep. I would lie about what I was thinking or change the subject. I did not want her to be feeling insecure or we would be arguing. I did have a little charisma and would be able to get on her nerves or make her smile. Then we would move on to something else.

It was that time again for the visit to the lawyer Mr. Pierce and I had the balance of the money to finalize the filing of the bankruptcy. It was on August 21, 1985, our bankruptcy was discharged. We were to accomplish that and move on to restore our credit. We spent about an hour and half at the courthouse. The lawyer Mr. Pierce stated that the final papers would be mailed to us concerning the discharge of debts. We shook hands and parted our ways. This was a happy moment for us driving home and talking about how now that there were only two months left before the baby would be born. So we made plans to make one more trip to Ohio to see the family, and everyone would see her pregnant, and that would be it. We also discussed that driving was not an option. Her belly was getting out there. The trip would have to take place in September, and we had to do more coordination between the school and our jobs.

Everything was going good with the planning to get airline tickets that we were able to afford plus a rental. We still had a few credit cards that we did not file bankruptcy on and were manageably under control. The airline agent told Adrian that before she could fly, she had to get a doctors' note. Adrian and I also discussed that in order to see my son Big Mike with Lynn, there would have to be other people at the house and not just Lynn alone. I agreed due to my past history. She wanted Lynn to know that she was pregnant. We did stuff like that to show off, and we would sometimes dress alike. At this time, we started to do everything together, and she would even come pregnant to watch me play basketball.

Everything went well at the doctors, and we were on our way. Once we arrived to the Akron-Canton airport, we rented a nice Lincoln Town Car with a military discount and of course to show off. I went to pick up my son from Lynn. They were outside on the porch sitting around. Adrian got out of the car, and Lynn came to talk with Adrian. They did not like each other, but they did talk. Then Lynn told Adrian that if she had a boy, she could not name him Michael because my first son was named Michael. Adrian told her, "Well, the last name would be different." I did not think that Lynn like that part. Those were the last few spoken words. I thanked God that the conversation went well and better than expected. This visit did not feel like their last conversation, and I was too glad that we had a short visit. Even though I was there to pick up Big Mike, oftentimes I had my gym stuff with me to go to the Akron Community Center East Market Street, just past the downtown and on the right side to play basketball, and Adrian was there to watch me play basketball and, on many occasions, to provide support to me. She was keeping a closer eye on me, especially while we were in Akron. I was glad that Adrian was there, but she was able to keep an eye on Big Mike play and watch him while I was playing basketball. I always kept allowing Big Mike to watch me play basketball. Then over time he would pick up a few of my basketball moves. At least, I could have been a small inspiration to my son. Those days of me sneaking around with Lynn were well behind us. Nor was I trying to make Adrian feel like I would cheat on her while I was visiting in Akron. I was really making moves mentally in my thoughts to get on the right track because that little baby in her belly had me in a better mindset. She was going all the way to term with this pregnancy. I was feeling pretty awesome! I asked myself what if he makes it to the NBA or the NFL? I wanted them both to stand out and do something amazingly outstanding, and I wanted to be there for them both. I believe it is a thought that most fathers have in making dreams for their children.

The reality of the dreams would be close and available as he gets older, always hoping for that chance opportunity. I knew that I could not plan either of my son's life, but I tried and continue to try to expose them both to as much as possible, and that is what I did almost every time I visit with him. I also had planned the same thing for new baby boy too. I thought for a while it would be easier to spend more time with the second because I was married to his mother. Time was short, and we were visiting everybody and stores too! Then we made it back to my sister Terri's house to spend the night but ended up playing cards all night bid whist and spades, but spades were played for money. Time does go fast while playing cards. After so many games, cheating and all, Adrian and I did have cheating signs, but we pretty much broke even. Then we were tired enough for bed. I had planned to play basketball and take my son to watch. One more day to go before flying back to home in Oklahoma City. While there, I did answer a lot of questions about being in the Air Force and what's it like. The questions never seem to end, but it was fun anyway. Sometimes I did a lot of thinking and was thinking about the length of time that I would be married to Adrian would be unknown, but I did make up in my mind that I would be there for both of my sons. Well, after the basketball time was over, I put back on my clothes and dry shirts.

At the next stop was to see Adrian's natural mother. We were to pick her up at Shelton's Temple off of North Howard Avenue and dropped her off at her shop/restaurant store about a mile up the road. It was obvious that Adrian wanted to see her mother again. She would deny it. Adrian always hid her true feelings. I believe that it would alleviate any surprise or disappointments, just in case the visit went into a different direction. We made it there to pick up Betty (her natural mother). We all greeted each other. As we were walking down the stairs, we were reminded in the fond conversation where Adrian and I was married here at Shelton's Temple for years. Anyway, while talking, Melody's name came up (Adrian's cousin and Betty's niece) on the tragedy of getting shot with a baby and still lived. What an awesome blessing to manage live after that. I believe her parents had planned for Melody to return home after she was well enough to have the baby. Then another conversation came about on Adrian not being raised up by Betty, I did not find out until later that there was a real beef or problem and hostility between Adrian and her real mother. I had seen it with my own eyes; they were way past mother-and-daughter issues. A few words were exchanged between Betty and Adrian. Then I heard Betty say, "If you were not pregnant, I would smack you," and Adrian's reply did shock me. Again, she was carrying my child inside her. Adrian, still quick on her words, replied, without a tremble, "Pretend I am not pregnant and come on."

I was in the middle of this and was not sure how Betty felt about me, and at the same time, I was in no way going to allow this fight or the stress of an argument to take place. So they calmed down a little, and I drove Betty down to her store and drop her off. Then the goodbye was a meaningless gesture. Then we would be on our way. That relationship between Betty and Adrian would never be anything more than hostile. The way I see it, Adrian never wanted to be adopted and always thought that there was a lie about her real father; nevertheless, Ben Thurmond did take that responsibility. At this point, it was hard to accept the truth from anyone. This was the day to leave, now on the way to see my oldest brother Cleottis (Junior). This was another quick stop, and we visited and checked out his spot, and he was very nice. I guess it was something that he picked up from the Marines. Anyway, we had some small talk, and I mentioned to him that he was the main reason that I joined the Air Force, being that the Marine Corps was my first priority. On the way out, Junior gave Adrian a watermelon. I guess because she so pregnant. Junior was nice like that! We greeted and left. We were to drop Big Mike off to Lynn. Then we were off to see my mom. Then back to Adrian's mom's (aunt) house. Boy, we were driving and moving. We ran in to pack our suitcases and off back to the Akron-Canton airport. The time was moving and no way to keep up, so we kept pushing it to get there, plus to turn in the rental car. We have made it. I was so glad we did not have to run. If so, it was not happening with a pregnant woman by my side. It worked out just surprisingly fine. Anymore rush then what we were doing would have jeopardized her to go into labor. Finally, we made it and was in the air going back to Oklahoma City. It was a pleasure to be headed back go home to our own space and carrying two watermelons, one in Adrian's belly and the green round fruit. It was sort of cute seeing a pregnant woman carrying a watermelon. This sight to see was truly ironic! After we landed back to the Will Rogers Airport in Oklahoma City, we picked up the luggage and headed home. This was a good trip and really made me miss home. I actually had fun, seeing and hanging out with my family.

This trip made me feel the love, and I realized that I was missing my family, and somehow too, I was missing home.

I wanted to get with James and Danetta as soon as possible. I wanted to ask him about the bootstrap program. So we set that up on the following Saturday, and I was able to pick his brain while we were eating dinner. I jumped in the conversation and sought James's advice concerning the bootstrap program. He did provide me with some insights and enough to encourage me to seek additional information. After dinner, Danetta started to show us stuff from the various places they lived. They had some really nice pieces and furniture and a lot of pictures. Also souvenirs and keepsakes, they had a bunch of stuff! The Kings gave us this cloth-like picture, very shiny stones in it, with a black velvet-like background, a nice keepsake for us since we have never got an assignment overseas nor yet to live over there. We had something to look forward to, just in case! They were awesomely nice people, and he was from Akron. That was a plus to him on our part. We really enjoyed knowing them; however, they were not the playing card type of people and definitely not for money. That card playing conversation had never come up. I am sure that we would have taken all the money, cheating or not!

On Monday, back at work, I was planning to find out about the bootstrap program. I cannot explain it, but it was on my mind to do so. I was in the Air Force, but that was not what I had seen for my long-term future. The words of Bishop Pope would come to mind, from when I was growing up and either I was with him hanging out and running errands or something I picked up from his teaching at church that stayed with me, and I had never forgotten. Anyway, he used to tell me or teach it to the church, "We only have once to live, and we have to make the best of it."

Of course, he would call me Mikey! Bishop Pope was one of the best influences I had in my life because my father did not spend much time with us, or we could never find him. However, the advice that I received from Bishop Pope was right on time. Whether he knows it or not, the foundation of the gospel or the Christian work he provided had always stayed with me. No matter where I were in life, I would always remember Bishop Pope and the Pope family, especially Anthony Pope too. I always remembered how his mother would chastise us both because we did get in trouble together. The Pope family will always be my other family; they were definitely the real deal! So I got to work and ran over to the orderly room. I saw SrA Donnie again, and he was still holding to he did not know what was going on. I just knew that he was lying because my wife found out from the rental office how long that it really took to get the referral check. He rushed away, and that was it. I felt that he was avoiding me for real! I knew deep inside me I would get it back. I decided not to report it to the first sergeant in the orderly room because it would be his word against my word. Pretty much a waste of time! I said to myself that I was not going to forget that he owes me $200 per our deal and would figure it out later.

Anyway, I made it to the orderly room to speak again the TSgt. Green concerning the bootstrap program. It was a good thing I did. He confirmed again that I could return back in the Air Force as a commissioned officer. Becoming a military officer was more in line as to where I wanted to be. It just took me a little longer to figure it out. The only catch was my paycheck would stop, and I would have to pay for all the college schooling all by myself and by whatever means necessary to get it done. The thing was time was of the essence, and my bootstrap program package would have to be submitted by October 30, 1985. If approved, I would be discharged from the active-duty military and would have to serve in the Air Force Reserve until my four-year college degree was achieved before returning back into the Air Force as an officer. Even before I joined the Air Force and while in basic military training, I served as a squad leader/latrine queen, and in military technical training school, I served as the dorm chief. I have always been in some type of leadership position. I went home after work and had a talk with Adrian, and at the same time, my mind was already made up. Anyway, she did not know much about it, but she did like the becoming officer part and moving back to Akron, and we both would go to the University of Akron for pre-med and at home at the same time. We would also have babysitting support since both of our families were there in Akron.

Getting Pell Grants and loans, we thought that we had a plan. With that thought, not liking Oklahoma City, Tinker AFB, nicknamed Tinker Stinker, I was all ready to move, no persuasion necessary. Now while working my regular and part-time job, plus school, we had a lot to do in a short period, and I would have an answer for approval, either yes or no within ninety days. To tell the truth, I had this feeling that I was doing a good thing and convinced about it. But the reality of it, I did not know what I was doing, how our lives would turn out, or how we would manage from three paychecks to zero. Anyway, the money was tight to manage in the first place. This one thing I knew: my mother did keep me in prayer! My faith was not really there, but her, my mother's faith, was, and I definitely believed that she was a real woman of God. However, Adrian did work up until the delivery.

The date was Friday, October 18, 1985. It was a Friday that I remembered. I was being nice to her and decided to send her some flowers. I sent them before we left for school. One of the reasons I got the flowers was that she did not give me a lot of grief about the bootstrap program in which I did get my package submitted and now awaiting the results from the review board for approval. Then I would find out the results! We ate dinner, watched a little TV, and we were probably watching some sports or *The Streets of San Francisco* (with Carl and Michael Douglas) or *Beretta* (starring Robert Blake). I also watched Marcus Welby MD or Quincy, the medical examiner. It was Friday. The TV went off the air, just like many nights. We got ready for bed, and that was it for the night. Things seem to be going well for us. That Saturday morning, we got up around 11:00 a.m. I was standing up, and she was still lying down, and as she was getting up, we both heard a *swoosh* sound. Yup, her water broke, the bed was just soaked with that fluid stuff, and it went everywhere. So we called the hospital to inform them as to what had happened. The nurse stated that there was no time for nothing, and that the baby could get infected or just drop out of her; therefore, we had to go. This was not the time to take a quick shower for us both; it was not happening as much as we wanted to. I had to go as we were, so we did just the opposite. No way, under any circumstance, does she go out before getting clean, but this baby thing was the exception, and we rushed, got my sweat pants on, and Adrian wore a blue-checker-striped sundress and went to Tinker AFB Hospital to have our first baby together. Since I missed my first son being born, I wanted to be there and stayed with her the entire time. The labor was not so bad with about eight hours of mostly mild pain to a short period of hard labor. I must admit Adrian was incredibly brave to have had a natural childbirth, no medicine whatsoever! The entire time, she did not get upset or curse me out as some of the nurses were stating how other women reacted as they give birth. I was glad she did not do that to me. I would have probably left, no doubt! But regardless she did well.

I was right there in the room. At 9:55 p.m. on October 19, 1985, this white-like baby was crowning and maneuvered out until the umbilical cord was cut, and he did not make a sound. The cord was clamped off, nor did he cry. They took him over to the other small baby table as I left her and followed to be with him the baby, and the nurses start tapping on him, cleaning out his mouth and nose with the suction. I was there as he opened up his beautiful eyes. It was awesome, as awesome could be. My beautiful son! It took a little while, but he briefly cried, and he was living in a new world. The boy weighed eight pounds and three ounces and about twenty inches long. This was my baby, as a little color was coming to his skin. He went from off-white (and chalky) to red, the top of ears was a little light brown. This was my second son. I was only twenty-three years old, and my sons were five years apart in age. Their mothers went from best friends to mothers and no longer the best of friends or friends at all. All over a man! Well, I've not seen my first child to be born in person. I was glad not to have missed this one. I had seemed to be connected to him in ways that I could not explain. Adrian and I had discussed what to name him in her birth room that she had all to herself. At first, she was not sure if I would agree what his name should be, or if he was to be named after me. I just looked at her and felt her heart to drop if I had said no. Instead, I told her that I did not care and that I would leave it up to her. The only thing I mentioned was that George Foreman named all his boys George, and besides, my two sons would have different last names. That was all I had to say.

Adrian decided to name him after me, his father. Just like my first son, which I was all over him (Big Mike), I did not want anyone to touch him, not even Lynn. I believe it is just natural for a father to bond to his sons, without question. This father-and-son thing, the bonding came natural for me! What a moment and a miracle this was at the same time! Wow! So I got off work early to pick up Adrian and the baby from the hospital. On that Monday, early afternoon, she was doing well. My new son, Michael II was just doing well too after he was circumcised earlier on that Monday morning. The great thing about Michael II that I noticed was he did not cry much. He was truly a good baby and did he sleep, yes, he did! His first day out into the world, once he left the hospital, we were headed home. Adrian was a little bold and spontaneous. She did not want to miss school, nor did she quietly want me to outdo her. So we took the baby to class with us, and the hardest part was to keep people out of his face. People and the teachers could not believe that Adrian came to class just after having a baby. We were at the last stage for completing our six hundred hours requirement to become registered medical assistants (RMA) in Oklahoma City. We were on our way, and we also thought that we could use our RMAs to get jobs in Akron, while we both were attending the University of Akron. We managed to take our newborn to class for about a week or so and worked fast to get a babysitter. Just like clockwork, we managed to find a babysitter in our neighborhood that was referred by the base and on the list of recommended referrals. She so happens to be in our neighborhood, a middle-aged black lady. The babysitter's price was affordable, and we both stated yes. What a lifesaver she was, and Adrian would also take it easy, and she headed back to work. The doctor mentioned that we have to take it easy between us, and if not, she would become pregnant again quickly, just like that. Those words were something that I kept true to. I could not at all afford another child. This was it for me, at this juncture in my life. I wanted to pursue my dream in becoming a doctor.

After seeing Michael II being born, I too wanted to do this and also wanted to be an OB/GYN doctor, that or ER doctor. I just knew that I really knew what I wanted to be. I wanted to work in the hospital! So most of my thinking were pointed at my dream job, and so my thoughts were in the works, starting with getting approved and accepted in the bootstrap program. I was only waiting for the news to come from our security police orderly room and by Lt. Watson. I done had my son, he was born, and my next step was to leave the Air Force and get transferred to the Air Force Reserve and attend full-time college. I was not anxious, but somehow, I was counting on the bootstrap program to be approved. The time in our lives kept moving, and we were so close to finishing the school. In a month's time, it would be done. For a place that I did not want to be in, the time actually went very fast. We got a better running car, the marriage had gotten better, schooling for both, and a brand-new baby boy—this was an awesome year of 1985. I thought if we could do all this in less than a year, plus I was working two jobs, what else could we have achieved? For the time in Oklahoma City, we could have been more successful. I truly believed that all by myself! In my heart of hearts, I knew I could never tell her the truth that I was hiding something. I knew I would have to be moving on one day, but I hung around and prolonged that day. At this point, I would have forgiven everything she had done to me. Really, I wanted to come clean because we were doing so good. I don't believe that I could handle it again for us to relive my truths that were before us, like in Dayton, Ohio, then for us to play the payback game. The difference now was we had a child, and I had to figure out when I leave, my son would not be in the middle or get hurt. I just had the thought of what I wanted to do. I just did not know how to act on it! This was one bridge in my life that I did not know how to cross. If I had left her at that moment, child support would have been my next challenge. So I kept my cool and not let my guilty conscience get the best of me. The past really has a way to catch up to you, especially me! I kept thinking that it was cheaper to keep her. I cannot count how many times I had said, "It is cheaper to keep her." Actually, it was sounding like a broken record playing around in my head.

The baby was doing fine. I remember taking him to his first appointment for the two-week checkup, and he just checked out fine and as healthy as he could be. The baby formula was doing him just fine. He did eat but was not greedy. I did everything that I could possibly do to be a good father to him. I would wash bottles, mix the formula for his baby milk, warm the bottle up, change the diapers, feed, and burp him. I gave him baths starting in the kitchen sink to rocking him to sleep. This was my baby, and I was his father. I was putting my time in. Michael II was definitely a daddy's boy! I have had plenty practice growing up in my family and changing and feeding the nieces and nephews growing up. My nephew Keith also gave me a lot of practice while I was growing up. I did not get it for the world for what I am about to say next. I thought and wanted to be a good father, and I wanted a family, but I was not a good match for Adrian or Lynn. How can you love your sons but not their mothers? I had plenty of chances not to have kids with neither one of them. Somehow, I found out the hard way that I was only foolish and not so smart for my age. I did the same thing twice and expected a different outcome. I would then place my heart in one of those Quincy Jones/James Ingram (on vocals and from Akron, Ohio) songs. "Just Once" was a healing kind of song for me. Songs gave me a way out of my troubled times, and it showed me that many times I was not the only one that wanted love. Even if it was within my reach, I still could not have it. This song spoke to my soul, especially when I would be hurting and never letting anyone—to trust them enough—to let them in. Also "Ben" was another song by Michael Jackson that displayed sadness in a very different way that I thought that I understood. Another song by Glady Knight, she sang that song "Midnight Train to Georgia," and I could not forget how many times I played that song by Natalie Cole "Keeping the Light." It was one of my favorites. That was how I was feeling through these songs, but I could not and did not show it to my wife. I realized that these songs and my most innocent love was with Deanna when I was seventeen years old. Lynette was the next phase of the love, but those two times made me realize that there was a true love out there for me! But how do I find it? I knew it existed. True love, I believe it really existed! I would promise to myself that I would not stop until I found it! Love!

This was working out just fine. Even on the class nights, she was the best. Studying was truly easy while having a sleeping baby. I was so glad that Adrian quickly went back to work after the travel. Our monies started to grow again, and the car just needed oil changes. We are now about to graduate for the United Technical Institute as RMAs. On November 20, 1985, we both received our registration certifications as registered medical assistants. We both did it with hectic lives and birth to a newborn baby. Wow again! I believe that Adrian had all Bs, and I had three As and five Bs with typing forty words per minute. Adrian was typing around sixty-five to seventy words per minute. She could go! We both did well and were dedicated to this cause. That was the one thing that I really liked about her. It seemed like the next day, on a Thursday, Adrian was acting a little strange and different towards me, kind of standoffish. Of course, I did not know what was wrong, nor were we arguing, which was a good thing. Anyway, Thursday and Friday were moving along just fine, with no more school to attend. We were supposed to be exceptionally happy for the success of our schooling, but not so. Something was definitely wrong! We watched a little TV, and I stayed up until nothing was on worth watching. Before going to work at Kentucky Fried Chicken on that Saturday, Adrian looked me in my eyes and told me these words, "I will never love you," and that was it. I remember taking out the trash and left for work. The baby was sleeping. Where did that come from? I thought I would get a "I thought I might be falling in love with you." Those words were not really spoken between us. We were there, we were nice to each other, and we had each other's back, but that was it. The word *love* was absent from our relationship, yet we yearned to share and keep sharing our lives together. I was kind of lost while I was at work but tried to keep my mind off it. After work I went home and asked her as soon as I was settled, "How could we just have a baby together, and you would say that to me that you would never love me?" Actually, that shocked me a little and caused my mind to be off balanced. I never knew women to be like her. I was so used to the tears. Not Adrian. Not to say that she never cried or she would cry when she got totally upset... Let's just say mad, which was the only time, I really seen her tears, but not crying. Adrian has never cried to be with me, and I didn't really understand it, but I accepted it because she, other than that one time, had left me! I did leave her these words, "You will love me!" The thing was that I was not sure why I said that. My mouth spoke those words, but my heart was absent to the feelings. I did not feel a thing at the moment. It was like I was just emptied or just caught off-guard! Nevertheless, we just did right by Michael II, went to our jobs, and stayed together, pretending to be happily married. In my observation, we did have a baby boy, which could not be denied. We had a piece of paper to say we are married (Adrian always called the marriage license a piece of paper), the fringe benefits of a marriage, without a lifetime commitment. Somehow, we both accepted that, and it worked for both of us. As there was nothing else to talk about, we did what we were supposed to be doing in our marriage relationship as she did her chores, and I did mine. No one could guess what we were doing other than being married, but we knew and accepted it as we were.

Things have moved to a normalcy for us. It was good and to make time the following week to check on the bootstrap program status to see if I were approved or not. Our life was in a sort of limbo as we were planning to prepare for Thanksgiving dinner on the November 28, 1985. I had to find out something, so, I went to work. I went quickly to check the status of the bootstrap program for me, and either way, I would keep thinking and moving forward on becoming a medical doctor and attend college in Oklahoma City at Oklahoma State University, and this was not an original thought of mine, but sincerely, it would have been a great idea. I just wanted to get out of Oklahoma City. Looking back, it was probably just me because I did not give Oklahoma City a fair chance. I just wanted to leave, and that was that! I would have just stayed in the Air Force and went to college. The only drawback that I had was to start college and get an assignment for overseas. Then I would be separated from my son, and my bills were too tight, just in case some like an PCS assignment would come about. Well, it did not happen like my mind was imagining things about Oklahoma City that just was not my reality. I was so focused to get out of there and not focusing on what was there. Moving forward, TSgt. Green looked for my boot-strap program approval and found it. I now had to talk with Lt. Watson for him to discuss with me the next phase of my military life, or the lack thereof. As he was reviewing the paperwork, Lt. Watson mentioned that he did not want to see me leave and that I was doing a great job. If only he knew about my finances and the bankruptcy I had filed. Anyway, as we talked, I told him on how I wanted to become a doctor and pursue that path. He said that I now had a requirement with the reserve unit in Pittsburgh IAP, Pennsylvania, at the 911th AW/32nd MAPS unit. He told me that I had to report to duty as soon as I had got settled in Ohio.

He provided me with my separation orders and moving orders. I was approved just like that, and now I had a month to be moved and on my way to Akron, Ohio, by January 1986. I was very excited to be separating from being an enlisted NCO on active duty from the Air Force. I thought that I belonged in the Air Force as an officer and a doctor. Looking back as things were beginning to fall in place for me, I knew that Oklahoma City would have been different for me, if I was partial to being there. But as I remembered the junior high school slogan: "Forward Ever, Backward Never!" I was not supposed to be going back there, to Akron and not without a job. Now, I have to go and share this okay good news with my wife (who did not seem to love me, and sometimes she did on the jealous side) that we were moving back to Ohio. Also we did not really have a place to live there in Akron, but I was not going to look back, so we kept it moving and forging ahead back to our old life, just six years later. We are back to where it all begun for us both, plus a new baby boy, Michael II. Six months ago, my brother David came down to help us move in, and we are still settling in, and now, we were packing to move again. Now, this was our third move in one year, and in six weeks, plus any leave taken, I would no longer have a full-time or part-time paycheck. My imagination would do its thing. I told Adrian that it would be easy to get a job, and also, we just finished our RMAs and who would not hire a military person and veteran. I was not sure what we were doing or going to do.

So I called my sister Terri, and she was living on 1596 Delba Street in Akron, a single-family pink house. She said if we could pay rent, it was okay to move in with her and her children. She only had three kids, two older girls and a young boy. Out of Erica, Tia, and Jonathan (JonJon), she would let us use JonJon, the baby's room. So now we had a place to live. That was sure enough backward, but we had to make it work. Everything we were to do at this point would be crucial for all of us. We discussed how I had got the U-Haul to get us to Oklahoma City. Now, we had more furniture and a baby. That type of move was not going to work. As I was out processing to separate from the Air Force to move and join the Air Force Reserve, I attended the briefing on the DIY move, and the military would move us. That was a no-brainer. That is what we did. They would send contracted packers over and pack us up, and the movers would load the truck and bring my household goods to Akron. This was an awesome benefit. We had to get through Christmas and New Year's first. I could not believe how things had gone in my life. My military career went from zero to sixty just like that, and I was on a brand-new path. This was incredible! The truth be told, I never thought that I was ever cut out for this lifestyle. It was the path that I had chosen to take to get out of Akron from humble beginnings to returning back to Akron worse off. I had more debt, more credit, and no full-time job. Nevertheless, I was following my dreams of becoming a doctor. I wanted this dream to be true. So I decided to follow it! I am truly learning the facts of life firsthand. I was learning that life is truly hard when we lack money.

Adrian and I talked and talked throughout December to continue cutting our budget spending, even though I was able get a few workouts in at the gym and just to keep working at Kentucky Fried Chicken as much as possible before submitting my two-week notice to be leaving. I was a very committed and dedicated worker and did enjoy the free food on most occasions, including the free desserts I just took. As we talked, it became obvious that the more we talked, the more we had to cut back. Therefore, as I realized that we were not going to have a big Christmas dinner or chitterlings and hog maws nor the soul food tradition from my mother for New Year's.

Now, this was the time that we started to get our stories straight as to what we were doing to go back to Akron. Plus, we didn't want, in no way shape or form, to look bad. We were going to be living with my sister and the three kids, but we wanted no one to see our struggles, if we had one. We did indeed knew that our finances were not at all together. This is not what we had in mind. We had a story (lie) to tell, and at the same time, from either of us, we had to say the same thing. Or no one would believe us! Now, at that point, I would be living two lies, and she would now just have to remember one lie. Then we had to decide what to do about SrA Donnie the security specialist that I was working with that kept avoiding me. He deceived me and lied about it. Adrian stated that she did not love me. I got it. However, she decided to agree me that we were going to pay him back, somehow. That was a real fact! We both were thinking of something. We knew that he was an Air Force Security Police. It had to be something short of a court martial, but we did not know what or how to get our money.

Meanwhile, my workdays were getting shorter and shorter. Well, in my mind, I really thought that MSgt. Roscoe and MSgt. Thomas were glad to see me shortly to be leaving but not more than I was. I was doing limited duty, and now, my main job was to out process from Tinker AFB since I had separation orders. I was really doing some running around. I was either taking Adrian to work or she was taking me to work. It was whomever had the most to do or was leaving work early or had to pick up Michael II from the babysitter's house. Every day, we were making it work for us and had no room for error. We were still running around like it was when we had schooling. The two packers were to arrive on December 26, 1985 (also my mother's birthday, I had to make sure I had called her that day), to bring boxes, paper, bubble wrap, and tape to get the entire house packed up for the movers to pick it up and load up the truck on the following week. Also the following day would be my last day of work at Kentucky Fried Chicken. That was on December 27, and my commitment for my last day was to never work at another restaurant ever again! The new car was doing well, and we were glad that the car was very reliable. I had to schedule the pickup from the junkyard to get the 1978 Dodge Monaco. This was the third car that I ever got on my own. Yeah, Lynette had taken me to get it, and now, I was getting rid of it for about $35. Well, I made $35 (cash) for a car that did not work, and the pick it up was free. I was not sad because we had another car to get around in. The sad part was that it reminded me of Lynette. I had to let go of the car and her!

On December 28, 1985, my car was gone. I gave the guy the signed title and keys. After he finished up the paperwork, he hooked up my car to the tow truck and left. I did watch my car roll away until it was gone and out of my sight. Really, I was glad to be driving another car. Of course, I was getting used to allowing Lynette to leave my thoughts and secretly face my reality all by myself. For the most part, I was dealing with Adrian and staying busy. It really helped me as unsolicited therapy. I was good and now still truly faithful to a wife that said she did not love me. I know what her words from her mouth said to me, but her actions still did not seem like it was not love. Truthfully, I think that she was protecting her heart, especially since we just had a baby together and she, not I, named him after me. Now, if and when I mess up again, I would remind her that she was not in love with me. That was now my biggest excuse to cheat again. I know that she was protecting her heart. Yet I remained faithful and just flirting at every possible chance. To me, flirting was not cheating. I can honesty state that I did not have any affairs in Oklahoma City, not one! Nor did I have time to! I would spend my last birthday in Oklahoma City in a way it was a present to myself because I was leaving. Adrian and I did not do much for my birthday on January 4, and that was okay with me. My thought was for my birthdays and special days to be meaningful, our relationship had to be special. Being special or having a "special moment" was not happening for Adrian and I. Romance we did not really have, only some moments here and there! We had one of those moments, and nine months later, we had a baby boy. I was now a father to my second son. Really, I did not want or would accept anything from her, birthday and Christmas included. To be honest, my best special moment with Adrian was on the day I left for basic military training for the Air Force, and she gave me her Snickers candy bar as a snack to take with me. We had moments to remember, and that was it. Really, on the other hand and in my confession in Dayton, when I was trying to find my back to the church, Adrian told me that when she went back to college, she had her share of messing around too. So it finally made sense to me that the only part where she was possibly true to me was the period of time between the engagement and our marriage up until the time I laid everything that I did on the table. I actually had a conscience enough to confess, but to me, she was just as terrible as I. We both did the same thing every time. We both were cheaters, or is that what she wanted me to think. Some kind of way, in my heart, I wanted to get her back. It was almost some sort of competition between us, but it was never mentioned or talked about. It was just there. I stayed the course, knowing that one day, I was leaving her for good.

All the time, these thoughts were like on rewind in my mind. I had made up my mind that the one time that I would have gave it all and to do it right was doing that church thing and for me to get it right. Sometimes, I would be deep in thought, and she would shake me to get my attention. I would say something believable, like I was thinking about my new son or thinking about us or something like that and totally not true. Adrian informed me that the movers had called and were coming on the next day to load the truck, except the things that we were keeping with us. Earlier that day, I was all processed out from Tinker and did receive another active-duty ID card that would expire once my remaining leave was finished. I was informed again to check in to my new reserve unit at the Greater Pittsburgh IAP, Pennsylvania, and to in process with my reserve unit. The location was a hundred miles from Akron and very doable. I did understand and confirmed everything and signed more forms for the separation. The thing was, I was going to lose all my medical and dental benefits for me and the family. I had completed my last physical, and everything was documented. Finally, I was glad to be leaving Oklahoma City. To what end, I did not know. The thing was I thought that I had a plan. I did until you don't have a plan! A foolproof plan, I did not have. I was planning to go anyway! I had to go! Again, I really did not know why, but being an officer helped for my inspiration to stay. I knew that we were on our way to Ohio in one more day.

That last night went by quicker than expected. We had called James and Danetta and informed them that we leaving the next day, and that was about it, except for the babysitter. The weather was beginning to get bad with the rain, sleet, and colder temperatures. I assumed that it, referring to the weather, would be like Ohio's winter weather, and I was confident that I would be all right driving in it. Right before the movers arrived, Adrian told me that she had another dream. We were talking again and very normal and had no sign of an attitude from her. That was surely a good sign. At that moment, it hit me, and I remembered how she had dreamed about Nancy and I fooling around in my last job at Wright Patt, and I did deny it at first. There was a lot happening in Oklahoma City as we were about to leave. Nevertheless, I remembered the last dream and was going to really pay close attention to all that she had to say. So I had told Adrian to go ahead and tell me what her dream was about. She said she saw me with light-skinned, long-hair, skinny girl and driving a candy-apple red car. "This girl that I saw you with was not me," she added. Then, Adrian dropped the bombshell on me. She really did. She said, "This girl that I would meet would be the one to kill you." At that moment, I was done, and inside my mind, I played it off. But I was really shaken up. I really thought that Adrian added that other lady in the dream that I would be with would kill me, but I started to think that she was the one that really wanted to kill me. Not knowing what to believe, I stayed vigilantly on my p's and q's forever, and I would keep looking for that woman in my wife's dream. Truthfully, before falling off to sleep, I made up in my mind that I wanted true love, and I was going to search for it and keep believing that this very woman was out there for me. I was really going to look for this description from my wife's dream: that I found the love of my life. She saw me with this light-skinned, long hair, tall, skinny woman, and driving a candy-apple red car. I also planned to act right and be faithful once I found the mysterious woman from the dream, so there would be no killing and especially the killing of me! Now, all the nonsense was gone, I assured myself again that the killing part of me would not be happening with the woman that I have never seen because I believe that we would be in church.

I vowed that I would follow Adrian's dream. I felt like there was some sort of connection that was unexplainable for me. The day before we are to leave Oklahoma City, she tells me this stuff. For a moment, I thought that she was making this up. I did not like or want to believe the words coming from her mouth. She was serious, and as serious she could be! She was not playing but knew because of her past dreams, this one was real to her too! For a quick moment, I almost wanted to curse her out, and it came to me why she really told me she would never love me about a month prior. That's where I begged the difference because in my mind, I really thought that she would not allow herself to love me and was protecting her heart. I knew something wasn't adding up. The way she looked at me and how she treated and cared for my son, Michael II, every time…it was as if her looking at me was a term of endearment, like she loved me, without saying the words. In her mind and because of the dream that she had, she really knew that she would never have me. The more I thought about her dream, the more I paid attention to it. Why would she lie? I would ask myself. Adrian, she didn't have a true reason to lie to me. I did not have anything; she would gain nothing! In my heart only, I knew that we were not going to be together. I knew she was jealous, so why tell me something like this. Again I could not make sense of it. My most intimate thoughts and a description of the woman that I wanted to one day meet came from her spoken words. Adrian did not know my thoughts. I had never shared that with her. Why would I? I had no reasons, not one! My ideal woman and wife was just that as she described, and she would be nice too. I had hoped to find her by going to church one day.

Right after I thought about it, there was another God moment for me. All this was happening in January 1986 as we are about to leave Oklahoma City. I was only twenty-four years old and living a very strange life. The mysterious events kept happening to me, and I could not explain it. I had asked myself, does all her dreams come true? My answer would be no as I run this through my brain. I did not know if I believe her because I thought it was true, or was it. I wanted this dream from her to be true. Nevertheless, I had thought of a woman like this for a long time. I had never revealed this to Adrian. How did she know? Now, I really had a lot to think about on our nineteen-hour ride home to Akron. Well, while we were talking, the movers pulled up to pack up the truck, and we were packing up the car and taking down our bed. We got the stuff out of the refrigerator last and the baby formula and the few food items that we had leftover. After about almost five hours, the truck was packed. The weather was changing and getting colder. Yet we were going to get on the road and go home to Akron. I then signed the packing paper for our household goods and provided the guy with a copy of my separation orders to stay with my moving records. Our furniture was leaving, and they were gone. My household goods would arrive about a week after we got there. It was all set! Then, we quickly finished up so we would be able to finish up before it got dark and then get the key back to office before they would close up for the evening. We were rushing like crazy, and I would keep taking the items to the car and keep the seat open behind me while I was driving. Then Michael II would be facing the back window. Our plan and coordination to get moved and packed and straightened up the townhouse a little. There was not much cleaning or sweeping that needed to be done. We did one more final check through every room and closet, and then we locked the front door. We were done! I rushed the key over to the rental office. Just in time again, I made it. Now, I was on my way back to the car, so we would drive away and leave Oklahoma City once and for all!

We were pulling around to get to the other side with a lane of cars parked in the middle. It was cold, quiet, and getting dark! As we were about to pass SrA Donnie's apartment, I saw one of his two cars, the older light-blue VW. The car was right there and cars on both sides, and the front of his car was close to the sidewalk. We suggested this was the time to get even for the $200 that he never paid to me. I had asked Adrian if she was going to help me flatten his car tires. This was the perfect opportunity to pay SrA Donnie back for his lies to me. Neither one of us had something sharp. I had to go the trunk to find some tools or screwdrivers to do the job. We got back in the car to discuss the plan, and the baby was doing just fine and quiet. Adrian took the passenger side, and I had the driver's side of the VW. I punctured the two tires on the driver side, and Adrian's screwdriver was not working for her. I told her to get in the car, and I did the passenger rear tire, for a total of three tires that I punctured. I wanted him to spend $200 that I did not get, and he would not keep it. I was so patient, and it did not work for me to get the money that we had shook hands on. I really thought SrA Donnie would be honest and keep our deal. I ran to our car, and we drove off to get out of there. We were gone and scared at the same time. We were trying to get to the highway, I-40W. We were looking and looking for the police and did not see a thing. We were home free, not a police car in sight. Then we did a sigh of relief and had a good laugh. But I noticed the more we drove, the worse the roads had gotten. The road was not salted and plowed like in Ohio. I was right in the Tulsa, Oklahoma, area, and I was in one of the worst storms ever for driving. We just kept driving, and as I was looking, it was icing everywhere. The roads were especially, icy in a moment's notice as I was in the left lane. I lost control of the car, and we were spinning on the ice. I thought of my baby in the backseat of the car. The steering wheel was not responsive to anything that I did. It was just about daybreak, and our car crossed the median on all ice. Then just as I could do nothing to steer the car, I could not even stop the car. I was pumping the brakes, and that did not work either. To our amazement, we were facing perpendicular to I-44E, and a semi-tractor-trailer came zooming by just as the car stopped on its own. Nothing I did worked! That car we were driving just like when we brought that car was nothing short of a miracle. I could not move a muscle. I was frozen still inside our warm car! For those few ten to twenty seconds, I could not breathe! It was so unbelievable! But it happened to me and my family! It was as if my life flashed before me, even all our lives! When I laid my eyes on that tractor-trailer, we could not stop. I just knew that we were dead, just dead! No way, we should have stopped at the brink of an oncoming truck and live! No way! This was another God moment for me, and still I did not know why. Same as before, this would be etched in my mind! Wow! I felt life move back into my body and knew that I had to back up in the median and get back on the road to I-44W to go to Akron. I was able to move again! Boy, was I scared and cautious all the way home. I slowed down until the roads had gotten better. I didn't remember taking a nap as the other times. I just kept it moving. I wanted to drive out of that ice storm. The sooner the better! Plus, I had a lot to talk to Adrian about, concerning her dream of me being with another woman. The tires we flattened. Then what just happened to us. We had almost died! Our lives were so busy, different, difficult, and strange! None of it really made sense as we were talking! We knew that we could not control the weather nor anyone's dreams. Parts of our lives could not ever be explained. These last four to six weeks has been mind-blowing. I was saying to Adrian, "Does things like this, the things that are happening to us, does it happens to regular people?" This question was only to be asked and not to be answered. One thing that I knew for sure is that God wanted us to live. I could never forget how the car stopped all by itself. We were in the car with no control of it. Then it stopped all by itself, on the brink of the highway, just before oncoming traffic. I asked Adrian, "Did you see that?" Adrian responded yes, like it did not faze her at all. I did not see her when it was happening, but I knew that she had to be scared too!

This was the type of miracle that no one would believe, unless they were there! But I would not wish that on anyone, not even my worst enemy. The way the car had stopped was just orchestrated by God! I told Adrian that I knew that my mother kept me in her prayers. This was another one of those times. I got it again! Still, yet I did not know what was in front of me and my life. We talked again about her dream and the girl that I was supposed to be with. So she just told me the dream again. Nothing changed. It was exactly just like she told me it was for the first time. Nothing changed, not one thing. The details were as clear as they could be. I was satisfied! We just talked little more, and then, Adrian was fast asleep. I just kept driving, even if she did snore just a little! My mind was just racing with thoughts for leaving Oklahoma City and the Air Force. I was second-guessing myself, if I had made the right choices and losing a steady paycheck. I would continue to get paid until my leave ran out.

The rest of it, being our life, we would have to figure it out. I must have driven about thirteen hours straight and was getting tired. At the next rest stop, we would stop and check the baby, feed him, and change his diapers. Then I would take a short nap in the car.

It was then about 7:00 a.m., and I must have slept for about four hours. I awoke, and we went again to the bathroom and checked the baby again, changed his wet pamper, and went on our way. The next exit, we were looking to get some gas and McDonald's to eat. We had just missed breakfast, but I was good with the fish sandwich. My nap did me good, so we started talking again. I said, "By now, Donnie should know that his tires were flat. He probably guessed that I had done it since I left, and really I didn't know and did not care!" I had wished that he had paid me the money he promised because we shook on it. I was disappointed! We were teammates on the same team, but I just lost all respect for him and his dishonesty. Well, we are back on the road and moving good. The highway had gotten cleaned and clearer to drive on, and we were making good time. With about six hours to go before arriving in Akron, I figured that we would be there around 5:00 p.m. We were beginning to get excited to be back in Akron. Not to mention, with the daylight savings time, it would be like almost dark outside. I wanted to get there earlier but knew to be better safe than sorry. We had enough spinouts when we first started out this trip to go home. As we were driving along, I was so hopeful that this would be the last time for me to drive to Oklahoma City. I did not want to go back, not for any reason, but I just knew, just in case. If I really had to go back, I would for a very good reason! The rest of the states on our paths were cleared up really good, and we did not have any other issues. Except for Michael II. This time, he made a mess in his diaper. Adrian and I would take turns, but you know this was a long trip. If you would remember each time you changed the baby, we would say things like, "I did it last time," and Michael II did not really care as long as he got changed, or we would know what was coming next. We would hear a crying baby until he got that pamper changed. And that was that! So I kept driving and driving. I did not want to get caught up in any more bad snow areas. We are finally almost there. I got really excited as the sign read entering Summit County. I was getting tired and kept pushing to I-76/I-77 and to my sister's house, which she did not live too far from where we were.

We had to get to 1596 Delba Street, off Route 261, also known as Wooster Avenue, on the west side of Akron. It was like I never left that place. I still remembered everything after six years of being away in the military. There was another Church's Chicken restaurant up the road and Rolling Acres Mall. It was a place I hung out from time to time. It was about three miles up the street. If you would drive in the opposite direction, you would end up at South High School, and it was where my oldest brother (Junior) attended high school. Also he ran cross-country track and wrestled. I thought that he was pretty good at both sports. He had plenty of trophies and ribbons. He was also a big part as to why I joined the Air Force. Anyway, I was back. I left Akron very single and a baby with Lynn on the way, and upon returning, I now have a wife and two sons in the same town. I thought that coming back would be something else, including the baby momma drama. I now did not have a check, whereas the child support would not come out automatically. After we got to Terri's house, pink in color, the nieces and one nephew were happy to see us. I did not like the house color, but I did need a place to stay and going back home to my mother's house was not going to do it for me. Also being at Terri's house, we would have more privacy. We unpacked the car and got situated and sat around to talk. I was too tired to stay up for any long periods of time. And we called it an early night. The next day, we had to find and pay for a self-storage unit to hold our household goods that would be arriving within a week's time. I did find one on the east side just off Arlington Street. It was about four miles up from another Church's Chicken Restaurant. This was also my favorite chicken place in the world. I would get a wing, fry, pepper, and an orange pop, also called, a chicken snack. That was my meal, good and cheap too!

My Aunt Beck lived around the corner, as I would often see her and my cousins—Mary, Gina, and Rocky—because we sort of grew up together. They are truly the closest cousins. Plus, I had many, many other cousins and family too that I really did not know. We still had some money until we would not. Plus I had to give my sister Terri some money for rent to live with her. I did not mind. She did have three kids. I totally understood! I had to figure out something because soon, my checks would stop. Next I went to buy a newspaper. I would pay the ten cents or whatever and grab two extra newspapers, just in case someone else wanted one. I got back to my sister's house and started my job search. I knew that I was done with the restaurant business, and I had to look for something else. I went to the moving company as I used to work for them, Cotter Moving and Storage, which was not hiring. I went to the factory that manufactures plastics and plastics jugs. I thought it was called Landmark Plastics. I took a chance to see if I could do this job, working in the factory. I did get hired. Nope, this was not for me! I was working, and this environment was not for me, plus smelling of plastics every day. I was not the one for this type of job. I had never done anything like this. I was thinking on how much I wanted to become a doctor. I just talked myself out of this job, and I really needed this job. I kept telling myself that this was not me. If I would have stayed there, my dream, and any dreams of becoming a doctor would be totally lost. It was not even a whole day of work. I'd just quit. My new job become my old job, just like that! I punched out and turned in my timecard to get my one-day check, and it was over. I have to seriously look for another job immediately and ASAP! The fact was not many jobs were hiring in Akron. I found out that the unemployment rate was about 11 percent of the population.

I ended up back home and without even the potential to get a job. The newspaper had become my friend, and I was at the unemployment office for job searches. In the evenings, I would be playing cards mostly spades with Terri and her friend or sometimes my brother Junior. They were as good as we were or just better cheaters. We were cheating too. I think that we all knew that anyway! When playing cards, it became, without question, may the best cheaters win! That was the name of the game anyway, so we kept on playing everywhere there was a game that we got invited to. We would play game after game and sometimes all night, shuffling those cards and with the high arch mix shuffled. We started playing again for a little money. I now had real bills to pay. without having a real job. We were good on the household goods, but we had to keep that storage unit paid up, or we would lose our stuff. Definitely not an option. We were now starting a new set of bills—rent to my sister, storage, baby items, and food and whatever else we needed.

Plus, I gave my mother what I could when I could. Every time my mother needed to go to the doctor, that was never a problem for me. I did not believe in charging my mother for gas money. While others did, I felt strongly against it because that was my mother. See my mother never had a driver's license. I truly believe that the time was never available to her for learning how to drive; therefore, it was taxis, close friends, my Aunt Beck (her sister), sometimes neighbors, some church folks, my cousin Mary, and then sometimes her children, if they were available. Without question, she did get around. We all wanted our mother to ourselves, and if my mother had a favorite, she tried not to reveal it to any of the other brothers and sisters. In our own way, we all care and loved our mother. Somehow, it would always work out for her to get to where she wanted to go. While I was in Akron, I would take her as much as possible. My mother's life was dedicated to her God, her children, and even the grown children. We all had our way about ourselves. My mother knew us all and how to deal with each one of us. I just think that I was hooked on Church's Chicken because of her. It was my favorite chicken too. At the same time, speaking about the chicken, my mother could fry herself up some chicken in that Crisco oil. It would be so out-of-this-world good! On multiple occasions, she would be still selling, pies, cakes, and dinners, and give the proceeds to the church. She did these things for the church before I left. And now, she was still doing the same thing, upon my return. My mother would work until she was tired, and still, she would take care of her children. She stayed busy and just enjoyed the simple things of life. There was one place that I knew that she dreamed of going, and it was to go to Hawaii. She would tell me and my brothers and sisters of her desire to go there one day or to become a nurse. For occasions like this, it was nice to be home again. I did spend some time with my mom. I just loved talking to her, and she was crazy about Adrian (my wife). The one thing that was so valuable to my mother about Adrian was when we were at the hospital visiting, and my mother had asked Adrian to watch her purse. From that moment on, she would call Adrian her girl like, "That's my girl." I just enjoyed seeing my mother so happy. My mother was definitely a churchgoing lady and a faithful goer at that. Sometimes, she would babysit my son, Michael II, and if she had him on a church night or a Sunday, this grandson of hers was going to church! She did have him a lot even though it started a little slow. By this time, Michael II was with my mother so much, they also gave him a new nickname, and I had already given him the name Ant after his middle name Anthony and my middle name too. But my family, Ant's uncles and aunts called him Pooky. I did not know how they came up with that name. So as time went on, while we were in Akron, Michael II, had two nicknames, Ant and Pooky. If you were to add all this up together to include going to the courthouse for her children to get them out of trouble and being faithfully to church as a member is why my mother never got her driver's license, nor did she get to go to college.

Her children changed her life to become their life. My dad was in the wind, and they had never got back together since back in the day when I was a child. Even to this day, my mother had always taught us to respect our father. I believe that she was telling all my brothers to be better than he was. She would always tell us stories about my dad and her life together or about her growing up with all her brothers and the trouble that they had got into. My mother was always the mother and the father. She was tough, attitude change and all at the drop of a hat. My mother was always a mother to me, not my friend, but my mother. I believe that I may not always tell her the truth, but my mother always told me the truth. I respected just that, the truth!

I now had two sons and never wanted to be their friend, but I loved being their father! Therefore, in my definition, I would always tell them the truth! If it was something that I could not answer to my sons, then I would not answer it! It was as simple as that! I would continue to make my rounds and see my family. As it got closer to night, we would be getting ready to go play cards. Most nights, we were making our way home to my sister's house. That was our thing of playing cards, doing that time of being there in Akron. The playing of cards became a new way of life for us. We were actually getting really good, and our signals to cheat were flawless. We were good. We were good at every game we played: tonk, spades, bid whist, and 21 (blackjack). But we did not know how to play poker. It was poker, the game of chance. Come big or not at all, but we had no skills at that game whatsoever! We put it on our list to learn and as soon as possible! So for now, we would just talk about it. Seeing the family and hanging out was good, and after a while, I was not moving forward. I was stagnated. I was stuck in life in Akron and getting more stuck or lazy. I was not doing much of nothing.

At this point, we knew we needed more money, so we decided on that next day. We would go downtown Akron on South Main Street (a building over from the military recruiting office, also on Main Street) and sign up for ADC Welfare Program. We had no more medical insurance since I left the active-duty Air Force, and our son needed medical care. So we stood in line and hoped that no one would recognize us while there. A few hours seemed like forever, so we sat down with the caseworker to fill out all of the papers. I was so glad that we took all our important papers. We were able to get approved, and now had to wait until they mailed the healthcare card, check, and food stamps to the house. In a few short months, I went from active duty with the Air Force to on welfare, and on that same day, we were approved for unemployment. The building was right around the corner on East Market Street. I knew it was illegal, but at some point, I had to survive and feed my family. My desires were getting railroaded, and my goals were moving to the left. I was a few days from reporting to my new unit at the Air Force Reserves. Now, I have to go to the storage to get some of my Air Force uniforms and shoes. I must report to duty and keep within my weight standards. I noticed that I have been putting on a few pounds. I was not playing as much basketball or running as I normally would, but now, I had to get it together, to make the weigh-in upon my in-processing. I had never been on the weight program (aka the fat boy program). I was good for weight anyway, but I had to get better and in a hurry just in case because there was no probation for me. I was cutting back on eating, quick, fast, and in a hurry! I was even running in the wintertime! Besides, I knew that I could get kicked out of the Air Force Reserve for being overweight. In my mind, this was not going to happen. I needed to keep my focus and on track. I needed that money too. It wasn't much, but it was a help every month, and also, two weeks out of the year, I would have to stay at the reserve base in Pittsburgh and do my time. I was dedicated as a family man, father, but it was hard to tell from the position that I was facing.

Being a family man was something that I believe in, and surely, I did get that from my mother. I always would remember the many times she would tell all of us to make sure that we would always have a bed for our wife. She did not want us to have some of the same experiences from her marriage. I did listen, and that became important to me as one of my family values. So I would leave for the weekend once a month. The drive to Pittsburgh IAP by the airport was about one hundred miles or so, going I-76E most of the way until the exit for the airport. The drive was not too bad, except for the tolls. There were a few tolls, and that was it. That was a good drive. It gave me lots of time to think, especially about what I was going to do for work. There was a closer Air Force Reserve unit in Youngstown, Ohio, but I did get the assignment to Pittsburgh because it was based on vacancies. I did not mind going to Pittsburgh. I was farther away because Youngstown was only about fifty miles from Akron. That was too close for me, just in case some young lady would catch my eye. I was assigned to that unit 32 MAPS since January 1986 and did not report for duty until February 1986. Everything went well. Pittsburgh was a lot like Oklahoma City. It was not a place to really get into trouble. I drink a little, but was not a big drinker. The military guys wanted to get together and go to the bars after work. I was not big on hanging out with the guys. I did place myself in the ladies' man category! As Ronny Light's song would say, "I'm a Lover Not a Fighter." I liked the odds for the best man to win.

I totally learned my lesson from Steve. We were buds and friends in Dayton that did not end right but on bad terms. I will never forget that he betrayed me! One time was enough for me! I would only

217

go out by myself or with a lady, and since I was married, we did not really go out. Adrian and I did plan to go to Harry O's club in Akron on the east side of town, but that was it. Anyway, I went to get something to eat at a nearby restaurant and then back to my room. I always chilled the night before I would get my uniforms ready, with a light press, if necessary or sometimes Adrian would iron them for me, especially the light-blue buttoned uniform shirts. She probably really wanted to be that good wife, but surely, we both betrayed each other. I knew that it was just a matter of time before I would be leaving for good. While I roomed at the base, I would think of things that I messed up and our lives got crossed up, and now, I was unemployed and trying to figure out life. One thing about Adrian, she was not the one to sit down and have a decent conversation. Her lightbulb would go off in her head if I thought of something to do, like cheat the system, pay somebody back to get even. I needed more than that. To me, Adrian was excited for the game and not the reality of life. Adrian was a little more hood than I was, even though we both lived on the same side of town, and she was definitely more ghetto than I was for sure! Let's just say she taught me a thing or two. Even though at first, I wanted to change her.

The next day was Sunday, and my last day for my February reserve duty. While I was there, my supervisor, SMSgt. Bob Simonette, an extremely nice guy and had a salt-and-pepper mustache, had told me that my weight and check-in went well, and then, he also informed me that I was getting a promotion. It would be effective by my next weekend tour of duty. Wow! I needed to hear some good news! My spirit was lifted up for sure! I was excited that I had the time in-grade (TIG) for the reserve. If I was still in the Air Force and on active, I would have to test through the Weighted Airman Promotion System (WAPS), complete the Career Development Course (CDC), and my Promotion Fitness Exam (PFE) all had to be done, plus a good Airman Performance Report, in order to get promoted. This time I did not have to deal with the PFE and the WAPS. I had everything else completed. I always believed in staying on top of my military training. This time, it paid off, and I did not know that the reserve promotion system was different than the active-duty promotions. I had to make it to the military clothing and sales to buy some new chevrons for my uniforms and make it to a dry cleaner in Akron and with a picture of chevrons on uniform sleeves to get them sown on my green battle uniforms and dark-blue short jacket. Now, I would be making a few more dollars, still not much, but moving in the right direction.

On the way back home to Akron because my tour of duty was over, I had wished that I had stayed in the Air Force back in Oklahoma City. Living there was better than my current situation. I did have my own space in the townhouse, and now, I had my household stuff in storage. I just did not know what I was getting into when I separated from the active-duty Air Force. Still, I kept it going with life! For some reason, when I had got my second speeding ticket in Dayton on the expressway, just before the bridge and entering the city, the highway patrolman had told me then that I should consider becoming a state trooper for the way I was driving. The thing was he complimented my driving abilities, tried to recruit me, and gave me a speeding ticket all at the same time. So I was thinking about the recruitment part of his conversation. I thought about becoming a fireman and/or paramedic at first, but I did not like the hours and shift work. I used to set fires, so that was not my thing that I had thought to do for a career. So I thought long and hard about the Ohio State Trooper. I was getting the feeling for it and decided to take the test. Why not? It was a decent job, and I would be back in uniform. The ladies do like the uniform. Plus, it would be a bit easier to live a double life as a trooper, if needed. My mind was working. I tried the post office as well, but it was not really my thing. I did that mailroom stuff back at Wright Patt and a little at Tinker AFB. Those two jobs did not thrill me either, but I would apply for them anyway. I was getting busy again and a great feeling about a new job I was hoping to have.

Anyway, while searching for a job, Adrian and I came across jobs that she and I could both apply. It was with the Central Intelligence Agency (CIA). They were hiring, and I was definitely interested, and so was Adrian. Because we really needed jobs. The interviews were like that next week in Pittsburgh, Pennsylvania, and we had to stay overnight. We got things in order and had my sister to babysit for Ant, and we were one our way. I believe that they paid for everything, even our travel. I thought that this would be easy to get hired since I was in was in the Air Force Reserve and served active duty. On the day we were interviewed and got processed, I believe it was a Friday. It was very rigorous, and there was nothing but interviews. We both thought that we did good, but not so fast. After all, we did do a lot of tests and polygraphs. Then we were done! And tired! They separately drilled us and drilled both of us, for hours. I guess we did not have what it took. We wanted a job that we badly needed. The thing was, I knew very little about the agency, and after it was over, we both knew that much less. We both were good with living with lies, and if they would have vetted us correctly, we would be perfect at living a lie. At that time in my life, it would have been perfect. And I possibly could have went to school to become that doctor. Now, I am dreaming because we would never know. Just to have the interview with the CIA was a badge of honor for me. I cannot speak for Adrian. Now, we will never know!

Well, I did take the time and signed up with the Ohio State Patrol to become a state trooper. The test was to be taken in person in Columbus, Ohio. The state trooper test was on a Saturday morning, and we were running late. Adrian and the baby were with me. I do not know how I made to Columbus to the testing site. Just under one and half hours, we just made it. I went in showed my ID and took the test. Well, to say the least, I did pass the exam, and the next step was to take the physical, which would be a few weeks away, so we would just come back down when the time was required to be there. Now, we have to drive back up to Akron using I-71N to I-77S and back home. This was not an overnight trip, but it was easy enough to do. That car was getting it. This was a good car we picked up that got us from place to place right on time! These jobs were not coming through fast enough. On the way back, we were finally on way back to Akron. Adrian and I were together most of the time. I think that she still had some trust issues with me and was not going to let me too far out of her sight. We were together so much; we were almost like twins. The radio sound was nice, and I could sing-along as necessary or talk with Adrian. It was good hearing Stephanie Mills or Teddy Pendergrass and The Manhattans. It was definitely a soulful sound that we lacked in Oklahoma City. We were jamming all the way there! The radio DJ then came out with the smooth jam by The Commodores, "Just to be Close to You." I remember singing to her and watching her cheeks blush. I was definitely on this type of girl diet and so-called faithful to my wife for my son. For the time being, I was definitely married and acting married for a change.

The weeks flew by, and it was time to take my physical for the Ohio State Patrol, part 2 of the exam. It seemed like the only way to get a real decent job is to leave Akron. One thing about becoming an Ohio State Trooper was that I could be assigned to post anywhere in Ohio, but I would be able to drive my state trooper car home. I was looking forward to getting this job. For now, I had to wait until the physical results in a few weeks. Meanwhile, we were still working on getting jobs. We were glad to be getting the welfare checks and unemployment checks and my Air Force Reserve check. My sister did want her rent and on time, so we had to keep money coming in. At that time, I was getting all my tax paperwork together, so I can do my taxes. I went to the post office and picked up all my required forms. I did learn how to do taxes for when I was stationed at Wright Patt. I also knew at some point my child support for Big Mike was not going to be paid once my Air Force checks were stopped. And the checks were already stopped. I knew eventually, the checks were going to catch up to me. I decided to keep it moving until it did. I was still seeing Big Mike and did explain to Lynn that I was looking for a job to start the child support back up. Every time I went near Lynn's house right behind our old house, Adrian was in the car and timing me too. The thing was at this time, Lynn and I were done. No, nothing was going on, and she had gotten a boyfriend. That did not bother me any. I was only interested in my son, Big Mike, and to get that child support reinstated to her. I believe that her mother made sure that I was able to see Big Mike as well. Lynn's mother Gertrude was a good old Christian lady and was truly nice to me all the time. She loved me like a son-in-law! Gertrude did give me a light version of the fifth degree about Adrian and why did I marry her. I thought they were fair questions. Still, she remained nice to me. Gertrude was definitely cool, and I always remember how she used to let me drive the blue Caddy. I always spoke to Lynn's brother Jeffery, and he stayed cool with me too, but now, we did not hang around each other much anyway. The rest of the family was very cool too! Gertrude and Adrian's mother went to the same church at Shelton's Temple. The same place Adrian and I were married at. I guess that was pretty strange for everyone at times.

In the evenings when not visiting family or playing cards, I would do any military studies that I had to do or get some other stuff done to be credited for the reserves. Or like paying bills or doing my state and federal income taxes completed and mailed off to the IRS. I did not play with that; besides, we did need the money. When things got really tight and until my check came, I was able to borrow some money from my mother (or she for borrow from friends or a lady store owner, she knew). She would find some money for me. One thing for sure, I would always pay her back with interest because she was my mother. At the time, my mother was the fiduciary for my brother Junior's Veterans Administration (VA) monthly check for his disability. She asked to me take it over, and it would pay me a $100 or so on a monthly basis to monitor and administer his VA checks and bank account to pay for any of his needs or bills. My mother's eyes were getting bad, and her vision was not what it used to be because of the diabetes and high blood pressure. I agreed and I also had to get bonded to protect his funds and account. I had signed some forms and turned them over to his trusted attorney. By this time, we were home at my sister's house, and as I opened the mail, I was ineligible and did not qualify for the state trooper position. That was okay. The letter didn't really say why. I was so disappointed. I did not want to investigate it to find out the reason. I decided to keep looking. I have been in Akron for several months, and nothing was happening too much. I did get a potential promotion with the reserves. Although that was a good thing, it was not enough.

I was checking for jobs with the Social Security Administration and thought that I could use my military service in the downtown Akron and nothing—not a job in sight. We had been in Akron about three months, and I still did not have a job. It was time to go back the Air Force Reserves for the weekend and to receive my promotion. I picked up my shirts with the new insignias on the uniforms for the rank of staff sergeant (SSgt). It was a proud moment for me. Now I had to go and get packed for my reserve duty on tomorrow. And get a little rest for the drive to Pennsylvania to do another one hundred miles each way. I was getting used to it because I did like to drive and I received the official promotion to E-5, staff sergeant. I got there to the unit all right again and headed straight to the dorms to get my room for two nights at no charge to perform my weekend military duties. I was by myself but never bored. I always had something to do or something to think about. I was always in thought, to figure my next move. Quiet time was relaxing me, and I appreciated every moment. Also driving long distance was relaxing to me and some-times too relaxing. I was always looking forward to the drive for my weekend duties. The active-duty military, all branches of services, have always called the reserves "weekend warriors." That did not affect me a bit, especially since I was on both sides. The reserve bases are normally smaller than the regular active-duty bases. And this one shared the runway with the Pittsburgh IAP for their commercial flight. The C-130 aircraft flew through there a few times. The cargo airmen would load the aircrafts, and I would tend to the computers and my administration duties. I was not that labor-intensive guy that had something to prove. Besides, I needed to keep my strength for any futures endeavors or whatever that would come my way.

I have seen a lot of guys in the military, moaning and groaning for the pain that their bodies endured for the military service. I kept all of my hard-manual labor to the most minimal point. I did not want my body to be broken down from all of the necessary hard labor. I did not like going outside most of the time in the winter. There were many hills there, and the snow and ice conditions were not always in the best conditions. I was not one of the ones to have had to shovel the snow; I was glad that I had a little rank that was given to me after a quick small ceremony. For the time being, this was good and the people seemed to be very nice, especially SMSgt. Simonette. Before leaving for the weekend, I had asked him if there was a possibility to work additional hours during the week. He said that that he would check into it and let me know. He was also an Air Reserve Technician (ART), where you could work as a government civilian and must participate as a reservist at the same time. I thought that would be neat to do as well. The thing was that you would basically have to wait until someone die or retires. I quickly crossed that off my list. Now I was standing by to see if I would be allowed to work the extra time. They were called military personnel appropriation (MPA) or MPA man-days, and there was reserve personnel appropriation (RPA) or RPA man-days. Both serves as an authorization to support-termed need of the active or reserve military force. The terms could be extended from days to years, depending on what the military needs were and if you had the skill sets required to perform the mission.

In my case, I would just need to get approved for the RPA mandays. So I was waiting and hopeful that I would be approved to participate in the that RPA capacity. My time was up for my weekend duties, so I just went back home to Akron. The good thing about Pennsylvania's highway was they were cleaned off pretty good and better than the Ohio streets and highways. Pennsylvania's Department of Transportation sure knows what they were doing. Those plow-drivers handled their business to get that snow plowed. The only bad thing about Pennsylvania's highways was there was always some type of construction going on for the roads or bridge repairs. You would get used to one lane for both sides and make no errors. Other than the barriers in the median or the other side, if you were to have an accident and move the barriers, the only bad thing about this was, you would have a big drop. To drive in Pennsylvania, the guardrails or barriers were not forgiving. Again, no room for error. And still, I may have to avoid the deer on the side the highway. Of course, avoid the Pennsylvania State Trooper, if you were speeding. Approximately 90 percent of the time, I would just follow the eighteen-wheelers and keep my hammer down. I would talk with them often on my CB radio that was something that I really enjoyed doing. I did know that there were a lot of mountains there, and your ears would definitely be popping from the elevation changes. This was something that I had to get used to. This I knew for sure and learned the hard way that each time you get off the I-76 toll for the Pennsylvania's turnpike, you would have to pay a toll. I did not like paying for extra tolls that I did not plan on, so I ensured that I always had my pop or juice and snacks and gas in the car. I had my trip to and from my reserve unit that I carefully and always planned to a tee. I did not stop unless I had to go to the bathroom, or I would try to catch a rest stop and not just the pull off. Believe me, when you have to go, you go outside too! Then I had to keep it going back on the road. Some of those stops and pull offs were just dark. I was always hoping that I did not see a mountain lion or a snake. Other than that, I was good. The few times I did make those stops, it did work out good for me. It was the driving back and forth from Akron to Oklahoma City or Dayton to Akron and now Akron to Pittsburgh that made me realize that I really enjoyed driving, and it never seemed to mind me at all.

Well, I made it home again and straight to see my son Michael II whom I missed and Adrian. I picked them up, and we went out to get a bite to eat. I was tired of the Whaler fish sandwich from Burger King, and I did lose some weight; it was time for me to get some Church's Chicken. I was so satisfied! I told her the good news that I was officially a staff sergeant in the Air Force Reserve, and that did not really thrill her. She tells me that she knew that already. My next trip down to Columbus was unsuccessful not because of the physical exam. That was not the issue, not at all. When we got there, the doors were locked, and no one was getting in. As usual, we were late and no excuse was accepted. Now if I wanted to pursue the state trooper route again, I would have to start all over, the writing test and all. So I told Adrian on the way back to Akron that I may get approved to work extra hours down there in the reserve unit at Pittsburgh, Pennsylvania. That news was good and not so good. I wasn't being trusted 100 percent, but I have been good for the past year, and let's just say that she did not trust me enough, but it was okay for the time being.

Now, once we were back in town, then we would be headed to meet at my dad's house on the west side of Akron too! My dad lived on Wildwood Street and his wife, and her name was Mary. She was cool and nice, but something was off about her, so I figured that she had got treated like my mother, and I knew that may have not been pleasant for her. Well, my dad was proud of me. I think that he loves me and all the children in his own way. My brother Junior was the first born and the oldest. I believe of us all, he was my dad's favorite child. The next to the oldest was my brother Robert and could fix cars just like our dad. Robert was just that good and probably to please dad. Still, Junior was the golden son and my father's favorite. I was probably my mother's favorite! I knew very little about him, my father, and he did not share that much. I knew what I remembered about him as a child and all that my mother had told us about him. That was it! Well, I was planning to see a lot more of him since I was in Akron. He met his new grandson, Michael II, for the first time and held him for a few, and I took him back. I knew that he could play cards from my mother and that he was good, but he was a better cheater. I wanted him to teach me, well, Adrian and I, the game of poker. I wanted to learn the game of poker and all of it. But I wanted to win fair and square.

The baby went to sleep, and we began to play poker for coins and dollars. We would play spades for a little money and back to poker. We held our own at poker, but if his wife would mess up, he would look at her so. And I would just change the subject. I did like my stepmother and felt sorry for her at the same time. There was another time that we went over there, and she had a black eye and tried to cover it up. But I knew! Anyway, we would leave my dad's house and go home. We would put the baby to sleep and get a deck of cards and play poker. We were learning all that we could know about poker. Several nights and weeks were beginning to payoff. Now, we thought we had it and were ready for the big league to play poker for real money and no table limits to sit down. My dad took us to the poker house on Lane Street (by Lane Elementary School, at 501 Howe Street). I had gone to that school for a brief time when I was younger) and then to Berry Street. You just cannot walk into these houses. If no one knew you, then you were not getting in. Period! I was impressed by my dad. He took us to these houses, and all we had to do was say our last name. Our name Gilcreast had weight to it in Akron. I never knew that. My oldest brother, Junior, did know because we played poker with him and his lady friend, and he taught me a few things too about the poker game. Well, some seats came open, and we sat down to gamble. These were after-hour places. They looked like regular, but it was more than just an ordinary house in a residential area. These houses would be playing poker as long as people had money to gamble. You could get food and alcohol there. Of course, you would have to buy it all. Transactions were cash only and no receipts. We were in just like that because I was my father's son! We had new money, which means new players coming to the game. My dad played a few hands, maybe about half-hour, and left the poker house. We stayed and were winning not big but enough! People were trying to get to know us better and to see if I was more like my dad or not. One of the ladies that came through there was Barbara. She so happened to be Adrian's cousin. That moment broke all of the ice, we were in there.

As we were playing poker, I was very careful of the playing cards that were in my hand but on the table under my hands. I did not want anyone to see what I had. Or the outside of the cards, just in case the cards were marked. Adrian and I were both fast learners. It was three hours later. We were still playing cards, and at times, we would be betting against the house. If the house called and lost, they had to pay up. There was no time for nonsense because almost everyone in there had guns. I was there on the reputation of my dad. Adrian and I were just fine! Since the ice was broken, we were not suspected of being undercover cops. We were talking to everyone and showing family pictures. Apparently, some of the older folks knew my family members, even when I was a child. They knew of me, and I did not know of them. Still, I did not trust any of them! I was about gambling first and not mixing the two. I did not believe in folks playing with my money. Not at all! The games were good and pleasant, but the speed of the game was a little slow, as in the pace of the game, but they kept the game moving. As we were getting ready to leave and as I called for my last hand, they began to tell us the schedule of the future games. Somebody was playing somewhere and finding a poker game was just that easy. The key was to stay within the crowd that you knew. We had to remember that not every card game was a good game to be around. I knew at some poker games, you could lose your life. For what, a card game? We played poker normally from Thursdays through Sundays and sometimes all day on Saturday and Sunday. It was weeks at a time. We were playing poker. The Berry Street poker house was the main house. We played a little on East Avenue and on Lane Street. Every now and then, we would go to people's private residence and play poker for birthday parties and such. Some days we would lose a few hundred dollars between the two of us.

It was on that following Monday in May, the weekend before my military weekend drill. We looked at the mail, and there was the tannish brown envelope, and inside was my tax refund. Outstanding, we did get our tax refund. I did realize that we had our hustle on. We were hustling, and we were playing the state lottery too. I had to put that money in our bank at the Ohio Savings Bank, off of North Howard Street. Adrian and I were planning a trip to Atlantic City, New Jersey. I had about four checks per month to come in. I had one check to serve as the fiduciary to manage my brother's account, unemployment, welfare assistance, and part-time in the Air Force for reserve duty. I was still trying to make more money. I did not count gambling or playing the lottery that were extra. My wife and I were expecting one more check from the state of Ohio for the 1985 tax return. That was not that much. Michael II was born on October of 1985 helped to boost taxes up, helping out the refunds. Once I got back from my reserve duty and on the following weekend Atlantic City, here we come. I was happy for all of the wrong reasons, hustling in the streets. I knew more about the streets than anything. I was hanging out with that street life and a few drug dealers that played cards as well and got high, smoking weed at the table. I was still in the Air Force Reserve and did not want any part of that. I was like one of the good guys, so it seemed that way. We, Adrian and I, were pretty good gamblers and held our own very well. To stay at the poker table all night is pretty good. We would go home take a shower and go back to gambling through Sunday evening. We would give my mother a few dollars to continue to watching, Michael II and to get something to eat, and then, we would go back to gambling. I did not smoke nor get high, but I may have sipped on a cold beer, every now and then, and take a shot of top shelf. That was it for me. The drinking was not really my thing, and I have been drunk a few times before, but overall, drinking was not for me. I was definitely about the money and making as much of it in that hustle that we were in.

I believe that I, more than Adrian, was getting hooked to gambling. I had that feeling over and again! I did keep it under control as much as possible because of my son. I did not want to leave him out and lose everything. I knew that gambling was becoming an internal fight for me. I could not stop gambling. I was loving that feeling of the "almost" feeling. You can feel the blood flowing through your veins. You can feel the intensity of your heart. That feeling was better than the legal drugs. That feeling had the worse letdown once you lose! Either way, on the high or the low, there's no feeling like it. You just will never like the lows. It was like being on the roller coaster without the amusement park. It was the thinking of my sons Big Mike and Michael II that made me a better gambler. I knew if I was to gamble correctly, I would not drink. I did not need a drink to take the edge off me. That edge gave me a natural high. It was my feeling toward gambling that changed my entire approach to money. I started saying, "Easy come. Easy go!" I was not going to allow money to become my God! I was learning that I could get money, but there was only one of me. And after me, the money would still exist! It was doing my gambling, which has taught me to never to become obsessed with money. Or drinking, then you would lose control. The thing was I did not like losing control. Now was a good of time as ever. We had some money in the bank. We were about to go to Atlantic city, New Jersey. Adrian and I discussed it, and then I told her that I had decided to buy a gun. The next day, we went to the pawnshop on East Exchange across from McDonalds, and I brought me a black automatic gun with light-brown wooden handles. And got some bullets too. And got a holster too! For all of the stuff we were doing and the people we hung around was about business. Plus, we wanted to feel safe when we won big. I was officially a small-time gangster.

By this time, I have been approached several times in the poker house with offers to sell drugs. The dudes were trying to recruit me. I was never interested. I wanted to become a doctor and never a drug dealer. I have tried drugs a few times, here and there, but never every day! Deep down inside of me, I want to help people and not selling them drugs. There had never been anything about drugs that excited me. I did not want to hurt people. I wasn't a doctor yet, but more importantly, I did not want to hurt people, even more black people! Me being black and as a person, I kept thinking how we kept hurting and killing ourselves. I did not want to be part of the problem by adding more drugs and killing my own. On the other side, I wanted to be part of the solution. Healing! And I was not going to give up my Air Force career just in case. I knew for sure that I had to get out of Akron! No doubt in my mind. I did think several times that school could be a possible way out!

Anyway, it was time to do my third reserve drill. No cards on the night before reserve duty. Plus I had to drive. I was excited to get down there. Just maybe, this would be the weekend to get the approval for the additional RPA man-days. It was my time when I reported for duty. SMSgt. Simonette told me that I could work one to two days a week. I was thrilled, to say the least. I would also be earning active-duty points that would help with me with meeting the time requirements once I was closer to retirement. I was thinking retirement, even though I was so far away from it. Anyway, I needed that good news. My mother must have been praying for me. Yes! Now, I was on track to make additional money for my family and provide better for my sons. I just kept it moving. So I had to setup reservations at billeting starting the following week to work additional days during the week, plus my reserve weekend. The most certainly was on time. That would then mean that Adrian would be seeing me that much less. We were doing good at this point, as far as the relationship was concerned. I was not slipping up anymore and calling her by Lynn's name. It was unbelievable that Adrian and I were just doing as well as we were. I was finally looking forward to going back to Akron to see my family. I could feel that things were beginning to change for me and the family. Well, this weekend went faster than the other two weekends. I had something working. Maybe I would be an ART, like SMSgt. Simonette, and become a combination of reserve and government employee. We shall see, and I know that these are hard positions to get into on a full-time basis, but I am hopeful and optimistic. I really did not know what to expect. For now, it was definitely working in my favor. Now, I had a real part-time job, and the money was much better.

We had some money for now and was to go to Atlantic City with my sister Terri and her friend, but when the money had gotten short and tight for us, we had to borrow money at times. Adrian would ask her mother, and I would ask my mother. Or my sister Terri with the three kids. Sometimes, we would pay bills or go and gamble to take the chance gamble with it, so we could pay more bills. We were doing everything to keep things together and the bills paid. I had some of the bills left from the bankruptcy back in Oklahoma City, and some of them were becoming past due. It became an act of desperation to rob Peter and pay Paul. I was maneuvering our bills to pay whatever bills when possible, even if I had to get it from playing poker. We even sold some of our food stamps at a discount price, just to play poker. Yes, I must admit, playing poker did help to pay our bills. There were even times we went to donate our plasma to get $15 to $20 at the blood bank on East Exchange Street as well.

Well, that week, I had to turn around and go back to Pittsburgh to do the additional reserve RPA man-days that I was approved for. In no way, I was going to mess that up. Well, we got reservations in Atlantic City for one night and come back home. The plan was for two days and one night. What a perfect plan, and it worked. We all spent a little on the Boardwalk. We shared some boardwalk french fries and just had a ball before we went to gamble. The hotel was pretty cool too, and for a night, we did not believe that we had our own room for a change. What a relief, just to get away for a night with the wife. Before going to bed, we went gambling. The casinos were very colorful and not a clock in sight. We spung the card wheels, played blackjack, poker, and then a few other games. I was really an amateur, and I then realized that we all were amateurs. There were bells, ring tones, smoking, and drinking everywhere. I really liked the slot machines too. When, we got up that next morning, awaken by the radio, I had set it the night before to the black radio soulful station. I heard the voice. What a song to wake up to. We did just that. "No, no, no way, I am living without you…" It was the first time we heard that song "And I'm Telling You" by Jennifer Holliday. That was a bad song. We really liked that song, especially Adrian. She liked it more! When it was all said and done, Adrian and I were down and out of about $500 that was too much for my blood. I was ready to go home! The bags were already in the car. If there's one big lesson that I learned, it was you can't win if you don't play, and you should not play, if you do not have it. I had to learn that all by myself, and I did that the hard way. I was learning as I was losing my money. One thing for sure, being in Atlantic City have already made me a better gambler just by watching the other players play the game. I was and we were ready to get on the road, get some food, and pay those tolls to get home. We all played a few slots machines on the way out, and that was the end of our gambling in Atlantic City. We talked about it and the gambling most of the way home. It was Adrian and I driving that ten-hour trip on the road and Atlantic City in our rearview mirror, the city lights and all. Akron, Ohio, here we come! I made up in my mind that I was never going back there to gamble in that place, not ever. That loss was too much for me. Plus, Adrian had me close hold and never let me out her sight. Everyone knew that I was taken.

It was a good thing that we stopped gambling, when we did and take the lost. I could clearly see now, how people could lose everything over gambling. Some of those people looked crazy and just out of it; you could tell that gambling was their life. As I was looking at them, it scared me to think that it could easily have been me if I stayed there at Atlantic City. If I would have stayed another day, I may have won, but the truth was I would have lost everything. We had seen folks on the street, and you could tell that they had lost everything. I did not want that to become me! For sure! Now, I know that I am not crazy nor was I addicted. I just enjoyed it because I knew what I was looking at was enough to motivate me to leave. I could not get to Akron fast enough. If I was seeing my future, really, I did not want any part of it. I was going to stick to our little hustle in Akron. It was working for us. We made a few stops along the way back to Ohio for goods and gas. It seemed like it was about the same stops as going to New Jersey. I had some moments to myself and realized that there was something good for me being in the Air Force and kept reminding myself not to mess it up. I really acted better by having that structure in my life. I did not really have structure in Akron, just a gun. The game of my life at that time was all for providing for my family and surviving. I just knew that this was not the life for me. I kept thinking on how Adrian only wanted to do bad things or stuff that would end us up in jail. She really wanted that gangster life. Plus, we always got along so much better when I would be falling into that life of a want-to-be gangster. Being in Akron, we arrive there safely and it has separated us even more. Sometimes, I think I would be in the mindset to want more with her and maybe just wishful thinking. She would say, "No matter what you had done to me. I do not want to know, and I forgive you."

You see, Adrian and I did not talk like that, not at all. Having intimacy in marriage is one thing, but to have intimate sincere conversations for our life just never happened, unless I pursued that direction of our relationship. I kept trying in so many ways to seek a positive life. Still, nothing happened. I did not believe that she would ever leave me, but she did not know how to share her innermost part of her feelings with me. Even though I knew Adrian as I did, I needed more. I was the one that needed the intimacy. I needed all of her, but without telling her. To me, love was sort of like gambling— all or nothing! I was living it with gambling but really did not know how to express it. I believe that gambling was an escape from love, and it was definitely working. It was similar to being drunk without the alcohol. When we were gambling, it was such a great escape from the relationship and reality. I was thinking too much, and we have to check on our son and pick him up. There was no gambling until the following weekend. We did hang out a little and played some cards, of course spades, and we called it a night. We did have a few more laughs and wishful thinking. If we would have won! I thought that it was pretty harmless to dream. I just wanted to dream on how to get out of Akron. It was not like Oklahoma City in which I did not like it there. But for Akron, I just did not want to be there, and for one, I wanted my own house. I did not have that in Akron, nor could Adrian or I could afford our own house. I did not want, nor did we ever applied for the welfare program—the urban housing program called Section 8. We would have been stuck in Akron forever. So I kept gambling to keep my mind off my jobless situation and thinking about my wife who would only have my last name and not my love.

I had to initiate everything in our conversations, our life, and really, she did not even try, but she did not want to let me go, and so we could go our separate ways! My nights kept being longer and longer. My mind kept racing in my head on how I wanted more in life and in a real relationship. I, most times, felt like I was desperate to be with Adrian… Somehow, I knew that there was more for me. Was I crazy or what? I kept trying to figure that out and would not give up on that search—that true love existed for me. I wanted to find true love but did not know how to begin. Again and again, I would fantasize to find true love. I had this burning desire to find her (a woman that love me and had her own self-expressions), this desire that would not be quenched. I did believe that it was a little crazy. But I had to keep chasing this fantasy. Anyway, I just had to keep it to myself. I didn't think it was fair for me to figure it out as I was doing over and over with Adrian. Let me say for the most part, I was home, and that was good for everybody else, but I was totally unhappy. Inside myself, I knew that I had let everybody down. How would I redeem myself? I did not know that answer either!

The next few months, nothing was changing. We were doing the same old thing. I was doing my reserve and extra reserve duties, and going back and forth to Pittsburgh IAP, I did a mail run for the office and met this fine young secretary. I can say that she was nice and gave me a smile. That was it. She was not in the military and only worked Monday to Friday. I was not about to press any way toward her. I just took the niceness and move on. I think that many guys had tried to hit on her, and nothing was happening. At least I was aware of where I stood with her. It was like nothing ventured and nothing gained, and it never would happen. I was fine for that.

From the month of July to August, Adrian and I were submitting and getting signed up for Pell Grants and student loans, so we both could go to the University of Akron to study premed to become doctors. This was the plan, or so we thought, but not so.

Something came up with my sister Terri, and we got into an argument of sorts. Adrian was leaving the baby stuff around the house, leaving food out, and enough was enough. My sister Terri wanted her house her way. At first, I thought that it was about money, but now I see how much I knew. One thing for sure, my sister who was a little older than I, then kicked me out of her house and started to bring my stuff out. This was not cool, but it was sure enough happening to me and my family. I called the Akron Police Department. They showed up only to let her do what she was doing. We had no place to go unless I was to go and live with my mother and younger siblings. I did not want them messing with my stuff. So the police allowed us to get out stuff, and we loaded up the car as best we could with our son and left. Adrian decided to ask her mother and father (adopted aunt and uncle parents), if we could live with them, so they gave us the attic, with a hot gas heater, connected to the house, and we had to keep a pot of water on it to keep the moisture in the air. We had to fill the water up once every evening. I could not believe that my sister put me out and my family out. What were we to do? Except move to the attic. There was a bed up there. We had more space, and we did have a crib for Ant, our baby. It was looking better; the rent was the best price. Free.

Going to college, this was an impossible task for both of us to do. We did get registered for school, and I had transferred some of my credits from Sinclair Community College, Wright State University, and the Community College of the Air Force. I was deemed a transfer student, and Adrian was admitted regularly. We had to meet counselors to select the program majors and to get the right classes.

This was unbearable. Adrian wanted to take all the same classes as I did. But it was not the best approach to do because we had different strengths. We did it anyway. I was definitely good at the math, chemistry, and biology, and Adrian had the English and psychology. The reality dropped on us. It was not working because I had to make the money too, and we had Michael II (Ant) to take care of. After less than two months, or maybe even less, we both dropped out and any unused money of the financial aid, and the student loans were returned us.

We had about $12,000 or more, and the student loans were building up from Wright State University. As long as you were attending college, we could get a forbearance to start making payments on the student loans, and we were in school and got our forbearance approved for six months at a time, or the student loan would go into default. She being Adrian held me back again, but I only blamed myself because I allowed it. I knew that she would have been too insecure to allow me the freedom to go to college without her. I was not paying the bills or the child support to Lynn for Big Mike! Still I was gambling and fooling myself to live a lie. At that present moment, I had accepted it until, as the saying goes, until my ship comes in! We wanted to give that poker life for what we were doing, a real shot to see if we could make some money from it. I was going to be in it to win! No doubt! We got with the dude, an older light-skinned black gentleman with white hair (out of respect, I will not put his name out there), and he rented the house on Berry Street for us. We did our thing, Adrian and I. Then my sister Terri and I had made up, and I had her to do my kitchen, selling fried chicken dinners, drinks, and alcohol. Then I would give her a portion of what money we brought in from the kitchen. It worked like this. We support other poker games, and they supported us. We would then pay the dude the monthly rent for our Saturday poker game night. Of course, you had to be carrying your gun, just in case. In that do or die life that we were living, you just have to be prepared for anything. I was in the thick of that life now, and the name of it was survival. On the streets, the language was kill or be killed! Right after we started to have our monthly turn, to run the after-hour, we started to get some of everybody to come up in there. The dudes were coming in there, trying to sell all kinds of items that they found (to me, they were fencing stolen goods, tapes, jewelry, and a chess board that I had gotten). The other side of it, if we were not interested, we would put them out and keep our games moving. I normally played the house, and I had to pay the table if I had got stuck out there on a bad poker hand. I did not play unless it was a sure thing. I had never operated like a charity. I only played to win! The chess set was marble, and I got it for a real good price. By this time, I got approached again to sell drugs, and again, I told the dude, "No, not interested." I told him again I appreciated the offer but still was not interested. I kept it moving. Selling drugs to my people was never my thing! Nor was I going to start doing drugs, at least not in this lifetime! I never trusted that guy anyway, him or his mustache. I just wanted him to play cards. That was it! This was the last time that he ever asked me again. I was so glad because I knew that if I was to ever cross that line, it was no coming back for me. I would have lost my soul! You know the following week or two, Adrian and I was at somebody else's game, playing poker. Another dude approached me to run the street number for him. I could do this. It was right up my alley and a little safer too! He was the numbers man for everyone and was recruiting someone that he could trust. That dude was me. Now, I can add "bookie" to my street résumé. I was a bookie for the street lottery, when the numbers came out. Now I was making house calls and finding new folks to gamble under the table. I was playing, too, about $25 a day or more! I was playing about the same for the Ohio State Lottery. I was gambling everywhere and hitting numbers too, hitting the small cash prizes for straight or boxed. I had thought that maybe, this could be a way out! Not yet! So I kept playing those numbers. I did have a limit to gambling. I never spent all our monies. We had some money in the bank and still more money coming in. It was not a lot, but we made it enough.

Our baby did not stay on milk long. My mother raises ten of us and knew a few tricks of the trade. Everybody just started to call Michael II, *Pooky*. He was just eating soft table food and teething. His first year went by so fast, and my mother had him, pretty much all of that time. Of course, I was paying my mother, and at that time, she was working on him being potty-trained. He was in a crash course of potting-training. My mother would tap his hand or behind, or he would be sitting on the potty chair. He was beginning to walk. I was so glad. We had him at Adrian's mother house. He would crawl upstairs to get his pampers and slide down the stairs to get to us with the pamper in hand. Ant was pretty good at it on the stairs, and we were scared for him. My mother was very used to keeping him and was bonding to him as well. Ant did not have much hair, so Adrian would put about four little braids in his hair. By this time, as the year was about to end, I was taking personal bets that the Denver Broncos would win against the New York Giants, even though Cleveland Browns just lost to the Broncos, with a score of 23–20. That year, the Browns almost made it to the Superbowl, and then, Cincinnati Bengals was my other team. Neither team were in the Superbowl. So I went with the Broncos because they beat the Browns. I was taking bets and had about $150 in bets total. I would be playing cards around all the holidays from Thanksgiving through New Year's, and even on the day before my birthday, I held a card game.

On this birthday, in 1987, I had turned twenty-five years old. Again, I was not interested in celebrating my birthday, and I never wanted a gift from my wife because I did not know how to accept a gift from Adrian. We had got the boys a few toys and clothes, and that was it for Christmas. Of course, I hooked up my mom. Plus her birthday was the day after Christmas, so I combined her gifts. I was not much for shopping. I would give my mother money or money with a card. I was labeled growing up and, even now, a momma's boy. I really did not mind because it was the truth. My mother and I had a very special kind of relationship. All I can say is, my mother was just a special lady. She was more than a friend, and she really was going to make it, regardless of who said what about her. My mother just did not care because she loved the Lord, the church, and her children! This was one attribute that I would really have to say: I got it from my mother. My mother kept our son most of the time and always kept him in church while we were in Akron. Every now and then, we had to find another babysitter, like my sister Terri and Adrian's Aunt Marion Shell did watch Ant for a few hours as we had to run to the VA hospital for Adrian's brother, and when we returned to pick up our child, I tried to pay her, and she would not take even a dollar for watching our child. My mother did most of the babysitting and even kept my other siblings' kids at the same time. While I knew that this was not fair to my mother, I was just stuck in a bad place, and I gave her money as often as possible, or I would just owe her because my credit was good with her. I did have some good things about me. Well, really, it was only one thing that was tangible, my connection to the Air Force and the other one was me.

I had a choice on how I wanted to live my life. I just had to find myself again, like when I left Akron for the first time and becoming a man! The life that I was facing was not the man I had hoped of becoming, and I was living a lie as a cheating husband. I would have cheated on her at the drop of a hat! I have not been this dry, with no women since living in Dayton, Ohio. I was admitting that I was faithful to a woman that I did not love but kept trying to love her since we were already a family. I knew and thought of it often if I was to only find anything, well, anybody that was somewhat close to love. I was going to leave her for good, regardless of my credit situation and the lack of a home. I wanted more! Somehow, I managed to keep myself together, but I was totally miserable! It was the playing poker that was my therapy in a group session. My mind was not on me or my family. We had held our game night, which was on. People came and left, and some of the folks ate or only came for the plate. Well, my sister could cook and the kitchen did well most of the time as well. We have some good nights on the poker table, as far as making money, and then, we had some bad nights. But when we put two and two together, we were in good shape to do it again. I was playing as the house since it was our night to host the poker games. At the same time, I was given tickets as the bookie. I made sure that I did not get the money mixed up. That would be stupid and a whole new story, especially if someone had hit the number. I would have been in some serious trouble. The one thing that I could do was count. I was never careless in dealings with other people money. The poker house was safe for the most part, especially since you could not enter unless you were vouched for.

We had a good night, and that night was gone. Now, Adrian and I just made the rounds again and kept playing poker. We went house to house and back to Berry street, and before you knew it, it was Superbowl Sunday. We were at the house as usual and gambling of course. I was not feeling good and all. I have over a $150 in foot-ball bets in favor of Denver Broncos. I had a fever, and my body was aching. I was coughing, and nothing was working. I had decided to go home and get some rest. As I was leaving, someone mentioned to get a shot of E&J Brandy and hung out for another half-hour. That drink was supposed to open up my pores. Boy, it did. I went outside in one of those Akron winter nights. I guess my pores opened fast once that cold air had hit my body. I went from okay (bad) to worse in no time! I was sick as a dog! I had a splitting headache, the cough-ing got worst, and my chest was hurting badly. I knew that this was nowhere close to normal for me. I was really sick. I could barely see straight. I thought that this was only the flu at first. We went to Saint Thomas Hospital, the closest one to us. Adrian was right there, not even thinking of leaving my side. I was looking pretty bad when we arrived to the hospital emergency room. I was not able to walk in. I did not sit in that wheel chair for long, nor was I able to. I was bent over and badly coughing. I have had sinusitis, a cold or the flu of this thing that was holding on to me and would not let go. I was getting sicker, by the minute! Now, nausea was setting in, so the nurse gave me a plastic pan to spit up in. I was thinking that if death felt like I was feeling, then I knew, firsthand that I was at the front door of death. I thought for real that I was going to die!

First, the doctor had the nurse give me a shot for the headache and to get some x-rays of my chest. My head started to feel better. On Superbowl Sunday, I was in the ER at Saint Thomas Hospital. Of course, I missed the game between the Denver, Broncos, and New York Giants. The Giants won with a final score for the New York Giants 39–20. The ER doctor told me that I had pneumonia. This was the very first time that I had gotten pneumonia. They gave some-thing to slow down the coughing and some prescriptions to pick up from the drug store. I was looking at death, and my life was spared again! I was able to go home and referred to follow up with another doctor. Being on welfare was definitely good in this case. I could have died. All I could think of was I was out of another $150 for the Superbowl loss. I had three bets and paid them all. I lost a bet on a team that beat my team. The Broncos were tough, and John Elway was tougher. I thought that Bernie Kesar was good with the dawg pound, but Elway was just better. I had always wished that John Elway would have transferred to the Cleveland Browns after Brian Sipe and the Kardiac Kids. That was a great era for the Cleveland Browns, my team! As we were leaving the hospital, I was so out of it and dazed from the medication, so Adrian drove us around the corner home to her mother's house. Out of all of my years, I had gotten pneumonia for the first time. Boy, I was sick as a dog. That was one drink of E&J Brandy that opened up my pores. I was outside and in Akron, and that same drink almost killed me. Never again!

We were going home to that cold attic. Boy was it cold. We filled up the pot for the gas oven, and I am sure the water helped the air quality, but we were breathing all kinds of junk in our lungs and the baby too. Sometimes, there would be scratching at the corners of the attic walls of a home that was built in 1907 and leaning over a little. We just wanted it to stay stable for us and everyone there. We did not know whether it was birds, racoons, squirrels, or what. We knew it had some type of wildlife happening in there. As this was an ongoing thing, we would hit on the walls or whatever. That next day, we were sitting downstairs in the living room as we had just gotten up. The phone rang, and Adrian's aunt told her mother that Adrian's aunt, Marion Shell, had died on that last Wednesday. It was just two days later. Another aunt (I believe it was her Aunt Rose, the mother's sister) called, and before the phone was picked up to be answered, Adrian said, right out of the blue, "Somebody else done died." That was exactly what had happened! Who does that! Exactly like that! My mind was blown, and my mouth was just opened with a profound look on my face. I just knew that Adrian was gifted. This time, it was her cousin that passed, trying to get to Akron from Chicago. Her cousin Elizabeth Louis had taken their aunt's death so hard that she died too. We did not know, if she had had a heart attack or what had happened. All we know is that the plan now was for two funerals. Lord, have mercy! I was also recovering from pneumonia back home on Superbowl Sunday. These were some exciting times, not knowing what to expect.

Anyway, we would eventually go back upstairs to get dressed to go out and still be hearing the scratching and such, but we never seen anything. Our living conditions was just that, a condition to live in. I could not keep up with the bills by gambling and hustling with the street numbers, welfare, and a few other things. I needed more money in a bad way. Plus, I had to pay for my poker game night. I thought about it. I tried to talk myself out of it, and the idea was to only borrow a little here and there and put it back after we would win. Well, sometimes we won and had gambling winnings. Then I would put the money back into my brother's account. I was bonded, and I really was not trying to steal anything. I was only borrowing the money. At first, it was a few hundred of dollars, and then, as the months went by, it turned into thousands. We had not paid the money back. That was my brother, Junior. He let me borrow his car, his clothes, and he trained with me to get in the Air Force. I was all messed up. We went to the Thistle Downs Race Track a few times with the guy that I was a bookie for (from Akron) to Cleveland, Ohio. I only lost more. I was playing numbers by the hundreds a day on the street number and the Ohio Lottery. I lost more and more. I did win on a regular basis, but it was not enough to pay my brother's account back. I even hit the street number 117 straight for $1,800 and forgot to back it up! Yet I hit. My luck was finally changing. Then I put a $1,000 back and kept the $800. My bills were further behind. I just said later for it and stopped paying those creditors, except a few of them. I could barely pay for the car insurance. Yet we kept gambling with the poker, and we did pretty good each time we played.

I remember it was a Monday or Tuesday at the beginning of May 1987. Michael II was one and half years old. He was playing in the living room around the solid brown wood coffee table in the middle of the floor. He slipped and fell before I could even think and his mouth, hit the coffee table, and all I could see was blood. It was bad with the blood. We rushed him to St. Thomas Hospital, and he would be fine, but we had to find a dentist to have some caps or teeth protectors placed over his two front teeth. Well, he was walking and getting into everything. I wish I had caught him, but I could not! We promptly had the caps placed on his two teeth on the next day at the dentist's office. Now, instead of gold, Ant had two silver teeth and still handsome as he could be. That was our baby, Adrian and me. However, he was totally a daddy's boy! The two silver teeth would fall out as his new teeth would grow in. The dentist had informed us of this. We were totally relieved and thankful for another blessing that could have turned out very badly. Well, spring was here before us, and the winter had gone! Now, the worst part was coming, summer! We did not need the heat and no air-conditioning for us. We did buy a few fans keep the air circulating. That attic was hot on top of hot, and the walls and the ceilings were hot too! It was just most miserable for us all! I could not wait to get out of that torture of a place for my family. I did realize that was the best that we could do for the time being, and we did! We did this every hot summer night and day. We took plenty of baths to keep us cool. Suffering like this, indeed, just kept me motivated to get us out of there! Plus, we both were wearing Jheri curls and the spray conditioner. Sometimes my sister would braid my hair. The middle braids going backward, and the side braids going down. And I had just gotten an ear piercing before going back to do my reserve duties. On my way to do the reserve duty for the Air Force, I had to pack my hair down and put a broom straw in my ear with alcohol, so the hold in my left ear would not close. I kept trying to figure out how to get my brother paid back.

As I was reading the messages on the bulletin board, it was one message that caught my eye. To travel to Warner Robins AFB, Georgia, to work for one month to assist the Reserve Headquarters for informational management in the publications section. It would be for the entire month of June. I was all over it. If you volunteered, it was almost automatic. Then the RPA man-days would get approved for your orders, and I would pick up my ticket that same weekend while there at Pittsburgh. I would get the airline ticket, rental car and hotel, plus per diem. The money was just right and better than what I was currently doing! This was a sweet deal! I left my reserve training in Pittsburgh IAP and headed back to Akron to tell Adrian the good news! When I got home seeing Adrian, this time was different. She was not smiling nor happy to see me. She then showed me the letter that came in the mail. This letter summons me to go to court. I was busted for spending my brother's money. I was looking at serving about ten years of jail time, if convicted. First thing I did was I drove over to my mother's house to see what she had to say. I could see the disappointment on her face. My only defense was that I was going to pay it all back. Of course, she would pray about it. And I had to leave, but she would watch the baby again. Well, my case was in this review board then a court hearing, and I had to sit outside the court room and await my disposition. All sorts of stuff were going through my mind. I thought that I would be going to jail. Adrian helped me to spend it, but I was the one that would have taken the entire penalty and serve time in jail.

On that court day and a week before, I was to report for the TDY at Robins AFB, Georgia. I was failing and yet trying to get my life back on track. My mother called me that morning before court, I was sitting in that chair outside the court room, awaiting my fate. My mother told me to read Psalm 70, the entire chapter, and it goes like this: "Make haste, o God, to deliver me; make haste to help me, O LORD. Let them be ashamed and confounded that seek after my soul: let them be turned backward, and put to confusion, that desire my hurt. Let them be turned back for a reward of their shame that say, Aha, aha. Let all those that seek thee rejoice and be glad in thee: and let such as love thy salvation say continually, Let God be magnified. But I am poor and needy: make haste unto me, O God: thou art my help and my deliverer; O LORD, make no tarrying." Then right before my mother went into the courtroom, she had written it out and told me to place it in my shoe… I then read the Bible scriptures again on the torn piece of brown paper bag that she had handprinted for me. For an hour and half I sat there in that chair, as uncomfortable as I could have been. I was just nervous because my life was in the balance and about to change with possible jail time for the mismanagement of fiduciary funds. The lawyer on my brother's side, he was the one that monitored the funds, along with my mother. He said that the only thing that saved me was the fact that I was bonded and my brother would get all the money returned to his bank account, and therefore, no charges were filed. I would have to relinquish all my access to his account. My mother's prayers again.

God heard her and saved me! Wow! I could not believe what had just transpired on my behalf!

To say that I was relieved would not be even close to what I was really feeling. Somehow, I knew this was just miraculous! Truthfully, I felt free again! Truly, just free! My brother Junior would get all of his money back because I was bonded. My mother was in that courtroom, but I believe that so was God! I was actually, holding my breath as the lawyer was speaking to me. Now, for real, the following week I would be going to Georgia. My brother was upset and upset with me, and he kept his peace because his money was returned to him. I know that he was proud of me for joining the Air Force on his advice, but I really disappointed him, now twice. Still, he did not hold it against me, nor did he treat me any differently. Especially since his money was returned to him. We never fuss or fought about it. I guess that is what big brother's does. I was encouraged to get back into the Air Force. Really, I wanted to make my brother proud of me again! He somehow knew or thought that my life would have turned out better, if I would have stayed in the Air Force and in Oklahoma City, and not to had come home. How was I going to get back out of Akron? This was one answer that I did not have but had to figure it out. I was going to do what I could while I was at the Air Force base in Georgia. In fact, I would be at the headquarters for the entire Air Force Reserve. I was on a mission. I was talking with Adrian throughout that week about how this was not the life that I wanted for our family. And that we had to get out of Akron. She then told me that she wanted to go to that temporary duty with me, to the Georgia, TDY assignment. If I would have responded no, she would had gotten suspicious of me wanting to cheat with other girls, so I agreed!

I was officially on lock down while in Georgia with my wife; therefore, I had to be a good husband and on my best behavior. We had planned to get my mother to watch Ant, our baby. We, mainly me, called my mother, and she happily agreed to do it. I believed that she enjoyed taking Ant to church as well. Ant was young, but he had a lot of church in him. I could feel it. After my court case, my life was changing for the good! I do thank God for my wonderful, faithful, loving, and praying mother! She has helped me so many times before and even now! I was a grown man, and yet I still needed my mother's help. What a blessing my mother was to me! Now to work on the rest of my life and get it in order. I was not doing hardly anything worthwhile. I could gamble and keep the Air Force. These two things were the bottom line within my life. They both were in conflict with each other, and I had to make a choice and stick to it. Then again, it all made perfect sense. I really only had one choice. It was to figure out on how to get back in the Air Force. I was now one step closer with this TDY trip with the Air Force. I had a month to make something happen. We were able to get a plane ticket for Adrian, so she could go with me. We played poker that Friday and Saturday. Then we were off to the Akron-Canton Airport onto Atlanta, Georgia, then to pick up a rental car and drive one hundred miles to Macon, Georgia. Since I had my wife with me, I was able to stay on base in the family quarters. The billeting was always based on space A or space availability. Once we arrived to Warner Robins, Georgia, I believe I procured to Best Western on Warner Robins Street, which was the main street to the base I would be working at the headquarters building # 210. It was located just past the gate on the left-hand side. It was a very large building with several floors and a lot of parking located around the building on the sides, and most of the parking was in the back of the building. It was very easy to get there in less than ten minutes as long as the gate traffic was moving.

That next morning, I left Adrian at the hotel, and I was off to work bright and early. I started at 7:30 a.m. or 8:00 a.m. The time to report for duty had some flexibility. I was okay with that! They took me around to meet the folks and showed me where I would be working. I was able to get there because they were a little short-handed and needed my skill set. So we had computers. At that time we used Microsoft Systems 2.0. Of course, I had to do the mail, but this time, I was doing data entry. The work was a lot more interesting. It felt good to be working again and earning a check. If I was offered a job there, I would definitely had moved there. The work was pretty interesting and busy too. I was never bored. I even drove the military vans to different locations to get work done too. I was working again other than it was for short-time. I felt great again. After I was off work, I went back to the room to pick up Adrian, and we would go and hang out. We were all over the place. The main mall there was the Houston Mall located at North Houston and Warner Robins Street. It was very easy to locate! Actually, it was easy to get to everywhere there. It sort of reminded me of Oklahoma City with much more greenery and landscapes. Every day, after work, we would do something different. On the weekends, we would check out a movie or go to the NCO club on base. I fitted right into that environment, and then, I made my way over to the gym. I was glad to be in the groove of the military life. If I was in Akron, it would be so different. Now, after being here for a few short weeks, I was not only motivated, but I was determined. The folks that I worked with were just nice to work with. I guess I got a little bored, and at lunch time, I would call the hospital OB/GYN and do a lot of obscene phone calls to their office. I was doing stupid things again. Yes, I must had called it twenty times and thinking I would not get caught. I only deceived myself. At least, I was smart enough to disguise my voice. I kept calling, and the secretary or nurse would just hang up the phone. I thought that I would never get caught.

Well, by the third day, the Air Force Security police shows up. What in the world was going on? I did not put two and two together. They were interviewing everyone in my section that used the phone in the conference room. Sometimes, I even used a payphone at the base exchange (BX). Now, it was my turn to interview with the Air Force Office of Special Investigations (AFOSI) and the security police. During the interview, they told me that they had my voice on tape and had evidence against me. Well, I knew they were lying because I disguised my voice. I was a suspect, but so was everyone I had worked with. So I did the only thing that I could do. I lied and lied! I said that it was not me. I denied their accusations, so they let me go and told me that they would be back on Thursday with more proof. We departed the room, and they called the next guy. The only thing they knew is that it was a male voice from what I had gathered. So that evening when I had got off work, I went to the hotel and explained to Adrian what I had done. I was just in trouble less than a month earlier and now this. I think that I was some sort of thrill seeker. I did enjoy the rush that came with it. Adrian told me that if they would have had something, that I would have been arrested by now, and that the police did not only interview me. She told me not to fall for the tricks and to keep denying it and say that I did not do it. I met with the security police and the AFOSI and deny every bit of it, and they just let me go! I did know that they would be watching that conference room phone from here on out. I did it and made a few more calls at the BX and stopped. Just to throw the police off. I am glad that I listened to my wife. I really thought that they had me on tape.

The rest of my time there went pretty easy. I am convinced that everyone was vetted in that office as to who could be trusted or not. Now, we would never know! But I knew! I kept my nose clean from that point, even though that was truly close, and I could have just really messed up. I must admit that was stupid as well. Certainly, it would be a last time for me. As the time went on, Adrian and I spoke of it a few more times and then dropped it. It was like nothing had ever happened. Well, it was nice to be getting paychecks again and this time with per diem and a rental car. It was almost like a vacation! This was a fun trip and duty for the Air Force. I realized that I was in the right place at the right time. Somehow, I am supposed to be there. The year 1987 was a strange one for me, yet we are in Georgia. We had decided to ride up by Atlanta to see my cousin on the last weekend there before my TDY assignment was completed. I had to get in touch with her and get the address. We also made errands to the BX and commissary to get a few personal items and some food items. The base had everything that we needed. Plus, it had bowling and movie theater, which we made it to do. Other than my little incident, this was a very productive trip. The people and my temporary job were getting used to seeing me, and some of them did not want me to leave. I should've been here, instead of Oklahoma City. I would probably still been in the Air Force full time. I really liked it there. Plus, the people were quite friendly. It was during my last week there that I came across a teletyped message that would have gone to all the reserve units in the world. By me already at the headquarters for the reserve, I was able to see it first. Normally, I would skim over the messages very quickly for sending them up for distribution at the message center. I saw the words "Seeking Reserve Recruiters for Shortage" or something along those lines. It really caught my eye, and I started to read it and made me a copy for myself.

It was for four weeks of training at Lackland AFB, Texas. I was originally there in July 1980 for my Air Force military basis training. I had to meet the time in grade of staff sergeant that I had just made in March of 1986. I had to work on my weight a little, and I would be good. There were not an *if* in my mind. I had to make it. I took the paper, folded it up, and stuck it in my pocket. I have never recruited anything and let alone a person. This would place me back on active duty as a staff sergeant. What a deal, I must say! I was feeling the positiveness ever since I was not charged for embezzlement of the money from my brother's account. I was now to be working on a way out of Akron. A place that I really did not belong. I knew it, and I knew from the moment that I came back in January 1986 that this was really a bad move. Plus I got put out of my sister's house. I made my first priority, to lose some more weight. I was good, but I had to get better. I did not want my weight to be the decision as to why I could not get accepted. I looked at the following: Ohio State Trooper, CIA, plastic factory, etc. All of them did not work for me, in one way or another. There must be a reason. Not only did I want to learn how to be a recruiter, but I had to be extra good at it. I really did not have a choice, or I would have to keep settling for the life that I had. We had to also get out of the hot sauna-like attic, even though it also would help me to lose weight. I had one more day to work. I was also missing my sons, so we had to be leaving. Even with the mixed feelings because we both missed this type of life that we were currently living. It was nice, plus the medical and gym was free, for my family, as long as I was on active duty, even if it was on a temporary basis of thirty days or more. I was beginning to believe that it was meant for me, or will be. Wow!

I was off work and could not wait to tell Adrian what I had found out to get us out of Akron, Ohio. I then showed here the paper that I took out of my pocket and informed her that I was going to lose some more weight and apply for it. I was so, so serious! We had two more times to eat dinner there before leaving. We wanted to eat at some place for dinner the last two nights and kind of nice, and that was it. Adrian did hold her excitement in, but that was how she was. I had so wish her to be different and much normal, but that was all I got. I did not like to live with her, the way she was. I was on my best behavior the entire time being there. I did not burn any new bridges! I did see a few honeys, but I was harmless. I must say that Georgia has a whole lot of beautiful women. I mean a whole lot of beautiful women and the best peaches and the orange meat watermelon. The night went by like a breeze, especially with the packing, and the last day came and gone. I said my goodbyes. Then I got all of my paperwork signed. I was able to leave at noon, and I called it a day. Adrian and I hung out for a while and just enjoyed that last day. We had heard that song on the radio by Tina Turner, "What's Love Got to Do with It." That song was right on time, every last word. I could identify with that song! Better yet, my relationship could identify with that song! It was right on time!

On Saturday, we drove up to Decatur, Georgia, to see my cousin Dorothy, and we hung out with her, talked about the family, but Dorothy had to make an errand, and we had to drive her there and then back. While at the location, I had realized what she did and did not like it a bit. I made an exception because she was my cousin. After the fact, I found out that she went to buy a bag of weed. I was trying to move forward and not let her take me backward. I told her that I could not be around that kind of stuff because I could go to jail and lose my career with the Air Force. That was not going to happen on my watch. I had to be more careful who rides with me, especially if I was going to be the one driving. I was learning very fast that some folks, even relatives, do not want to do the right thing, and that includes disrespecting you at the same time. I only wanted to spend a little time with my family and a cousin that I have not seen in a while. I did not like that at all. I would know better for the next time. Another fact was I was in a strange place and did not know a thing. Well, I was protected with my gun that I used to wrap it up in foil and place it in my luggage on the airplane. It was the way to travel. I liked to always feel safe. I knew nothing about Atlanta, or Decatur, Georgia, where we were at. The thing is when we got back to her house, she had told Adrian and I that she was robbed for some cash that she had to deposit for her job. I was always interested in Atlanta, Georgia, anyway and wanted to get stationed when I was on active duty for the Air Force, at Dobbins AFB, not too far from Atlanta. Well, the time was moving on, and we did have to catch a flight back to Akron to go home.

Now, once we get back, I had to check on the recruiting stuff, which sounded like a great opportunity. As always, we were running a little late to the check-in gate after we dropped off the rental car. The flight was a little bumpy for the turbulence while leaving the Atlanta area, and after that, it got better, and the flight got smoother. Now that we were on the plane, it seemed like we had something to look forward to. Nope, that was only our imagination, and nothing had changed. Except our little boy, Michael II, would be turning two years old in two months and we wanted to plan something for him. I thought that he was a little too young for a party, and that he would not remember it. Normally, through our disagreements, we would argue, fuss, or fight, and we have not done that in a while. Plus, we did not argue at her parent's house. For one, they were old and would not be having it, and I respected them, just for being old. And her dad threatened to shoot me if I mistreated Adrian. Well, we had a last option that was not discussed and settled it the democratic way. We would play spades or poker (the most wins out of so many hands) for who would get what. For example, if Adrian wins, she would get the birthday party for Michael II. And if I would win, then she would have to do laundry, or we would play for other things that were obtainable. It was the playing cards that worked for us on several occasions, throughout our marriage. I was not a sore loser because there would be times when I would win and other times I would lose. Well, I lost the card games, and it was official that Michael II was having his first birthday in October as he would be turning age two. Now the next piece that I had to get my sister to agree to was to use her house to host the party. Adrian had to find the clown for the party. We had a little money with my Air Force TDY, because we just returned from being in Georgia.

Now, we are back in the groove, and the birthday party was settled that Saturday evening. Then Sunday, we would find a poker game to get into. I remember the following Friday, we were going to play poker on Berry Street. I was hanging out with my brother Robert. I did not see him much. He was always gone and driving those big 18-wheelers. Anyway, we were drinking some Bartle's and Jayme's wine coolers, normally in a four-pack, the lime or wild berry flavors. That night, we decided to mix it with another drink called Cisco wine cooler (aka liquid crack). I may have drink two and then another Bartle's and Jayme's. I was not a real drinker. I was driving and did not remember much, except driving to the poker house on Berry Street. Adrian and I went inside, and all I remember was the doorway. I did not remember going past the doorway. Adrian mentioned that Robert, my brother, left us and decided to go home. As my wife was telling me, I was remembering bits and pieces. I was stone-cold drunk! This was worse than being drunk with Mad Dog 2020 and Irish Rose put together. I became violent to anyone in my path! At the doorway, I just went off on a dude. I was drunk and all I know was I just kept cussing and cussing and then threaten to kill him. This guy must have been six feet and four inches and about 280 pounds, and his initials are JR. Then I remember going to my trunk to get my gun. I saw the guy and his friend leaving. I was just torn up with anger. I got to the trunk of my car and somehow opened it up and pulled out a pair of jumper cables. I remember him driving past me.

Somehow, right after that, I drove to the crap house to play some dice. I remember vaguely stopping the car each time, just past the stop sign. Mind you, I have never played dice in my life. Nor did my father teach it to me! I was just drunk! I do not remember arriving to the house or leaving it. I just remember playing, and the guys were playing it on the floor. So I put up $20 and lost it just like that, and then, I did it again and lost another $20. The only thing that I remember about playing craps is losing the $40, and that made me even more upset. I wanted to get my money back. Again, I was in the car, and somehow, I was on the passenger side when we arrived to the house. Adrian woke me up to get out the car, and I bashed up the dashboard with my fists. The only thing that I remember when I had awakened was that I lost my $40, and I wanted to get it back. I did not remember going into the house or upstairs or getting in the bed. But I was there! I was in the house and in the bed. The next morning, Adrian was telling me everything, and I could not even think. My head, I mentioned! My head was splitting painfully with a headache. It felt like I had ten headaches at the same time! All the things that I remember vaguely doing. Adrian did clarify everything with me. I took like three or four Tylenol pills for my head. She said that I cussed that guy out really bad and for no reason. Adrian stated that if he would have just blew on me, I would have fallen over. The good thing was that he did not know that I was drunk. Plus, I was only carrying my name reputation. Then I wanted to get the $40 back from the dice games, and that place was dangerous, so she got us out of there.

I really did not know the depth of the danger that we were in. I could have really messed up by trying to get my money back. Looking back, that would have been a big mistake. Then she told me that she was the reason that we got home and put me to bed. Then I remembered drinking that Cisco wine cooler, and on the street, it was called Liquid Crack. I found that out firsthand and how dangerous of a drink that was for me. That Friday night, on August 8, 1987, I could have died three times as I was looking back at the stupid incidents that I was involved in! Getting drunk was not something that I did as a normal, at least by choice! I did not have a death wish. It was just that fast life I was living. Indeed, my mother's prayers did and was keeping me from death. That was something that I knew or just a feeling that I could not explain, nor could that feeling be denied! I would think of her prayers often! In reality, that Cisco wine cooler really took my choice from me. Yes, I was guilty of drinking only two bottles of it, but I did not know the consequences of what I was doing. I, for the first time in my life, did not have control of my decisions. Then I told Adrian that I could have killed a man (with initials of JR), been locked up in jail, and I would not know why. Really, I could have killed an innocent man that did nothing to me for no reason! I did not like that feeling, nor that feeling becoming my end result.

From that moment on, I vowed to never get drunk again, nor would I ever drink another bottle of Cisco wine cooler. I did not know that 20 percent of alcohol volume that was in that Cisco would do that to me. I am one that could normally hold my liquor, but that Cisco drink, I did not know how to explain it. I did not like that at all! And that would never be me again. My brother Robert was smarter than I, he went home and slept it off. I was not that smart, and it would have been so simple to go home and slept it off. Now, I was even more determined to get out of Akron! In one night, I almost had thrown everything away and would not have remembered it. I almost lost it all and my future. For now, I had to do what I had to do and keep my hustle going. But getting back from Robins AFB, Georgia, I came across that Reserve Recruiting message, so at the same time, I would be working on an exit plan to leave Akron and to get out of Ohio. I had to get it together and real soon! Meanwhile, I was able to get Big Mike and take him to the gym, or he would try to run with me on the streets or on the tracks at a local school, either on the north side or the west side of town. The Akron Community Center was a favorite place of mine. I just had to keep losing that weight.

Once I would apply for that Reserve Recruiter position, I had to be in tiptop shape, or I would get disqualified, and my application would not even get submitted. I had a few things to do, see the family, see my sons, train and get in shape, run the numbers, play the lottery, and of course, play cards. For weeks, I kept this same routine, and my mind was getting focused better. I would take a drink every now and again. I was never the same after the Cisco wine cooler incident. I was not a drunk, but being and staying sober was a new priority for me. I have to be in control of my livelihood and not the alcohol. September was almost over. As I thought that everything was good, the family was good, and everything moving forward. Except for I was not paying the child support and getting much more behind than I wanted to. I did buy Big Mike some clothes and gifts, every now and then. I knew that it was still not enough. I kept hoping for the best regardless! I did my reserve duty for September 1987 and thought that I would submit my recruiting package on the following month, being October 3. This was my plan, and it was working! Anyway, it was all doing well. I had a plan. For the life of me, I was a man trying to do better and keep my family together. Well, I can only explain my side of things as we were driving on East Tallmadge Avenue, and yes, we started to argue with our son in the back seat, and we were still arguing pushing and pulling and not what I was expecting. As I was pulling her back into the car, she kicked the window out on the passenger side, and all the little pieces of glass went everywhere. Even as you will touch the glass in the window, glass would fall everywhere. What a mess. I was so upset. I was even mad. We were making so much progress, and my life was changing for the better. Without thinking and no thoughts were moving in my mind after Adrian did this. I just wanted to die. Yes, I wanted to die!

As I was driving off, she jumped into the car. As I was moving while driving the car, I was on my way to kill myself. This was the day I thought in my mind to die. So I made it pass the Kroger Grocery Store, onto North Main Street to Saint Thomas Hospital, just past Olive Street, and there was the Y-Bridge. I was going to jump off the bridge. As I was running toward the bridge, Adrian was running and crying after me to stop. She was crying, "Don't do it! I am sorry." In that moment, she shocked me and changed my mindset. I was just approaching the bridge and could see the houses down below. Somehow, her words stopped me in my tracks. I was going to actually jump, and my mind was made up to end my life. I stopped and walked back to the car that was not parked and in the middle of the street. I drove off, feeling empty. I needed for those moments to believe Adrian was telling the truth, and to this day and after the fact, my mind will not believe that she was for real. That song was on the radio, "Just Once." I needed that song, "Just Once" by James Ingram! This was like the second attempt on my life, for me to die, but to commit suicide!

Once I gathered my thoughts, then I was good again. I did not consider myself to be suicidal, but somehow, I had to keep crossing that bridge every time I approached that empty situation in my life. I know it would be easier to shoot myself, but never would it cross my mind. I wanted to do better for the family, and Adrian kept setting us back! I wanted to do more for the boys, and Adrian sometimes, she seemed to compete with Big Mike, my son! I did not know how to get Adrian to want more out of life. She only seemed to enjoy the hustle, playing cards, and the bad things that we did. She was so difficult to understand. She would not say that she loved me. But she would not leave me. Sometimes, I thought it possible for her to love and forgive me, regardless of what I have done! Adrian was just the opposite. It took a few days. Then we were back to normal. I had got the window fixed with the insurance claim, and we were back in business. No way, could we be roaming around in Akron with a broken car window. The insurance company had the window company come to the house and fix the car window. I paid the deductible, and that was it. Really, I did not like her working against me when I was trying to give her a better life for all three of us and then visit my other son on occasions.

One way or another, I was going to try to make our relationship work. I had not cheated with another woman. I just was working and hustling. I did not know at what point I would stop trying and just leave her! In my present status, she was it. For one thing, I did not have a place to live. So I kind of figured that I owed her. Even though, I knew that something was missing between us and in our marriage. One thing for sure, I never thought that I was foolish because we were married. I felt that if I looked bad, then she would too. And vice versa! I must admit I was not the best husband, but I was a good father and provider under the right circumstances. Also we kept gambling because we were pretty good at it, and we kept getting better. While I know that I may be leaving Akron, but just in case, I did not get approved for the Reserve Recruiter position with the Air Force. I decided to get a backup plan. So I saw this ad in our town newspaper, the *Akron Beacon Journal*. It was a few jobs there, and I did not want a driving job. It was some other jobs in the paper, but I was just not interested. This one job caught my attention, and I thought why not? I already was carrying a gun. It was at the Cleveland Police Department. They were looking for new recruits. I was definitely contemplating it. However, it was not the Ohio State Trooper, but it was a job and only a backup plan. So I called to get a copy of the application sent to me and to see what would happen just in case I may really need this job. Then I was back and forth of what if this or that. I could not totally convince myself if I truly wanted to be a policeman in Cleveland, Ohio. This would be my second potential police job, and it was a long way from becoming a doctor. Besides, Cleveland was a whole lot tougher than Akron, anyway!

Well, I turned my attention to the folded piece of paper that I brought back from Robins AFB, Georgia. I started to really read and dig into the message to better understand what was being required of me, if I had applied, and my application was accepted. All applications had to be approved by the commander and submitted not later than October 3, 1987. I had roughly less than three weeks to get everything done, approved, and submitted. I was excited and not really anyone to share it with. Adrian was not that kind of wife. I was a lonely married man and very faithful these last few years. I had not cheated. I was really trying to do right just in case Adrian would have a change of heart and truly become my wife. I watched very little television while in Akron. Nothing there felt like home! It was really good to be around my family, but my mother and my two sons is what I really enjoyed out of Akron. I was married to Adrian only for convenience. Adrian was not coming around as far as being a real wife. I did not count the benefits from each other. I wanted the relationship full of love and trust. My reality with Adrian was that I was only fooling myself. To think I was going to kill myself. I did not see it at the time, but now, to think suicide was the answer that was so foolish. I am glad that I was pulling my brain back together. I stayed on the track and changed my diet a bit. I had to do a photo shoot in my service dress uniform for the Air Force. I had to write an essay. I was in the military and have plenty of forms to fill out and get approved by my military supervisor and/or the commander. I was a little down anyway because I had gotten out of the Air Force in Oklahoma City and really did not know why. The reason that I thought to go to the University of Akron and become a doctor. I was not even close! I should have thought about it and got my head examined by a doctor to find out what was wrong with me. It was just a thought because I had never been seen by a head doctor (shrink) because I thought that I was crazy for getting married.

As I was getting it together in my mind, I had to get my Jheri Curl cut off my hair again to take my official uniform photos for my Reserve Recruiting package. I thank God that I was not crazy, just out of my element. I just wanted more to include a new wife. I just kept it in my mind and start to focus on what I truly believe. It was not a fantasy. The more I was trying to get my life in order, the less I wanted Adrian. I kept trying to be with her and kept wishing that she would change. She never did! The weeks went past. Adrian stay the same. I needed more! I was sort of going through something. The more I was seeing that there was an opportunity on the horizon for my life to get better, the more I stopped wanting us to be a family. I just wanted my son, actually, both sons at that to be with me. I messed up horribly! I had two ex-girlfriends, with two kids, and I did not love either one of them. I was a family man, and only wanted the boys. That was it! At that present time, it was not happening, so then I could only live with Ant (Michael II). That would be good for now because it was working. Well, playing poker and numbers were my main gigs, and they were getting old. I didn't want the thrill of gambling anymore! Doing it for a way of life was not truly pleasant! I was beginning to get tired of it. I just believe better was coming. I just had to get the recruiting job with the Air Force Reserve. I just had to make it! This was definitely a lifeline to my future. I was only in Akron, now going on two years and almost lost my life. Each time I was at the Pittsburgh IAP reserve unit, I was working on my package. I was making the most of all my time, and my part-time RPA man-days were also getting shortened, so, I was working less. I was working fewer days, but that was alright. I would gamble more, and I kept focusing since I got my package together, and I did submit it on time with hopes that all that hard and quick work would pay off. I did my write up. I took the pictures from the military photo shoot for my package during my September reserve duty and during my RPA man-days.

The thing is, the pictures were to be returned to me, just by the October reserve training weekend. It was a little close for comfort at times, but everything was going as planned. Once I was back home, Adrian and I begin to argue a little more. So I did more duty as usual. I was back at the Pittsburgh IAP reserve unit around the middle of month, and I got the mail after getting back to the unit. It was in the mail. My approval was in there. I was approved to attend the Air Force Reserve Recruiting School Training in San Antonio, Texas. My orders for the recruiting were also inside the envelope, and I was to leave on October 18, the Sunday after my son's birthday party and report to San Antonio, Texas, at the recruiting school that Monday. And no rental car was to be authorized. Everything was planned to perfection. I was just ecstatic! My heart was racing with joy. I could feel my heartbeats! Every one of them! When I returned home, we picked up where we left off. I just kept my focus. I know she proba-bly did not like the fact that I had to go to San Antonio, Texas, again for the Air Force Reserve Training since I had got selected. I have not been there, in Texas, since my ENT nose surgery in 1985, like two years ago. I kept reassuring her that there would be no time for me to fraternize with the ladies and that there would be no time for that. Really, I did not care if she believes me or not, I was going, and my plan was to do nothing less than to pass and succeed. I was on a mission to survive and stay alive. With her or without her!

After I made my point to her several times, she settled down. On the other hand, I was trusting her too by leaving her in Akron. We both had people there in Akron from our past. After I did not commit suicide on that dreadful day, I did not care if she cheated or not. I would have not care for her even more. Somehow, we cleared the air and started getting along again. I proposed she realized that I was telling the truth or possibly even leave her there. I did think about it, but I did not want to leave my son with her. The majority of the time we spent in Akron, we did not provide care for Ant that much. My mother did. My mother had him potty-trained and walk-ing in no time at all. We saw some of the baby steps but not many before he was actually walking. My mother did a great job. I was not worried about it anyway. She did raise ten of us and mostly without a father. Just awesome, she was and she knew all the tricks to raising children! It was awesome for my son Ant to experience some of his grandmother's childrearing gifts too!

As soon as I returned home from that reserve weekend on October 4, we were on the move planning the birthday party for Ant. We were so glad that my sister Terri agreed to let us use her house to do the party. Well, Ant had his first birthday party at age two. Plus Terri had a little boy too, Jonathan, and they both were as happy as the both of them could be. We did take some picture, and the weather was a little chilly but nice. The clown did a fantastic job, with the balloons, tricks, and games. The children just loved everything; it was about twelve of them. That day for his birthday party was also our sixth wedding anniversary that was on the Saturday, October 17, 1987. This worked out well because there was no way I was going to celebrate his birthday and wedding anniversary, with or for her. This birthday party was the perfect coverup, not to do anything with Adrian. Many times, I thought about ending her life and mine too. But I could not. I just thought it over and over. I would not bring myself to do it. This feeling was another fight that I held inside me. Other than that normal stuff married people do, we were to feel some intimacy, you know the touch and feeling. It was hardly any of that, and I did not mind at all since I would be leaving. Well, the party was a success.

A week after I returned from my reserve weekend, it was on October 10. We decided that it would be our last poker game that we rented the house for. We did not mention it to anyone just in case, and we would still be playing poker. I was trying to clean my life up. It was the last hand of the next day. We played poker all night. There was this light-skinned brother who wanted the house (that's me) to pay him for a hand that we did not know that he was in. We had never had any issues previously at our poker games. He wanted to bully and make threats, and we held our ground. He was upset, and so was I! We were at a standstill. We were cussing and all. I did not want to pay. By this time, it was daylight. So Adrian called my house, and my oldest two brothers came, Junior and Robert. I was the one brother that they did not want anything to happen to, nor did they want anyone to mess with me. So I compromised before my brothers arrived and just gave him his money back for that hand. I did not want anything to get in the way on how I was trying to change my life. I did not need a police record, so I just kept the peace. But one thing for sure: I was not going to be intimated. I had a possible chance with the Cleveland Police Department and an application that I decided to put in the trash because I was going to see what the possibilities were with the Air Force. I did just that! I was leaving and had to pack and get my uniforms together, then do some running around to get some items needed for the trip and a small briefcase. I would have to share rooms again in the dormitory, and that was okay. Just think, if I did not make staff sergeant, I would not had been qualified. I'm saying that it came right on time. I had to leave Adrian with the car, and she mentioned that she would still be going to play poker all by herself. I did not like that part (I was kind of overprotecting). I just let it go, but I knew that she was able to handle herself. We did play poker on the next day after the party and again that following weekend, just Friday and Saturday.

On that following day of October 25, I placed all my luggage in the car, and Adrian drove with me to the Akron-Canton airport. I was so glad that Sunday was here. We talked some, just last night, but the conversation was very short. We barely kissed and hugged goodbye, and it did not feel real at all! Now that I was on the plane, the questions in my mind was, "Could I trust her?" I did not know. My other question was, "Did I trust her?" Still, I did not know, nor did I care, really. I was not sure where I was on this topic, so I just avoided it in totality. I really just tried not to think about it. I was in the next class to start on October 26, which was my son's original birthday, exactly one week earlier, which was October 19. I did not miss it is why we celebrated, the actual date earlier. This was actually new to me in becoming an Air Force Reserve Recruiter. All I knew was I could not fail or go back home. I had to be focused. I did not try to chase, entertain, or pursue any of the ladies. I did not care to do anything less than succeed. I had to graduate! I was genuinely focused, even though the weather was cold. I did prefer a warm body next to mine! I thought that in San Antonio, the weather would be hot or warm, but not in October through November, for the time I was there, all I have was a light-blue Air Force jacket for my uniform, with the chevrons. And my coat that could not be worn with my uniform. So I stayed cold, and each time, I could not wait to get inside any building for warmth! I decided that all my energy was to go into passing this course! Plus, I still had it within me to pursue my life's dream on becoming a doctor. I could not let this go at all!

Anyway, we arrived at the San Antonio airport and had to go to the USO office, and there were signs Air Force people were holding up and pointed us in the direction of the bus with our luggage to load onto the bus. This reminded me of that date July 1, 1980, as I left Akron to join the Air Force to the same place. How ironic! Well, this time was different, and I had a little rank! Actually, that was the big difference for being at a military training base. Well, we got settled in, and I put my stuff up as I was getting to know my roommate. I did keep it vague because I wanted to stay focused, and I was not about going out or hanging out. I was not going to do anything other than studying. The night had come and gone. We got up, got dressed, and walked over to get something to eat. Since we were getting per diem, we had to buy our own food. Believe you me, I was not eating that much. Some mornings, we were scheduled to get up and go to physical training (PT), and that was good too. I actually looked forward to those days. I was beginning to miss my boys and my mother and a little for Adrian. It was not enough to change my focus. I did stay in the books and studied profusely. I was not going to fail. I wanted to know all the basis and recruiting techniques, inside and out. I wanted to master the art of persuasion and get those continuous agreements, with the head nodding yes. I was learning all the materials. They were doing a lot of classroom teaching. It was mostly male instructors, but one of the female instructors told the entire recruiting class that if we were to get this same training outside of the military, it would cost us about $25,000. I could not believe it. I was getting some serious knowledge. She also told us if you were to compare us to all the other military recruiting services—Army, Navy, and the Marine Corps—the Air Force office would mainly have one recruiter, for the most part, and surely, not more than two. It would definitely be a rarity. I was totally pleased that I was getting some valuable training. I was actually beginning to like this training. I was also making a little more money to go with the welfare check that I was getting. I would call my mother and check on her, and then, I would call Adrian to see what was up too and to ensure that she was not messing up the money. I was glad to hear that she was doing okay, and sometimes she would break even playing poker. I was okay with that.

A week later at the recruiting school, that Monday, we did impromptu. Boy was I just everything but good. Actually, I was just the opposite! I was really terrible! On the second day or the next day in the following week, we had another impromptu, and I had gotten worst. I was stuttering badly! I did stutter from time to time, especially when I got nervous. I was nervous! That day, we had two instructors for that class. The unthinkable happened to me! I just could not believe it. I was sweating from under my arms. I could feel the sweat rolling down my side. The lady instructor, I believe she was a master sergeant, was very stern and serious. While I was talking, I did not see her as she was behind me. Then I heard a loud noise while I was trying to talk. I then turned around and saw two large books on the table in front of her and her hand was on top of them. My arms sweated even more. She actually scared the sweat out of me. I thought that I was going to fail. For real, I thought that I was going to fail! Believe you me, it was everything but that. Again, it was just the opposite! From that moment forward, I would never forget it. At that moment, when I heard the slamming sound from those books, it was truly a blessing in disguise. This is the truth from the bottom of my heart. I never stuttered again. I was healed! The stuttering had left me, and so did the sweating from my armpits! That was truly a miracle, and the best thing that could have happened to my public speaking. I was ready to speak in public and in the classrooms at a moment's notice. I was truly healed! While what I thought was over for me in that I did not speak well, it was only a beginning and a new one at that! I was talking very good and started performing the classroom exercises very well. I did gain some more confidence in myself while attending this class. In less than two months ago, I could have been dead over stupid stuff. I was glad as I was thinking of it that I did not end my life.

The classes would go on as normal. I was passing all my classes. I would be studying every night. Still, I was not planning to fail. My failing was not an option for this recruiting course. I was born to succeed! It was a very important reason that I was there. I was beginning to believe that nothing happens by accident. And speaking of accidents, I almost died in one that I had no control over, but I am still living to talk about it. One day, as we are nearing the end of the recruiting school, I was looking around the classroom and noticed the makeup of our recruiting class. The class demographics were made up of on thirteen people, a small class size at that. We had one black female and myself. Everyone else were white for a total of three women and ten males. Together we were not even 50 percent of the others, and actually, together, we made up just over 15 percent of the group. I was the only black male and if there was a quota, I made it. It was in class that I started to notice that the higher I went in life, the fewer the blacks and especially black men that were there with me. Even in basic training and now, I was there at that same place that I performed my basic training, and my class consisted of forty-six men—five were black, one was Latino, and one Asian. We together made up of just over 15 percent of my squadron back in 1980. I just knew because the way the deck was stacked up against me, I just had to be that much better and work that much harder than other folks.

Sometimes, I have never blamed the color of my skin for what I did not have. I always knew I had to be better, and I would always have to do more. My faith had to get stronger in my abilities to succeed in life. One thing that I did know for sure was, it was a white lady master sergeant in the Air Force that enabled me to talk better. This same lady helped me to get my confidence back, and I was learning. I had the skills but did not know how to use them. I was better, and a white lady had helped me in my speech! For that and other things, I had always refused to hate white people. I do believe that in this world that we lived in, we need everybody. I mean everybody to work together! My mother always told me that I could talk the ginger out of the gingerbread. Now, I am able to understand what she was telling me all along!

This class was nothing more than a sales class, and our product was the Air Force Reserve. I was learning and did learn the art of persuasion. The government spent $25,000 on me to learn a major part of it, which was the art of persuasion, and I learned every bit of it. Of course, this is my interpretation of what I was learning. The military only called it recruiting school. By the way, the one name that I did remember was the black woman, and it was Monica Walker. She was tall and pleasant to my eyes. I must admit that my eyes did wander a few times and even at Monica and even the other two white military women. At best, I could only place these thoughts in the normal attraction category of life. I was strictly harmless. This entire trip I still decided to remain faithful and be a good husband, not that it mattered that much. My family may have been broken with the wife that I had selected, but family was very important to me, and I wanted for myself to maintain the structure of it. Even when we go our separate ways, I had to keep the value of family locked away in my mind. It was not an easy way to explain it, but I was doing what I needed to be done. Besides, I had too much studying to do. Success was always in the forefront of my mind.

There's no way I'm going to mess up this opportunity for me to change my life, which would entirely get me out of Akron, Ohio, and my life back on the track. I was looking forward to not living with anyone. There was one more week of class and the final written tests and presentation that I had to work on constantly. I had plenty of times of performing my presentations of looking at myself in the mirror as I gave my presentation to the audience of one myself! The beginning of this recruiting was tough, even for me. I was normally pretty good at classroom work, and especially, involving studying, I normally held my own. I did keep my focus to get through this recruiting course! The last day of the class was upon me. After all of the studying and practicing that I had done, I was ready as could be. Then I gave my final presentation after the written test in front of the entire class. My nerves came at first, and then they were gone as soon as I started to talk. I gave the introduction, I talked about each example from the introduction and then, I summarized it to bring it home. At the end of the class, I was notified that I had passed and did a great job. I was officially an Air Force Recruiter as I received my certificate that read, "L3AZR99500-002, Air Force Reserve Recruiter Course, PDS Code RHZ, 152 Hours, 3290th Technical Training Grout (ATC), Lackland AFB, Texas, Dated on November 20, 1987. Signed by Colonel Frank Capone, Commander. I now had a new AFSC (Air Force Specialty Code) of 99500. I passed!

Now I was able to leave Akron, Ohio. I will also have to say, "Thank you, Jesus!" This was a meant to be moment for me! I said earlier that "I was beginning to feel that my life was changing for the good!" My life was changing indeed! I went to get me something to eat and call home, spreading the good news. Adrian was not as enthusiastic as I had hoped, but it was better than nothing. I guessed! Anyway, my mother was happy and excited! I became happier that my mother was happy. I did not want to disappoint her and keep disappointing her. I was going to be back out of Akron. I went to pack up my things, so they would take me to the airport on the Air Force bus. So I could take the flight back to Akron. Yes, indeed, home again. I had some money, and we did go to gamble playing poker that Saturday night! That was my celebration or not! But I was gambling and winning! It was a good thing that I never expected anything much from Adrian. I knew or thought that in the back of her mind, she knew that I would leave her. She was correct, but I would do it anyway when the time was right. Anyway, I still had to do my reserve duties at Greater Pittsburg IAP until my assignment orders would arrive to place me back on active duty for the Air Force Reserve and obtain my PCS orders. I had to also do another swearing in for the active-duty assignment once the orders would arrive. I was no longer down and out anymore. Truth is, Akron was not good for me, my pockets or my mindset! Actually, it was truly unhealthy for me! It was sure nice to have a little money now, even after I was sending some Adrian's way too for what she and Ant needed. As I was thinking about things that needed to be done in Akron, prior to leaving, and wanted this place to be in my rearview mirror, I thought that as soon as I had my orders, I had to be sure that I had gotten off the welfare system, for me and my family.

As usual, I was sure to give my mother money for watching my son. I was so glad that I was not a selfish guy, and I normally like to help people and people in need. With a majority of faults that I had possessed, I did have a big heart in giving, just like my mother. She was the only person that I could have gotten it from. Ant was just two years old, and we were touching our thoughts of getting him something small for Christmas since I did not know when we would be leaving. Playing cards was a sort of therapy for us to keep our mind off everything else, and for me, that child support that I still had to pay had become behind in my payments. The IRS would snatch up my tax returns still, and then, I would file the injured spouse form, year after year, so we could get my wife's tax portion returned to her. The tax season was just around the corner, fast approaching, and was gearing up for it, keeping up with all my receipts for filing. With as much as we played poker and the numbers, and the state lottery, I was not able to gamble at the racetrack in Cleveland. I had to give that up once I was caught with my brother's money. I do remember that I almost went to jail, but I had a praying mother. We barely had time for anything else. We also made time for the things that we needed to get done, or it was important to us. However, we did have my son when we were not gambling. When my mother kept him, Ant was there in church. By this time, Adrian and I started to call our son Anthony. This child had a multitude of nicknames. I was so glad that Ant was not affected much by the situation that we were in because he was only two years old. We did have some making up to do for him once we were situated at the new place. I only stayed because I did not want to leave my son.

This year's pace was completed fast. The card games were going faster and faster with the back and forth at the reserve unit in Pittsburgh going just as fast. That weekend, unexpectedly, I received a lot of kudos for successfully completed the Air Force Recruiting school. I did appreciate that recognition because it came from people that were truly genuine. My military supervisor, SMSgt. Robert Simonette, I would miss him the most! He wasn't a country boy but a genuinely good guy, a good human being. But I must continue to do my duties until my orders came. I was excited for leaving and not know where the family and I would be ending up. I am leaving my reserve duty again since the weekend was over. Then Adrian and I would go Christmas shopping for the two boys and something for my mother. That part would be easy because that would normally be money for Christmas and her birthday. We normally did not do anything for each other. That was cool too! In no time, I was back in Akron and shopping as planned. I believe that we did manage to get tickets to bring in the New Year's with The O'Jays, Stephanie Mills, Anita Baker, and of course, Luther Vandross. He would normally give roses out at the concert to the ladies. I did try often to sing Luther's songs, but it was a mild, mild comparison. I did try, but to no avail! It was an awesome concert and a definite best! The concert was good, and we, Adrian and I, had an awesome time. That was a good New Year's celebration and a time to remember! That was awesome the entire New Year's weekend. We had the concert Thursday to Friday and played poker on Saturday and Sunday.

Then on Monday, I celebrated my twenty-sixth birthday. This was a great time of the year for me, from passing the recruiting school and to that fabulous weekend. I finally had something positive about me that I was satisfied for. Within the things that were in my control, it was going to plan. Other than playing the lottery, a few street numbers, and playing poker, I was keeping a low profile and was not planning to mess up anything and except for a beer here and there. I stayed peaceful, even with Adrian. Plus, it was the winter, and the snow was in plain sight. It was the driving in the snow that I did enjoy doing in Akron. There was no place like it in the world! I was so used to the snow, cold, and ice. I had gotten used to it. The streets were pretty clear, and the plow trucks did a wonderful job cleaning up the snow and salted the roads and highways. It was good, bad, and different as I was on the road to Pittsburgh IAP to perform my Air Force Reserve Duty or training. I did not like to miss an Air Force Reserve weekend as it was my own personal getaway! The Pennsylvania highways and mountains were not as clean as the Ohio roads. I really had to be careful, but I did manage to stay safe the entire winter, and sometimes, I was fearful enough to believe for God to keep me. And God did just that! I do know that if he did not hear my prayers, then I just believe that he had heard my mother's prayers. Again, the driving in Pittsburgh, was never a joke, you had to either respect the curves on the mountains, the construction on the bridges, or the deer on the side of the highway; being sleeping was never an option. I had to stay alert even if I had to roll down the window in the winter. I was going back and forth to Pittsburgh IAP, and Akron, Ohio, I was so glad to be safe to this day. Well, as things were getting in order, even if I had nothing to do with it, the chips were falling in place. And much to my disbelief, I did not know when or how I would be provided a second chance at life and even with the Air Force. The thing was that the gangster life that I was living was going away. Just think if I would have been so pressed for money that I had decided to sell drugs each time I was approached. I would not be leaving Akron at least on my two feet.

I was fortunately blessed. I do appreciate the fact that I knew that I could be more in life than to sell drugs to take my own people out. I believe that the drugs were a mechanism to keep impoverished people, blacks and minorities, down. I love all people regardless of race, but I also recognized that society as a whole will always be unfair. I have even dated other races and cultures, hoping for a good relationship. I was never raised up by my mother to hate nor to hate people. I was raised up to respect all people. I myself believe that the value of love exists in all people, regardless of where they are from. I was taught to love people and hate their actions. As I was understanding life as I got older, I held true to that. I had to love everybody, even the people that mistreated me. I was not quite there, but I was headed in the right direction in life! Well, it was February, and yes, it was still cold, and we kept getting snow that was sticking to the ground. I made it once again to Pittsburgh IAP, to do my reserve unit and that would be my last duty there. I had finally received my orders to PCS to Hartford, Connecticut, one of the New England States. I had no idea as to where I would be headed. Like Oklahoma City, I knew nothing of the modern times in Connecticut, except that it was one of the sixteen colonies, and the Boston Tea Party in Massachusetts, and the NBA Hall of Fame, in Springfield, Massachusetts. But my biggest question was not, what was there, and who was there? I wanted to know if there were black people living there? I guess I would find out soon enough when I get there. I will have to go to the Traffic Management Office (TMO) to arrange my furniture and family moving requirements. I could not wait to the end of day on Sunday to get back home. We had less than three weeks left to live in Akron and then less than two weeks to move into the military housing once we checked into the base at Westover Air Reserve Base (WARB) located in Chicopee, Massachusetts. The Reserve Recruiting Headquarters was there for that region.

Once I had arrived, I had to report in to the senior recruiter, CMSgt. Ron Koper, SMSgt. Jim Lisanby, and the base commander, Brigadier General Frederick D. Walker (aka General Mike Walker). It was located about thirty miles from Hartford, Connecticut. I knew that I would be living in Manchester, Connecticut, which was about eight miles from Hartford, Connecticut. Plus, I would be driving my own government vehicle to do my recruiting duties. I was really looking forward to getting there. I just could not wait! So I rushed home to Akron after my last reserve weekend. We were running around to get everything in order. Once I had got back, I picked up my wife and son. And we went once again to my mother's house to tell her the good news. She was really happy for me. I believe that it saddens her that we would be taking her Pooky and my Ant from her, and she would miss him dearly. Still my Ant was a daddy's boy! My other son Big Mike was definitely a momma's boy. I did not hold it against him. I could not because I loved and wanted them both! Now, I would be leaving him once again. I was also thinking about getting that child support back on track. Things would definitely be different and better, and I would be making more money, in the not so distant future, and I was looking to get another promotion in about a year! Wow! I am not there in Connecticut, but I am on my way. We were playing cards, running around, and saying our goodbyes. I know that my mother was glad for me, but you could just feel it in your heart that no one really wanted to see me leave. I do wish that they could feel what I was feeling. I just had to get out of Akron. I know if I would have continued in that place, in that destructive lifestyle, somebody would have ended up dead, and just maybe me! Just like our last poker game that we hosted, and I was on the money bag as the house. Things could have gone terribly wrong, but that time, it did not!

That type of lifestyle that my father introduced me to was not for me. My dad was a bad boy anyway, having served in the Vietnam and Korean wars. My mother had told us of the story when my dad had gotten shot in the stomach with a .22 caliber gun, and then, he took the gun from the man that shot him and then shot him back. Plus, he used to go boxing and was pretty good, so I heard. However, for Adrian and me to be gambling, it was a means to an end! One way or another! I was able to hold my own. My dad at the time was only fifty-six years old, and for one reason or another, I just believe that he had my back too! My dad knew women, cars, electronics, and could fix pretty much anything. Also he could fight, drink, and could hold his own. I was definitely a not a true drinker. I did not particularly like the violent part of drinking and not remembering. That one time taught me a valuable lesson for a lifetime. Now, I have a chance to move on and get it right. I just wanted my family to know that I was truly suffocating in Akron, and I just wanted more. I truly wanted more, and I was in search of it. Plus, if I would have stayed, I would have disappointed everyone. After getting out of the Air Force the first time, and then returning, I feel that I let my family down and me too! I had never told anyone how I truly felt until now. Actually, I did not know how to say it, but I wanted to show it! I had to leave again, and this time for good, except to visit everyone. I could show everyone on occasion and especially my family that I could do better. And they could too! Just think, without that promotion to staff sergeant, I would not have qualified for that recruiting position. Now we are down to the wire and getting out of that cold attic. We had received our last welfare check on the first of March, healthcare card, food stamps, and check. This was the last one.

A few days prior, around the last of February, we told the welfare that we moving away on the fifth of March. They informed us that the March check would be the last one. We picked up the truck that Friday. We got with my younger brother David to help us to pack up the truck from our storage unit off of Arlington Road. So Ant stayed with Adrian's mom (auntie), and she was able to watch him since we were leaving. Then Adrian, David my brother, and myself drove the truck to the storage place. We got to the unit, and mind you, it is a little cold, but all right as for the temperature. As we were moving our furniture around, we saw this big rat running across our furniture. I was like, "What in the world is going on?" But I saw it too. So we had to figure out how to box it in, and finally, we did that so it would not get away. My brother David was a big tough guy, and he decided to step on its tail and then step on it, and that is just what he did. There were rats' droppings everywhere. I mean everywhere. Thank God that it was only one rat and not a colony of them. I said, "There goes Ben," and like in the Michael Jackson song in the movie. Yeah, I was sort of a jokester at times! This was one of my jokes! It was funny, but not that funny! And we did laugh, after it was dead! But I was not sad at all! I just could not believe this was pretty much, new furniture that we had to get clean, I was so glad that the mattresses were in protected boxes. Well, our clothes, dishes, towels, and mostly everything were in boxes, except for the new living room furniture. We still had to clean everything with Lysol and Pine Sol just to get rid of the smell, once we got to Connecticut. I was glad that my brother was there. I would have found something to kill that thing with and made a bigger mess. While we were packing the truck, we saw a box with food in it and found out that rat was eating our saltine crackers, no wonder the rat was camped out in our storage unit. I wondered how that thing had got into our storage unit, and the bottom of the unit was sealed tightly. Just as I looked upward, there was an opening between the top panel and the roof. Which means, that storage place had rats anyway. And we had to pay for the unit anyway. So unfair! I was so disappointed, but I'm glad that rat did not have a colony of other mice. If that were the case. Then I would have just left everything there.

We just kept on packing while it was daytime. It got colder at night. We definitely had our work cut out for us even once we had moved to Connecticut. I guess good and bad can happen at the same time, as it did in my case. We packed up everything, and we were a little tired, so we drove the truck with the car dolly on the back. We got something to eat, took David home, and then took the U-Haul back to Adrian's parents' house. We took some of our stuff from the house and placed it on the back of the truck, so there would not be much to do for when we would be leaving. On the next day, we then parked the truck in the field with the big extra master lock that I was holding onto. Everything was safe and sound. We went into the house and sat around and talked a little while. As in the past, we would talk about Ant and laugh at some of the stuff that he would do and his trying to talk was so cute. He was a character at times and enjoyable! After a few hours passed by, we gave each other the signal, for it was time to go. Of course, it would be our last day to play poker. This time, we could not play all night. We did not see her dad (Uncle Hosea) much. He was at the Laundromat most times and stayed there until closing, around 10:00 p.m. and normally walked home, if he did not get a ride. He preferred to walk most times anyway. About the time he would arrive home, we would have been gone and the baby would be back with my mother for the last night. Besides, I wanted her to spend more time with him. Now on the way to play poker, we stopped by my dad's house to say goodbye. Then, that would be it. I did have some advance travel pay with me to get to Connecticut that I received from the Air Force in Pittsburgh IAP as part of my out processing per my orders. We were not going to mess up any money because we had a limit, just in case we did not win.

The one thing that we both could do well after all the practicing we did while learning the game did pay off. We both won and left around 1:00 a.m. with the winnings. We both were excited. We went to pick up our son. I gave my mother extra money, and we called it a night. That next morning, we awaken to get up, but while lying there, Adrian was telling me that she had dreamed that she had a little girl, and I was awaiting to hear what was next, knowing how badly I wanted to have a little girl. She shocked me again. We were about to leave for Connecticut. After what she said, I should have just left her in Akron and in her mother and father's attic to live. She said she was holding her baby girl, and she was not mine! Again, I was not the father! I had heard her loud and clear, no doubt, every word! Nope, I did not like hearing that nor did I want to believe it! For some reason, I just could not deny it! There was no denying her dreams until they failed to come to pass. I did not get upset but wanted to. How could I arrive to anything less than content from what she had mentioned earlier as we left Oklahoma City. Again Adrian mentioned her second major dream involving me. Adrian said that I found the love of my life. She saw me with this light-skinned, long-hair, tall, skinny woman, and driving a candy-apple red car. Anyway, I had gotten some good rest to cover the drive of 550 miles to Hartford, Connecticut, and the eight hours plus it would take to get there. This drive would be a whole lot easier than the drive to Oklahoma City. Much better all the way around, except there were some tolls, especially through Pennsylvania and New York! Yes, we did talk about her dreams to get some type of understanding, even though it never made really good sense since we kept getting back together. Wow! I only had to drive from Akron on I-76 East, through the length of Pennsylvania, to New York to I-80 East to I-84 East to Hartford, and then onto I-384 to Manchester. Once we arrived, we spent one night into a hotel, probably a Holiday Inn, that was our normal, most of the time and to receive hotel points. It worked! We got up the next day and got some McDonald's and drove up on I-91 North to the Westover AFB, Massachusetts. I took my family and went to meet everyone SMSgt. Lisanby, CMSgt. Koper, and General Mike Walker. They seemed pleased to have me to work there. It really was not bad for a blind assignment because I did not know where I would end up after the recruiting school. Now, I do know that I had done very well in recruiting school to be able to open my own office in Hartford for the first time! I must have passed some type of private test too. Once I would in process to the base, then I would have the rest of the week off to get settled and moved in. I went over to the housing building to sign up for military housing. I gave the lady a copy of my orders and filled out the paperwork to get the military housing. My new address was 27 Nike Circle, Manchester, Connecticut 06040. We had our own single-family home, a little rambler-style home, with three bedrooms and one bathroom, kitchen, dining room, and living room. The lady gave me the keys to the house—excited, yes! I was just ecstatic again, happy and overwhelmed! Finally, privacy and no sharing! We could not wait to get back to see it.

But first, we had to take the truck to the truck station to get weighed for my DIY move that we did for the military PCS move to Connecticut. The weight of the truck with my household goods would determine the amount that we would get back for the move, then onto our new home to unpack. We had a house, our own! This was a forthcoming brighter day. No more laundromats. We had our own unit in the house. All the recruiters for all of the services lived here, and there were government vehicles everywhere. It was quite shady with a lot of trees there. This place was sort of hidden. Our house was on a lot all by itself, on the right side and a dead end. I soon met one of our neighbors. He was an Army recruiter that lived across the street with his family. There were about another fifteen to twenty other military housing on the opposite end of Nike Circle. The Nike Site was left there by the Army in the early 1960s and operational from 1956 to 1961. They handled radar and missile silos. I did not care. This was home, and I had planned and vowed to myself that I was never going to live in Akron again! I was back in the military. I did not have any help this time to unpack the truck, but I managed. I had my own dolly, and it was really working for us. Most of the boxes were labeled from the movers, so we knew pretty much where everything went. It did not get as bad as I thought. Plus I was a pretty solid dude anyway and was not afraid of a little thing. Adrian only really helped me with the sofa and the love seat. We quickly went to the store after everything was moved in. Manchester, Connecticut, was established in 1672 but rather more modern. You can tell that it was more money there! The highway, I-384, was looking pretty new itself. This place was way better than Akron. It seemed to be very progressive to me. It was very difficult to get around, and the roads were far different than in Akron, which meant better! Later that day, I used the truck to go to Kmart and picked up an outside shed and lawnmower and some gardening tools to maintain the outside since we were required to take care of our own lawns, but there was no outside storage, so I had to cover that.

Then it was time to take the truck back to the U-Haul dealer, so I got all my paperwork together to turn in on that Monday as I start my official duty as a recruiter for the PCS move and to receive the last check. We were rushing to put the house together to make it a home. There were blinds and shades already on the windows, which were a good thing. The windows were covered. I started to set up the baby's crib first thing, then our bed, in the bedroom. As I was doing those things, Adrian was washing down the kitchen and refrigerator and then the bathroom. It was smelling pretty good in there and clean versus old. We got used to no carpet and had to get a few rugs and bedroom slippers. As long as we had heat, the floor was fine too! In this place was the first time that we experienced not to have gas or electric heat. It was oil heating, and the tank was located outside on the left side of the house. The costs were included from my base quarters allowance (BAQ), but we had the number to call it in once the oil/fuel was low. After the beds were up, I started to hang up the clothes and pull my uniforms out and get them ready. Adrian would wash, starch, and iron all of my Air Force shirts for me. Then I would add my name tag, ribbons, and the jacket, or coat chevrons, and I set them aside for the new job that would start on Monday. Sometimes, she could be the best wife, with no problems to think about, without the jealousy stuff, and then, with the jealousy stuff, just the worse. She was like two different people. She always said something like I was the one that made her jealous. I was not sure about that one because she wanted to know the details of everything I did...from their names and all the details. Then she would hold it against me. That was not fair to me. For now, we settled for that bit of good and excitement of moving, that was happening for us. I was not going to make her jealous, and she would not get on my nerves with her insecurities of jealousy. I was glad once again that it was working good between us. We now had a new life to get used to and new neighbors once again. We had a black army staff sergeant that lived across, and it was a kind of on a cul-de-sac, and the cross street separated my house from everyone else's. It was a very wooded and secluded area. I had no garage but a driveway. It will work, no doubt! After where I came from, it was definitely going to work! I can say this much, we were not in the hood, and surprisingly, we did not see a lot of black folks. Manchester was in the suburbs in comparison to Hartford, Connecticut. We did some driving around to get familiar with the area to see what the area was all about, including Hartford, and to see my new duty location and area at 233 Pearl St., third office on the left as you enter the building. We stopped by for a brief moment to see the office building.

That Friday coming, we were able to get the cable and telephone hooked up. We laid down a few rugs and pictures and the third bedroom. I made it a little office for me and a studying space. The next day being Saturday, we went to Sears for a Magnavox floor model television. Now, our little home was shaping up. We were like living in a different world. On Sunday, we would run more errands to get a few more things and stack up on some of the baby items, clothes, and snacks. And of course toys! Our baby was happy. We would often be playing around in the living room or our bedroom. He was getting bigger, and soon we would not be able to shower together. Ant and I would share the same food, drinks, and desserts. He was my little man and did everything I did. If I was fixing something or putting something together, even if it was for him, he would run in his room and get his little plastic tools that we had brought for him and pull them out to help me. He did this most of the time, and sometimes, I would tell him to go get his tools. It was so cute! Each time, Ant really brought joy to me. He went everywhere I had gone; he was right with me. I carried him a lot of times on my shoulders. Then he got used to it, but as he was growing, that boy was getting heavier. Most of the time he won!

By now, it was time to double-check everything for my first day on the job as a recruiter, even though it was training for the first few days. I was still able to play some basketball at Westover because they had an open gym that was also active. I took my gym stuff too just in case. The next morning, I left home and took I-384 West to I-91 North and followed the signs to Westover AFB. I would pass each time the Bradley Airport, and just as I crossed into Massachusetts, on my left side, I would see the Basketball Hall of Fame. I made a mental note that I would visit that place before leaving. It was on! Okay, I have arrived to Westover and pulled out my ID card to show the military police, and then, I would be allowed to go onto the base. Once on the base, I found parking and made my way to the recruiting building. These two days was not much for training as I supposed. It was more of me dealing with SMSgt. Jim Lisanby, assistant senior recruiter. He was giving me the tools of the trade, my recruiting badge that I had to wear daily, keys to the office and the commercial office building. Then he gave me the keys to 1987 White Chevrolet Citation, four-door and hatchback, with government license plates, and the monthly garage parking pass card that they would pay for, including a government credit card for the vehicle. There was no styling and profiling. Strictly serving the business of recruiting!

We had to have special circumstances to drive the vehicle home. Therefore, I knew already that I would be driving the vehicle home as often as possible. I receive the safety briefings, and being in this type of business, when I was stationed at Tinker AFB, I was the monitor for sexual harassment, but to my amazement, there was not a single item of a class on sexual harassment. Not even a brochure. I went home for the day. The next day, Adrian drove me up to get the rest of my recruiting supplies, so she dropped me off. I picked up the remaining posters and brochures. I still remember the Air Force Recruiting phone number. It was (800) 257-1212. I also got a new Air Force Reserve Training Cassette Video that video was really good, and the rest, I assume would be easy. I could talk and now could talk better since my recruiter training. I had finished loading the government vehicle, and then, I was on my way to unload the car at my new office. I just took my time driving to Hartford, Connecticut, to Pearl Street. I was excited and ready to go. What a change transformation that happened to me. I quickly found out that Hartford's newspaper was the Hartford Courant, which was the major state paper and was home to the largest insurance capital of the world. In comparison to Akron, there were jobs there. I did introduce myself to the other Air Force recruiter. It was two desks in the front and one desk in the back, and the door was closed. I then brought in the rest of the supply items and materials and then parked the car around the corner, within the same block, in the parking garage. I locked it and onto my office. I opened the back door to see how nice my office was. Boy, was I surprised! SSgt. Bill Vincent was a nerdy white dude, but he was pretty cool and helped me out. I did most of the work. He kept what he wanted, and we put the rest of that old stuff in the dumpster in the back of the building. My to-be office was sort of a storage room with a desk and phone. Well, I did have my own phone. Bill had an answering machine, so I had to get one too from my senior recruiter the next time that I had to go to Westover AFB. Well, at least I had the back office. It looked like I was in charge with the perception. And in reality, I was only in charge of myself. At least I did have the privacy to lock my door at the end of the day.

Bill was telling me that it was the first time that there was another recruiter in that office in Hartford. Bill had told me that there was a Civil Air Patrol person that volunteered one or two days per week to assist with the mailings and answered the phone. SSgt. Vincent called him by his last name, Armstrong, and he was very talkative, when he did show up, just so I would know. We figured out that I was the very first Air Force Reserve Recruiter in that office ever. Bill was telling me about the demographics of the area and some schools needed more work than the other schools, with the lowest ASVAB testing at school and harder to get into the military, especially the ones closest to Hartford. My plan was to hit all the schools. He was showing me around bringing me up to speed on how the things work around there. As I was being introduced to all the other recruiters for the other services, I noticed that the Air Force had the least of all recruiters per office. I had also noticed that some of those recruiters were my neighbors on Nike circle in Manchester. The one recruiter that I had always remembered was this tall slender Marine by the name of SSgt. Riddick. He stuck out in my mind because I had always wanted to be a Marine. What a coincidence. He seemed pretty cool. The Navy Recruiters were four in number. The Marines Recruiters were three. The Army Recruiters were about ten to twelve. They, the Army, had the entire other side on the first floor. For the first official day of work, I now had an office, all clean out and ready to go. My wife picked me up from work the first week. Most times after that I just drove the government vehicle. I was not supposed to drive it home daily; however, I was a one man in a two-man office but had separate office but was assigned to active and reserve office in Hartford. Perfect! He minds his business, and I handled mine!

About a week later, I had talked with MSgt. Ben Occhino in which he covered the Hartford area at first, along with Milford, Waterford, and Bridgeport and New Haven. He provided me with a few pointers, and that was it. I really liked how Bill and I worked. We had nothing to do with each other. I was truly on my own! Plus, Bill did not live in the same place as I did. For me to drive the government vehicle home on a daily basis was not a problem. I really was like my own supervisor. I had total independence! This was incredible and unbelievable! I was on my own! I did notice that when I drove in to work and parked the car in the garage, then walked to the office. One thing that I had notice is that every morning, I would speak to people, and they would not say a word, black or white… They were rude! I mentioned that to Bill, and he informed me that it was their culture or way of life. For the New England way, he let me know that you have to had been there for a while, and then the people would speak to you. Don't get me wrong, very seldom, some people would surprise me, and they would speak! I had to learn not to take it personal. After a while, I stopped speaking and saying good morning. Then it happened. They would speak! That was the weird New England way!

A month has passed by and no one. No one has come to visit me nor sought information on the Air Force Reserve. I was getting bored! I had to get something popping, and then, after the first quarter of being there, I would be placed on quota's just like everyone else. I was doing cold calling folks out of the phone book, asking parents if their sons or daughters have an interest in joining the Air Force. I did not like getting the phone hung up on me. I did not ever get used to that part! We had a list in the office of all the old ASVAB scores that high school seniors had taken during their high school years. Then I would match their last name to that name in the phonebook and just asked for that high school senior by name that was more personable, and I did not get hung up on as much. Or sometimes the phone number would be on the students ASVAB score. I had to talk to a lot of kids to retake the ASVAB test again, which was a hard task by itself! Sometimes, it worked! Then, one day the students and sometimes adults would just walk into our office. After they found out, if they wanted active duty or reserve Air Force. I liked the ones that knew what they wanted and if they lived in the following areas in my recruiting zone: Hartford, Windsor, Manchester, West Hartford, New Britain, Elmwood, East Hartford, Bloomfield, Wethersfield, Windsor Locks, Newington, or Enfield. Generally, they were good to go, and the test scores were generally higher, which made it easier to get into the reserves. The thing was, it was just harder to recruit from the middle to upper class or the low-income communities just had to work harder to make the right scores. I did not care. I just wanted bodies to join. I did not recruit with bias because I was not raised that way. I wanted everyone to have a fair chance as I did. I already found that out that life was not on an even playing field. I was there and the only black male in my recruiting class I just recently graduated from. I was the first black Air Force Reserve Recruiter to recruit in Hartford. In which, I found during my recruiting efforts that Hartford was a melting pot.

All kinds of people lived there. Those areas had the money and the better schools and higher ASVAB scores, but those kids, well, high school seniors, were very indecisive and spoil and much harder to persuade. Well, I started to put folks in, but the biggest market like myself to get into the reserve were the prior service folks. I was able to put them in the Air Force Reserve from any of the other services. I did, even though a few of them may have needed a waiver or retake the ASVAB to get into a different career path. Sometimes, I called MSgt. Ben O at the Milford, Connecticut, office or my supervisor, SMSgt. Lisanby, to receive guidance if I had a question or gotten stuck. I was figuring it all out and working those packages and taking them to Westover AFB. My quota varied. Some months, it was two, and but for me, presently, it was just one per month. I was actually making quota before it was required. I may have had some personal issues within myself, but I was always to do my job. I remember one afternoon, I took a walk the opposite direction. Actually, I took a left turn as I would be walking around to see what was around there.

I saw a fire station on the same side as our building, but it was just across the street. I then crossed Ford Street to Bushnell Park, and I saw some food trucks and vendors there for lunchtime and a left on Ford Street. It turns into Jewell Street, and you would see the majority of the food trucks. The park was nice and not rundown, like in Akron. So I started walking over there often as possible. Just to get a break and check out the females. People would be running there too! I would sit on the benches too and just chill while in uniform. When at home, we would go to West Farms Mall on Farmington Avenue. This was a well-to-do area and mall. The black and Jamaican or Trinidadian folks lived mostly on Albany Avenue, just past the Stowe Village, a project housing development, and the Latinos lived on Park Street.

The dynamics of Hartford was totally segregated. I had learned a lot as we were doing some sightseeing and to get some Jamaican food and punch. I had learned a lot about the area from recruiting. I had to know the demographics. Being in Connecticut was definitely growing on me, and it was definitely better than Oklahoma City and Akron put together. As we were headed back to Manchester, it was like being in a different world. The quality of life was much better than Hartford. But at least I knew where the hoods were in Hartford. We were close to it but lived in a different area. We did enjoy hanging around our people. I wanted to recruit as many as possible. Adrian was enjoying the area too and did find a federal job with the social security office downtown on Main Street. She worked about a mile from me, and then, we decided to drive in together, and I would drop her off and park the car in my garage. It was much easier that way. We then we were able to put Ant into KinderCare Daycare. It was working fine. He did not like it the first few times that we dropped him off. After that, we were an afterthought. He liked it and being there at KinderCare all the time. Life was beginning to be good! What a change in such a short time.

Back at the job, I set up visits at Bulkeley High School (predominately Latinos) and Weaver High School (predominately black). Those were the only two schools that I had visited. Personally, I wanted to put my efforts where my assistance would have the most impact. I even went with my white counterpart; besides, he felt better by going to the schools with me. After now, working in Hartford, Connecticut, my doubts have subsided that no longer would I wonder if Hartford had black people. As I was beginning to see and learn how the world works, I can now say black people and all cultures of people were living everywhere. You see, I had never been around all types of people this close up. I was learning of other black cultures, other than black, and it was not from the television. I wanted to help all the minorities. I thought of it as a sort of giving back. This part of the job was very enjoyable for me. Plus, it kept me busy! I had to stay busy! The job was good, and nobody from the recruiting headquarters came to check on me, not even a surprise visit. As long as I was making my quota, I could do pretty much whatever I elected even for my hours. There was no such things as being late or staying late.

I do remember around September that a young man came into my office and sat down. He had gone to Bulkeley High School. I believe his name was Pierre or something close to that. He had graduated and had a bachelor's degree. Awesome, right! After he had taken the ASVAB, I was so surprised and wanted to help him find the job. I wanted to help him. Because of his excitement, he showed me after watching the training aid video. He was pumped, and I sold him. His scores were so low. Anyway, I explained all the requirements prior to going to the take the physical and what clothing to be wearing, so I sent him to Military Entrance Processing Station (MEPS) for the physical. I found out that the only job that he was eligible for was to become a cook in the military. I tried my best to get him more, and when I had told him what I had found out, since he had a degree, I thought that he would be hurt. No, it was just the opposite. Pierre wanted to only serve his country. What a patriotic thought! I was so relieved! I realized the people can surprise you at times! He would come to visit me from time to time to express his excitement. I was so glad!

One thing about me was I did not want to deceive anyone that wanted to join the Air Force Reserve. My recruiter had never deceived me! Adrian's job did not let her see me at lunch or during the day unless I made time to run by her building or something. I was not doing anything, but this was good. I would tell her of some of my recruits and high school seniors that wanted to join and the funny stories too. When she had asked me about the female's recruits, she started to become insecure. In this type of job, she had to trust me with the ladies. She would ask to know all about them, age, hair, color, and then we would start to argue a little. I did not want this to start again the arguments. This time, other than looking, I was not doing a thing. Not a thing. This time I was innocent! She sometimes gave me surprises and just popped up unannounced to my office, just to see what I was doing. Adrian was even accusing my female recruits. Not a chance I would mess up a qualified applied applicant and miss my quota. I definitely separated the personal from the business. That really didn't matter to her. All female in Adrian's book were guilty. She was really slowly pushing me out the door again, but Adrian did not know it. I was tired of being falsely accused.

That same day, I received notification letter from the Child Support Agency that my Air Force check would be deducted $100 per month to pay for the child support—$80 for Big Mike and $20 for the back child support. They caught up with me just like that. Not two weeks later, right before Ant's birthday, on October 19, I received another letter in the mail from the welfare department. Yup! As I suspected, while I was opening up the letter to see several pages and as I started to read each line, I did not want to believe what I was reading. Yes, I was reading the letter correctly, and I was doing so good on my job. They knew, the fraud section of the welfare department, and they punched my ticket! I was caught red-handed of receiving unemployment and welfare at the same time. I had to payback over $3,500, but the beautiful part of the whole thing was that inside the letter, one of the pages provided me with a payment schedule that was more than doable. I could not contest these findings. No way did I want this information to get back to my senior recruiter or the general who I really worked for as my overall supervisor. So I just paid it monthly, or I would have been finished. Besides that, I was already paying the bills from the bankruptcy that was discharged in August 1985, plus paying the regular bills.

Well, I was doing the right thing, and I was even making more money. Then in February, I would make my next promotion. Even though I did not pay them the full amount and as long as I was paying something, they did not bother me. Not at all. Overall, to include the babysitting for Ant at KinderCare, we did just fine. With Adrian working, it made things even better. We were not struggling anymore like in Oklahoma City or Akron, Ohio, with the hustle going on. The good thing was we had money left over per each paycheck. We did want to make a few trips to Ohio to visit, and I would be able to see Big Mike, and this time Lynn was getting the child support payments. I was never a fan of child support, but I did not mind taking care of my son. I did not like giving the money to his mother because I did not like how she spent the money, nor did I like the clothes he wore. Each time I saw his clothes that I had brought him, even when I was in Akron, I would be so disappointed. It really upset me each visit! I always thought that all child support should be monitored more closely. At the same time, I just knew that this was not going to happen. I could not do anything anyway; it was automatically coming from my check. An old saying goes, when it rains, it pours! All this stuff was happening at one time. For now, I had to put going back to school off even longer because recruiting, family, and schools were never going to work for me, and I had to accept it. I was stuck for a time and even in a good way because I did have a job versus not having a job!

Back at work, I found out why the other recruiters were so nice to us, the Air Force, and me. It was for anyone that could not get qualified to join the Air Force or Air Force Reserves. The other recruiters that belonged to the other services, they wanted to have a chance for Bill or me to send the rejected referrals to them. My recruiting technique was not to play games with all the prospects, as this was their life that could possibly change everything for them. I had always wanted to ensure that the recruits were making the best decision for themselves. When someone was on the fence and could not decide which service would be there best for their future. I would stop the interview after I had shown the recruiting video. Then I was gathering their personal data. Next, I would advise them to seek advice from all the other services. Then after the prospect has gathered all of the data, when they can make an informed decision, they can then see me. I wanted the prospect to be sure that they understood the mission for all of the services. And once you have determined that the Air Force was a fit for you, come back and see me! Right after that about a week later, I was sending this young lady to Springfield, Massachusetts, for her MEPS physical and examination. She had good ASVAB scores already. In order to see if she was indeed physically qualified for the military, I informed her of the items to take and provided her with a bus ticket on Greyhound free of charge. As she was getting ready to be leaving, this young lady had asked me a surprisingly question: "What if I do not wear underwear?" She had shocked me. They did not teach me that type of question in recruiting school. I hesitated, not knowing how to respond, and yes, my mind went left. Totally to left field! I was a little embarrassed and responded as if it was an everyday thing. I said, "You will just have to buy you some underwear!" Truth is, she was beautiful and Italian. As tempting as it was to pursue her, I remained focused on making my quota for every quarter. She was my only female recruit, thus far. I really did not like to mix business with pleasure. Besides, Adrian did pop up in my office from time to time, as she did with one of my recruits that I was working with.

Her name was Cecilia (aka Cece). Cece was a sweet young lady, just out of high school, just as cute as a button, and that was it. I had just started to work with her, and my wife walked in. Adrian did not even greet her. She assumed that we had something going on, or she believed that Cece had a crush on me. That was the furthest thing from the truth. I did not care. I just wanted to make my quota. I did not see that coming. Anyway, we had gotten all the application stuff and set up her testing. I was so glad that we, the Air Force Reserve, did not chauffeur the prospects and recruits around as the other services. I wanted to distance myself as much as possible, and I wanted to keep and maintain a professional environment. That young recruit passed everything with flying colors and enlisted in the delay entry program while at MEPS. About a few weeks later, I finished up her paperwork and took it up to the recruiting headquarters at Westover

AFB. I was busy from that point on. I started to hear the rumors between the different recruiters of messing around with the prospects and recruits from the others services and some news articles for recruiters not being honest. I was still glad to be there and to have this recruiting job. After all I have been through and sleeping in the attic, I decided not to ever harass or have any type of relationship with any of my prospects for applicants. I wanted to be an honest and professional recruiter. I actually thought that I was getting to know the job. I decided to have my own code that business and pleasure does not mix!

Once I was at home and would share my story of the day with Adrian, I would only tell her that the female recruit had mentioned that she did not wear under garments and that I was surprised. Then Adrian would ask a ton of questions, so I learned I had to give her less information about the day and the recruits, and then, she would be fine. I think not. Adrian and I argued several times over Cece, and she had no idea what I was going through about her. We definitely argued a whole lot, and this time, I was innocent. I was so glad that Cece was qualified for everything and was scheduled to leave in the fall. However, she did come to visit the recruiting office, and we talked on and off until the time for her to leave for basic military training. I would not go anywhere with any prospect or recruit to get paperwork or whatever they needed or forgot. Once I was able to trust myself to just be a recruiter, then I would be able to go anywhere with them. I was busy. The next day, I was working with the prior service Army gentlemen by the name of Sgt Leonard. He was just awesome to work with and was very grateful. Sgt. Leonard was the first prior service guy to cross over from the Army, another service and to be put in the Air Force. I had to request his test scores before we could move forward and take the physical at MEPS. My job was growing on me, and I would take those walks to Bushnell Park whenever possible just to clear my head or take a break. I would see people walking, talking, smiling, and some were even holding hands. Those were the times that I realized that I was truly missing something that I desperately wanted.

I was married and just so unhappy as I was thinking never had that "spark" or the "flame." What I had with Adrian was not love, not even close. It was a good thing that this job came along as I was learning the art of recruiting, and it kept me focused enough not to focus on Adrian. I believe that I was beginning to hate her. I was thinking of the words of the song "It's a Thin Line Between Love and Hate" by the Persuaders. As in the song, it was more of me instead of her. I found a way to maintain because of my son Ant! As I was leaving the park, I knew that this marriage was getting too toxic for me to stay in it. I just did not know how to leave or part ways. There was something good between us, but it was never love for a relationship. I think we should have just stayed friends. We started everything for the wrong reasons and way too fast! We just bypassed the friend part, and I just realized that as I opened the door and walked into my office. Anyway, I could not believe who was waiting for me once. I returned to my office. No way! I was already being successful as a recruiter. I was looking at two, not one, but two beautiful friends that wanted to join the Air Force Reserves. I said two! Wow! I was thinking to keep my promise and to be a good recruiter. They were from East Hartford, Connecticut, and their names were Felicia and Tonya. They were friends that wanted to join the reserve together. They were not the normal black females that I was used to seeing. I could not compare them to anyone from my past, except for Lynette, Pam Ringer, Teresa (at Church's Chicken). These girls were just beautiful, classy, cool, well-spoken, and could handle themselves. They dressed nice too. They were in there mid-twenties, and Tonya was just a little older. If they wanted to be just noticed, my attention was in their direction. They had it together, and I mean all the way together! Looking back, and truth be told, if the opportunity had presented itself—but it did not, and I definitely stayed professional—I would have broken every rule possible at either one of them. I remember Felicia getting her identification out of her purse, and she had a three-inch switch blade. After seeing the knife, now I can add mysterious to the list. I was sure it was an accident, but I was definitely not going to make any first moves, but I would have not turned her down. Actually, not either one of them. We were able to finally fill out all the paperwork. Besides, I was asking a lot of questions because I did not want them to leave. Even though I was in some deep thinking on my break at the park. These two ladies actually made my day! I had informed them to check-out the study guide from the library, if needed and to take the test, and we would go from there. As they were leaving, Tonya's hair was just absolutely long. She had the good stuff. Now I was confident that I would be adding two more to my quota. They would put me on track for making goal. I was glad my wife did not see those two!

In Oklahoma City, she said that she did not love me and could never. Then nothing made sense. The jealousy contradicted her love for me. I don't believe that she really wanted to lose me. Besides, her jealousy would not allow her to care about my quotas. Well, Adrian really kept coming at me, especially since it was time for Cece to leave for BMTS in Texas. Two days prior to Cece leaving for the Air Force Reserve training, SMSgt. Lisanby called me to the headquarters office at Westover AFB. When I arrived, I met the new senior recruiter, Chief Doug Winter. Now, I have to answer and give a reason why should I not take Cece to the airport. I blatantly made up some lie because I could not tell them that my wife Adrian kept arguing with me over Cece. The bottom line, I was ordered to take her to the airport. The new chief kept looking at me very suspiciously, and I was still innocent, and my wife falsely accused me again! Frankly, Adrian has never caught me doing anything with a woman. Never! They told me to be careful and to watch myself. I called Cece once I was back in the office and told her everything. I also dropped her off at the airport. Cece was so understanding, and she and I remained friends. While I never expected Adrian to do such a thing and not like or accuse my recruits, all I wanted was for Adrian not to chase them away. Then again, my wife never met these two new ones because the confrontation may have changed their mind. Somehow, I did not see Felicia or Tonya backing down from Adrian! Well, at the same time, I believe that it worked out for the best. A week or two later, I had gotten the results of their practice scores, and they both did well, Felicia and Tonya. I made them an appointment and had them back to the office to schedule the actual ASVAB test.

Now, I was thinking that Connecticut has a lot of beautiful women, and I was really beginning to enjoy my stay there. Besides, Connecticut really had some beautiful women there. Yes, indeed! Not to mention the ones that I saw in the park by my office. While back at my desk, I was going through the mail from the last time I was at the recruiting headquarters at Westover AFB. I noticed the annual Air Force Reserve Recruiting conference in Destin, Florida. Now, we were looking at a week in Florida with the family. At least, we would be on good terms for this function. That's it for the day, going home with Adrian today! It was not every day that we rode home together. Her job was going good for her, as well at the Social Security Office. I was taking hold of the recruiting job and making my quotas. It was one of the very few things we had in common, but some things we are very compatible and can be very normal, in every sense of the word! We were riding along. As I was driving, I had asked her if she wanted to fly to Destin, Florida, and she said that she did not mind. Then I told her that the job was having a recruiting conference there on October 24–28. We had to leave that Sunday and return on Saturday. Plus, she had to take a week off work, which was not a problem. In less than one year, we had our first quasi-vacation, plus a formal Air Force dining-in. My first priority was to return to work on the next day and to get Felicia's and Tonya's results from their physical. Once they walked into my office, even though it was strictly business, my day was definitely brighter. They elected to bypass the free bus ticket to the Springfield, Massachusetts, and drove instead. So I had informed them of all the requirements in order to take the physical and just nothing phase them at all! These two ladies were just serious about every step. They knew exactly what they wanted to do! I told them that I would be out town with the Air Force and would call them upon my return. I wish them both well and walked them outside as they were leaving.

I know we should have done something for Ant's third birthday but only got him a little toy, and he was happy to get that! Packing was the next agenda item. We were not the best at having birthday parties, actually for none of us. Plus, I did not want anything from her. I was never feeling it. Adrian's jealously and misconceptions really got the best of us. We would argue, and she would say that I made her that way! That would be entirely true, if she did not have that payback attitude, instead of just forgiving me. That may have worked better for us in Dayton. I will and we will never know! Because, one day, I will have the strength to just leave. I always said that I would leave someday, but would never do it. I kept taking her with me! Now we are going to Florida and just put on another front, which means we are having marital problems and no one would know it! Most of our lives was lived just like that, even in Akron, when I was being honest!

Truthfully, trust would always be a major issue for us as long as we were married. I believe if our being together was more for convenience, and of course, it was definitely cheaper to keep her. So true! I am thoughtful for remembering what Smitty had said back in Dayton at the base as to why buy the cow, if you can get the milk free. I just did not listen because I rushed and did not do it for love. It's a little too late, but now, I am learning later the facts of life! Being in Florida was exciting! During the day, Adrian was mainly in the room with Ant and sleeping. She did not mind sleeping, not at all! I would be in recruiting workshops, classes, and briefings. And Commander's briefings! It was always something to do and fun times with the baby. I was glad to see at the pool that we were not the only ones that brought children to the conference. They had setup a babysitting daycare for the dining in at a cost of $20 for a few hours. It worked like perfect. The night before the dining in, we were all by the pool with the other families, a few beers, and loud music. I was in the pool, and the sun had just gone down. For some reason, as I was walking in the pool, the bottom had dropped off and was immediately over my head. I panicked! I mean really panicked, and somehow, I almost drowned. I vowed never to drink and swim. That combination did not work, at least not for me! I was so embarrassed that I never said anything until later on. Not a word! The good thing was at the time I survived! The last day here, and I was glad to be alive! We were done with all the recruiting meetings and had time to spend with our families. At the dining in would also come the awards and the top recruiters. I did get a plaque award with gold letters and a gold plate on it for my performance. I was truly surprised! My wife was looking really quite lovely for the evening, and she was smiling. Now, I was surprised again! Well, I told her that three smiles are a charm and that we shall see! Again, at times, we could be good together, but rarely did it last long.

The night had come and gone. Now to get packed and ready to take a taxi to the airport, we headed back to Hartford. I realized that Ant had flown before he was born and just did not know it. I wasn't too keen on going home because Destin, Florida, was just gorgeous! I did enjoy it except for the almost drowning incident. However, it was very beautiful there! I would come back in a heartbeat! In just two or three hours, we were home at the Bradley Airport. I know the first thing that I was going to be doing was filing for my travel voucher on the DD Form 1351-2 to get reimbursed for my expenses and to receive my per diem. What a great system we had, and I was always about getting my paperwork completed and submitted. I was the same way with my recruits. Well, we got home and unpacked, and I would do the father thing and spend time with Ant. I was able to be a big kid at times. We really had a lot of fun together. He was my little man and just growing! He was also getting taller! Most times, I would put him to bed, with a song. First, we would repeat together the "Five Little Monkeys" song that he learned at KinderCare daycare. Then we would sing the "Good Night, Sweetheart, Good Night" song and replace it with his name. It went like "Good night, Ant. It's time to go. It's been fun. I want you to know..." Finally, before leaving and turning off the light, we would say, "Now lay me down to sleep," pray, and that would be the close of the night for us. The most beautiful part of it all was when he started to learning each the songs and prayers on his own! Just beautiful!

On Sundays and most weekends, I tried to watch sports as much as possible. In this case, before going to work, it would be football. I was a die-hard Cleveland Browns fan, and since living in Connecticut, I also took on most of the local teams and became a New England Patriots fan for the time I was there. By doing this, it kept my interests in sports. Even though I was always for Ohio State, I took on the UConn Huskies for the college level basketball team.

Nights were getting to be pretty interesting. Sometimes they were too long, if we were arguing and too short, when we were getting along. We did have that rollercoaster of a marriage! It was full of the highs and the lowest lows! Somehow and sometimes, we made it work between us. Then again, sometimes, I would purposely make her jealous, just to get back at her. I was so glad and elated that we only had one child. I don't believe that I could have handled more children with her! The night went quickly, and I was so glad. Boy, was I glad to be going to work! I was looking for a way out! A way out was always somewhere in my mind. Besides, I was looking forward to my Monday appointments, starting with Felicia and Tonya. I just wanted to find out if they had passed the physical and all. Normally, I would have appointments with the recruits or just walk-ins, but not one time can I remember a parent or any parent to have joined the meeting with their high school children. Well, the meeting with Felicia and Tonya went well. They were always on time. They were good to go and all set to leave for the next BMTS class in San Antonio, Texas. The appointment was over quickly, and they would only call me now if they needed something. I just had to take their recruiting packages to Westover AFB. The next time I would go and also file my travel voucher from the Florida recruiters conference trip. The holidays were fast approaching.

Anyway, Ant had missed a few good holidays, and I wanted this time to be special, especially since we missed his birthday, sort of. I was in the thought of doing Christmas for my son. Everything was on track. We had the three things mostly needed—love for him, some money, and a place to live. Now, I was going home to talk about it. I was sure it was something we could do. Truthfully, Ant had just turned three years old, and this was his first Thanksgiving and Christmas since we left Oklahoma City and Akron. I was feeling a little bothered and wanted to do something for my baby boy! When I arrived home, most of the time, Adrian was there before I arrived and sometimes not, especially if she went shopping or had to make a stop at the grocery store. Well, this time, she was there, and as I was changing my uniform and throw on some lounge pants or cutoff shorts and a T-shirt (which was my normal, unless we were going somewhere), we would be talking. I was expressing my thoughts or the guiltiness of my feelings and wanted this holiday plans for our son. I must say, we did not argue this time. She agreed! Our yard was really looking good and the shed that I put up in the rear of the house. But not understanding that it was not time for the winter season. I was glad that I was already used to the cold and snow. So I knew what to expect, but I was not prepared. In a sense, I had to go to Sears or Montgomery Wards to find some shovels and outside salt for the snow and ice. Plus, we had to get a fake Christmas tree. For the reasons of my sons only, I was in the mood to do Christmas. I would have to buy Big Mike something too and take it to him. Other than not getting along sometimes, the best part of our marriage was making up. We did not have much of anything else in common. Our conversations was not much about nothing, so I tried to stay busy with life and go to Westover AFB and play basketball as much as possible on the weekends at the gym, and it would be free for me to do so! These things helped me to keep my sanity because, literally, sometimes, she would just drive me crazy with her jealousy. But the kicker was, I was not doing anything. While we would be driving in the car, on the way to the store, Adrian would watch me like a hawk. For real! Even in some stores, you can look but not touch! I kept explaining that it was just like watching the television, and it meant nothing. If it was not for the making up, it would never work because I did not want another child with her.

Anyway, since we were at the BX at Westover AFB, I found a six-foot evergreen tree and took it to the front of the store and continued shopping with Adrian. The BX prices were a whole lot cheaper. Now we had to continue on and get the decorations and a few gifts. I knew that year, I was being safe and brought her a perfume set, a robe, and slippers, which she needed anyway! I was trying to be nice again! Since we discussed to do a gift exchange for each other. When we got home, it was good and feeling like Christmas. I too was in a good mood! I cannot remember nothing that was celebrated on Thanksgiving. It was like a normal day, except for the football game. It was Dallas Cowboys losing to the Houston Oilers with a score of 25–17. Herschel Walker did get a touchdown, but Warren

Moon and Drew Hill gave them the beatdown! What a game! The next day, Ant and I were putting together the Christmas tree with the lights and star on top. While we did not believe in Santa Claus, I was in the moment! It was the allowing Ant to take pictures with Santa at the mall, and riding the train, he was so happy, and we were too! This was so exciting, and we were not going to burst his bubble. We were giving Santa all our credit. It was shame on me, but we did not care! My leave was finally building up, and I put in to take four days and go to Akron for the New Year's. The recruiting work was slowing down. I had some potential recruiting prospects to look into after the holidays, and most days, I was leaving earlier than usual. The holiday season was like for me of being on my own. My senior recruiter was not bothering me. Nevertheless, we kept getting ready for it and buying gifts. I was glad about that! It was Christmas, and the greatest time our family had ever seen. The house was smelling good with the ham and chitterlings and hog maws. There was also greens and macaroni and cheese. We had some good soul food. Adrian even called her mother for some of her recipes, and I made some sweet potato pies and also called my mother for the recipes. It was soul food all the way!

We were celebrating Christmas, like we never had a Christmas before, ever! Somehow, it brought back memories from a Christmas in Dayton when we lived there, and this day made me remember that we did have a Christmas dinner in our apartment. I distinctly remember Adrian cleaning and cooking chitterlings and hog maws and sweet potatoes and stuff. It also was good! Somehow, all the arguments clouded the good thoughts for me not to remember. My Ant was just as happy as he could be. We had him a big racetrack for cars and placed it under his bed that we had recently got for him. It was so cool. We were going to let him open it up after we returned from Akron. After working that week, I decided to leave the government vehicle in the garage at the job. I did not want to leave it at the house, just in case! Since I was on leave the following week, Adrian was able to take off from work too. It was getting colder as we packed our clothes and loaded the car. We had made a stop to get some gas and food, then be on our way. Going through New York and just before crossing the George Washington bridge, we saw cars everywhere on the highways, with no tires, wrecked or on fire. For the brief moments of going through Brooklyn, the cars were worst off. People were actually selling items on the highway in New York while we were going to Ohio. Get this, they were on the highway selling tapes, jewelry, and everything else. It was guys even washing your windshields, if you let them. Some of them were even drugs addicts and all! I was always driving and being on alert while in New York. The key to the whole thing was not to pull over, not to stop, no windshield washing, and stay alert. Really going through New York was like a scene of the 1981 movie *Escape from New York*. That futuristic film definitely came to life in 1989. Finally, we made it to New Jersey and quickly onto Pennsylvania. Then Ohio was the next state. This drive was a lot shorter than the one to Oklahoma City. It was just that the New York highway was nothing to play with. However, if you had seen something that you liked, you buy it, and that was it!

It was good to be in Akron and see my family. My mother was happy to see me and the family. I also found out that my mother was giving Adrian some cooking tips. Now it all made sense why the food was so good. Wow! I was glad to see my mother's smile again! She was glad to see that I was back on my feet and holding my own. We made our rounds to see everyone, no attic this time. This time, we stayed in a hotel. We did hear on the radio that the O'Jays were performing at the Tangiers on West Market Street to bring in the New Year's. We just had to get some tickets so I would not miss the songs "Stairway to Heaven," "Brandy," "Cry Together," and "Forever Mine." The Brandy" and "Forever Mine" songs would remind me of Lynette back in Dayton, Ohio, when I was stationed there a few years back. Oh my! We got there just in time and in time to play some poker too. What a New Year's for 1989. Wow! I was really enjoying myself, and this was as close to a birthday celebration that I would get. We were in Akron for the week, and all was well, especially hanging out with the O'Jays! I played a few lottery numbers in Ohio and did not win a thing. Not even a box number but the poker games went over well. Sometimes we broke even, and the other times we won! We could gamble well together and never lost that! We also saw my dad, and he was glad that I was back in the Air Force! I told him that I was to make technical sergeant (TSgt, E-6) in two months. I had all of my training done, and the job was good. Therefore, my next promotion was on the way! Truthfully, for the first time in a long time, I felt alive again in Akron, Ohio. I thought about how I almost lost it all for nothing! Nothing! I am finding out that life goes on! So was this week and including my twenty-seventh birthday.

As far as I was concerned, the fourth of January was celebrated with the O'Jays. I was well pleased! Adrian did tell me happy birthday out of guilt, I think, but for me, it did not matter anyway. We kept making our rounds seeing my mother, and she was glad to be keeping Ant, but they all still called him Pooky. I was not broke, like not without money. What a feeling! We had left early enough on Sunday to get home and to get unpacked, getting my uniform ready for Monday. It was not a bad drive. We had to get used to New York as we did. We had to learn that was just New York. Well, we did not like paying those tolls, which were also distracting. The other good thing was that we did was not get caught in the snow because the winter was upon us, but it was soon to arrive. I definitely made sure that there was fuel in the tank outside our home. The one thing was that I did have to keep an eye on was the fuel tank. After work for that week, since everything was slow in the office, we had planned to go downtown Hartford for the after Christmas specials. We were there. Adrian and I were walking in the downtown area.

We passed by the little liquid store to play some numbers and the pick 6 lottery. I was not really playing the numbers in Connecticut as we were doing good getting back on our feet from our days of living in Akron. I did not play much, and Adrian played a few numbers herself. I must have played about only $10, far less than was I used to playing while in Akron. I also played my usual six numbers, and I got a quick pick 6 lottery ticket to go. It was on! We got home and put everything away! I was hanging out with my little man Ant, and we were watching the television. The numbers were coming out on the television while we were watching. I had nothing on my favorite numbers and the pick 6, but that quick pick... I noticed that I had one number, then two numbers, then three numbers, then four numbers. I called Adrian into the living room with us. Then I had five numbers, and the last number was off by three. If I had 22, then the number was 25 or vice versa. All I know is I had missed the last number by three digits. Well, for five numbers, I was paid a lump sum of $1,000, and that was enough because it was the limit of my winnings. I was glad to get that and disappointed at the same time that I did not win it all. To be truthful, I was a little disdained that I did not win it all and had got over it as I went back to the liquor store place to collect my money! We were then able to pay some more bills! That winning was truly on time, and we made the most of it!

From the rest of January through February, I had to work Saturdays for the first time. SMSgt. Lisanby paid me a visit in my office. Seeing that my office was pretty active, but the overall region for the recruiting headquarters were low and they were not making goal, everyone was penalized! I thought that this practice was not fair, and my Saturdays were no longer free weekends. Instead of going to Westover AFB to play basketball, I was driving to the office. This was the first time anyone from my office had paid me a visit, and since I was producing, probably the last visit, I played like I was actively looking for recruits, making cold calls, trying to get appointments set up. As soon as he had left after a few hours, I did nothing and went back to my normal routine and waited for the phone to ring. Within a week or two, I had two high school friends to come in to join. They were also out of high school and a little silly. Sometimes I thought that they were flirting. That did not really bother me. I was sort of getting used to it. After showing the video on the Air Force, we completed the paperwork, and I got them set-up to take the ASVAB test as part of getting qualified. Their names were Angie and Laura. We talked for a few, and they were on their way out the door, but I did take them home. We also had scheduled our next meet. The ride to their house was quite interesting. They would never finish talking and laughing. I do thank God that we were there at the house, and I did meet the parents. They had a nice family. My home life was pretty fair, with the extended hours, plus the penalty of Saturday. I did not mind the longer hours in the office.

Right before the February ended, it was half over. It was like the third Saturday of February. I could not believe that this happened to me as I was the only one in the Air Force office. I was already going through something with turning twenty-seven years old. It was like I kept thinking of how close it was for me to turning thirty years old. I believe after the life that I was living, my midlife crisis came early. My turning thirty was always a weird one for me! I was going through something! And then, this happened to me on February 18, 1989. On this Saturday, my office was slow and no people traffic at all. This young female just walked in. Was I dreaming? Was it my midlife crisis in action? I just lost it! My mind was not on recruiting at all. She was just beautifully sexy, thin, light-brown skinned, with short hair. Her smile was alluring, to say the least. I have never seen a young woman like this! Somebody needed to hit me or slap me for real! She wanted to find out how to join the Air Force Reserve. Of course, I was okay. After she started to speak, I was just watching her mouth softly speak her words. Then she told me that she wanted to join and was from England! Her English and proper accented enunciation was just beautiful. I just loved her English accent! I should have known that she was not an American. Nothing about her fit an American profile of a woman. However, the bad news for her was that she didn't qualify based on not being a United States citizen. Somehow, her bad news was my good news. I was about to leave for the day, anyway, so we struck up another conversation about London, England, and I did not take my eyes off her. I could not because I was hypnotized by the mystery that made her beautiful. As we kept talking, before I could react, she was in my face, and from the first time, she kissed me. It changed me. It was like being resuscitated to live again. For the first time in my life, I was caught off-guard. That day, I slid into second base, and really, I almost hit a home run, figuratively speaking! While I do not remember her name, I will always remember that day!

Again, that day made me want to be free from Adrian. I no longer wanted to cheat on her. I wanted to leave her, for good. For real! This young lady made me realized that I was still alive! I now love London, England, for all the right reasons, plus her accent! England must be for lovers! Now, I was not sure about any American woman

because of my list of bad experiences and relationships! I did not
want to go home at all! So I had called her after we went our separate
ways, so we could meet again. She was there visiting some family or
a grandmother, but she was not able to get away! I have never spoken
to her again! I kept wondering, was it my midlife crisis, or did she do
something to me. I was way past being mesmerized. That day, after
our meeting, I would have gone to England! Just to be with her! I
had called her on a different day, and I was not able to ever speak to
her again! Not ever! Now I am sure that that occurrence would be a
one-time episode in my life! That English lady helped me in more
ways than words can say. For a long time, I was truly hooked! When
I arrived home, days had passed, and still I was thinking of her being
in England without me! Adrian could not even get an argument out
of me. My mind was truly in England with that mystery of a woman!

After a few days of my solitude, I was back at work. It was amazing that before February was over, on the twenty-seventh of February
1989, this young lady named Kendra and her guy friend wandered
in to my office, seeking reserve information. I only processed her
paperwork and to get her setup to take the ASVAB test. Kendra was
tall and barely light-skinned, and she was just cool, with a personality
of being very down to earth. Her friend Alex was cool too, but I was
under the suspicion that he was flirting with me. I could not believe
it, but I made it clear the I was strictly for the ladies and that I was
married. I didn't think that he really cared. The best thing that I did
was to keep it professional. Besides, I had to make quota, which was
my first priority, and I had just gotten off probation for the Air Force
Reserve not making the quarterly quotas. The probation was sort of
a bonus after meeting that lady for England. SMSgt. Lisanby called
while I was interviewing Kendra and informed me to bring in my
government vehicle to Westover AFB and to pick up my new 1989
Chevy Malibu on Tuesday. It was a tannish brown color with four
doors. Now, I am getting a brand-new government car. I could not
believe it. It looked like my numbers would be back on the rise and a
new car. Besides, Kendra knew what she wanted and was more on the
serious side. The good thing about her was she knew that her mind
was made up, and I was glad too! I try to be nice to everyone, and if

they were not able to join, then I would ask them to refer some of their friends and families in my direction. I was always the forward thinker, and Alex was no exception, and I stuck to my bottom line and requested that they would send me some people to join.

Once I returned to the office, I put things away and went on about my business and called it a day. On the next day of work, I found out that Chief Koper had retired, and now SMSgt. Lisanby was just my immediate supervisor and no longer the acting senior recruiter. CMSgt. Winter was here now. Now, I almost had no supervisor because SMSgt. Lisanby had the acting senior recruiter position and would be doing the work of two people. I was still on the grind and putting folks in the Air Force Reserves. While I am now working with several people to get tested or retested, it was rocking for me. Then I was trying to space everyone out, so I could make goal for the next two quarters. That was awesomely plan, and it was working. So Kendra had to retest or something to do over, which played perfectly into my plan. I was with Angie and Laura, which had to retest and past. I could not get these two qualified for nothing. So now, they both were disqualified. I figured that I would throw my mack or rap down on Angie. She could not get into the Air Force Reserve, so I decided to make her one of my ladies. She was cute and sort of short. We talked and talked. After a few months of that, I just gave up! Now, I had lost twice with Angie with no quota gained and no girlfriend on the side. Let's say that I recognized Angie was a good girl and did not do married men. We did not have enough attraction like the lady from England for me to get a divorce on her behalf. So I had to keep it moving. It was now late in the summer, and I took a few days of leave to go and visit the family in Akron. We were on the road again. We made it through New York, and it looked about the same. Except there were a few less cars on the highway stripped of their car tires. We passed New Jersey just fine, but when we started driving through Pennsylvania, the Mercury Cougar, my car, was not performing right. Something was entirely wrong with the engine, so I thought at first, this car would not go over 50 mph, unless we were going down the hills in the mountains. I could get the speed up to about 80 mph only going downward. It was like that all the way there to Ohio. Of course, it had taken us much longer to get there and back. We stopped by my dad's, so he could look at my car and verified the problem. He said that the transmission was beginning to slip, and eventually, it would fail, but I could keep on driving it until the car would just die on me. Or I could put in a new transmission, which was not a viable option at the time. So we decided to just keep driving it. Not to mention that Adrian had already hit the side of the car on the roof while parking in the garage.

We made our visits for a few days and left. Really, I preferred to be closer to home, just in case the car breaks down. We really did not want to get stranded in Akron or on the interstate. We kept driving our car with the variation of fast speeds, but still slow. It was frustrating to drive our car at times, but we made it work. Sometimes, I would get these moments over at Bushnell Park or just sitting at my desk. I would fold my hands and just think about life. I would think about my life in particular, and I was getting older. All of a sudden, I was getting fearful of my age. I was getting closer and closer to thirty years of age. I often felt trapped in life and marriage. I thought that recruiting was not what I wanted to do, and I felt stuck as well. This is where I desired a younger woman, and I wanted it to happen before I was too old. I felt old when I was with Adrian. I no longer wanted to go home. I was beginning to blame her for how my life was turning out. I was almost thirty years old, and I wanted *love* and true love at that. Now, I did not want to be a recruiter anymore. I did not want this life anymore. I need to be free before I got too old to do anything. I was thinking that my body would stop working, and I needed to have someone younger. My mind was all over the place. Was this a midlife crisis that I was going through? I did not know! All I knew was that I wanted to get my age back, when I was eighteen to twenty-five years old. I know mentally I was not thinking correctly for my age of twenty-seven years old. I was going home every day, and it was not interesting anymore. I was a father and a husband, yet I was always empty of feelings. Somehow, we picked the right weekend to drive that broke car back to Akron. In a strange way, we both missed Akron. While there again, we managed to see another concert. It was Stephanie Mills singing "Home," Luther Vandross singing "If This World Were Mine" and "A House is Not a Home" and "Since I Lost My Baby," Anita Baker singing "Caught Up in the Rapture." The concert was just breathtaking and memorable!

We did our visits, and came back to Connecticut. As soon as we returned, we needed more money, so Adrian and I started gambling again! This time, it was a total new game that neither one us have never heard of it. The game was jai alai. The very first time we played this game, a coworker of Adrian told her about the game, and Adrian told me about it. Then after asking our little boy, he gave us our very first winner number of 347 (we hit it straight and box), and we won that number for over $5,600. Thinking I would hit it again, I played another $1,000 back into it. I was glad with the winnings that we paid off some major bills first! From that point forward, we both were hooked to jai alai. After getting a friend of Adrian to babysit Ant, we were on our way! We even drove to Milford, Connecticut, to play jai alai and lost even more. We did not know the players at the time; we just wanted to win. We needed to win! Then gambling was helping us cope again but only for a short time. I could not stop daydreaming and wishing for a new life! I did not know how much time I had left on our car transmission before it had stopped working. Sometimes, I used the government vehicle to do some of the grocery shopping or when our car did not act right. Or I would use it to go to the Laundromat when our washing machine was broken or to take Adrian to work.

My government car was right on time. I believe it was the norm because the other recruiters did pretty much the same thing. This was around October, and Ant was turning four years old. And still he was a daddy's boy! He was definitely the reason I stay married so long. I did not want to leave my son. I had only wished that I had not cheated on her. Then again, I would be glad I did cheat because I was so empty. We were so messed up with gambling and writing bad checks, and the manager would always show up in the grocery stores and would not accept our check. The businesses and people were always chasing us down and now the bill collectors again. At the same time, we were going back and forth at the Manchester Superior Court, located at 410 Center Street, showing up and getting continues until August 1990. In my thought of private sessions of thinking, I messed up, and at the same time, we both messed up. I had so many regrets that I had kept suppressing. Truthfully, we were truly broken and could never be fixed. My debts, child support, and bills were just terrible and adding up. I knew it was matter of time before these collections would affect my Air Force recruiting job, and I had decided to get out of recruiting. I was good, but I had to quit in the upcoming months! My mind was made to leave a good job because of all of our bad debts. I realized that Adrian and I could never prosper! Nothing that we have ever done has worked out! Nothing and that kept bothering me!

Sometimes like, what I was going through, I had to call mother. I expressed my true feelings to her, and she understood. I always knew that my mother have me covered under the blood of Jesus.

Anyway, another day in the office, and the day was going pretty slow. I was looking up from my desk as this young woman walked in SSgt. Scott (he took over for SSgt. Vincent) and was talking to her about the Air Force. One thing about the military, once your orders come, you are done and gone! Well, she was interested in the reserves, and he sent her into my office. She introduced herself at Millicecia Farrington (aka Suzie) from Saint Thomas, Virgin Islands. She weighs just under a one hundred pounds and about five feet and four inches and brown-skinned with short hair. She had the cutest smile. After the weight and the processing of the paperwork. She was eighteen years old and just out of high school. It was all official, and we were having a real good time together. This young lady really wanted to join the Air Force Reserve, but first things first. While she did catch my eyes, I kept focus on making the quota first! I sent Suzie on her way for the testing, and also, I had to get Kendra paperwork finished and to get her sworn in. Kendra and Sgt. Leonard were my next two to get sworn in. I was slow rolling their paperwork to ensure I had made goal in this next quarter. It always seemed like when I would make contact with Kendra, her friend Alex, in which I cannot say for sure, but I would get prank phone calls from a guy dude. I did not like this at all. This got to me, and then, I started to think of what I did on the phone to others, with the phone calls that I made to the hospital in Georgia on my temporary military assignment. How ironic. I had received several of these types of obscene phone calls from a dude. Wow, did I learn a valuable lesson!

What goes around comes around. I was so glad that I was growing up! I never reported it because I realized that I was getting my payback! I just never expected it from a guy! Anyway, Kendra was on the right track, and my quotas were good. I had recruited people, left and right. Now, I'm here for about eighteen months so far. I just did not know their names guys and girls. I was recruiting and doing well! On the other hand, my marriage was all but over. I did not like coming and going home. I only tolerated everything to see my son. So many times, I did not want to touch her or for her to touch me. Going to work was my peace, and staying busy was keeping my mind busy. Now, more bad news. Another potential recruit did not pass the ASVAB. Therefore, Suzie was disappointed, and now, she did not want to take the test again. I did all I could do to calm her down. So we decided to become friends. I had hopes to get her to test and study to pass the ASVAB in six months or so. The friendship was working great! I had no plans on the summer, and the car could not make the drive to Ohio, again without dying. But we still could go anywhere locally. That worked fine! Now, in September was the big Westover AFB Air Show, and we had to do an Air Force Reserve Recruiting booth there and pass out flyers. I was able get Adrian to come and also bring our son, Ant. I just completed my hour at the Air Force Reserve booth and spent the rest of time with the family. I took my little man Ant and placed him on my shoulders, and he just had a ball, and I took him to see the C-5 aircraft on the inside and was given one of the stats to understand that that C-5 could carry up to eleven buses. We were enamored for the facts finding details and about 23.5 million golf-balls could fit on the aircraft. These planes even had passenger seating! I was glad that Ant was having a blast!

The following month, we did another Military Air Show and the Air Force Thunderbirds would do a flyover, just like at Westover AFB. My family did not go to this one because it was for two days and we had to go, back-to-back to the Air National Guard Base there. The recruiter for that area was MSgt. Carl Frantz and he showed us the ropes for that area. To say the least about Rhode Island, it was like one of those gangster types deals. They had dudes standing in front of certain establishments and anyone could not gain access. I believe Rhode Island, was definitely, not a joke type place to be! These were the only two days that I have ever set foot in that place. I was wondering where the money was. Even the police cruisers were old and beat-up but drivable vehicles. Bottom line, the police needed to have their police vehicles newly replaced! I was driving a brand-new government vehicle. Wow! It was about a few weeks later, and we had to go to Lime Rock, Connecticut, to the Lime Rock Racetrack to do a photo shoot for one of the race cars that the Air Force Reserve had sponsored. This was a busy time serving the Air Force Reserve as a recruiter. I was not getting any per diem on these trips because I was driving a government vehicle. No fair! I thought what a waste, but these trips were messing up my daily work schedule! Now, back at the recruiting office, it was almost like a second home because the gambling and bad checks. We were writing checks everywhere, they just kept bouncing.

I was to meet another young lady. Her name was LaDana. She was just out of high school. She was just beautiful, sweet, and kind. LaDana was very quiet and did not talk much. She was smart but distracted. I really did not know what to make of her. She was ready to test and physical and be gone! She was probably my most mysterious recruit of all times. She did everything I asked her to do. LaDana was very disciplined and very nice at the same time. We talked a few times, and everything stayed business. I would say in less than a few months, LaDana was on her way to BMTS in San Antonio, Texas, and then technical school. She had promised to see me on her return from all the training. Since LaDana had left for training, a lot of this transpired within my life. The holidays were not celebrated at all. I did manage to buy Ant a few things, and we allowed him to believe in Santa Claus for one more year. It was the year of 1990, and I had turned twenty-eight years old. I had just left Angie's house from dropping off some recruiting paperwork to her at her parent house. Then I had left for home. It had gotten darker faster, and I arrived home around 6:00 p.m. As soon as I walked in the door, Adrian was going off, accusing me of cheating. It was not true! I was not cheating at all, but I had wished I were. Adrian was really going off, and I could not take it anymore! I had had enough! So the sofa was there to the right of me. I laid my stuff there on the floor and then laid on the sofa.

In my mind, if I were to go to the bedroom, I would had killed all of us. I had to lay on the sofa and go to sleep. That was how mad I was. I had decided at that point that I was leaving. I knew that at that moment, Adrian would have been dead. I went to work on that Friday and called Suzy. We were friends. She was still eighteen years old, and I had just turned twenty-eight years old. I mentioned to Suzie that I was having issues within my marriage and had to get away. At that moment, I found out that she had had a crush on me. This girl was from St Thomas, Virgin Islands, and yes, I just loved her accent too! She agreed for me to move in with her on the next day, which was Saturday. So I had packed my things up. Adrian was still going at it. So I had got a cord and tied her up in the closet and left. Adrian had asked me just before I left. *Why don't I want her?* The thing was that she did not allow me to want her. All she kept doing was driving me away! And I figured that she would get out of it when I was gone. So I finished packing up my new Chevy Malibu up with my things and left Adrian with our car, the Mercury Cougar.

Adrian had called me, or I called her. Either way, she had told me that she at the hospital. So I rushed over to see her. Adrian had broken her wrist from getting untied in the closet. I really was not trying to hurt her, which was the main reason that I had left her tied up in the closet. Now since I was really gone from her life, it seemed like, per our conversations, she wanted me back. I thought about it. Adrian was going to be turning twenty-nine years old in the upcoming June, and Suzie was only turning nineteen years old in the months to come. Plus, I did not have to deal with any jealousy issues or arguments. When I had arrived to move in with Suzie, she had her brother living with her on a temporary basis. She asked him to take his stuff and move out. So the next day on Sunday, he got his clothes and shotgun off the closet shelf and left. He understood since I was there. He had to go, and they were cool like that. I did not know what I was doing or getting myself into. All I knew was to get away from my wife or kill her. Wow, what was I to do? Adrian kept spending the credit card funds that we did not have. I needed to get away from her. Now I had no one to turn to, and Akron was not an option. I did not want to call my mother for something like this situation that I was in. I would tell her later on, once things had cooled down for me. I could not believe that Suzie and I hit it off just like that.

I had left the military housing to Adrian as well, even though I was still responsible for it. But I knew that her being there was a short-time solution, especially since she had my son. Suzie was just wonderful. She could cook, and she was clean. And at this point, she was so happy to be my girl. I did not know if it was an island thing, but Suzie was proud to be with me! For the first time in a long time, I was feeling appreciated. A long-awaited feeling that I had been missing for a while in my life. I did not have to pay rent or buy food or any bills. I still gave her some money too, not much, but a little here and there. I could not believe that Suzie was glad to be with me more than I could ever imagine. She allowed me to handle my other responsibilities with Adrian and my son Ant whom I was truly missing. But I could not take living like that with Adrian anymore! Suzie and I started to go out more, like shopping and grocery shopping. I cannot remember us going out to dinner, not one time. Besides, she did cook well, and going out was never an issue. She was not materialistic, nor was I. We did enjoy seeing each other and spending time learning and understanding each other. Suzie was looking into my eyes and told me that if I was ever in Saint Thomas, the girls would go crazy over me and my American brown skin and bowlegs. We were making plans to take a visit there and for me to meet her family. She was saying how her family was well-to-do down there in the islands.

Right after our talk, she called her mother in the islands and allowed me to speak to her. Then Suzie asked her mother to send a few lobsters to her from the islands. She wanted to fix me a special meal and plantains with vegetables. I remember that Suzie fixed some saltwater cod fish on top of the stove, and it was the bomb. That food was awesome. I had never tasted Caribbean food like that!

I found out Suzie was doing nursing in the medical field and surviving on her own. Suzie had great work ethics, and surprisingly, she trusted me just like that because I was married and left my wife. She was never suspecting that I would be unfaithful to her. However, I was faithful to her, and to a point. But I still had a wife whom I just could not live with anymore. She did treat me like I was all hers, and I never compromised her way of thinking, not even once. Suzie was falling in love with me. I knew that this was not a final stopping place for me. Truthfully, I did not know how to tell this eighteen-year-old that all this was temporary. I was always at a lost as her eyes would light up when she had seen me or I came in from work. Every time, all I would do was hold her tight and tell her that I was glad to be with her. Sometimes, I would call her Adrian. But she had never said anything back to me. I found it amazing on how much better Adrian treated me when I was gone, and she wanted me back. We were crazy living together and civilized living a part! She was working me and trying to be nice because Adrian wanted me to come back home. I really did not think the reason would be because of my son. I was not bulging a bit. Finally, I was definitely in the driver's seat and had the best of both worlds. I found out that this time gave me the most control over Adrian. It was the leaving her that made her hurt the worst. She humbled down a whole lot. Now, I had two women to want me. I was beginning to like the feeling of this. I truly have real power over both of them. I just could not believe that it took me so long to figure it out! I did not know what I wanted or if I could stay with either one of them. I was in a good place, but truly, I was still not happy but was in an intriguing situation.

So Suzie and I started to go to jai alai from time to time but not often. There were a lot of folks gossiping because they had only seen me with Adrian, my wife whom I was now separated from. The people had these funny stares at us because they did not expect to see me with another lady and much younger at that. Now, I was figuring out that I was truly a dog, but I did try to be nice about it and wanted to respect women, especially since I had never liked the tears, which was a soft spot for me. Anyway, I held Suzie closer and went on about my business to keep gambling. Well, Suzie did not know what was going on, and I just kept it that way. She was just glad that I was holding her. Besides, she had deserved my undivided attention because she was taking good care of me. I was about to be without a job that I had to eventually tell her about. I had to slow roll it for as long as possible. Suzie and I did not do much of nothing but work and stay home, pretending to live like married folks. That was good for her. In reality, we really did not have much in common. It was June, and going into July, we had no summer plans, just our normal schedule that was working for us.

While I was back at the office, to my surprise, LaDana, came walking into my office, and I had all but wished that I was living with her. She stopped by to let me know that she had finished all the Air Force Reserve training, including BMTS. As I was talking to her, she wanted to tell me something. I wanted to think that she had a crush on me, but it did not feel like that. I was totally surprised to see LaDana because most of my recruits didn't return to visit me, very few! That look on her face said more than her words. But she would not talk. I really could not figure it out, and when she had left that time, I did not see her again. Normally, after putting in almost twenty-five recruits in my two and half years, very seldom did a recruit return to see me, as I stated earlier! I was a good recruiter, but against my better judgment and having too much going on! Leaving the recruiting job was best for me! Besides, I did not want to tarnish my career in the Air Force! I allowed Adrian to persuade me to make many terrible decisions with my life. Not to be funny, being with her and married to her, it almost felt like I was cursed! I could not break away from her. I never understood why she wanted me back, and then, she took me back. Were we both sick, crazy, and cursed, with each other? I don't know exactly! How could I still be missing her, even though I was creeping around to see her with more women!

I knew deep inside my thoughts that Adrian was no good for me. Did I just like making her jealous? Was that my real control over her? Sometimes, when I was alone, I would sing that song "Thin Line Between Love and Hate." I really was not trying to cross that hate line for what she did to me and messed up the credit cards. Adrian did pretty much the same thing to me over and again. I would always say, "You can take the person out of the ghetto, but you cannot take the ghetto out of the person!" I did not believe she was that ghetto to get me before I got her! This was the only thing that I was thinking that totally made sense. Anyway, I had to get ready to do my reserve duty at Westover ARB. The base recently went from Air Force Base (AFB) to Air Reserve Base (ARB). Then part of the base was being downsized due to governmental budget cuts and sold off to commercial interests. I know that to process in as a reservist for the second time, from being at Pittsburgh IAP, in Pennsylvania and I was getting used to the routine and the RPA Man-Days that would come from time to time, to get extra assignments and duties. I was already onboard! This time, it had to get sign off at legal, and I would be issued new uniforms for my reserve duties. After, processing in, I would then go to my assigned unit. Well, while I was at legal, I met this Air Force Public Affairs Officer by the name of Maj. Rick Dyer. I was assigned to her 439th Base Information Management Officer. I was the assistant information officer under the supervision of MSgt. Jackie Davis. I was glad to be carrying the rank of TSgt. Now, I was no longer at the bottom of the military ranks. I did not think Jackie liked me much, but I was really into her. Jackie never even looked at me twice. I had thought that she was on the wild side because mostly, all they talked about was who could drink the most or how drunk they were the night before. Jackie was between a blond and brunette and nicely built. Sometimes, I guess she would wonder about her and me from time to time, and maybe, that was why she gave me a hard way to go. Other times, I must have found the soft spot in her heart because she would normally let me do what I needed to do. I did really enjoy working with Jackie, Sue, Dave, Pat, and the other folks. Plus, we handled military messages and Freedom of Information and Privacy Act stuff and of course the base mail system.

Suzie did let me use her new car, the Corolla, most of the times. To go to the reserves or whatever, I would drop her off at work and pick her up. Or she would drop me off at the reserve unit at Westover ARB and pick me up. We had a good little system going and right on time. A few days after, I returned from my first reserve duty. I went to see Adrian, and she was living at the hotel. Things were pretty bad, she and Ant were eating the cup of noodles with hot sauce. Also Adrian was about to take Ant out of KinderCare because she had informed me that her emergency voucher had arrived, and they were moving to a low-income housing at Bowles Park. Living there had beat the projects at Stow Village. Stow Village was no joke. It was straight-up ghetto. I had to arrange for our furniture that the military were holding in storage to be delivered there. Our new address would be on Nahum Drive at Bowles Park. We had road by to see it, and I did not want my son to live there. All the apartments had bars on the windows. It was straight-up ghetto. Thanks to Suzie, now I was hanging out with my wife too. Adrian also told me that we had to go to court on the twenty-first of August in Manchester, Connecticut. I took them back to the hotel in Manchester and went home to Suzie. I had informed Suzie on everything that was going on and on how I needed to use the car. Suzie was nice about it but did not like me picking her up late sometimes. I told her that I would work on getting better to settle things down between us.

About that Saturday, on the eighteenth of August, it was surely a hot day at that, as the other August days, Adrian called me and told me that the car just stopped running. It would not move. She just left it around the corner from jai alai at 93 Weston Street and Jennings Road, in Hartford, Connecticut. By the time, Suzie and I had arrived, the car was towed, to the gas station. I got that information from the policeman that was there doing the report. By the time I had got to the gas station, I could only get some cassette tapes, Atlas maps, and a few other items. My coin change and CB radio, with the magnetic antenna, were all gone. Somebody stole it, and when I had inquired, nobody had it. So I just left the car there with the bad transmission. Now, Adrian did not have a car to get around in. Now Suzie could never find this out—that I had Adrian in her car! Boy, was I living on the edge and with no car of my own. Besides, Adrian will now be riding the bus and taking taxis to get around, go to work, and drop off and picked up Ant. I did help out on occasion with some of the errands! Now, I was beginning to miss Adrian again. This feeling was something that I could not explain. Anyway, it was Tuesday, the twenty-first of August. I had dropped Suzie off to work, picked Adrian and I up some McDonald's breakfast, and we would be on our way to court. We were planning to get another continuance and appear to court at a later date. I was to appear to the court room with nine counts of check fraud and on three different dockets. I did not recall what Adrian's count were. I did not know that many people from Manchester. Of all of the people that I knew, I would have never guessed that I would see someone there from the Air Force Reserve at Westover ARB. It was no other than Maj. Rick Dyer whom had just met him only two weeks earlier. I was so glad that I had stayed in the Air Force Reserve and did not quit. This was one of those times that I knew my mother was praying for me! Maj. Rick Dryer. I introduced my wife as herself.

Then Maj. Dryer asked what were we doing there. I handled him my folder with my wife and court documents in it and the charges. He took my folder and told us to wait right there! By the time it was over, not only did I not have to attend court, but he had gotten all my charges null and stated to only pay the restitution when I could and told us both to go home. My case was settled. Wow! Then, he told us that he was a lawyer in Manchester, Connecticut, and a small claims judge! I was just baffled and just could not believe what had just happened. I did not have to take him to dinner or lunch. My court case was done! Over just like that! I could not wait to tell Suzie what transpired, and believe it or not, she was happy for me, unlike Adrian would have been. So that night, we went to jai alai to celebrate my victory. By the time September rolled around, I had not found a job, but I was actively looking. Of course, after this court case that I had just won, I was done writing bad checks. Most time I was home at Suzie's house after dropping her off at work. I was watching the news, and they said a black man was found dead in the yard at his home in the Hartford, Connecticut, area and expected foul play. I did not do much for the holidays, nor my two sons' birthday. I was not seeing them much either. Especially Big Mike in Ohio. Of course, I was not liking the situation, that I was in being there once again—no job, except the reserves!

I would see Maj. Dyer from time to time at the base, but he never mentioned my check situation ever again. He was one white dude that did not see color with me. He will always be remembered by me! Forever! I had finally called my mother to tell her that I had left my wife and my son did not have milk or food. So she had sent me a money order, and I received it a few days later. I had called Adrian and told her it would be coming soon—money from my mother. Adrian had to find another babysitter, and she did. She also changed jobs and started working for the Department of Labor (OSHA). Adrian had really learned how to get around in Hartford. I was glad that she had not quit. Actually, she was stronger than I had imagined! It was a few weeks later and earlier in November, Suzie was talking to one of her Jamaican female friends. I heard her say that LaDana was dead. I beamed into the conversation to see if it was the same LaDana that I had recruited. And it was! So I tried to quiet down until Suzie had finished talking with her friend. Then I just kept butting in. Suzie was relaying to me for what had happened to LaDana. Here it was as Suzie was telling me. The Jamaican friend was saying she and LaDana were friends and that LaDana's boyfriend had them all at gunpoint, and no one could leave. He then had killed or shot LaDana and before killing himself. He had told the Jamaican girl that was friends with Suzie and LaDana that he had killed LaDana's father in the yard, and I remember the news that I had heard. He would let the friend live, only if she would tell the story. She had agreed, and then he killed himself!

I was just at a loss for words. I had recruited her and recently seen her. I know for sure that she wanted to tell me something. I believe she knew the situation that she was in and did not want to get me involved. I knew that she wanted to tell me something! Now, I would never know because she is gone forever! I do know this. Without any doubt in my mind and no reservations, LaDana was truly faithful to or scared of that dude in her life. Her death was a total disappointment and shock to me! I was glad to had known her. What little time it was. I wished she had gone active-duty military, and I believe that she would have still been alive! I know that death will remain constant, and it is so unexplained! My life was so abrupt in the decisions I have made so far. The death of people, family, and friends often makes me think as to what I was doing! I was thinking about Suzie and if there was a future. I believe that she was falling in love with me, if she was not already. I really wanted to be there, back with Adrian to really be there for my son. I did not like him living in Bowles Park, in those apartments. I missed his fifth birthday and I missed my son. I just had to figure out how to deal with his mother. This was not going to be a good move, but I felt that it was something that I had to do. My mother would like the fact that I would be back with Adrian. My mother just loved her, but she did not know what it was like mentally for me! Adrian, regardless if it was for love or not and whatever the costs, she does not like to lose. Adrian did not want to lose me to anyone. I mean to anyone! And for that reason alone, I could always go back to her! I know that Millicecia (Suzie) was living her dream with me, and I could not continue to live like this with her. Suzie was giving me everything and all her heart. I did not know how to let her down easy.

My oldest son was turning ten years old on the tenth of December, and my youngest son was five years old. Suzie was less than twice the age of my oldest son! My point is I did not know how to let her down easy as she was only nineteen years old. My dilemma was not to keep doing what I doing by allowing Suzie to keep supporting me. I did not enjoy that part. Still Suzie was happy for me being with her! I really liked Suzie. I could not settle down with her, and the longer that I would stay, the harder it would be for me to leave. Plus, I was not going to chance her getting pregnant. That was never an option! So I left that morning, on the fifteenth of December, because the week prior was my reserve weekend with Suzie's car to see Adrian to confirm our moving in together again. Adrian had met me on Sherbrooke Avenue at Suzie's apartment in a taxi. Adrian wanted to come into her apartment to help me get my things and have the taxi wait. I told Adrian that I would not allow that to happen. And finally, Adrian agreed because I would have changed my mind. Then I went inside to let Suzie know that I was leaving, and my wife was outside waiting in a taxi. Suzie just grabbed me and held me so, so tight and started to cry. She wanted to do that makeup thing! And I was prying her off me. I was thinking that this would have not turned out well, if my wife would had walked in. I have to get my things. This is why I did not tell her upfront that I was leaving. After I finished getting my things, I returned my key to her, we kissed, and almost…but I walked away. Those tears, her crying, was just so innocent! I actually was feeling Suzie's pain too. I did not want Adrian to touch me! At that moment, as the taxi driver was going to Bowles Park, I felt a little broken. Those tears just kept doing something to me. If Adrian was crying, I would have never taken her seriously. But Suzie, I too was feeling her pain! I carried Suzie's guilt with me for a while because I knew that she loved me! We were only together for about six months, and even for that short time, I was not faithful to her. Adrian was not going to let that happen! Not at all!

Adrian would ask me out of the blue, if I loved her, Suzie. I would not answer her or change the subject. I would just ignore her or act like I did not hear her, even though I did only like Suzie. I knew that it was not about love for me. I was not sure that I was truly capable of love after all the stuff that I have been through with Adrian. Sometimes, I would mistakenly and on purpose call Adrian by Suzie's name. Adrian would ask me what I said. Then I would state that she was only trying to start an argument. By calling my wife by Suzie's name proves that she had touched me, just a little. We arrived to the apartment, and I was glad to see my son when the Adrian's friend brought him over. I was home with Adrian again and just glad to be with my son! We did not celebrate the holidays much because of the limited cash flow.

Our Thanksgiving and Christmas was pretty sad and not much of a celebration. On New Year's Eve, the best thing that I remember was shooting my gun several times in the air to bring the New Year's in. That was my fun for the beginning of the year! Adrian had the only real full-time job, and I was still in the Air Force Reserve, and we had no car. Adrian had already learned how to ride the CT Transit bus since I had left her to be with Suzie. Now, I had to make contact with this guy that I had met Westover ARB back in December. I believe that he was a staff sergeant (SSgt) or SSgt. Charles Hudson. We exchanged numbers and agreed to ride to Westover ARB together. Boy was this right on time. I now had a ride to go back and forth. I could not have planned this connection better, even if I had wanted to. Sometimes, I would think that God was truly watching over me! Anyway, I had a ride. Charles had taken me over to his house after our reserve duty, so I could meet his wife, Carrie. They both were truly nice people, and they were becoming friends with me and planned to meet my wife. I was able to stay in the Air Force Reserve because Charles was kind enough to give me rides. I knew that he was a true friend because he would not charge me for gas. Not at all! Or just maybe he did not charge me because I lived in Bowles Park. He had probably figured that I did not have the gas money anyway! Really, that conversation never came up. Charles was there for me. Charles and I would hang out from time to time, mostly talking. He really loved his wife, Carrie. They really had a special thing going on that I had only wished for.

The conversations with Adrian and me were mostly vague, and I stayed on the surface. It was good for me to talk with another guy since 1981. I had kind of lost that perspective and trust since my best man had betrayed me. And I told Adrian everything that I was doing, and it turned out to be true. For Charles, I did not feel that way. I knew what he and his wife had was real. We were not doing any of the watching and wishing to be with the other ladies. Come to find out, Charles was a churchgoer, and he sang in the choir. I believe that he was a deacon and inspiring to become a minister. Charles did mention that he went to the same church as NBA basketball player Rick Mahorn's mother on Blue Hills Avenue, in Hartford, Connecticut. Charles definitely had made some impressions on me and my life. Every reserve weekend, I had always enjoyed carpooling to Westover ARB to perform our monthly weekend reserve duty. This brother was about God's business, which made me to want to be around him even more. We even did our two-week annual tour together at the base, so I would still have a ride there and back. I just knew there was something different about the guy. Now, he had me engaging in conversations about the Bible, God, and life. I was wanting to talk with Charles all the time. I was learning more about the Bible. Other than Anthony Pope, I grew up with his dad. He was my pastor, Bishop JE Pope! Knowing Charles was my only other person that I could really call a friend! I did not talk to him about my marriage and my extra martial affairs because I just could not tell him anything different.

I wanted Charles to think that I was a good person. I had much respect for him. Besides, he was a mentor to me and did not know it! Charles did impress me and especially on how he treated his wife! They were a beautiful couple and in the church. I wanted that for me too but had not an idea on how to get there! It was sometime in December. I was looking in the Hartford Courant newspaper in the job section. Boy, did I see a nice-sized advertisement for CT Transit. Yes, it was the same bus that I, or Adrian and I, did ride those buses. The advertisement stated that the training was provided and paid to make about $15.50 per hour for one month of training, and thereafter, about $16.75. It was way less than working full-time in the Air Force. I figured that having a job making less money is better than not having a job or making no money. I had to apply for it because I really enjoyed driving anyway! Plus, I needed to make restitution on those checks and catch up my regular bills. I was still paying child support, and now, back child support was added to catch up the arrears. Then we were trying to get a forbearance on our student loans. Between the two of us, I was the responsible one. I was always striving to get debt-free. It was hard to do that with Adrian. It was a good thing that all the credit cards were mostly maxed out, and some of them were closed but still had balances that were sent over to debt collections. We were getting mail all the time or the phone calls from the bill collectors. We both avoided them at all costs. We would even answer the phone and tell the collectors that we were not home or they had the wrong number. It was like a full-time job just to avoid all the bill collectors on a daily occurrence. While I was waiting to hear back from CT Transit to see if I would get the job and to get a copy of my driving record, which was good anyway.

Adrian heard of a poker game that we went to after getting one of her friends to babysit for a few hours. We took a taxi. Boy, was it cold! We then rode the bus to the poker game off of Albany Avenue at the bottom close to downtown Hartford. We found it. We did stay for a few hours, and while there, everyone was talking about how they all got robbed. Not only were they robbed, but the robbers made everyone take their clothes off. And then they took all the money. To me, it seemed like an inside setup. We decided that would be our first and last time there. From that point on, our poker days were all but gone! The risks were too high and the stakes too low. I had made up in my mind that I did not want to lose my life or take someone else's life over poker. So we left to pick up our son and took a taxi home. It was tough getting around. Taxis and the bus system were our major means of getting around, except when I preformed my reserve duties on the weekends. We even took taxis to pick up takeout. Our life had taken another bad turn and seemed to be getting worst. Our gambling at jai alai was also like nonexistence. If we did make it, it was for very short periods of time. Believe you me, it was not working. There was no way that she or I would get rich quick or anything remotely closed to that. It was my son I felt who suffered the most, and yet he still loved his dad. Both of my sons on different occasions have experienced multiple times of waiting for me to show up to pick them up, and I did not show! Then they both would be disappointed! I learned this later on by each of their mothers.

Now, I could see one of my sons and not the other. Still, we had no car and could not afford one. I was glad that I could watch sports on the television because I was not able to do much else. I was bored out of my mind most times! Now I was missing Suzie and how clean she kept up her home. Adrian did not wash every day, nor did the dishes. I would be complaining all the time as to how messy she was! Our laundry was lying everywhere. The washing and the dryer were both in the kitchen. I did not know how much more of that I could take living like we were living! Adrian was absolutely lazy! No doubt in my mind, Adrian was just lazy! I was a twenty-nine-year-old, unemployed, but a working reservist. That was how I saw myself, just shy of being homeless! But on the first of February 1991, I received the call from CT Transit and the lady offered me the job to become a driver for the local bus company. It took me about six months to get another job, but never in my lifetime did I imagine that I would be driving a bus! However, the only way to get to work from Bowles Park was to either walk, find a ride, or take a taxi. I had to figure it out quickly because the bus driving class started on February 5. I had to also get ready for the winter's crazy and crazy cold outside weather, most of the time! I got a job and had to go to training at CT Transit bus company! We had to get fitted for uniforms too! The training was to learn some of the state laws, rules of CT Transit, safety, and to obtain a commercial driver's license (CDL).

Whether the weather was cold, raining, snowing, or on a good day, I would sometimes show up wet to work and just hoped that my clothes would dry quickly. This was an everyday occurrence to walk over four miles to work, which took almost one and a half hours. These walks made me to want a car even more, which was only wishful thinking because we did not have the budget to get a car. The thing was that I had to walk past Keney Park every day, and the nickname for Keney park was Murder Park. Several people were murdered, or their bodies were just found there. I was always on my P's and Q's. I had to always watch my back because I never trusted walking in that area. I always had to keep it moving, even though that was the shortest route to get to work. Every time I walked by the park, I walked in the street and also to avoid the debris, weeds, and the trash as well. That area of Keney Park was known to be a place for the Hartford Police Department to really find dead bodies. I was so glad that it was safe for me every time, and I never had one incident. The worst part for me was the weather. My hands, nose, and toes were the coldest parts of my body. Getting home was easier because I could catch the bus homes during training because I was only working Monday through Friday. I would then go to jai alai on Fridays after work, and Adrian would meet me there from off the bus or taxi. I hate to say it, but some paydays, I was still losing my money and staying broke after playing jai alai within a half-hour after getting paid. My money was gone! Just like that! I was desperately trying to get out of debt and pay our bills. I was hooked like a dog chasing the carrot. Plus I was playing the lottery and lotto. I would win from time and again. Still I wanted and needed more! I felt myself getting addicted to gambling, but I always thought that I could win and did sometimes!

Adrian jealousy was still too much for me. The arguments were too much for me as well. I saw that she started to gain weight, even though we walked together at Weaver High School. It was around the corner from where we were living in Bowles Park. On the warmer days, we would go up there and walk or run. Since I was running all the time, I was already doing good and losing weight. We changed our diets and ate more salads and stuff that was good for us. I kept losing weight, but she was gaining. I could not understand it. One thing for sure, I hated to be lied to. She never stopped eating. Adrian used to sneak and eat in which I had found out in one of our arguments. I just kept working out and running as much as possible because I had to stay in shape for the Air Force Reserve at Westover ARB. I was glad for the good days, sometimes cold, but yet it was still good enough to go to Weaver High to run on the track. Weaver High School was one of the schools that I tried to recruit some of the high school seniors from. I was really liking the lifestyle of Hartford, Connecticut, but not with Adrian. I was trying to take it and man up. It was just getting to be too hard to do. My mind could not conquer the matter with her. However, I was able to pass the bus driving course and obtain my first ever commercial driver's license (CDL). I was to drive that bus like it was a car, keeping that right mirror aimed at the rear right tire. That was the trick Ronnie taught me and to drive by knowing the landmarks and to always know where I was at, verses to remember streets and street names. He was an awesome teacher and driver!

Now I worked for the State of Connecticut, Department of Transportation, CT Transit. I was now an official bus operator, badge number 1492, and low seniority. It was the lowest seniority and equaled the worst bus schedules and routes. That was me, and I signed up for it, and I was in the local union. For the next two weeks, I was a ride-along and student driver. I recalled Ronnie Blank as one of my trainers. If I was running behind the bus time schedule, Ronnie drove to catch me up and then give the wheel back to me. Anthony (Tony) Charles was my other trainer, and he taught me that back tire trick again. I did get it rather quickly because I wanted to be a good driver too! The two weeks were over, and I was driving my own bus route and driving my own bus. Tony was from Trinidad, and his nickname was Trinidad Tony. Then, we hit it right off and exchanged numbers. These boys (men), Tony and Ronnie, could drive some buses. They were just bad, as in good! Since I had my own route I felt that I had learned from the best! Tony told me to think and drive it like a car, and I was doing just that! I had past my CDL on the very first try, like I really had a choice. I did not have a job. While driving my route, I was remembering everything they taught me. I was remembering the landmarks, just like Ronnie taught me! I was wearing my own CT Transit uniform. I went from one uniform in the military and to another one, both of them blue, with one exception, I was making a whole lot less money!

Nevertheless, I had a job. As we passed other drivers, I noticed we always waved our hands, which was a bus operator norm, and I had no choice but to get used to it. The bus rides went pretty smooth, and the driver's seat was comfortable too. I did not trust other drivers as far as cleanliness. The driver's areas were dirty, and I had to wash my hands often. The other thing was when using the bathroom. The only options there were to pull over with people on the bus and stop at the gas station or like a McDonald's or wait to the end of the route with an empty bottle on the back of the bus or hope the end of your run is at the mall or something close to it. Because I never knew. I always kept an empty bottle with me. Also no longer do I sit on the back of the bus! Since I was on the low side of seniority. I was normally on the K-route or T-Route to Albany Avenue and Stow Village. It was definitely a ghetto to the Blue Hills Road onto the city of Bloomfield. On the other side, I would go up to Park Street was the Latino side of Hartford (ghetto for the Latino's) to Prospect Street to New Britain Ave. It was pretty ironic. The farther that you would drive the bus out, the nicer the neighbors. So was meeting all kinds of people. Sometimes, Adrian would surprise me and show up on my route to the mall with my son Ant. He was soon to turn six years old. While I was glad to see him, I knew that she was only checking on me. I had to keep my cool and never to make a scene because it would be easier to lose my job. I was always nice, even if I did not want to be. So I played nice to her for my son's sake and mine too! I did give her free rides and transfers to get home. In that case, it was a win-win!

When I drove my bus route, I was driving the a split shift of four hours in the morning, four hours on break, and four hours in in the afternoon. I would get off work between 9:30 p.m. to 11:00 p.m. Of course, there were no buses to get me home. For all my bus runs, I would always have a thermos of orange juice and a bottle of water, some M&Ms and maybe a light snack. I could ride the bus back to work on my split shift and pick up my bus run from another driver on the downtown Hartford route. When I would go on my break after the first four hours, I would take their car back to the bus terminal and leave the keys in the car. That was safe to do because we had armed security at the gate. Sometimes, I would hang out at the bus depot and play pool or try to take a nap. It was the best that I could before the next split shift. Or I would just go home! I was beginning to meet and make friends to get rides home, a lot of times, but not all the times. Sometimes I would walk or take a taxi, depending on the weather. It was working out and going pretty well. I was getting a few phone numbers too. Girls would just drop their phone numbers off to me with little or no effort. To be honest, some of the women should have just kept their numbers because I never called. Now I had to keep Adrian from finding the other girls phone numbers. So I would mix them in with my CT Transit bus paperwork. I went from taking naps to living on the pay phones at the bus depot/ bus company.

It was sometime in March 1991. I had just relieved a bus operator in downtown Hartford and drove his car to him. I noticed this young lady as soon as I was putting my things away on the bus and adjusting my seat. The weather was getting better. I had on my gloves with the fingers out, my tinted glasses, and a CT Transit baseball cap with my jacket on. To say the least, I was pretty cool and was getting a lot of smiles from the ladies! Yes, I was flirting too! But this brown-skinned beauty with long curly hair smiled back at me. And I could not take my eyes off her as I was preparing to drive the bus! I believed that I had embarrassed her totally! She had on this leather coat and just looked awesome! As it was time for my route to begin, I paused again and looked at her and asked for her phone number. I did not know her name at the time, and right before the second stop, she, this beautiful young lady ringed the bell to get off of the bus. These were older buses, and the bell was kind of loud. As she gathered her belongings to disembark the bus, she placed a piece of paper with her phone number into my hand. It was just as soft and gentle as ever! I had a moment. Whatever it was, I had that moment! I was totally interested, totally! Once everyone had exited the bus and new passengers paid and got on, I was beginning to move again. I did the most unthinkable thing in that moment! I did not learn this in my bus training in my aspirations to becoming a bus operator. This is what I did. As soon as I saw her and made eye contact, I opened the front door to the bus and watched her hair blowing backward in the wind, with her leather coat that fitted her body, just right. And most importantly, she gave me the biggest smiles ever. I had not seen a smile as such since I met the young lady from England. At this point, I really did not mind walking home today. I wanted to take my time! This girl was just beautiful!

Being married to Adrian was no longer a priority for me. My interests were only in my sons! That's it! As I was driving my route toward Albany Avenue, I was thinking on how glad I was to get her number because there was a good chance that I would never see her again. This girl had me on cloud nine after blowing my mind! I was just ecstatic and beyond happy! I could not wait to get to the other end down Park Street. Park Street was a very narrow road with cars parked on one side. This street taught me to drive with instincts and skills, and it got easier and easier. I never panicked, not once! I was confident to drive that bus anywhere on the road. At the end of my route in Bloomfield, I had a ten-minute break before I would allow the people on. If the weather was bad, I would let them on sooner, depending if I had to use my bottle or not. So I looked at the paper she gave to me. And it was true. Her name was Denise, and I now had her phone number. I said I have liked another Denise or dated girls by that name before. I made up my mind to call Denise after I drove to the other end of my bus route. First, I had to go back downtown and to Park Street onto West Farms mall. I had drove other routes too, but I stayed on this bus route most of the time.

As my seniority was growing, I was able to get better bus route times. Once I arrived to West Farms mall. I took my fifteen minutes for a break, went to the restroom, and then for the time I had left, I called Denise. She answered the phone, and we talked for a minute and had to hang up because I was running late to back downtown for the bus lineup. We had to be on time for that, so I had a little time to make up. Once my shift was over, I made back to the bus depot, and this guy named Kendall Fisher noticed that I have been walking and offered me a ride home. We had good conversation and exchanged phone numbers too. Sometimes, I would ride with Mario on his motorcycle, and he would start teaching me Spanish. I was making friends with other bus operators. However, Kendall and Tony were my only real friends. We started to talk more and more. Then I had Charles who also was my friend and gave me rides to do my Air Force Reserve. The money I had was on the low side, but my life was beginning to take shape again. Plus I was playing pool again. My biggest challenge was to try to setup a date with Denise. I was getting that feeling again as to when I had first met her, and I just had to see her again. So Denise allowed me to come over to her place. My first visit was after my bus shift was ended, and I caught a ride with Kendall over to Denise's apartment building. I was a little nervous, not knowing what to expect. I was there in a strange building on South Whitney Street in apartment number B-6. I did not expect to see this handsome light-skinned brother knocking on the door. Nevertheless, he was there, and so was I.

At this point, I had to find out what was going on. I almost turned around, not wanting any domestic confusion and stuff because I had my own issues with my wife going on! So anyway, the dude and I had spoken, and I knocked on the door too! I did not care if this was a setup or not because I was definitely interested in her. Besides, I come too far to just turn around. Plus I had to walk home and then walk to work the next morning and not wanting to miss my shift. It was four miles to home and four miles to the bus company and an hour and a half walk either way. At this point, it was either leave now and walk it or take a taxi. That was not happening, but it did cross my mind! I knocked and said, "It was Mike," and she opened the door for me to let me in, and they had a few words, and he left. She explained that it was her ex-boyfriend Mark, and it was already over before she had met me. Then Denise told me that he had wanted her back. She had reiterated that it was totally over, and she had decided to move on. I believe that it was to the point of being unfaithful or something close for me.

Denise had quickly left that conversation and wanted to know more about me. I was just captivated by her beauty and kindness, having a little country in her voice. I had checked out Ms. Denise Burkes and put her at 118–120 pounds, twenty-four years old, which she was, and from Albany, Georgia. It was almost perfect. I believe that she had worked at a company called SYSCO, a distribution food processing company. She was enjoying the attention that I was giving to her, and I needed the attention that she was giving to me. I was not used to it! I would sing bits of that "Midnight Train to Georgia" by Gladys Knight. The fact was Denise was my midnight train to Georgia! Until I had met Denise, I was almost on empty with all the negative things that were happening in my life. If I did not just have bad luck with Adrian. It was pretty close to being over. I was explaining everything to Denise on our first date. I felt like I had nothing to lose. I had almost lost everything already. I had told her that my credit was messed up, my car died, bankruptcy, married with two kids, by two different women, etc. My list was long, and that baggage that I was carrying would have run her away. I was just brutally honest! At the same time, I told her that I was trying to figure out how much I wanted my dream to come true on becoming a doctor. I then told her the next possible opportunity that I was planning to leave my wife. It was like the only thing that she reacted to was that I was planning to leave my wife. Denise seemed too happy about that fact. Denise was not focusing on my past but any of our conversations that would put us together. It was at that moment. I knew she would be my girl! I just knew it!

The thing was that I was leaving Adrian anyway. Denise came along to know me and assist my plans to leave. It was almost midnight, so I decided to take a taxi home. I had such a beautiful evening, and then by the time I reached home, Adrian was just mad and upset. She had thought that I was with Suzie, and I was not. Suzie and I had totally stopped communicating. I told her that I had a lot to get off my chest and needed time to think. Adrian did not believe me, not at all! So we argued more, yet I had to get up in the morning. I did not get much sleep but did not mind. I was still on cloud nine! I was tired, yet I had to drive that bus. Denise showed up at my downtown bus lineup and brought me some lunch. She was only going to drop it off to me, and since I was on my way to West Farms Mall, I convinced her to stay on the bus. Then I had convinced her for me to drop her off to home on the way back from the mall. Besides, I needed her company because I was just tired. I was telling Denise at the end of the route for the few minutes that we were able to talk that I was into arguing most of the night and had wished that I had a place to go. She looked back at me and gave me the biggest grind that I have ever seen and agreed that I could move in with her. The old saying goes, April showers brings May flowers. It was definitely raining good on me. I was to move in that following day on Sunday. We had this connection that I could not imagined how to explain. Denise did not seem to care if I was married or not! Her focus was just on me. I believed that we just had to be together. Denise told me on how much of an impression I had made on her when we first met, when I stopped the bus and gave her all my attention!

With that one incident, I had stolen her heart! I was truly flattered! We touched our faces together to seal our agreement. I then dropped her off, finished my bus shift, and was able to get a ride home. I went home, and we argued more. Adrian would not stop! I knew that I was leaving, and Adrian probably knew it too. I was trying to be silent and avoid her because I knew that I would be gone on tomorrow. We got up about 10:00 a.m. and more arguments as we were trying to get dressed. We made Ant to stay in his room. I just had enough. We were fighting, smacking, pushing, and holding. This was the worst it has been between us, and I just snapped. I had had enough! I started to cut up the furniture. I cut up her clothes, and then I held her and cut her hair off. Mentally, I was just hurting, but I was not feeling any remorse or love from Adrian or myself. At this point, I was just on empty. I could not take any more of the jealousy, false accusations, insecurities, etc. I was done, and she knew it too! I then packed up my clothes, shoes, uniforms, and important papers. When I decided to leave her again in less than a year about eight months. We both knew it was over! I do know if she would have called the police, I would have…let's say it would have been over for her! I was not going to jail. I had found out that she would had never called the police on me because she still wanted me back. Adrian just hated to lose and especially me. I still did not understand it all. Adrian stated that she did not love me but I thought that she did, even though she never wanted to let me go, even after I cut off her hair. The part that I did not remember was cutting her hair! The taxi came, I took my things, and just left after kissing my son good-bye! This time I knew that I had to leave and not look back. I knew that Adrian and I were just too toxic to stay together! I knew at that point that the next time, Adrian would kill me or I would to her! I had to leave because there were no room in my mind for her to stay. I wanted to just leave.

Denise was a blessing for me in disguise. The timing of our meeting and hitting it off was just impeccable. I made it to Denise's house, unloaded the taxi, and explained the argument with the fewest details. Denise was a brand-new start for me. She gave me the keys and told me to get comfortable! Denise was as nice as she could be and taking a leap of faith to be with me. I was definitely smitten with her! This was the second time that I had left my family, and only now, I was missing both of my sons! I had issues with their mothers and especially the woman that I married. This time, I knew it was over, and being with Denise made it less difficult for me! I had asked Denise about her ex (Mark), and he had left her alone after he tried calling her again. She told him that we were together. Now, we had to truly get to know each other and start our future together. I was still in awe for meeting Denise, and now, we are living together. This woman was just unbelievable and incredible at the same time. The more we talked, the better it sounds, and the better I felt. She wanted to help me to get on my feet and my life back in order. She was the first woman I have ever known that I was her interest. Then Denise told me that she wanted to help me get a car. I had told her how my wife just left my car in the street when it had broken down. She comforted me and wanted me to heal by getting over Adrian! She really did not want to hear about Adrian! Denise wanted to be there for me! I was totally not used to a woman of this caliber! Denise was just fantastic. I kept wondering if this was for real. Denise had interest in me. I had kept questioning the facts! But could this be true? Denise was not going to let me go back to Adrian. I believe that her mind was made up as soon as she knew that I was married. She saw me doing better and from a perspective that I have never encountered before. Not ever!

I was definitely at a new level in relationships. This girl was just simply too good to be true! I kept trying to find something wrong with her! I had terrible credit, and Denise wanted to assist me in getting my credit back together, so I could get a car. I was so tired of walking to and from home, getting rained on, or being late to work, and sometimes, I did not get paid for the day. She had my attention, and I was definitely her man! I was exclusively committed to her. This girl just blew my mind! Adrian could not touch what Denise was putting out! Plus, we had way better conversations!

Now I had to get to the bus company to sign up for my new bus bid on a new route that was based on seniority. A few days later, when it was all said and done, I was able to pick up a different bus route. Now, I was able to go on later by catching the bus, right outside her apartment and relieve the driver downtown. The thing was, I would work until closed and then, if possible, catch a ride home to Denise or walk. My life was getting better already. The second shift was working much better for me. A few weeks had passed, and Denise's ex was still giving it another try. Then she had told him that we were living together! That did it, and he decided to press on! I had never suspected her of anything. For one, she was definitely invested into me and carrying most of the weight, bills, etc. Denise was pushing me to save what I could and that she would add to it to help me get a car. This went on for a month or so, and I was able to convince her to go to jai alai to try to obtain more money too if I was able to hit a few numbers. We caught the bus there, and I would win from here or there. If I had won anything over $500, there was this guy there that would cash people tickets for a small fee. I was winning from time to time, and Denise would push me to leave. Again, people would be looking at us kind of strange. This was now the third woman that I was with, and she was not my wife. Again, I did not care! You would not believe who I ran into. Adrian and her friend Howard, we met and went our separate ways! I had not talked to her since leaving, and she let me know that my son wanted to see me and I had some mail at the house! The conversation was going on. Then I placed my arm around Denise, and we were on our way. Denise had kissed me unexpectedly to show me her approval. Wow! Denise did not mind having this married man. Now, I was wondering if her ex was married. I had asked her, and she stated no. I must say as I was thinking of the guy that Adrian was with, I could not get jealous. Actually, I know that I am a dark-skinned brother, but Howard was black and purple mixed together. He was definitely darker!

Based on Adrian's reactions, there's one thing I knew for sure: Adrian did not like Denise! Adrian and I had a promise that if we ever left each other that we would do better than we were currently doing. Well, let's just say that I kept my end of the deal! Because I knew that she was jealous. I knew that I could always get her back! Adrian did not like to lose, and that was probably the reason she was not one of the best gamblers. Well, she wanted me to see my son and pick up the mail. That was really code that she wanted to see me, even if I was only passing through. I had Adrian hook, line, and sinker! Adrian would get all dressed up and bring my son as a pawn to ride along on the bus with me. Adrian wanted me to come back home without saying a word. I would only pass through and spend a little time with her and be on my way. I was not about to leave Denise and become miserable again. I had finally had a peace of mind. I remember I was driving the K-route on the bus, and this little boy got on bus eating an ice cream cone, and I had denied him and his mother to board the bus unless they got rid of the ice cream cone, so she threw it in the trash outside the bus. This lady was furious with me, and I just drove the bus anyway with people continuing to board the bus. There was Adrian and Ant to ride the bus. My son Ant was eating an ice cream cone, and they got on the bus and pretended to show me a pass and boarded. I could not tell my son to get rid of the ice cream. I thought that the lady was going to call the bus company on me, but I did not hear about it. Not at all! On the way back from the mall, I was routed to Albany Avenue and Stowe Village. Anyway, this guy had gotten on from the mall and decided to put his feet on the seat in front of him. This lady came to me and informed me of what was going on. I popped the emergency brake and walked to the back of the bus with my cap and half gloves on and told the people we are not going anywhere unless he removes his foot off the chair. I was about to radio it in and call the police. Then I said, "Take your foot off of the chair or take your feet off of the bus!" Without hesitation, he moved his foot, and I jumped into my seat and we proceeded to downtown for the bus lineup! Sometimes, I did have days like that and even to call the police and then cancel it because it worked itself out. Well, that day, Denise was not suspecting me of cheating on her with my wife since I had to go over there during my four hours break that day. So we hug and pressed on! I vowed to myself that I would never be Adrian's husband again. At some point in our relationship, Denise was wanting to go to Atlanta, Georgia. She had family that lived on Cleveland Avenue, but we had to wait until we had a car, which we were working to save for. We were saving, and I had almost $500 toward getting the car. I wasn't gambling much. I was doing the day-to-day stuff. We were going to the grocery store and very little gambling.

Denise pretty much gave me an ultimatum. Either don't gamble as much or she would not help me to get a car. Well, sometimes I gambled and lost my check, and we would walk four miles home. And other times, I would win, and we would leave in a taxi. I did not like or appreciate ultimatums, so I called her bluff. Most times I had won, and she was able to get me to leave. I had kept my same bus route because it was working. In our relationship, we were doing pretty well, and Denise got quite the love bug. Yes, she was falling in love with me, and still she was helping me to get the car. What Denise did not know even though I did not want to, but if I wanted to, I could still always go back to Adrian. Since things were really well between us, I did not want to mess it up.

One day, I saw Kendall at the job and had asked him if I could borrow his car. It was a nice and clean sporty VW Jetta. He had asked if I could drive a stick shift, and I told him yes. I was glad that Lynette had taught me to drive her stick shift back in Ohio. Kendall was my friend forever! He was the kindest guy I had ever known. He allowed me to use his car. It was like a Thursday night that I was off. I went home to pick Denise up, and we were on our way. So we had decided to go to Red Lobster in East Hartford, Connecticut. It was on. The weather was quite pleasant. I must say that I was not the total best a stick shift driver, but my parking skills still needed a little work. We were in the car, smooching in a much serious way and the car, started to roll in the parking lot. We felted it moving just in time for me to panic and hit the clutch and brake at the same time right before, just inches away, I would have hit the parked car in front of us. The stopping time was just impeccable! That moment of time that we shared sealed the deal between us.

Denise was totally in to me, and we were making our own history! She was liking everything that we were doing. Denise was cooking, cleaning, washing clothes, and all. And we were not married! Why would anyone get married when the milk was free! This is where it all messed up for me! She was totally into me, and I was still healing from a broken marriage. My mind was not even close to right, especially for one woman. Let's just say that I had the big head and did not want to settle for one woman. No, not yet! I needed a ride to Westover ARB to do my reserve duty for October, and that weekend, Charles was not available. I was stuck and had never missed. Plus, I needed the extra money. I just had to find another way. Denise had called her best friend to give me a ride, and her name was Doria. And Doria worked for Congresswoman Barbara Kennelly in downtown Hartford. This Doria, I felt that she did not like me much because Denise had told me after the fact that Doria only did the favor to take me and pick me up. Doria had a nice light-blue Opel, and it was almost new. On the way there to the base, I had asked Doria if she could make as stop at Adrian's house in Bowles Park, as I had to drop something off. She agreed! I went in the house for about fifteen to twenty minutes. Adrian was getting dressed anyway, and I could not believe what was happening while Denise and Doria was in the car waiting from me, and I was already in my Air Force uniform. Let's just say that I handled all my business with my wife as she was still my wife. I could not believe that Adrian still wanted to be with me, but I knew that I would never go back to her on a permanent basis. I was just done! I quickly got myself together, fixed my uniform, and walked to the car. Denise was just beautiful, awesome, and trusting, which I did not deserve. If she had only knew!

I had come to the conclusion that it was the time in my life that was a little off for me to be totally exclusive as Denise was! She would even sometimes bring me lunch on the bus doing my drive on the bus route. But I was just not ready for the full commitment thing! So I played along for the ride! Still with a good woman, I was not ready to get married again, just yet! Plus, I had to get a divorce first! I knew that Adrian would have given me a hard way to go if I had tried to divorce her at that time. Adrian and I still had our thing going on! See what Denise and I shared was too good for me to go back to my wife. Denise was helping to do better and want more. But somehow it was putting distance between us, not much distance, but some!

One day I was showing Denise my gun. She held it and seemed to be scared of it. She wanted me to keep it away from her. I thought that that was good for me that she was not the violent type or crazy female. This made me to relax around her even more! Now, I was back at work and driving up Farmington Avenue on the E-route, and I saw this just beautiful, beautiful Latino female (and a Penelope Cruz lookalike) get on the bus. I kept asking myself to stay faithful to Denise! I told myself not to do it! And before I knew it, I smiled at her and asked her to sit in that seat adjacent to me, as it was empty at the time, and normally, the senior citizens would sit there or close to it! This beautiful specimen smiled back at me and took the seat that I had asked her to. I was doing the small talk with her every chance that I could get while driving and keeping my eyes on the road. I did not know how I would be able to see her! I didn't have a clue! I just had to try! As she was leaving the bus, she gave me her number that I had asked for earlier and told me her name as she was exiting the bus. Her name was Florence as she softly spoke it! I did not know where all these beautiful ladies were coming from. I had to be smart about this and memorized all phone number and set up a code for each one as needed. I could not afford to get caught, and I had just showed Denise about my gun! Not smart! I did not know that I would meet someone else so quickly. Now at this point, I knew for sure that I was not going to settle down—not with anyone! And not anytime soon! I had just learned very quickly that driving the bus was more than driving a bus. It was a chick magnet and in every sense of the word! I was picking up women left and right. Let just say, I was getting phone numbers and holding the numbers. I could not pick them up yet because I did not have a car. I was twenty-nine years and felt like I was nineteen years old again. My body felt pretty young as well. I guess, I was in my prime or did I have another ten to twelve years to good! "Right?" I asked myself. I was definitely on my way to finding out since I had passed ages eighteen to twenty-two!

About the time I got off work and reached home, I had downplayed the day, as if I was only thinking of Denise and could not wait to see her. Really, my mind was on Florence. Nothing more and nothing less. I stalled on calling her. I wanted to see how she would respond to me by being married, but separated and having a live-in girlfriend. Meanwhile, I had to find me a car and needed Denise to help me to get it as we talked about it. So I brought up jai alai to try to get the money faster. Denise was not totally down with me gambling. She would go with me but did not want to stay there for long periods of times. She also told me to keep looking for a car and kept encouraging me. Denise was just so nice to me and part of that southern hospitality. On that Friday at the end of September, I found a dealership in the newspaper that help people with bad credit, and they would not turn anybody away that wanted a car. It was like no reasonable deal would be refused! How were we going to get to Andover, Massachusetts, to the dealership? That Saturday, we decided to take the train to get there. We only had to buy one ticket because I was in the CT Transit local teamster union, and all I needed was my union card. I tried it on the train, and it was all good. We were on our way. I was thinking that it has been a few weeks since I had met Florence and made no contact to call her. Now, that I was getting a car, I had decided a give her a call.

After the train ride and a taxi, we were at the car dealership, and I only had about $500, and that was it! We walked around at first, and it was only two cars that I was interested in, and they were the 1986 black Chevrolet Monte Carlo and the 1987 Cadillac Sedan Deville. It was charcoal gray and four years old. Both cars were about $14,500 each, and I was no longer interested in the Monte Carlo. The only catch after we had the test drive we were sold on it, and missing the down payment. I still needed another $1,500. No way I could not believe it. I had asked Denise if she could make the down payment, and she said yes with a smile! The finance guy was telling us about the financing terms and that their program would help people like me to start building my credit back up because the car would be in my name. What a deal that I had and a very nice girlfriend. I was well-pleased, and the payments were about $416.83 split in a bimonthly payment! This car was in mint condition! We talked all the way home planning a weekend trip to Atlanta, Georgia. Denise kept her promise in saying that she would help me get a car. Now, once we were back home, I spent some quality time with Denise, and then, I was all over the place a few days later. Denise knew that I had made some friends, and I blamed the time that I was away from her, on them. I was with some of my friends from the bus company. I had finally called Florence and was able to meet her at her house on Farmington Avenue, in which she lived in a two-bedroom apartment. Very nice place! We hit it off immediately. I was honest and told her that I was married but separated and had a friend that I lived with but was leaving.

Florence told me that she was from Puerto Rico and spoke Spanish to me from time to time in a flirtatious way. She had mentioned that she was twenty-three years old. When I had told her that I was in the Air Force Reserve, she also mentioned that she was considering joining herself, but nothing came of it. Sometimes, there were days that I would get upset with Denise and spend most of my time with Florence. Florence had a child, a little girl about three years old named Eliana. She and the baby's father had broken off their relationship a while ago! This was the second time that I was at her house and had just got there. This dude, her ex-boyfriend and the baby's daddy, was banging on the door. Florence would not open the door. I wanted to open it, so he would know that I was there. Florence would not allow me to. So we waited to get serious and engage in our time together. Florence was everything else that Denise was missing. I wanted to have them both to be completed! Now, Florence was my girl too. I had told her the truth about my situation, and she was cool with it! I really wanted her and was just intoxicated with their beauty and her long jet-black hair. While back at work, I just kept driving the bus and tried to stay out of trouble with the ladies.

One day, I had told Adrian about all my ladies, so she wanted to know everything I was doing and who I was seeing. It was sort of therapy for me, so I engaged in telling her. Plus, I did not care if she got jealous. So eventually, Adrian was also at this stop where Florence usually gets on the bus. Adrian and Florence were getting into it, so I popped the emergency brake on the bus, and to settle them down, I then asked Florence to catch the next bus. Adrian got on the bus with me, and we were off. Boy, I was in an awkward situation! Yet I kept doing the same thing and kept chasing the ladies. Now, after work, I had to go over to Florence's house to make up for her meeting mess with my wife. She wanted me more. I could not believe it, and from that day forward, she referred to me as her Stallion. I thought my plate was getting full. I went home later that day to Denise. That next day, Denise went to work, and I had a day off. The last week of October, we both were planning to take time off and spend it in Atlanta to see some of her family. Also in that October month, I was home alone, watching the news and come to find out, people was writing bad checks from congress. I could not believe what I was hearing about this congresswoman. I distinctly remember the name of Congresswoman Barbara Kennelly, and other congress folks were bouncing checks. The news was calling it bouncing checks! I was not the only one writing bad checks and could have almost went to jail! The thought that the legal system was not fair to all. I could not wait until I could tell Denise about Doria's congresswoman supervisor, especially since Doria was not so fond of me. She actually thought that I would take advantage of Denise. Even though it turned out to be true, but really it did not start like that.

I was truly genuine, and Denise wanted more from me than I wanted to give her. I was damaged goods, or that was the way I saw myself. At least until I was able to heal from my wife Adrian. Something was just broken inside me. What I allowed Adrian to bring out of me was not a pretty sight. I would have killed us and for what. I was so glad I realized that it all was not worth it and so much easier to leave. I did find out that it was more devastating to Adrian for me to had just left her. It was the leaving, which caused her the real pain! I knew that Denise was not the one to help me initiate the process from within for healing. Every last one of my relationships had started well, but there were no fairy tales in sight only to end that relationship and start another. Somehow, I was able to hold on to everyone and then some. Since I had a full-time job, I was able to give Adrian a few dollars for Ant's support. Adrian had never put me on child support while they were drawing money out of my check to pay the support for Big Mike. I also had to find some time to see Big Mike because I missed him as well. I had to plan two trips to Akron, one trip with Denise and one trip with Florence. I wanted to keep both of these women for long-term. That way, they would think that I was getting serious and be more relaxed in our relationship. I went to a jewelry store and got a brochure and just wanted Denise to see it. She did not get it that nothing could happen until I had got a divorce more sooner than later. I thought that I had game, so I was working it!

Well, it was time to go to Georgia for a few days. We both were excited to take a minivacation together and plan another trip to Ohio. It was almost halfway there when we got to I-95 South. Traffic was as thick as it could be. I did not like it at all, and then, I said I would never live here in Washington, DC. I really did not enjoy being stuck in traffic. This was just terrible for our vacation! I had never seen anything like it. Cars were everywhere, bumper to bumper! I had to drive all the way there because Denise did not have a license. I was trying to teach her some things on driving and let her drive sometimes. Even though I was slow rolling it because I would not want her to drive my caddy anytime soon and not to think about messing up my game. Let's just say I was a little selfish and had some ulterior motives going on with my other ladies and more to follow. Anyway, I was trying, and she was happy, always smiling and being happy! We finally made the sixteen-hour trip, and I was tired. I actually felt like the cold/flu was coming onto me because my body was aching all over. Later that night, I had determined that I had a cold/flu that was in me, and it was winning. Denise was trying to comfort me, without any soup and ginger ale, but I had those chills and shakes, and I was not feeling well at all. This trip was a disaster for the first few days, leaving I was down for the count and not going anywhere.

The Tylenol was beginning to help break my fever after I took a hot shower and then wrapped up in some clothes to help break my fever. This was a shorter trip because of my illness. At least I had that Kaiser insurance with my job, and I did not even use it. As I was feeling better, we did manage to see her family on Saturday in Atlanta off Cleveland Avenue. They were very nice! Denise's uncle kissed her on the cheek and said that he always kisses the ladies and shake the brother's hand. We laugh and kept it going for about three or four hours! I did manage to get in touch with one of my cousins that lived there that I had seen before. Her name was Dorothy. Yes, our mothers were sisters! Dorothy had seen my wife when I was there the first time a few years ago. I had told her that I was separated from my wife and really serious about Denise. We talked a little about our family pasts and made mention of going to Six Flags over Georgia but did not have enough time as we were leaving soon and headed back to Connecticut. I did tell my cousin that Denise and I were planning a trip to Akron to see and make a formal introduction to my family! In my mind, this little episode was only a formality. I was pulling out all the tricks, just until I found my own place that I was not quite ready for either. At this point, our little love connection was done and over. I had totally decided that I was never going back to Adrian, and I needed to pass this time with Denise. We were together, but it was over.

I could not get Florence, my Latino girl, out of my mind. She called me her Stallion, now that really stood out to me! While I really wanted to be with her, I still need to keep Denise. I wanted both of these ladies to continue to take care of me. Yet I still was thriving for more. I did know this that each one of my ladies was fulfilling my mental capacity. I was satisfied! It seems once again, we made it back faster than getting to Georgia. I was kind of speeding with the flow of traffic. While Denise was sleeping, I could only think of the time that I had spent with Florence. This girl had me tripping at times! I would ask Denise if she wanted to go and see me play basketball at one of the local elementary schools that another bus driver's friend had access to. As usual, Denise would be tired and not wanting to go anywhere. So I would call Florence to see if she was to go with me. She was thrilled. I was showing her off to everyone, and I did not worry about getting caught because Denise didn't like to go many places. She was homebody. I did have it made! Absolute freedom! I was driving the bus and noticed this older Jamaican lady would always say something, mumbling something under her breath. Once she saw me get a phone number or two, she would exit the bus through the front door and roll her eyes at me. Two days later, the same thing happened again as I got this phone number from an attractive island girl. I was all into her as she sat across from me. She was just a soft-brown-skinned woman about the same color as Denise. This day, I was driving the U bus route, and I was so glad that I was. On these routes, I did not have to worry about Denise or Adrian and Florence sneaking up on me or bringing me something to eat. I did not need any distractions.

I was just fine admiring this young lady named Yvette. She had the sexiest eyes and smile combination going on! It did not take me long to get her number. It was like she was waiting for me to ask for it. Yvette was nicely put together and long thick hair. I would take this young Jamaican lady over that other one anytime, and that was what I did. I met up with Yvette as soon as I got off from work that evening. Now, I was up to three women and plus a wife. With Yvette, I could not believe that I was with her. We talked, and I explained my situation. The thing was that I was totally honest! I told her that

I was married but separated and had live-in girlfriend, and we were not getting along that well, but actually we were! I made sure that all of the women knew that same story, so I did not seem like a liar or a dog. Still I called my self a puppy dog. The moment I kissed her. I knew she would be committed to me! I really believe that I could have stayed the night, but I had a standing obligation with Denise and wanted to be there for her. I did not like to disappoint her at all, nor did I want her to become suspicious of me messing around. I do believe that she would have known. So I just left Yvette hanging until the next time! In order to be there and spend time with all these women, I would pick an argument with Denise and just leave. Then I was able to see my other ladies. Then as the opportunity presented itself, it would be Denise and me, or sometimes I would go to the jai alai.

At times, I would lose my entire paycheck within an hour after receiving it, and Denise would again be there for me. These were the times that she would get all my time and attention. I would not go out much because I would have no funds! She even paid multiple car payments for me! Wow, she was really in love with me! It worked like a charm every time! The other times that we would go to jai alai. I would be winning, and Denise would say, "Let's take that $500 or $1,000, and she would do all possible to get me to leave. Then I would play on the way out as we were leaving. Denise was very supportive of me, regardless of how many times I had gotten upset with her. Denise always wanted to make up or start over again! She was sweet like that! Denise and I just keep on living on her income until I would get paid again. I didn't have a bank account, so I would hide money here and there and watched it start to grow. I was cashing my checks anywhere I could. I had to do something different because I knew that one day, I would be leaving her! It was starting to get cold again with the weather and the holidays around the corner. I was making my rounds with my ladies and keeping my distance in order not to buy gifts. Too many women and too little money. I had to be smart. I was not the type of guy that would spend all his money on women. Having a married wife was the only exception. It was around the middle of November, and my cousin Rocky called me and wanted me to pick him up at a truck stop around Newington, Connecticut, but his tractor-trailer eighteen-wheeler had to stay there. I was not busy and brought him up to see Hartford. First, we went to our apartment so he could meet Denise. Then about a half hour later, we went to Florence's home. This was where I did my entertaining, at least for my cousin. Rocky is the same cousin I kept missing in Atlanta when visiting our cousin Dorothy. We would always miss each other, and now, we are together in Hartford. I did see him from time to time when visiting family in Akron as he lived in Akron too. Florence would fix us something to eat. Some very good Spanish dishes and recipes, red rice and all that she had gotten from her grandmother. She was so glad to cook for the both of us. It was still early, so we talked and played catch up. An hour or so later, I had taken him back to his truck, and it had a bed inside. Rocky was impressed and wondered how was I able to be around such beautiful women and had it like I did. I told him that there was another one, plus my wife. Rocky said that I was the man! We then did our hugs, and I was headed back to see Florence. This was a no-brainer because Denise had thought that I was with my cousin Rocky, but Florence was where I really wanted to be. Then, I was with her for most of the night until around 3:00 a.m.! I went home and grab a shower and held Denise so close, as if I had missed her. The next day, I had told her that I had wished she was with me. She just smiled!

Now, all was back to normal, driving the bus, flirting with the ladies, making my rounds, and planning a trip to Akron with Denise for the first time to see my son Big Mike for his birthday. I made reservations at the Holiday Inn. I was glad to be seeing Big Mike too. I had not seen him for a long while. I called and told Lynn that I would be stopping through and to see my son. He was just so excited. We had a pretty quiet Thanksgiving, and it was not much of a Thanksgiving Day meal, but it was a meal. Denise could fix a few things good, like chicken, gravy, and rice, and it was good. But that was all that I could remember. Now Adrian could cook that soul food at times. I was not missing her food that much to leave Denise. Besides, I planned to get some leftovers anyway from Adrian as I would see my son Ant! It was now early in December; my reserve duty was on the first weekend and, I would be in Akron the second weekend. As for my reserve weekend, I was running really late, and if you were late, then you were red line, and I would not be allowed to perform my reserve duty for that weekend. I had gotten dressed and driving like I had lost my mind. I was moving up on I-91N to Enfield, Connecticut, and then, Chicopee, Massachusetts. I was still running super late from my normal time of leaving. I got to Westover ARB; the gate was a long line of cars going through the gate on Westover Road.

So I did the unthinkable and drove my caddy down the side lane at about ninety miles per hour, and I could not believe who had seen me. It was none other than CMSgt. Joe LaFrance (most CMSgt. are also known as Chief). The way he looked at me I could feel the steam from his nose. I had just made the time and thought that I was in a great big deal of trouble. It turns out that the base had no jurisdiction on Westover Road. I just knew that I was on his bad boy list, and I made every possible way to make sure that I had always stayed out of his way. That dude did not play, and I never really seen a smile. I had stopped over to see my son that Sunday after my reserve weekend, and then, I hung out with Tony Charles. Then he turned me onto some Mauby Tea, which was tree bark. Kendall was the other guy that I would see. They were my boys! The other good drivers that I was cool with were Jay, Blake (retired Army), Guy, Johnny, Robert, Mario (he taught me Spanish that I shared with Florence), and Ronnie Blanks, and he knew everybody's business. Well, everyone believed that Tony was my brother but had different mothers. While it was not true, we stuck to the story. I was still in uniform and turned down getting high. I did not like getting high and smoking. I did meet Tony's lady friend Dawn and his older son! Tony taught me my way around the bus company. I started to think about applying to become a supervisor. It was just a thought for now!

Meanwhile, between shifts, we would play some pool, and I would be there with Jay most of the time and a few others. I was about to take off on December 13 to 14 and blame it on my reserve duty and took military leave from the bus operator job. Meanwhile, Denise and I would be in Akron. I wanted to really be there for my son Big Mike's eleventh birthday. We had planned it to a tee, as the saying goes, and it all worked like something awesome. I did not let Denise in on what I was doing because then, she would be hip to my game. Besides, it was a win-win. Denise thought that I was intending to marry her, and I wanted to see my son and family. We had packed and ready to go to make that nine-hour trip. At least, I had a reliable car this time! This is the first time that I am bringing another woman to Akron, and she is not my wife! All I can say is that it felt a little strange at first, but I got over it fast! I just kept driving and paying those tolls! Going past the George Washington bridge in New York was the same. I had gotten used to it, and it became normal. Every now and again, I would let the dude wash my windshield. I would always think when I help people, even now, that could have been me, then I would keep it moving.

Getting to Pennsylvania was always the tricky state because you never know what to expect when it comes to the weather. The temperature was good, so I just pressed my way. Denise and I were talking and had some pretty good conversations, concerning our future. She was all in, and I was glad. I did not want any more drama, so I kept playing it cool. I kept saying that she was really a beautiful girl, but something about us was off. The only thing that kept playing in my mind was that I was not in love. That love stuff was giving me too many mental issues. If the truth be told, with all that she had done for me, I would have never returned the favor. I just have to be in love. For the number of women that surrounded me in my presence and others that I could not name. The word *love* was not the name of the game that I was playing. We arrived to Akron again. I knew my way around pretty decently, except my sister Terri and her family had moved to East Avenue on the West Side of Akron. We met my mother first that evening on arrival, and my mother cosigned and said that Denise was a pretty girl! My mother lived on East Avenue, too, but farther up the street, closer to Copley Road. I gave Mom a few dollars, and that was it. Akron was changing and the kids, my younger brothers and sisters, were getting older, married, and moving out of the house. Then eventually, Mom would have to get something smaller to live in. Her health was changing for the worse, with the high blood pressure and the diabetes. She would mix up our names sometimes. But still, my mother was going strong! We left and went to Church's Chicken to get a bite to eat before going to Terri's house. Denise did like the Church's Chicken after trying it for the first time! Once arriving to Terri's house, we all talked, and they gave Denise the third degree of questions, and she answered them. We then started to play cards and talked. I did not have a partner like my wife to play with because Denise did not know how to play spades but a little. I did not like to lose, and let's say we were not winning, and I was getting loud at times with Denise. So we finished that game and quit. So Terri and I were catching up, and she asked about Pooky (Ant), and I said that they were fine. Then she asked about Adrian.

Denise was feeling left out and did not want to hear about my wife, even though I was still married. Get this, Denise had gotten upset while we were talking and unbeknownst to me, she had taken the car keys, took my car, and drove off. No, she did not. I was thinking and could not believe it, but it was happening to me! I guess that I had taught her too much on driving and just enough for her to take my car. I was just furious. We all were outside looking for her and the car. That was not the area of town to just be hanging out and chilling. Finally, about fifteen minutes later, she saw us and then me, causing her to slow down. Denise was driving, but she did not know to stop the car first and then put the gear in park. No, Denise did the opposite by trying to place the car in park while moving. The car was in one piece, and I was glad about that! I thought that I would lose my transmission. I was too upset to do anything else, so I grabbed her up in her collar cursed her out. That was a first! I knew at that moment I would be leaving her ASAP but did not know when. That was so selfish for Denise, and I did not do that to her when we were just in Georgia to visit her family. I just thought that I had too many ladies to be a "yes man." I was thinking that I was not the one! I did not know what Denise was thinking! This was total nonsense! So we had left for the hotel because we had to get Big Mike on tomorrow. It was getting late anyway, so we had left for the Holiday Inn to check in. I was just upset with her and could not believe what she had done!

While she was trying to make up, I would not stop talking, and then, I kissed her back! Denise wanted me all to herself! No way that would be happening in this lifetime, but I played the game for the time, and we stayed together! Why not?

The next day, we had got up late and got dressed and went to pick up Big Mike. Then we went to Swenson's to get something to eat. Denise was impressed for that kind of service on how the guys would run to your cars and take the orders. We were doing much better, and Denise promised to never do that again and take the car. Big Mike was eleven years old now and was growing up a bit too fast. Big Mike was a quick study and admired Denise too. They got along just fine. I was happy about that. He just did not know that she would only be temporary. We shopped at Rollings Acres Mall and just kept shopping at other stores, getting him some outfits and some sneakers and ice cream and more stuff. I was just happy to see him and that they were getting along. The next thing Denise did really surprise me. I was not sure if she was still trying to make up with me or trying to buy me. At this point, I was only marking time in our relationship. Anyway, Denise just brought Big Mike a kid's boys' twenty-inch bike that we had to fit in the back of the Caddy. Big Mike sat upfront with me. It was a nice move, and my son was just so happy! Let's just say, I started to become nice to her again, and now we would have a normal relationship again because for the most part, I did not want much to do with her. Let's just say that I made it clear that she could be replaced. I did not appreciate on how she showed out over my sister's house! I was not dating a ghetto chick. I kept telling her how special I thought she was and was totally disappointed that she acted quite ghetto. That hurt her feelings, which I was trying to do. Don't get me wrong, Denise was a classy young lady that had a moment of bad judgement.

I was just cussing, showing my frustration, and in fact, I was only missing Florence and Yvette. Besides, this episode, I was already making plans months earlier to bring Florence to Akron as well! I had Denise right where I wanted her on making this trip! I was ready to go, and we said our goodbyes, and we were gone on our way back to Connecticut. The more I made a big deal about it and stayed upset with her. It then provided me with the freedom to leave the apartment and time to think. Then I could make my rounds to see my ladies. I was missing my two ladies with the kids, and Denise had no kids. But Florence and Yvette seemed like they both understood me better than Denise. It was easier to relate to the both of them. Then again, maybe I started to think that I was selfish as well, like Denise! But I was in the driver's seat for all of the relationships! The times that I was not able to see Yvette, I would explain that I was tired from working, serving in my military duty or that I just could not get away from Denise!

Yvette was just so understanding and never demanding of my time. Yvette was just a real sweetheart! I thought about it, and the thing about what I was doing. I could never accept it if the shoe was on the other foot! I have always had a double standard, and people have relayed their opinion to me on several occasions. My double standard and a little charisma was working for me. And I knew this because I was doing it and living it. Because of these four women, I was turning more and more ladies away. I was really besides myself. And at the same time, I did not want to lose control or put myself in a situation, whereas I could not keep up the pace with my ladies, including the wife! Just before Christmas, a few days or so, Deborah, Denise's sister, came to the house to take Denise to her hospital. I decided to go too! They did not want me to know that Denise may be having a miscarriage. I did not know what to think. Then my ex-wife Adrian missed her cycle! Florence missed hers too and Yvette thought that she may be pregnant. I would have thought this was a conspiracy, but that thought was very much inconclusive. They did not know each other. I thought that Adrian was playing a game because she knew everything about everybody. I mean everybody! And Adrian wanted me back even more. I just did not know what was going on, but I knew that I had to get smarter by definitely not making any more babies. It was hard enough trying to take care of the two boys that I had already had! It was a flat-out mess, and no one knew it! I had to spend Christmas, the New Year of 1992, and my thirtieth birthday, wondering if Yvette was pregnant with my child.

Now, I was beginning to be more careful. It was pastime to do so! Literally, I was not able to afford more children and four more children at that! No way! My nerves were on high alert! No one received anything for Christmas from me, except for Denise. I had got her a card and a perfume set! Thankfully enough, while at the hospital, we found out that Denise only had missed her birth control pill. Now, I believe that she was too, like my wife, was trying to get pregnant. I was a nicest bus operator at this point and very courteous to the ladies. I was not going to be calling any numbers that were dropped off to me from the women upon them exiting the bus. My reserve weekend was just completed on January 11 to 12 at Westover ARB. I was planning to tell the job that the following weekend that I had another reserve duty to complete, so I put my paperwork in for military duty and got my excused absence approval. Then I had informed Florence that I was going to Akron and wanted her to go with me. She happily agreed. I had taken Florence everywhere with me, even to play basketball. I would always show her off. This Spanish young lady was just beautiful, and I felt alive and special from being with her. She had given me all her undivided attention that was missing from my life. We had some special moments together that I never wanted to let her go. I had to take a few of my uniforms for the Air Force, so Denise would not get suspicious. We kissed and said our goodbyes…

I mentioned that I had wished she could have gone because it was not possible anyway. Denise had to work. Then I headed over to Florence's house to pick her up and her luggage. But first, we had to drop off her little girl Eliana to her mother's her house while she would be out of town. They (her mother and stepdad) had to meet the guy that was taking their daughter on a little trip. Florence's stepdad was also a black man, which surprised me a little. It was a real short stay, and then, Florence and I were on our way to Ohio. I really wanted my family to see this girlfriend, and she spoke Spanish fluently. I was her Stallion and that I enjoyed how she spoke it to me. I did not think we had any hidden agendas, but other than what we had, which was great, we never talked of something more permanent, and I just never pushed it because I did not want to go too fast because she had a baby daddy, but I was in her hooks. I was emotionally fixed on her for real! Florence kept me pretty occupied on the way to Akron. Going through New York was hardly noticed as were going through it. We did manage to have some fun on the way there, making our own history. I do not believe that we had a dull moment. Florence always had this spark about, the smile, beauty, just everything was on point. I really enjoyed being around her. Somehow, I was beginning to let my guard down allowing me to become more fonder of her. She was a breath of fresh air with the softest smile. At this point in my life, having a child that was not mine was a deal breaker that I could not mentally handle. We were perfect, almost! I was not sure on previous visits, if we ever stayed in the same hotel room at the Holiday Inn, but we did have a nice place to stay. I had to skip seeing my son Big Mike on this trip because I did not want to set a bad example to him by me having so many women in my life. It was in Akron that I found out that Florence's religion was on the Iglesias Pentecostal side of her faith and was in line with my faith. My family enjoyed talking with her. Everyone tried to get their words pronounced in Spanish!

This was a fun trip, the family just enjoyed her, even my mother! By Florence being in the same faith as I am was a great plausibility for her. But my question was, could I love her with that man's child? I was prepared to find out! This was my main reason to come to Akron. Florence had accepted my two boys, my family accepted her, and the religion was a must, and now, could I accept all of her? I avoided to ever find out. I only could keep my interest, focus on Florence and what we shared together! I took her around to meet my cousins as I normally do. We ate at some of my favorite food places, and that was it. Our time that we spent together was the most valuable. Plus, I was able to get my head on straight for all that I was going through with all the possible pregnancies. I must say that miracles can happen as it did for me. I was facing a bona fide disaster, and my life was facing ruins with no recovery in sight. I was looking to have at least six kids in total, but so good so far! Now it was time to head back to Connecticut. This was a great trip. Florence and I really enjoyed our time together, which was quite productive. This trip was to play no cards and no gambling. I was back to driving the bus, and everything was back to normal for me, even Yvette.

That following Tuesday, on my bus extended break, I was called into the office of Tom Crispino, manager of bus operations. He was the small framed white dude but very nice and people friendly. At the same time, Tom meant business. I thought that I was in trouble or something, or someone had called me in over a complaint. I was a little uneasy, not knowing what to expect. I then thought I had damaged a bus mirror and did not report it. I would never report it anyway because the bus company policy was to charge it to you as an accident, but it did not go on your driving motor vehicle record. Tom relaxed my mind by saying my driving performance was out-standing, and I had just received a safety award for my driving. The meeting was short, very short! Tom told me that I was not fired, but I did not belong there as a bus operator. His point was that I was not a fit! It seemed to me that Tom was implying that there was more for me than driving a bus and I should go and find out what it was. I was already seriously thinking about becoming a bus supervisor. After leaving his office, I thought that this was the weirdest meeting that I have ever encountered. I was a good driver that did not fit in the bus company. I tried to put it bluntly, but still, at a lost. I wondered if I had taken too much time off, for my military duty. Really, I did not know what to think, but his words stayed with me, from that point on. I knew that in my heart that I wanted more! I had only wished I knew why he called me into his office and then maybe, I already had the answer.

Now, it was the end of January, and I had to go and visit Yvette after my bus route was completed. Yvette had told me that it was an honest mistake. She was the only one that I believed. So we hang out until about 3:00 a.m. and then, I went home. Denise knew that I did not like what she had done, by trying to get pregnant! Denise and I were truly falling apart. Yet we were trying to fix it! I kept playing my part until I had another place to live. I was not happy at this point with her! Anyway, I went to my reserve duty in February and signed up to do some extra RPA Man-days, I wanted to get some money together to leave Denise and find my own place. Denise had taken care of me long enough, and now, I wanted to be on my own. I came across another military message requesting reserve support. I quickly volunteered for it and was easily approved for it, per my past performance of being on temporary duty and did an excellent job! I was approved just like that and would leave on February 29, 1992, with a report date of March 2 at Robins AFB, Georgia. I had to cover over a thousand miles in sixteen hours, all by myself, down the I-95S corridor, with no tolls. Let's say I was used to it from my drives to Oklahoma City. I told Denise once I had got settled in, I would send for her to visit me. She was smiling and excited. It has been a little while since she has smiled like that. I just hit a home run, again! She was all for it! Now I was glad twice.

Denise and I were cool, and I had no baby with her on the way! I had about a week before leaving and put my notice in to the CT Transit that I was leaving again for military duty. Since it was for almost two months, I had given a copy of my orders. I think this is what Tom was talking about, that I was taking too much time off for the military. Yet I was not breaking any laws, and by law, I could be excused to attend military duty. I kept taking military time off for personal leave, as well. It was the law to be given the time off. I had just abused and stretch the rules a little! That week had come and gone. I was packed, and on my way, Denise held me extra close this time as I was leaving her for duty. This time, our goodbye felt different. I had also headed over to see Florence and told her that I would send for her as well. I then saw Yvette and told her that I would see her upon my return and that we would stay in touch by phone. I was all good! I visited my son last, and Adrian I informed her that I would be sending her some money for Ant. I also had made arrangements to receive advance pay from Westover ARB for my per diem and travel. I decided to drive this time since no rental car was authorized. I had already told the other bus operators that I was leaving for military duty again, and now, Hartford was in my rearview mirror. I will tell you that caddy was one of the smoothest air rides that I had ever experience and I was moving with the flow of traffic. When I had got tired, I pulled over at the rest stops, and kept it moving. I kept drinking those orange sodas from McDonald's and M&M candies, and I was good and ready to be driving. I was remembering Denise when we had passed through Washington DC and of course the traffic. I remember driving through Columbia, South Carolina on I-20W around 10:00 p.m. to get some gas and go to the restroom. It was sort of the ghetto too. I never expected to see it a little rundown, but everybody was cool. Nevertheless, I had my piece in my luggage and was not taking any chances in these strange lands. I was seeing places that I had never imagined to see. I was seeing hoods, ghettos, and cities that never had I thought to see! Nobody bothered me—nothing! Unlike me remembering driving through Peoria, Illinois, and was called a nigger. Some things I will never forget, and that word was one of them.

This was truly a pleasant drive, so far I wanted to get back on the road. The closer I had gotten to Georgia, the more alert I became. I was getting anxious to get there and get some real rest. I had about three hours to go and was pumped for it. I kept it moving and arrived about 2:00 a.m., in the morning that Sunday. I was glad that I was already familiar with the area. However, this time, I would be there without my wife. I was feeling like a married bachelor, living with my girlfriend. And now, I am in Georgia, a place known for beautiful women. Wow! I also thought about Denise being from Georgia. I just knew that my hands would be full. It took me a little bit to get a room. The first room had a naked guy lying across the bed sleep and seemed to be intoxicated. This Best Western Motel was a place I stayed before and my new home for two months. The clerk apologized and gave me another room upstairs overlooking the parking lot. I got my stuff from the car, then took a shower and call it a night. I was just tired! I slept until noon, got up, and unpacked my uniforms whatever else that I could and was comfortable as it was going to get. I did wish it was a Holiday Inn available, but it was not. I had to get refamiliarized with the area and find the gym. I had missed working out and basketball for about a week or so. I wanted to establish a routine of things to do, so I would stay busy and my mind active.

I found a payphone and called Denise collect. She missed me and was looking for my call. I would never be able to talk on the phone long because it was a collect call. Nevertheless, my ladies always accepted the calls from me, or so I thought. My first day of work was pretty good, the majority of the folks remembered me, and we struck up conversations, quite easily. Plus I knew my way around. I had to keep my nose clean on this one and to stay out of trouble. I did my job and worked with everyone just fine. I believe the main folks that I was working with was Bill, Joe, and JoAnn. They were a nice group of people and a little country. I really did not care; besides, they liked me and were pretty nice to me. That was all that mattered. I was doing my job and assisting in the publications backlog for the Air Force Reserve regulations. There was a ton of stuff to do there, and I was busy a lot but not all of the time. The good thing about these types of duty for being on active duty was that I was racking up on my active-duty points for retirement, and I and my family had full military benefits while I was performing military service while I was on active duty. I did not mind doing this because I was not driving the city bus. I was getting tired of it. Truthfully, I wanted to be back on active duty. Plus, I was making a whole lot more of money. It was much easier to pay all my bills and the child support too. I had to figure out how to get back on active duty. I just did not know how I was going to accomplishment such a task at hand. I could just hope for now! I was thinking that my ladies were in Connecticut, and I had an empty bed in Georgia.

Since I was a little older, I was not about to drive around look-ing for the ladies. I did not want to appear desperate. Besides, I was driving a Cadillac, meaning women came with the territory. I showed up at the NCO club on base, and the ladies were a lot younger. Meaning I had my work cut out for me. The NCO club was a little dry for the older, over-30 crowd, and it got me to thinking. I did learn that with the ladies, they were not interested in you unless you were with someone else. Therefore, I desperately needed a beautiful decoy that would fit the bill. I had called Denise and set it up for her to fly down to see me on the following weekend. I was all over her when she arrived. We went everywhere together and then to the NCO club after I was off work again. I learned that women overall love the competition. I made sure everyone noticed Denise, and I ignored all the ladies in the club. Out of all the fun Denise and I were having, including a movie, the one thing I knew that would not happen again, birth control pill or not. Denise would not be getting pregnant by me. We had a real nice time. I had called Florence and worked out the same deal for the following Friday. After work that Friday, I was at the gym when she had arrived. I left for the airport to get her. She was just beautiful getting off the plane on the tarmac. I was there to see her get off the plane. Florence had on this lime-green rain/trench coat and stylish! We went back to my hotel and got changed for the club. Again, the same thing. I was showing her off to everyone. Now, I started to notice the other ladies, and they were taking notice of me. I managed to get a few winks in, here and there. Yet I remained close to Florence. I thought that everything was cool between us. The next morning, we got up and got a quick bite to eat for breakfast, and I took her with me to the gym. We went sightseeing. I showed her a few of the historic military aircrafts. We went to the Houston Mall. We got something to eat and got dressed to go back to the NCO club.

I did not think the fast life was the scene for Florence. She had indicated that she wanted to spend more time with me, and still once again, I ignore it. I knew that I could not give her any more than what I was doing. If she had no child, I would have dropped everything for her. Florence wanted more from me. Still, I could never really feel comfortable with a lady that had a child with another man because I thought about what I had going on with Adrian. There would always be feelings when a child is involved. I was the example for what I was feeling. And then, there was doubt in my mind, on if Florence tried to get pregnant without my knowledge. I had a trust issue with her as well. We did have a good time, and I had planned to see her once I was back in Connecticut. We were all in each other faces with caressing and said our goodbyes, and she went in onto the airport terminal. I was missing her already. I was now looking at week three at Warner Robins, Georgia. I was still working at the Air Force Reserve Headquarters for a little while longer. This was a great duty assignment, and it helped to pave the way for my military career to become better. I checked on Florence, and she said that she had a safe flight. This time, she did not mention that she had missed me. That seemed to be a little off for me as I tend to notice the little things! Anyway, the job was pretty routine, except for the backlog, and I kind of knew what to expect since being on duty there from before. The food was okay on the base, and parking was iffy at times, but I always seemed to manage my timing pretty well. I was even building up some leave time, that I had only planned to cash it in, once my TDY was complete. This is my fourth week at the club, and I was talking to this young lady. I did manage to get her number before she had gone. She was not as young as the other ladies, but it was worth a try. I had called her and talked and got her address to meet. She was divorced and full of drama. That was not my scene, and after a few days, it was all a waste of my time. I was trying to see her during the week, so she would not mess up my weekend to get something going on at the club. I had talked with Denise on most days and also Adrian. I stayed in touch with Yvette too. But Florence would not accept any of my calls. I was concerned but still did not know what was going on. I did not know what she was doing and did not want to believe the obvious. Regardless, I just had to wait until my military tour of duty was over, so I would be able to see her again. I was getting used to being at Warner Robins. It was growing on me. I had my routine pretty down pack. Playing basketball and staying busy were the key factors, which prevented me from getting into trouble.

I was focusing on not to do anything stupid. I was getting through each week for the weekends to look forward to. I had three weeks to go and counting the weeks left in April! I went to the NCO club that Friday, chilling as normal. This time I had a slow gin fizz to drink. I was mellow and relaxed until I had noticed this tall light-brown, medium hair, and slender built, and just beautiful being of a lady. I did not know if I should approach her because I was flying my girls in to keep my company with and make solid our relationships. However, I had not seen this one before. Still I was contemplating to meet her or not! I could not stand the suspense any longer. I finally decided regardless of how it would turn out, in my introduction, even if she had said no. It was worth the try! I was thinking nothing beats a failure, but a try! So I approached her and introduced myself,

"Hello, my name is Michael." She was young, so my confidence would impress her, so I thought.

She replied, "I am Kimberly Hayes, but people call me Kim, and I have not been out in a while." I made eye contact and said, "The closer I got to you, the more beautiful you are. I just had to take a closer look!" When I saw her hazel-brown eyes that did it, I was in and her smile told it all! I could not believe that I was a little nervous, but I was. It was like the very first time for me! I asked why she stayed hidden, and she stated that she was in college at Fort Valley, studying to become a lawyer. She was telling me all about herself and being from Nebraska and had just won the Queen for Miss Fort Valley State College (FVSC). I was impressed again, and she was going to be in *Ebony* magazine in the April 1993 edition almost a year later. I was in shock and caught off guard a little, and I was thinking that this is as close to a celebrity that I had ever came in contact with. I played it cool and said, "Now, I know why you have been missing in action. Because you were crazy busy and to include going to college." I told her that I was impressed that she was a black woman, medium-good hair, beautiful, and smart. She smiles again! I wanted to find out more about her, and that was what I had planned to do. Then she had asked what did I do. I had decided to tell the truth again! The thing was that I was tired of lying! I had told her that I was in the Air Force on reserve duty, special assignment for a few more weeks, and worked for the State of Connecticut in the Transportation Department (there was no way, I would tell her that I was a bus operator). I also told her that I was thinking about going back to school to become a doctor, my lifelong dream. By this time, her roommates and friends were leaving and had asked her if she was going with them. Kim then had asked me for a ride. I happily obliged her and said yes! Then, I grabbed her hand and wanted to dance to a slow song by Whitney Houston called "I Will Always Love You." That song was right on time.

We left the club, and I took her to the college dorm, which was in the boonies, with a lot of trees and country roads. Then we just sat in the car and talked. Kim was only about nineteen years old going on twenty. I had told her that I wanted to do this right because I was attracted to her. Kim agreed, and I told her that I was married but separated and had a little boy. I continued on telling her that I lived with my girlfriend, and we were breaking up very soon! As we kept talking, Kim wrote down her number and gave it to me. Then she had told me that I was different. I was thinking that this was a good thing! She allowed me to kiss her, and she got out of the car waving at me. At this point, I was the happiest man in Georgia. Now I had to call the payphone in her dormitory, and then, someone would have to knock on her door to get her. Now, I was talking to Kim more than Denise daily after I had got off of work. Kim and I were in sync, really getting into her each time. We had talked and had some chemistry between us and really going on full blast. I kept telling her that I could not wait to see her! My workdays were a breeze. I could not get Kim off my mind. We were talking most days and had planned to go back to the NCO Club at the base on the upcoming Friday. I had planned to pick her up around 7:00 p.m. from the college. We had another date and my being married did not scare her off. She was so mature at her age.

Thinking back from my early Air Force days in Mississippi at Keesler AFB, I was getting to know this white young lady by the name of Jamie, and she was from Nebraska. What a small world, and our relationship was short lived. You see, Kim may have been from Nebraska, but I was really into her. It was like I was hooked, and nothing had happened between us. Wow! I was all dressed and ready to go. Now I had to follow the signs to get to FVSC to the girls' dorm. I don't know if I am ever going to get used to the country roads and all the trees. Some of the area, I remembered from the other night and was remembering the landmarks, like driving the bus. Anyway, I made it. I was there and got out of the car and went to the lobby and asked one of the young ladies to fetch her for me. After a few moments, I was wowed again. She was beautiful, with medium-length hair, those hazel eyes and her long legs. I could not believe that I was going out with a beautiful young lady that was to be featured in the *Ebony* magazine. This has never happened to me before not ever! We made a stop and got some chicken and then hit the club. It was very difficult to drive and keep my eyes off her. The club was not that interesting. It was cool, the music and all, but I totally had Kim's attention. We then decided to go to my hotel room. I did all but pray that my room phone did not ring, not even for maid service. We were there, and I opened the car door again, and holding hands, up the steps, and to my room. We got comfortable, lying around doing nothing but talking. She started to talk more and begin to confide in me, telling me some very personal things. I just listened. I was enjoying just to hear her speak. Kim had a very nice voice and very proper. Then she would tell me again that I was different, and I thought maybe because I was just older and knew a little more than she…

Then, as the time faded away. I was having the best time ever in Georgia, including that night we were together. There was nothing like it, not even close, until things had calmed down with us. Then she had asked me later on if I was trying to get her pregnant. Then I saw the tears drop from her eyes. What just happened, this was totally new for me? I thought that it did not matter because we were so into each other. Everything was just perfect. Then Kim went silent until the morning and wanted me to take her back to the dorm. I had no problem to take her, but I had to get my shower first. Kim was just upset, with no explanation, and I was totally disappointed. Then I realized that getting her pregnant would mess her up for college. That time, I truly was not thinking, but I truly wanted to be with her. I was totally vulnerable and would have changed to be with her. It seemed like it was over as fast as it started, and I did not want it to be over. I took her to the dorm, and she did not say goodbye! I was in total confusion and lost in my emotions at the same time. I got back to the room and noticed that Kim left her earrings on the nightstand. I was glad because I would see her again, so I kept calling her dorm. I figured that she had left her earrings on purpose and wanted me to beg to see her. I was not that guy! I wanted her. I really did but never would I beg for anyone!

I could not play that game. Besides, I had less than a week before my assignment was over. Then I would be returning to Connecticut. I did manage to talk with her roommate to bring her the earrings and had hoped to see her again. I was really hoping to see her. It was like a piece of my heart was missing! Kim and I had something real, but I probably scare her too! I had opened the door and slowing walking to my car. I was feeling something awful. In that short time that Kim and I were together, something happened to me. And I believe that something was almost love. It just had to be! One thing about knowing Kim and that night… Let's just say it was something special! That last week at Robins AFB, Georgia, was the longest week ever. I just could not want until that Friday came, and I had got my orders signed off. I was already packed, car loaded up, and ready to go. As I was leaving, I decided to call Kim one more time, and no one answered the phone at her dorm. Maybe, she was in class. I guess that was a sign, or so I thought! So I just left and drove to the highway, not looking back! This was one of my best drives ever for driving all by myself. It was just what I had needed! I know that this would be my last assignment there in Warner Robins, Georgia. While driving, I had a thought that I was all by myself and had approximately sixteen hours of driving before I was home to see Denise. I had pulled over to call Denise and told her that I was on my way, Denise seemed glad about it. So I got back in the car and kept it moving. I knew that I should arrive early Sunday and back to driving the bus on Monday. Boy, my mind was racing, and Kim was in the thick of my thoughts. I had no way to reach her, and now, I was over a thousand of miles from her once I arrived to Connecticut. Just to think about everything was not easy task to accomplish. I just don't believe. I got so messed up over a nineteen-year-old beautiful woman. I could not wait to get back to Connecticut to see my ladies to mask my pain. I thought that maybe I was getting some of my payback even though Florence was not talking to me either.

Now, I was down to three, and if Yvette did not have any children, she could had been my number one. It was still hard for me to be a father to someone else's children and not to my own. I did not know how to rationalize that in my thoughts. I had had to love my two boys first. This was my biggest issues with women that had children. Therefore, I only wanted to get serious with women that had no children. My mind was racing at one hundred miles per hour with all of my thoughts. I was not sure what I was going to do. But I had to do something, and I knew now that I was done with older women. Kim, she was way younger than I was, but what I felt was so real and innocent. The first time it felt like this, I was in Dayton, Ohio, with Lynette, but I was not faithful to one woman. Somehow, I knew that I wanted somebody younger for me. Kim did that for me. I did not know what I was looking for until I met her. Kim had helped me to find myself. I just wanted to be me with her. Boy, I just kept missing her, and once I was back in Connecticut, I knew that there was no substitute. Nobody I knew had come close to Kim. Once I had got home, Denise was glad to see me. I smiled and hugged her, only wishing that I was with Kim. This I was feeling was not easy to detach itself from me.

At this point, I no longer wanted to live in Connecticut. I needed a fresh start and had to keep trying to find it. I had already planned to keep searching for that next temporary assignment. I had to keep believing that something else was going to happen. I just did not know what? And when? And most definitely the who? I was now looking for my next wife. I knew that I wanted to be married again! Kim did more for me in the few weeks that I was gone than I had accomplished in the past ten years, including being married to my wife. Secretly, I had to find me a wife, and I just kept believing that I would find her! While I would yet hang out with the ladies, I wanted to find my wife. Day in and day out, my life was pretty routine! Except for trying to get in touch with Florence. Finally, we talked. I had called her from the bus yard, and she told me that we were over, and she was with somebody else. Come to find out, it was a white dude. I could not believe it, and it was like a slap in my face. I was upset and hung up the phone on her! I kept saying, "Me for a white dude?" I thought that I was her stallion. I had to accept it and keep it moving. I guess her patience had ran out for waiting on me. I must say that Florence was truly patient with me, and I was also married. I must say, "Life goes on!" I really liked having her. She was a beautiful sidepiece.

Of course, I had told Adrian all about her and Kim. Adrian wanted to know everything I did and with whom. It actually kept me balance by talking to her of my escapades. Or maybe it gave her a permission to have a cold heart for what she was doing. Adrian even told me that she had sort of dated one of the guys that I was in basic training with. It actually did not hurt me because I really did not care! Denise and I were hanging out pretty tight, and I would sneak away to see Yvette whenever possible. Yvette kept getting more serious on me and started to cry when I would leave. I was sure that I could move in with her because she never wanted me to leave. While that was well and good, I just had to get my own place. Denise was helping me pay some of my bills, so I was not that quick to leave her. I went to jai alai less and lesser because I wanted to get my own place. I had a little credit union account with CT Transit. It was growing, just not as fast as I wanted to. I was trying to focus on Denise so she would not be so suspicious. Sometimes, we would argue. Then I would go to see Yvette. I could only think of the song by the O'Jays, "Your Body's Here with Me." I needed to be free.

The months were just going by, and I received a summons to be in court for Big Mike's child support. I did not know if Lynn was pursuing or what because the support was still in arrears. Anyway, Denise could not get off from work on a short notice, and neither could Adrian or Yvette, so I took Ant with me. It was just he and I, so we were bonding a little. Ant always got excited to be around me, and I was good with that. I was running late as usual, and the traffic was hit-or-miss but still busy. I had to do an eight-hour drive in seven, give or take, minutes. Let's just say, I was doing at least above and beyond the highway limits until almost to Pittsburgh on I-76W. I was moving. I looked up in the rearview mirror with two flashing red lights on top of his white cruiser. I probably could have went to jail, but I think that having my son Ant in the car just saved me! I had a ticket for over $200 and still had to get it moving again Akron to make the court on time. I was about ten miles out of his way and punched it again. That caddy was a smooth riding car. The speeding did not feel like speeding in that car. I have to paid the tolls too. Then when I finally arrived, I was still fifteen minutes late. The clerk did not want to see me, so I had got noisy because of what it took for me to get there. Finally, the caseworker agreed to see me. I had explained again that it took me almost eight hours to get there. Plus,

I had got a speeding ticket. She had begun to sympathize with me, and I thought that it would be good until she had spoken the words, I did not want to hear.

She has to raise up my child support payments by double of what I was paying. Believe me, I did not want to give Lynn another dime and not one cent more! I had always thought that she would be spending it on another dude and not my son, Big Mike! I told her that it was not possible. I only drive the bus and pay child support on Ant, car payment, and did not have my own place. I then told her that I may as well, just kill myself. The lady told me that I did not have to talk crazy, and for me to keep paying what I was paying until my next review. I told her how much I appreciated it and that I really did not have it. I think that she was glad to see me leave. I briefly saw the family and took Ant to see his brother. We had got some ice cream together at Dairy Queen. I dropped Big Mike back home. And we had to hit the road before I had gotten too tired to drive. Even though we took a quick nap on the Pennsylvania turnpike, I had to get back Connecticut and get some rest, so I would be able to drive the bus on the next day.

That was a tight schedule, and it had to be done. Just think, if I would have missed that court date, my child support to Big Mike would had doubled. Denise was truly there for me. I would had not got the car, if it was not for Denise. I was starting to appreciate her a little more. I was feeling guilty and had a conscience. We had got back safely, and I took Ant home. I was so tired that I could barely keep my eyes opened. I took my shower and hurried to bed. I just made it to work on the next day, and I was driving that bus, so I was unusually tired. There were times that I was sleep at the light and played it off, like if was thinking! That day, I was killing those M&M peanuts and orange juice to stay awake, and it worked. I survived that day with a few near-misses with the bus. They were truly close calls. I had promised to never do that again. The bus was no joke. I was glad that it turned out the way it did! That following weekend, on a Saturday, I decided to take Yvette being Jamaican, to the Jamaican Day Parade (West Indies Parade) by Albany Avenue. This was the most fun that I had had all summer. Yvette and I had never smiled so much together. We were dancing very provocative and Jamaican style. I was doing it too and having much fun. This was my first time taking her out. Still she never asked for more than I was giving her, but her tears, her tears, would tell the story of her heart. I too could feel it, but it was 2:30 a.m., and I had to get home.

Denise was asleep when I got in, so I showered and got into bed too! The following week, I had to cut her sons' heads after I had returned from Westover ARB early on a Sunday evening and then over to Yvette house to cut her boys' heads. Those boys were so proper and nice to be around. It was strange for me to be around her sons, which only made me miss my two sons as well. Still, I was doing my regular reserve weekends, hanging out briefly with the fellas, but I was all about the ladies. Or ladies' man, that was my true identity! In September, while I was doing some of the RPA man-days, I had come across two more military messages, requesting volunteers for a special assignment, concurrent. I was down for both of them. It was for two months at the Pentagon in Washington DC and thirty-three days at Hickam AFB, Hawaii. That was a no-brainer. I did not even have to think about it and volunteered right away! The commander approved it without hesitation since I had just returned from Air Force Reserve Headquarters, Robins AFB, in Georgia. I gained automatic points from the commander for going to the headquarters buildings. I was in just like that! I had done another military leave at the CT Transit for just over three months. I knew Tom Crispino would not like it, but he probably knew that I was working on getting out of there. On the true side of things, I really did not have any plans of leaving. I was only playing it by ear. Well, one reason that I had kept going on the trips for TDY and special assignment was that I was only hoping to get back into the Air Force. I had truly messed up when I had got out in Oklahoma City. I had just over a month left to say my goodbyes and make my rounds. I don't know why, but I still had a soft spot for Adrian, and we made plans for her to come to visit, and of course, Denise would come to visit too. I had to finish up in Hartford, Connecticut, with driving the bus. Yvette and I, mostly me, was becoming distance. I had to start breaking away from her. I was fighting the feeling and did not want her two sons getting too attached to me with me going to Washington DC. This was the break I had needed, and I felt this course with her had come to an end. I just did not want to see any more of the tears. Her tears were just real. I was truly feeling her, and I felt her tears. Yvette was so gentle with me as even her eyes, and my heart was trying not to break! This had to be my last time seeing her! A week later, I found myself wanting to see her again, and that was the most of it. A thought!

Denise was keeping me close because we were going to look at rings. Still, I found myself thinking about Yvette. I did not want to let her go, and I knew that I could not keep her because my life was not going to settle down. I was not ready. Kim would be the only one that I would be ready to settle down with and at a moment's notice. But that was truly wishful thinking! Getting back to the rings, I only wanted her to think that I wanted to get her ring size and that was it. Well, and again, I did not want her to put me out, so I decided to string her along for the ride. I was planning to stay with her until I had enough funds to move out. I wanted my freedom, and most importantly, I needed my freedom for total independence. I was paying child support on both of my boys and doing better with my bills. I really slowed down on the gambling. That was messing me up, all the way around, but I was managing the gambling pretty well. Plus, I could not leave her yet. I have a little credit union savings account, and everything else was by cash or money order and one good visa to my name. That was it! Something was happening to me, my life was changing, and yet I was trying to hold on to parts of my past life. I thought often of the words Tom Crispino spoke to me, implying that I did not belong there. I really did not think that he was the least bit prejudice, but genuine! Those words, his words really affected me more than he could ever imagine. I had to think of doing more than driving the bus. I kept thinking and asking myself, would going to the Pentagon change my life? I did not know that answer, but I made up in my mind that I was destined to find out!

On the other hand, Denise now gets me part of the time, and now I was going out of town most of the year or at least three to six months of the year because I kept volunteering for special duty assignments. I really wanted back in the Air Force, and no one, I mean no one, could imagine that more than me! I wanted out of Connecticut, and I definitely needed a new start. Denise and I were getting a little edgy, but we avoided any conversations to acknowledge anything bad. So we denied it and played like all was well! I believe that the only thing or the only control that I had over her was that she thought that I may marry her. I was living with Denise for almost two years and had more in common with Kim in about three weeks. Kim was something special. We had something special. My meeting Kim woke something up in me that only scratched the surface for what I shared with Lynette in Dayton, Ohio, even though Lynette lived in Middletown! Kim was something special. I was thinking as my eyes stared off into space! The days were approaching fast, and now, it was time to go. Another drive away from home. What was I doing! I was winging it, and really, I was lost for words. I hugged Denise as the right thing to do, but I was empty, and my heart was numb. I did not want to hurt Denise too. I will always remember Denise because if it was not for her, I would not have had a car, a place to live, food, and she had helped pay my bills. Denise did not allow me to fail. I just had to figure out how to let her down easy. Really easy! I had packed up in my car, military uniforms and all, I was ready to hit the road. I held her and touched her lips again and told her that I would be sending for her very soon! I was glad that Denise did not have a car because I ran over to see Adrian and say goodbye to my son and then I told Adrian that I would be sending for her to come to visit.

Adrian was playing tough and doubtful that I was serious, but yet she agreed. I did know that I would never love her again, so we just had this understanding that we both agreed upon, and that was all we could ever have had. Let's say it was working! This was a very quick stop, and I was on my way to Washington DC for the next 350 miles and about six hours. I did not remember if there were tolls to pay or not. If so, it was only the George Washington Bridge in New York/New Jersey area. I had my advance and advance pay from the military, and I was good to go. I was holding almost $2,000 at a time for my travel and advance per diem. Plus, I would get a paycheck. And I had a check come in from driving the bus. I was doing pretty good, making it a lot easier to pay my bills. I now had the desire to cleanup my credit for real. I have no issues paying my child support. I had to pay $80 per month for Big Mike and $40 on my back child support and unofficially $200 for Ant. Adrian had a friend that gave me a unofficial copy of what I had to pay, if she had enforced it. So I kept cool with Adrian for the times that I was not able to pay the support. I stayed in her life, and she would not place me on child support. At least, that was the way I saw it! It was a win-win for the both of us! This was the same path that Denise and I traveled when we had gone to Georgia, a year earlier. I was remembering the states: New York, New Jersey, Philadelphia, Delaware, Maryland. With a stop in New Jersey and again in Maryland at the rest stop, I was there. The whole way down there, I kept saying that I was going to Washington DC to find me a wife. I do not know why I had said it, but I kept saying it: I was going to find me a wife in Washington DC. I could not and would not stop saying it until I had believed in what I was saying! I was in disbelief for the welcoming I received in the DC metropolitan area, actually it was in Arlington, Virginia. I was on Wilson Boulevard and Fort Myers Drive, I looked in my rearview mirror and notice the flashing lights on top of the police car. I was doing nothing, no running lights, no speeding, no weaving, no aggressive driving, I mean absolutely nothing. But the police just had to stop me and pull me over, because I was driving a 1987 black Cadillac; mind you, it was dark, the car was dark, and the windows were just a little tinted. Plus, I was a black man that looked-like a suspicious person, per the police. The only question that the police officer had asked me was, "Where did I work?" I stated: "The Pentagon!" Then, the strangest happened, the officer then stated that "I was the wrong person." Fact is: "I had to be!" It was my first time in Arlington, Virginia, and I had Connecticut license plates. I then figured that by working at Pentagon kept me out of some made-up trouble. I then only thought to keep it moving and to watch my back. They did not want anything! Absolutely nothing! Some things you just don't forget. Such irony, when I was sixteen years old, and living in Akron—I was driving my car illegally on a learner's permit only; I had my younger brother in the car, there was an incident just

ahead, get this, the police just waived me through. I could not believe
what had happened. My bottom-line was to really let it go, so this
negative event would not to spoil, the remainder of my time there,
but I would still remember this happening to me both times!

Finally, I had arrived at the Pentagon. I walked there since it
was in walking distance from the hotel. Even the parking lots was
gigantic. There were loads of cars there. I showed my military ID
card, and I was in the building, just like that and walked through
the turnstile. There were a lot of police there too, so I had asked one
of them where the room number that was listed on my orders. Get
this, I was truly on a special assignment. The beginning of my orders
read, "By direction of the President." I had mandatory card blanche
orders. I was working there at the top echelon for the Department
of the Defense. I even saw General Colin Powell on the concourse!
I could not believe my eyes. I was at the Pentagon! Never once had
I ever imagined that! This, me being there, was never in my wildest
dreams! I was there! I finally got to the office, SAF/FMBI, 4D110,
and first met Mrs. Carol Anderson, the Secretary. Then I had met
Mrs. Cathy Sparks, senior executive service (SES), appointed by the
president, and also, equivalent to a general. And finally, Colonel Paul
Huegel. They were the nicest people ever. I was treated like a person.
A real person. I was a technical sergeant (TSgt) and now assigned as
the acting executive to Ms. Sparks (SES). This position was awaiting
a major to come in to fill the billet for his next assignment. I was
in a major's billet. I quickly found out that the real power was in
that office. I would have colonels, majors, GS-15, GS-12, captains,
and anyone from our subdepartment come to me immediate from
a phone call to pick up budget investment packages to be corrected.
Also on the first day, I learned by Carol to say that Ms. Sparks wanted
it and that would give me the control. I actually had respected power.
I decided to learn everything about Ms. Cathy Sparks. She was a role
model to me and did not know it. Having that kind of power was
not a big deal to her, which impressed me even more! Ms. Sparks had
the power, but she was humbled. She respected everybody, even me!
A black man! When I was around her, for the first time in my life,
I did not have to defend my color, race, or culture. To Ms. Sparks,

I was just a person. I was chauvinist all my life until I had met Ms. Sparks! She was the reason I stopped thinking like my father and other men that I have known and realized in working with her and not necessary for her, that man and women are equal. This woman was bringing out the best of me! She had no idea how she changed my life. Ms. Sparks was the kindest gentleness giant that I had ever known. Carol and I ran everything for her and Col. Huegel. I did not drink coffee, but the office rule was the first one in that unlocked the door and turn on the lights made the coffee.

By the second week, I beat everyone in the office and made the coffee. Well, let's just say that my first pot of coffee was my last. I was banned from making coffee. I did not know how many scoops of coffee to add. I had no problem with that and became the small joke on making coffee for the office, but it never became a big deal! In that second week, Carol suggested that I would take the Pentagon tour to learn my way around, and the tours were given every hour downstairs with a little film and would take about an hour. So I went and learned as much as I could. I did learn that all around the outer E-Ring was over a mile long and over twenty-two thousand people worked in that building. Also there were more officers there than enlisted folks. That place had stores, drug stores, restaurants, cleaners, hair salons, barbers, banks, credit unions, post offices, clinics, Department of Motor Vehicles (DMV), and you could even play the lottery. There was no reason to leave the five-sided building, also known as the Puzzle Palace! My life was changed already, and I had an active-duty green military ID card. I was in the money, so to speak. The office I was working in managed part of the Air Force budget allotted by congress in the amount of over $40 billion. I was getting the hang of things and was handling the office as the acting exec, not with the big head, but I was the man.

I had to understand how Ms. Sparks wanted things and meet the expectation. Carol taught me a lot of that stuff. Carol was quite awesome and we became a great team! I had things under control even while she had taken leave and was away from the office. Ms. Sparks would come out to talk to us about the sightseeing tours in Washington DC, the Baltimore Aquarium, the Washington

Monument, and a list of other things. Even things that she wanted to attend, then, she said that she was going to get tickets discounted, upward to 50 percent off the regular price. That shocked me! I was not used to that…saving money! She was making over six figures and yet talking about saving money. Now, I just learned another valuable lesson from her on how not to throw money away, regardless of how much money you made. I became a sponge to Ms. Sparks! I started changing my spending habits. And then, I went to Air Force Recreation Services and to see what they had available. Get this, they even had discounted movie tickets. I was now hooked on having some fun and saving money too! Believe you me, I have plenty of money racking up. Still, I was at the Pentagon in my second week. I had never expected to be in such a place or expected to live my life as such, even though it was temporary. I just had to figure out a way to make it permanent! Somehow, I know that I was in the right place to do just that! They even had a full-gym, swimming, basketball, track, weights, and all and it was free for me to go. I was able to get two and a half-hour to work out! Being at the Pentagon, just kept getting better and better. I was walking back from the gym and saw these Army women walking on the concourse by the jewelry store. I was told that the women in Washington DC outnumbered the men by eleven to one, and what I was seeing at the Pentagon was just that! Before the second week was over, I *pssst, pssst* with my lips to get her attention, and they both turned around. I had pointed to the lighter one and waved her over to me, so she came to me with a partial smile. This girl had single written all over her face, I just knew it. I had asked her if we could get a movie or something. And then I had asked for her name and told her who I was.

I had just met Sgt Georgetta Bradford from Louisiana around the New Orleans area. She was a very nice looking and attractive young lady, about twenty-four years old. I had my first date set up in less than two weeks. Then I went back to my office to check in. Then I quickly ran out again to pick up movie tickets. That was it! Georgetta (aka Getta) and I were doing everything together, movies, tours, and shopping. We just had fun! Getta was attached to me, and just like that, we just hit it off. The first day that I saw Getta with her hair down her back, I was just in awe. She had really long hair. I needed this change. During the week, I would be at her apartment in Alexandria, Virginia, or she would stay at my hotel. I had told her too that I was married but separated and lived with a girlfriend but was leaving her, and that was one of the reasons that I was in DC trying to start over. The DC part was only wishful thinking, but it sounded good at the time! The girl was really fun to be around. I truly needed this break and this new experience. I really and truly felt alive! I knew that I was on the search for a wife and did not want to be tied down, just yet. I had arranged for Denise to get down there in the middle of November around the twelfth.

Back at the Pentagon, I was meeting all kinds of people that we were working with, Annie Barnes, Reggie Howard, Byron Strickland, Delores, MSgt. Debra Bowie, Maj. Barbara Gilchrist, Mike Novel, Eddie Pagan, Lt. Col. Greg Brundidge, Cindy, Maria, Mr. Robert (Bob) Stuart, SES, Mr. Robert Zook (SES), Pat Z (SES-select), Lt. Col. Cindy Deese, Lt. Col. Sandra Gregory, and a host of others. I would go to the offices of Byron, Reggie, and Annie B. We would be hanging out most of the time. Reggie and I had more in common. He was also in the Air Force Reserve, and his dad was a SES at Wright Patt in Ohio. A place that I used to be stationed at with the Air Force and actually my first duty assignment. From what I had gathered, Ms. Sparks, Mr. Zook, and Mr. Stuart, all started together with the government at GS-5, and they worked their way up the chain of command to become SESs all of them. I was truly impressed and was glad that I was there! As I was back in the office, luckily, I found a brochure for hotels and furnished apartments in Arlington, Virginia, I had called a few of them from my desk, as I was getting tired of the hotel seen. Finally, I called Cortland Park Luxury Apartments (a Dittmar Company). There were furnished units that ran about $1,700 per month and much cheaper than paying almost $3,500 per month for the per diem that I was getting. This was a no-brainer, and I did just that. There was no security deposit and a $500 rebate, if I would move in in November and a $500 referral fee. I applied and got approved and moved in just before the end of the month. This place was just luxurious, and I was getting paid too.

It had underground parking, pool table, swimming pool, concierge, that took messages for me, daily maid service, a phone in front of the toilet, and full kitchen. This place was loaded with folks from the embassies stayed there! I just could not believe it!

By this time, I met another young lady at the Pentagon, and we were just passing through to get to work. Somehow, I just caught her eye and got her attention. We started to talk. She was a cute little thing with short hair and totally stylishly cool. We talked for a few minutes before going to work and introduced ourselves. Her name was Tracey Coleman, and she lived in Maryland with her brother. Yes, I got that number, and she was kind of in control. She was a little older and knew what she wanted. I was on the fence with her. She was saying all the right things, but there was something about her that I could not trust. I just had this feeling that would never leave me, and I never could shake it. Let's just say that I was intrigued. Her approach was different and forward! She invited me out to dinner in Greenbelt, Maryland, to Jaspers restaurant with a soulful-type environment. I had immediately canceled plans with Getta and have a date with Tracey. The attraction and chemistry between us was just off. I could not put my finger on it. I kept having the weird feeling about her, yet we were hanging out together. Our first date, we went out to Jasper's, and afterward, I followed her to Laurel, Maryland, to her place. I met her brother there, and all was well. He then left the room so we could have some privacy. So Tracey and I just talked and holding hands. I had all her attention. Her eyes stayed focused on me. I decided to burst her bubble and take control back. I felt that Tracey like having control. I told her I was married and had two kids by two different women. Then she asked, "Why did I not tell her that I was married?" I stated, "You asked me out, so I figured that it did not make a difference." Now, I was back in control of the relationship and on my terms!

I was not about to play that cat-and-mouse game, and she would be the chase! So then we were at a standstill. Tracey told me then that she believed in equal relationships. She stated that whatever, a man could do, she could too" I told her then that she had just reminded me of my wife, and that was why we were separated.

Now she knew that I was separated. I changed the subject and told her where I was staying and asked her if she knew of anyone that was moving, and that I wanted to refer them to where I was living. Then she said she was thinking about moving closer in Arlington, so I gave her the information. Now, I was the mouse, and she was the cat in the chase. I would know it for sure, if she moves to my building. I was there for a few hours and decided to leave. I ended up finding a payphone and calling Getta and went to see her for the evening. Getta mentioned that sometimes she would be outside my hotel room door spying on me, making sure that I was alone. At the same time, I did explain on how it bothered me for canceling, and I just had to see her. As I was leaving the next day, I told her that the next two weekends that I could not see her because my wife was coming down from Connecticut. In all actuality, Denise was coming down on November 12–15 and Adrian from November 20–22, 1992. It was all set! Anyway, on November 7, that evening after leaving Getta, I went to the Classics Night Club in Suitland, Maryland, and then, I went to the Ritz Night Club, on E Street, NW, in DC. I had to check them out and see what was happening. I had met this dude at the Ritz and told him that I was visiting from Connecticut and trying to find the happenings. He was a cool brother and gave me the card to call for special tickets, and for one ticket to the Washington Bullets, NBA Team, afterparty.

Again, I could not believe it! I was in the mix and in the DC game! So this is what I had decided to do. I went back to work at the Pentagon, and it was on. I took a break and went to the Air Force Recreation service office and started buying extra movie passes and food vouchers. I started buying basketball tickets for a few of the games for Getta mostly to go with me. Then I had got a set of tickets for Denise and me to go for her visit. The Air Force had purchased annual games seats for its Air Force members in Portal Box Six (6) at US Air Area in Largo, Maryland. They were good seats too! I believe Denise came in on the train, so I picked her up at Union Station, downtown DC off North Capitol and First Street, NW. There was so much to do there, so we stopped by Fat Tuesdays and got a fla-vored liquor shot. They were good, and then we had got some fried mushrooms and fried chicken. I was really trying to impress her and showing her a good time, and she was falling for it. I showed her the Pentagon at night, and the next day, we went to Bolling AFB, so I could work out and play some basketball. Plus, the guys were checking her. I was just showing her how much I missed her. I even told her that after Thanksgiving, I would plan to come home to Connecticut to pay her a visit, like every two or three weeks, when possible.

The next day, on November 13, we saw the Bullets beat the Knicks by two points (Denise was not a big sports fan, but I liked her on my side). I was a fan of Mike Adams and Rex Chapman (Rex stayed hurt, but he was very good). And that Saturday night, we saw a comedy show with Joe Torry. We had so much fun, and I did all this to have a temporary place to lay my head and to keep my things there. Denise was having flashbacks on how it used to be when we met. Even though we had some nice moments, I still wanted to be gone, but I was sort of suffering through it because I did have the benefits too, which was not too bad! Denise was beautiful at that, and I did like seeing her hair going backward as the wind was blowing. We chilled after that and played a few games of pool in the recreation room in my apartment building. The time came and gone. Plus I had to be extra careful and was glad that no one had called me. That Sunday came, and it was time to take her to Union Station to ride the train back to Connecticut. To be honest, I did have a few mixed feelings, but she had to be going and to get back to work. That entire next week, I was keeping a very low profile and pretty much just talked some with Getta to get me through the week. Getta was really cool and never tried to mess up my game. I did not trust Tracey enough to keep a low profile. My work week was getting much better. I had started to review, budget investment packages, and proofreading them too. Then I coordinated them to the next level after Ms. Sparks had signed them off. It was the working at the Pentagon that I actually felt like I had belonged there. I had fitted right in there, like I had been there all along.

I remember my first day at the Pentagon, and I was in the bathroom at the urinal standing next to a one-star general (this was a white dude). I said to myself that we put our pants on the same way, and we go to the bathroom the same way. I thought at that moment that he was no better that I was. I said that people are people and was glad that this had happened to me. Once I dismissed the hype, I soon realized that this was just another building. After this event happened, I had really liked being there! Now, I had to get ready for Adrian to come down for a visit on Friday. I just wanted to see if she could ever change. I was also expecting her on the train. The cost of the train tickets roundtrip was a pretty good price. Plus, this was a first time on the Amtrack Train for Adrian. I was really on the move and barely had time to do my own laundry, but I managed because I needed to have clean underwear and socks. I was not the one that could ever get used to smelling my funk. I had to have clean clothes and a clean body. I truly think that was offensive to the other partner not having good hygiene. Or should I say that by not having great hygiene would be a deal breaker for a future with me. I was glad to have the stackable washer/dryer in my temporary apartment unit. I kept thinking about going to Hawaii for the first time after this TDY was complete. I did also had the best commute to and from the Pentagon, just by jumping on the train from Courthouse to the Pentagon. I only had to catch two trains, to and from. It was the orange line to the blue line and vice versa, and the entire trip was about fifteen minutes. The Metro train was just awesome, especially since I did not have to drive to the Pentagon every day.

I did think that I was the man in Connecticut. I now beg the difference since being in DC, but the Pentagon is actually located in Arlington, Virginia, with a DC address, a fact that most people are not familiar with. Anyway, back to the drawing board and the hustle and grind of work but steady. While I did stay pretty busy in the office on most days and still took breaks as necessary, it was the ladies, all the day long! I had found out when I had gone downstairs to the bakery, and I saw this girl at the register with a name tag on that spelled Chineta. She was light-skinned and fine and plain cool. This girl knew me, without really knowing me. We had just met. I liked her because I could not have her. I knew the first day that we could only be friends. It would never be a fly-by-night kind of thing. If I wanted to have half of a chance with her, I had to put my time in with no games! I did plan to keep cool with her anyway and build up the friendship side of things. The things were that I really did not have many lady friends and decided to change my approach. The Pentagon was a place, that I actually felt like I belonged there. It was a place that I had never imagined and everything I did not know that I wanted.

Anyway, back to the office to finish out the week and then off to pick up Adrian. She was fortunate to leave Ant with one of her friends at her job for the weekend. Like Diana Ross singing the song "Ain't No Mountain High Enough," Adrian had always found a way for us to stay friends. I really should change my habits, I was thinking, "What if Denise surprised me and showed up for a visit?" I would have been busted for picking up my wife. I was glad that it did not happen. While I had like variety of relationships, I had also enjoyed the spice of it or living on the edge. There she was Adrian. I could see her holding back her smile, like she was not impressed, but I knew she would be. Why else would you ride on a train from Connecticut to DC? Unless you wanted your husband back and the best that I could offer her was friends! My last trip to Georgia with Kim and now in DC gave me hope, and I did believe that I would find a wife there. Yes, even though I was married! I could not shake those emotions. I was totally hooked on the idea and not moving from it! Not a chance! Now, I was looking at other women, and this time, Adrian could not do a thing about it. Normally, we would be arguing as pastimes. I only wanted to show her that I was free! Totally free and to set her free as well! We started off a little rough at first, and then it got better, especially after she had seen my apartment. I think she was liking it too, to be in the DC area. There was so much to do.

At the same time, I knew it was over between us. Even the conversation had come up. I had a problem with trust. As I was told by her, no trust, no relationship! Plus, I still had my double standard as far as relationship goes! I could do whatever, and if you tried it, I would just let you go. That was the biggest reason I never trusted Tracey. She was sort of like me, and she thought that we could only be equals. I was very cautious to not get set up in a web of traps and someone gets pregnant. I was not taking any chances. Especially now that my wife and I are only friends that had a separated marriage and by paper only. Adrian and I were chilling. She tried to argue to see if I cared, then tried to make me jealous. None of the nonsense worked. I had already moved on and really didn't care what she was doing. So she saw that I was serious and had really moved on in my life, and I was giving up my ladies. Still, Adrian wanted to know everything that I was doing and who I was doing it with. We had talked into the night, and before we knew it, it was daylight. We had gotten dressed and went to get some breakfast, and I had to go to the commissary. I showed my orders, and because she was my still my wife, she was able to get in. We were in the dairy section of the store, I would not forget this day as Getta was walking around the corner, and we caught each other's eye. As soon as she saw me, she turned around quickly and was on her way to get out of there. I remember when that happened with Teresa in Dayton, Ohio, and she got out of there. I was glad that we had cleared that up just the day before. I was not her man or husband any longer.

Then Adrian had asked if that was one of my girlfriends. I said no, we were just friends. Denise was my only girlfriend, and everybody else were friends. I was using being married as my advantage for everyone, except my wife. That way, I did not have to be tied down or stay tied down in a relationship. There was no promises whatsoever to be made! I had the perfect freedom! And it worked! I would had given it all up for Kim back in Georgia. I thought of her often and on how I made of mess of things. Adrian had to hold her peace, and now she was in my world. We had planned to go out to the NCO Club at Bolling AFB, DC, and then, would be leaving the next day. She knew too much about me to hang out any longer. It was just a fun weekend, nothing more or less. I was glad that we both knew that we did not belong together. I changed the subject as I always do and told Adrian that Michael Jordan was coming to town next month, and I was getting the tickets once they go on sale with the Air Force. However, now back to our friendship thing was better than being married. For real! Before going out to the club and playing a few games of pool in our downstairs recreation room. As we were going upstairs to get dressed for the club, she reminded me that of her dream, that she had a little girl, and it was not mine. We were not together. I was wondering if she was telling me that she had really decided to move on, and this would be my last chance at her. I was good because I had already moved on.

As we were back in my apartment, Adrian continued to tell me again of the other dream that I had heard so many times before. She started again, saying that I found the love of my life. She saw me with this light-skinned, long-haired, tall, skinny woman, and driving a candy-apple red car. Except this woman would kill me! I did not like that part at all! We were talking, and I said the only way she would want to kill me is if I would be cheating on her. My biggest challenge would be is to find a way, not to cheat! I did not know, if that was a solution not to cheat or a question not to cheat. I really did not want to find out! As part of my game plan, I would always show up at the club, with or without a lady. The other ladies always took notice, especially if I had flirted or winked my eye. The other women always welcomed the competition. I was all over my wife, so we would seem like we were really close. Nope, it was all for show until I showed up at the club the next time! I was back to being me again. The morning came and gone, and Adrian was on her way back to Connecticut. I had to do my laundry and clean up my apartment. Then the maid would bring fresh linen the next morning, vacuum, and clean the rest. Now, I was back at work, and things were going smoothly. I took a break and walked around the building. I decided to go and see what the Army Recreation Services had offered for basketball tickets before purchasing them. I decided to go to the Air Force Recreation Services offered for basketball tickets. I was excited to see that my favorite basketball player of all time would be coming to DC with the Chicago Bulls. It was none other than Michael Jordon. Folks called me his lookalike, which made it even better. I did not care. I was planning to get two tickets once they go on sale.

I had to keep checking and eventually asked Getta to go with me. Getta was nice to be around. I really liked her too, but this might sound a little crazy, but since Adrian reminded me of her dream, I started to chase it again. I was looking for that girl, even if I would never find her. Adrian's dream was the exact woman I had hoped to find. I somehow wanted to believe that that dream was true. I often wondered how could she dream the woman in my mind. It must be a God thing! Nothing else could explain it. Besides and to the point, she was batting a thousand in my book! I just had to believe her and this lady existed in more than a dream! She was in my mind! I also would second-guess myself, stating that I had too much baggage, kids, no money, bad credit, etc. Yet I was all throughout the Pentagon, looking for this imagination in my mind! Could my ex-wife be playing me? That did not make sense because she still had feelings for me! Well, I shall see what the future holds! I just remembered again that I said I was coming to DC to find me a wife with love and all! If I was dreaming, this was definitely a good dream!

Adrian had gone back to Connecticut a week before Thanksgiving. Anyway, that same Thursday, I had gone to the Classics Night Club, as it was ladies' night! I wanted to see the ladies but did not get any numbers. I was there for a short while and had two drinks as usual because I had to get up for work on the next day. I was tired on that Friday morning and getting dressed for work, and my eyes were burning too. Then I had my green parka on top of my uniform because it was really cold that day. Once again, as I normally do, I walked to the Metro train, took the escalator door to the platform to catch the train, and got on the orange line to Rosslyn metro stop. I saw this light-skinned young lady. Her hair was down with a little hat and a black leather coat with a hood that she was not wearing. Therefore, I could see her face, and from what I saw, not seeing her face and hair together, I had concluded that she was nothing less than gorgeous! As she walked by me, I just had to say something, so I said, "You are a sight for sore eyes." It was actually a true statement from the club night partying the night before! I then said to myself, *I just have to have her!* I was starstruck for real! I could not get her out of my mind. Then I had got to the office, and I was late opening up the office. The first thing I did was, I grabbed a Post-It and started to write, "Hi, my name is Michael. As you can see, by catching the metro, we don't have much time to talk. If you are unattached, call me and give me a day phone number." I flipped the Post-It over and continued to write, "Also I may get tickets for the Thursday, Chicago Bulls game, and I want you to be my date. Thanks, for your time. My number is (703) 875-XXXX."

What was I thinking? I had never done anything close to this. I had planned to carry that note in my pocket until I see her again. The following week, I saw her again on Tuesday and gave her my note and was looking for her to call me. I jumped on the blue line the train that she had got off, so I could get to the Pentagon. I kept being late to work, hoping to see her again. Nothing! I would check with the concierge for any phone messages, and there was nothing. That Wednesday, I have picked up the Chicago Bulls tickets, and after work, we only worked a half-day because of the next day would be Thanksgiving. As I was about to leave for Connecticut to be with my girl Denise. She was still my girl but only for a little while longer. I was confident that I would be leaving her for good! As I was almost done packing to leave for Connecticut, Tracey was at the door! I had let her in, and she came to the bedroom as I finished packing. We talked, and we kissed, and as soon as we stopped, the lights went out. There was no power in the building. None! I could not believe it. I don't believe that Tracey wanted me to leave for Connecticut. But her game did not and was not going to work on me. Tracey could not control me. I truly believe that was our attraction. She could not have me! Anyway, that is what I believed! Well, I know that she did not want me to leave because what she did next shocked me! I did not trust this woman for some reason! Plus, I needed my strength for Denise. Somehow, she would had figured that something was up with me. I was thinking that I did not want to make Denise suspicious of me, not in any way!

Tracey did the most spontaneous thing that I could had never imagined. There was no power in the building, but she checked the water, and it was still hot. So she then went in the bathroom, cracked the door so the sunlight would provide some light for her in the shower. I had a dilemma to join her or not! I could not move. Everything said no, and I would not do it. In fact, I did not want to. I did not trust Tracey, and I did not want to disappoint Denise! I was leaving Denise but cared more for Denise than Tracey! Tracey told me after the fact that I should have joined her! I had her. Tracey now wanted me more because she could not have me! Believe you me, I was so tempted. I just felt a trap coming my way! There was something about her eyes that I could not trust. In a weird way, it felt like somebody else was in the picture with her, and I would not like that at all. I had a double standard, but I was honest as to what I was doing as far as relationships. So I allowed the chase between Tracey and I to continue. I was not going to get with her. I did not like to be pursued. I had to be the pursuer and felt it was part of my manhood. I never had that with Tracey. Everything would be her idea, even the first date at Jasper's restaurant. I then informed Tracey that I had to be going and made way with the little light that we had. For the first time, the temptation with Tracey did not get the best of me! I did not want to upset Denise, and she would put my stuff on the streets! I really believe that I had made the right choice, even though it was a tempting situation that kept playing over and over in my head! Plus, I did not want to get on the road and be very tired! Getta and I agreed to hookup once I got back in town! I would be home for a few days plus stop over to see my son!

I did mention to Denise that this lady in the building tried to flirt with me, but I had told her that I was with someone. Denise was glad to hear that, but I kept her on her wits about herself, so she would think that I was still into her! It was working. Yes! We, Denise and I, watched a little television and soon went to bed. She cooked a little meal, and we called it Thanksgiving. Her funds were kind of low from helping me to get on my feet, and I was saving to get my apartment to move out, and I was sure that she would not understand! So I thought to never bring it up! We had a good time anyway! In spite of my secrets, I thought that she would have a secret or two that she kept to herself. I would make some rounds and see my son and a few friends. Denise and I would see a movie together and try to make the most our time. We only touched on marriage subject just to keep the conversation going but nothing serious! I believe that talking on marriage was really the only string that was keeping us together! Then, from time and again, I would mention to her to practice writing my last name! That was it! I was glad when it was time to go back to DC. I could not wait to see Getta. Our relation-ship was not about stress and no talk about marriage. I was really not ready again to get married. I am off and headed back to DC. Once I had arrived back and settled in, I had got my uniforms ready for Monday and back at the Pentagon. Things were going pretty well. I would wave to Chineta in the Pentagon bakery and Dorothy Tucker worked in one of our FMB sections from time to time. It was during one of my breaks, I had injured my leg at the Pentagon in the POAC playing basketball. This guy went for the rebound and then came down with his foot kicking my right knee. Boy, the pain was unbear-able! Well, playing basketball was out for me for about a month. However, the crutches and leg-splint slowed me down a little, but I kept moving forward.

I was meeting a lot of people. I started to talk more with Annie Barnes (aka Annie B). This was just as awesome woman, and she was a good friend and full of wisdom. Annie taught me not to call people my boss, but supervisor. She said that a boss owns everything and that my only boss was God! Annie did not like that word *boss*! I respected that, and that phrase has always been in my thoughts! I would even walk to the cafeteria with her. There was something about Annie. I always wanted to be around her. I also enjoyed how she talked about her husband Grady and on how she loved him to death! I really appreciated those moments of her sharing with me, including her daughter Danielle! She really loved those two people! I sort of wanted that too but was still figuring my life out! I had figured that I would call that dude that I met at the Ritz and get a ticket to the Bullets afterparty. The dude came to my apartment and dropped me off a ticket. I was in there, and everything was private. I could not believe it. These guys were in the mix could be around and ladies everywhere. I saw Rex Chapman, Michael Adams, Harvey Grant, Brent Price, Pervis Ellison, and just could not remember everyone, but the ladies were everywhere.

I was talking to one young lady, and she was about business. Karen stated that she was in the import/export business. With those few words, I knew that Karen was out of my league. Well, it was a good thing that working at the Pentagon, and my rap was good enough to get her number. It was the next best thing since none of the NBA players were at her table. I was glad to have experience that got me out to the afterparty. Those ladies were about money and my $50,000 year, and child support was not going to cut it. I had quickly left after I got her number and called Getta to hang out with her. By this time, when I left work, the concierge had a message for me from Melody. I said Melody had called me and left no phone number. I was puzzled, not knowing but one Melody, which was my wife's cousin in Akron. I had thought why was she calling me and that I had never gave her the phone number. Then I had called Adrian to see why Melody would call me. I had thought Adrian was playing a game! So I decided to call Melody in Akron myself. I had asked Melody on how she was doing and asked why was she calling me? Melody had denied calling me. There was nothing to it, no connection at all! Then it hit me! The lightbulb went off in my head, and it was that moment as soon as I hung up the phone. I realized it was that it could have been that girl on the train that I gave the note to! I was so excited that Melody had called me!

I remember the black leather coat and hood with a soft beautiful face! Wow, she may have called me! I wanted to find out if this was the lady in my wife's dream that she kept reminding me of. I just had to find out, but not having her phone number made it almost impossible for me to get to know her. I finally figured out that the only way was to go straight home after work and hope the phone would ring. Then one day at the Pentagon, I decided to go to Pentagon City Mall for lunch at the food court and by myself. I did this just to change the scenery a bit. It was well… It turned out to be a pretty good move. I ate a steak sandwich and fries from Old Fashion Burger place and then walked around the mall trying to do a little shopping. I met this nice-looking young lady, and I saw that gleam in her eyes as soon as we made eye contact. Her smile followed, and I was in there! As I was talking with her, she seemed to be so happy! I do not know if she was impressed by my Air Force uniform or what. But it probably was the uniform. Wow! We introduced ourselves, and her name was Angelique Jones. Angelique had told me that she was a medical student at Howard University. I was just admiring her long hair, thin medium-built body, and she was soon to be mine, as I told her just that. She had given me her phone number as I had to get back to work. The only thing was that she wore glasses, but I figured to let that slide since she had everything else working for her. She had mentioned that she was twenty years old, and my age never came up, even though I had ten years on her. I was trying to figure out how would she fit into my plans, and now I was back to making rounds, like in Hartford, Connecticut.

Angelique became a priority for me since she was new. I wanted her to feel important, and then I would tell her that I was married and planning to leave my live-in girlfriend. It worked again! I was using the same line on all these females and in two different states, not including the two other states that I was living in. Angelique and I started to conversate, and she wanted to see me, only at the Howard University dorms, so it did not interfere with her course schedule. I agreed as she had a place to herself. The first time that I spent the night, everything went well, except when I got back to my car. I had got a parking ticket. I was not happy about that. I guess based on the sign, I just had to leave earlier. Anyway, I had to get back to my apartment and kept wondering why I got a parking ticket on a Saturday. We had to get this thing we shared between us changed to my place. Then Angelique would have to catch the Metro train to my place. I had told everyone that they must call first, just in case my girlfriend surprised me on a visit from Connecticut. It was a perfect plan and was working precisely. Doing this time, while at work, I had gotten notification from Westover AB that it was time for my annual military dental exam and cleaning, and I was to go over to Bolling AFB, DC, at the dental clinic.

My appointment was on the next day on Friday, December 11, 1992. It was just Big Mike's birthday the day before. I had promise to send him a toy and a football. He was twelve and did not say much but was always glad to talk to me! I just could not see him as much as I wanted to. Anyway, I left work early and caught the blue military bus from the Pentagon to Bolling AFB. What a great system, it took me right to the dental clinic. My name was finally called, TSgt. Michael Gilcreast. I followed the dental assistant to the dentist for my examination. All went well! Then I waited for a few more minutes to get my teeth cleaned and the fluoride treatment. This fine Latino chick called me for the cleaning. She looked just like the dancer/singer Paula Abdul. They could have been twins. After she had finished cleaning my teeth, it was time for me to go. Somehow, I mentioned if she was going to the Chicago Bulls game, which was the biggest news in town? She was a senior airman (SrA), and I was a technical sergeant. One thing for sure we are not supposed to fraternize with the younger troops. I thought maybe I was a little exempt since I was still in the reserves. This girl went berserk and crazy excited. She said that she was from Chicago and just loved the Bulls, and her favorite player was BJ Armstrong (#10). I told her that I had two tickets and the person that I was going with had just canceled. I had got her number, and now, I had an unexpected date. This girl was short. Paula Abdul, beautiful. I could not believe what just happened! Her name was Ana Ramirez and about twenty-one years old. It was time for me to leave and catch the bus back to the Pentagon.

Once I had got back to the Pentagon, I had made up my mind to tell everyone (Getta, Tracey, and Angelique) that I would be out of town from December 17 to 20, so no one would be looking for me. Another week was moving but not without a major issue that was on the horizon. I had about three weeks left on my tour, which would take me to the second week of December. Ms. Sparks contacted the Air Force personnel office and had asked if I could get some active duty MPA man-days, and they told her no. And she asked, "What do they mean no?" Ms. Sparks then called director of personnel, and after that conversation, I was now getting new orders to extend me to the end of April 1993. Ms. Sparks had appreciated the work I was doing and had asked me to stay longer until the major had arrived. I mean nobody in my entire life had ever gone to bat for me as she did. Ms. Sparks treated all people as people, regardless of where they were from. I thought Ms. Sparks was one great humanitarian, and I had always been honored to had worked for her! It was just that simple! This was a SES that no was unacceptable! I had to get my job extended with CT Transit and my apartment in Arlington, Virginia. I knew that this place had felt like home! I had new orders coming my way that begin with "by direction of the president." I was now getting to be more self-confident. This was truly a busy week, and tonight was December 17, 1992, and my brother Ernest (Ernie) birthday as he had turned thirty years old. Yup, we both were born in the same year! I could not wait to get off work and pick up Ana from the dorms at Bolling AFB and head to the game. This was our weekend after the Friday workday. I picked up Ana, and we were headed up to US Air Arena in Largo, Maryland. We both were Bulls fans, except Ana liked BJ Armstrong, and I was for my twin, Michael Jordan. I knew that the only thing that we really did have in common was our first names. Even though I still was called Jordan on the basketball court! This would be the first time that I would be seeing him person on the basketball court.

I was and we were thrilled! We had got some snacks and found our seats in the Air Force Portal Box Six (6), Pentagon leased seats. While I was interest partly in the game, I was mostly interested in Ana. I tried holding her hand, and that was okay, and then, I touched her thigh, and that was okay! Now I could focus on the game. I had to first know that I would not be wasting my time. It was on, and it seemed like we had something going on, but I would not call it attraction. The game was awesome. As we were leaving, I was able to get my arm around her. Yes! Then we walked to the car, talking about our victory. That Bulls win made our date that much more special! Michael Jordan had 29 points and the most spectacular blocked shot by the opponent's basket and the side corner. He ran down the court and just blocked that ball out of the court. Michael had another block shot after that one. I saw every bit of that awesome block shot! My other main man was Scottie Pippin, which ended up with 19 points. Then Ana's favorite player, BJ Armstrong, finished with 11 points. That was an overall, a great basketball game. We were driving to Bolling AFB, holding hands and making some plans to go out for Friday and Saturday. Ana was a lot of fun, and we did have a lot of fun. I was looking forward to seeing her beautiful face again. Let's just say that I was definitely interested but wanted to control the relationship and told her. I had to first see, if we were going to get serious or not. I just felt that there was some potential between us!

After work I went home to shower and change, then on to pick her up around 9:00 p.m. My time with Ana was pretty good. We did things together, talked on the phone, and planned another night out. I kept wanting to get to know her, but she wanted the fun times, and yet she kept reserved. I really did not know what to make of it. Yet I still saw the Ritz Night Club was the place with dancing on every floor. We were dancing, drinking a little here and there, and hanging close the entire night. I almost felt like she could be my girl. We left about two o'clock in the morning. I took her back to Bolling AFB to the dorms, seriously hung out in the car, and she went to her room. I was not sure how long I would keep an empty bed. I chilled and went home and watched some TV, showered, and hit the sack. We talked on the next morning once I returned from the gym at Bolling AFB and very seldom I would go to the Pentagon and play some basketball on Saturdays. I had no problems finding a gym to play ball. Some of the other courts were at Andrews AFB, Anacostia Naval Station—on the other side of Bolling AFB, which I liked that floor the least, Fort Myers Army Base, Henderson Hall Marine Base, and Fort Belvoir Army Base, but Bolling was my favorite. I felt a little better playing ball with the Air Force fellas, including the few that I knew. I got my laundry done, washed my caddy over at Bolling AFB by the Hobby Shop, and picked up some snacks and miscellaneous items for my apartment from the commissary.

I was living the responsible life and with my little gold stud in my ear, thinking that I was pretty cool. As much as I had gone to Bolling AFB, I had never run into Ana but was definitely check-ing everyone else out! No one at the base could match up to Ana. I had to call Adrian and tell her about Ana and on how we met, and I ended up taking her to the Bulls game, instead of the mystery young lady that I had met. I had tried to forget about her since Ana came into the picture. I had told Adrian that I was not a 100 percent sure, but her name could have been Melody since it was not your cousin Melody that lived in Akron. Adrian and I were becoming better friends, except for the child support, even though I was send-ing her money. Yet she wanted more! I was telling Adrian that I still had to find out if her dream would be true. After we hung up from talking, it was time to get ready for going out with Ana. On the way to get Ana, I stopped to get me a bite to eat and pick her up thereafter. Once I picked her up, out of three choices—the NCO club, The Ritz, and Classics—we decided on the Classics Night club in Suitland, Maryland. The club was cool and all, but our company that we were keeping together was beginning to get better, and I was beginning to feel the chemistry. Finally, we were beginning to bond! Ana agreed to go to my place! We had got out coats, and I had helped her with her coat first, then mine. We were holding hands and all. I must say that I always had a personal goal to achieve for—that was to strive for the home run in less than one week and was holding that record, not always, but pretty well! I was thinking that Ana had a three-date rule. Somehow that Saturday night at my place, let's say it was on! We got comfortable and started in the living room to the bedroom. It was on, and Ana was in control of the whole situation. It was hot and steamy that seemed like forever, and all of a sudden, Ana stopped and jumped up, sat on the bed and began to cry.

What in the world just happened? I knew that it was not me. I was totally 100 percent committed to those moments, my best moments? How could this be? She was not a pastor's daughter, and we both were in the Air Force on free time? We both were single. At least she was. She finally slowed down from crying and told me that she had just had an abortion. The whole mood was gone, and the room was deflated. I was buffooned! Totally lost at the same time, I tried to be empathic and obliged as Ana wanted to go back to the girls' dorms at Bolling AFB. Ana kept apologizing, and I told her that I understood. But I did not! One thing that I truly knew for a fact was that we were done! I was on my best behavior and a gentleman too! I was willing to take my time with her because I like the direction that we were moving into. I was there and not at the same time! This was almost a great weekend, but we were done! I did appreciate the silver lining between Ana and I that there would be no baby to blame on me! I would always feel and believe that Ana deceived me and was glad that it was over!

The next Monday at work, I was kind of in a zone and a little broken up from the Ana thing, yet I found a way to tell everyone that the weekend was great because the Bulls won, and I saw Michael Jordan play ball. I decided to go out that following weekend all by myself. I needed some me time! I had gone to the NCO club at Bolling AFB, hoping to see Ana, but she was nowhere in sight. So I decided to take it slow and just be out. I had a few light mixed drinks and stayed until the club was closing. The DJ was announcing the last call for alcohol and then to slow jams. The Commodores were on the turntable playing "Just to be Close to You," and I wanted to dance. I looked around until I saw the four ladies sitting at the table, then caught the most beautiful one there! Let me tell you that this girl looked like Holly Robinson from the TV show *21 Jump Street.* I was truly over Ana, just like that! We talked on the dance floor and found out her name was Krissy Jones from Maryland. She had good curly hair, nice to hold, and had all my attention. We danced the next slow jam and walked over to her table and met her friends. As they were getting their things, I had asked Krissy for her number as she was writing her number down. I went over to my table and got my full-length leather coat, and it was very warm. I had also asked Krissy if I could walk her to her car. It was cold and a little icy too. She agreed! As the gust of wind hit us as soon as we opened the club doors and the ladies were not wearing coats. I decided to do the gentleman thing and then took off my coat, cuddled Krissy, and walked with them to their car. After she was in the car, I put my coat back on and waved goodbye. I knew that I had scored major points with her that night. Then got into my caddy and went home!

Now I had someone new to think about, and she was beautiful as well, but not Hispanic, like Ana! I had called Adrian and gave her the updates on what just happened with Krissy whom I had just met. It was as crazy as it seemed. I was looking for the woman in my wife's dream! I had to know if it was Krissy. Will this be my next wife? I just wanted to know. I had to know! Then I had called Krissy to talk to and set up a date for when I returned from Connecticut after the holidays of Christmas and New Year's. I did miss another call from Melody, the mystery lady. But I still did not know what to expect. So I had taken leave to be with my girl Denise, Adrian, and my son. The money that I was making was good, and I was saving some of my money to move out, but not soon enough, and not enough money! I had to buy Denise something for Christmas because she was still my girl. I had hoped that she was not expecting an engagement ring because I did not want to disappoint her. I was sure that I would get by again. So I had told all my ladies that I would be out of town for the holidays. These ladies made it so easy for me to have my cake and eat it too. Plus they all knew and accepted my story. It was true, of course, but they all made it so easy for me to cheat and each one thought that they had a chance to be with me! I would had not been so naïve! Yet I was only looking for one woman that my wife had only dreamed about!

By this time, I really believed her and the dream! I could not wait to get back to Krissy! Denise and I were together by a strongly held thread. Denise wanted more, and I told her that I am back in ninety days and would be finished with these types of TDYs of staying away from her. I had told her that I would bring her a little money for rent, yet I mentioned that was paying for my trips to and from Connecticut. Plus the child support was beating me up. She agreed to be a little more patient with me, not rushing me into marriage. I kept telling her that it would get be better between us while still missing my bachelor type of life back in DC. We did not do much for the holidays. The money was still tight, and therefore, no Christmas decorations, and the food was just regular food. I could not wait until the holidays were over. It was getting depressing, and I wanted to breathe. The day after Christmas, I went to see my son Ant and take him a few little gifts. I really like to have Christmas with my kids as a family, but it was not possible for the moment. It was cold and snowy, and the days were going slowly like a drift. I had gone to see Tony to catch him up my situation. He was telling me that guys at CT Transit were talking much about me and on how I kept a job, being gone all the time for military duty. They were just jealous! I had nothing to worry about since it was the law. I was on military leave. I did take more than my fair share of it. Even when I was not on military leave, I had told Tony about my life in DC, and he kept saying, "Man, you are lucky!"

The truth of that whole matter was I had forgotten some of their names! Now, that's bad! Then I told him of all the ladies at the Pentagon. Well, I had a few days left to give to Denise. So Denise and I did a few movies and went bowling. We made the most of our limited time, and I did miss her a little. We shared some good moments and talked about our old times too! I had told her that I could not wait to get back to her! Well, it sounded good at the time, even though it was not even close to the truth. Those few days were coming to an end, and the next day Sunday, January 3, 1993, I would be leaving for DC. I did call Kendall and Charles to say hello! I was so glad that Denise knew nothing of the military, and I could tell her whatever I wanted. I did just that! That is one reason why I never want to marry a military woman. The military motto goes, "What you do TDY, stays, TDY, which means, never talk about it!"

While driving back, I noticed the cars in Maryland, in the median, off the road, and nobody was behind me. I was moving on the highway, and I suddenly slowed down because there was too many cars off the road, and still, not one was behind me. So I made a stop on the highway in the middle of the road. I opened the car door and touched ground and noticed that road was all ice. I was not sliding, but I slowed my caddy down and took precautions, and I decided to drive right. It took me an extra two hours to get home to my Arlington apartment. It was almost midnight, and I was tired! I quickly unpacked my luggage, got my uniforms ready, showered, and then, my bed was calling me. The next day, I was to turn thirty-one years old. While working that morning, Carol was acting and little strange, and come to find out, she and others were preparing Ms. Spark's office up as the Grim Reaper as a theme for my surprise birthday party, with cake! What a surprise! All of the department gathered around, singing happy birthday to me. I was surprised and truly happy at the same time! I had never had anything like this to ever happened to me and at the Pentagon! I would have never thought that I could deserve anything close to this day! The thought of everybody thinking of me meant the world to me! I was lost for words. I was only at the Pentagon for less than three months, and I received a birthday party! Wow, things like this has never happened to me! I was totally caught off guard! I was truly happy! A day that I could never forget! Never! Throughout the week, folks kept wishing me happy birthday and talked about the party. I did not go out that weekend. I just stayed on the phone, and on Friday, I managed to set-up a date with Krissy. We agreed on Red Lobster on Auth Rd, in Suitland, Maryland, for dinner that Sunday. Krissy mentioned that she was about twenty-four years old and had a little girl about two years old. Krissy was from Maryland and single. Even though she was too fine to be single, she was just that!

On Saturday, the following day, I talked with Getta, Angelique, and Tracey to let them know that I was back and missed them all. Tracey and I would just catch up since we lived in the same building! Getta had informed me again that I called her as a last resort if my other plans did not work out. Yet Getta was always there for me whenever! She was definitely on my reserve for a last-minute thing. I would call her to go out or hangout! I told Getta that she was wrong, and I just stayed busy. Anyway, Getta and I made plans to see each other later that night for a movie and then hang out at my place because she had to leave in the morning. It was win-win! When she had left the next day, I had got up and dressed and decided to straighten up the place and washed my clothes. After, I had made me an omelet, bacon, and toast. It was Sunday morning about 11:00 a.m., and the phone rang. I had said hello. The soft voice on the other side said, "Hello, my name is Melody." I responded, "Melody?" Then she explained the note and the Chicago Bulls. I knew exactly who I was speaking to. Melody stated that she had only called to apologize for not letting me know that she was not going to the game, and that was all she wanted. As she was about to hang up, I quickly shouted, in a low voice for her to hold on, and then, I said, "Let's go get some ice cream." I knew it was in the middle of winter, but I had to see this woman even if it was for ice cream! Melody then informed me that her co-worker Sabrina, saw me pass the note and had asked if Melody had called me. At the time, the answer was "no."

We started to talk, and the conversation just went on, even talking about what I had made for breakfast. I could not believe that she was like me to have never heard of an omelet. We laughed! I did tell her that I could cook and that my mother had taught me and all my siblings. Then she took a quick break from the phone because she was not feeling well. I did find out that she was born in Wilson, North Carolina, and had just turned twenty-three years old, on the past December 23, 1992, so our birthdays were twelve days apart. She had told me that I was not her type and thought that I was an old man in my Air Force uniform with a green parka on to keep warm. Melody had mentioned that she did not like dark-skinned guys. Now, I thought that I just had to be the exception, so I just had to keep her talking, then wanted to prove her theory wrong. I had nothing to lose, so I continued to be honest. I kept telling my same story—separated from my wife and leaving my girlfriend! She then had asked what type of car did I have? Then, I said, "A beat-up '64 Volkswagen." Then she said that did not matter. "A car is a car," she said. I was only testing her to see if she was materialistic or not. As we kept the conversation going, I then mentioned that the type of car I had was a 1987 Cadillac Sedan Deville. Melody said again that the type of car did not matter. I was impressed as she continued to talk with me. To say the least, she had my attention, so I asked for her phone number. Then she changed the subject! So I had asked for her number again, and she did not feel comfortable and that maybe she would call me again.

Was this a joke or what? I was thinking, I had other women that I could be with, and she was holding on to her phone number? I was outdone, but I stayed nice to her anyway! At the same time, I was truly intrigued! I was thinking that this Melody was not desperate, but my curiosity was at its peak! I had to meet this woman! I mean no one had ever done this to me, not ever! I was the man, so I thought! After I got off the phone, I finished putting my clothes up, got dressed, and called Krissy to let her know that I was on my way to Prince George County in Maryland to pick her up for our first date. I went in to meet her mother and a few family members. Everyone seemed nice, and their home was pretty decent. While I was waiting for Krissy, I had met her mother. Then Krissy showed up just as beautiful as ever. We said our goodbyes and opened the door and left. I even opened the car door for Krissy, and we were on our way to Red Lobster. While at Red Lobster, having dinner Krissy was mainly quiet and very shy! She did talk some about her child and her job. She worked for the DC Army National Guard as a government employee. I had talked much about how I have traveled a lot, but I liked the DC area and wanted to settle down there. But for me, it was all wishful thinking unless I found me a job first! I kept holding her hands, and then Krissy mentioned that her mother had told her that it looked like I had a lot of women.

It was so true, but of course, I denied all of it! After dinner, we decided to go over to my place to hang out! Krissy was curious to see my place. So we were on our way. We only had a few hours as she had to get home to get ready for the next workday. We both ate until we were satisfied with the Red Lobster food and then decided to go chill in my apartment. Everything was going well. I was just impressed with her that she was one my girls in the making. The night, everything was just beautiful. We spent a romantic time together. Then one thing led to another. In a matter of seconds, we had made it to the bedroom. The only thing that I had wished was that she would have talked more. So it was beginning to get late, and I had to get Krissy home, so we got our things together and coats too. She double-checked everything to ensure that she did not leave anything behind. I just wished we had more time to cuddle. Plus I had to work the next day too! It actually felt like we belonged together because we definitely had the chemistry in common. Now, I was too busy with these women, and what about Melody. She had my real attention. Melody was a priority in my book. Plus she was very different from anyone I had ever met. So I started going straight home after work not to miss Melody's call. I talked with the other ladies over the phone, and Tracey would stop by, but nothing still was going to happen between us. Every day for about two weeks, I was going straight home after work to catch a call from Melody, if she was going to call me.

What was I doing? I did not understand this at all, but I kept doing it! Finally, I reached home, and this day Melody called me. I was doing all this that she was not aware of, and I had never really met her, but I had that quick glance in passing on the Metro train! I wanted to meet this Melody that much more! We talked again, and she was to do some type of modeling fashion show. I told her that I wanted to see some pictures as I was not invited. I figured that she was testing me out first before she would even meet me. This girl was different, secretive, mysterious, and what I saw in those briefed moments on the metro platform, she was absolutely beautiful. I was so used to having my way with women, but not with this one, not at all! This time while talking on the phone, I had once again asked for her number. Then she decided to give me her number. It was like I actually worked hard just to get a phone number, her phone number. It was a real honor. I actually felt like I achieved something for the first time. Now, I just had to see her again in person! I wanted to feel the full effect of her presence. I wanted to see her almost vehemently! Even though I had her phone number, Melody was in no rush to see me. She was playing everything cool and safe; it was almost like she had an instructional dating manual.

That next conversation ended, and I was finally making progress. Well, I knew that she would not be seeing me for at least a week. So on the following week, Getta and I went to the game where Milwaukee Bucks, lost with the score of 121–98. The thing was anytime the Bullets won and scored over a 100 points, and the Bullets did just that, so all the fans would receive Wendy's food coupons. I held on to the coupon for a future use. So the game was on Tuesday. I worked during the week and worked out with basketball. Then I spent the night at Howard University dorms, so I could see Angelique and catch up. And that next morning, it happened again. I got another parking ticket. I was not pleased, not at all! That was the worst part of staying overnight at Howard University. Once I arrived home, I showered and got dressed. Then I called Melody to see what she was doing. Well, not what I was expecting. Melody's mother had answered the phone and said, "Hello, who is this." Before I finished saying, "My name is Michael. Don't worry about it, you will meet me and at the same time…" Melody had picked up the phone and said, "No, you won't!" Then I had asked Melody if she was busy for the Saturday night. So I had asked, "Melody, how are you doing?" I asked her if she wanted to go get some ice cream with me? I was trying to be funny with a little sarcasm. Of course she said no because it was wintertime. I finally was able to secure a date with this mysterious beautiful woman. Melody was holding all the cards. I have never met a lady like her. She was in control of me and my time. I was changing everything and dates with other women just so I did not miss a call from her. I finally had the opportunity to plan us a little date for her to come over to my place to check it out. This would be our very first date!

Then we had plan to get something to eat first. We were all set. I just had to get to her. I drove over to pick her up in DC by 58th Street SE to 5929 Central Avenue, Apt #804 by Addison Road and the Capital Heights Metro station stop. It was the rough side of DC, gun shots, bars on the windows, and all. I had never seen anything like this in DC before. You had to be ready for anything to pop off! And I was ready too! I parked the car and took the elevator up to the eight floor. As I knocked on the door, Melody's mother introduced herself as Mary Kent, and I told her who I was. Melody came out of the room. Then my eyes had locked on her. This was no comparison to the first time that I saw her at the Rosslyn metro station in the lower level by the back escalator. The very first time and the second time that I saw her did her no justice. This girl was everything that I had been looking for. She was described by my wife to a tee, and all that I knew of her was right in front of me! I instantly thought that she was a mixed between the young Janet Jackson and Chanté Moore. Melody was, at my first sighting that night and for the third time, gorgeous and beautiful. She was so fine! I was trying to treat her like everybody else, and seeing her was no big deal. But it was a big deal—my big deal, and I just could not take my eyes from her. I was hooked and to see her that night was worth the wait. She was finer than wine! Just gorgeous! I could not believe that Melody was 100 percent single! I was feeling like I had hit the jackpot! Then, as we were leaving, Melody wanted to make a stop downstairs to her sister's apartment number 206 for me to meet them. So we went in to meet. I had met Linda Harris, Robert (Butch) Scott, and her daughter Von. I had told Linda jokingly that I was taking her sister back to Connecticut with me as the date, and Linda said, "Over my dead body!"

Well, I knew at that moment that she loved her sister, Melody. I thought the gesture was nice! Then we left again. We walked to my car, and I opened the car door for Melody, and we were on our way to our first date to hangout. The funny thing was that I could not see without my glasses, and I never wore a seatbelt, except on base. It was not against the law, so I did not want to wear it. I thought that I was too cool! I did not want her to see me with my glasses on. I was squinting my eyes just to see the street signs. I could see close up but not far away. On the far away signs, I would take my best guess, and if I missed my turn, I would play it off, like I was trying to see something else. Yet everybody that rode in the car with me never knew that I could not see very well. How funny is that? Well, we were almost there to my apartment, and Wendy's burger restaurant was right there in the middle of the road on Clarendon Boulevard. I mentioned to Melody that I had a coupon for a free burger from Wendy's that I have got from the basketball game. The Washington Bullets gave out these coupons every time the Bullets would score over 100 points. Melody said this was nice and emphatically said, "You are not taking me to get something to eat off a coupon for our first date!" Then I saw the Pizza Hut that was adjacent to Wendy's. I said, "What about Pizza Hut?"

She agreed, but now, I had to get some more money! It was a good thing that I opened a savings account at the credit union but still could not write checks and still had ATM privileges. So I did make a U-turn to the ATM that was across the street and ran to it. Then we went to Pizza Hut. Again, I was not going to deny her because she was so beautiful! Truthfully, I was not the type to spend big money now or any money on women. I was not the type, but for Melody, I made a quick exception. We began to talk at the table booth that were we in. Then I had told her again that I lived in Connecticut and had an apartment there too and would be leaving in March or April timeframe because my assignment at the Pentagon would be over. I was trying to gear up the conversation to plan some type of future for us or to see if we had a future together. The waitress came and took our order. We ordered the pizza and drinks and kept talking. Melody still had all my attention. I wanted to hear everything that she was speaking about. And before we knew it, that waitress brought the food to us and left. I was ready to dig in and grab my plate.

Melody said, "Aren't you going to pray?" I said, "You pray!" I normally did not pray over my food, and I thought that I was cool for what I did. So I did it! So softy, without hesitation, we bowed our heads, and Melody was praying. It was just beautiful that prayer! I was not even close to being used to that. Then just before Melody finished praying, these words just came out of my mouth. I could not stop my mouth! My brain, feelings, and emotions had taken over my lips, and the words were flowing! How could this be? At the end of Melody's prayer, and this is no lie. I said, "And Lord, let her be my wife." Yes, I said it and did not back down from it! I then looked at her, right into her beautiful eyes, and we had a moment! I believe we connected! What was I doing? The fact was as true as these words, I had never done anything remotely close to this, not anything. I was emotionally connected to her. I believe from the first time that I laid my eyes on Melody, I was in love! Love! I just knew she was the one. I would have married Melody right then and there! I was in love, at best! I wanted to be on top of the world. I have never felt like this before. I did not know that she would not be willing to kiss on the first date! We had got to the car. I had to immediately turn on the heat as it was truly cold outside. I was about to take her back home and asked her if she wanted to see my apartment again? She agreed! Well, for starters, I knew that I had to be a gentleman as Melody had already set the tone for the evening. Melody did not allow me to have my way with her as I have treated my other ladies. She made me want to respect her. That was so, so different for me. I had never really had boundaries like this before. I wanted to be with Melody even more because I could not have her. What was happening to me? I was beginning to think with my brain this time and figure out how to really romance her, with real romance!

This woman was so beautiful. I had begun to thinking to myself that I had to be original, sincere, and then, it hit me. I had to be romantic. I have never been romantic in my life, but I did try it before. We made a quick stop over to my apartment, and Melody had liked my apartment after I had showed her around, and we continued to sit in the living room and just talked. We were about to leave, and I wanted to take some pictures because no one would believe that I was seeing and dating a woman this beautiful. So she did not mind the camera or being very photogenic. Then we took the elevator down to the underground parking to the closed-in garage, with the breezy see-through bricks to the outside. I opened the door for her first and had plan to make a habit of it. I was really liking this girl! Once we arrived back to her apartment, we sat in the car for a few minutes, and then, I walked with her to the apartment door. As she opened the door, I had wondered if I would get a little kiss. No! But at least, I had hoped to have kissed her! I was still happy anyway just to have had the date with her! Ecstatic! Now, I was beginning to think positive and thought maybe next time, for every date, I still had a chance. I just had to treat this one perfect! Well, in my case, almost perfect because to eventually get rid of the other ladies was in the plan! Somehow I knew that I was changing because of Melody, and that she was in my life for good! I was so pleased just to believe that! I had just a short time to get the ball rolling for us! I had to keep building up this relationship, and now, I really had my work cut out for me. Romance it would be for us!

As I was driving home, I could not wait to tell Adrian about Melody and to discuss her dream again. Adrian's dream was no joke about Melody! Wow! I was a true believer in dreams! I kept thinking that Melody just had to be the one! Once I was back in the car, I finally put my glasses back on, and now, I could clearly see the road, lines, and all the signs! What a feeling that I was having of not having my way with Melody on our date! I was totally clueless as to why I did not have that first kiss with Melody! I did not know what to think. Wow! I was not the kiss-and-tell type of man, so really it did not matter. I never shared my experiences. Therefore, I had no one to tell, except for my memories! I had always felt that what was understood need not to be explained, especially when it came to anyone that I was dating. Regardless of what I did or was doing on the side, I respected my ladies. Anyway, I always tried to be discreet! I had place everything on hold. I had no time for my other ladies, Angelique, Getta, Tracy, and Krissy. My hands were full on trying to get to know Melody. I spent every waking moment with Melody running through my brain. I could not wait to see her again! This new Melody was stopping all my action! I was going to church with her in my off time away from the Pentagon. I was meeting her friends, Brenda and Randy, and then Ralph and Carol. Then we were becoming an item, Mike and Melody. We were well on our way to becoming a couple! If Melody got busy with going to church or going to participating in her church, like dance ministry or prison ministry, only then would I see my other ladies. To be truthful, I was never bored and was having the best time of my life ever since turning eighteen years of age. I could have never planned this chain of events, even if I wanted to. I was going to church more and more, just to be with Melody. I was meeting her church friends but was only interested in being with Melody. I did meet the pastors at Harvest International Ministry (now called Integrity Church in Landover, Maryland) that they had moved into a vacant movie theater on Varnum Road in Mount Rainier, Maryland, which was, converted for their church use.

The pastors were Pastor Jim and Jean Thompson (aka Pastors Jim and Jean). They were nice too. I had joined, and that became my church as long as Melody was attending there. I could not believe that I was going to church again, but that was not it. I was going quite often! By this time, and still there working my TDY assignment, my replacement had showed up into the office and was to serve as the executive to Ms. Sparks. Well, Ms. Sparks had him to work in an office upstairs in one of her other sections until my time was over. That was remarkable. That lady just kept me amazed in her leadership style. I had learned and adapted so much from her leadership style to my own style. She had truly respected and accepted everything that I was doing. I was only temporary and a technical sergeant (TSgt) at that, and my replacement was a major. I was still impressed and humbled! He was just a nice guy too. I really liked talking to him too. Maj. Greg Sato was from Hawaii, and boy did I ask him a lot of questions. It seemed kind of funny because I was supposed to be there already, but my orders were canceled as I continued my assignment at the Pentagon. The other thing was Maj. Sato was from the place that I wanted to go to. Now, that was pure irony! The winter months was going by the wayside, and the trees were beginning to bud before the leaves come. I thought that nature was pretty cool, in itself. Nature knows exactly what to do. Truly amazing! Like the old saying that goes, time flies when you are having fun, and I was having a lot of it with Melody! My time to leave was closing in on me. I was not ready to be leaving, not even close to it. As I left work again, Melody and I had another week looming to its end.

We had church again that weekend. The gospel singer was Helen Baylor. I had never heard of her, but I was about to find out. Melody was on the dance ministry, and I was there to support her as she danced for Helen Baylor and the church congregation. I really liked that song "The Testimony." It really touched me, and I was so moved by her singing. Now that I have seen Helen sing, I could not help but to remember her from now on! We saw Helen perform two days in a row. I was beginning to start liking church again. I also like the other song she sang. It was "Can You Reach My Friend." it was very nice. I was definitely experiencing something new for a change! The Pentagon was by far the best place I have ever worked, and Melody was by far the best woman I have ever known. Most importantly, she taught me how to respect her and take my time with her. My other time was getting shorter, and I needed to spend more one-on-one time with Melody. I was barely thinking of the other ladies. Melody was beginning to fill the voids of my emptiness. The time that we were spending together was just priceless, even if it meant going to church. The more that we had talked and spent time together, I learned that Melody was not the "going out and clubbing" kind of woman. As fast as the conversation came, it never had got any traction. Going out was not her thing. I did accept it for her only! I was okay with it because I just wanted to be with her. So I then asked her if she wanted to go to see a movie. She agreed. I already had some old movie tickets. The tickets were from the Pentagon for the Courthouse Multiplex Cinemas right by my apartment building. Melody then took the metro rail to my apartment, and I would walk down to meet her, and then we could go to the movies together. Nice plan, and it worked.

Well, we got to the movie theater, and I had no ideas as for what was playing. We went inside, and I presented our tickets. I wanted Melody to pick the movie, and she wanted me to pick it. I was already a fan of Al Pacino, so I picked the movie that he was in called *The Scent of a Woman*. I thought it was appropriate, and I did have Melody's scent of attraction to her beauty because I was chasing her for one, and she was smelling so good! Al Pacino played a blind man and sort of romantic. It was the perfect movie, including the popcorn, candy, and drinks! What a fun date, except that I could not get too close to her. I had put my arm around her, and after five or ten seconds, Melody would take my hand and put it on my lap. I would then place my hand on her thigh that was right next to me. This time, it was quicker, as soon as I did it, she took my hand and placed it once again on my lap. After a few more times, I was frustrated, disappointed, and had to quit trying. Melody had made her point. So being determined, I held her hand. I knew that holding hands would be the limit for this evening. Even though I was a little frustrated and disappointed, somehow, I wanted her that much more! I had to have her but not like I treated everyone else. So I started to think even though I already knew that I was not her type! If I really wanted to get and keep Melody, I had to do something that I have never did, and it was. I have never been romantic with any woman, including my wife that was living in Connecticut! I was planning to go all out for this sweet young lady. I just had to have her! I was also learning a lot about respect. Then for me to respect Melody became a personal choice. It was my desire, and I wanted to respect her. It was that simple once you have learned something new and accepted it! I had one more weekend and several people to let them know that I was leaving but would be returning. I still just did not know when and how.

One thing for sure, I knew that I would find a way back to Melody. This last week, I especially knew that I would miss my honeys and Tracey too but not as much as I would be missing Melody. I did manage to see and spend some real time with the three of them and saw Tracey on and off until the last day. I kept saying how glad

I was that Melody never surprised me and came over to my place. I would have been so busted. Melody and I were growing, but she was keeping our relationship and the serious stuff at a distance. I truly respected that and still had my own thing going on. Melody and I made plans for her to see me before my departure back to Connecticut. My last day on the job was celebrated with a luncheon at Tivoli Restaurant in Rosslyn, Virginia. I received a gift and of course a free lunch and my first Pentagon picture with all of the signatures. This was an exciting time for me, and quite frankly, I was not ready to be leaving. Everybody was there—Ms. Sparks, Carol Anderson, Annie Barnes, Reggie Howard, Byron, Betty, Deborah, Cindy, Maria, Pat Vestal, Delores, Maj. Sato, and a few others. I could not believe the turnout, just like it was at my birthday celebration. The Pentagon, just working there, did wonders for me. It was wonderful and in a class all by itself! Well, I left early that day. My orders were signed for the entire day. Plus I had left a week early to take the remaining of my leave. Well, I decided to leave a little later, just so I would be able to see Melody last to complete my day. Well, I was all packed, the car was loaded up with my stuff, and now I was sitting around just awaiting Melody's arrival. About 6:30 p.m., I heard a knock on my door, and yes, it was my Melody. I had hugged and kissed her without thinking of her rules and boundaries. I think that she was beginning to grow onto me. It was that kiss! That kiss said it all! I knew that it would be all for now, but it was enough to make me want to come back to DC. Somehow, I just knew that I would find a way to see her again. We had talked for about a half hour, and she gave me this big bag. I looked inside the bag and pulled out this basket and brown bear. Inside it was a message on the bear that said, "Hugs and Kisses," along with a sandwich and snacks for the road. Who does this? No one. I mean no one—not my wife or any of my girls had never done anything remotely close to this. I was at the least impressed and well-pleased at the same time! What a surprise on my last day! We kissed again with tight hugs, and I walked her back to the metro rail as I did not want her to get home too late and that I would call her from the road to check to see if she arrived home. I just could not stop thinking about her. I could just see her face clearly even though she was not there with me. The drive home was refreshing. However, I was finally going back home to my other girlfriend Denise as she was waiting for my arrival and was hoping for a proposal. I had to figure something out and quickly.

When I had reached home, I was a little tired but had to unpack the car. We lived in a pretty decent neighborhood but still you had to watch your back. While I was bringing my things in, Denise quickly asked me about the brown bear in the weaved handbasket. My mind was incapacitated, and I straight up lied! I told her how much they loved me at the Pentagon, and it was one of my gifts, and I had thought it was a nice gesture! I also told her that they wanted me to come back, which was my desire only. My assignment was totally done, over! We hugged and kissed, and I told her how much I had missed her. She could not stop grinning. I just had to think that she believed me. I did call her several times, and we talked. Well, I had to get my uniforms ready to go back and drive the CT Transit bus on Monday. Yup, everything went back to normal, my bills were getting paid, my child support was on time, and I was feeling pretty good about that. I still had my two credit union accounts to work with. Now, I had to sneak to call Melody from the pay phones, using calling cards. I could not allow her number to show up on Denise's phone bill. A DC phone number would just convict me in a heartbeat! I would never want to take that chance. And I did not! For the times that I did talk with Melody, I could tell that she was missing me!

Melody had mentioned that the church dance ministry was keeping her pretty busy and a few modeling jobs and photoshoots she had to do. She also mentioned that she had to do the rehearsal for her friends Carol and Ralph's wedding. Then she told me about how her ex-boyfriend Ron tried to go out with her to get a bite to eat. Well, she had thought about it just to be nice but declined nevertheless. I said I had thought that Ron had gotten married, and she said he was still married. I then told her that I was glad that she did not go because he was probably up to no good! Well, that's was my way of thinking too because I would have been guilty as charged! The rehearsal went on as planned, and that was it. Now, that was that!

This was now April, and the following weekend, I was back on to doing my Air Force Reserve duty back at Westover ARB. I was here and there, always on the move. Well, I had got some good news, but it would be not so good news from MSgt. Jackie Davis. My name came up to complete the Senior Non-Commissioned Officer Training Command Academy at McGuire AFB in New Jersey. Military training was a must for the Air Force with courses like advanced leadership and management, advanced managerial communication, and advanced military studies. It was mandatory training and another TDY. I was glad to do it. If I did not attend, not only would I not get college credits, I would also not be eligible for my next promotion. The bad part was that I was to leave in one week on the April 18, 1993, to report on April 19, 1993, and the class would continue onto the graduation of May 20, 1998. I now had a week to leave for McGuire AFB. I could not have planned this next thing that just happened to me right after I got home from driving the bus. My caddy transmission was gone out! The car would barely move, but the reverse did work.

When I had slowly arrived home, I immediately called the car dealership where we got it from. The service manager stated that since I was still paying for it, the motor and transmission were still under warranty. What a burden to be lifted from off me. I was totally surprised! I was thinking and questioning myself was it because I was going to church in DC? Was it my mother's prayers? I was glad, for one thing that I knew for sure was that it was God's doing! Because I knew that I did not have the money to get it fixed. And Denise did not have my back this time. Actually, I blamed Denise at first that she had did it. The last time when she got upset in Akron at my sister's house and took off in my car and did not put the car in park correctly. I was so upset with her! But Denise remained calm because maybe I was correct. Anyway, they sent a flatbed tow truck to get the car to replace the transmission, but the work had to be done in Andover, Massachusetts. I would be away in training from my car for the first time while the transmission was being repaired. The only catch was I had to find a way to pick it up when the repairs have been completed. I did not have to worry about it until my class was over, which was another five weeks. Now, I had to get around again without a car, but at least, I was already capable of doing that. It was only for a few days of driving the CT Transit bus, and I was out of there for about a month. Denise and I said our goodbyes again with far less intimacy. She was disappointed, and I knew that we were almost done. This part of being gone for training would be a real strain on our relationship. We were good for the most part, but the love from her was truly missing, and she just played it off! Well, the base at Westover had arranged a bus ticket for me because I did not have a rental car authorization on my order to New Jersey, so I took the Greyhound bus to Trenton, New Jersey, and the military academy folks from the base came to pick me up with the other new students. I did not enjoy either ride. There was no girls to talk to, so I slept most of the way to help me pass the time. Well, it was a little cool, but okay, we were having that iffy spring weather.

Anyway, I was all checked in at the base with my room assignment. The only bad parts were that it was an old base with old furniture. I had to share a room with this cool white dude, and I had no car, which meant I had to make a few friends, so I get some access to transportation. We all had access to the base bus taxi system or call your own private taxi. That's why friends were important. I was really into sports for the college and pros. Plus I watched a little tennis and golf to pass the time. All I wanted was to get back to DC to see Melody, and I was about halfway there already. What a true coincidence? There were no holidays for the extra time off, so I had to make the best of every weekend. I had my gym stuff, so my next stop would be the gym. I just had to play me some basketball. When I had got to the gym, they were balling, girls and all. These two girls came to play. They played just like dudes, which had reminded me of when I used to play one-on-one with Carmen. I had next game and picked my team. When we got on the court, I had to check this girl about six feet tall with a nicely shape body. She was in good physical shape! She was backing me down like I was a dude with the sweat and all. No way! I had to push my pride to the side and had nothing to lose. She was a tough opponent, but I did hold my own. While I did not know her name, I remembered playing basketball against her. She and her friend could have easily went pro, if there was a pro basketball team around for the women. Carmen too! If I had thought of either one of them as a girl, they all would had made me look very bad, and that was not going to happen. Because deep down inside me, I did not like to lose! Not at all!

Okay, I hung out at the gym for a while and tried to meet some people and to see what was going on in the area. I did find out that there was a Six Flags amusement park close by. It was a thought, but I had no interests in going by myself or with dudes. I was good to stay in my room and watch the games in playoff mode. So I got showered and ready for the night. I had a quick thought that I was trying to slow down a little. I had a new lady interest in Melody that was in DC. And I was really trying to change and start settling down again. Denise was sort of upset with me because I was not supposed to be taken any new assignments. Plus I did not propose to her over the holidays. I really did not care. I was just playing the role, so my stuff would not get sat outside. Besides, I still needed a place to stay for a little while longer. I was promising Denise over the phone. I promised that this was the last long trip that I was taking. I also keep telling her that I was wishing that she was there with me! I keep lying through my teeth! Then I had called Melody, and this was the real deal. The more that I had talked to her, I felt that we started to miss each other. She had told me that her friend's wedding was in a few weeks. Melody had invited me to the wedding, but I had no mode of transportation. I did consider taking the train or a bus, but their schedules did not work for me. So that was out! Melody did not have a car and had just got her license. Ralph had helped her to learn how to drive until she had gotten her license. I kept thinking on how I could get to DC, and nothing came to mind.

Meanwhile, I was actively hanging out at the gym and eating around the base. The NCO club did have some pretty okay food. That was better than nothing. The next week at the gym, I was playing ball and saw these two brown-skinned girls there doing a little workout. This one dude was talking to one of the young ladies, and I was talking to the other one. I was talking to the younger one, and she was about twenty years old and smiled often. Her name was Tori, and

I had forgotten her friend's name. She was just too nice of a young pretty young thing to pass up, so I had taken interest, and we were talking like there was no tomorrow. Well, she had a car, but I would not be there long enough to use it on my own! Well, it looks like I have a new lady friend. She had liked my conversation about having a job with the State of Connecticut and wanted to become a doctor. There was no way on this God's green earth that I would tell her that I was a bus operator on the city bus. That worked in Connecticut but not on a military base. Not at all! I had got her number and plan to see her again in the very near future. I was not trying to be mean, but she was a little naïve, anyway I was not after her brain or her to become the mother of my child. By Sunday, she was in my dorm room, watching the games with me. My roommate understood the need for privacy and left the room as needed. I was glad that he was cool like that. We really did not have any rules anyway and a lot of freedom! I was only going to be there very short time, and I was not planning to get into any serious relationships. No way! I was trying to get to DC. I finally caught up with the other dude the next day between our military classes. I don't believe it—another Tony but from Maryland.

In our friendly conversation, I came to find out that he was going to Maryland the following weekend to see his girl. We were just talking to the other two girls at the gym. Except he did not get the phone number, but I did. We just had a grand old laugh about me getting the younger one's number, and now, we had a few things in common that we were not totally faithful. I told Tony that I had another young lady in DC, and that we had just started seeing each other and moving toward the serious side. But I had to figure out how to dump Tori whom I had just met. I really got to know her pretty well over the past few days. Well, after the classes were over, I had mentioned to Tori that I would be out of town, to DC, for a few days until Sunday. I told her that Tony and I were going together. What did I say that for. It was like she heard those words before. She had made plans for us, and I was not going to be there for her. I thought that, us being together and there were no strings attached, but Tori was upset anyway. I just could not tell her my heart was in DC. I was so glad that she was upset with me. Therefore, I did not have to see any tears! So I told her that he and I were going to visit family. Tori was not buying it and called me a liar! Well, it was the truth, and I was lying. So I cop an attitude and told Tori that it would be best that we go our separate ways. Now, we both were upset and went our separate ways. It was fun while it lasted, but that relationship was over almost as fast as it started. I just needed one more week, and I would have her car keys to go see Melody in DC. I was glad that Tony showed up just in time. I could had not planned it better if I wanted too! I guess it was meant for me to see Melody because I knew that I would not be going to that wedding. I was placing every one of my ladies on the backseat. Melody was a priority for me. I still thought about Kim from Fort Valley on how she had taken me for a loop. Well, now it was nothing in comparison to what I was feeling for Melody. Absolutely nothing! I had an "I don't care" attitude for Denise, Tori, and not even my wife received special time from me. We were never going to be good again. All I could think about was Melody! We were so close but yet so far in distance! I did have the thought several times to have her move to Connecticut. She had already told me that she would come for a visit one day. I was thinking out of all of the ladies and girls that I was seeing or dating, not one of them could came close to what I was beginning to feel for Melody.

On that Friday, on May 7, we were released from class a little earlier because it was Friday. We took our things to Tony's van, not a car, but a van. It had seats in the back and pretty spacious. Well, it was a ride, and that was all it mattered. It took about two and half hours to get there. Then Tony wanted to make a stop to the Gentleman's Club, on the northwest side of DC, in Georgetown, to get a bite to eat. I too was hungry, and I agreed! Out of all the places that I have visited, this was a first for me in DC. My second time in my life to visit the Gentleman's Club. The first time was in Mississippi during my technical training school for the Air Force. Call me crazy! Now, I know why I never liked to visit places like this before. These unclothed dancers were just beautiful and wasting their lives. They smelled really funky with all of the smoke and sweating too. What was I going to say to Melody, that I had a free ride and we went to get something to eat at this place. How innocent was that! Regardless of how I felt about places like that, we will always have these types of places, but not for me. I always wanted a real woman to become my wife.

Tony was ready to go, and I was right behind him as I had been ready to go too! Well, I finally arrived again to 5929 Central Avenue, and the only difference about this time, I was taking my luggage out of his vehicle instead of my car! Melody had allowed me to stay at her place for the weekend with her mother and the sister and boyfriend lived downstairs. While I thought that I would be staying on the sofa or something as innocent as we were trying to be, Melody was changing and drawing closer to me. I had to place my things in her room. I was not interested in staying in DC but you quickly get used to it. Her mother was cooking, and the apartment was smelling deliciously good. I remembered eating some of the tendonous beef roast that I had ever tasted. It was good, and if it was not for Melody, I would not had eaten it. Because I was not in the habit of eating other people's cooking. Anyway, her mom had passed the test because that food was very good! After we finished eating, we just sat around and talked. Her sister and boyfriend came up too from their apartment that was located downstairs. They spent an hour or so and left. Melody's mother shared a lot about Melody's childhood and on her growing up and on the modeling stuff that she was doing trying to get famous and to make a career of it. She even ran track and was the co-captain. Melody was fast, and she was the Douglas Junior High School team captain for the cheerleading squad! This girl was bad. She even had more trophies than I ever had! Wow! Well, it was about that time for bed, and it was getting late. Then at times, you would hear the gunshots throughout the night. That's how it was in southeast DC! Somehow, I did get used to it. After a while, it did become very normal. Hey, I had to see my baby even if it was in the hood.

Like always, I had to take a shower, or it would be very difficult for me to rest throughout the night. I was in the shower, fighting with the roaches and trying to keep them off the soap and me. Then

Melody's mother had to go to the bathroom. I mean immediately! She said, "I will just be a minute, so don't look out of the curtain, and I won't look into the shower." I could not believe that she was serious, but she was. So we laughed and I agreed, which also seemed pretty reasonable, so I just kept taking my shower. Really, I was too uncomfortable and still could not believe that she came into the bathroom with me. I was so glad that it all went well! Now, in my mind, I knew that I had to watch that old lady! In spite of that, everything turned out all right. Ms. Mary was pretty cool and told it just like it was. Well, we were sitting on the bed talking, and who could have known that the phone would be ringing. Well, the phone did ring, and for a few seconds, Melody was talking to a dude that was a photographer and on the phone line. He had asked her what she was wearing. Then, Melody just handed me the phone. I was upset to say the least. I really cursed him out. He was saying that he did not know that she was with somebody, and the conversation ended. And that was that! Melody explained that it was nothing other than to take pictures for a photoshoot. I believed her, just because she handed me the phone, but from that conversation, I knew that he was a fraud and wanted more. It was the right thing to do, so I gave him a piece of my mind! Besides, Melody had never given me a reason to feel uncomfortable with her. Bottom line, I really trusted her! I did not really trust any woman, except my mother, because I was so bad with women. But I trusted my Melody!

Well, I knew and that night, it was confirmed, the one thing that I did not like about apartment building—roaches and mice. I was glad to have only see them in the bathroom and had wished that I had never seen any of them at all. Well, that was a very interesting night. When I had showered the next morning, I my made sure that the bathroom door was locked this time. Once was enough for me and not a big deal for Melody either. Okay, it was time for the wedding of Carol and Ralph Williams at Harvest International Church, also Melody's and her friends home church. It was kind of my church too, but I was only there for Melody. That was it! Anyway, Brenda Griffin (Melody's best friend since elementary school) came to pick her up since Melody was one of the bridesmaids. Then I had gone to the second floor of the apartment building to hang out with Melody's sister's boyfriend Butch. I don't remember eating until the wedding. Then after, everyone was dressed, and we all rode together to the church, including Melody's mother. Butch's tan Camry was loaded with people. I did not want to get my gray suit wrinkled, with the mauve color shirt, no tie, but too late. I was in the back seat with Von (Melody's sister child) and Ms. Mary. I was really missing my caddy, and then Melody would have been riding with me. Maybe next time.

Well, we all have arrived safely, and so did everyone else. We had to find our seats on either side; it really didn't matter what side we sat on because Ralph and Carol were friends with everyone, including Melody's ex-boyfriend. I decided not to make a scene and mess up their wedding. Melody had made sure that we did not meet, and we did not. I just saw him from afar, and that was enough. It was clear to see that Melody had move on with me! Besides, I really did not have any place to talk, and they were over before she even met me. I just did not like the fact that he was trying to hang out with her again and played like it was innocent. I just refused to believe that in any fashion so that was what I was thinking. My situation was not above board anyway, but I was trying to get better! It was hard not to like Ralph and Carol; they were nice to everyone! They loved everyone! These were some special kinds of people. Well, the wedding was going well. Everything was right in place. Absolutely everything. Then I noticed Carol, the bride. She was definitely a beautiful bride, and Ralph just blew my mind. As she was at the altar, Ralph was saying that he wrote a song, and right on the spot, Ralph serenaded her with his song. It was just beautiful as I remembered it! That boy could sing! He was just outstanding, singing that beautiful song! Bravo! The wedding was awesome. I have never seen a wedding as such. That was my first time! At the reception, I was at the table with Melody's family and mainly with Butch. He and I were getting to know each other. Butch was a cool brother as well! He never said anything about my gun that I had showed him. So I knew then that he could be trusted. Now, Butch was dating Melody's sister, Linda, and I was dating Melody. Butch and I made a no money bet to see who would get married first between him and me. So it was on! So the wedding and the reception was over, and I had thought that Melody would introduce me to her ex-boyfriend. To my surprise, she did not. Melody was a class act. She had told me that she did not like to focus on the past nor talk about it. Melody was a progressive woman and was all about keeping it positive and moving forward. She never even commented on my suit that was missing a tie. Well, after all, it did not matter. I was glad to be back with her.

After she stopped by Linda's apartment to pick me up as Butch and I were in our own conversation. I had just found out that the actress Kellie Williams was his cousin. Well, this day was about over, and I had one more night with Melody, not knowing when I would see her again. Somehow, we both knew that we would see each other again. We knew without saying it! Melody was a beautifully and gorgeous bridesmaid. At every awakening moment, I would just look at her, even stared, but I just could not help myself. This was a woman of my dreams and beyond the imagination. She was just so gorgeous to me! I was just, for the most part, mesmerized! I was just not used to someone like her being beautiful and nice! I have never met that combination in a woman, not ever that I could trust! Once again, that day, we talked about Proverbs 31 as we did earlier that day. I just did not know the Bible that well. By this time, her mother, Ms. Mary, just walked into Melody's room. No knock and then said, "Excuse me." I was glad that we were reading the Bible. Anyway, that night, the shower for me went well with far less roaches this time, which was a pleasure this time! We stayed up to talk until we both fell asleep! It was morning, and we missed church the next day because I would be leaving once Tony came to pick me up to go back to New Jersey. I did not want to leave my Melody. She was growing in my mind, and I was feeling something different within me, new and exciting! I was looking at her and into her beautiful brown eyes. She was right in front of me and I was missing her. My heart was missing her. My heart was feeling something weird like I wanted to cry or something. The phone rang, and it was Tony. He would be there within the next two hours. I needed something more of her. I was able to get a few more pictures. I told Melody that when we had talked on the phone, I could look at her pictures, and when I go to bed at night, I could look at her pictures again. I had about an hour left to go before leaving. Melody had something on her mind that she wanted to discuss. Normally, she was quiet, but this thing was bothering her as she was aware that I was married, but separated. And yet there was Denise, and we were still living together. The Denise part of the conversation would had been a problem, if I was planning to stay there for a longer period of time. So it ended up in the conversation that I would have six months to save my money and to leave her, so it would be exclusively Melody and me.

I was so glad that Melody was giving me a chance that was more than reasonable, which I never expected. Six months! She was so sweet about it, no arguments, no ultimatums, nothing. I was left with the option to leave Denise and had six months to do it. It was now the month of May, and I had until the month of November 1993. I did feel that even though she was so nice about it. I truly felt she meant every word that she softly spoken to me. I just saw the sincerity in her eyes and that she was falling for me! I kissed her again and again and said that it was more than fair, and I would start looking for my own place as soon as I got my car back with the transmission repairs completed. So I had called to check on my car since I was thinking about it and talking from Melody's apartment. The great news that I had heard was that my car was ready for pickup. I had planned to pick it up on Saturday, the next day, after I had returned back to Connecticut. The best part about it was they had told me there were no charge to me, whatsoever! I just had to keep making my monthly payments on time, and I was already doing that. Special thanks to Denise for helping me in so many ways. I promised to find me a place soon, and then I kissed Melody again! I really could not believe that she was in my arms! It was this day as I was leaving that I knew in my heart that I did not deserve her. I knew that I was not right, but I was trying to figure me out. I knew that even though I was feeling some kind of a strange way, I knew without a doubt that I did not deserve her at all. I told her that a few times, just in case she had decided to move on. I said to her a few times that I did not deserve her and that she was too good to be true. No, that was not the case. She did not want to hear any of my words. Melody's mind was already made up and wanted to wait for me to return to her. She just knew that I would. I just knew that we connected at all levels, and this was too strange for me. No way this girl was blowing my mind. I was beginning to feel guilty for my selfishness. I pushed on to deny what I was feeling that Melody was changing me. I could not control it—that feeling I had all over my body almost to have goose bumps that I could not shake. But I tried to and all that I could think about was Melody as I was gathering my things.

It was time to leave and I had told Ms. Mary goodbye. Melody had walked me out, and I did not want to let her go! I thought once again that Melody was as pure as a gem, and yes, priceless! Now I had more pictures to hide from Denise once I reached Connecticut again. Tony and I talked all the way back to McGuire AFB, New Jersey. This was definitely a great weekend for the both of us. I was grateful for the free ride and appreciated making a new friend. I showed Tony a picture of Melody. He and everyone said that she was beautiful. I was just as excited to respond, "Thanks!" I was showing her pictures off to everyone that I had come in contact with. At least, I knew that I would be on my best behavior as we arrived back to the base at McGuire AFB, since Tori and I were over. I only had eight days to go before graduation. I was never this focus! Never! This training was much easier than recruiting school. I had picked up some additional leadership styles and still plan to implement them, without losing the objectivity of being myself. I just had to be me! That final night, there in the barracks (dorms), which were so old, either way, after packing and setting up the government taxi to take me to the bus terminal back to Trenton, New Jersey. After I had got something to eat, I spent almost two hours on the phone with Adrian. I had a lot to say about Melody, and Adrian was glad to hear that her dream came true. I told Adrian that her dream was definitely this Melody that I just started dating. I just knew it would be her. Melody was the only one that made sense out of all the other girls that I had met, especially how I was feeling about her! Still, the whole experience was a shock to me, and part of me was just numb!

Adrian had told me that Ant was doing good but misses his daddy, so I spoke to him for a few. And then I was back on the phone with Adrian. Adrian said that she did not know how to tell me something. Then, we were going back and forth. Finally, she said, "I will just tell you I had another dream about Denise." Adrian kept on saying that she had seen Denise with another guy, kind of brown-skinned, but it was not you. She said, "I saw the guy give her some flowers, and that was her dream." I did not know what to think! I downplayed it and said to Adrian, "No way. She thinks I am going to marry her. I even had some pamphlets for wedding rings to show her to get an idea on what she liked." I said again as I was sure of myself, "No way, Denise would cheat on me!" In reality, I was upset and could not wait to get back to Connecticut. I was furious as I had to ask myself, "How could she cheat on me!" I told Adrian that I had to go to bed, so I could get up in the morning. Somehow, most of the night, I could not sleep! The next morning, I was up and ready to go and saying my goodbyes to everyone. Then I would be on my back to Connecticut first thing in the morning after breakfast. The base taxi got me there on time with a half hour to spare. The bus pulled up and the announcement came, and we loaded our suitcases and boarded. Then off we were riding to Connecticut with several stops in between, including a few stops in New York. After that long drive, and the multiple stops, I was home, got my luggage, and took a taxi home. Once I had got all my things out from the taxi and into Denise's apartment. I greeted Denise like I was glad to be home and back with her. I took my things to the bedroom and started to unpack. Then I got this feeling to look around the apartment for the flowers as I was remembering Adrian's dream to see was it true!

Wow, when I opened up one of the closet doors, there were some old dead flowers in a vase sitting on the floor. I instantly grabbed the vase and took the dead flowers to Denise. With all kinds of cussing words departing my lips, I then said, "What is this and what is going on?" I said, "I already know that you were with somebody. You know I have all kinds of friends." But really, I was only referring to Adrian's dream. I did not believe that she would believe the dream things, so I just replaced the dream with friends. It worked! Denise had told me how she was feeling lonely, and that I was never around anymore, and that I was gone with the military for the past seven months. Still, I was just so mad. Then without thinking, I twisted her up in her collar and pushed her on the sofa! I stopped because I knew that I was leaving her. So I played the part like I was so upset that she would do this to me. I then showed her the jewelry books with the wedding rings in there. I said that I had thought that she loved me. Then I just tore up the three books that I had right in front of her face. Now, she was upset too! In her defense, she told me that nothing happened. Absolutely nothing happened, but he tried to kiss her, and they had gone out on a date, and that was it! From that point on, I could not and would not trust her ever again. Even though I still had my double standards! But I still had that little situation that I needed a place to stay and was still upset with her. In my mind, I would definitely be paying her back. I then told her that I would be picking up the car tomorrow and get a free ride on the train because I was in the bus union and could ride free.

That night, we sort of made up, and I had decided to still be mad or play like I was hurting with betrayal from her. Well, I had gone to sleep, got up the next morning, showered, and called to train station to see the next train times that were leaving for Andover, Massachusetts, so I arrived to the train station by taxi to catch the 10:30 a.m. and arrived by 12:45 p.m. After dressing myself, I did notice that my gun was lying on the sofa, but I thought nothing of it. Then before leaving and her going to work, Denise made it a point to mention to me that last night, she had got up and got my gun, and held it to my head. Denise went on further to say that she had almost shot me but changed her mind, with her hand on the trigger. I did not know if she was serious, so I told her that she should have killed me, and then I had said, "Just don't miss." I could not have thought that since we were so close last night like nothing was wrong. Wow, was I so deceived by kindness, niceness, and beauty! I truly know that if she was telling the truth. There is truly a thin line between love and hate! Regardless, I played like I did not believe her. So my taxi came and I left. I made it and was on the train. It was a nice ride and better than riding the bus but for free. I had to make this trip all by myself, and I was glad that I did. I knew that as I was thinking on the way to get my car that I had to leave Denise before something bad would happen. Besides, I thought that Denise could had been telling me the truth. I did not want to be shot by my own gun! It was no longer important to find out if she was telling the truth. Plus I was trying to think of something as to how to pay her back. I just had to get her back somehow!

Anyway, I had taxi over to the dealership, got the car, and it was repaired with a car wash, so I signed the papers, and received a full tank of gas, which was nice gesture of them, and I was on my way. I had asked to use the phone to call Melody to let her know what Denise had done to me by holding a gun on me while I slept because I had caught her with some flowers from another guy. We had agreed that I was supposed to be leaving her anyway and to find my own place as soon as possible! Melody was happy that I was leaving her anyway. Before we hung up the phone, I mentioned that I would be looking for a place as soon as I had returned to Connecticut! I told Melody that I would call her back once I had found something, and then, we hung up the phone. Well, I must say that it felt good to be alive! I was thinking while driving back that Denise had moved on and was only waiting to see if I would propose to her. I started to think that Denise was playing the same game that I was playing. I knew that if I did not know about the flowers, I would had never known that Denise was seeing someone else. This was another time that I knew that my mother was praying for me! My caddy was riding nicely once again! I was thinking, all the way back from picking up my car, that I had to find a way to leave Denise. Maybe the next time she would just kill me! One thing for sure, that would be my last confrontation with her! Let's just say I was beginning to believe her and take her seriously. I will always believe the old wise tale, for most people, "If you will cheat with me while I was married, then you will cheat on me."

The first thing that I did once I arrived to Hartford, Connecticut, was to buy me a *Hartford Courant Newspaper* and start my apartment hunting for any possibilities. I did not have much time before everything would be closing. I was in the front seat of my car looking and searching for at each and every available apartment in Hartford, Manchester, East Hartford, Waterbury, and a few others. There were a few vacancies. I did use the payphone at the gas station to call a few, and some were no longer vacant. I then noticed this one in East Hartford, Connecticut. It was about $850 per month, which was a price that I could afford. All by myself! I had the security deposit in my credit union account but not the first month rent. I have been paying my child support and my bankruptcies bills and trying to build my credit back up. The apartment rental place that I was fortunate to find was about to close, so I made an appointment for the upcoming Monday to see the apartment between my bus route (split shift) as I was to start back driving the bus again since returning from my military training in New Jersey. I had to bring the application fee and the security deposit, regardless if everything would work out.

Right after I hung up the phone, I had called Melody collect. My back was against the wall, and I had no one else to turn to. But I had to move fast and was out of calling cards and no time to get some more. Melody had accepted the collect call and I had told her that I had found an apartment in East Hartford, and I had the security deposit and the application fee, but I did not have the first month's rent. I told her that I could try to win the money from jai alai, Melody did not want me to gamble. Really, I did not know what to expect, then, Melody went quiet for a moment and then, just like that, Melody stated that she would give me the money for the apartment because she wanted me out of the apartment with Denise! The sooner, the better" Then, I just said, "Thanks." Then I replied that I was able to beat the six months deadline that she had gave me to move out. She laughed! The arrangements were made for me to receive the money, and I was all set. After hanging up with Melody, my mind was thinking of how to get Denise back. Denise was there when I had arrived home. As planned, I was very nice to her like she was nice to me when I had returned from New Jersey the night before. I apologized a few times and then suggested to start all over. Then I told her that it was my fault for being gone so much. We then planned to go out that Friday when she got home from work to the mall to pick out the rings and get her finger sized. She was changing her tune and relaxing. Really, we just made up and just had the best time for the few days that I would be there! There was no way that I was going to mess that up. Plus I was staying home and not running the streets as usual!

I gave her all of my time because I was leaving. On the real, I was going to pay her back. I did not like that gun action from her. I wished Adrian would had told me about the gun being pulled on me. But it was working out for me anyway. I would call Denise on my breaks, and this other guy she tried to see had to second-guess himself. Because I was on my A game, and he did not have a chance until after Friday if she did not already cancel him. I made up in my mind that I was just going to break her heart a little! That Sunday passed by, and Monday was here. I did not have to get a ride or take a taxi because I had my car back. Great! I was anxiously driving the bus and waiting for the first part of my bus split shift to arrive, and it did. I drove the relief driver's car to the bus lot. Then I jumped in my car and off to see the apartment on the corner of 55 Burnside Avenue in East Hartford. I parked and ran inside. I filled out the application as this was second time since 1982 in Dayton, Ohio, that I felt like I was sort of single again because I would be moving into the place all by myself. Then the rental lady showed me the one-bedroom apartment on the second floor. It was nice and spacious, but I did not have any furniture. I immediately liked it. As we were leaving, she showed me the washer and dryers' location and the dumpster. The apartments came with the intercom system for privacy, and everyone would have to get buzzed in. I was thinking that was perfect! Just perfect and less chances for me to get busted, just in case!

Well, I had to wait a day or two to see if my rental application would get approved. I did not know what to expect because I knew my credit was bad, but I was paying on the bills for Adrian and myself for the bills that were in both of our names. I just hoped that I would get good points for being in the Air Force Reserve and working at CT Transit. Now, it was Wednesday, and I would call after my break to see the results of my rental application. The lady on the other end said that my rental application had gotten approved. What a milestone to be conquered in my unbelief as I was holding it in. I was ecstatic and excited at the same time. I just told the lady thank you! She said that I could stop by to pick up the keys and I would be able to move in starting that Friday because the apartment would be ready then, and since it was Memorial Day on that following Monday, my first official day would be on the first of June. So that would be my first stop after hanging up the phone to sign the papers and pick up my apartment keys! I went to see it again since I had the keys and the apartment was clean, and I did not see any bugs! Yes! Then I had drove down the street to the U-Haul place to reserve me a small truck for Friday. Since starting back, I now had Fridays and Sundays off. It was just perfect! I was all set as Friday was my payday too and no jai alai. I was not going to mess up at all. Melody was helping me to do better. Not all but a lot of my choices was not my norm. I was becoming a little different, and I knew that I was changing for the better. My mother was there for me always, but now, this was different.

I was looking to Melody for comfort! Just the sound of her voice made things better for me. My life was better with her in it. I just knew it! You know now that Denise and I were at a good place, and we shared that it reminded us on how it was in the beginning of our relationship. I must agree. It was nice, and we were having a very good time. We even went out to get a bite to eat that Thursday night. In actuality, it was the night before the storm, and I just knew that I would miss the tears, her tears, and seeing the outcome of my revenge! Boy, did I ever want to see her face, regardless. It was my Friday morning to leave her, I even woke up to see her off to work. We kissed and hugged. I told her that I could not wait until she returned home from work. I was so glad that I knew her schedule, and she did not have a car. I then immediately got up, showered, and was on my way. I grabbed some McDonald's breakfast and drove to East Hartford to get my U-Haul truck. I got it and left my car on the lot. I rushed to do everything just in case Denise would return early from work. Boy, I was moving like I was on a mission, and I was because time was of the essence, and I had none of it to lose! I purchased a few more boxes as some of my stuff was already in boxes. I loaded up the truck with only my stuff. I did not bother any of her things since she had helped me out tremendously. Nevertheless, she had left her memory etched in my mind forever on how she pulled my own gun on me! This was definitely the right time, my time to leave. I would have never married her anyway because of the flowers, and she was seeing another guy. Even if Denise and the guy had never done anything and for her words to be true, I could had never trusted her again! It was definitely over, and I was gone, so I left my keys and locked her door. That was my payback!

Right now, I had a new girlfriend in DC named Melody and a wife that I was separated from, and we just stayed friends. I had two sons that I was desperately trying to get them back into my life! This time, I wanted to find that love and happiness! For real and having Melody in my life was a good start! Then, I went to Kmart and brought me an air mattress, sheets, towels, things for the kitchen, a frying pan, and some pots, including soap and a plate set that came with silverware! That was enough for me to get started. I was glad to have blinds, so I washed everything down and called it home. On Saturday, I worked on the bus, and during my split shift, at the bus garage, I had signed up to work overtime for Monday, the Memorial Day. I now had some seniority and would get a bus route for sure. I thought getting the double-time would help me to get my apartment together and put me a mattress and box spring on layaway! I did just that! I had boxes everywhere. I was able to get my own house phone too and stop a lot of that payphone action. Melody was still very active in church and with the dance ministry and crusades. Sometimes she would be modeling, doing some fashion shows. That was perfect too as I would still have some freedom. Because I just had to stay busy! So I started going back to Westover ARB, to play basketball on Saturdays. I also would sign up to work extra RPA man-days on my off days during the week from my bus job. I have to get my money together, so I could see Melody again and have money for when I would take off to be with her, but the downside is that I would not get paid from the bus company. Everything was in motion and doing well. I was able to start seeing Ant again. He would come over to spend the night with me. I had to also make sure that I always had cereal too for him. Other than seeing my wife here and there and seeing my son and a few friends, my social life was pretty slim, and nothing else was happening.

I was able to start talking with my other son in Ohio, Big Mike! I was promising to see him soon as Melody and I were planning to make a trip there, so she would be able to meet my family! I had to first figure out on how to leave my bus job again for military duty. Then Melody and I would drive to Ohio. My life was finally moving in the right direction, and I was learning how to become happy again. My life was now simple and mundane, and I really needed some excitement in Connecticut. My wife Adrian and I were doing good, and I was not going to mess with that. We had figured it out, and it was working well. The following week, I had to go to Westover ARB to do my weekend drill. I would have the weekend, well, really only Sunday, because I worked mostly on Saturdays. It was that following Saturday when my shift was almost over, except to do our last bus lineup from downtown. I was running a little late and had to make up some time from the mall. I had less than ten minutes to get there. I was moving really fast. I blew by this one bus stop, and everybody on the bus said, screaming, "Stop the bus!" Well, if you know anything about buses and air brakes, I could not stop that bus on a dime. No way! So I stopped about fifty yards up the road, and this person seemed to be running, and I was about to leave. They shouted again, "Wait!" This beautiful young girl got on the bus, out of breath, and was looking frustrated at me! I apologized and said, "I did not see you for real. I pointed to the seat across from me and said, "Sit right here!" I said again, "My bad. Do not pay. I got you." She smiled, and I melted! She was just beautiful, with a tiny black mole on her nose. She was a doll. Still I had a choice to make and could not help myself at the same time! I was at a lost, so I asked her name and called dispatch and stated that I would be a few minutes late.

Now, all the other buses had to wait until I had arrived, so we all could leave at the same time. Plus, my riders could make their bus connections. I had asked for her name again, and she said "Patrina," and I said, "Beautiful like you!" I told her my name and had asked if she would stay on the bus because I had one more route to do, and then I would take her home. She agreed! Once I finished my route,

Patrina rode back with me to the bus garage, and once inside the gate, I dropped her in front and, told her to wait for me. I had come out, and we walked to my car. I took her home. I had guessed that she was about sixteen years old, but she was actually eighteen years old and about to turn nineteen years old in a few weeks, and she was from the Virgin Islands. She told me that my age of thirty-one years old was not too old for her. We talked more, and I had got her number. She kissed me and left. She was nice! I was stuck again! I am now between two women that I really liked, but Melody was definitely winning in my mind! What was I to do again! I was so stuck! For real! I had every reason to leave her alone, except one: I did not know how to say no! Her attractiveness outweighed my reasoning to stop! We talked on the phone a few times, and then, within a week, I had picked her up from her grandmother's house by Albany Avenue, in Hartford. Patrina had introduced me to her grandmother, and she gave me a soft hello, but I was feeling that she did not like me. So her granddaughter and I had left to get a bite to eat, and then Patrina would be hanging out at my apartment for the weekend. Patrina knew that I had a girlfriend in DC and a wife in Hartford as well. I kept being honest to a point, which made our relationship to my advantage. I would be able to keep my freedom from the nonsense that came with real relationships. We had a reasonable understanding that when Melody would call me, Patrina would know to be quiet. I had not one problem with her. I really did not want to do her like that, but I was stuck in a pinch.

Patrina and I became a public couple. I would be doing everything with her. I would take her with me to the Westover ARB to play basketball or outside at CT Transit on their basketball court. Patrina would just ride the bus with me, and I would be play basketball with the guys after I dropped my bus off. By the end of June, I met two more honeys on the bus. One was this Muslim young lady named Aisha. We met at my apartment and hung out for a short, short while. And someone was ringing my apartment to get in. There was no way I was going to answer the door. I do remember her light skin and red freckles and was shocked at the fact that I had her attention. I would had never guessed that I would ever have a chance. I remembered that even though we were hanging out, she was still faithful to her belief. I did respect that she was faithful to her religion. I do believe that if our relationship would had grown, I may have ended up checking it out—the Islamic religion that was as close as I ever been to knowing that faith because it was interesting. I do know that because if she was truly faithful, we would have no choice but to part our ways. That time was gone and that thing we had, just like my meeting her had never happened. We quickly lost all contact, and I never seen her again. However, the other shorty about 5'1" or 5'2", and she was just explosive and tailor made and attractive. My nose was wide-open about the time I called her. I was able to pick her up on the same day. I did not believe that she was eighteen years old too and just out of high school. By the time I had picked her up, she just loved my black caddy. Normally, I would get something to eat, and then we would hang out at my new apartment.

This girl was named Vivian, and she just love my car. Let's just say we almost lived in that car. She barely wanted to go to my apartment. The other times that I was able to see her, the car was the best option because time was of the essence sometimes. I had asked Vivian, why was the car so important or why was the time so important. She finally told me that she was living with her boyfriend and she was not really happy with him. So I had that in common with Vivian by each of us having a side relationship, except I was her side-piece. She wanted her boyfriend and me too! I was now learning that women stepped out on their men too! The bad part was Vivian was possessive of me and did not want me talking to anyone else. She was jealous too! When I would have Patrina over to my apartment, she knew to be quiet I had a phone call. This time when Patrina was over and I was talking on the phone to Vivian, I was telling Vivian about my friend, Patrina, and Vivian wanted to speak to her. I had asked Patrina if she wanted to talk, and she agreed. I had put her on the phone and could not believe my ears for what I was hearing. They both were on the phone arguing over me! Unbelievable, but true! I had told Vivian that she had no rights because she had a live-in boyfriend. I just took the phone back. One fact I know is that women have gotten jealous over the other woman that was with me in a relationship or something, but I have never witness two young women arguing over me! There was a good chance that neither one of them were going to end up with me. I was able to keep both of them. Regardless, I just wanted to pat myself on the back, but instead, I just chalked one up there in the air!

Now, I was back at work to end the week and approaching the Fourth of July, and then I started preparing that Friday to go to Westover ARB for another one of my reserve weekends. I finally made contact with Charles Hudson again. Him and his wife were doing well that he explained. I had to tell him about Melody and showed him a few of her pictures. I also told him that I was making plans to see her the following weekend and go to Ohio for about four days. He told me congrats, and that was it. We were trying to make plans to see each other again, but our schedules were conflicting. Now, once back at CT Transit, I had to take off again for military training but not really for training! While driving the bus that week, I met another young honey and Jamaican born this time. I knew the accent! She was riding the bus with her mother and very proper. I could tell that she loved her mother, but I kept distracting her and made her blush! That was it, and I just knew that she was single! Truthfully, she had that look about her, saying I am single and available! Again, I just could not pass this opportunity up, plus she was Jamaican. Until I had met Melody in DC, I was almost to give up on American black women! I was looking at and flirting with all white women and any culture but black women. I was about to give up on meeting black women because of my experience with my wife. But meeting Melody restored my hope in all women, including black women. I realized that one bad marriage does not void a good relationship with another black woman. This would be my second Jamaican woman to conquer! I had asked her name on the bus while driving, and she was totally embarrassed and blushing as she said, "Jasmine." I said this aloud, "Your name is just beautiful like the flower and you!" This was my fourth new girl in less than two months in Connecticut. I also had the other three in DC, plus Tracey waiting until I had come back to DC. I was being presumptuous and counting Jasmine too because she passed me her phone number on the way out. I was not going to call her until I was back from DC and Ohio with Melody. Plus the making her wait to talk to me would give me more of the advantage, and that she would want me more!

No longer was I mundane, but I was living on the edge! I had told Patrina and Vivian that I would be out of town with the military, just in case they ran into other bus drivers, especially Patrina. I had to keep my stories straight, and I had no room for errors! I got packed, permed my hair, so it would be wavy, but it did not take. I put a hat on and left anyway. Then I saw my son Ant on the way out. I was on my way to DC to see my baby! Yes! I was on my way and decided not to tell anyone that I will be in DC. Melody was definitely priority number one, and I did not want anything to mess it up. As soon as I had got to DC, the traffic got heavier. And I knew that I was almost there. I had my blue Atlanta Braves baseball cap on over my perm with the A/C on in the car. By the time I had reached Melody's apartment complex, I was glad that it was still daylight. I went up to her apartment on the eighth floor, to speak to her mother, sister, and help with her luggage. Once we put her things in the car, we were on our way to Akron. Her ambience was so pleasant, set by the radiance of her smile, had set the tone for our entire drive to Akron. I was so happy! By the time we were close to Breezewood, Pennsylvania, I was getting tired and sleepy. So we made a pit stop, for gas, restrooms, and got some ice cream from Dairy Queen and pizza from Pizza Hut. On the way back to the car, I had asked Melody if she wanted to drive because I was getting tired. I knew already that Melody had just gotten her license and really did not drive much. I really did not know what to expect, so I had told her that she would only be going straight on the highway and nothing to worry about!

Oh, and to watch the speed limit because I had gotten a ticket once before on the turnpike. We had finished eating in the car and she started to drive. It was about fifteen to twenty minutes later. I was sleep. Melody was taking the curves in Pennsylvania, left and right. This girl was moving! On the real, she only knew to drive one speed, which was fast. I was so scared out of my mind and very tired and still could not drive. I had to just sit there on pins and needles and trust her driving. I did not like her driving at all, but I had to get some more sleep. I told her that I was going to kiss the ground on our first stop, and I did. Even though Melody's style of driving scared me, she was getting it, especially to be a new driver in Pennsylvania. I definitely kissed the ground as we both laughed as that was too funny. Melody was driving very close to the jersey barriers. I was so glad that I had got the wheel back.

Once we arrived to Akron, we went straight to the hotel. Once we checked in and made our way to the room, I had told Melody that she had scared me but had some great potential in driving! Then, she hit me on the arm! As we were settling in, I took off my baseball hat. Then Melody said, "What did you do to your hair?" It was straight, and my hair was going everywhere, and no, not one curl or wave! I told her that I was trying to get my hair like my dad's. But I was not even close. I agreed with Melody, so I took my clippers, went into the bathroom, and cut it all off. But the clippers could not cut me bald. And that was okay. Melody had to help me with the back of my head to make sure that my hair was evenly cut. She was liking that, and now I had no hair. I knew that once it had started to grow again, I would go back to the fade haircut. After I showered and got ready for bed, we were in for some much-needed rest. The next morning, we got cleaned and dressed to go and meet my family and oldest son. We went to the Country Buffet that was in Akron and then off to see the family. Even though my poker days were about over, Melody and I had a lot of fun. I had showed her where I used to live, on 10 Manila Place, but the house was no longer there. Then we went to the northside and road the go carts and went bowling. We grab another bite to eat from Swenson's drive up restaurant. I was turning her on to places that I used to go to. I really wanted Melody to see how I grew up and where. I wanted her to get to know me. This was a first to me. I have never done this before. Not even with Denise! I really tried to make everything that I had done with Melody a first time.

Melody was really growing on me, and I tried hard not to disappoint her. Then we went to my mother's house on East Avenue. Everybody just loved Melody! They were looking at her in awe. She was beautiful. Some of my siblings said look at Mikey's girlfriend.

Again, she is pretty! My mother greeted her and smiled. My mother had that proud look on her face once again, and she just knew that I was happy. My oldest brother, Cleottis, my mother, and I had got a photo together. Melody had brought us some African t-shirts. I was wearing this orange T-shirt with an African design on the front of it with some jeans on. We had a good time, and I was so amazed that we got along so good! There were other photos as well. I was also getting into photography as a part-time hobby. One thing for sure, I really enjoyed taking photos of my Melody. Well, we all were talking in the other room with my other brothers, and I cursed in the conversation and did not realize it at all. It was just a normal conversation. I had gone into the kitchen to get some water as we were about to leave. Melody met me at the doorway and said softly to me, "Why did you say that?" She was talking about my cursing, which I quickly denied, and walked away. I played it back in my mind, and boy, she was correct! She was changing me and not by forcing me to change! I had nothing to argue about. Melody was so sweet about the whole thing. I did realize that I had cursed, so I quickly told her that she was right after replaying it back in my thoughts. She was right!

After leaving my mother's house, we stopped by my Auntie Beck's house and to see my cousins Mary, Regina, and Rocky! Again, everyone thought that she was pretty. We stayed for a little and just talked. Then we left to get some White Castle's hamburgers. The next stop was over to my sister Terri's house. As soon as we got to enter into the house, my little niece blurted out, "Another one!" My niece had meant that I had brought another girl for them to meet. I replied, "Yes, but I am going to marry this one!" I looked over to Melody, and she just smiled. I was so glad that it was not surprising to Melody to have heard that, or I would have been in trouble! It was so cute and funny. We all just laughed at it! Boy, was I glad that I had already told her that I had brought Denise (ex-girlfriend) to Akron almost a year earlier. I was so in the clear because I had told the truth and just was glad that everyone was laughing, even Melody! After a quick few days of seeing the family, we had to be going. I had to get Melody back to DC and me back to Connecticut. We had said our goodbyes, and then, I stopped over to see my mother to give her a few dollars. I was just glad to be getting back on my feet. The drive was going well. Melody and I were talking about my family, and right around the time we got to Pittsburgh, I was beginning to get sleepy, staying up and playing cards with my sister Terri, and Melody and I were partners in the spade game.

By doing that, I was just tired, and it was catching up to me. I just did not want to let Melody drive my car again. As quick as I had spoken these few words, it was a no-brainer that I did not really have a choice. I needed some sleep. Then I pulled over on the side of the highway as the cars were zooming by fast as lightning. She was driving again, and before I knew it, we were in Breezewood, Pennsylvania, which was our normal stopping point, gas and pit stop (restrooms and food). Melody was wide-awake, and her eyes were wide-open! I kept waking up when she would hit those curves and tell her to slow down. This girl knew fast driving and did inform me that this trip was her first time driving distance travel. It was still scary for me, but she was getting it! I guess I was the one to teach her this, and it was apparently working. Melody was not scare to drive. I was impressed, but I think that she wanted to impress me too. Once we had gotten to I-495 south, I had awoken, and we traded places again. I had said it again and did it. I just had to kiss the ground, not believing we made it. But we thankfully did make it back to DC! I had one night to spend in DC with Melody and would leave by 2:00 p.m. on Sunday. It was hot and sweating for that long weekend trip. I could not wait to get into the shower. We both were getting ready for bed to call it a night. Still we had a few loose ends to get-together from my past and the big topic of getting a divorce was one of them, along with the child support. Melody was wondering why I was separated so long and had not gotten a divorce? Then the response of my timing was just impeccable! It suddenly came to me in our conversation. It has never been important until now! She gave me the biggest smile. I think what she really wanted to know was that if I was ready to divorce my wife, or did I still wanted to hold on to her? I just told her to wait and see! Then I told Melody that I knew that it was past time that I should have been divorced a long time ago. I just had lost the initiative.

It was then I had decided to work my jobs harder and do more hours every chance I had between the Air Force and CT Transit. I did not want my divorce to be a part of our future. I had to and wanted to let go of my past. The next day, we got up and slowly gotten dressed as I really did not want to leave and be so far away from her. Besides, it would definitely keep me out of trouble. This time, I spent all my time with Melody while visiting DC again. Melody was growing on me and I, her. We were wanting to be together, more and more. My other big priority was to eventually get rid of all of the other women and divorce them too. I also thought that it would work itself out. I was thinking to myself as we were getting showered and dressed. Melody had already known that I had many lady friends in Connecticut and DC, but she was not aware of the four new ladies since I had my new apartment that she had helped me to get. I did not want to lie to her, and I don't believe I could have told her exactly what I have been doing. So I decided not to tell her, so it was not lying, but it was a part of my reputation that she already known about. Boy, I was in a tight space for my feelings with Melody, and my plan was to never get caught. I had to let my new past die. I was living a double life with my new girlfriend and still had a wife. I was in this weird predicament in which I was falling in love with Melody and really liked Patrina a great deal. I was sort of torn between the two of them. They were the same two I given most of my attention to.

Truth of the matter was I have never been faithful to anybody. That real love kept slipping through my fingers, except for these two women. But Melody was still somehow winning my torn heart right from Patrina. You see, Melody and I had a chemistry when we were together. That felt totally like my destiny like we are meant to be! I did not have that same feeling with Patrina. I thought of Adrian's dream, and really, they both could have easily still had been a tough choice based on her dream. Somehow, Melody was the only one that I kept protected from everyone. I kept asking myself, was Patrina too young for me? Then I thought that Melody was about church and Patrina never mentioned church. Suddenly, that would probably become the deal breaker. I really wanted to be in church myself, even though I was doing all these things and had all these women. Yet I felt God pulling at me! I truly wanted to believe that God was the reason that I had found Melody. The thing was he used my wife Adrian to help me with her gifts because God knew that I would believe her. I wanted to go back to my roots in which I was raised up in the church for most of my childhood and still was desiring in my adulthood to get back in church and a secret that I only kept to myself!

Melody was the only one that could have made that a reality for me at this particular time in my life. But if Patrina and I would had had that church conversation, I would have definitely been confused. I was so glad that Patrina and I did not have to cross that bridge. I had taken some of my stuff down to the car, and Melody had helped me with the rest of my things. I said bye to her mother. We loaded the car, and Melody sat with me for a few minutes. She kissed me a few times and got out of the car. It was at that moment that I knew that she would be waiting for me, and I felt that she was hooked and our relationship was going to the next level. This was my girl. I started to sing parts of that song "My Girl" by The Temptations. For I was feeling some kind of way. I was really on cloud nine. The traffic was pretty decent, but the weather was hot, and I had made pretty good time getting back to Connecticut and to my own apartment. I did not like coming home to an empty apartment. I had gotten used to somebody being there for me and all the time. But there was no way it was happening this time or the next. I had called Melody to tell her that I had made it home, and we talked as I was getting tired. I also reassured her that I would be working on my divorce. I wanted Melody to feel secured with me and in our relationship, and that we were moving forward. So after we hung up the phone, I had called that Jamaican young lady named Jasmine. I had to see if my hunch was correct, to see indeed if she was truly single. While it has been a little while since we had met, I called her, and we talked. As I was talking to her, she had mentioned in the beginning of our conversation that her mother thought that I was a handsome man, and she did too! Well, I knew right then that she was single, twenty-four years old, and available. She said that she was not sure if I would call. I had told her that I had to see her again as I had just gotten back from out of town visiting family.

As soon as I asked her out for next Friday to chill at my place, she agreed. I now had a limited time to get ready to take the air mattress back to Kmart for the third time, and this time, it was for a full refund. Then I went to my get my mattress and box spring from off layaway since moving in, and that was exactly what I had done on my day off and payday. I could not take that air mattress any longer. I went to the warehouse to pick up my layaway. The guys tied them to the top of my caddy, and I was on my way. I even got the free bedframe to go with it. I took them and drove off, which it was a good start because I really needed a bed. Then Jasmine would understand that I was just moving in and getting on my feet. It all had worked out, even though the bed was the only furniture that I had to sit on. Because I normally stood up and ate at the kitchen counter. After the week was over driving the bus, I went to her house to pick her up and meet the family. The next payday, I had planned to get a vacuum to get all the crumbs off the floor. I did have boxes everywhere, even the television was still on a box. I was so amazed that none of my ladies ever complained about the shape that my apartment was in. I must say that my apartment was still neat and clean, even the bathroom. As I was talking to Melody, it was mostly Patrina or Jasmine at my place rotating on and off. They always stayed in the background, quiet as a mouse, and never gave me any issues after I had hung up the phone. Even if I was talking to some other lady or one of them. They just gave me space and respect. These two ladies could have easily messed things up for me and did not! I was making plans to take Patrina and my son Ant to the movies on an upcoming weekend. After I had returned from my August, Air Force Reserve weekend duty and also planning to go back to see Melody in DC for my earned weeks' vacation from the CT Transit bus company. Well, at least, I did not have to lie this time on the Air Force for a special duty assignment. I have the perfect cover and never to get busted.

Still, my main agenda was to seek every opportunity to make plans to see Melody every chance I got! I had talked with Adrian to pick up Ant and take him to the movies. I had gone to Bowles

Park to pick up Ant, and then we would go and get Patrina from her house. No way was I going to take Patrina to pick up my son. I wanted to avoid drama at all costs. Anyway, that was the start of it. We then picked up Patrina, and we are all off to the movies. The biggest theater around was the Multiples Cinemas in East Hartford, Connecticut. Once in the theater, we were trying to decide on what movie to see. Well, Ant decided on one movie, and Patrina had decided another one. What was I to do? It was tug-of-war between my girlfriend and my son. She was nineteen years old, and he was eight years old. My son got upset, and Patrina was upset, and I was in the middle of two spoiled people that I cared about. This was a first time for me. I had to play it cool as Patrina was going to stay the weekend with me, and my son was going back home to his mother. Wow! Well, I decided to be the adult and got upset with both of them, and we just left the cinemas altogether. There was nothing left to do but to leave, and that was exactly what we all did. I took Ant to McDonald's and then took him home. Then Patrina wanted to stop for snacks and then, back to my place. I had a few old movies and a VCR player. When we reached my place, I got comfortable and laid across the bed. As I was lying there, my mind drifted off as I was thinking about the cinema incident between my girlfriend and my son. It became evident that Patrina and I could have never attained beyond what we had. I knew that if I was to ever get with anyone, my sons and I were a package deal! No exceptions! I really needed for Patrina to be, at that moment, the bigger person and not to have competed with my son.

From that moment on, we were only hanging out and passing time together. I really enjoyed her company and the times we spent together. I had really liked her too! I mean really as to say there was a little struggle within me to keep holding on to her, but this little incident made my choice quite a bit easier to eventually let her go! Still I did not want to let her go so fast as I was emotionally attached to her. Yes, I really liked her a lot. Right as I was about to get up off the bed to start the movie, Patrina asked me what I was thinking, and the only thing that came to my mind was her. So I told her that I was thinking of her and how I was feeling. It was hard to look at her young and innocent eyes and not feel the connection that we had. As I looked back at her and into her eyes, I knew that Melody had my heart. Melody was the only one person stopping Patrina and I from having a more serious relationship. It did not matter who I was with or hanging out with or what I would be doing. Melody always found a way to be on my mind. Our weekend between Patrina and I went well. I did tell her on the way to taking her home that I would be gone for about eight or nine days for some military training in DC. The good thing was that she was never in the military, and she did not understand what I was talking about. I could not tell her that I would be with my other girlfriend in DC. The real one! So I had to lie about in my absence that I would be on another military assignment! Well, at least, she and the others would be missing me for the time that I would be away.

I could not believe that I was between two women that cared about me in two different places, but my heart was only with Melody. I knew that I wanted to be married again, but I did not know how I ever become seriously committed to one woman! I did not have the answer to that unknown question that lingered into my mind! I had a few days to spare and wanted to see Jasmine once more before leaving, but we had to meet during the week. I had also seen her on the bus with her sister that was visiting from New York. I now had another problem. It was her sister Felicia, light-skinned, intriguing, and full of life! This girl was just like a bad, sexy girl for real. We were flirting with each other on the bus, right in front of her sister. I even got her number to talk as "friends." I would have traded her with Jasmine in a heartbeat, but that reality could never be. I think that Felicia wanted more of the attention for herself than anything else.

I was telling Jasmine about how I liked her sister too. Then Jasmine told me to go for it and started to cry. What did I just do? Then I told her that I was just playing, and I was interested in her. Then we made plans to hangout after I had got off work because I just had to see her! I could not understand on how she could be this into me in such a short time. She was so there for me and into me too! To say the least, I was at a loss! I really did not understand her at all and this connection that she had with me. You would think that we had been together for years, but it was only weeks of time spent together. As we would talk on the phone, she would really open up about herself. Then I would remind her that we had to take it slow as I still had a wife in which I always used as a convenience. I must say that Jasmine was definitely a sweetheart and as nice as she could be. I did know that what we had shared together was all I had to give to her, and my heart would never to be included. I was not letting Melody go nor did not have any strength to ever leave her anyway. I was not leaving Melody for anyone, and my mind was made up! Well, Jasmine and I hung out for a while at my place, and I had to get her back home because I had one more workday. I was on my way to out of town to see Melody in DC! I had packed (to include something for church) and planned to load up the car on my bus midday split shift. I knew what I was doing was totally wrong, even though it did not make me feel that it was wrong. Again, I am living this double life, but when I was with Melody, I did not think of my other ladies. But when I was with the other ladies, I only thought about Melody!

Once I had arrived to DC again, I stayed at Melody's apartment again. They must have sprayed the bathroom this time. I did not see not one roach! I was more relaxed this time. We did everything this week, especially since it was summer. I could not see enough her. I had got tickets to do a DC tour, and we rode the tour bus for Washington DC. Then we had got off by the Washington Monument and decided to take the elevator to the top of the monument. The elevator ride was long like forever! But we finally made it to the top. As we looked out of the windows, I took a few pictures. It was totally unbelievable up there! While still on the top floor, you can feel the movement of the monument sway from side to side. It was a little scary but well worth the while. After we had returned from all the DC touring, we want to get something to eat. Well, we had decided to walk the neighbor and find a place to eat. We walked, just over a mile, to this place called the Shrimp Boat located at 4510 East Capitol Street, NE, Washington, DC, and we could not find anything that we wanted to eat. The walking was cool, holding hands and sometimes hugging. It was so nice as I was not used to this type of romance of any sort. Melody and I were actually sharing our thoughts and feelings and spent real quality time together. We ended up driving down to Long John Silver seafood restaurant up on Central Avenue, and the restaurant was on the right-hand side. Every moment that we shared together blocked out the rest of the world as if no one else mattered.

Well, the next day, we got up and hung out at the Baltimore Aquarium in Maryland including taking picture for our keepsake. There was so much to do there even at the Baltimore Harbor. Everything that we did was a first time that we ever had ventured out like we did as a couple. We were creating a lot of first times, and Melody was the first and only person that I had romanced like this. I was even trying to take her on a helicopter ride in Maryland, but it never worked out for one reason or another. After touring the aquarium, we walked around the harbor. We were so involved with each other and observing the different shows and events. There was a lot to do at the harbor. We almost got on one of those water taxis for fun but did not want to take a chance on getting wet. We spent the whole day there and then made our way back to DC.

The next day, we shared a Kentucky Fried Chicken picnic at Hain's Point in DC, another public and popular park in the area. It was a soulful kind of place with a few picnic tables, family bonding, and a host of other things to do; folks were even playing on the grass. The biggest attraction there was the seventy-foot giant aluminum man in the ground sculpture by the artist Seward Johnson entitled "The Awakening." This thing was truly a work of art and just awesome. I had never seen anything like this, so we decided to take pictures of it, and we took pictures of the sculpture and some with us in it. I did not think that we wanted to miss this park memories without the pictures. This week kept being a surprise to us as I kept making efforts to impress upon Melody to be a first time for everything that we did. I wanted everything to be memorable at every turn in our relationship. The more I spent time with Melody, the more I was becoming disinterested in my other ladies. I kept getting these feelings and chills or goosebumps that couldn't be explained. I knew that there was something about my Melody in the way she was not easy for me to have. Therefore, I had to keep working to impress her. She was well worth it. I was doing whatever it took for me to see her, even if I continued to lie and took off from my CT Transit bus job. In fact, I would easily do it again in a heartbeat. It felt to me that she was worth every day of pay that I had missed, just to see her again. Melody was so beautiful to me. Some moments, I would just be lost looking at her with amazement. I was overtaking by her niceness and had a lot of getting used to someone like her. I was getting hooked on her, and that was nothing to complain about. The more I looked at her, the more I had to be with her.

These moments were not just time spent together; it was so much more. Melody and I had something truly special. Melody then suggested that I should go over to the Pentagon and talk to my new friends to try to get another assignment there. So after I had arrived back to the Pentagon, I parked illegally, and I went to see Annie B. I then told her that I wanted to get back into the building, meaning the Pentagon, to work there again. Immediately, she took me over to introduce me to this major in the Air Force by the name of Barbara Gilchrist. This sister was short, nice, and cute! I mentioned to Maj. Gilchrist that I had used to work for Ms. Sparks the SES, and she would be able to ask her questions if needed. She was about business and a good listener. I was intrigued by her last name, and thought that this could have not have been a coincidence. If not, what was it? I truly believe that her name was sign of sorts. She told me that she would see what she could do and let me know. I left her with my number. We shook hands and was on my way. I also spoke to Reggie, Byron Strickland, and a few other folks. I even said hello to Ms. Sparks at her office, even though it seemed very productive just to stop through the Pentagon. The name of Gilchrist was all over my mind, and I could not wait to tell Melody about her and that there may be a chance I could get another assignment.

Once I had got back to Melody's apartment, she was glad to see me, and I was glad to see her! We were missing each other in that short amount of time! I then told Melody everything. The last few days were about Melody and me. We were growing together and bonding like non other. I was beginning to feel that feeling again when I first arrived to the Pentagon—that my life was about to change, and it was unfolding right before my eyes! Melody and I took another walk just to be walking, and she was showing me around her DC/bordering the Maryland neighborhood area. Even though it was in southeast DC, our walks were peaceful together. And all that I was truly interested in was my Melody, and she was my song! That is what I would call her from time to time! The next day, we drove over to meet her best friend Brenda and her husband Randy McCain. They had a dog named Domino, a German shepherd. We stayed over to her house for a while. Randy and I had talked about the military and basketball. I was not sure if he had game enough to play against me, so all we kept doing was talking. Then we went to get something to eat, and that ended our day! My final day came so quickly. We did not do the helicopter or the air balloon ride, but every moment shared was something special. I was actually getting to know Melody as my friend and not just a relationship. Her, Brenda, Randy, and I were talking about sports and how Brenda and Melody were cheerleaders and ran track—both holding captain or co-captain positions. I also learned about their track coach Mr. Bobo at the McKinley Tech High School in DC and of one young lady that was faster than Melody, and her name was Gracie Brown. Not only did they both started together for track and cheerleading at the Douglas Junior High School, they were the best of friends with their other track friend Lisa Todd. They were a tight trio of friends. I could tell that these ladies were really close based on the passion in their conversation!

Well, it was beginning to get late. We were about to leave. We greeted each other, and I said goodbye to their dog Domino. What a beautiful dog, I was thinking. But I just let the thought past through my mind since our dog Misty was attacked by my former next-door neighbor. My childhood memories will always be a void in my mind. Misty will always be the memory that I could ever imagine to call my dog. At all costs, I will never be close to a dog again! Anyway, we made our way to get some chicken and go back to the apartment. This was my last night there after a very productive week in DC. This was the best week that I have ever spent with anyone, and I was really falling in love with Melody. I knew that I had a messy life with the ladies and all, but I had a lot of mixed up feelings, and I just knew my strength to let them all go was just something that I had to deal with, especially how my feelings were growing toward Melody. I knew I was so wrong, and I could not tell her without the risk of losing her.

One thing was for sure: I wanted to figure out a way to eventually tell her of my other escapades without losing her. I could not afford to lose her, and I could not stay with her without telling her the total truth. I could not really do the lie thing as it was with my first wife, and I refuse to do the lie thing with Melody. I just was able to keep telling myself to wait. I was falling love with Melody and could not bear to hurt her at all. I was so fearful of the pain that it would cause her to know the truth about my affairs. I just kept asking myself that I was still married, so how is that more cheating? This question to myself was enough to put it off for a while longer and not to say anything. Many thoughts were roaming through my mind, but I was not going to say anything to Melody. But someday, Melody would know the truth because I would have to tell her. Once again, I was living a temporary double life! Telling her the truth was just something that I just had to eventually do! This week made me realize that I now have hope and a conscience! I have not spoken about the *love* word to anyone. I never even wanted a divorce from Adrian until I met Melody that is the God's truth! That divorce would be the first priority to be resolved once I return back to Connecticut. Melody and I stayed awake and kept talking, staying close until we drifted off into the night. The mornings always seemed to come faster when Melody and I were together. As we were about to arise to start the day, I told Melody this little poem similar to something that I heard growing up. It went something like reminding us of eating her mother's cooking, and it was funny too. Here it goes: "I love you once. I love you twice, I love you more than your mother's beans and rice." It was my little saying to Melody that brought us both much joy every time that I would mention it. We would just laugh at it! And then, each and every time that I would blow a kiss her way when we were at a distance, Melody would pretend to catch it and put her hand to her lips. This was one lady that I most definitely wanted to be the mother of my baby! These two things that Melody and I shared were also a first from me to her! I wanted her to always remember me and us being together.

Well, we made our keepsakes together and had to be getting dressed, so I could get back to Connecticut to be back at work on the following day. I really wanted to stay, but by now, I know that I needed to have my own place. Now, that thought made it very easier to leave this time. Because I knew that I needed to have my own place. I was packed up and ready to roll. Of course, once again, Melody saw me off, and while walking back to the car, I noticed that I now had no hood ornament in the front of my caddy and the one in the back that covered the trunk keyhole. They were both gone. What a disappointment. Wow! Somebody was upset with me or that was a term of endearment to say, "Welcome to the neighborhood!" Nevertheless, my caddy ornaments were gone, and I did not like that at all. Well, I thought it was still a caddy and pressed my way back on the road. My mind was full with thoughts going back home, mostly filled with the time Melody and I shared together. The only damper to the whole thing was that I missed my hood ornaments to my car. So I moved my thoughts to about working the extra hours to get my divorce.

The drive was so pleasant, so I was moving in my car get back to my place. A long drive felt short because my thoughts toward Melody, and our lives that were taking shape. I really didn't mind the drive nor paying the tolls. I would do it again in a heartbeat to see my Melody. Well, the long drive seemed short, but my mind was filled with good thoughts. Just like that the drive was eventually over, getting a divorce was on my mind, and nevertheless, I was home again and to my own place. I had no one to come home to, and trust me, I did not like that feeling. But I did have thoughts of Melody and decided to call her. We talked for a minute because I was missing her in some kind of way. Plus, that empty apartment did not help me at all. I was also telling her that I had to figure out on how to get back to the Pentagon. I was hoping my meeting with Maj. Gilchrist would also work out. While we were talking, I had made up the bed with clean linen and changed the bathroom towels. I got my bus uniform stuff ready as well as it was time to take my shower, set the alarm clock, and go to bed. I got up the next day, showered, got dressed, and for a first time in a long time, I showed up a little bit early for work. During my break, I got a newspaper, and when I reached home, I pulled out the phonebook and looked through the newspaper to find a lawyer for a dissolution of marriage or divorce lawyer. I really wanted to be a free man. I was so glad that I did not leave Adrian for Melody.

Instead, I left my girlfriend for Melody. Now I wanted to do the right thing and get a divorce. I was still a crazy and wild married man that wanted to be free in which I truly figured out why I should have never gotten married. I was nowhere close to a real relationship until my dream girl came along. This will always be weird for me as my wife dreamed about the second wife, and Adrian was okay with it. She had accepted that she and I were done. Truly, I do believe that Adrian would have never divorced me. The reason that she would not divorce me, I would never know, or maybe, I may be in denial. I had found this one attorney in Hartford, Connecticut, named Mr. DiFazio to represent me for my no-contest divorce for under $400, and I was allowed to make payments. The only thing we had together was debt to pay from the 1985 bankruptcy and our son. I was paying her about $200 a month child support that we had agreed upon. The attorney Mr. DiFazio and I had set up a meeting later in the week on my day off to meet and sign the necessary paperwork. I am finally doing it and really getting a divorce. It has been long overdue!

As for my game, the wife and girlfriend thing (the line that I was using) had worked for me as I would pick up women. Now that I was getting really serious about Melody. It was not so important anymore for me to still be in the game. I was not seeing my other ladies as much only here and there. Adrian and I were still friends and such, and we would continue to work together in raising Ant. Time was not about to stop because September was almost over, and I now had a court date set for the divorce. This part was unbelievable for real. The date was set on October 19, 1993, which was also my son's eighth birthday of all days. I was excited to be getting a divorce and disappointed that it would be on my son's birthday. I had never been comfortable with that date. Not ever! I had to meet at the Superior Court Judicial District of Hartford/New Britain, Connecticut.

It was a Tuesday, and I had to change my work schedule to attend the court. At the same time when I had called Melody, she wanted to come and see me and look at Connecticut, just in case our future was moving in that direction. I completed my Air Force Reserve on the first weekend in October. I was glad that weekend was over, and Melody was coming up to spend some time with me. But now, I had to make everyone else scarce by the time she had arrived to Connecticut with me and my son. The thing was I had to go and pick her up. It would be a lot of driving, but I would figure it out and get it done during my days off. Adrian and I had made a plan for her to meet me on my bus route to bring me Ant so I could take him with me. So I took Ant (he was glad to spend time with me) with me to DC on October 7 after my bus shift ended. I went home to change, and we were on our way because we had just had new bus routes, and I was off on Thursdays and Sundays, and since following Monday was the celebration of Columbus Day. I would be off and get paid for that Monday anyway, and no money would be lost. We would have to spend one night there, and Ant would meet her family. I was thinking and feeling guilty on the drive to DC. I did not want my two sons to keep seeing me with all these women. I let Big Mike met three of them, and Ant met about five women that I was dating. My two sons were working on my conscience, and they were not aware of what was going on. I just knew that I was setting a bad example for both of my boys, and I had to start changing. Actually, I was already changing. I wanted a better life and to become a better example for both of my sons. It was two months ago that I was in DC, and this time, I now had my son with me. Ant and I stopped by Krissy's job in DC at the Army National Guard Headquarters. She was glad to see me and meet my son. It was while I was talking to Krissy that Ant snuck off without drawing any attention to himself. All of a sudden, we heard this loud noise of sirens going off. What was it? Or who done it? It was my little man that was kind of bored. He had pulled the fire alarm. People were running from everywhere, and that was a huge place. The commander had come out, and I did explain that my son pulled the alarm. He understood, and all went well. There was no concerns thereafter. Wow! After the long drive and a stop, I was getting tired and wanted to rest. Ant was to sleep on the sofa, and I took a shower and getting ready to laid down. I was down for the count and just plain tired! The next morning, we had got up a little late. Ms. Mary had fixed some breakfast. We all then just poked around for a short while and started to gather our things. My son Ant was ready to leave as he had nothing to do. After he had mentioned it a few times already, we started to gather our things to get moving back to Connecticut.

It was late when we had arrived, so I knew one of the first things that we had to do was to get some gas before getting on the road. I had to get some gas, and a Mountain Dew soda, including some snacks. I also wanted to see how Melody and Ant would act together around each other. I did not want another Patrina and Ant action. I did not know what to expect. On the other hand, Melody and Ant were doing well together. Yes! I was so glad that it was working out between those two, and there was not a competition between the two of them. Surprisingly, Melody was actually good with kids. She mentioned how she spent some time with her nephew Dawain and took him to the circus, and other places. I was glad that Ant had come with me to DC, and everything was working well. Okay, now it was time to be head back and get on the road. We had taken the stuff to the car and went back in the apartment building to say bye to Linda. Once Linda let us into her apartment, and she had just instantly fell in love with Ant. She found some candy to give to him because she had to give him something. This time we left Linda's place; once again, we were on our way. I was glad that Melody would get to see Connecticut because I had just told everybody about her. I also knew that she would back me up driving if she had to. After a few hours of driving with a few pitstops, it was going well. We had plenty of conversation too. We have passed through other states and now New York. Then Connecticut would be the next to get us home to my apartment. I was so glad that the dealership fixed the transmission to provide me with reliable transportation again, especially so I could be able to see Melody.

My life was coming together with someone that I actually cared for. My life had changed so much since I met Melody. Once we arrived back to Hartford, I took Ant to his new address on Raymond Street because I only had a one bedroom and would make plans to pick him up again. One of my motives was that I wanted to see Melody's interaction with him and also his response. This part was very instrumental to my relationship. I really did not want to be blindsided by love and always wanted everyone to know that my two sons and I were a package deal, and I would never deny them. This was something that I kept to myself because our family's true acceptance had to be a natural response from Melody and not prompted, which was also very important to me! Melody was a winner, and she had helped me to feel alive again, and because of her, I was beginning to have a conscience. I was beginning to care about love again and that it truly existed for me. When I looked at Melody and would think that if there was ever a fairytale that was true to me, this one would be it. Melody was my fairytale dream girl that came true! If knowing her was a dream, please do not wake me up!

Well, it was Friday, and it was just us two, and I was getting that jai alai itch and wanted to do a little gambling and to show off my new lady. When we were walking into that place on that Friday evening, all I can say is that all eyes were on us, well her! I had never had that much attention ever! She was the showstopper. The people I knew and introduced her to would all say that she's beautiful! It was countless times, and that was all that I had heard: she is beautiful! We did not stay long at all. I don't even remember if I had won, but this time, I did not lose much. Melody had asked me why I had to gamble. I thought about it and could not find an answer, but what I had found instead was guilt. I was beginning to feel all kinds of regrets and guilt in just over a few words Melody had spoken softly to me. I had finished that round of jai alai. I gathered my things and left because I could not answer Melody as to why I was gambling, and in actuality, I was hooked in a bad way. It was the way she asked me why I did it, the gambling. All I knew was that I was cured! Just like that, we left that place, and I never gambled at jai alai again. I had truly lost more than I had ever won but gained a new reality for jai alai. I was cured, and I promised to never go there again! My true cure was Melody's question to me, and I never had to go to a Gamblers Anonymous, not one time. I was cured and had my life's control back. I could breathe again all because of Melody! I had promised Melody that I would never go back there again. I was alive again!

Melody and I had a nice quiet night of talking and chilling, and it was very nice. She was so easy to talk to and to be around with. Our lives were clicking together, and we were really bonding together. You could feel our love growing together with each moment that we were there together. It was like I could feel her thoughts, and she did not want to leave my side. We watched a movie and continued to chill. Melody was so sweet, and her sweetness alone was like therapy for me. My life was changing, even more than I could have ever imagined right before my eyes. The thing that was strange about all the things that I was doing was her kindness. The fact of the matter was that Melody and I did not argue nor did she try to force me or anything of such. It was all my choice to do the right thing. I really did not mind doing none of it. The divorce was soon to come, the gambling has stopped at jai alai, the cursing was getting lessened, and the other ladies that I was seeing were slowing going away. I wanted to make these changes, and I did it own my own. We shared laughter together. I was happier than I have ever been before.

On Saturday, we got up, showered, and got dressed for the day. Melody had on this outfit with like a Navy type of military service hat, but it was really a lady's type of fashioned hat. This outfit was bad as in good, and she looked as if she had stepped out of a magazine. She was just gorgeous! So we ate some cereal and was on our way. I had to go and pick up Ant as he was to spend the day with me, and now Melody as I drove the bus on my route. So I dropped them off temporarily and went to the CT Transit garage to pick up my bus for the day. I picked them up on the way to start my bus route downtown Hartford. They both rode with me for two trips, end to end. On the next leg back to the West Farms Mall, Melody and Ant was going to stay at the mall while I had to drive the other next two legs of my trip. That was her first unexpected babysitting gig that she did by watching my son. For over the next two and half hours, I could not wait to see how it turned out.

Once I had arrived back to the mall, I had one more end-to-end bus trip to do on my bus route after picking them up. Well, I was pushing that bus a little to get to the end of the route, so would have a few extra minutes with Melody and my son. Ant had got away from Melody at the toy store and went outside to wait for me at the bus stop. Melody was coming quickly behind him and told me that Ant was good except for the few times that she could not find him. Also Ant was impatient on getting the ice cream that she promised him, so he left and ran outside. As for my regards, Melody did well, and Ant was beginning to like her as well since he could not drive her away from me. It was almost great, but it turned out pretty okay. Well, to be honest, it turned out better than I had expect it to. Ant was a little spoiled by me, and that did not help her at all. I was glad that little experiment was a one and done to never be repeated. I now only had two more round trips to do, and my shift would be over for the day. They stayed on the bus for the remainder of my shift. I was glad about it that I had company and my pretty woman to see.

Just like that, Melody was able to see my day-to-day bus route. I had one more trip to the mall and to Blue Hills Road to Bloomfield. Well, once we arrived downtown to the lineup, the folks exited the bus, mostly from the mall, with their bags and stuff. Then I allowed the folks waiting to get on the bus using their passes or transfers. As the end of the folks getting on the bus was almost done, and then, I noticed Patrina at the next to the last person to get on my bus. I shook my head as if to say, "You can't ride the bus with me today." She quickly got out of line and went to the next bus. I was busted bigger than day! Melody looked me dead in my face, and we stepped off the bus to talk as I had a few minutes before leaving. I had told Melody that girl, I had nodded away was one of my ex-girlfriends. Then I pointed her out by my description of her, so Melody could see what she looked like, and I would still see her from time to time! I was glad that she was attractive because I could not say anything more because they both were my present girlfriends. It turned out that Melody did believe me and took my word for it. That was too close for comfort as I did not want anything to jump off on my bus, nor me to get busted for a real domestic scene. They saw each other briefly, and it may have been too much because I did not deny what I had with Melody, and we were going strong and getting stronger! I kept taking risks and decided to take another one. After the last bus run was over for the day, I was headed to take the bus back to the garage with Melody and Ant.

It was beginning to get dark, but we had some sun leftover. I decided to let Melody drive my bus to see if she could handle it. What did I do that for? Was I crazy or what? Well, Melody got us about one hundred yards on the road before slamming on the brakes. Ant and I did not know she was going to do that so abruptly I immediately grabbed the rail to brace myself, and Ant grabbed the rail by the farebox, just in time or he would have gone through the right windshield. Ant had some quick reactions to hold on to the railing. It was almost a catastrophe, and it became fun for us instead after it was all over. We were all fearful and laughing at the same time! That was a moment never to be forgotten. I jumped back into the driver's seat, and off we went to the garage. If I had gotten caught for letting Melody drive, I would have lost my job for sure! As I went through the CT Transit gate, I had dropped them off at the lane by my car and then took my bus into the garage. I parked it and went to meet up with Melody and Ant. We stopped to eat, and I then took Ant home. That was a fun-filled day and most memorable! Now, I wanted to spend the remainder of the time with Melody before I took her home. We spoke a little on my upcoming divorce that was a week and a half away. Then I would be a free man. I was hoping that she did not ask me to marry her or bring the conversation up on marriage, which would have ruined all for me.

I had never thought of her as the asking kind of woman, but I had to be the one to ask for her hand in marriage. It was truly a win-win because the conversation never came up. Melody was just glad for me that I would be free. We then talked about her driving the bus and on how she felt about keeping my son. She did say that he was spoiled rotten. It was fun for all we did, especially the part of me not playing jai alai anymore! That was good all by itself. We just talked and enjoyed our time that we had left because tomorrow, she would be returning to DC. Melody mentioned that she did think about surprising me and just showing up at my door. While it was not a wise decision, and our relationship would have been totally over. I just told her I was glad that she did not do it. The drive would give us more time together. She agreed! I was thinking that her heart would have been crushed, and I did not want to do that to her at all! I know that I have cleaned up my act a whole lot, but I still was not totally there yet. I took her back to DC and spent one night. Our relationship was really growing fast, and we were getting very serious in our going forward. We both felt that we had something real, and I was feeling it. I was connecting to her family as well, especially to Linda and Butch. I had assumed that Melody was getting positive feedback from everyone because I was still there with Melody. We were almost inseparable.

Once again, that night and the morning gone and came too fast, and I had to be leaving again. I was in a very long distance relationship, which was not fun at all. Neither one of us enjoyed the distance, and I was hoping for another assignment at the Pentagon. We shall see! I kissed her several times and held her tightly close. Then off I went into the day, with the sun shining in the brightness of the day. If I had looked back, I would have turned around to see her once again. I don't believe it. It was totally harder to leave her; in fact, it was the same for the both of us. Once I arrived back to Connecticut, I had called Patrina. There was no answer the first time, so I called her right back! This time Patrina answered, and the way she answered the phone, I knew that something was wrong, and I did know why, but I played innocent. She had asked if that was Melody. I replied yes! After seeing me with Melody on the bus a few days ago, Patrina no longer wanted to be in the background. I had to make a choice, and I did not want to do that either. So Patrina stated that she would not be able to see me again, and it was over between us. I totally understood, and this was our last conversation ever! Now, I was down to two others, Jasmine and Vivian, plus my soon to be ex-wife. Without saying anything, Melody was my choice, hands down! I knew that eventually everybody else had to go.

Sometimes on my off day, I would take Adrian to run a few of her errands, even though we were getting a divorce. We stayed friends and all for the sake of our son. She even came over to my place, and we would hang out for a while. Then she would have to leave to pick up Ant once he returned home from school. This day before Adrian had left, we had a little argument, which meant to me that she still cares. I could not give to her no more than I was giving. Another relationship was nowhere in my sights. As we were about to leave, I just had to tell her again that this was the reason for arguments like this that I wanted a divorce. That little argument reminded me all over again why I was divorcing her. It was this day a few days before the actual divorce. It was the last time that Adrian and I were ever close again as husband and wife. But we would always be friends! The month of October was not playing; the days were moving so fast!

It was October 19, 1993, and it was my son Ant's birthday. What an unusual coincidence. I remember being in the courtroom, and my lawyer Mr. DiFazio was speaking on my behalf. We all paused by the judge's direction to wait for Adrian to show up, but she never did. I know that this divorce pained her so bad, which is why I will always believe as the real reason for her not to show up! Regardless, the divorce was then granted. The judge then added in the child support (with normal visitation to our son) was about $476 monthly, with a $1 alimony per year. Then we were to split the remaining bills. The caddy was not included because I had obtained it while we were separated. I really did not know how to explain this, but at that moment, the gravel hit the wood, and the judge said that the divorce was granted! I felt like the entire world just lifted off my shoulders. To put it simply, I was totally relieved. I was also happy too! After the divorce, I went by Adrian's job. I officially wanted her to know that we were officially divorced. Her demeanor never changed like she really did not care, but I could beg to differ because she kept my last name. Now, Adrian and I were no longer husband and wife. Now, being platonic friends was our new normal. I did not know what to do with myself. About a week later, Vivian and I just stopped everything. It was too hard for us to schedule time together. Plus, I was tired of being the other man, and we were sneaking around trying to see each other. I was a free man and just refuse to sneak around anymore. Life was getting better. I was now known as a free man and no longer married! What a feeling! It had seemed like with Melody in the picture, all my other relationships were disappearing. So I tried Jasmine first, and she had a prior engagement with her mother. I did not want to be by myself, and I could not be with Melody either. So I had called Denise—yes, Denise—the one who was going to shoot me in my sleep. Anyway, Denise had agreed to see me! One thing I knew for sure: she had not moved on with the guy who gave her the flowers. I had picked her up, and she was in my apartment in East Hartford.

Well, about ten minutes, after we had got to the apartment, the phone began to ring. I should have had it to keep ringing, but I picked it up and had asked for Denise to keep quiet. Patrina was the best at it for keeping quiet. Well, it was my Melody from DC calling. I went into the other room and sat on the floor, and we just talked for about fifteen minutes! As soon as I got off the phone, I had told Denise of who I was talking to. I thought it was cool, and I just had it like that. Nope, I did not! Suddenly, Denise grabbed all my keys and ran out of my apartment, down the stairs, and out of the building. I ran too and was chasing her on the sidewalk, down Burnside Avenue, and part of the pavement had some gravel on it. I was moving too as I could not afford for her to take my car again like she had done in Akron. No way! So I reached out to grab her shirt and jacket collar to slow her down, and as I did that, Denise slipped. And at the rate of speed that we were going, I fell on top of her, and we skidded on the gravel. This was not good as Denise took the brunt of the fall and skid as I had landed on top of her. Denise had skid, and gravel did a number on her. She had injury from her face to arms, stomach, and legs. When I had helped her up, she could barely walk or move. I just got in the car with her and took her home.

We had plans for that night at my apartment, but when Melody had called, all plans were truly diminished in its entirety! I thought on how Melody was keeping girls away from me, even though she was in DC. Now, that was weird! That night I was alone but did not want to be alone, so I called Jasmine again, but she could not go anywhere because her allergies were acting up, and she did not feel well. So we just talked on the phone for a while. I was learning more and more about her as she was quite interesting to talk to, and she told me so much. Sometimes the conversation had gotten emotional, even involving her tears! I was watchful that I was not going to get to emotionally attached to her; one attachment was enough for me. The more that I have listened to Jasmine, I knew something was off. Our conversation went into a different direction altogether. She was getting too seriously involved with me and was loving how I was treating her. I could not believe that this girl was totally mine and really wanted to be with me! Wow! It was getting late, and I had to get up for work. I had to stay busy and only see Jasmine when I could. Even though I had thought about her at times, but I still had Melody, and I was not trading what Melody and I had shared together. Well, it was working, so Jasmine and I were able to hangout a little more since she was my only girl in Connecticut. All ties with other females were gone. It was on the third of November, just before my reserve weekend, and on my break from driving the bus, I received a call from the Pentagon. Wow, I had forgotten all about it.

I had got the call anyway, and boy was I surprised. It was Maj. Gilchrist on the phone line, offering me a three-month assignment to assist on the Air Force budget. I had immediately accepted the assignment as she would be sending the authorization for the orders to my reserve unit at Westover ARB. After we had hung up the phone, I called Westover ARB and talked with MSgt. Jackie Davis. She told me no, I could not go. I was in disbelief. I had put so much into trying to get back there to DC, so I called my Melody and told her. Melody wanted me to call my mother, so we could all pray together on the phone. I did not know how to pray like them, and Melody was praying and keeping up with my mother. We had got off the phone, and all I know is on the next day, on my day off, MSgt. Davis had called me to say that my orders were approved for me to go back to the Pentagon for six months. Then I could pick up my orders on Saturday and do my orders processing.

One thing that I knew for sure is that prayer works! On Saturday, the sixth of November, I became a local celebrity at the base for going back to the Pentagon. Not only did I have to pick up my orders and then, out process for my travel to DC, but I now had to do an interview too, with the Public Affairs office, and a writeup for the base newspaper. It was none other than MSgt. Gordon A. Newell from the Public Affairs. This interview was to be featured in the Westover newspaper called the PATRIOT, 439th Airlift Wing, Air Force Reserve, Westover ARB, Volume, XX, Number X, November 10, 1993. I was to be on page 4, of the *Patriot Newspaper* entitled "Westover Reservists Chosen to Assist Pentagon Projects." They took my picture and all, so the interview and the picture were right there on the page. This was actually great news because my life was coming together, so I would be closer to Melody. The ladies and I were going in separate directions anyway. Besides, I was always leaving town with the Air Force for long periods of time. Relationships of many women were phasing out for me. Melody was the only good thing that was constant for me, besides having two sons I was crazy about and loved very much, plus the owed child support. The prayer of my mother and Melody allowed me to be back on my way to DC. It was not until now, with Melody in my life, that I continue to see my life was turning around to the good.

I was only down to one other woman in Connecticut. I could not get too close to Jasmine because she was falling in love with me. I knew that I did not love her, but I did like her and only wish for her sister too. Of course, that did not happen. It was only wishful thinking. I had gotten packed up again and had everything done. I finished that week out at CT Transit and took another military leave. This time I had given them a copy of my orders. For the way things were happening for me, it felt like it was meant to be for Melody and me. There was so much that was happening to me and around me that I could only accept it and not explain none of it. All my ladies were out of the way. I had seemed to be done with cheating or the relationship just broke off for various reasons. It was kind of strange or weird in a way, but it was real because it was happening to me. For real! I was growing up, and since the divorce, I was actually happy, especially since I could now see Melody full-time. I knew that this time, thinking to myself on the drive to DC, that I did not want to mess this thing up with Melody because it felt too real. Also I knew that this time I was moving to DC, if I had to, Melody was my main focus.

Deep down inside me, I really wanted to be married again, and it was easier to become an honest man. I knew that I had to be married to the right woman, and Melody was the only closest thing to me that was a perfect fit to my thought. Well, once I got back to DC, I had to get my act together with other ladies, so I stopped by to see Krissy on my way to the apartment's that I was staying at before. I had told her that I was passing through and wanted to see her but did not stay long. She was glad to see me again. I mentioned that I would be back at the Pentagon and could not really see her like I thought I would. I had told her that I was now divorced and making a go at it with my girlfriend, and we were pretty serious. I was sure not to tell her of a brand-new girlfriend that I was serious about. I gave her impression that it was Denise and not Melody. I hugged her and left. I did the same thing for Getta, and she was a little hurt. She kept saying, "Michael, it should have been me." What she was looking for I only had enough for Melody. I did tell Getta that she was truly a sweet person, and we could stay friends. She was about to cry, so I told her that I had to leave. If I had gotten a little closer, it would have been harder for me to leave, but I had to leave or I would have stayed. I had to fix all my loose ends, or I would have gotten busted. I, in no way, wanted to hurt Melody that I cared deeply for. The only one that I did not talk to was Angelique, but we kind of faded in the distance, so I thought that there was no need to call her. Plus, I did not want any more parking tickets for overnight stays at Howard University dorms.

I was free for the remainder of Saturday and Sunday. I had to be back at the Pentagon on Monday to in-process, all over again. I was glad that I still knew some people and was not a stranger like when I first arrived in 1992. Almost a year later, I cannot believe that I was back in the Pentagon! Even one better, I was full of joy this time and falling in love with Melody. I wanted everyone to know that Melody was it for me. I was doing a lot of changing myself, just to have the perfect opportunity to make a real impression to her. As I was leaving the apartment garage on Saturday to go to the store, I saw Tracey out by her car. She did not know that I was back, and I did not know that she was pregnant and still living in the same apartment building. Tracey was very, very pregnant, and I was not the father, and I knew that for a fact! I was thinking of asking her just that: "I thought that you could not get pregnant." But she was, in fact, all the way pregnant. I was happy for her and happy that it was not mine. I have always kept my innocence with her because I always had trust issues. My sneaking suspicions were all the way correct. Anyway, I had missed her and was rubbing on her belly, and I had pulled up her dress to see her stomach and rubbed it again. I missed Tracey in a very different way. I guess it was always a friendly tease, at least on my part. Well, I had to get to the commissary and the BX before the store had to close. So we greeted again and left. She had planned to stop by later on, and I gave her my new apartment number.

I was off to the base to pick up a few groceries and milk. I was back at the apartment and first had to wipe down everything, so I would feel as comfortable again as my stay there before. It was about three hours later, and Tracey had knocked on the door. Before I knew it, we were in my bed and were about to… I just stopped due to my wishful thinking, and I could not do anything because that was not my baby growing inside her. Then I was thinking that I was the fall guy because her dude was nowhere in sight. I was not going to pick up the pieces to her life and mess up my life with Melody. I was not going to do it! So I calmed myself down, and we started fixing our clothes up and went back into the living room. If there was no Melody in my life, I would have never stopped. I was ever so close to messing up! But I was glad I did not. I had this sneaking suspicion that Tracey would have found a way to make me regret it ever had happened. I was so glad that I had the strength to stop. In all reality, I could not believe that I had any strength to stop and not to engage any further. We were so close, but my mind could not go any further. Even then, Melody was on my mind. And I was not going to do anything more with Tracey to jeopardize my up-and-coming relationship with Melody, even though I never told Melody this story. At the same time, Tracey kept coming over to my apartment since we lived in the same building. Or she would be ringing my phone. She wanted to sneak around Melody's back. I still was not going to do anything further and in Melody's face at that. Melody started to come over more.

Then shortly afterward, like in a few weeks, we were practically living together. Not even Tracey could come between us. I was beginning to get stronger and settle down with one woman. Tracey kept trying. We would meet for happy hour after work, and she would try to make plans or something. Still nothing! I figured out afterward that maybe she was trying to get me in a compromising position or just catch me off guard to show Melody some proof that I was cheating. I was not that stupid to let my guard all the way down. Getta and I stayed platonic friends for the longest time. It was one night in November. Melody and I were in my apartment chilling about to call it a night. Then there was this knock on the door. I got up to answer the door, and it was Angelique, the premed student from Howard University. She was a nice young lady, and we just dropped off from staying in touch. I pretty much thought that we were done anyway. But her knock on the door proved otherwise. I even moved to a different apartment since returning to DC, but still Angelique found me and wanted to surprise me. Instead, I surprised her, but I was surprised because I had never expected to see her again. I was honest as Melody wanted me to be with my past life, and I mentioned to her that I had company, and I wanted Melody to hear me because I wanted Melody to see that I was changing because it was true. Melody was changing me. Angelique was immediately upset and turned away walking faster to the elevators. I quickly put on my shoes and ran after her. I did not know until I caught up with her as to how she really felt about me and was waiting for me to contact her. Angelique got tired of waiting for me to show up, so she came to my new apartment. I could only figure that she received my new apartment number from the concierge but really did not know. While I was playing the fields, these ladies were getting serious with me, and I really did not truly understand why and the same with Patrina and

Jasmine in Connecticut. With the exception of Patrina, I really did not spend a lot of time with these women.

I then told Angelique that I was in a serious relationship. I then softly said goodbye as she was leaving, and I saw her holding back her tears as she quickly walked away from me to catch the Metro train at the Court House Metro and then back to Howard University. I went back upstairs to my apartment and told Melody what had transpired with Angelique. I told Angelique that I had moved on, but she was still waiting on my return in which I did not know. I really did not mean for that to happen like that, and I could not fix it. Melody understood me and did not get upset but held me instead. I was thinking if I had known that, I would had talked to her like I had told Krissy and Getta—that I was now in a serious relationship, but indeed, I truly missed that opportunity to have fixed it in advance! I really did not understand how I could deserve such a classy lady like Melody who accepted me with my checkered past. Yet to my disbelief, Melody has never held my past against me. Even though I had a sultry past, I too was into Melody and had always thought to myself and told her aloud that I did not deserve her or she was just too good to be with me! I was ever more intrigued to change and become a better person because of Melody. Still, Melody and I did not go out to the clubs. There was no need to go out anymore nor a desire to do so because we had each other. We just loved sharing our time being together! To be honest, this was all new for me, to be with only one woman, and I was just loving every moment too! Melody was just differently good all the way around her. Yes, she was some kind of special! I just wanted to keep going and growing with her. Melody kept seeing me constantly growing and letting go of my past. I knew that this area in DC and Virginia would become my home, if this temporary duty assignment did not work out. I decided to give it my best shot and to try to get a permanent assignment at the Pentagon or somewhere close to her. I kept telling myself that I did not want to lose Melody. The distance was too much for me. Plus I knew that I would just mess up again. I must admit that I was trying to become an honest man. Because on the real side of things, I have never even wanted to try to become something close to honest until Melody happened to me! Still, I will tell her that she saved my life. The freedom and the trust that she gave me made me want to be honest on my own. I think often as to how I would have never afforded to her the same relationship type of opportunity she gave me; I just knew that I did not deserve a second chance! This woman gave me undeserving love. Even though at first, she was not even attracted to me. Who does that?

Melody kept trusting me as we kept growing together, and I did not even trust myself! I think that she was determined to not only change me but assist me in turning my life around. I just could not believe again, her commitment to me and to us. Slowly on my part and we were growing together, Melody was teaching me to trust again. Since women came so easy for me, it was truly hard for me to trust women at all. Yet Melody kept standing out above the other ladies. Then I would say to myself, all my other lady friends were gone out of my life, except for Melody. Maybe Melody was really the one for me. Sometimes, I would think that I was somehow insecure by having so many women. Yet again, I felt secure with Melody! I could not answer why I felt secure with Melody. Even I could not answer that question concerning my relationship security. All I knew is that it was that, I never wanted to lose her. I kept noticing that the more that she trusted me, the closer I was drawn to her. Now we were moving on as our relationship was becoming pretty tightly knitted together. It was around Thanksgiving holiday, and her church had a program that Melody was to participate in the praise-dancing for her church in the dance ministry. I really did not mind because it was another opportunity for me to see and spend time with her. Plus, I realized that my club days were just gone, and church was the new direction that I was heading for. She was exactly what I wanted, and it was happening right in front of me. Privately to God, I said I was asking for a wife, and I wanted her to be in church. The thing was that Melody was already in church; we had kept going to church, but Melody had backslidden. There was not a doubt in my mind, but she was still dedicated to the church.

The thing was that we both were attending church, and we both were backsliders. I was a backslider since age sixteen, and Melody had backslidden at age twenty-three, but we never stop going to church. I knew that one day I, well we, would be back in church. Melody and I had made plans to get my sons Ant and Big Mike for the Christmas holiday and part, going into the New Year's. Besides, they both would be on winter break from school. Ant was eight years old, and Big Mike was thirteen years old. I really enjoyed being around my sons and just loved being dad. It was my belief in God, my new girlfriend Melody, and my two sons were the special components that made me to want more out of life. These three people made me want to live again and make something special out of my life. I really wanted my life back; one thing that I knew for sure is that my sons were watching me and looking up to me, which became very import-ant to me because I, in no way, shape, or form, and by no means, wanted to let those two young men down. I always wanted them to do their best on the first time. I wanted to set a standard in life that they could follow or come back to, and there was nothing other than God! I wanted God to be my standard in life! I knew that it worked because I was looking for a wife in DC, and Melody was the only one that made sense. Plus, it was all working out!

Well, next I called Adrian to see if she would be able to take Ant to the airport in Hartford, Connecticut, and she would have if I had paid for it. Money was better since going back in the Air Force on this temporary reserve assignment at the Pentagon. We were all set, and Lynn also agreed to allow Big Mike to stay with me for the Christmas holiday, but I was going to pick him up and take him back. We had planned it that way so the boys would be able to spend good quality time with each other. One of my biggest priorities was my family, which meant a whole lot to me. I have always believed in keeping families together, especially my family. I really think that this weighed heavily on my priorities since I was a child and my family, including my brothers and sisters who were almost separated while we were in the Akron Children's Home on Arlington Street. My mother fought so hard to get us back and keep us together. Family will always mean a great deal to me! Well, I had plenty of time off during the last two weeks in December from the military. As long as I would stay in the area, I would be off most of the last two weeks of December.

It was perfect. We were waiting for Ant to fly into National Airport and then to pick him up. It was about dark but visible, and cars were everywhere. The National Airport was a busy one.

Well, we gathered Ant's baggage and went to the car to go back to my apartment. He was excited to see me as I had not seen him in about two months and Big Mike in about three months. Now, that Ant has arrived, all that was about to change. We were leaving that night for Ohio to pick up Big Mike. As we took the exit to leave the airport, the car in front of us acted like he was taking off to the highway toward Route 1, and then, all of a sudden, he just stopped, and I could not stop in time. I hit the rear end of his car. My car suffered the brunt of the damage, and then after checking, he and his wife were okay. So it seems. Then he gave me his card. As I looked at it, the card stated that he was a lawyer. Then I was in disbelief as he was a lawyer to my surprise. He and his wife were doing just fine, as they got out of their car, looking at their vehicle, for damages, but there were none. I had a little dent on the passenger side fender that I was able to push out with a crowbar. Absolutely nothing to see! My car took the worst of it, but I quickly fixed it. No police were called. We all seemed happy that no one had gotten hurt. We exchanged information and left the accident scene. We added this little trip incident to our conversation on the way to Ohio. We were only about six hours away, and we planned to make good time. It was only a one-day trip with a night spent at the Holiday Inn. We knew that the majority of the time would be spent like a family at my apartment in Arlington. Christmas would be happening at my place, and I was just ecstatic to be able to spend time with both of my sons and my beautiful girl. Along the way, I cracked my window and played my music and ate my M&Ms with peanuts with a Mountain Dew. I was good to go. They were sleeping, and I had gotten used to that. I did not speak much to Melody and Ant unless we had to make a pit stop or gas the car. Just like the last time that we stopped on the way would be our normal stop in Breezewood. We were pretty close to Akron but too late to do anything, so we went straight to the hotel and got some sleep. We did have the roll-a-bed too for Ant. That bed barely had fitted in the room, but nevertheless, we made it work. We got up and got dressed a little later than I wanted to, and we kept it moving. This would be another quick trip to see my mother and a few of my brothers and sisters. Pick up Big Mike too. I did stop by Adrian's house so her mother could see Ant that she missed and meet my girlfriend too.

Everything went well. We had left and stopped by the gas station and then Church's Chicken for some food and we were on our way back to DC. My boys were excited to be with me as well. They got along too, another special moment for me as well. Big Mike was the one to stay awake, but he still did not talk much unless he wanted something or to eat. The trip back was pretty decent. I was pretty happy. Melody had mentioned to me a few times as to how easier it was for her to love me because of the way I looked out and cared for my sons. I had showed them around the apartment and the pool and pool table. They mainly hung around me. We cooked a meal for Christmas dinner and opened gifts. We gave Ant a much-wanted Gameboy, and we got Big Mike some sneakers and clothes. I was fooling Melody and had her to think that I did not get her anything. So I took the boys in the room with me and got her present. Then I gave the little gift-wrapped box to Ant to present to Melody while we all watched her open it. It was a K-Mart's finest diamond tennis bracelet with gold trim. It was definitely a first for me, and it was the best that I could have afford at the time. She had liked it a lot and kissed the boys and saved the biggest one for me. That was a good Christmas. By the way, I received my first real Zeigler and Zeigler, custom tailor-made athletic-fit suit from Melody. I found out shortly thereafter, the suit that Melody had went all out for was only a setup as part of Melody's plan to get me in church. She was really tired of the clothes that I was wearing and was working undercover on me a new clothing wardrobe, and of course, with church in mind. It had all made sense that Melody's major plan for me was to get me into church. Then we would be in church together.

Well, that Wednesday, the twenty-ninth of December, I already had the four basketball ticket, for us all to see the Washington Bullets play against the Sacramento Kings. The Kings won 103–97. Great, I was never a Bullets fan. This was not a winning season for the

Bullets, and I had really liked the overall game and mainly routed for the other teams. That became fun for me at the games. We had gone sightseeing through the DC streets. It was so much to take in, and the boys were loving it. And on that Friday, after hours, and New Year's Eve, I took them all on a private tour of the Pentagon and showed them my office. The boys were so impressed and outdone as that were their last day. So we then took Ant to the airport to catch his flight home back to Connecticut. Then we drove Big Mike back to Ohio on New Year's Day. We then dropped him off at home, and we spent the night at the hotel. We got up the next day because I have to be back to work at the Pentagon on January 3, 1994. Once we got to Ohio, and after I had dropped off Big Mike to his house, I was feeling somewhat sad and a little empty. I was missing my boys. That was one of the best times we ever had together, and I wanted more of this for us. I had wanted them to be with me on a full-time basis. I had never imagined that I would ever get that chance now after seeing my family again and just briefly. On that Sunday, the sky did not look right, and I didn't want to get caught up in any bad winter storms, so we wasted no time to get out of Akron and back to DC. One thing that I knew for sure is the weather storms in Ohio could become unpredictable, and getting stranded was not a luxury that I had. Now, it was just Melody and I all the way back to DC, hoping the weather to be good.

That little Christmas break with the boys, Melody, and me touched my heart in some kind of way. Briefly, those moments felt like we were a family. Unbeknownst to Melody, I had put a wedding ring on layaway at Service Merchandise in Connecticut; it was a marquis diamond set in gold with two little diamonds, sort of slanted. No matter what I was doing in Connecticut, my mind was always on Melody. I just could not tell her anything, except that I wanted to marry her as I felt when we had our first date. We only talked about us and what we were going to do next. Naturally, going to church or staying in church was probably most of our conversations. Or great debates over the Bible. Melody knew way more than I did hands-down. So I would tell her to prove it to me that it was in the Bible, and then I would actually be learning. She did not know, not one time that I really did not know. It was a great plan that kept working! The conversation of marriage never came up in our relationship. I knew that every moment that I spent with Melody, on the truth, I could never get enough of her. The drive back was just fantastic! Melody kept complimenting me on how well I treated my sons. She just loved the times that I spent with them and never felt that I was neglecting her. That was amazing as we were sharing our conversations. I never gave her any indication that I wanted to marry her, but we had that magic between us. That really was something special. We can just call it euphoria and beyond! My Melody was something pure amazing. I had no one in my life except for her. And really, it was because of her, Melody, there was not room enough for them too. I was becoming an honest man for the first time in my life. I had told Melody as to how I was feeling as I was holding her hand. I had told her that I have never been faithful to anyone, ever, until I met her. Melody had known about the others women that were in my life, but none of the ones since I had moved on my own. There was something about her and how she looked at me. It was like she knew that we were going to be together. We never even argued about the other women that were in my life because she knew that they would be gone.

Once we had arrived by to DC, I dropped her off at home and went up her apartment, and we talked in the living room for a while. I went home too, back to Courthouse. I was back home and was thinking that I had to fix the Tracey thing. I wanted to put a freeze on what she was trying to get me to do with her. So I called her and told her that Melody and I were pretty serious now, and I had to distance our time spent together. I could not jeopardize my relationship with Melody. Getta and I kept the friend side of our relationship going because we decided to just remained friends with no benefits! Anyway, I knew that I wanted to find a wife in DC, and the time that I had spent with Melody, I just believe that she was the one that I wanted to marry, with not one doubt in my mind. I knew that I had loved her even before I really knew her. I could never get the urge to stop talking about her. I wanted the world to know. I was telling everyone about Melody and showing her picture, and then, I kept telling folks that she was not only beautiful, but she was nice too—a combination that was rare to find in a woman. But I did find that woman, and her name was Melody! I was telling Annie B a record of all that had transpired between us. Then Annie said this verbatim, "Out of all of the women that Mike G. knew, Melody had just put the brakes on everything."

This happened on my birthday, and I wanted to get married to Melody. I was just so excited that I could not believe any of it. I had even called my ex-wife and told her that her dream was right on, and I was going to get married again! Adrian just surprisingly said, "Congrats!" She could even tell that I was happy too! Adrian had told me that she would have never thought that I would give up all the women and settle down. Melody had come by the apartment to see me and to bring me a birthday gift. It was truly a surprise to me as I was not used to getting gifts for my birthday. It was a gold ring from Gordon's Jewelers, with my garnet birthstone in it. It was a total surprise. I was nowhere close to receiving expensive gives from anyone. She did not stay long, but she wanted me to know that she was thinking about me. That was another first. She did that and was drawing me and us closer together. I was so grateful, without words to express how I was feeling. Awesome. The next day, at work, I went to play basketball for lunch at the Pentagon, POAC, and ran into Curtis. He was one of the guys that I referred to my apartment building earlier on.

Just as I began talking, the Valentine Day thing popped into my head. So I told him that if he was not doing anything for Valentine's Day, maybe we could double-date, and I was planning to do a proposal to my girl, Melody. He wanted to get back to me later on. He had met Melody, and I had met Angie. We even went out too. Well, later on that afternoon, I was talking to Annie B as we were setting up the meeting for the budget review groups (BRG). This meeting was where the Air Force budget would be discussed and tied in to the president's budget, also called PB. We also set up the slides in a book call slide facer. Annie B designed the slides. She was a natural and very good at it! Overall, we stayed pretty busy on the job during the PB cycle! I talked with Capt. David Zorzi. I remembered him because when he eats fruit, he eats the core too. Lt. Col. Sandra Gregory, she was a very smart lady and married to a general named Tom Bradley. Capt. Otis Hutchins, Christina Klink, and a few other folks on our team. Later that afternoon, I had told Annie B that I was going write a poem for my proposal to Melody. I wanted to have something to do around beans and rice. In which I always teased Melody about her mom's cooking, and I would tell her a poem like this, "Roses are red, and violets are blue. I love you more than your mom's beans and rice." It was corny, but I would laugh because it would be funny to me. Then Melody would laugh too. That was one of our jokes.

Anyway, later that night, I went home to work on that poem for my proposal. After several start-overs, I had it. it read on the front, "Melody, Be My Valentine," and on the inside, it read, "To the one I love, this is my first poem but...not to be my last. You're a great work of art, mind, body, spirit, and soul. With all of this, you could never be cold. I'm thankful for everything we shared, and when I see your million-dollar smile, I know that you care. God gave us the knowledge to love each other more. That's why this Valentine's Day will be more special than before. As I look into your eyes, now I can say to you, with all my heart: I love you once. I love you twice. I will love for you to become my wife. Melody, will you marry me?" I put a lot of time into this writing of the proposal poem, but it just had to be right.

The next day, I had given it to Annie B, and she took a week or so to make to perfect folding card for me. So we kept working, and I had giving her some space. Meanwhile, someone, a nosey person, maybe a coworker, was in my marriage story and had the story all twisted up. Some person ran to General AD Bunger and told him that I was getting married and that I was already married. So let's just say that I stayed diplomatic and responded correctly to every question. Then I asked the general why would I do such a thing and get married. I then told him that my divorce was final last year. Now, I only have my suspicions of who would do such a thing. Then I realized that it was not that important. That was so low-down even for the Pentagon personnel! I was almost sure that I knew who the person was. The fact was that nobody was going to stand in my way.

Not even the general. I was in love, all the way single, and kept my life moving forward! By Friday, I had left the job a little early. By the time I reached home, I had a message from the concierge. I had a little small talk and went to my apartment. When I had returned to call, it was the lawyer that I had the car accident with at the airport from picking up my son Ant. The lawyer told me that he and his wife were injured. I said, "No way, you both were fine on the day that it happened." I then told him to take me to court and have fun because I had just filed bankruptcy (it was actually nine years ago; I had my own response to his scam). He had quickly got off the phone, and I had never heard from him again. Those types of scams did not work well on broke people, like myself. I was glad that this one seemed to be over. I was working so hard to make this wedding proposal right. I was with Melody on most weekends or picking her up for church. She was definitely a constant fixture in our life and a positive one at that. I was doing so much better.

Well, the following weekend was also a Martin Luther King's Holiday on that Monday, January 17, 1994. I have to go to Connecticut to pick up my copy of the divorce decree (in order to get a new marriage license, per DC law) and take the ring out of layaway. I as trying to be back on Saturday, so I would be able to see Melody on Sunday and Monday for the holiday. Well, before leaving Connecticut, I stopped by to see my son and to show the rings to Adrian. She said that they were nice and congrats. She could tell that I have changed and now in love. I kept thanking her for telling me the dreams and on how it was so real. I hugged my son, Ant, as he this time said, "Bye, Daddy." That moment was so sweet for me. I was glad that we had shared some time together. I was all packed and ready to head back to DC. All I knew was it was cold, and the big snow was coming. I was doing good for timing until I made a pit stop for gas and the restroom. It was at the Maryland House Travel Plaza by Exit 93 off of I-95 south. In my case, I was just stuck. The car would not start, no clicks for the battery or nothing. After getting the car jumped and then disconnecting the battery, everything dies again. I knew then that the battery was good, and the alternator was not working at all. I had a free trial of AAA Auto Club and called them. Since I was trying to be honest now and one hundred miles away from my apartment, I decided to do everything right and leave the other girls alone. So I just waited for AAA to show up. Then I had called Melody to meet me at the apartment by taking the train. I could not swing by to pick her up because my car was broken. She agreed! It took almost an hour. Then we tried to jump the car battery again, and I had him tow it to my apartment to be parked in the front. The tow truck driver was moving on the highway making time. However, he noticed that one of the j-hooks had come loose and punctured my gas tank. The tow truck driver stated that the impact of the puncture could have blown up the whole car.

We were now safe, and my car had no gas. It was a full tank. The next morning, I had gotten up and called the tow truck person, and they came and picked up the car and took it over to Lindsey Cadillac dealer service department, in Alexandria, Virginia. The gas tank was getting replaced on my caddy by the tow truck company, and they would cover the cost plus a full tank of gas. They also told me that the alternator would be another $400, and I then told them to bring my broken car as I did not have the money to get it fixed. I started to reading auto books and taking notes from the auto parts dude. I then called my dad and explained to him what was going on. He walked me through the whole thing, and I fixed it that same day for under $150. I loosened the tension pulley to the belt, disconnected the alternator, switched it out, and I was back in business. I then put everything back, except I had to keep the special tool for the tension dolly and took the alternator core back to the store for my $20 deposit. I was back in business. I just changed my first car Cadillac alternator. Now, I was back on the road. This car handles very well in the snow and on the highway. Now, Melody and I could go to Chesapeake Bay Seafood Restaurant by Bailey's Crossroads, off Columbia Pike as she had planned with her sister, Linda, Butch, and Von. We used to plan to go there or in Maryland at least once a month or every other month—for the all-you-can-eat crab legs and shrimps. I had never eaten crab legs until I had met Melody. We never got tired of this restaurant. I was bonding with her sister, Von, and Butch, and I almost felt like family. Melody and I even had a seafood feast at my apartment for us all. We all had great times together mall shopping and going bowling sometimes at the local military bases. I had finally figured out that special thing that I wanted to do for Melody on Valentine's Day. I had no doubts in mind that I wanted to be with her and only as my wife. We had a lot special moments and created a lot of first times together since we have been dating. It was so amazing that I was able to get another temporary assignment at the Pentagon.

My life was never boring, and so unbelievable. Again I say, like a fairytale, but it was for real! I was in love again for the first time. Nothing could compare to what I had at that moment with Melody. It had been a few months, and I have been faithful! What a surprise to myself. I always thought that I did not deserve her. I did not know still if I could trust myself, but Melody trusted me. I just could not understand what I did to deserve her. Then I would remember Adrian's dream and the wish that I made coming to DC to find me a wife. I said it, and when I had asked, God allowed me to find a wife in DC. I said it, remembered saying it often, but I still did not believe it. I was the pinnacle of unfaithfulness to anyone. Even with my thoughts, she was different and most committed to me. I had all the baggage, and she had none, and no way in the world was she desperate. Melody accepted me at face value, and it was not for the money. I did not believe in the horoscopes, and I knew that it was not that. The last time I checked was when it stated that I am compatible with Virgo as I was a Capricorn. Well, I put that to be untrue because Lynn was a Virgo, and we did not have a future, nowhere in sight. Melody was a Capricorn, and it has nothing to do with nothing because we were in love. We had another awesome weekend as she got ready to go home, so we could both get ready to go back to work on Monday. So I walked her to the Metro train, and we did our goodbyes. I would await her call once she arrived home, and then, we would talk for a little while longer.

On my way back to the Pentagon this time riding with Curtis, as we very seldom ride in on the train together at the courthouse metro that day, but we did. I told him my plans for Valentine's Day, and he agreed to go in with me for half. We were to do a white stretch limousine that I had on hold and got our tickets for the Spirit of Washington Dinner Cruise. It was a go. All I had to do was find me a tuxedo from Today's Men Clothing Store! Curtis and I were able to get tickets from the Air Force Recreation services that was on the fifth floor of the Pentagon. Then I could not wait to see the poem that Annie B would have completed by now. I stopped by Maj. Gilchrist's desk, and I would talk as she would share stories about her two kids. I even sometimes played basketball with her husband who was in the Air Force Reserve and a pilot for United Airlines. He was pretty good and fast at basketball, but I was the better shooter. I had much respect for their entire family. Then I went back over to Annie B, and she showed me what she had done with my words… Totally awesome!

January ended with snow. Then the government and school were closing. At the beginning of February, around the tenth of the month, more of the snow came and had the normal openings for the most part. Melody stayed with me through Sunday to get by the snow storm, and then I took her home. It was very cold too as I did not want her to walk to the Metro. The roads were pretty treacherous but passable. I just took my time. That caddy was cruising just fine on the snow, slush, and icy roads. Therefore, not knowing until the last moment if the Spirit of Washington would set sail on Valentine's Day, I confirmed with the limo company to pick us up at my apartment. At the last possible moments, everything was a go, and I was on cloud nine with plenty of confidence. I was so sure that I was doing the right thing proposing to Melody. Actually, I had no nerves at all. I did not worry about what if she would have said no. I was not going to allow my mind to play tricks on me. This was our very first Valentine's together. We both had the next day off from work. We both worked all day, faring the cold and snow. When we had spoken earlier, Melody was going to meet me at my apartment. The Valentine dinner and limo were surprises. I had let Melody in the apartment and went back in the bedroom to get dressed. I did not want her to slow me down as we had a limo waiting and on the clock. I told Melody to let me know how she like the suit that she had brought me as I came out of the bedroom. I had a fresh haircut and was just all-around sharp. It so happened that I was not wearing the suit that she had gotten for me. Instead, I wore a black tuxedo with a white bow tie, wing-tip tuxedo shirt, and a white vest, including the black shoes. I secretly placed the proposal poem and the note inside my tuxedo jacket. It barely fitted inside. The note was to be given to the captain on the dinner cruise ship. The note read, "As soon as the ship's departure, please call me up, so I can do a marriage proposal."

Upon coming out of the room, I definitely surprised Melody with that tuxedo I was wearing that evening! I was dressed, and we left the apartment. Once we arrived to the elevator, and as soon as the doors opened, there was Curtis, with his black tuxedo and black bow tie, no vest, and Angie was on his arm. It was cold with snow on the ground, but no way were we going to wear coats. After we had got on the elevator to press the button for the lobby. Curtis said, "Mike, are you driving?" I said, "No, Curtis, you are driving." Then at a moment's notice, Melody blurted out, "Y'all know that limo downstairs is waiting for us." Then she went on further to say, "I saw that limo at the entrance of the building on the way up to see you." That part was no longer a surprise, but the dinner cruise stayed a surprise until we had arrived to the dock for the dinner cruise ship. The limo driver has asked Curtis and I if we wanted to take the scenic route. Of course, we both said yes! It was on! We took in some of the sightings, and some things were still snow covered, yet still the sights were nice to see. The ladies, Angie and Melody, were trying to guess where we're all going all the way there. Still, Curtis and I did not say a word! Meanwhile, we took some really nice pictures, pretending we were on the phone inside the limo. Melody and I opened the sunroof and stood up and took more pictures. In a few of the pictures, Melody was looking at me with such proud amazement. She was just happy and in love. I could really see it! I was too! We felt like we were on top of the world in that Valentine's night. It was so special. The moments we shared together and with our friends. The pictures turned out a little dark but still nice.

We had finally arrived, and it was cold. Well, the ladies had never guessed where we were going. They were still surprised as we pulled up close for the special limo parking. The dinner cruise ship was called *The Spirit of Washington*. This was my first time in a limo and the second time on the Spirit of Washington. I went the first time on it for a going-away for someone that retired from the Pentagon. Well, as the limo driver opened the door, people looked at us as if we were celebrities or something. But we were not. We were only regular people who were in love! We were embarking the cruise ship and we followed the hostess to our table. I slipped my note to the captain. It happened just like I planned it. I did not know that my plan would go so smoothly, but it did! We also had a surprise to all of us. *The Spirit of Washington's* Valentine's surprise to us was there was a live radio show there. The radio station was called the Oldies WGIG-FM or BIG 100.3. Then the hostess had called me up about five minutes after the ship's departure. I shook Curtis's hand and then grabbed Melody's hand, and we walked to the dance floor. I was going to just read the poem and do the proposal, but the radio station BIG 100.3 played the song, "When a Man Loves a Woman." I loved that song "When a Man Loves a Woman" by Michael Bolton. It was right on time, so we had a dance first. Then there was silence, pure silence, so I begin reading the poem: "To the one I love, this is my first poem but…not to be my last. You're a great work of art, mind, body, spirit, and soul. With all of this, you could never be cold. I'm thankful for everything we shared, and when I see your million-dollar smile, I know that you care. God gave us the knowledge to love each other more. That's why this Valentine's Day will be more special than before. As I look into your eyes, now I can say to you, with all my heart: I love you once. I love you twice. I will love for you to become my wife. Melody, will you marry me?" I knelt down on one knee.

She had on this beautiful black formal stylish knee-high dress and with the nice hairdo and the biggest smile, showing all her teeth. She then said yes! I placed the diamond ring on her finger. Then we had the biggest kiss ever! Wow! We walked to our table. Curtis and Angie greeted us again. Then BIG 100.3 came to our table and gave us two of their radio station T-shirts for keepsake. We were so thankful as the radio personality started playing oldies music again. Before we were about to be served, we took more pictures. Then people, strangers, were walking up to our table congratulating us multiple times. One lady said that she had punched her husband and had asked him why he did not propose to her like that. We all thought that comment was funny. That moment would be forever etched in my mind. We talked, ate, watched the performers, and went upstairs to go outside to take more pictures. It was so exciting, and we all had a great time. I was officially off the market, and so was she. I was getting married again and was happy to be doing it and to really be in love. We were cruising on the dinner cruise on the Potomac River. It had some beautiful sights that we were taking in. That two hours went quickly. It was time to disembark, and the limo was waiting for us. As we all quickly walked down the ramp, it actually had gotten colder, and I had given Melody my tux jacket, and she had the poem in her hands. Melody was enamored with the poem that I read to her. It was now a keepsake forever! We rode back to the apartment and exited. I was the last to get out, so I could tip the driver. It was a first class and excellent date for us all. Melody and I both had the next day off. I was officially engaged, and it was as real as it gets. Nice but still I could not tell her that I have been unfaithful since I had moved in the Connecticut apartment. There was no way that I was going to mess up her day—our day. I only could wish that I would have waited prior to my first marriage because I was still just wild. My identity and my existence did not make sense until Melody came into my life.

This was as close to love and happiness as I had ever known. It all made sense once I looked into her eyes. I was in love! Still I was living a lie! I often wondered how long would it last. I did not know, even to the point of questioning my sincerity. My biggest question to myself was, "Would I last, or remain faithful?" I did not know that answer, but I did not want to break her heart without me being broken. I actually felt the true feelings of hurt of our love with Melody for the first time. I would look into the innocence of her face, her eyes, and could not hurt her with the truth. I was not sure of myself and did not want to lose her at all! I just could not tell her the truth, and it really bothered me. I have learned that neither telling the truth nor lying makes you feel better. I eventually, will have to tell the truth, if I wanted to keep my first ever true love! I had to decide when. I was not going to say anything until after the wedding. Adrian knew most of it, but her lips were sealed. She was not going to enlighten the woman that stole my heart. I was not going to risk losing Melody at this point. I just stopped thinking, and I just held her. I wanted nothing to mess this up. Nothing! I was truly getting better with being faithful because of what Melody and I shared together. I was planning to just keep her and us together! Still, I say that there was no way I was going to break her heart! I truly meant it!

The next day, before I took her home, we discussed a wedding date. I wanted sooner, and Melody wanted a longer date. I finally convinced her of the sooner date, and we set it for July 2, 1994, the first Saturday in July. I did not believe in long engagements. I am the type that loves family and marriage. Plus, I knew that I would be so much better in a long-term relationship. The next step was to get a job and move to DC from Connecticut. I truly did not realize that I was at the headquarters of all headquarters for all of the Department of Defense for all military branches. Since I was able to get back there, I had to make the most of it and contact everybody that I knew. I had a plan to talk with everyone that I knew and have known since 1992, almost two years earlier. So I told Annie B what I was planning to do, and being newly engaged, I wanted to stay in the area. Annie B pointed me to Ms. Sparks the SES since I used to work for her. I went to see her and was able to walk right in her office. Ms. Sparks had gotten the ball rolling and pointed me to Lt. Col. Sandra Gregory whose husband was a general and the brother-in-law too. They both were generals. I was told to go the Headquarters Air Force Reserve Office in the Pentagon and get a package to include pictures and submitted it as soon as possible. I got started on it immediately. I was able to work on putting my package together for an Air Guard/ Reservist (AGR) for active-duty tour. It was very similar to regular active duty but would be a statutory tour of active duty in the Air Force and appointed by the president of the United States. This was a great deal and opportunity. If I was successful, I would be entitled to an active-duty retirement with an immediate annuity. This last trip was my best trip, and everything seemed to be working out for me.

It had taken the rest of February and part of March to get the package complete. In the midst of getting my package completed while I was working directly for Maj. Gilchrist, Colonel Don Henney was the next level supervisor (he was the nicest person to had ever worked for), and he wanted to see me. I could tell that this guy did want anything to do with confrontation of any sorts. I could not imagine what's in forever for I just did not have a clue. Well, he had a concern that someone had told him that I was living in my TDY apartment with my fiancée. First of all, I denied it and returned a question back to him. I asked him how could I live in two places with a move-in guest and my orders would be completed on the next month in May. Then, I mentioned that I could have guests, and it was not one's concern, nor was it illegal. Col. Henney agreed, and we dropped the subject, but I had always believed that this jealous, nosey person was a dude, and I only had an idea on who it was. This happened twice with General Bunger and now Colonel Henney, and nothing came of either conversation. I did not know why that nosey, jealous someone was all in my business. I had a revolving door to my apartments from 1992 to present and just knew that it was not illegal. It was totally nonsense! It was during this same time that Melody was working on the wedding, invitations, dress, food, place and all. It was thanks to Brenda McCain, one of her best friends, who convinced her that it was possible to get the wedding done. Brenda even got her church folks to pitch in, cater and all. We had also got signed up with our church, at Harvest International for the marriage counselling classes. We were assigned marriage counsellors from the church, a husband-and-wife couple. They were Bro. Ralph and Sis. Diane Ferguson.

Our first session, was on March 18, 1994, at 9:30 p.m. We had used the workbook *Called Together* by Steve and Mary Prokopchak, of Dove Christian Fellowship. We also used another book called *Before You Say I Do* by Wes Roberts and H. Norman Wright. We had all kinds of homework assignments to complete before the next sessions. We had our premarital classes about every two weeks for almost eight weeks. It was in this first class that I first really learned about love and how I must first love myself before loving Melody. Everything that I thought I know about marriage, family, relationship, roles, responsibilities, and love was wrong. I had to understand that God is love, therefore dismissing all my other bad habits. The more I was learning and by doing premarital lessons, the better I treated my commitment toward Melody. This was all in my first class! Wow! I was changing me all over again! My Pentagon days of working were full to include briefings, meetings, budget review groups for the Air Force programs. Still, I managed to work out at the gym as much as possible because leadership encouraged us to be physically and mentally fit. My evenings and were full as well, spending time with Melody for the wedding coordination, plus attending church on a regular basis, especially since the church was providing the premarital counselling. It was sometime doing our apartment hunt that Melody had mentioned that her co-worker Sabrina, saw me give her the first note. It so happens that our wedding date was also, her birthday. Wow! I was in awe! What a coincidence! I guess this was meant to be.

Colonel Rodney (Rod) Wood was the senior leader of our section SAF/FMBP, and this guy rubbed me the wrong way because of what he had asked me to do. I really thought that he was a skinny, evil, racist mad man. Well, it was not what he had asked me to, but it was the tone in his voice, the look in his eyes, and he did not care how. It just had to be done! To be honest, my first mindset was to catch him outside the Pentagon, blindfold him, and just beat him down. Colonel Wood's tone to me was just condescending and full of hatred. I was so glad that Melody was in my life, and I was getting married again. I had to calm down as it took me about two days to get to it. It was on that third day I decided to clean out this old refrigerator that was unplugged, and it stunk up the entire office. There was slimy green and black mold from old food and liquid spills, and to say the least, there was a lot to clean. I found some old towels and rags in the janitor's closet and the janitor's bucket. Even though I was in my Air Force blues, I used my bare hands and started to wring out the liquid with the rags one after the other and kept doing it until I was done. I only did as I was instructed to do. I did not wash it down afterward. So even though it appeared clean, it was not. I believe that somehow, there was a lesson to be learned from that experience. After it was over, I became humbled again because I had loved Melody enough not to mess that up by assaulting this colonel. I remembered saying that it humbled me, and it was just not worth it to break me! That was the only way that I did survive, and it helped sharpen me to hold my peace in uncomfortable situations. I believe that there was something inside me that needed to be changed. I must admit that cleaning that refrigerator has assisted me in holding my peace. The one thing that I did learn from that experience was I could not change people, which was an important lesson to be learned. I did not allow this experience to break me nor did it define me!

This one event truly hurt me, and then, it humbled me to rise above it. I knew that I needed an attitude adjustment, and this refrigerator duty given to me truly taught me not to kill every ignorant person that I come in contact with. In fact, I used to jump out of my car at a stoplight. Another time, the light would change to green up by Glebe Road and Fairfax Drive. I would then honk my horn for the car in front of me to go and move on. Instead that person would give me the finger. That was not acceptable. I would jump out of me car with my stick like the movie *Walking Tall* and go after them. Of course, they would take off. Yes, I knew that I had a temper and needed some cooling off! My girlfriend would be in the car with me, and she would tell me that I cannot do that and to keep my cool. She said, "I am not sure if you know this, but people in Virginia are allowed to carry guns." Even though I did some stupid things, I was indeed a fast-learner! One thing that I learned was that I would never be a fan of Colonel Wood, but he was the reason that I had to learn humility. He was definitely not on the invite list to my wedding! I did learn a good thing from that refrigerator cleaning, but I wished that I would had learned it without that vibe feeling of hatred from him! I was definitely feeling the hatred, right from the beginning of that tasking, and even now, that feeling that I had would never be forgotten! Nevertheless, I remained focused and kept the important things before me, like putting the list of names together that I was planning to invite to the wedding. The list would be comprised of people that I knew from the Pentagon, CT Transit, Connecticut, and my family in Akron, Ohio. If I did not have an address, I would hand-deliver the wedding invitation. I had to invite Chineta and Tracey because we had no intimacy and would remain friends. I must give credit to Chineta because she would only trust me to the length of a distance friend! As far as Tracey, my suspicions were correct. She would not be interested. I did not really know a bunch of people on a long term, but many folks showed interest, including Ms. Sparks and Carol Anderson. I even remember Ms. Alice. She was a nice, nice lady too. I was getting a lot of positive interests and feedback that people were genuinely planning to attend.

I also remember, sometime in April 1994, going home to my apartment from the Pentagon. I was in a happy mood and singing this new song that I had heard on the radio. It was "Baby, Hold On to Me" by Gerald and Eddie LeVert. The timing was just perfection. I was still singing, and to my surprise, as I walked around the corner with my gym bag in hand, I looked up. Wow, Melody was at my door waiting to surprise me. Immediately I was lost for words! What a beautiful and pleasant surprise, and I was totally caught off-guard! I was singing that song and thinking of Melody. Wow, and how appropriate! We had just completed our premarital counselling sessions. The previous Sunday, we were at church try and see the Thompsons, our pastors, to see if they would do our wedding. It was out of the questions to see them because we had to go through the administration staff, and it turned out that I had to be a member for so long or something along those lines, plus my recent divorce. The request was denied! We had to wait until I had enough time in, including a longer engagement, or find someone else to do the wedding. I went back to the Pentagon that following Monday and found an Air Force civilian chaplain to do the wedding. It was quickly decided at our meeting that the Reverend Carlton A. Powell would gladly do the ceremony at Bolling AFB, DC. Then we booked the date to include a wedding coordinator for a small fee as well. The use of the approximately a thousand-seat church, and since I was in the Air Force, its use were free to me. We just had to give the reverend a love offering. And right after, we left the main base chapel. He also referred us to the Air Force Morale, Recreation, and Welfare Service. Then we quickly booked the reservation for the recreation hall for the reception. The total cost was about $200 in which the dinner would be catered by Brenda's church hospitality friends. We were all set even though we were told no from our church, but it worked out better than we had ever planned and much cheaper. The remaining funds went toward our honeymoon trip to Hawaii. I had to get my sons, Big Mike, Ant, and my brother Shawn's tuxedo sizes as soon as possible and get mine too since I would be soon leaving in less than two weeks.

It was that same Friday that I was to be fitted for my tuxedo. I had just returned from the two-and-half-hour lunch/gym break at the POAC. Well, to my surprise, it was about 2:00 p.m. I received a set of my orders that my four-year statutory tour was approved from the HQ USAF Reserves by the direction of the president. It was all working out, and I would finally be moving to Washington DC to live and work at the Pentagon permanently! This was a dream come true to be with Melody, on top of everything that was going on, and the planning of our wedding. Then Melody and I had to find a place in DC, Virginia, and Maryland to live in. Because of the receipt for my new PCS orders to move from Connecticut. This was all of a sudden, and we had to choose fast. After a process of elimination, we both decided on Virginia, and we want to be near the Pentagon and her job. Plus we could commute together. We took a few days off toward the next weekend to find a place to live and make appointments for viewing apartments and townhouses. I could not believe the timing of everything; it was truly amazing. It felt like it was meant to be. You know, since I have been with Melody, my whole life got better in a short amount of time. I was moving to DC for good and to be with the woman I loved and truly needed! Just by being around her, I was continuing to make better choices and my life was getting on the right track! For real! She would tell me from time and again that because of my past, she saved my life. Even now, still, I felt that I really did not deserve her! Yet we were looking for a place to live once we were married. These few days off were so tiresome, trying to find a place to live. Actually, it was getting discouraging, disappointing, and negative, and at the same time, we were being charged application fees each time from $30 to $55 per occurrence. The answer was the same: disapproved because of my credit and bankruptcy. I did not want to move in with Melody and her mother in DC. We really needed our own space. Besides, I have been there and done that back in Ohio!

My time was running out, and my options were less than few. That next day, I had made an appointment with Robin from Terrace Townhouses in Annandale, Virginia, to see a vacant townhouse. I remembered that day because of how hot it was. Melody and I were at the main office, close by the townhouses and across the street. We checked it out on the tour and looked like it was kept up really good, and the neighborhood was quiet on Perry Penny Drive. After going back to the office to complete the paperwork, we waited for about a half hour. Just before, Robin could have easily said no. Instead, she told us that she was recently divorced and understood how difficult of a time that we were having in obtaining a place to live, especially on a short notice. It turned out that Melody's credit was good, and I was the problem child, and it seems that regardless of my situation. Robin said that since I was in the military, she would go ahead and take a chance on me. I was so relieved and about to give up because we were out of options! Now we had a place to call home. We then paid the last application fee, and then, we both would sign the lease on June 4, 1994, and pick up the keys. Well, that was the last Saturday that I had before my TDY orders were over. I had a few days to works, out-process from the Pentagon, moved out of the apartment and head for Connecticut to work with CT Transit for about three weeks. Then I would get a U-Haul moving truck to do the move with.

On my last day of TDY there before returning to my permanent duty station, I had to pass out my remaining wedding invitations to give a special thanks to Annie Barnes, Maj. Barbara Gilchrist, Lt. Col. Sandra Gregory, and to a lady who became my friend to whom I gave my last wedding invitation to, Ms. Cathy Sparks. I was having the best time of my life! It was time to leave Melody for the last time before our wedding. Once again, Melody came and saw me off that Friday as I would be driving the bus for a few more weeks and that would be it! As soon as I got home, I started to pack because I was so, so excited. I was leaving. I saw Adrian and Ant on that Sunday to say that I was leaving and want to see my son as much as possible. Adrian and I were cool, and nothing happened between us ever again. We were now only friends and no hard feelings. Adrian and I always talked about her dreams and on how she was now pregnant. Her little girl was due in October 1994, again, just like her dream! I had invited her to the wedding to see our son in it, but she declined the invitation because she was pregnant. I was happy for her too, and there was no way that I could have been the father! Again, so amazing! We both knew beforehand and accepted that our lives would be spent with other people. I stayed for a minute and met her friend. I was glad for her because I was not looking back and had no regret. My only regret was that I did not have full custody of my sons. I now had to head back home to get ready to drive the bus on the next day. As I headed toward work, I was full of excitement and was engaged. Once I arrived to CT Transit, the guys were glad once again to see me. I was happy to see them and happier that I would be soon leaving for good.

The following weekend would be my final reserve duty prior to doing my out-processing. Anyway, I had told the fellas that I had got engaged and moving to DC to work at the Pentagon full-time in the Air Force. My manager Tom Crispino was correct. I did not belong there, and finally, my time had come to be leaving. We cut the conversations and the picture showings short because we had to get the buses on the road or we would be written up. I had a short time left, and I wanted to make a lasting impression. I was planning to drive without an attitude! Sometimes, I did have an attitude or a chip on my shoulder, except with the ladies! I had only two and a half weeks left and was planning to be good and leave all the ladies alone. I was just nice to everyone whether they had enough money or none at all. I just told them just get on the bus. And when the folks got off the bus, I told them to have a nice day! This was my new norm, and I was happy just to think about Melody, my beautiful bride-to-be. That week was almost done. I just had to get through Friday and Saturday—only, two more days! I was coaching myself and saying repeatedly, "You can do it!" It was now Friday, and I was just going to hang out after work and play some pool, then go visit

Kendall, Tony, and Charles from the Air Force Reserve. I was doing everything to stay busy plus be a kind bus driver. I was talking with Melody every day and sometimes twice a day or whenever possible! I was truly missing her. I knew that for sure! Well, this week was almost gone, and now, ten more days to drive the bus, not including my normal time off work and the last two days of reserve duty that I had get completed.

I had the split run on the U-route, and as I was headed to downtown Hartford to pick up the line of people waiting and going in the direction of Hartford High School. People were paying the fare and getting on the bus, taking their seat. I could not believe it. There was this young lady who reminded me of Jennifer Lopez. She was beautiful with her infant child. I was trying to be good, and but then, the words came out of my mouth, "Can I get your number?" I was shocked that I said such a thing. I was in love with Melody and in lust with Olivia, with her little child who was about four months. Olivia gave me the look like she was available. I was at a loss, and this time, I had a conscience! I did not want anything to do with the kid at all! As soon as I got home, I called her, and she talked for a few moments but had to get off the phone. I did not know as Olivia had told me that she lived in with her boyfriend, which was the baby's father. I never knew if the dude was black or Latino, but I did know that she was not happy being with him and wanted to leave him. I began to figure I was her exit. Once I told her that I was moving to DC to work at the Pentagon, I just hit a home run. So I rolled with it. Even though it was difficult for us to be together, the plan was in motion and soon to happen. But there was a catch, she had to bring the baby with her and with us and she had to sneak away from her boyfriend. Because I kept telling her that I had to see her. I was just crazy busy packing, seeing friends and my son. I also was passing out a few wedding invitations and trying to get Tony to become my best-man. Tony agreed for a few days and backed out at the last moment because of a personal matter. I was stuck and quickly decided to ask the one friend that had always been there for me, so I finally had decided to ask Kendall to be my best man, and he was thrilled to accept. Besides, Kendall had family in Baltimore, Maryland. I told him about the tuxedo, and it was on. Kendall had always been there for me!

It was my last day to drive the bus, and I was all set to leave the CT Transit bus company and would clean out my locker and get rid of all the phone numbers, except Olivia's, Tracey's, and Getta's. I did not have too much stuff and loaded the U-Haul all by myself and had the car dolly on the back of it. It was not too bad. The weights, television, with the stand, the mattress, and box spring were my big items. As I was packing and finishing up, my phone rang. It was Olivia and she wanted to see me before I leave, but I had to go pick her up and her baby too. Now, the bed is on the truck, just in case, and I had no plans to bring it back in. I had been pretty good! I stopped everything on that Friday, June 3, 1994, and then I went to pick them up. Why did she want to see me? Why did I go and pick her up? I just did it without thinking. We went back to my apartment that was almost emptied, and the stuff was on the truck. I had finally asked her where she was from, and she said that she was from Puerto Rico. We kept talking as she was holding her baby, and the stroller was in the back of the car. I had to pick her up walking the baby, so the boyfriend did not get suspicious. Anyway, now we were in my empty apartment, and there was nothing to do, except to get to know all her thoughts. Once she laid the baby down, she kissed me, and I have forgotten that I was leaving Connecticut! Then, once we got cleaned up, Olivia wanted to come with me! That was not my plan of thought. Plus, I could not afford to help her until I got my stuff together. She understood, so we made plans to stay in touch. Then I had taken her home. Well, almost home because she had to push the stroller. While Olivia and I had some nice moments together, that was it, nothing more. I still was not going to leave Melody, not for her beauty or her baby! At most, she would have to take care of herself and remain my side piece. That was all I could offer.

After dropping Olivia off, I rushed back to quickly shower, finished packing, turned in my keys, placed the caddy on the car dolly, and hit the road, heading to DC. That was my last affair in Connecticut, and I was not looking back, except to see my son Ant and a few of my friends Kendall, Charles, and Tony. My ex-wife

Adrian did not count because we were just cool. I had a lot to think about on the way to DC, and my conscience was making me feel a little guilty. I was good the entire three weeks except for the last day. That one day, I knew when she had called me that something was going to happen. Why did I not say no or not answer the phone! I did know neither. I was just lustfully greedy, and my conscience bothered me and kept me alert while driving the entire time. I just could not tell Melody anything. I kept thinking that I was not going to break her heart. That trip went fast even with checking the belts and car dolly for the tightness and getting gas. My conscience had bothered me so much I had to tell Melody something. Therefore, I did make Melody a promise that I would always be faithful to her once we had got married and would always tell her the truth! She looked into my eyes and agreed to what I was saying. I was so, so relieved! I was so glad that trip went fast, so I could get that off my chest.

On that Saturday, we got up and loaded Melody's things on the truck, her bedroom set, mostly clothes, and all. After that, we were on way to Annandale, Virginia, to sign the lease, pay the first month's rent, and pick up the keys from Robin. So Melody grabbed the cleaning supplies and started in the kitchen to reclean the apartment to her satisfaction. I was bringing in the stuff from the truck and placing the items in the different rooms. I was glad to see that we had window blinds already for shade. Once Melody had gotten to the refrigerator, there were roach trails and eggs all over it. It was nasty and disgusting. I was looking at Melody as she frowned her face. I said, "Well, we just had to clean it real good." There was a big hole in the wall under the sink with a few mouse droppings. My mind was on finishing the unpacking and go to store to get some Raid bug spray and mouse traps. We only had to live together for twenty-four days, but her plan was to spend the night out on the night before the wedding. So our townhouse was taking shape and missing living room furniture but were planning to get some. We had cleaned and unpacked what we could, but it was getting late, and we had to be getting ready for work. This time, we would carpool together. I would sneak and call Olivia a few more times and had to let her go. We both realized that I was no sugar daddy nor could be her baby's daddy. I have two kids of my own! Really, we both knew that there was no way that it could work.

Olivia and I were over and had to end this distant thing we tried but could not work at all. This breakup was on as I completed my first week working for the HQ USAF/REO office, also known as the Air Staff for folks working for HQ USAF. The secretary Ms. Deborah (Ann) Johnson showed me the ropes as my desk was parallel to hers. She was a cool sister and could sing her face off! Ann was kind of tall and walked with pigeon toes. I could always hear her singing this one song, even when I was not around her. It was a John Denver song "Take Me Home, Country Roads." Then I started to sing that song too. It was sort of addicted to sing it. But Ann, she was that good and a funny comedian! Carol Anderson and Ann Johnson were two awesome coworkers that taught me everything. Carol taught me to be nice to everyone because tomorrow, you don't know who you could be working for. That was the Pentagon mentality. Also anyone that worked in the front office with the big-time executives and the generals, everyone, were nice to you. The front office was one of my favorite places to work, just like when I used to work for Ms. Sparks. Just awesome! This time by the time that we arrived home and checked the outside keyed mailbox. I took the mail inside our townhouse and opened it from Bank of America (Melody's Bank), and it was a preapproval check for exactly $20,000 to purchase a new car. The Toyota Camry was a very popular car, so we started there first. The car salesman at the Alexandria, Virginia, dealership told us that we would never find a car for that price because he wanted more money. This brother was greedy, and we did not trust him! As we were leaving, Melody paused and then told the salesman that he was wrong, and God was going to do something better for us! The guy said, "Good luck." Then we left the dealership. Next, we on to the second place headed to Passport Nissan, on Auth Way, Marlow Heights, Maryland. It was getting late, but we kept going. We got there. This brother was patient as he was trying to help us out. We took it for a test ride, and I drove. I still had to get used to Melody's driving! Then, we sat down to talk and told the guy that there would be no trade. We then showed him the preapproved check, and he hesitated and left to see the sales manager. We were playing the game that I was not used to as I had never purchased a brand-new car before. I did learn persuasion from recruiting school when I was in Texas. I was a natural, so I thought. The guy came back the desk and asked how much could be put down. We both said at the same time, "Nothing!" I then was to call his bluff, so I took the check off the desk and nodded to Melody. "Let's go!" He then said, "Let me check one more thing."

After fifteen minutes, he said that they could do everything including tax, title, and registration, but it was cost us $0.02 over. We shook hands and agreed. Then we completed all the financing paperwork. It was about 10:00 p.m. Melody followed me and drove our new 1994 Nissan Maxima, and the color was hunter green with beige interior. Once we got home, we talked about how the first guy stated that it could not happen for under $20,000, but he was totally wrong. Now we were driving two cars. The next day at work, I was still inviting everyone to my wedding. I did not care how long I knew them. I was inviting everyone. On June 11, my mother was in the area, so we had planned to pick her up to get her dress sizes at the fitting. My mother had taken a church bus trip from Akron to DC but stayed around Greenbelt, Maryland. We were planning to see Julie (Sew-It-All). She was from Ghana, Africa, and the same seamstress that was making Melody's wedding dress. On the next day, my mother spent some time with Melody's mother, so they could get to know each other. Melody's mother and her Aunt Angeline had made breakfast before we all left to get the fitting. Her sister Linda, Von, and Butch, all followed us to Julie's house to do the measurements. She had made all of the dresses for the bridal party, plus our mothers', as she was very talented and was Melody's friend. Then later that day, we all made it to the church to do the one and only wedding rehearsal. We actually skipped the rehearsal dinner because everyone had tight schedules. We did not mind saving that cost. We had to head back to my mother's hotel, so my mother could join back in with her church group.

As we were saying our goodbyes, my mother mentioned that she had a good time, and I was glad too! I had less than a few weeks to go before the July 2, 1994, the wedding date. My new coworkers were excited for me, and some of them had planned to come. I do remember giving one to Lt. Col. Bob Stice, Capt. Fred Roys, Lt. Col. Chris Mears, Lt. Col. Steve Leyva, Maj. Mary Ann Miller, Ann Johnson, Julio Sotomayor, Gary Hopper, TSgt. Barbara Stewart, Col. William McLoughlin, and a few others. I figured the more folks came, the more gifts and money we could have, including new friendships. I had not an ounce of shame. I had to get comfortable, being that I would be stationed with these operational types of folks for the next four years and even longer, if all went well. These folks were a lot on the wild side, and it all made sense once I found that most of them were Air Force pilots, navigators, and in space programs. I was the right hand to the colonel. Everything went through me before reaching the colonel. I had the power, and I knew my stuff. It was always a pleasure to see folks waiting at my desk for me to arrive the first thing in the mornings. I was thinking on the way home before picking up Melody from work how I stayed current on my child support for Big Mike because there was a court order involved, keeping Lynn cool with everything. Still, I was dealing with Adrian, and all the deals I made with her to pay different child supports amounts to pay some of my bills, even though I missed a few payments. Adrian would still threaten me all the time but never officially placed me on child support. Adrian even had a friend that worked for the child support system, but I was still good! Once we reached home, I can still remember playing songs by Stephanie Mills, Luther Vandross, "If This World Were Mine" or "A House Is Not a Home" or "Since I Lost My Baby" and other favorites by Anita Baker or the O'Jays.

On Sunday, while at church, I would have on the gospel radio for the church music. I was not going to make Melody look bad around her friends. I was never like that much into church once I had become an adult and would go to church for Melody. On that Sunday, I heard this one church song as we were parking the car across the street in the gravel parking lot. The song was just bad. We did not get out of the car until it was over. The song was "Fully Committed" by Kingdom. And I just had to learn that song and right at the moment, right then. I wanted to sing that song to Melody on our wedding day.

I have found the cassette tape of it a few days later. Really, I was learning that song! I played it over and over again! I had to get that song. After many times of trying to sing it, I made it fit me to sing it at the wedding. That was a bad song and suited for me! I did not have a lot of time, but I was determined to get it! The time was getting so close to the date, and I had to pay for my mother, brother Shawn, and son Big Mike. They were two of my groomsmen, flying down from Ohio because they were in the wedding. My oldest brother Cleottis did not make it to the wedding but insisted on buying our wedding cake. My brother buying our cake was another big relief toward the wedding expenses. Then we flew Ant down too from Connecticut as he was our ring bearer. I was off work and on leave for the next eleven days, taking advance leave that was approved.

Then returning on July 14, I had much to do, back and forth to the National Airport in Arlington, Virginia. My sister Terri drove down with Shawn's girlfriend Meeka and her daughter Erica on the day of the wedding. I had all of the family with me on the way to my house. I had to stay focus on the wedding, and by Sunday, on 3 July 1994, everyone would be gone because we were leaving early on Monday morning to Oahu, Hawaii (Waikiki). On July 1, 1994, Melody got up, got dressed, and I dropped her off over Ralph and Carol's house where she would spend the night, get dressed, makeup, first photo shoot, and then take the limousine to the church at Bolling AFB. Emmanuel was Ralph and Ron's friend (Melody's ex-friend) from before meeting me, but he played the saxophone. We only had that one little piece of time to do a quick rehearsal. So we did! Ralph was a musician and was assisting me with the background "Fully Committed" music and voice pitch. Then Emmanuel would do a solo piece by playing the saxophone. It was turning out okay, but we had very little time for perfection! After saying goodbye to Melody, I was left to get everyone else to the church on Saturday and on time. But I had to first get home to do haircuts on my boys' heads since I was getting pretty good with the clippers, being self-taught. My mother, brother, and the boys talked most of the night after eating. I was not the one that usually dreamed. But I had told Shawn that I had a dream about him. I told him that I had dreamed that he had gotten shot in the head and his blood was everywhere, running down his face. Then looking at him, he had a scar on the top front of his head. He then told us that he was in an incident with someone and the person had broken a bottle over his head, and the blood went everywhere, running down his face.

On the real, dreams were actually making me somewhat scared because I did not understand them or how they actually work. The scary part was the truth was so close to my dream. That was amazing! That dream was strange and real at the same time! Then, it was bedtime! That night, I will never forget it once I showered and got into the bed. I could not sleep the entire night. I tossed and turned over and again or just lied in bed awake. I had nervous insomnia, and part of it was my cheating conscience for the entire night because I was about to get married. The next day, I was not even close to tired or sleeping. I was just full of energy. The boys and my brother got up showered, got dressed, and then, we all ate cereal and milk! Then for our first stop, I had to go to the barbershop at Bolling AFB, my normal place to get a haircut for $6 with a dollar tip. Next, we had to pick up the tuxedos, then back to Annandale to get dressed. I had about two hours to spare before getting dressed and had to leave. That's when my sister pulled up from the Ohio drive, just in time to get dressed. So I let all the ladies get dressed first, then us. We had already had my mother's dress from Julie to Melody given to her at their job.

Anyway, we were all dressed to the max, and we were decked out and ready to go in our new Maxima! This was our wedding date, July 2, 1994. It was definitely here! We were on our way to Bolling AFB! I had met my best man Kendall at the church. Also I saw the other two groomsmen, Butch (Linda's boyfriend) and Melody's brother Vernon. Then I went over to talk with Freddie and Grace. They were Melody's father and stepmother. I was talking to everyone, and a lot of people had mistakenly thought that Melody's sister Linda was Melody because they resembled a little. I had to keep letting them know that Melody had not arrived there yet. Then I saw another coworker Alice Bell and her daughter. I was too glad to see Alice from the Pentagon as she one of the nicest people one could know.

People were coming in left and right, and the wedding coordinator was nowhere to be found. Because I did not know where things went or who was to sit on which side nor where to place our wedding gifts. The little that I knew, I did. I almost felt like a celebrity, but I just could not answer all the questions coming my way. However, I kept noticing on how the church was filling up with people, and it was sort of empty when I had first arrived. I was at my new job at the Pentagon for less than thirty days, and some of them were there too. Most of the folks that knew me for a short time came from the Pentagon, and no way I could name them all. Of course, some came to the wedding and not the wedding reception and vice versa. However, that I was aware of. Wow! Truthfully, I was a little nervous, but I played it pretty cool and had to keep it that way because I had to sing to my bride as she walked down the aisle, but for now, I went to the back with the groomsmen, best man, and Reverend Powell, and we talked a while. I had no choice but to be ready even though I had not a wink of sleep. So Reverend Powell had asked me if I was ready. I had no choice because I wanted to marry her. Of course I told him that I could not wait. He nodded his head as well.

They did come and tell me that Melody was running about fifteen minutes late, so we had to chill for a minute. I just talked with Kendall (my best man) and my brother Shawn. He kept me laughing, talking about folks, just being silly! It was a good thing because the time went by rather quickly. Then the wedding coordinator finally showed up. I then found out that she was trying to coordinate two weddings at the same time. I did not want to hear that, but anyway, they started to line us up and play the music for the groomsmen to walk down the church aisle together, and halfway down, they would pick up a rose and present it to their bridesmaid and bow. She would hold his arm and walk to their place. And then the next one, and so on. The best man Kendall walked with the maid of honor. Then it was myself, the groom. I was just smiling, walking down the aisle shaking hands, hugging folks, and I saw my sister Terri too. I was so relaxed doing that. Reverend Powell was last. Then Garence (from Akron, Ohio, and my ex-wife classmate), Melody's coworker rolled out the white runway, his foot was all bandaged up from that morning's injury, but he pulled it off limping. It was a sight to see! Then, her little girl cousins walked down the aisle, dropping the rose petals. And then the ring bearers, my son Ant and Melody's nephew Dawain. The colors were red and gold. It was so lovely. Everything was turning out so beautifully. You could not tell that many things had gone wrong in the preparation of the wedding ceremony.

Then the moment that everyone was waiting for has arrived. There was silence. The wedding coordinator was in the front and had directed everyone to stand up as she had motioned with her hands. There must have been about two hundred people there, and people were still coming in. Most of the people there were there for Melody, being friends and family. I just could not believe it! There she was, as beautiful as could be and her father, shorter than her, right by her side. I was truly stunned! I could not imagine her any more beautiful because I would have been so wrong. The way she had looked—it was way past gorgeous. She had looked like she had stepped out of a magazine, and that was exactly what I was thinking. I actually was frozen because she was so beautiful. I truly could not believe how Melody was transformed! It was sort of angelically amazing! I was lost for any words for me to speak. I was just shocked! Then I had given the nod to Ralph for the music and to play the song "Fully Committed" by Kingdom with Emmanuel playing the live saxophone in the background. Ralph had the sound system on point that sounded as good as live! I finally begin to sing to her as they walked down the aisle. I was doing just fine, and as they were about halfway down, I turned toward the Linda and Brenda, the maid/matron of honor to compose myself as I was about to cry and felt the tears in the wells of my eyes because Melody was so beautiful. Then I was able to start singing again. Then at that time, the only music left was my little rap piece with the saxophone, and the song ended with the saxophone. For it was my first time doing such a thing, and it had turned out quite well! I was so pleased! Then I walked down and her father gave Melody to me to walk her to the alter for our wedding vows and double-ring exchange. This wedding was off the chain and so beautiful.

Once it was over, we had the photo shoot as folks left to meet us at the reception hall. The photographer had taken so many photos with different poses of us and family members and then pictures of our rings. After the photos, we took a ride in the limousine. My two sons wanted to ride with me and Melody. Melody said no, and I wanted to expose them to more. Melody reluctantly agreed, and then she was okay! Shortly after looking back, I had realized to never do that again because we had no privacy in the limo. And I did drink some of the Champagne anyway to relax me from having no sleep! Ralph and Emmanuel had followed us to continue the video-taping. Another beautiful part was it had rained while the wedding was going on, and it stopped raining while we were driving around Bolling AFB a little before going to the reception hall. It was almost movie-like! Once we had arrived to the Bolling Recreation Center, the photographer was ready to take more photos. Then the other hostesses and coordinator Lynn (Melody's coworker) was there for the reception. Lynn started to lineup the bridal party to walk in to sit at the head table. Of course, we were last to walk in as everyone stood up. There were people everywhere! The photographer was taking pictures, and Ralph was doing the video as a wedding present to us with music from Kenny G or BeBe and CeCe Winans in the background. I was definitely a Kenny G fan! After we had sat down, Kendall had brought my eight-year-old son to me crying. We made room for him at the head table, and he still would not stop crying. He had never told me why he was crying; it only stayed a mystery.

Then just as people had stopped eating, I had turned backward to toss the garter belt that I had taken off my wife's leg. My brother Shawn was the fortunate one to catch it. After that, my wife turned around with her back to the ladies. She teased them, with the motion of throwing it at first, and finally Melody had tossed it, only to have fallen on the floor. Then Winnifred (Melody's coworker) picked it up, and that was it. Then Melody and I walked around in different directions to meet and greet everyone. Ralph was doing interview pieces to add to the wedding video. That reception was a class act! By the time I had got to speak to Ms. Sparks, she seemed a little ticked off by her husband, Colonel Tom Sparks. Ms. Sparks face was so serious, yet she was pleasant to me. As they had to be leaving, we greeted again, and they left. By this time, my dad had shown up in an off-white leisure suite, with my ex-wife cousin Melody. They were late, but they made it. Then they took a seat, and the hostess had got them something to eat. Brenda's church did the food, and it was awesome. Those ladies were awesome representatives of their church, Greater Revelation Baptist Church in Fort Washington, Maryland. We did have some Christian music playing in the background but not distracting. We kept greeting folks, and by this time, we took a few more pictures, right before the cake-cutting ceremony to feed each other. That cake was the bomb that Ever had made, and she also attended Brenda's church. And then a few more pictures...

This little white dude was almost glued to my wife, and by this time, during this stage of the reception, he had to be on overtime that was not included in the contract. He did not care! He was just captivated by Melody, and from out of nowhere, he told her that she was one of the most beautiful brides that he has ever seen, immediately followed by his blindsided kiss on the cheek! I went to grab her right then and did not want to make a scene. This guy did not care even if I would have knocked him out! He just kept telling her how beautiful she was. He also knew that it was his time to go! I could not believe that he had kissed her cheek without asking! Right after that, we kept greeting and saying bye to our friends, family, and coworkers. It was time to leave, and the wedding ceremony was officially over. We had to clean up our part, and good old Kendall stayed behind to help with everything. Kendall was just the best friend that anyone could ask for. Then we loaded our car with the gifts and presents. It was too much, and then Kendall loaded his car too, the Jetta that I used to drive. My mother was so proud of me as we all hugged, and my sister Terri drove everyone back to Akron, our brother Shawn, and my son Big Mike. My dad and Melody (ex-wife's cousin) wanted us to spend our wedding night with them to do some sightseeing, and I only wanted to be with Melody and I had Ant. Plus we were flying to Oahu, Hawaii, late that Sunday night, and Ant was leaving on Sunday morning. My dad got upset and told us that he was going to give us a hundred dollars but was going to now keep it. I was so disappointed and just left. Nothing that I could have said would have sounded right, and I was not going to mess things up for my wife. While it did hurt me, I just played it off to Melody like it was not a big deal! We were headed home, and Kendall followed me. As heavy as it had started to rain, Kendall helped me unload everything until it was done. Before he had left to go back to Baltimore, Kendall had left me with these words: Melody complements me, and I complement her. I had always kept his words close to me and remembered it. They had life! We hugged and he left. Kendall was my great friend! I had to put Ant to bed as we had an early day on Sunday.

One thing that I had learned about weddings was that guys were to never pick the wedding date, and now I truly know why. That's it! It was the excitement of marrying Melody that had got the best of me, and I still did not want anything to change. The sooner we were married, the better! Now, it was quiet again. My boys and family were gone, and Ant made it home safely. We did not have much time to pack and leave later that night. I was thinking that this was the worst possible time, because I was holding it in long enough. I just had to do it! I then got Melody's attention, while in the kitchen to tell her something important. We then continued to stand, as I had to just come clean for when I had first moved into my apartment in Connecticut. I had told her that I was still seeing other women. I then promised to be faithful and totally stopped, since we are married. Melody stated: "That I had waited until we got married to tell her this" Then, she was quiet and disappointed. I was not sure what she would do, but she did forgive me! Because the integrity of her vows and faith were very important, she believed me and agreed to forgive me. This was truly incredible and unbelievable, but I was truly living with this miracle of a woman. No further conversations came off it and we stayed the course. Wow! Our honeymoon was still on! We hurried out the door from home and made it to the airport on time, just barely making it there, but we did have to rush. We were on our Delta Dream Vacation on the way to our first stop to Dallas Fort Worth, Texas. Then we were onto the extremely long flight to Waikiki, Hawaii. This was another first and our first time flying together. We both have only wished that we could have taken this flight first class, and the flight was a little rough or bumpy just before we landed. But it was not first class this time! However, we were enjoying each other's company. I had my favorite seat by the window, and Melody was next to me. It was just magical, and then we started to get sleepy. We both were so tired from all wedding planning, and excitement. Plus I missed a night's sleep, the night before the wedding. We did see some fireworks between the sleep, eating, or going to the restroom. I kept thinking on how being with her and being together was so beautiful all by itself. Sometimes, we would wake up enough to smile at each other and then go back to sleep. We could not wait to go to bed to get some real sleep. We had about six hours to go and to sleep and eat as much as possible. Melody definitely slept more than I did. Sometimes, I just wanted to watch her sleep. Her peace and beauty were just so amazing, and I was really enjoying myself. I went back to sleep with Melody on my mind. Melody seemed so relaxed and comfortable with me. We kindly gathered our things.

Once we landed to make that connecting flight, we were so tired and could not wait to get to the next gate. We made it just in time as the announcement was made to begin boarding, so we decided to take turns watching our things, and we took turns going to the restroom. As we began to board, at first glance, this plane was big, with five or six seats in the middle. I have never been on a plane like this before. We ate again after the take-off and went right back to sleep. Being tired was least of our concerns. We also had a time zone change to get used to. Then about seven hours later, we were there and was forced to wake up before landing to adjust our seats. The view was just fabulous looking out the window, and I did get a few pictures. As soon as we were off the plane and walked to the terminal with no windows, they placed these necklaces around our necks. Later, we found out that they were called leis. This was the Hawaiian greeting. The people were so beautiful and nice, and the weather was gorgeous! Both of our eyes were burning, the tired kind of burning. We went over to get our luggage, and there was just so much to see. Next, there was a person holding a Delta Dream Vacation sign and pointed us to the delta bus transportation to the hotel.

Once at the Outrigger Hotel, we had to place our luggage in the hotel. I believe we had a bellman. And then, we had to rush downstairs back to the bus for breakfast and an island tour presentation by Delta Dream Vacations. After the breakfast was the presentations for what to do, information about the islands, and tours to purchase. We did the shopping tour, a luau for couples, and an island tour to include the Pearl Harbor Memorial. We did these things on different days with the luau being on the last full day, which was Thursday. We were just having fun. Then the shuttle took us to the ATM to get money to pay for our tours. Then back to the hotel as we had the rest of the day off. In Waikiki, everything we needed was in walking distance. So we first went to the Hale Koa, the military hotel, plus it had a mini-BX for any extras that we needed to buy. I was able to get me a few Mai Tai drinks. I was not really a big drinker, but these things were good. Melody did not want the alcohol. And I did not have more than that. Melody did not want me to drink anything with alcohol in it. Besides, it was the very hardest thing to tell her no, without feeling bad within myself. Her sweetness did get the best of me.

Thereafter, we both drink virgin Mai Tais, here and there. They were still good to drink, so it worked out for both of us. Once we left the Hale Koa, we walked along the beach areas, and just kept walking. We eventually ran into some guys holding some parrots. With a glove on and for $5, we could hold the bird and take a picture. So we both did it! Then we brought a picture of Hawaii as the sun was to set! We had a little bit of daylight left, and you could see the sun was to start setting. It was beautiful, just like on the *Hawaii Five-O*, television show. To see the sunset was as mind-blowing as it could be. It was truly a sight to see! We wanted to catch every one of the Hawaii's sunsets! So amazing! We did learn that day as we were beginning to walk back to the hotel that on most days in the morning, there is a mist or light rain, and then, the sun comes out. Then the beautiful weather remains for the rest of the day. The next day, after breakfast, we saw the pineapple plants, then the place where Jurassic Park was filmed, and went shopping. We did pick up a lot of leis that was just given to us, and then, we brought some others and souvenirs. Once we got back to the hotel, we took a taxi to the Sato's Store, and they also sold shaved ice that we had got free, plus some other items. We had stopped by there because Maj. Greg Sato, the one who took my place at the Pentagon, working for Ms. Sparks who also referred me there to meet his parents and stop by their store. It was on this trip that I realized how much my new wife had like to shop. She could stay in the stores for hours and not buy anything. Shopping did not really bother me because we were together. We just enjoyed each other company. Hawaii was truly a paradise in its own right!

The next day, we saw the Pearl Harbor Memorial. That was an amazing special place. I remembered this strange feeling that came over me when we were there. You could just tell that something happened there! The tour guide told you the story, and we understood that it was like a tomb in the water. Then that feeling I had suddenly all made sense. Let's just say that I was glad to leave. That night, while at the hotel, we decided to go back out to see what was happening in the evening. To tell the truth, the streets of Waikiki does not sleep! There was something to do each and every entire night. We even saw this man with an all-silver outfit on and could look just like a statute. There was even a guy, passing out ninety-minute tours, and you could make a $100 just for taking the tour, plus a free dinner cruise. Melody looked at me those googly eyes, and the $100 would not hurt to get a few extra souvenirs. It was our very first time-share presentation. We signed up to take the tour on tomorrow before the luau. We were planning to make the most of the last two nights there, and it was always something to do. One of our greatest pleasures was walking together, and holding hands were sort of magical for us. Each moment that we shared together was just priceless, and our relationship was really taking shape, after the bad news I shared with her before leaving. Let's say that we were bouncing back. We were loving and sharing every moment together. I have never had anything close to this—what I shared with Melody. I have only seen her happy, but surprisingly to me, Melody was truly happy being with me. I kept always feeling like I did not deserve her, but she was happy, just being here with me! Yet Melody was so special to me. I did not really know how to dream until Melody chooses me back. I was her choice too! We were in Hawaii together, the woman that I love, for the first time.

I really never thought that it was possible for me to even be in Hawaii. And we were there! I truly felt liberated and free! I too was happy as I could be and never thought it could be! I thought if I was dreaming, please do not wake me up! I truly had a happiness that was real and lasting on a good note! This was the best honeymoon trip in my entire life. Each day that we shared, I could only want to be with or think about my Melody! Well, it was time to walk back to the hotel and call it a night. We had got up earlier that next morning to do the time-share tour after the free breakfast that was included. After the tour, we chose to buy what ended up being time-weeks, and we choose the plan where we could have the option to make payments up to eighteen months for the Embassy Suites Resort, and the payments for the introductory package was about a $1,000 for two full-week stay and one per year, including breakfast. This deal was something that we figured out and decided together to get it. The best part was that the payments would not start until sixty days later. Once we filled out all the paper, we collected our $100 and dinner cruise vouchers. We all boarded the bus and got dropped off by Waikiki beach. We had some free time and decided to rent a two-seated moped that drove like a car, steering wheel and all. We were all over Honolulu with that moped. We did not only see the stores, but we made our way to the residential areas, as well.

Boy, the fun that we were having only made us want to pay this new trip off come back as soon as possible. The fun that we were having was not rated on any chart. We really had the time of our lives; however, we did wish that we had an extra day to stay there, but it was not even remotely possible. So we just kept enjoying the moments together, pictures and all! This was our last night, and we turned in the car-moped and had a little time left over before getting dressed for the luau for couples. We hung out for a while and decided to get dressed, not to miss the bus. I had to wear a shirt with no tie or a Hawaiian shirt, and Melody had on the Hawaiian skirt set that she had picked up. No matter what she had worn or how she dressed, Melody was just beautiful! For real! We made the bus and onto the luau. We were finally talking with people, especially me. We hung around a lot of couples that we met in various situations and outings. And they too seemed to be so in love. We had got quiet for the Hawaiian ceremony to begin on the ritual for the pig cooked in the ground and cover with fig leaves. The food was different for us and surprisingly really tasted good! The people were just so friendly; the entire trip was so worthwhile. After dinner, we watched the after-dinner show, hula girls and all. They were really just awesome!

Once it was over, we were allowed to talk and take photos with them. Wow! We had a good evening, and then we return to the room and went walking one more night to get a little exercise too! We were really full from dinner! Now, it was time to shower after we had finished packing. Our last night there, and Melody surprised me once again since the first night. She gave me another massage. It was something that she wanted to do, and since being married, this was just her touch of class. I was just lost for words. I did not know what to say other than thanks! That last day, we got up a little late and got dressed. We had to leave our things and the front desk holding cage. Then we got the city bus to go shopping again. We took as much stuff back that we could pack from Hawaii, even some macadamia nuts, keychains, and post cards. We finally made it back to the hotel to catch the bus transportation to the Honolulu airport and await the 12:45 p.m. flight to take off. Finally, it was time to leave. What an enjoyable honeymoon trip it was. Now we are on the plane and headed home. Still, we were on our honeymoon for real. I just never wanted this mindset that I had to leave me. I just wanted to keep this feeling going on. This was a very long trip with a short layover in Atlanta, Georgia. We had just a short layover in Georgia, and just as we were boarding the connecting flight, I realized that I had forgot my blue, black, and red Atlanta Braves baseball cap. I was just lost into my wife, and I did not want to lose my hat. I even called the Delta airline's lost and found to no avail. My baseball and favorite cap was gone.

Now that we were back in Annandale, Virginia, with a few more days off, I was in the advance leave status of minus eleven days. We had to get her identification (ID) change, plus her dependent military ID card too. Never a dull moment. Now that I was married again and in love, having the best time of my life. Plus, my child-support was current and my bills were current too. We were also saving money together and not just Melody. I was so glad that Melody shared everything with me as she was not materialistic. Neither was I! I just did not have a whole lot at the time, and Melody did not mind! She had always told me that I had potential. That word *potential* have always meant something to me and provided me with an obscured value.

One thing that I had found out in a hurry was that Melody did clean the house, and we did some chores together, but Melody could not cook too many food items but did okay for the most part. Jokingly, I had said that if I did not already know how to cook, we probably would have been a frozen dinner type of family. I did know how to cook and would help teach her everything that I know, and then, of course, she would call her mother for all other recipes. Let's just say, we did have a plan. If not, we had cereal, french fries, and peanut butter and jelly sandwiches. As the days were progressing, I must say that we were eating pretty well in that she did prepare a few new food items, which some foods stuck to pan or just tasted funny, and that was all that I remembered. July and August were very hot months and very dry. By this time, Melody's mother, Ms. Mary, took ill and had to be hospitalized for problems with her pancreas. After she had recovered, she had retired from her job and moved to North Carolina and then brought a double-wide trailer to live in. Then we did most of our shopping of Fort Myers and seldomly at Fort Belvoir Commissary. Everything was pretty normal, doing our day-to-day stuff. It was sort of mundane, but not at all boring for us. Because we just did everything together or sometimes with her sister Linda, Butch, and Von. Melody and I really enjoyed being together, even if it was just doing nothing. I did have on my screen saver at the Pentagon the words *marital bliss*. I was so happy. Just before thinking about going back to school, Melody and I made it up to College Park, Maryland, Abstract Studio, off route one, to pick up our wedding photos and a large portrait. Boy, the pictures and the portrait were outstanding. Great work! Then, it was at this time that I decided to go back to school and finish my degree with the Community College of the Air Force. I had also registered at the local community college called Northern Virginia Community College to finish up my associate degree. Once I had sat down with the counselor to figure out my curriculum I went at it full speed. I was in the flow of things and not at all chasing the women. I was this time happily married.

My life was perfect for going back to school. I really wanted to succeed. All was going well. Other than talking to my boys on the phone, I was not able to see them as much, except for once or twice a year or a week in the summer or on spring break from school. Anyway, we did go to Goldsboro, North Carolina, to see Melody's mother and family. On the way down there, Melody's aunt Angeline rode down there with us. It was good for the trip down there toward the end of September. Once we got there on Thursday night, I met all of the family, and since I was again, active-duty Air Force, we stayed at the Southern Pines Inn, Seymour-Johnson AFB, North Carolina, at the discounted military rate. Everything was going well, and somehow, the conversation went left, and for one reason or another, I was upset and told Melody to come on. As soon as she was in the car, I drove off. We went to the room to get our things and checked out. Then we immediately drove back to Virginia. I just left her aunt Angeline stranded. I had never done anything as such. Melody was quiet the whole way back. I could tell that she did not like it either. But I was in the I don't care mode! I was not sure when we were going back to North Carolina. My school classes were back in, and I just kept busy. Melody would most times quiz me on my tests in the evenings and back and forth to work. She was really good, and I was getting it rather quickly. I did find out that Melody's family were totally upset with me for leaving her Aunt Angeline. We did find a little time to eat a piece of the year-old wedding cake and put it back in the freezer. Still, I had to just ignored it and kept my focus on my studies. It did take me a while to get used to Melody's side of the family. We did go to visit her mother and sister Linda. I was still cool with Linda. No one on Melody's side of the family would mention what I had done, but I was sure that the talking was being done behind my back. Moving forward, we were finally able to get a new black and gold living room set from Marlo Furniture Store. After having such struggle, with getting the sofa in my townhouse, my neighbor in the downstairs townhouse, this big Afro American gentleman came out to help me. I had never seen him before. I had thought that he may have been watching me through his front windows. After finishing, we talked for about fifteen minutes, and that was it. He had told me that he worked at Georgetown University and Allen Iverson was in attendance there. He was telling me on how the players were partying at Georgetown all of the time and at night. I had told him that I had worked at the Pentagon. I also mentioned that I had worked with a colonel by the name of Mike Mitchell and his wife, who was in the education arena, had tutored Allen Iverson (AI). I was definitely of fan of AI even with all the controversial issues that was in the news, concerning AI. AI was definitely a force to be recognized with! I did not care. That boy could play some basketball! We both mentioned that we lived in a very small world.

The conversation ended between my mysterious neighbor, and I never did see him ever again. Moving on with working at the Pentagon, which was a big part of my everyday life, plus dropping Melody off at her job at Computer-Based Systems, Inc (CBSI). It's a contract company for the Environmental Protection Agency (EPA) in Arlington, Virginia (Ballston section of Arlington). It was about this time in November I went on a TDY trip to Arizona with a few of the pilots to Air National Guard Air Force Reserve Command Test Center (AATC) to see a night vision demonstration. I was also trying to get a test flight in the A-10 training aircraft. This trip was only for a few days and just full of information. The evenings, I stayed to myself, and it was a little boring. So I decided to go to the BX to pick up a few items. While there, I ran into this young white female sergeant in the Air Force. We somehow struck up a conversation because I had told that I was on TDY and not from there. I really was trying to be good. I had my own hotel room and rental car. There a military saying, "What you do TDY stays in TDY." Pretty much, don't kiss and tell! I was really trying, but she was flirting with me and wanted to go to Phoenix, and we were in Tucson, about 115 miles away, to see a friend. After shopping, I decided to be a nice guy and take her.

Her name was Jamie or Janet. Anyway, we were on the road, and then I started to flirt back with her. Then by the time we had arrived, she was in a rush to get out and knock on the door. This chick was pretty cute, and as soon as she saw this dude, I immediately knew that I had wasted my time. They had locked lips at a moment's notice and hugged immensely. Then she introduced me as her friend that drove her up there. We were only there for about twenty minutes and parted back to Tucson. I was totally used! I had thought just maybe, she and I would have the night together, even though it did not stop me from trying. This was a lesson to be learned by me: do not cheat on my newlywed wife. Believe you me, once we had got back, we had parted ways. I just did not know why. I did not just leave her there, but I did not. This was the first time that I had ever fell for someone flirting with me, but it would be my last time.

The next day, Melody had picked me up from the National Airport. It was just cold outside, and I had got off the plane, and there she was as beautiful as ever, her hair was down, and I do remember her wearing this long trench coat. Boy, was this a beautiful surprise, and I was surprised that she did not catch a cold! I could tell that she had missed me, and I was glad that nothing happened between Janet and myself in Arizona. But it could have very well been a close call! This was my first secret that I had kept from her since being married, and I dare not tell her! The holidays were approaching, and my leave was beginning to grow a little from the honeymoon trip, but we were not planning to travel anyway. Just before our first, being married Christmas, I wanted to do something special for Melody, other than put up the Christmas decorations as she was turning twenty-five on December 23. At a spare of the moment, I had called Brenda, one of her best friends and help me pull this off—a surprise birthday party! So I invited family and friends: Brenda, Carol, and her husband Ralph, Linda, Butch, Von, Betty Artis an Air Force coworker and friend.

Melody was okay trusting me with me having female friends too, but she had to feel comfortable and kept informed. I also had Chineta order the cake for me at the Pentagon, as well as Brenda meeting me at the Pentagon to get the key to our house, so she could get it decorated with streamers, balloons, and all. Plus I had to order the pizzas. The birthday party was a success! We did not do much but did some cooking together and brought in the New Year's watching the celebrations. Plus I was getting ready to start the winter semester. I was so glad that the Air Force education program paid for most of my education's tuition. Sharon in the education office was definitely the best and kept me on target for all of my training needs. Sharon had also informed me that I was eligible to take the DANTES test to CLEP (bypass the actual classroom studies) and still receive six free college semester hours. What a deal! I had gone for it because math was my strong suit in regards to my studies. Now that the DANTES Algebra II Examination was scheduled, I had got the book from the library and study some more. I really had no time to waste or play. I was very busy, even though my thirty-third birthday just passed, and there was no time to celebrate. However, Melody scraped up some time to bake me a cake. The thing was that in all my years, this was the first real birthday cake that I could ever remember, other than at the Pentagon. Melody made a cake just for me. I was just looking at my birthday as another day. Then somehow, Melody made me feel so special. She actually touched my heart. Again, I had that feeling that she was too good for me, and I did not deserve her.

Not once did Melody stop believing in me or us! She was totally one of a kind and just an incredible human being! I must say that even though I was drastically changing and made some nice milestones, but I could see in her eyes and the way that she looked at me that she believed in me and us! How could this be? But it was! I did ask myself over and again, Could I be faithful to one person? Or could I stay faithful? I really did not know either answer. Once back at work, I met with Sharon again in the Pentagon Education Office to check on the DANTES testing. I still had a short time to finish preparing for the DANTES testing. We were just everywhere on our schedules, plus the going to the store, dry cleaners, including the house chores, coupled with washing and drying the clothes. Melody was studying with me like it was her second job. We had just stop going to church as well! The distance that we traveled to the church was too far, which made it easier to let going to church just phase out!

Going to church was no longer our first priority. So I did run out and brought a twelve-pack of Miller High Life beer. I had decided to stop perpetrating that I was totally in church and I was not even close. In my heart, for what little that I knew of God, I did not want to continuing playing being saved and in church.

I was just sinner and a hypocrite churchgoer at that. This had to stop! There was something inside me that would not allow me to play with God! I just could not continue to do it, and in my mind, it was settled! I was not a big drinker. I just wanted some beer in the refrigerator, just for beer to be at my disposal. Through all this, I was in fact studying to take the test on January 24, the day before my brother David's birthday. On Monday, I did work out and then studied at the Pentagon library. I was as ready as I could be on Tuesday. I showed up to the education office on that morning as ready as could be. I could take nothing into the classroom, except for water, pencil, and paper, which were provided. Sharon did proctor the examination for quietness and us to stay awake during the exam. I must agree that it took all of total time of all most three hours to take the examination. After it was over, I did pass with flying colors. I just CLEP six college credits for Algebra II. I passed! I was so, so happy and in the state of shock! I could not wait to see Melody once I have picked her up from work! I was glad to see her and to tell her that I had passed Algebra II. Melody did have one of the biggest smiles on her face, then kissed me!

Then I had told her that I was slated with a few more courses to complete. Then I would graduate in August 1997 with an associate degree in personnel administration from the Community College of the Air Force. I was just charging away with excitement in obtaining my first degree and the first person in my family to do so. I did not want to let anyone down. My family back home did not say much, but I knew that they were counting on me as well! I knew that time was still of the essence for me. And it was February 1995. I remembered to order Melody some roses for our one-year anniversary and that I had proposed to her and sent her some flowers to her job, with my signature flower in the arrangement. I also included a card, and it read, "Happy Valentine's Day, Melody! Forever…that's how long I'm going to love you. Michael." The card had a red rose on it. The more I kept changing, the more I kept doing these types of things. I would not even think about it. I would just do spontaneous things like little gifts under her pillow or on the car seat because of the way I was feeling about her. It kept happening at a moment's notice! Still, it was truly a struggle for me to change from the old me to the new me that was truly happy, being in love with my Melody! I still remember that we had an evergreen tree in the front yard close to our townhouse which caught on fire all by itself. It was good that the building was brick. Other than a little scorching to the brick, there was not much damage. The fire department arrived within minutes. I must say that that was pretty exciting because we were very quiet in the neighborhood. It was a very diverse neighborhood, and the people just stayed to themselves. We just kept it moving and exploring the neighborhood, stores, and Landmark Mall. Then we still did most of our shopping of Fort Myers and seldomly at Fort Belvoir Commissary.

I would still be saying bad words, but not as much. Plus, the gambling was gone, and my other females too. I did not miss those ladies or the gambling for the simple fact it that I got tired of staying broke, without money. My mind was in a good place, with the focus on school, and soon to graduate and obtaining my first college degree. Meanwhile, I had to agree with Adrian to get my son Ant for the summer. Our finances were getting better, so we had to fly him down to us for the summer. We also had to drive to Ohio to pick up Big Mike and my niece Tia for the summer too. I had one month before graduation. This was also our one-year wedding anniversary. Since Tia was the oldest and my niece, she would be tasked with babysitting my two sons who were also her cousins. Melody and I had our one-year anniversary planned for a romantic getaway at the Wintergreen Resorts, nestled in the Blue Ridge Mountains. We left them food in the house, money, and phone numbers, and we were gone as soon as the car was packed. We had a four-hour drive ahead of us, and we did not mind. We had about four days and wanted to make the best of it. I was also glad that my leave was building up as well. We had everything to look forward to. I wanted to keep being romantic, so we had talked about doing an anniversary trip every year. It was a good plan, and we decided to give it our best shot to make it happen for our future anniversaries. We had so much to look forward to even on this trip once we had arrived, from my favorite of horseback riding, mountain bike riding, outdoor jacuzzi located right into the mountain, and dining. The rooms were on the natural side of things, and mostly, everything was made by hand. All was working well, except for the second night at dinner. We had tried to eat dinner at the Clubhouse Restaurant, and neither one of us played golf. It looked like a nice place until we sat down for dinner. After a while, we started watching people coming and going after us, and then after two-hours later, the manager came to the table and apologized, also giving us our meals free.

While there, the conversation about church came up. We agreed to start looking to going back to church. We also noticed that there were not many, if any, people of color there. Then the lightbulb went off. We were purposely left there at the table ignored, and no one would come to the table each time that we had asked for service. We literally watched people that came in after us eat and leave. Wow! Until that experience at the clubhouse restaurant, we had not experienced any racial negativity at all. One thing for sure was that we knew this would be our last trip there. We truly and really enjoyed this spot, except for that one racial incident. We also decided to enjoy the rest of our Wintergreen Resort trip and never visited that restaurant ever again! The walks in the mountains and the horseback riding were just the best, and of course, the balcony to our room was a nice added touch hidden by the forest greenery for us to experience nature at its best! Over all, we both really had a nice first anniversary in spite of the racial nonsense! It was now time to leave. We were packed and ready to depart the resort down the mountains. We were just in love as could be. I must say that Melody was smitten and in love with me! It seemed as if the drive home was the easiest drive that I have ever made. We were really enjoying each other company. Once we reached home and decided to relax after unpacking, the kids decided to sing to us a song to celebrate our anniversary. It was "I Swear" by John Michael Montgomery. Big Mike, Ant, and Tia really tried hard to impress upon us and to give us a love song upon our return. It was just so thoughtful and beautiful. Just beautiful! We really enjoyed the presentation, and it was so fitting and special to always be remembered! Melody and I were just outdone on this surprise song! Children are just so special! For the time that they had remaining, we took up some sights in DC, and I had given them a private tour of the Pentagon afterhours. We rode the Metro train to some the DC sights and did some of the blue paddle boats. We had food, so they ate well too. It was the end of the two weeks, and it was that time to take Big Mike and Tia back to Akron on the next day. I did not have much time to waste as I had to get ready for the fall semester. Akron was a quick trip, and I spent only one night there. I saw my mother, and we hit the road back to DC (the metro area).

Ant was nine years old and was about to turn ten years old in October. On the way back leaving Akron, he decided that he wanted to stay with us and not go back to Hartford, Connecticut. I did not count on this nor did either of us planned for something like this to happen. How do I tell him no? I had no babysitter, and what would his mother say? I did not know the answers to any of this. If he was to be here for the next school year, he would attend the fifth grade. Next, and surprisingly, Adrian had said yes. I had never expected that response from her, but she did agree! Not having a babysitter was my biggest concern, so we checked out the government details on the age that a child could stay home by themselves. The guidance was in our favor, and we made it happen. I was not ready to take on this task to have my son down for the school year. In August, as I was preparing to graduate for my associate degree. We also had to get Ant enrolled in Columbia Elementary School. My graduation with the Community College of the Air Force went over very well, and the ceremony was held over at Bolling AFB, DC. I had invited Brigadier General John Bradley, Ms. Cathy Sparks, Annie Barnes, my wife, and a host of other folks. I was so glad that these people took time out of their day for me! I was again overwhelmed in obtaining my first degree! Melody and I had to learn all we could about the Child Latch-Key Program. The few things that I really did not like was the latchkey program. He would be staying home by himself, and he had to cross the busy four-lane highway, Route 236, twice on every school day. I do thank God that he was an obedient child. We did a few practices runs together, and then he was on his own. I was scared every day, but he was a very safe and independent child. I had plenty of rules for him, and Ant followed them to every detail. Ant did not give me one problem, so I was sure to reward him accordingly. I was so glad that my son had some smarts about himself and showing maturity. I was so glad that Adrian and I had raised him to be independent, and it was paying off.

Now we were all set to have him registered for his elementary school. I too had to get register for school. I still had the driving desire to become a doctor, so while working on the job, I had taken a break to call Howard University in DC as they had a physician assistant (PA) program that caught my attention. While that was on hold, I called George Mason University in Fairfax, Virginia. They had a chemistry program that I wanted to see firsthand. I then made an appointment for the next day to meet with the professors and take a tour of the campus. On the next day, I had taken an extended lunch to go and check out the campus. The thing was, if I was going to continue on the path to become a doctor, and having a chemistry background would provide me with a stronger foundation as a doctor. I did remember that from my premed teacher Ms. James back at Central Hower High School. I had to first get the approval signed off from two professors in the chemistry program and the dean of chemistry to ensure that I had a strong enough math and science background. I think being in my Air Force uniform may have given me a few extra points. A few hours later, while still at George Mason, I had got everything approved and submitted with my transcripts and associate degree. Now, I was registered in George Mason University chemistry program officially as a transfer student. Once back at the Pentagon, I dropped my things off at my desk and signed out to the education office to see Sharon.

While there, I was reading some material and brochures from the University of Southern Illinois University at Carbondale (SIUC). They had a satellite office at Bethesda, Maryland, National Institute of Health (NIH). The materials were for the health care management, bachelor's degree program. I had changed my mind in an instant and immediately signed up for the program, plus the course date for classroom was in line with my schedule. This program would also line up with the direct-commissioned officer program. I was all in! I could not wait to get home and let Melody know what I had done all day. Once I had informed her of all I did that day, and the decision that I made and why, Melody only wanted me to be happy for my choice and to do my best! I then went to talk with Ant to see how he was doing and to check on his homework. He had most of it done because that was his priority once he was home from school. We were a temporary family and almost there because I had one of my sons, and I really wanted both of them. Everything was working like clockwork, and Ant was crossing the street every day safely. Every now and again, one of Ant's classmates Mohammad, who lived directly in front of us, would knock on our door and ask, "Can the little boy come out to play?" Then, Melody and I would get a kick out of it because he was a little boy too. We just had a little laughter together!

Moving forward now, we all had a lot to do as the year was coming to a close. Melody did make it to one of Ant's parent and teachers conference meeting. and his teacher made mention that he was doing so good, and she did not want him to transfer out or to go back to Connecticut. That was really nice of her as our home was disciplined and structured. My days in the military were coming to the surface because having structure was the one thing that I knew how to do as it was very much a part of me. I was really focusing on school myself, and Melody was right there quizzing me and helping me to study, ensuring that I was to get good grades, as well as my son. Just before the holidays of Thanksgiving and Christmas. I received my next promotion to master sergeant (MSgt), and with that came my biggest ever pay increase. Now, I was considered one of the enlisted top three and a great place to be in. The saying was, "Rank has its privileges!" Now, we were celebrating another Christmas, and this time, I was only missing one son. We did start putting up a small Christmas tree and decorations. Melody was talking about church again, then more and more, so we started looking to visit some churches in Maryland and DC, hoping to be led to the right one. The first church that we visited was New Mount Olivet Apostolic Church in Seat Pleasant, Maryland, with the pastor as Bishop Hopeton Mair. After parking the car, I stood in the middle of the road on the now James Farmer Way. I was looking at this little white church with red trim called True Apostolic Church. I stood there and told my wife that this Sunday, we were going to New Mount Olivet, but next Sunday, we are going to True Apostolic Church. I could not believe what I was saying. Then I said to her, "I am drawn to that church, and I do not know why, but I felt that I had to go there."

That next week just zoomed by, work and all, and I had gotten my homework done, and Ant did too. Melody would also quiz me on my college courses for SIUC on the way to church and back. We had a great Christmas, and my son and Melody were happy as well. We had started going to the other church, and it was small but friendly. We were first greeted by Mother Twilley and Sister Faye Harris, and I remember as we entered the church doors at True Apostolic Church (TAC). The first words that I remember Mother Twilley saying we were just like new money! I was very flattered and felt very welcomed. I had never been greeted as such from any church that I or we have attended thus far. One thing for sure, this church felt like home. From this point on, Melody and I started to go back to church again, and now, Melody was just like me, a backslider from the church!

On that next Thursday, in January 1996, I was turning thirty-four years old, and my mind was made up to get back in church for real! My heart was changing to get right and for God to forgive me of my sins. Melody was as happy as she could be. It all felt right! Just three days later, on Sunday, on January 7, after Pastor Charlie Plummer had preached. Then the altar call was given for visitors to become members, so we went up, Melody and I. We did not just go up there to take the right hand of fellowship to become members, but we decided to be rebaptized again, just to be sure that this time, we both had known what we were doing for ourselves. Immediately, the church had baptismal robes and clean towels for us. Then we went into the back of the church, and there was the metal horse trolley, being filled with water, the singing started with "Take Me to the Water" by Nina Simone. It was an old church song that I have heard many times. We both were happy to be baptized once again as my son Ant looked on at us. This time was very special for Melody and me because we did this religious act together and had brought us closer together. This was our new church home, and everyone greeted us as we were leaving.

We talked all the way home as to what just happened, and I did not get any studying done that Sunday at all. Now, it was time to eat to get ready for school and work. The pastor's wife started to call us and check on us. Her name was Mother/Lady Flossie Plummer. She had really kept us encouraged. She may have called one or two times that week. Now, Melody and I had to figure out on how to attend Bible study that was taught mostly by the pastor's son and assistant pastor, Elder James Plummer. This dude I had admired right from the start. He was so wise and very astute in the Bible knowledge. I was totally impressed, and he had my attention to learn more about the Bible. It was also a compliment to me because I was already in college and writing plenty of reports and papers. I wanted to know more about this Jesus. Elder Plummer was so eloquent and passionate in the presentation of Bible teaching. The more I was learning and understanding, the more I wanted to learn. It was that simple. I was hooked for knowledge of the Bible. Then in February, I went on another TDY to Melbourne, Florida, to see a space rocket launch. The winter here was cold and snowy with ice on the roads. As we had gotten ready to fly out, things were beginning to clear up just a bit. The worst part about the snow days were back at our townhouses, it was open parking, and if you shoveled out your parking space, it was open for anyone to take it. That was not fun at all but just the opposite! I really had to learn and keep my patience. So everyone placed all kinds of items in the snow, just to hope it would hold your parking space that they and myself had dug out.

This was the second year that we're doing this, plus having one sink in the bathroom that Melody and I shared was beginning to get to us, especially me. So after winter, we decided to find a realtor and would look to see if we could afford a house to buy with a double sink in the master bath and a must-have two-car garage. Well, it was time to leave for Florida to see a space launch with Pentagon VIP treatment. The folks from my office that I went with were Col. Scott Nichols and Lt. Col. Mike Collins. First the visiting team had to find me a flight suit and some patches. We went on to get the safety briefing followed by meeting some of the pilots and astronauts. Then the VIP treatment was to take a flight in one of the Air Force HH60 helicopter flight around the area and then ending up at the launch-pad restricted zone, within two to three miles from the launchpad and the space shuttle. I could not believe that I was right there! Just before we had landed, the helicopter hit an air pocket and dropped like ten feet, just like that. What a scary moment. Plus I was taking pictures! Then, we were all driven over to the viewing stands to see the launch and were about two miles away to see the space-shuttle take off. This was set for a long-drawn-out day. Someone from the Florida team suggested that we go over to Hooters Restaurant to get some wings. I was not sure what to expect being my first time there.

While I thought that the wings were pretty good, I figured out that the main attraction was the ladies in the short shorts! That really was not my kind of place, and I did plan not to go back. But to be honest, those ladies were pretty attractive and still not my scene. I just had to resist this temptation! I am a one-on-one type of person and never to compete with the other guys and have them get jealous of me. Plus, this time I was planning to stay faithful. Truly the temptation was right in front of me, but nothing beyond that. I just could not wait to leave after that. I was not driving. This time, it was much easier to be faithful to Melody and not having any close calls with the ladies. Those ladies were just not my style. I truly like a classy and beautiful lady, and I already had that taken care of. Besides, I was nowhere close to desperate. On the next day, I was glad to be leaving to fly back home, hold my wife, and get my pictures develop. Once I returned home, still busy as ever, with school and now, trying to buy a house after the winter. Now that the snow was gone, we kept trying to see different things, and the realtors were very unhelpful and unreliable. Even though we kept changing realtors, we did not like anything that was shown to us. Because we were so busy, we went to church less. Well, Mother Flossie Plummer just kept calling us to see how we were doing. It was not any pressure at all! She was a very nice lady. Then one day after we got home from work, we caught up the details of Ant's school work, changed our clothes and my uniform. Then I turn on the television. I like to watch the public service announcements to see what was happening in the local area. I then saw this one ad for real estate presented by Rick Saunders.

So I took the number down to call him and setup an appointment. I was tired from after two winters at this townhouse and people taking my parking spot that I labored and shoveled was a bit too much, including sharing one bathroom sink with Melody. I decided that it was time to expand. I was making more money as a master sergeant, and my bills and bankruptcy items were current and paid off. We were still working on Melody's hospital bills with just a little left. We were almost debt-free, except Melody's credit was better than mine. Our income was looking good, and it was time. I noticed that my whole life was just better since being with Melody. It was the beginning of April 1996, and we had an appointment in Falls Church, Virginia, to meet with Rick Saunders. All three of us went to the appointment, and Ant was bothering things and distracting me from what Rick was saying. Anyway, we completed the paperwork, paystubs, and all. We now had a realtor that seemed legit and better than the other folks we were using.

We had planned to go out and look for houses on next weekend on that following Saturday in the late morning. We then followed him over to Fairfax, Virginia, to a place called Atlantic Coast Mortgage. Since my credit was not the best, these were the people to assist us, especially me. We met Lisa Nattania, her fiancée' Larry Rice, and Gale Goodwin, the loan processor. We filled out more paperwork on the financial side of things, so they would compile everything and let us know before next Saturday how much house that we could afford. I was at work, and Lisa called me on Wednesday and stated that we could not go over $200,000 and wished me happy house hunting. That was more zeros than I had ever imagined. It seemed as if the more that my life was changing for the better. Yet, we stayed away from the church that we had recently joined. We were staying away from God. I even went out a got a six-pack of Miller beer in the can. Mother Flossie Plummer would still call us to give us encouragement. Sometimes, we wondered why she kept calling. But we did not know how to answer or make an excuse. Really, we just stopped going to church. We were going to church for a good four six months, and things got really hectic! Also by this time, we were able to get two Motorola cell phones by Bell Atlantic. They were pretty big and heavy.

My schedule was still plenty full, and I had very little time to do anything. These courses were taking a toll on me. We had a cheap computer but did not own a printer, so I could not work on my school stuff during the day since my job was pretty busy. So I would go to the Pentagon (a norm for people in school) in the evenings and on weekends just to print my papers. Sometimes I would take Melody and Ant with me. Other times, I would go to the Pentagon library to print my paper report and do some background research. After I arrived to the Pentagon in a controlled tour, our directorate was under the leadership of Maj. General Robert A. McIntosh. This guy would always call you by your first name. I was always impressed by him to be a busy general at the Pentagon and still remember my first name. At this point in my classes, I had to do a paper on leadership change, and I had to pick a leader to interview in order to do the report. I then approached Maj. Gen. McIntosh walking in the hallway. I then told him my pitch for a college project and wanted to interview him and mentioned that he had impressed me. He was honored to accommodate me. I just had to schedule a time with Cindy for the general's calendar for a few days. I wanted to pick a leader that had already made it. I had learned a lot during my interview with him. The single most thing that I had learned from Maj. Gen. McIntosh was that *change is constant*. I did not know the concept but would always remember it. Another point from him was to know people names! I believe that I had an A for that interview and paper. I also remembered the professor that was the most demanding. It was Professor James Hall, and the other one was Professor James Justice. This guy was just awesome and knew his stuff. I believe that I had learned the most from his style of teaching. I worked much harder for him than any other professor, including Professor Anita

G. I remember writing so many papers, and the research was altogether too much. While at work, we had just had a going-away for Ann Johnson. She and I would stay in touch, especially to talk about antiques, which was her favorites. Then I was responsible to hire the next secretary. So after all the interviewing, I hired Ms. Alberta Ross. Alberta was a very nice lady and hard working. Now another weekend was here to look for a house to buy.

Rick took us to South Riding to view some very nice homes. These houses were just enormous and gigantic. We went inside these model homes with stairs up one side and down the other side. We just loved these homes. Ant and I were playing hide-and-go-seek. We actually could not find Ant for a few minutes because the houses were just big. Rick gave us a dream, and he wanted us to see ourselves in a house as nice as this. I really believed him and the entire story. I have never ever had any dream as close to the house that I was standing in. It was just too amazing for me to dream that big! Rick taught me something doing that trip to view homes. That was my first time and our first time ever in a house that big! Then Rick was taking us west past the Dulles Airport. There were mountains and was quite scenic. We finally got to an area in Virginia called Exeter, and they were building homes. Nothing had been completed, and the sales folks were in a trailer doing business. When we arrived, no sales agent was available, so we had to wait. When it was all said and done, we were working with one sales lady, and the other guy was Jim Graves with long frizzy, salt and pepper hair. He always drove this yellow corvette, which was parked outside. This was a cool realtor dude! This dude just knew that he was good. He really knew these houses. When Jim was finished, we had spent $197,000 and only brought a design and layout on a piece of paper. The house was not even built yet. Our first buying experience was to buy an idea on a piece of paper. Rick and Jim both were good and awesome! The house would be completed in October 1996. Melody and I were buying our first house, and the name of it was called the Dominion.

That following Monday, I had told Alberta that Melody and I were buying our first home and the location in Virginia. She was very familiar with the area, and she was telling me everything and about all the new developments, and come to find out, that Loudoun county was one of the fastest growing counties in America. Everything that Rick had mentioned to us was right on point and even about the Greenway extension to the Dulles toll road, which was also home to some of the top school districts in the country, which were Fairfax and Loudoun counties. One selling point that stood out for me was to be in a location that had good schools. I really was interested in that point, just in case, my sons were able to move down from Ohio and Connecticut to live here with me. That would be one exciting day for me! Every day at work Alberta and I had so much to talk about as she and her husband had just had their house built. At this same time, I took an interest in the workforce diversity programs, special emphasis program, and blacks in government (aka BIG). Since I was a black man, and have experienced some setback, with the various mindsets that I had to work with, I knew the silent struggle of diversity firsthand. Then by working at the Pentagon, I wanted to find a way to give back. I wanted to set all people up for success, not just for the blacks, but for all people to have a level playing field. I know that life is not fair, but I wanted to believe that I could be fair, and I could make the difference for someone. I reflected back on my own life's struggles and wanted to figure out a way to help someone in their life. I also volunteered to work with the program director Margaret Wilson on one of the special emphasis programs. I then became the chairman for the Air Force Pentagon Mentoring Program.

Now, I have my own committee as well with about five people on it. I remember Toy Jones (vice chair), Karla Hunt, Joyce Void, and one guy, Dick Fidelman. The committee were a diverse group, and I had to stay on my game. Most of the time, they were always there. At some point, my wife did meet them all, and the one that was the most interesting was Toy Jones. She had seemed to have a little office crush on me the most, and I pretended that she was just friendly. I knew that this time, nothing was going to happen because she already had a son and a friend that she was getting serious about. Still, she kept trying to make plans to go get some drinks at happy hour, but it never came to fruition. I was avoiding every encounter with her because I was really trying to be and stay married. After a while, it seemed like more was going on with Toy and I, then it really was because we were always talking or in the hallway together. But I was apprised of everything that I was doing or she was trying to do, and I was going to do absolutely nothing! Toy did have a son, so a little office friendship was all that I could manage to do.

I had to stay nice to everyone to get my agenda on my committee accomplished. Margaret also had got me involved with the Washington Chapter of Blacks in Government (BIG), and I would be able to travel on TDYs for this program. By this time, I receive the Air Force Achievement Medal at the commander's call. I was also getting awards for the Air Force Pentagon Mentoring Program and the BIG program. I was very active and part of my giving back. My life was ever changing before my eyes and especially since meeting and marrying Melody. She was definitely the best thing for me. Our life was full and interesting with fun. We kept going back and forth to Loudoun county to see the house being built. I did notice that doing the framing phase we were able to go upstairs and the master bathroom door was hung on the wrong side. We went over to the builder's trailer to let them know. Jim told us that he would get that fixed and informed us that the model home was being built at the same time across the street. The following weekend, we took a weekend trip to North Carolina to see Melody's mother. Her health had gotten a lot better since she had moved down there. They also just loved Ant and treated him as part of the family. I guess I was forgiven and no one mentioned anything about me leaving Melody's aunt down there. It was all cool. I was relieved and glad. I was really trying to do things right. We were telling Melody's mother that Ant had passed to the sixth grade but had to be back home in Connecticut the following weekend, just before school was to start for me and my son. Ant was doing so good, and the teachers did not want him to leave. But Adrian wanted him back to help babysit his sister Rayashajaney (Rae) Johnson.

We had gone to see her cousins Mike and Lisa Sutton and then Terrell and Durwood, the Sutton brothers, and then it was time to go. Melody did give her mother some money, and we had left back to Virginia. One stop that we always had to make was Parkers Barbeque

Restaurant for the pork barbeque sandwich and some chicken wings. We did make it home and another busy week to get things ready for Ant to go back Connecticut. We did not want him to leave. We had all bonded together and became a family unit. Working was good for us both, and our funds were growing still, and the credit was getting better. However, Gale had called from Atlantic Coast Mortgage Inc. and left a message with us on the home phone once we returned home from work. Right then, we had called Lisa back instead of Gale about the issues that came about on our loan. My credit was not where they needed it to be. She wanted to use Melody as the primary on the loan, but I had made more money. I said okay, and forget about it, and we hung up the phone. Less than a half hour later, Lisa had spoken to Larry, the vice president of the mortgage company and her fiancé. Then she said that they had figured out a way to make it work and got our loan approved.

Next, our rates were to be locked in. It all was a go, and we were buying our first home! We had to go in and sign the papers with Gale on the next day after work. Awesome! We took Ant home to Adrian. Then we spent the night at Kendall's place, and he gave us his bed. My best man was in a class all by himself. Kendall was always a gentleman! He gave me the updates on the bus company and was telling me that he was planning to move back to Baltimore. I was happy for him. I had told him that I was still trying to become a doctor and still back in school. We said our goodbyes and headed back to Virginia. Melody and I were going back to Virginia to pack. Melody had found a cheap quick trip to Nassau, Bahamas, one price included airfare and hotel for each of us. This was supposed to be our second anniversary trip. It was an okay trip once we arrived. The landing was hard and bumpy. Everyone shouted and clapped their hands for a happy landing as they were ready to gamble and party. We made it to the hotel and decided to shower and checkout the island. Now, the worst part was the tub and shower because the water had gone past her ankles. Melody did not like that shower nor to be in that water. I was okay with the shower, and as long as I was clean, it was not a big deal. Melody just kept reminding me of that shower. So we had called housekeeping once we had returned. Let's just say that it had gotten a little better. It was just great to get away and be together. God knows that we really needed this break from the world. We had gone to the beach to walk and take some pictures. After that, we took the Pat and Diane Tours to do some scuba diving and to see some coral reefs. I tried the scuba diving for the first time. For some reason once I was in the water, my mask did not seal properly, and all of the saltwater was getting in my mouth. I had two choices: to swim back to the boat where Melody was or to keep choking and drown. I had thought that the boat had anchored and stop moving. That was not the case; the boat kept moving and literally, I almost drowned because I could not see and breathe. Plus I was choking. That was a scary moment for me. So as the people were beginning to get back on the boat, the party got started, and I sat down and drank water. Then I partied a little. I saw Melody doing the Spanish dance called the Macarena.

I almost thought that my life was almost over! That was a scary moment for me in the water, and I was glad to be alive! Then, on the last night there, Melody had found this seafood restaurant that sat on the beach. We had got dressed up and called a taxi to get there. They had our seating on the screen-in patio as you would see the waves rolling off the water, the setting was perfect and a bit romantic. This was a very nice and classy place as we had lobster for dinner. Still, we have conversations about that restaurant. On tomorrow, we left the Bahamas Island and wanted to make the best of that night. The night setting was so beautiful and peaceful and gone too quickly. It was time to get ready to turn in. This one night there made up for the issues with the water in the bathtub. Now, the whole trip was a worthwhile one to be remember! The only worse part for me was the off-brand air plane flight, and I was not looking forward to the trip we had to make back. I could have messed up badly, but I was glad to had confessed of the escapades that I was involved in. I am only grateful to Melody, for the life that I almost missed out on. Wow, I had almost drowned too. There must be a God somewhere! I believe that falling in love with Melody and we had stopped going to church was really getting to my conscience. I would just look at how happy she was with me and did not want to mess things up between us.

Once again, I hugged her, and we talked about the trip as we began boarding the ghetto plane. It was not the best plane, but we made it back to Virginia. I was so glad to get off that plane. Never again!

Now, we had to get home. It was now just us again. Ant was gone, and I was missing him dearly as I looked into his room. Melody and I were yet doing well and staying busy, and yes, being in school was keeping us up at night, but mostly me. I had to get those papers done! By any means necessary, I was getting those papers done whether I was at the Pentagon Library in my office printing or home. I was getting those papers done! Nothing less and nothing more. I was meeting or exceeding every college assignment! In the evenings, out of everything that I was doing and we were doing. I would be talking with Melody and would confide in her that something was still missing in my life. Melody would then say, "It's God." I would get upset with her and deny what she was saying. I did not want to believe that it was God that I was missing. I kept telling Melody that on many occasions that it was more than that! Once again, I denied to her that I was missing God! And then I would walk away. I have accomplished more in two years of being married to Melody than the entire twelve years of marriage with Adrian. Plus, we were buying our first home. I just felt that something else was missing. Still and even to myself, I did not truly believe that I was missing God because I did go to church, even though we had just stop going again.

After a few more weeks of school and work, we took many trips to see our new home that was being built. It was taking shape. It was just beautiful to look at even with no porch. I saw the two-car garage doors and just got excited. Rick met us there with the paperwork to complete the final walkthrough. We went through every room, checking the water, sockets, and placing painter's tape on the walls, cracks, windows, doors, etc. for areas to be touched up or fixed that day before we were to get the keys. We all signed the paperwork for the home and headed to the Chantilly, Virginia, office to do the closing. We also brought our $291 cashier check from the bank for the settlement closing costs. After the closing, Rick Saunders had added a touch of class and provided us with a gift basket to seal the deal. Rick even had our garage insulated and finished, just because of a misunderstanding that we had. And because he went the extra mile, Rick would be the first person that I called if I ever needed to buy a house again. Now, we had to pack up our townhouse after just two years of living there. It was the one sink in the bathroom and the shoveling snow in the parking lots for someone else to take your parking spot—these were all the motivation I needed to get out of there. We were awaiting the arrival of my brother David to get there; once again, he was to help us move to Loudoun County, Virginia.

I was completely done! David had finally flown into Baltimore Airport, Maryland (BWI). It was on. We went to pick up the U-Haul on the next day. I really did not trust a lot of guys, during that time, since what Steve Witherspoon went through the ordeal with Adrian, my first wife. So my brother would always be there for me, and David had done my moves on several occasions. We had the truck loaded and ready to go as soon as we double-checked for our final clean up so we could get the security deposit returned to us. We knew that we would be deducted for the light fixture cover that got melted, and that was it. We turned in the keys and were on our way. I drove the U-Haul, Melody drove the Maxima, and David drove the Cadillac. The thing about this trip to moving, we now had to pay tolls. To go back and forth to take Melody to work and I would then drive to the Pentagon, we also added an additional twenty minutes to our daily commute. Life just got better. We now had mountains, country roads, and the real suburbs, including our own house. My brother David was with us for a few days for us to get settled, and he was to get back to Akron. Plus, I still had to go to school on the next day. Boy, was I tired! I was just tired and exhausted from the move, but I had to get that degree, just in case I was able to get a commission in the Air Force as an officer! I was on a mission!

Once I returned home from school, we took the U-Haul truck back. David was working completely hard for us. We took a few minutes to talk here and there. He was so into church and an inspiration to me. I believe that he was going to First Apostolic Faith Church on Easter Avenue in Akron. David talked a lot on how he appreciated Pastor Samuel Hampton. I was just excited because he was excited. I did not know that people could love the church the way my brother did. Then he put up the other bed, hung the curtains and the cheap blinds. He unpacked a few boxes, we were set, and he was ready to get back home. The next day, on Sunday, we unpacked a few more boxes after eating, and the time had gotten away from us. We were now actually running late to get him to BWI airport. I was moving in the caddy. Yes, we barely made it. After getting back home, I finally realized that I had a life to fight for and strive to give it my best. I was on track to completing my bachelor's degree in less than one year, and after thirty-five years of age, I would then need a waiver unless I could obtain a medical commission. I did not care. I just wanted to get a commission as an Air Force officer. We did Thanksgiving dinner and Christmas in our new home with the tree and all. I even cleaned some chitterlings and hog maws, which took forever to do. Our first Christmas and dinner turned out well. The house was looking good too. I notice when I took out the trash that one of our evergreen trees were just gone. I took a closer look, and it was surely sawed down to the stump. It was not even considered a Christmas tree. It was a white pine tree, per the police, and we made the police report. We also went to the model home and reported to Jim Graves and the other salesperson, Renee Blackmon, what had happened, and they had their landscaping company to replace the stolen white pine tree. Now, our concern had turned into joy! We did not like what had happened, but now we were more watchful of the neighborhood. Now, we could enjoy our new home once again. But we were watching those trees every chance we got.

Now, January was rolling around, and for me, an another birthday was on the horizon. and I was about to turn thirty-five years old. No birthday celebrations for me at work or home. I was studying and did not want to lose my focus; however, Melody did give me a birthday card. It was at this point going back to church was beginning to cross my mind. I had started to attend Bible studies, at the Pentagon. This Air Force Lt. Col. Ron Holloway had got me interested in attending. So I started to go on and off. Then suddenly, it got interesting, and I started to go every Thursday at 11:00 a.m. For the first few months, I did not say much. The winter months were ending, and right before March 1997, the BIG were having a conference in Los Angeles, California. I wanted to go and learn more, and I wanted my wife to go too.

By this time, Alberta and I and our families became friends. Alberta even taught me how to save money on the toll roads for the commute. Then she had told the office that she had found another job. That was truly quick and short notice. Now, I had to hire another office secretary. My job title was the chief of computers and information manager. I ran everything in that office and the righthand man to the colonel. I was the go-to man for the office. One of the good things about my job was I was like my own boss. I even took two and half to three hours for lunch most days to work out at the POAC. I was into so much stuff at the Pentagon, and then, I received an Air Force Accommodation Medal for all of my hard work. From the life that I had come from, I could not believe the life that I was living. However, I had got this feeling of fear that I could not explain. I could not shake this feeling that I was having for days. I was feeling that if I had gone TDY without getting right with God, then something would happen to me on that flight to California for the BIG conference. I made up in my mind that I would not get on that plane until I got my soul right with God! I told my wife that I was going back to church on that next Sunday. That day we were on our way to church after getting dressed. Melody and I were having little arguments about this and that, but nothing major. So I decided that nothing was going to deter me or get me upset. I was going to church to get my soul right with God because I could not shake this feeling. Bottom line, I was in fear that I was going to die!

That was the feeling that I could not shake! No arguments for me. I did not care what Melody was talking about. I had to stay focused, or I would have changed my mind. That day, Elder James Plummer had preached. He was also the assistant pastor. I did not care about the message preached that day. I was waiting for the altar call. I knew that I would be saved that day. After I had gotten saved, my voice was gone, my voice was hoarse, and I staggered from the spirit of God! For real! I knew at that moment God was with me! The people kept hugging me and congratulating me, and then, it was time to go back home. The first thing that I did was to call my mother and gave her the scripture 2 Corinthians 5:17 (KJV): "Therefore, if any man be in Christ, he is a new creature: old things are passed away; behold, all things are become new." Immediately my mother knew exactly what had transpired with me and know that I was back with the Lord. I then told my mother on how my brother David and sister Marsha were ministering to me on the last time that I was in Akron and on the phone as to how good God was to them. I wanted some too. I wanted and desired what they had and on how their lives have changed!

I then told my mother that I had wished that I had come back to God and gotten back in church a long time ago. My mother then said, without hesitation, that *it was not my time!* I got it just then and needed to hear those very words. Those few words hit home in my brain, and I immediately stopped regretting the guilty feeling for what I had missed over the years! She said that it was not my time! I then was calling everybody, including Marsha and David to tell them that same scripture, 2 Corinthians 5:17! I was trying to tell the world that I was back in the church. I was that happy and excited! Now, I had started to change this time for real. I was watching everything that I was doing at work, school, and home. I tried to live a Christian life. It was not the easiest thing to do as I could not stop cursing or using foul language. My mouth was just that filthy. I still had it so bad that I did not know that I was doing it, using bad language or foul language. I then offended myself. I was like how could I now be saved, and my mouth was still so foul. I did not know what to do or who should I talk to. I was just stuck! But I really wanted to stop.

From that point forward, I tried to pray on a daily basis. I would ask God, "In the name of Jesus, please take this cursing, and bad language from me!" I just kept praying for about two weeks straight to change the way I was talking because I knew without a doubt that I was totally wrong for what I was doing, and I wanted to change. So I kept praying, and I never stop praying! Never! I just kept believing that God would deliver me, and I just kept praying the same prayer! I believe that this was my first test from God for me to know that prayer works! Prayer works! Then, I was playing basketball at the Pentagon during my lunch workout break, and I had got in a heated discussion with one other basketball player. We were about to argue and fight. I had never had a problem using curse words or foul language, but this time was different. I could not even think of a curse/cussing word to say. Not one word would come to mind! Not one word could I frame in my mind! I knew that God had delivered me!

At that time, I no longer desired to use foul language again. I was delivered, and I knew that prayer did it! I did believe that prayers worked! God had delivered me. He changed my mindset and my mouth, and I did not even know that my deliverance was already done! I was delivered and excited and could not wait to express it to my wife what God had done for me! Melody was happy for me as well. She never liked for me to use such choice of words and foul language! It would be times like this, when I was being ugly with my language or me telling Melody of some of the bad things that I had done with Adrian, Melody gave Adrian and I the nicknames of "Bonnie and Clyde." Melody had teased me with this nickname several times in our relationship!

When everything was done and over for that week, it was time to go back home. On the flight back, this is when I knew of that feeling that I had before—that something was going to happen to me. The announcement came on over the air to us passengers, stating that there was bad weather and thunderstorm at the Chicago Airport, and the plane had to sit on the runway with us onboard. The thing was, we all sat in that plane on the runway for just over two hours. At that time, I was glad to be back in church. I knew within me that I really did not have an option or choice. It was like I belong to God before I actually did. One fact that I know was that I could never believe that the feeling I was having. The thunderstorm in Chicago, and we are sitting in California on the runway was no coincidence. I truly believed that God had chased me and that I had chosen him at the appropriate time before my trip. That was the only thing that made sense because it didn't make sense. Nevertheless, I have been changed! Now, we were truly busier than ever. I decided to stick with church this time. I measured the mileage, and it was fifty-one miles one way. If we went to work, home, and then church, it was about two hundred miles a day. After thinking long and hard about it again, Melody and I did agree to do it! I needed to be in a good church, and Melody wanted me in church as well! About two weeks later, Melody was backsliding because of hanging out with me. Then we married. Melody rededicated her life back to God and was now saved in the church too! We knew that we both had to be in church and on the same page in life. I was doing well at everything and no time for play.

My schedule was a complicated one—with work, school, church, and marriage all going on at the same time. I was still writing papers and doing my printing at the Pentagon, and sometimes I was allowed to study my college materials while I was at work. Still, I had a few months remaining before I would be taking the final and graduating with my bachelor's degree in health care management, and this would be my second degree. Wow! Since I was really back in church, it seemed as if my grades had gotten better. I knew it had to be that I was going to church because I would be falling to sleep in some my college classes, and yet believe it or not, I was still getting As and very few Bs on my exams. I had less time to study, and I seemed to be doing much better. Melody and I were staying up later, just to study, and there was a lot of material to go over. We were going over everything and my notes. Melody just kept on pushing me and pushing me, causing me to get the material in my brain. I was not going to quit at all because I had the best support system in the entire world—my wife! I was doing all I could to push. I was not going to let her down in any fashion. I just had to pass my exams and write some more papers for a final or two as well!

Those past few months were very well less than easy, and I did finish all my courses and turned my work in. If I did well enough to graduate, it was to happen at Bethesda National Institute of Health (NIH) May 1997. This was the day as I received my bachelor's degree in health care management from Southern Illinois University at Carbondale. I also made it on the dean's list too with a 3.68 GPA. I was done with school for now. I was considering going to medical school. I was also looking at the program at NIH called The Aqua Medical Diversity Program that would assist me through medical school. I could not decide, so I proceeded to go the direct commission route and skip medical school. I had one chance to obtain a commission without an age waiver. But I had to find an officer personnel billet that I could get a commission in. Well, a number of weeks went by and nothing. Then I finally found someone to interview me for an officer's military personnel billet. The position was located at Fort Belvoir at the Defense Logistics Agency (DLA), and this Lt. Col. Thorpe Murrell was a black man and seemed very serious. I did not want to get the job based on my race. I wanted to get the job based on my merit.

I graduated from college on the dean's list, which means I worked hard for that degree! Lt. Col. Murrell was impressed by my tenacity and merit. I had to feel like I belong in that position because I had earned it. I was a master sergeant in the Air Force and just completed my bachelor's degree. Not only did I have to find a position first. The next step was to get approved and acceptance for Officers Training School (OTS), which was not an easy task to do. Because age thirty-five was the cutoff unless I could obtain a medical commission, which would be a direct commission. I even had to have my age waiver preapproved, just in case my package was delayed in the process. I had all of this going on, plus we were committed to our new church. The year was closing fast, and we are right in the middle of summer. We also had to skip getting the boys that summer, for obvious reasons and had planned for the following year. It was our anniversary. Plus I need a break. We also tried to trade in our Nissan Maxima for a new 1997 Toyota Avalon after it was all said and done. Not to mention the fact that Melody kept telling me not to buy the car and we could not afford it. The salesman took our car and gave us a loaner until the new car arrived. We went home, I recalculated the bills and Melody was correct. Melody and I had to come up with a plan to get our $500 deposit back, and our car returned to us. Once we got back to the dealership, they took us to the new car that we purchased. Melody and I looked over the burgundy car and nothing would be missed. We had to get out of that deal by any means necessary. I then saw what appeared to be several scratches. My wife and I then showed the salesman.

The salesman took a napkin and rubbed it lightly to remove the mark, and he said that it was only mud splash from the transport. Nothing that he could say that would change our mind, so we kept asking for our car back and for the manager to cancel the car transaction. First, the manager lied and told us that our car was already gone or sold to auction. We did not believe him, not even for a moment. After almost an hour later, the car runner brought us our car back and gave us a deposit back. My wife did not argue with me or nothing. She did not even make me feel bad, for the bad decision that I had made. That was a lesson learned that taught me to consult my wife and her with me before any big items are purchased. We did convince our salesman and manager that they looked like scratches that was on the new car that we were about to purchase. It was a blessing to get out of that deal because we really could not have afforded it. It was now funny to us as we drove back home. That was a valuable lesson that I had learned. And to say the least, never again! Now we had to celebrate our anniversary a week or so later. Melody had found some cheap airline tickets, so we both took a week off work and were heading to Los Angeles, California. We stayed at the Hilton Embassy Suites for the free breakfast and had to do a ninety-minute presentation for the four-day hotel stay. Plus we paid for an extra night with a military discount. We also signed up to become Hilton members to build points for free future stays.

We were off to the airport once again to take the five-hour flight to Los Angeles. Melody was looking forward to going to Rodeo Drive to window shop, and we did go into a few of the stores just to look. We had our phone and camera to take photos, not wanting to miss much. We both were posing and taking pictures everywhere. We did a lot of sightseeing and walking. We did manage on the next day to find a restaurant on the corner called Pink's Restaurant. They had some good burgers and hotdogs and fries with messy cheese. It was all good as long as there were plenty of napkins. Of course, we found a few malls to shop at and to get some different kinds of ice cream. The malls were mostly outdoors, very unique for us. We were beginning to learn our way around LA and Melrose Avenue or Melrose for short. As we were about to leave, we did the tour to look at new properties for Hilton, and we did not buy a thing, and we already had something we brought to stay at the Embassy Suites in Hawaii. Besides, we just brought a new house and were just satisfied all the way around!

When I would go to work, I was so focused on what and how I would be able to get an Air Force commission. I was also doing interviews to hire a new office secretary. I did not want anyone to outside of normal, whatever that meant. After a few weeks of searching and interviewing from the certs, I had selected Ms. Tina Bise. She was a young married white lady and in the Air Force Reserve or the National Guard. She interviewed quite well. She was nice but never there. Tina was not what I had expected. I did not want to hire anymore civilians, only military. I just had to figure that part out on how to make it happen once Tina was gone. It did not take her long at all. Tina was ambitious as I was trying to be, but she was better than I on maneuvering around the job. I was just glad that we did get along. I had an appointment setup for an interview with Col. Donna Martin in the AF/REM, Reserve Medical Director. She too was looking to hire someone as an assistant to her. She could have said yes, and that was it. Instead, she told me of a black guy that used to work for her and on how he was good at what he did. Bringing the conversation to sometimes, somethings are not meant to be. I did not like the direction that the conversation was going. Col. Martin had told me in a few different ways that came to the same end point: no. And she was very diplomatic about it only to let me know in a very different way that there was another path that I should be at. None of what she was saying to me made true sense, but it had something to do with church.

As soon as I left her office, I was just devastated and broken and had that feeling all over my body. I immediately had that feeling of rejection and to cry. I was in the Pentagon hallway and in my Air Force uniform. I was hurting and holding back all my tears! I was broken! My heart was broken! I then found the men's restroom at the end of the hall by the E-ring on the second floor. I rushed into the stall, and I could not hold in my tears any longer. I put my folder in the crack behind the toilet paper roll and grabbed some tissue to wipe my face. Those tears were flowing from my eyes. Just because she did not say yes because I knew that I was qualified. I just stood there and cried. That pain was something that I was carrying inside me for years—all the hurt and rejection I received possibly because of my race. I really wanted that job and did not want to believe that I did not get that job as a health care manager and a direct commission to lieutenant. It was now around November 1997, and my window to get promoted to the officer ranks were dwindling for every day that passes by. I now only had one shot left to get the job with Lt. Col. Murrell at Fort Belvoir. The next officer's class would not begin until March to April 1998, and I would definitely need the age waiver. I had submitted everything and just had to wait for the results.

My hands were tied and waiting was the best and only option available to me. I had promised that day that I will never experience that type of hurt ever. I did not want to really start all over again in my life by becoming an officer. I did reflect back on what my newly promoted coworker Colonel Bob Stice, and soon to be leaving, always said to me. Why would I want to start all over again to work my way up the ranks again? It was like I was getting signs from God that becoming an Air Force office was not meant to be for me, and I just had to accept it. Just maybe, Colonel Martin with the Air Force and Tom Crispino from the CT Transit were both correct that my life's path was better served with God. This was only a thought that I had had and could not prove if it would be true or not! Now, I guess I would never know. Still, I had to at least try until all my options were exhausted. I had no choice but to give it my best, so I would know that I tried! While the rest of my life was going forward, and pretty good with the two degrees that I had just accomplished. However, my main focus was to become an officer in the Air Force. One part of me wanted to still become a doctor, and I was only counting on one option.

Then by Christmas, just before my thirty-sixth birthday, my age waiver was disapproved. That was it with the disapprovals. I can't say that I was not disappointed because I was truly disappointed. This was the pinnacle of my life where I had to just accept this misfortunate. God knows that I tried but to no avail. I just had to find the peace in it all and move forward. The one option that was not really an option: live off student loans and go to medical school. Since I had already had issues with credit, I did not want to go down that path. Other than having my degrees, there was nothing else that could be done, except go for my master's degree. I only pondered the idea, but nothing came of it. Just quick recap of the past four years. I had got married, brought a house, and a new car. I finished two degrees and had my son live with me for a year. I also realized that my biggest accomplishment was when my life was cleaned up, and I was back in church.

If I only had to pick two things, I would have to pick church and getting married to Melody. I will always believe that God used Melody to save my life! Actually, my life was kind of up in the air, with not much of anything going on that was worthwhile until now. Now, I believe that I have a faithful wife. I had unexpectantly achieved more in four years than the past eighteen years of life since graduating high school, and this was during my second marriage too. I do not believe in luck, but if I did, Melody would be my lucky charm. Now, I have to submit my reserve package to remain on active duty station at the Pentagon because in less than five months, I need to get approved to continue on my tour for another four years. Right before Col. Bill McLoughlin hesitated before signed off my package. I did not understand the reasoning. I informed my wife, and we both prayed about it. Two days later, he signed my package for the tour renewal. I was so glad because Melody and I had just brought a new house. I decided to talk to the Col. McLoughlin a bit more and found that he either worked for the stock exchange, early in his life or just knew a lot about it. I was learning about different stocks and the calls and puts. It was the "options" the caught my attention. It was during this conversation, I was remembering how, I was instrumental in the coordination efforts to turn Curtis onto the same AGR program that I was working in. His application had got approved and somehow, we became co-workers.

Between Col. McLoughlin and my friend Curtis Webber, who was with me when I proposed to Melody, we also served in the Air Force together and now in the same office, I found out about oil stocks, K-mart, Walmart, Rite Aid, IT companies, etc. Shortly thereafter, I had opened up an account with Scottrade Inc. for about $800. I was holding steady. Nothing fancy that I was doing because I was still learning the market and on how to invest. I was absolutely a nobody in the stock market. So almost daily, I was checking the stock market and develop my tickers for a quick look at the market. I did go on with my regular military duties, and for the most part, I stayed busy even at work. It was beginning of summer. Loudoun county was small and quaint, a town in the post-Civil War era, but liberal. Loudoun County was one of the fastest growing in the nation with great school districts. They were building department stores, grocery stores, malls, homes, restaurants, and schools. There was a lot going on. I since realized that the more that buildings were erected, the traffic got congested and slower. I then started to meet my neighbors, Russ and Robin two doors down and Dave and Sandy, across the street. My next-door neighbors were schoolteachers about to retire and move to North Carolina. Our neighbors were really nice and caring. We were a pretty diverse group of people and just likable! Church was going well, except for the distance that we kept traveling. At some point, for all of the miles, we did join the choir, and I also joined the men's choir and brotherhood group. Now we had to drive extra on Saturdays to make the rehearsals. Not at first but I even picked up a few leading solo parts. The choir director was none other than the pastor's daughter, Sister Brenda Plummer, their baby daughter.

This girl was just awesomely bad. She had out-of-sight moves that would just make you dizzy. Not to mention that we had a pretty decent sound in praising the Lord. Brother Charles Terry played the guitar/keyboard, James Plummer Jr. (the grandson) on the drums, and Tre Harris (their cousin) on the organ. These boys were just awesome too! The church was made up of mostly family, but I never had the feeling of nepotism. They made everyone feel welcomed and you felt like you just belonged there. Melody and I had never felt like outsiders, not even once! Now, we were beginning to give our tithes and offerings to the church with a new mortgage and car payment at hand. We also had a vacation planned to Los Angeles, San

Diego, and Tijuana, Mexico. We were going with Melody's friends who were becoming my friends. We were spending time together often between them and Brenda and Randy every chance we were able to do. I did inform the assistant pastor James Plummer and his mother, Mother Flossie, that we would be out of town on travel. We finished up the packing for our trip on Sunday evening and tried to get a good night's sleep on Monday morning to get up early and meet with Ralph and Carol.

For one reason or another, Ralph and Carol were running late. Therefore, we all missed the flight. Now panic set in, and I did not want to mess up our planned vacation too. At first, we knew that we were at a loss, and we knew that God was with us on this trip. Ralph and I with our wives went to the Delta reservations desk, explained what had happened, and just like that, we were on the next flight to LA, about one hour delayed. We were all happily shocked as we knew that what just happened was a blessing from God. The flight was our biggest expense. Once we arrived, I don't know how he did it, but Ralph did 90 percent of all the driving, so he drove from LA airport to March Air Force Base, California. It was located in Riverside County, California, about seventy miles from LA airport. I was able to get rooms at the base for the week in the Temporary Living Facilities, which were mini apartments for traveling families. The units roughly cost about $20 per night each. We were catching good deals on everything. On the next few days, we were back and forth to LA to see Hollywood.

On the way to Hollywood Walk of Fame on Hollywood Boulevard, we stopped at McDonalds or close thereby for the restroom break, and come to find out, you had to pay to use the facilities, which was a big culture shock for us. People also kept asking us for directions, and our famous line became "We are not from here." Then, we were on our way to the Hollywood Walk of Fame to take pictures with different poses. Then we took pictures with the background of the "HOLLYWOOD" sign in the mountain, also pictures at Paramount Picture Studios, and we even took pictures of Moesha stage door at the Sunset Gower Studios, just before going to Roscoe's Chicken and Waffles Restaurant. We did more pictures of the million-dollar homes in Beverly Hills, and there was an instant where Ralph even talked with the police while we were taking pictures of the homes, sitting on the dark green Dodge Intrepid rental car. We then took pictures on Rodeo Drive. Then I saw a yellow Rolls Royce convertible. It was just beautiful! Wow! We went to dinner back by the base to a Dave and Buster Restaurant and also played a few games after dinner. The next day was planned, and we all were ready to hit the road. I know that Melody and I were singing church songs every morning in the shower. It was really just a happy relaxing trip. Ralph's personality just made the trip extra crazy relaxing fun. Ralph would just talk to anyone at random. Anyway we're off the next day.

We're off to get on *The Price Is Right* with Bob Barker. This was an all-day gig in the heat of a California Day. The lines were long, and the interviews were slow, but we had made it. I had only wished that I had worn my Air Force uniform for an extra shot to get my name called. Mostly Ralph and I were talking to folks to see what was going on around LA. We did find out some good information that we all were going to discuss later on. We gave a lot of excitement once we were in the filming studio, and when the "Applause" lights came on and talked with Bob Barker during commercial and intermission. Still none of our names were called. We then went to Pinks Restaurant (this was my second trip there) to get something to eat. We were all hungry on *The Price Is Right* television show. We talked about going to the Keith Sweat and Norm Nixon's Restaurant to go see how it was. First, we all were going to see the outdoor mall and then on the LA beach by Malibu Beach, which was the same place where *Baywatch* the television show was filmed. It was also in close proximity to OJ Simpson's house where Nicole Brown Simpson and Ron Goldman were murdered. We just had to see the infamous house, where it all happened. We did get some pictures on the beach as the sun was setting. It was such a beautiful sight. This area on the beach as the sun went down did remind us of being in Hawaii. We were killing time on the evening that we were planning to come. We did a little more shopping, and then, we headed for some kind of Keith Sweat album release party at his Norm Nixon's Restaurant. As soon as we arrived, it was early enough to get the Keith Sweat's orange T-Shirts with black letters on them. We had to find parking too. We all could not believe who walked up to our car and stuck his head in the window. It was none other than big Tommy Lister Jr. He had on this all-brown sweat suit and a large wad of money in his hand and asked our wives, "Are you all movie star?" Then he asked my wife Melody which movie she played in. By this time, Ralph had enough of the Tommy conversations to our wives, and Ralph had told Tommy, "Them ladies are our wives." Then Tommy backed off and went about his business. We had finally parked the car and went back on the sidewalk where everyone else was at. We were getting Keith Sweat music CDs. Then, Magic Irving Johnson walked with us and spoke to us, and of course, we could not help ourselves as we had asked to take pictures with him.

Once Magic Johnson took pictures with us, everybody else obliged us like Tommy Lister Jr, Eddie Griffin, Robert Townsend, Howard Hewitt (like me, also from Akron, on the East side of town), and his new beautiful wife, and Jaleel White (Urkel). This guy was way out of character as my wife Melody told me after the fact that he had placed his hand on her behind. I had asked Melody why she waited so long to tell me of this. Melody said that she knew how I was or would react. Yes indeed. That would have been the one time that I would have forgotten that I was back in church. And to tell the truth, it would have definitely been on between Urkel and I. That little boy had disrespected me and my wife! To this date, I am still waiting for Jaleel White to apologize for his reckless behavior! I really wished that he would have just denied taking pictures with us altogether. Being disrespected was not worth the photos. We even had gotten everyone's autographs for keepsake! In spite of the Jaleel White incident that became known to me after the fact, we had an awesome time. Robert Townsend had invited us to one of his shows. We also were invited to Shaquille O'Neal's party too as he had played for the Lakers with Kobe Bryant! Well, we had tickets for everything, but Ralph did not bring any clothes to go out in or to dress up.

So we all decided to not leave our friend hanging and found something else to do. We have heard that Las Vegas have a lot of all you could eat buffets. So on the next day, we all went to Vegas and got a room for one night at Harrah's. We had decided to spend the night because we were all packed and did not want to drive back to March AFB. It turns out that it was not the place for a bunch of Christian people like ourselves; sightseeing was the most of it. We did see a Christian Mission Church, trying to minister to people that was on the street. This I knew, and we all did realize quickly that the food was overrated. I just knew that I could not wait until morning to leave there as soon as possible! I was not even tempted to gamble again! I know that I have been changed and delivered from gambling. The one thing I knew for sure being there in Vegas, and it totally felt like none of us belonged there. Unless we were there to do some type of Christian work. That next morning, we got up and put our things together and met in the lobby to get out of there. We all agreed to get something on the road to eat.

Believe it or not, people were still gambling as we left that place. I had a thought that when I was in Atlantic City to gamble. I did not feel guilty about it. Since I had gotten back in church and was now in Vegas, I felt very uncomfortable being there. Never again! Now, we were on our way to meet up by Camp Pendleton with Melody's first cousin, Kelvin Sutton, and his wife Trecie and their two kids (KeJalen and Keonna). We were on our way to Tijuana, Mexico, to shop, take pictures, and of course, eat. Once we arrived, we parked our cars on the American side and walked across the border and through the gates into Mexico. We all had to have an ID in order to return to the United States. The walk took a while to get across the border, but we made it. Now, we all shopped and bartered with the local vendors. I was getting some really good deals. One guy even tried to buy my brand-new Atlanta Braves blue baseball cap. I told him that it was not for sale! It was totally a poor country. I had an apple and orange that I had brought with me to eat it later. I then saw these kids that looked hungry, and I could not eat my fruit. I called the kids over and gave them my orange. Not to be negative, but immediately they swarm around us, the children came to us from everywhere. It was easily thirty to forty kids surrounding us, so I gave up the fruit. I looked at Ralph, and we both had some $1 bill singles. We both were giving out US dollars like candy. We continued our touring, taking photos, and shopping. We saw this lady on the steps breastfeeding her child. That was truly a sad, sad sight to see. I gave her some money too!

Then, Melody had got this nice black and brown purse that went from $200 to the barter price of $40. We then went over to see what everyone else was buying. Trecie was buying a whole lot of stuff and souvenirs. As Trecie was about to pay for it, Melody whispered in her ear to let me get the price lowered! So she did. I told the guy that was too much money to pay for the items. I then told Trecie to leave it there and let's all go! Trecie looked at me like I was crazy! The guy wanted to stop me as we were going back and forth. Nothing! Then the guy said, "How much?" I said, "$40!" I mean that Trecie had a bunch of stuff, probably a few hundred dollars' worth. He finally agreed, and he kept saying, "No, Señor." And then, we left. Feeling a little hungry, a few of us had got something to eat, and we did not know really what to order. We just went by the pictures, and that was it. So we had made our orders. Once the food came out to the table, everything looked okay, but Ralph's food did not and his food did not, let's say, smelled fresh. Ralph's food really smelled awful! We tried to do the American thing in Mexico and send it back and not pay for it. Wrong! We saw one guy with a machete and another guy kept shouting, "Policia! Policia!" That interprets to the police. We decided to pay for the food and left in a hurry.

None of us wanted any trouble, and we decided that paying for it was the best course of action. It was getting late, and being military, we were not allowed to be there after dark. Kelvin knew of this too because he used to be in the Marine Corps. It was all fun up until that point. Once we all got back and crossed to border back to the USA, we decided to go to the restaurant Anthony's Seafood Grotto in Seaport Village, in San Diego, California. Get this, the restaurant sat directly over the water. It was just amazing on how it was built that way. We were also to fly out of there to go back home. Everyone trusted our judgment since Melody and I gave that restaurant high ratings since we had been there before. As it was getting dark, we were eating and talking about the fun and the possible police incident. It was all fun. Overall, that was the trip of a lifetime, and we did not have one sad moment the entire trip. We had a little fear in Mexico, but that was it! We all hugged, and then Trecie and Kelvin took their tired kids home. We all decided to go and check in the hotel.

We decided to take our wives on a romantic walk down the pier and look at the water. We must have walked about a half mile down the pier and back before getting into our rental car to onto the hotel. It was our last night there, and none of us wanted that night to end. The air was fresh. The night was still kind of young, so we started to look for a Denny's Restaurant for dessert. I had remembered a commercial for a new caramel ice cream dish they were offering. It was the perfect solution. However, San Diego was peaceful other than the big rat that ran across the street by the railroad track. Regardless to that, San Diego was an enjoyable town. I was thinking that if the possibility existed for me to move to California, then San Diego would be my home! The next morning, we sort of took our time. We had an early afternoon flight back to DC. So we went to breakfast in this little place in the Gas Lamp District. I remember that there were plenty of birds around us while we were having breakfast outside, just before the sidewalk. It turned out well anyway. Now, we have to turn in the rental car on the way to the San Diego airport.

From breakfast on, none of us had stopped talking about the trip. Now, we all were laughing about the food incident in Tijuana, Mexico… It was so funny as we were remembering it! Once we checked into the airport. On the way to the gate, I just had to have a picture of this dome-like shape waterfall. I thought that I was pretty cool with my dark-blue Fila warmup on with white Nike sneakers and my blue Braves baseball cap. Now, this was an awesome Christian trip of friends; there was no cussing, lying, drinking, or smoking. A lot of our conversation was centered around the Bible and church—also the new church that we had joined. Also we mentioned Raine, the Williamses' golden retriever dog. We made good of the long flight, and we safely arrived home. Then we went our own separated ways. We were just excited as ever to be home from a real exciting vacation! I could not wait to get the camera rolls developed. Now, we had to get ready for church on the next day and then back to work for the both of us. Now, we have to get on track to plan our next trip and get the money saved. We both knew that vacations were very important to us. Now, a few weeks had gone by us, and Melody and I happened to be outside and saw Dave and Sandy. They were a middle-aged happy husband and wife. We never saw any children. They were the nicest couple, and to our surprise, while we were talking, Sandy asked if we wanted to go to get some wings at the Wing Factory Restaurant in Ashburn, Virginia.

The thing is, if we knew that they were paying for the food, it would have been a no-brainer, but we did not know. We quickly declined as we had just returned from travel. The wings were a no-go! We really wanted to go, but the truth of the whole matter was that we were at a point that we would not afford chicken wings for real! Yet we kept pressing forward. Then eventually, we started talking to Russ and Robin. They had a son. The ice was broken! I did not think that we would fit in that neighborhood, but we did even though we both were from the hood. I was thinking that maybe sometimes my neighbors would see me sometimes in my Air Force uniform, and maybe, that made it little easier to talk to us. We just enjoyed talking to Sandy. She alone was our neighborhood watch person and all by herself. I don't remember if Dave helped her or not. Really, if you needed to know something or find out was going on around the neighborhood, Sandy was the one-stop shop! We really enjoyed talking to her. Plus, I had other things that needed more of my immediate attention like getting more involved with church. Also I was trying to figure out how I wanted to give my tithes to the church. We wanted to definitely be good Christian example. We wanted to be in church for the right reasons and serve God the right way! Now, I am on my second military tour at the Pentagon, and I was keeping busy as ever. Boy, did we still need some money.

One day while at work, in the office, I overheard the coworkers talking about homes and refinancing. Wild, I thought. What a concept. I did not know that you could take money out of the home that you lived in. I had called Gale Goodwin, the loan officer at Atlantic Coast Mortgage, to find out about how to get a refinance or Home Equity Line of Credit (HELOC) done. Okay now, Gale had discussed both programs to us, but the more attractive one for me was the HELOC. I figured that if the HELOC gets out of my control, then I would roll it in back into my mortgage, if I have any issues through another refinance. I already knew that we had equality in the house. For some reason or another, we had to get the HELOC from an outside lender. So we decided to go to another bank like Wachovia. I believe that we were banking there at the time. We had gotten the appraisal done, and we got the approval in a short time as well. This money would take us out from all our debt. We would be able to catch up our tithes at our new church and then some.

Even before we even got to this point, I even had my back child support paid off to Lynn. Things have been looking up since meeting Melody and going back to church. Besides the obvious and to my point, to me, it all made sense. Melody is definitely the right one, and I did not want to mess things up, so I would remind myself over and over on how well I had it with Melody! And on how my life kept changing for the better. In fact, I was not even for sure if my next four-year tour in the Air Force was even going to be approved. Then we were awaiting the HELOC to be approved and all the paperwork later. It was. Now, once the funds came in, we were handling all our business to focus on just paying the HELOC back. This was a great plan, and it worked like a charm. We even had a chance to catch up our tithing for our new church. It was something about owing God that just did not feel right! I just have to make it right with God and as soon as possible. While at work, I was finding out about military HOPS or also known as HOP. It is when you are able to fly on a military aircraft from one location to another worldwide. I was trying to find out as much information on HOPS as possible, just in case we were able go on a cheap military flight. Now, I wanted to travel more and collect gospel music.

I was also listening to folks like the Winans, Hezekiah Walker, James Cleveland, Yolanda Adams, Shirley Caesar, Dawkins and Dawkins, Mighty Clouds of Joy, and the Canton Spirituals, the group called Anointed and many more… I started to follow gospel and collecting gospel albums and tapes as I used to collect the R&B records. Now, in my new life with the Lord, I was all about collecting gospel music. Also at this time, I was trying to sing gospel music, and

Ralph was a musician, and he had a studio as well. We had discussed on our trip to California and Mexico and to start writing and laying down some musical tracks. We started meeting a few times a week. In February, my wife and I went to get dinner with the assistant pastor James Plummer and his family at the Red Lobster on Auth Road in Maryland. Before leaving, I mentioned to Assistant Pastor James that I felt that the Lord was leading me to get more involved in church and the ministry. We would plan to talk about it more later on. Around March 1999, Ralph and I, with our wives, went to a music writing and gift workshop with Vicki Winans, Donnie Lawrence, and Richard Smallwood. We wanted to understand the music aspects of the industry. They all shared their experiences with us as well. Not long before, I have become a deacon. I had a vision one Sunday while Pastor James was preaching. I saw me preaching. I had even told Pastor James of my vision. Pastor James had seemed to believe me because now I was becoming a deacon. Wow! Then on March 21, 1999, at the Sunday service, I was ordained as a deacon along with two other deacons. They were Pierre Lockett and Kenneth Bannerman.

We had also invited Melody's sister, Linda, Butch, and Von. We also met with Elder Plummer because he was the assistant pastor under his father. We had explained to him our commuting woes between work and church. Therefore, and at most times, we were doing two hundred miles on church days. Pastor James had that military mindset since he was prior Air Force. He only told us that he needed us there at church! Pastor James was serious, and we understood and complied. I could tell with our conversation that Pastor James was about church business! We decided to do our best possible, and that conversation was over. I could not wait to call and tell my mother that I had made it to the Office of Deacon in the church. My mother was so excited for me. She had called me right back within the hour after she had talked with her pastor by the name of Robert Palmer, Ebenezer Apostolic Assembly, in Akron, Ohio. Pastor Palmer wanted me to be the guest speaker. So the following Sunday, I talked with Pastor Charlie Plummer to make sure it was okay for me to go. He agreed! I was just so excited. I believe that the following weekend was the Pentecostal Assembles of the World (PAW) Council to be held on Dix Street in DC at Greater Morning Star Apostolic Church. It was pastored by Elder Charles Johnson. The PAW overseer or prelate was none other than Bishop Wesley Weeks, Sr. It was during this council that I had gotten signed up for the minister's training classes. The main Bible instructors were the late Pastor/Dr. James Graham, Pastor/Dr. Hurbert Adams, Minister Carol Williams, Minister Yvonne Pendleton, Pastor Sam Briscoe, Bishop Arthur Coleman, and a few others.

Now, once again, my plate was full. Every day and almost every weekend was gone, just like that. Plus, we stayed faithful to the choir rehearsals. By the time that I was back to work, Tina Bise was gone. I needed a solution for an administrative assistance and fast. I decided to get approval to bring in a reservist for thirty days to try it out. It was within a week I had an Air Force female reservist slated to come in from Oklahoma. I was just hoping that she would be a hard worker. It was during that same time that Lynn had call me about Big Mike and that he no longer wanted to go to school. Now, Big Mike was eighteen years old in the tenth grade. He had pretty much given up but not on my watch! I had planned to go and pick him up and get his school records. Then Melody and I had decided to go on a fast for both of my sons. Then I met the reservist to work on thirty-day RPA man-day tour in my office to assist me. Her name was SSgt. Rolanda Allen. She liked it so much that she wanted to move to DC. I was then inclined to help a sister out. Meanwhile, Melody and I had took a weekend off and drove to Akron to pick up Big Mike. All of the time worked out so I was able to be the guest speaker for the Friday night service. My mother was able to introduce me and as happy as she could possibly be. I was just glad that she was with some of my brothers and sisters were able to see me preach. I will never forget it that my mother introduced me as Minister Michael Gilcreast!

After I was done preaching and church was dismissed, I received a lot of compliments! The amazing part was that I was a totally new deacon and preaching for my very first time, but the thing that really caught my attention was that people wanted to touch me! I thought that I was a nobody! Wow! I had truly learned a lot as a member of

True Apostolic Church as they were preparing me for times like this! As soon as we returned from Ohio. The first thing that I did was to look up the word *deacon* to make sure that I was called the proper title; therefore, a deacon is also a minister. I was now relieved not to offend God by having the wrong title, knowing that was very important to me! Not long thereafter, Ant had called me and want to come down because life was hard for his mother to properly take care of him and his sister Rae. They had barely any place to live and eat. I was so upset! I had money now and was ready to take Adrian to the probate court. I had wanted both of my sons way before their conditions had worsened as the facts known now. By the time that I had got to Hartford, Connecticut, we all had gone to the probate court, and Adrian had just signed Ant over to me. Before the decision would become permanent custody, there was a home study to be conducted by Department of Children and Families Services for almost a year. Ant had very little to bring back with him. I did not want Adrian to pay me child support because she had never placed me in the child support system. We had to hurry back from the one day of leave that I had to take to pick up Ant.

Then I had to take another two days of leave to get them registered for school. I did not plan for any of this to happen. We only fasted and prayer and immediately our whole life changed. Then back at the job, I hired another reservist who was from Maryland because Rolanda had moved on to find another job, so I hired SSgt. Alisha Jones. Let's just say that she reminded me of my ex-wife with a lot of attitude! I wanted to get rid of her on the very first week when she started. Alisha had befriended Lt. Col. Denny Stephens, and through him, I allowed her to stay for the entire thirty days. I was so miserable because I could not find her half the time. I found another young lady by the name of Sgt. Katrina Rivers who was already working in the Pentagon and in another office, and her RPA man-day tour was ending. I was thinking that she was a little young cutie! She was working there with her friend, another sergeant by the name of Allison. I had just allowed her to overlap tours with Alisha. I too was off here and there to get my sons school life in order. Now Sgt. Rivers was a good fit for the office. But she was a little flirtatious, to say the least. I tried and chose to ignore her and just keep it professional. This one I had to tell my wife about her, and I really needed her assistance in the office. She already knew everything to do, which made my life so much easier. I did manage to get Sgt. Rivers' tour extended to a few extra months with all the turnover that I was having with keeping people in the office. My wife also made a surprise visit to the Pentagon to see me and the folks in my office. Curtis Webber, she had already met, and a few others. Then I had introduced her to Katrina. Even though it had felt a little weird, Melody was very nice. I sort of expected a scene, but there was none! I had walked with her to leave out of the building by the concourse. We kissed and she left. This time I was really trying to do the church scene and not to mess up anything or my marriage. I was not used to Katrina's reactions toward me. Almost every response she had given me had these sexual overtones. Whether it was the way she bit her bottom lip or to say things like "My pleasure!" It was actually becoming tempting to me.

One day for lunch, she went to the movies with the male Air Force officers that worked in the back. They were all white males and one black female. The entire office was won over by her personality and smiles. One of the majors by the name of Michael Landry was single and seemed to have a crush on Katrina. I did not want to go, so I stayed behind. I had no time to get caught up in some girl mess. After they finally returned, Katrina and I started to talk about movies, and we both had seen the movie *As Good as It Gets* with Jack Nicholson. Then, "as good as it gets" became our secret code. I was fighting to stay away for her! The thing was, Katrina sat right behind me. She would bump me, fall onto me, touch me by accident, and lean over me constantly. Once Katrina had met my wife Melody, she kept turning the "as good as it gets" to another level. She would wear a skirt and turn around with her legs open or prop her feet on me! I had touched her knee and thigh to move her leg off me. That did it! It went from an innocent touch to feeling. Then I could not resist her! A week later, we had an office picnic. The guys wanted to take Katrina, but she would only want to ride with me! I must say we were so close many times, even on the way to the picnic. I just could not close the deal! I had the biggest war going on between Katrina and betraying my wife and sons!

While at the picnic Katrina was mainly around me, but Maj. Landry must have had too much to drink and was trying to openly flirt with Katrina. So I had to take her home! We both were flirting with danger and adultery. Still, I was fighting not to do it, if you know what I mean! I was a mess! I went home and started to get upset with Melody, and we kept arguing. Then I wanted to leave. Katrina and I were planning a trip to New York for the upcoming weekend. Not thinking in my right mind, I was messing up my beautiful marriage and really did not understand why. I then told Melody to leave and get out! She told me that she was not going anywhere. What? I thought. Melody had no intentions to leave me! None! The next day, I went to work, and Katrina had just bought Hanes pantyhose from one of the Pentagon's stores. While I was at my desk in the front office, and people were working in the back on both sides. Then she comes out in her military blouse and underwear that was it to get her bag with the pantyhose! I was in disbelief! I went home to tell my wife Melody what she had done! I was trying to make Melody leave me or even jealous! It did not work. Melody would not even talk to me! Not knowing what Melody was planning or what would happen next, I had plans to leave the following weekend.

It seems as if Katina was trying to get me to leave everything that I cared about. I was still in minister's training school, doing very well, including going to church and everything else, while yet falling away from the church, and looking for another church closer to home. Melody and I agreed to get the pastor's blessing prior to leaving the church, especially after a two- or three-week time span. We would drive to church and get a flat. We put air in the tire and took it to Sears Automotive for the repair. A week later, the same thing happened again. Another week later, this time, the tire was going flat but only had a slow leak in the tire. Then back to Sears for the repair! I found out that the tire valve was loose. Melody and I also took this as a sign for God that it was time to leave and find another church. I am not the typical believer that things just happened. Meanwhile, Pastor James was handling most things administratively since his dad, the pastor of the church, was getting older. So Pastor James had a meeting with us, and we told him that we were leaving. Pastor James blessed us and told us that he did not want to see us leave, but he understood the commuting issues. With so much going on, we checked out and found a closer church to home, first thing. Then we all moved to that church a few weeks later. The only thing was that it was on Catoctin Street in Leesburg and located inside the fire station. Those sirens at times were noisy for our church services. The name of the church was Zion Pentecostal Temple under the leadership of Pastor Samuel Riley, from San Antonio, Texas. As soon as we both arrived and already in church, Pastor Riley made us both Sunday school teachers, and I was also promoted to the minister of music. I was already writing songs with Ralph for our little group, singing and learning how to play the keyboard that I brought with me to the church services.

Anyway, getting back to the job, the more that I was around Katrina, the weaker I became. God knows that I was fighting this one and not to cheat on my wife, but I wanted to have another child. The thoughts were racing through my mind on how difficult it would be for Melody to have a child, based on what the doctors was saying because of the previous miscarriage. Having a child with Melody was one of our biggest disagreements between us. We did see plenty of doctors, but the answers were the same: in vitro fertilization! I was praying and trying desperately not to hold it against her. No way I could have my cake and eat it too. Katrina's timing was so convenient but wrong all at the same time. I was being weakening by her temptation day after day! I was officially on my way to losing this temptation fight and on my way to becoming a church hypocrite, about to cheat on my wife! That same day, I found out that while I was at the gym playing basketball, my wife had called Katrina at work, and they had a conversation concerning Katrina's intentions with a married man, me! Melody had told Katrina that God would get her for what she was doing and that she would place Katrina and I in God's hands! That was it! I must say that the Lord does work in mysterious ways! That same evening, everyone was gone, except for Katrina and I had to lock up and secure the alarm to the office. While we were still talking, one thing led to another, and she began to unzip and remove her pants. She suddenly stopped! Katrina just stopped, zipped up, grabbed her things, and ran out the door! Before I realized what she had done, it was over.

If she had not moved as quickly as she did that evening, we would have consummated our relationship to adultery. It was not until she left that the lust was just gone, and I had never felt more guilty. But this time, it was different. I remembered how Joseph ran from Potiphar's wife, which was also in the Bible. I said that the same thing just happened to me once before! I must say that I was bewildered! This was the second time that this has happened to me. This girl Katrina ran out for no reason unless that conversation with my wife had put the fear of God in her. It had to be! The first time was in Dayton, Ohio, with Pam Ringer (Bishop Eugene Ringer's daughter) and I was married to Adrian, and now, almost again with my second wife Melody! This was no coincidence. I was thinking instead it was nothing less than a God moment! I had locked up the office, and when I had got home, we prayed as normal with the boys, and they went to bed for school on the next day. Melody and I stayed up to discuss that day events and on how she talked to Katrina earlier that day. Then Melody calmy got the Bible and had asked me to read only one scripture. It read, "For by means of a whorish woman a man is brought to a piece of bread: and the adulteress will hunt for the precious life" (Proverbs 6:26, KJV).

After reading that one scripture, I had interpreted it to mean to me that God was going to kill me if I had committed adultery! This scripture had changed my life the moment that I read it! I had apologized to Melody for what I had put her through and then said that I was going to cancel my weekend with Katrina and leave her alone! I had promised to be done, but I was really in fear of my life from God! That one scripture convicted me. I then told Melody that what almost happened between Katrina and I earlier that evening after work, but Katrina had ran out just before!

Now, Melody had known everything. Then I stated that I have never cheated since we were married. Melody then said, "Yes, you did when you had desired Katrina." This was an incredibly complicated situation for most people and understood that Katrina pursued me at first, but Melody still loved and forgave me, so we could move forward! Wow, I never expected that she would still love and trust me!

I had just started working for a new colonel by the name of Colonel Robert Shaw. To me, this guy was nice, nasty, and shrewd. Col. Shaw was not to be trusted by me! I just had that feeling. Still, I had to work with Katrina, just a few weeks longer for obvious reasons. She just had to go! I was now glad that nothing more serious had happened between us, yet my conscience was bothering me to repent, and at times, I would barely be able to find rest or peace! Now, I knew that I had to talk to Pastor Riley, my new pastor. I knew that I wanted to move up into the ministry. I just had to get it right! After preaching at my mother's church, I just had to repent because I knew that I was supposed to preach. Plus I had already seen me preach in a vision at Pastor Plummer's church while Pastor James was preaching on one Sunday! I have really seen me preach, and now I was chasing after it because I just knew that it was supposed to be! It was on a Sunday after our church service. I had asked Pastor Riley for some time with him to discuss an important matter. He agreed!

I had informed him of my little escapade with Katrina, but no consummating of the relationship, nor did I commit physical adultery, but I almost did! Pastor Riley provided me with spiritual counselling and set me on the correct road. He also let me know that a lot of times when we repent, God would had already forgiven us, but we are hard to forgive ourselves! These were the exact words that I needed to hear! This talk with him really did wonders for me! Pastor Riley really helped me to heal because I was really in a fight to do right and not sin, but the temptation almost got me! I had finally forgiven myself and eventually was able to move on in the Lord and church! I do thank God for songs like "This Battle Is the Lord's" by Yolanda Adams and "It's Okay" by BeBe and CeCe Winans and "I Been in the Storm Too Long" by the Canton Spirituals and "Near the Cross" by The Mississippi Mass Choir and "I Don't Feel Noways Tired" by James Cleveland and my all-time favorite "Lord, Remember Me" by the late Frank Williams. These were the songs that got me through these types of rough roads in my life. I would play these songs over and again throughout difficult periods within my life. I would always add new songs that would help me along my way. Now, getting back to Pastor Riley, I did think that he was going to sat me down in the church, but I was not. It did not happen!

What a blessing from the Lord, I was on the path of forgiveness and now able to move forward! It was not until this had happened to me with Katrina that I have come to realize that temptation was nothing to be played with! On Katrina's last day, I walked her down to exit the Pentagon building, then unexpectedly as I turned towards her, she surprised me with a kiss on the concourse and did not want to end our little escapade. But it was totally over, and I stayed honest to Melody! Now other than the normal things like school for me and the boys, work, church, and basketball, I had to get my house in order with my sons newly living with us. My first priority was to lay down the ground rules, such as no company whatsoever, we eat together, and no staying out late, and most definitely, everyone goes to church. We took a trip to the Pentagon one Saturday afternoon, and I gave them a private tour plus satisfied their curiosity and let them see my office too. Then we went to the Wharf to hang out and get some seafood and T-shirts. I have these boys, or should I say, young adolescent males with me, and there was this lady. Mind you that she was really nice looking, to say the least. She had on this black see-through fish-net sundress on and nothing on underneath it! Wow, more temptation from what I just been through! So I showed the woman to Melody and told her that the boys could not see this, so we gathered them up in a hurry and left! That was a close call! And also I did not allow them to have company at my house! Ant was still getting the belt to his behind on days that he got in trouble, but Big Mike was eighteen years old and too big for the belt form of punishment. So the other form of punishment was awesome in itself. I would make them write minimum of five hundred times for the solution to whatever offense that they committed. Every time, if they would give me or Melody back talk, I would add an additional five hundred. and if more talking back to me, then another five hundred times to continue writing. They figured out very fast that I was not going to be playing games with either one of them. Also if they were to get suspended from school, then I would to take a day or two off with them, and they would work around the house, cleaning up and washing walls. I had always taught them to do it right the first time and also to work hard and play hard for our family. Then we started to bond together as a family. To say the least, my sons did not do much writing as a punishment. Since they both were doing pretty well in school, Melody and I wanted to plan a vacation for all of us to be together. We had talked about it to be discussed at dinner a trip for all of us to fly and go to Walt Disney World in Orlando.

We knew that they were a little old for the trip, but we all still wanted to go. Besides, it would still be a first time for us all. Melody and I did grocery shopping together after work at Fort Myers mostly and sometimes at Fort Belvoir. Since the boys have been there with us, our grocery bill skyrocketed to over $800 per month and a few shopping carts, not counting the weekly odd and ends. We were able to afford everything since the child support for Big Mike was paid in full, and Ant was now living with us. Having my sons living with us just made me and us very happy. Melody had already accepted both of my sons as her own. You can see that Melody was a pretty amazing person that had always shown me that she was 100 percent in love with me! I had never imagined that this could have been the life that I was living could have ever reached this point. *Grateful* was the only word that I could have thought of that I was truly feeling! While at the Pentagon, I had picked up our Disney World tickets and hopper passes, and a coworker gave us free parking passes from a family member that worked there. We were on our way flying to Disney. We went to two of the parks Magic Kingdom and EPCOT. We did ride a few of the rides, but the ones that stood out were the Test Track, Thunder Mountain, Space Mountain, and the Elevator Ride in an ugly building. It was pretty scary. I was able to participate in one of the shows we saw, which I had dressed up as one of the pirates that was chasing Indiana Jones. I believe that Big Mike played another part. We also saw the dolphin show too. The next day, we went to some type of reptile farm. We watched a show where the trainers wrestled with crocodiles, which was exciting to see. The final day, we rented an airboat and hung out in the swamps, hoping to see alligators. It was an awesome ride because we did not see one alligator. We finished off the day with some lunch and shopped for some souvenirs. For dinner someone gave us a coupon book, and everyone wanted the all-you-can-eat shrimp and lobster restaurant. I think the name of it was Boston Seafood Restaurant. It was on and very inexpensive, a price that we could afford. I must say that we had eaten so much food, and Ant by himself had eaten every bit of eleven lobsters. Everyone was so happy, but not more than I! This was a great trip and our first trip as a family!

The next day, we were flying out of there. What a great vacation! The next day, we ate breakfast at the Embassy and off to the airport. After we boarded the plane and was seated, the stewardess, out of nowhere, approached us and asked, "Since there are several vacated seats in first-class, do you want to move to first class at no additional charge?" We gladly obliged her request. That was just icing on the cake for the boys! Wow, we could not have taken a better trip! We would get home in time for church on Sunday. I really did not like to miss church much. Plus, we were small, and I wanted us to be there in the service to help it grow. School was about to start, and we still had to get a few things for the boy's school. Big Mike would be starting his senior year at Loudoun County High School. That was the deal the we had worked out with his counsellor, and he would now graduate at nineteen years old. That boy was fortunate enough to have just enough credits. Then Ant would be going to Harper Park Middle School and attending the eighth grade. After his first few weeks of school, Ant was having difficulty with his math teacher. We immediately handled that situation. His story just made sense, and this was also a new school and full year for him. All I wanted was to set him up for success, no excuses. We went to the school and had his math class changed. It was certainly good thereafter. Also during this same time, I had started to attend Bible study classes at the Pentagon on Thursdays at 11:00 a.m.

The instructor that talked me into going was an Air Force Lt. Col. Ronald Holloway. He used to always challenge me the differences in our faith and religion, including my belief in miracles! I was thankful that he did not last there long because I was going to stop going to the Bible class. Then Ron Holloway was reassigned, and a Baptist preacher had taken over. He was there for a short while and went out sick. Now, there was no teacher for teaching the Bible class. It was still vacated for a teacher. I started thinking that maybe I should teach the class, so I prayed to God to see if I was supposed to be teaching the class. Pastor Riley always wanted us to get involved in ministry outside of the church. So I decided to go to the Army chaplains office to get signed up as an instructor. I was just following the path that just opened up for me. Let's just say it just felt right for me to be there, yet I did not know exactly what I was doing or getting myself into. One thing for sure, it made me study more and read the Bible, plus other study books that I wanted to have for my library. I have already preached at my mother's church, teaching Sunday school at church and in minister's training school. My life was moving in a different direction, and none of it was planned by me. Still, I think on how my ex-wife pointed me in the direction of my current wife Melody, including both of my sons living with me and going to church with me. I was truly living in a dream! Please just wake me up! I did not plan any of this, but internally, I was being drawn to want to know more about church, Jesus, heaven, and most importantly the truth! I did not like all of the different religions, yet we were serving only one God! This did not make sense to me, not whatsoever!

So one day, I decided to ask my Bible class group, "Why do you all come to my Bible class called the Hour of Power and we have different religions?" They answered me and responded that I taught them the truth that was understanding to them! This was why truth is so important to me! Some of the brothers and sisters that attended my Pentagon Bible class were Sister Jan Robinson, Sister Kathy Sheppard, Sister Toni Callendar (my wife and I attended her church a few times), Sister Penney (from the mailroom), Sister Devalle, Sister April, Sister Beverly Fenwick, Sister Annette, Brother Maurice Cromer, Brother David Garner, and a host of other military and government civilians. That Bible class was so blessed, we would be praying for promotions, healings, etc., and it was happening! Brother David Garner and Brother Ted Agnew became good friends in the gospel. They would even teach the class for me in my absence. God was definitely in our Bible classes! The class was growing as such. They were being held in the auditorium on the fifth floor as the other classes. I could not believe that people were coming week after week, and the notification listing was growing as well. It was truly a blessing to be teaching these Bible study classes because it was aiding me in presenting my presentations at my ministry training classes. I did not know that even my college speech class, all helped me for what was currently doing. Like I keep saying, I had never planned for any of this to happen on my behalf. It just did!

Ant just had another birthday. And as the year was closing, we all had our first little Thanksgiving and Christmas together as a family unit. Every now and again, I would take Ant and Big Mike to my rehearsals over Ralph's house, and then I would be up most nights studying for my exams for the minister's training school or reading chapters in my books. Not only did I want my sons to do better than I did, but I always wanted them to see me working hard. I always believe that working hard would someday pay off! We did manage to get Ant to play basketball in the Loudoun County League for the winter of 1999, and Ant wanted me to be the coach (Daniel's dad and my son Big Mike were my assistant coaches), so he could get more playing time but without saying it! Our county basketball team name was the Knights! We had our practices on Thursdays at Simpson Middle School on Evergreen Street. The players I remember were John Shippey, Ryan, Daniel, Paul, Ant, and a few others. From my practices I only had three good players, and they were Ryan, my son Ant, and John. My computer and printer that I had finally gotten, were always working with little issues connecting to the worldwide web. I had taken one of the bedrooms and made it into my office. That year, I had made an effort to get a snow blower from Sears. It was a Craftsman. Plus I had my boys outside to assist me because there was a lot of snow to remove! Melody and I was closer than ever. Somehow the episode with Katrina brought us together closer than ever.

Our relationship was as solid as it could be. From the time that I married her, I was trying to be a good and faithful husband. Now,

I can add godly husband to that! Melody was happy as well! She was just quiet, and still almost every night, Melody would give me a massage. The massages had never stopped even when we had trouble! How did I ever deserve her or the good treatment she was giving me! I know for certain Melody had never stopped being my wife, and still, she never wanted to get a divorce! Amazing! Now, weeks had gone by, and there were no wins for the Knight basketball team, and we only had one team game left. The game was on a Sunday, and as soon as Pastor Riley was done preaching and church was dismissed, we headed to the game with our church suits on and all. I was coaching the team and my son in my suit. I really felt like I was doing something. Well, when it was all said and done, the basketball season was over for us, and we did not make the playoffs! The good thing about that last game is, we left for the game immediately following church. We put God first, and yes, we won our last and only game! The kicker was a smart remark from one of the coaches. They had said that we should have worn suits to every game. While it was meant to be funny, ironically, it was so true! At the championship game, I did end up with a coach's plaque with the team group photo on it! Melody would still assist me with my studying and word memorizations… She was so dedicated to me and to our marriage. She always told me that her vows meant something special to her, and she would always honor them, including forgiving me. Still, I spent time with the family as a whole and all decisions or family talks would be held at the kitchen table, with no exceptions! Now that I was thirty-eight years old, the caddy was having some electrical issues, and it was past time to get another car.

At this point in my life, I had never brought me a brand-new car. So we go looking for a car as a family that we had discussed at the kitchen table. Our family made it to Tyson's Corner for some shopping, we started at the Jeep dealership, then Toyota, a few others, and finally we ended up at the Isuzu dealership. After a few test drives, I brought our first ever, brand-new white 2000 Isuzu Rodeo V6, 4×4, SUV and a six-disc CD changer. Ant and Big Mike were happier for the extra leg room in the back seat. The next big thing that I had to do was to pass my final exam. Plus I had to write a final paper. It was all well and good, except for one question that I really did not understand. Anyway, I decided to call Pastor Graham, one of the course professors. I asked him for some clarity, and he did not even provide me with one inch of direction. I mean nothing! Pastor/Dr. Graham pretty much told me to pray about it! That was it, and we hung up the phone. Now, I was back to square one. Anyway, on test day, I had turned in my paper and sat down to take my written test. After all was said and done, I passed! It was not until the convention where the graduation was being held. The ceremony was at Greater Morning Star Apostolic Church on Dix Street in DC. Bishop Thomas Weeks Sr. was the PAW presider.

Anyway, on March 16, 2000, I was graduated as the first male valedictorian of the PAW—DC, Delaware, and Maryland Council. I had to give the speech for our graduating class and the latter part of my speech read, "Only what you do for Jesus Christ will last… Preach the truth, teach the truth and don't take down for nothing!" (I had kept that last saying from my spiritual father in the Lord, the honorable Bishop JE Pope, in Cleveland, Ohio—to this day, he is still my spiritual father!) My sons were looking sharp that day, with suits, trench-coats and all! I was just too busy, plus writing and singing music that I wrote, coupled with working with Ralph. I only wanted, but never expected to become a full-time dad. Now getting back to the minister school that I was doing, I told Melody a few times that I only wanted to do just enough to pass the courses; Melody encouraged and convicted me at the same time, and I will never forget her words that inspired me to do better, she said, "You are supposed to give God your best!" From that point on, I sincerely strive to do my very best. At the same time, there were not arguments, she only provided me with kind words to give God my best!

I believe that my wife, Melody, was the real reason that I made valedictorian for the program. Better yet, I could not had gotten it without her! Shortly after my graduation for my ministry class graduation. Sister Patricia Plummer invited us to one of their Friday evening revival services on March 24, 2000, so we took the boys and went to the service at our old church. They had had a guest speaker from Greater Cross Tabernacle, 1140 Williams Road, Columbus,

Ohio, and the pastors George (Awesome) and Karen Dawson. That night, the speaker was Pastor Karen Dawson. It was a drive for us to get there, but we made it. Once all the singing was done and the preaching began, shortly after that, the preacher Pastor Dawson did not know us, and we have never met her. She proceeded to call my wife from her seat. She said, "Come here, First Lady." Melody did not know of who the preacher was referring since she knew that she was not a first lady. So Pastor Dawson asked for her again, and this time, the pastor pointed and said, "Yes, you," and she said for me to come up with her! Pastor Dawson began to speak into our lives—from my wife's sickness that no one knew of except for me, the building we were in and that we will not be there long, and regarding not filing a complaint on my job. I had my doubts, but if she, Pastor Karen Dawson, was a fake, she would have got one thing right, maybe, or nothing correct.

This woman of God had gotten everything correct because most of it was private and never shared to our former church. It was as if Melody started to cry in slow motion, and her tears came forth from her eyes because no one knew of her pain and suffering or the number of doctors visited. This experience was nothing less than divine intervention from God. Melody and I knew at this time the she truly was a real woman of God! That night, we made sure that we had got a copy of the cassette tape for proof! We truly believed. Wow! Getting back to Melody, not one time did she ever leave my side but only supported me and been there for me! Wow, my Melody only kept giving me her best as well. She did not just love me, but she loves me the agape unconditional way! Well, since my sons and my wife had hung in there with me, I wanted to do something big for them all. Not to mention that Ant was doing pretty good in school and taking German as one of his classes. I had preferred Spanish because I had taken it, but I let him decide, and he wanted to take German, so he did. Mike wanted to play football but was ineligible due to his age in his senior year. Melody and I did discuss a trip overseas, but none of us had passports and needed to get them processed at the post office ASAP. We decide to take a military flight over to Europe and stay at various military bases while there for our summer vacation. The plan was that Melody was to go with me, and the boys would watch themselves for the week, and I would leave them some money as well. About a week later, we had heard on the radio the Stephen Hurd was doing a gospel music workshop in Maryland. The musician, Stephen Hurd, already had a hot album out in 1999 with the song "Goodbye, World." It was hot, with a Caribbean sound to it. And I did purchase it too! Ralph and I was trying to learn as much as possible before we launched our first album and start our business in gospel music. We wanted to try producing other people too! We even talked with radio personality on the AM radio dial Matt Anderson, who we had talked with for him to master our gospel sound track once we had completed. He agreed! It was by this time that I wanted to leave the military and pursue this career.

Again, Melody was right there, and she had asked me only one question concerning my leaving the Air Force and get a civilian job. Melody asked me did I seek the Lord before I had made my decision? My reply was, I did not even ask Him! That had settled it, and I was no longer wanting to get out of the military. My real frustration was that I could not get promoted, but I had watched folks that came in after me with the same rank, and yet in a short time, they were getting promoted. Yet I was writing e-mails and letters to everyone, trying to understand this promotion system that kept changing, every time I wanted to get a deserving promotion. I had written to the generals, colonels, and to personnel people. Still no promotion. I did notice one peculiar notable fact that I sought out about promotions on my military job; it was the true fact that I kept getting promotions and several times in the church! I was beginning to see a pattern that really could not be explained because it didn't even make sense to me. Then it just hit me to stopped trusting the Air Force promotion system and started trusting the God system because really I was getting promotions in the church to different positions and to start trusting God for my promotions. Still the days could not go fast enough as we were awaiting the passports through the mail, I kept saying that I have never been assigned an overseas assignment in the military, but now, I am going over there for vacation and out of the country for the second time, counting our visit to Mexico.

A few days later and in the nick of time, they arrived around the August 10, 2000, and we would be on our way in two days. We still had a few things to tighten up. I was teaching Big Mike how to drive, get my leave approved from the job, a few errands to do that Big Mike would be driving, and of course the packing! The true fact was that I was trying to expose my two sons to the world. Plus, I was making ups for lost time, which I did learn the reality of it is that those years will never come back. Of which, I was broke, I gambled, made bad choices, and yes, I was a dead-beat dad! I did figure out somehow that the only best dad impression that I could leave with my two sons was now in the present time when they both came to live with Melody and myself! I have three things going for me: military, church, and loving my family! We were all packed and ready to go to Dover AFB, Delaware.

That was the plan; however, once we were at to take the military C-5 Galaxy aircraft to Italy, we learn the rules the hard way. First, the only cost to us was the $10 meals per person to be paid on the plane. Next, we had to get on the waiting list based on military rank and status. It was like seven priority status, and we were in the second priority, but we had to be ready at a moment's notice. Next, we had to sleep in the car and wait for fourteen hours, waiting for our flight to Italy. It was such a small price to pay since the trip was basically free. So each time we would wake up in the car, we would go a check on the status. Then off back to the car for more sleep at the back of the Rodeo! I must admit, we let the back seats down to the cargo area, and with the rain coming down, we did not get very good sleep, and the rain did not make it easier for us! Finally, it was daybreak, and we went back inside to terminal and hooked up with the boys. It was about an hour later, and our names were called to go get in line for boarding the C-5 Air Force plane. We boarded upstairs for the seating, it was pretty decent but no windows; however, we were facing backward. Melody and Ant knew of this already from the previous air show that we had visited. We really wanted to sleep and eat and also get used to the six-hour time change in front of New York time. After the long arduous flight, our first stop was Aviano Air Base (AB), Italy. We did not care where we ended up. We just wanted to go overseas for a family vacation. Incidentally, we passed up the first trip to Rota AB, Spain, because I allowed another military family to go before us. We had no destination in mind but to just keep taking military HOPS until it is a location that we wanted to go to. We were taking in the sights of viewing the snow-top mountains in Italy. Then since we had already known, we added our names to the list each time we deplaned. An hour and half passed by, then a C-9 Med-Vac aircraft came through that was headed to Ramstein AB, Germany.

This would be our next flight next flight out of there on our continued vacation. I did have an opportunity with a promotion to move to Germany, but I had turned it down. I never wanted to be stationed overseas, only to visit. If I would have had my first assignment here in 1980 before the fire. I believe that I would have had a difference of opinion. Now we were at Ramstein AB, and I just thought that we would check in to billeting (military temporary housing for families and official business); however, that was not the case. What a disappointment that was not factored in to our vacation plans. I did not know that it would be a remote chance that billeting would be full. All we have was our passports and luggage and the absence of a car. I could not let my kids see me on the panic, but I had not a clue of what to do in a foreign land. I was at a total lost. Most of the hotels were out of our price range. A stranger on the base saw us and suggested that we tried a bed and breakfast. So we did! The phones and the phone numbers were different for us as well, but we gave it a try anyway! The first few called were either full or no one would say anything. Then my young son Ant said, "Let me try to talk." So we did!

To everyone's surprise, Ant said in German from what he had learned in his eight-grade German language class, "Sprichst du Deutsch?" Meaning "Do you speak German?" It was our thirteen-year-old son that broke the ice for us to get a room. It truly worked! Then, the German gentleman on the phone spoke English. Ant gave the phone to me, and we had got a room for the night and took a taxi to get there. Mercedes-Benz cars were used as taxis. They were everywhere! That was one of the strangest places that I or we had ever spent the night in. The guy that checked us in was tall and strange-looking! Right from the start, once we checked in, then the elevator, that only a few people could fit at a time, and you pull the two doors close. That was a scary few-minute ride up. The elevator made all kinds of noises. We had rooms next to the boys, but everything was very weird.

Even the running water made funny sounds. That place surely put me in the mindset of the *Addams Family Television Show*! Those strange noises kept wakening me throughout the night! I could not await morning. They sat us down to breakfast, and we put our luggage to the side. The breakfast bar was plentiful, food for days; however, cold-cuts, cheeses, fruits was not the meal that we were aiming for, but we were finding out that it was the German way! Anyway, after fifteen minutes or so, we excused ourselves from the table and asked to use the phone. Melody had found a rental car business, and then we had called a taxi to take us there, and we were on our way. We got the last car on the lot! I was the driver, and Melody was the map navigator. Once we had the car, it was a five-speed Ford Focus Hatchback. We were on the move to find a McDonald's. We had made it to Heidelberg, Germany, to McDonald's. A few doors down, on the same side as McDonald's, was the hotel called the Ibis Hotel. We immediately checked it out, and it was like an American Best Western Motel. We all liked it and would be our home until we left. Once we had the car and hotel, things were looking up. We were blending in and finding out things to do. We found a little place that sold bratwurst sandwiches and with sauerkraut. This food was definitely a German thing. Their meats and even at McDonald's tasted differently than the foods in America. McDonalds's ketchup packages were even larger than what we were used to!

The next day, we drove to Paris for the day, and on the Audubon, I was pushing it 90 to 130 miles per hour most of the way. I had never driven as such before! This driving was just too fast! What a rush and not one single inch of room for error! We did get stopped just after we passed the countryside and the awful smell of manure in the air. The air-conditioning did not help the air quality at all. Plus, it was during the time of the mad cow disease! We were ever so careful not to eat beef, if any! Then as the sun was beginning to set and the sky was darkening, we thought that we would not make it back to Heidelberg and would have to spend the night in Paris. As we were fast approaching Paris, we were stopped by the police at the gate. I told him that we were on holiday, showed our passports, and then we were again on our way to Paris! It was getting late, and we were driving everywhere in Paris to find a hotel. We found one without any type of air-conditioning, and it was just too hot! We had to deal with a few flying bugs, but it was not too bad. We were still hungry and went to see the concierge to find a place to get something to eat. Except the concierge did not speak a speck of English! So she decided to write us a note, but it was in French after signed the motion to her that we had motioned to her that we wanted something to eat.

We then got change to ride their Metro train to find a place to get something to eat. We walked to the platform to catch their Metro train. As we all were awaiting the trains arrival, we watched this big rat walk onto the platform and was bold enough to just walk around before leaving. Here is our train, according to our note. The train had made several stops and began to slow down. Then the lights and the power were off! In our panic, we all started to press every button and pull every lever available. Suddenly, the doors came open, and of course, the train driver did not speak English, so we showed her the note. She motioned for us all to sit down, and she put up one finger, and then the lights came back on, and we started to move again. What a scary moment we just had to be locked on a train, but we made it! The doors opened, and we followed the note to the location! As we were crossing the crowded street, I saw this dude reach out to touch my wife. I could not catch up to him without leaving my family. I figured that it was the best decision and for my family's safety. Anyway, we made it to another McDonald's and then back on the train to return to the hotel. The boys were in the room next to ours, so I went to check on them. We took our showers to cool down, and then we went to their room for prayer. We left back to our rooms and turned on the television in our room and noticed an "Explicit Adult Entertainment Channel." It was free of charge. We decided to just leave the television off, in our room! This time had to trust that my boys would do the right thing, and not watch those explicit television shows!

The next morning, we were up an excited to leave the hotel but more excited to see Paris and the Eiffel Tower. We then drove closer over to the Eiffel Tower and parked the car. Then we started walking and found a little restaurant since we did not have any breakfast, so we tried some crepes. Since we were on vacation, our diet restrictions were totally out of the window. Then on the path to the Tower, we took some pictures with the tower in the background and having the year 2000 inside it. Then we just kept walking to see the tower up close. On the way, we kept stopping to see what merchandise that the street vendors were selling. Thus far, we did not purchase anything from them. Then all the vendors must have been doing it illegally because they were quickly rolling their merchandise up in the blankets and take off running. The police were everywhere chasing them down in every direction. I had never seen anything like it, except for the television. But we had front-row seats as it was unfolding! We did not see anyone get caught and arrested! Since we had to purchase tickets first to see the Eiffel Tower, we just took a few more pictures. We had figured one more hour there in Paris before driving back to Germany. The tower was one of the places that we had to see. Next was to see some of the architectural structures and a various amount of nude art of people. This was pretty normal of life there in France. Well, we had enough excitement for one day and definitely time to be leaving. So we got back to the car, Melody pulled out the map again, and we were all on our way back to Heidelberg, Germany. The autobahn was nice, but the smell of the manure was terrible, and still the countryside was breathtaking as we were driving through!

As we arrived back to Heidelberg, Melody did a great job of navigation with the map. We did not get lost not one time. It was still early so we took some time to explore Heidelberg to see what it had to offer and to see the sights. So we drove around to find some dinner too. The next day, we were off to catch the bus and ride with the locals and went to the Heidelberger Schloss (English is Heidelberg Castle) about 785 years old, so we saw the castle and the dungeon as we climbed the 315 steps. It was laborious and had taken us forever to climb. Big Mike and Ant stayed in front of us for the most part, and then when we had gotten to him, Big Mike realized quickly that he was stunned by a bee. I did not think that he would cry, but he was in obvious pain. He was tough, so we kept going. Big Mike's bee sting was memorable but become funny as the trip continued on! On the last day in Heidelberg that Saturday, we went to Mannheim, Germany, and had fun all day at the amusement park and plenty of rides. Not only did we ride the rides, having fun. Also, we had plenty of fun watching the Germans kids have fun. We could tell that they too were having fun, but we could not understand what they were saying. Still, the fun was in that place! Big Mike neck was a little swollen, but he was just fine! The last day we packed up the car and checked out of the hotel. Then we made a beeline to McDonald's for a quick breakfast. Then we went to fill up the gas tank, return the rental car, and got a taxi to Ramstein AB, Germany. It did not take long to leave at all. We were on the first flight out with the priority that we had by signing up early. We all boarded the C-5A aircraft to Mildenhall, Marlborough, England, as our first stop at the Air Base (AB). We were there for about four hours, then we boarded again to Dover AFB, Delaware.

The flight was good, except for the seating that was in the opposite direction, backward. As we were deplaning, I did notice a few caskets draped in a flag as they were dead bodies coming home for whatever reason. Anyway, the plane food was good, but moreover, we were glad to be home. It was the reflecting back on the trip with Ralph and Carol a year earlier that made this trip and vacation more enjoyable. Both trips and vacations consisted of no plans whatsoever. Everything was done ad hoc. I must admit that I did learn and credit this new attribute from Ralph because he knows how to travel. Now, I have that flexibility and spontaneity when I travel or travel with my family. Since returning back from our trip, Melody and I discussed having children again. This was not one of best subjects as we had tried to get pregnant so many times, just short of in vitro fertilization, which was not an option for us. The multiple birth thing would not be an immediate resolve for us. Neither of us wanted this way to have a baby. We finally decided to leave the whole thing into God's hand. We agreed that if God wanted us to have a child, He would let it happened. We did not blame God, but believed God for the results! Then we looked at Ant and Big Mike and said that God had given us two children anyway and that we all were living together as a family. The greatest part was that Melody had always accepted and claimed the boys as her own. That part of Melody was just too amazing. At that point, I could not ask of her anything more.

God knows that I was pretty hard on her, and all she kept doing was love me back! I do not know how Melody was able to be so strong for me. She never stopped loving me. That part of our relationship only baffles me because I have never been strong like her. Her love for me enables me to be strong. I do believe that the love that Melody gave me on a daily carries us both. I could not help myself but to love her back! I will always credit her for teaching me on how to love back! I just don't believe that Melody would have ever quit on trying for us! She was just incredible like that, and I was the fortunate one! Our life was really lining up for marriage to be successful. Not even Katrina was able to break us up because the Lord was on our side. Now, I believe for the way Katrina ran out of my office that day, God would have never allowed me to commit adultery. This trip to Europe with all the family had made our church life better and our marriage relationship even stronger! For sure! Moving on, I was now trying to go through the mail, and I noticed my student loan debt that was in default! I had to do something—sacrifice and pay that bill. So I started to pay $25 to $50 per month and kept promising to pay more later on! I had to get this debt taken care of. It had gotten better for us financially because the IRS was no longer taking child support from me, so I would be able to pay on my student loans. We were beginning to save money and traveling and now this. I was so motivated to get this default taken care of soon, and this student loan would become a thing in our past. Yes, by far, it was easier said than done! So the truth was it just became a lower priority than I wanted it to be, but I would get it paid off in time and travel at the same time.

Melody and I were able to get away for one more weekend to fly up and back to the Cleveland-Hopkins Airport to attend my twentieth Central Hower High School Class Reunion in Akron, Ohio, at Urban League spot off Vernon Odom (Wooster Ave, Route 261). I did the opening prayer to start the reunion dinner off. We were having all kinds of fun, photos taken, and those back-in-the-day conversations! It was truly a blast! I had left Melody at the table all by herself so I could catch up with Phil Anderson and Kim White. Kim had asked me who was the young lady that I was with or was it my daughter. Well, like always, I had thought of it as a compliment and gladly told them that she was my wife! They really thought that I was lying! I was gone for more than a half-hour and figured that I need to get back to her. She had not notice where I was at, but I could see her. The dancing was about to start, and we had to leave to catch an early flight not to miss church the next day, which was Sunday. That was short, sweet, and fun. I even spent a little time with my mother and the family before going to the class reunion. Anyway, we had made it back safely in time for church.

On the next day, school was back in session, and everything seemed normal the classes were just fine. Ant was in the ninth grade and turning fifteen years old in October. Ant was beginning to try me from time to time to see how much he could get away with. In short, not much because I held my ground. Then Ant was writing more and more! Since all was well, Melody and I talked to start looking for a car for Big Mike to start driving. We wanted him to have his own car once he was graduated from high school since he was a senior. I also wanted to keep him motivated other than going to church. I did not want to turn him off from church but to have a well-rounded life and by putting God first. Was it working? I don't know, but Big Mike was pretty balanced and very quiet. Still, he wanted to play football but was too old. My boy had an awesome arm on him for throwing the football. Wow! For Ant's birthday, I believe we had got him some sneakers. Then it was Ant and Big Mike attending Loudoun County High School together. But it was Ant that was able to play junior varsity (JV) football for the high school.

Then we agreed with Ant that the three of us would come to the home games when there were not any church services. Going to church was definitely a priority for us! I remember we all attended one Friday football game after school. I was on the field, but on the sideline with my family, I was rooting for Ant to go! Ant had two carries back-to-back, with the gain of about fourteen yards. It was doing the second carry that Ant did not get up as the other players. I ran onto the field and carried him off the field. We all jumped into the Rodeo and rushed Ant to the hospital ER. He had left the hospital with crutches and a bad sprain to his ankle. He was looking much better once we left the hospital and were on our way home. I was glad too. In fact, we all were happy to see Ant doing better! After a few days of recovery, Ant had given up any aspiration to ever want to play football again. The thing was he could had recovered and kept playing the game. Besides, he was running pretty well for a beginner! I was impressed, then I tried to push him to keep playing, but I wanted it to be his decision! The holidays were upon us again. Big Mike had picked up a part-time job at McDonald's. We wanted Mike to start saving this own money, but to our surprise and when I looked at his bank statement, Big Mike was eating everything up and not saving but a few pennies! Mike did pay his tithes and was not ready to take care of a car or pay for car insurance! I had to figure something out fast!

So I was planning to make him pay rent and hold that money to give back to him once he was to move out. While we were celebrating the Christmas, I had another dream. I had dreamed that I was in the desert with my family, walking in the sand, and no one was around us! The only thing that I could take from the dream is that we were going to be alone, and that was it! Then Ant and I had some type of disagreement about a school function, dance, or something that he wanted to attend. Ant had gotten upset with me. I could not believe it. After all I had done for him. Ant and I used to sneak off and go to the Nike Outlet at the Leesburg Outlet Mall, and we would buy sneakers and warmups. Melody would get on me not to waste our money like that and keep spoiling Ant. She was 100 percent correct, but I did not see what she was saying at first but understood later on! Anyway, getting back to Ant, we had found out that Ant had run away because of our disagreement and my rules. It was cold and snowy outside everywhere. Then finally, about three hours later and calling the police, the phone rang. On the other end of the phone line was Pastor Riley! What a surprise! Pastor Riley had talked to him and called me to pick him up from his home. Pastor Riley had told me jokingly that Ant had picked the coldest day of the year to run away! We laughed, and we gave our thanks! Let's just say that I did spank him once we had got home, and then, he had to write again. Ant knew at that point that he had two choices, and they were to obey my rules or leave as he did! Let's just say, from that point forward, Ant did not run away again! The New Year of 2001 was here, and as the few days had passed, I had just turned thirty-nine years old.

It was a few days earlier that Pastor Riley had decided to ordain me to Elder on the first Sunday in January. I had a little time to invite a few of my friends and Elder/Dr. Graham from my minister school. We invited Pat McNeil, Ted Agnew, and a few others. Elder/Dr. Graham was able to assist with the ceremony. While I was excited, I knew that somehow this was tied to my dream and my reading the Bible book of 1 Samuel, the third chapter. I believe that all this coming together at the same time could not be a coincidence! No way because I could not shake it! So I begin to keep following my dream and the vision that I had had of me preaching when I was at Pastor Plummer's church. I just knew that there was something to it! It had to be! I was not going to let it go. I talked with my wife, trying to figure it out! Then I started to think that I was supposed to start my own church. Elder Riley even left me in charge to preach, as he was out sick for several weeks. I was not going to let this go! Like God was calling Samuel out in the Bible, I had truly believed that it was me, and the desert dream meant that I was going to be in a church alone with my family! I just could not let this go! Even with all this happening somehow through my whole life, I knew that God had chosen me to be right where I was at! I just had to see if it was truly God's desire for me to become a pastor. I then wanted to talk to Pastor Riley! At this time, I was listening to songs like "Order My Steps" on the *WOW Gospel* album (I still have them and over four hundred more in my collection) or anything that Kirk Franklin or Fred Hammond was laying down on tracks. Even though I was writing and singing gospel music with Ralph; all of gospel music became my main genre. A lot of times before I do anything major or make life-changing decisions or even preach or teach, I would always play some gospel music. It soothes me greatly and helps my focus, especially a song like "I'll See You in the Rapture" or "Near the Cross" by the Mississippi Mass Choir helped me to stand strong. Before I met with Pastor Riley, as January 2001 was ending; I had told him my dream and on how I felt that God was leading and guiding me to start a church.

I must say doing the conversation, Pastor Riley was a bit disjointed with my conversation with him. I could tell that it caught him by surprise and he was disappointed. I too felt bad about the entire ordeal, but I just believe that God truly wanted me to move on. Truly, I did believe that God was leading me, and I had to keep going. Pastor Riley did guide me through some of the processes to get the church moving and gave me the lawyer contact information to get things setup with the Article of Incorporation and the bylaws. Right after that, just before February 2001, we were no longer members of Praise Temple Pentecostal Church. We went our own separate ways! Just like my dream of the desert, it was just my family in starting the church. I did get the information from Pastor Riley as to where to order the Sunday School materials. It was from that point on we started our own church in our home, teaching Sunday school only and trying to figure out a church name. We had used our own finances to get things going and for paying the lawyer. The lawyer was attorney Michael Mahoney out of Fairfax. He was a great help to our ministry and helping us with advice for the IRS forms and opening up bank accounts for the church. Through prayer, we had to decide for a church ministry name of Michael Gilcreast Ministries, Incorporated and one of the doing business as (DBA) name of New Life Praise and Deliverance Church. Another thing that I had learned for Pastor Riley, other than how to teach better, was to make me some flyers and business cards. I did not just want to be a pastor, I wanted what I had learned from the military; I wanted professionalism in the church ministry. To put it simply, I wanted the church to be in order and have true integrity, including morals! My personal foundation in my ministry was only one word, *truth*! My favorite scripture is 2 Timothy 2:15 (KVJ), which reads, "Study to shew thyself approved unto God, a workman that needeth not to be ashamed, rightly dividing the word of truth." Finally, our church's theme scripture is 2 Corinthians 5:17 (KVJ), which reads, "Therefore if any man be in Christ, he is a new creature: old things are passed away; behold, all things are become new." It was these two scriptures in the Bible that has taught me that I had to learn something new, let go of my past, and start over!

Melody and I were doing well at our jobs, but Melody's job was talking about a layoff but not yet, and I was planning to attend the BIG conference in Los Angeles in the summer. Most evenings after work, if I did not have to practice our songs with Ralph, I would play basketball with my sons and their high school friend named Kerry Williams from Trinidad. We also would play 21 or two-on-two. It was a lot of fun because I was keeping up with them young boys! I did share with them that when I played basketball at the Pentagon. My nickname was Jordan, as in Michael. People did say that I favored him (MJ) or Evander Holyfield. Mostly of Michael Jordan (MJ). I did like the MJ comments, and that was always the one guy that I wanted to play against because MJ was my favorite basketball player, period! It was on March 13, 2001, that we, our church New Life Praise and Deliverance Church (NLPAD), received our certificate from the Virginia State Corporation Commission. We were an official business and with the IRS paperwork approvals, we could operate as a nonprofit church. It was totally official, and I was so ecstatic too! On March 16, 2001, at 09:30, I had sent an e-mail to our entire AF/RE Directorate, about a 150 in total, as I had just had enough. The e-mail read exactly this: "This is only a request! Please read with an open mind! For the ones with children can understand better than others, but overall, I'm sure we all do understand. As children grow up, we always try to guard what they see, hear, and say, but overall, this can be viewed as their environment, and we should try to keep it as positive as possible. Sometimes for our environment—the workplace, we (as a people) sometimes negate the facts that some people such as myself are sensitive to hear or use language that may be offensive to someone in the same environment or lifestyle."

When most of us go to church, we watch everything we say and do when we talk with the chaplains, priest, ministers, bishops, pastors, presidents, the secretary of defense, house representatives, senators, appropriate two letters and even our own children, we can say whatever we need to say using a better choice of words. Right! Remember, the same people that go to church are the same people that make up our environment, workplace, family, neighbor, friends, etc. Being a pastor myself, I will leave you with one scripture that I hope it will aid you in your future conversations. James 1:19 states, "Wherefore, my beloved brethren, let every man [meaning man or woman], be swift to hear, slow to speak, slow to wrath." Seems as if since I have become a pastor, the words that I used to use now offends me. How ironic that God has truly changed me! Colonel Joe Viani had me to promise to never do that again! At the same time, everything in that office, my office was managed by me. The choice was nothing less than simple but to restore all my privileges by me, since turning off my account for the fore-mention email! Two other Christian women that attended my Bible study from the job comforted me. They were Evevon Rollins and Cindy Quilliam, but I never got in trouble for my actions! Wow! Amazing! I smiled as I thought God is truly good! Now, I started to look for a building to host our church services and move the services out of our home. My wife and I had thought to relisten to that tape again that we had forgotten about, and we found the words of Pastor Karen Dawson to be so spiritually true! We had gone to her church in Columbus, Ohio, just to fellowship with her about six months ago—to attend a women's conference and told her on how God used her to bless us. We had got her number to stay in touch! It was so ironic as we both reflected on how hard it was to believe, but it all became true! My wife, Melody, was now a first lady and me a pastor at NLPAD! Only God could have made this to be because my past was so terrible!

Now, I always say that God is good! It was by April 2001 that Pastor Riley had closed the church doors of Praise Temple Pentecostal Church and had planned to move back to Texas. I stayed in touch with his sister Queen and niece Venus that had gone to his church with us. Pastor Riley's son Sammy was a hair stylist and used to do my wife Melody's hair. I can sometimes still hear him call me black man! Sammy was a cool dude, so I did not mind him calling me that at all! But only Sammy because he was so down to earth! By May 2001, we still did not have a church building. We checked with schools, store fronts, buildings, and finally I took a day of leave from the Air Force to find our family a church building, and I still believe that God wanted me to continue to pastor a church. Doing that day of leave, I was to look at three places. My wife and I went to the VFW, and the answer was no. The second stop was Douglass Community Center located at 407 East Market Street, Leesburg, Virginia, so we went in to speak to the director and her name was Judy! We also met the assistant director, Jon. They were just the nicest people, including the other staff members, Nick, Shanay, Janice, and another person or Nick would open the building for church use for the weekend hours. They were nice but did not have space for us unless we wanted to use the gymnasium. It was too big and cost more money. However, as we were about to leave, Judy stopped us and told us, she had heard about the church that was in the building would be a good fit for us was leaving, and she had provided me with the number to talk with Pastor Bailey.

We had left and went home with a pretty good lead and did not explore the third option at Stonebridge High School in Ashburn, Virginia. I had felt that this one was it as I had relayed it to Melody! It was about an hour later. I had called Pastor Bailey, a member of the United Pentecostal Church International (UPC). We were talking and comparing church notes only to find out that we both were of the same faith and doctrine. Pastor Bailey had told me that they would be done by June 1, 2001, as the contract with Douglass Community Center would be completed. Pastor Bailey had told me about his assistant pastor, Brother Ray, and of the new location that their church would be moving to. The timing could have not come at a better time, and as always, God is always on time! I had taken the contract and the application back to Judy at Douglass Community Center about a week later with the deposit. Judy had mentioned to me that she had just gotten off the phone with another pastor that had tried to get the same space, and she informed him that she was holding the space for our church. I then realized that God was on my side, and I was glad that I was following the voice of God! Just think if I had waited an extra day or week, I would have missed everything! God was truly leading me! Wow! We were using the monies that Melody and I had provided to the church to get started to buy the books, Bibles, music equipment, podium, excreta. Ralph had taken me around to pick up keyboards, speakers, mics, and all. To say the least, Ralph was truly a blessing to our ministry!

On June 3, 2001, we waited for the doors to the community center to get opened, so we could have our first church service on *Pentecost Sunday, as* New Life Praise and Deliverance Church. (Note: Currently the church name had been changed to Higher Hope Apostolic Church, located in Charles Town, West Virginia.) It was a success! Now, we had to get some street signs made up so people would know that we were there! We did get visitors here and there, but we knew that we had to saturate the community with flyers and handout through evangelism. Other times people would stand outside the door but would not come in. A few weeks had gone, we just knew that it would change, and the people would eventually come through those doors! Melody would be singing and doing the praise and worship. I would have to play the keyboard, sing, and preach. This I knew for sure, whether people came or not, one thing that we knew for sure was that we were definitely called by God to do this church, and we were committed enough to know that we would not be quitting. I made it a sure point that I would not look at the number of people attending the services with us. Then we met a brother by the name of Frank Paige. He had told us that he used to sit in the car to see our faithfulness before coming in. Then Brother Frank informed us that that it sounded like we had more people than we actually had in attendance! That was an amazing observation to Melody and me, but we knew that it was God's blessings to our church ministry! The church ministry was moving in a good direction, and I was working to get a church website going, and my wife was making the flyers and Sunday programs. To date, I no longer have any office assistants, working with me at the Pentagon. I would try at least one more time, so I hired the young man by the name of SrA Delano Burnett Jr. I had him to work on a long-term assignment. This guy was just awesome and polite. We just worked very well together! I needed him in place for my BIG conference at the Staple Center in California. My wife was going with me, and my sons were staying home with the rules by themselves.

Off we were to Los Angeles, and I believe that I had the government rate at the Wilshire Grand Hotel. It was pretty nice for Melody and me. The next day, I was registered for the conference and took my wife as well with me to some of the venues at the BIG conference. Then I would go to separate meetings. The best part of the whole thing for me was to hear Judge Greg Matias speak at one of the seminars. We did a lot of sightseeing on this trip, plus we had to go to Roscoe's Waffles and Chicken, one of our favorites. There was a lot to do at the Staples Center, plus the street vendors and some of the clothing district. After attending a lot of the seminars and seeing Judge Greg Mathis as he was the main attraction, I had heard him speak and found him very relatable in comparison to my life. Judge Mathis's story, his words were inspiring to me and my life as well. At the end of his briefing, Melody and I were able to take some photos with him. I even provided him one of my pastor's church business cards to stop by our church, if it was possible when he was in town. But I truly believe that it would have been a one in a million long shot! I was glad to see that I was not shy nor ashamed. No guts no glory was the way I had seen it! This was another good trip, and we were on our way home. As we were flying home to DC, I realized that Melody had never stopped loving me. I did feel fortunate to have her! She only loved me and never held me accountable to my past. I did not want to disappoint her ever again. I was really faithful to her and as a pastor to the church. Boy, did I come a long way!

Now, when we got home, we promised the boys another vacation to Florida, but this time Universal Studios. They were excited too! Ant wanted to go back to that Boston Seafood Restaurant for the lobsters. At the job, Delano was doing well, so I signed up to take leave for my family vacation to Orlando, Florida, at the Westgate Resorts, plus we had to do a timeshare presentation, to stay at a nice place for a cheaper price. I was able to teach a few Bible classes and get a few practices in with Ralph in Maryland. The good thing about our church was we always may it back in time for church on Sundays, even though we had missed the prayer on Tuesday and Bible study classes on Wednesday. That worked out too! Now, getting back to the trip, we had a deal, and we were on our way to fly down there. What a blessing that we could go and afford the entire family! Wow! The thing was it was a one bedroom that sleeps four. They had to share the sofa bed that they were just a little too big for it. Somehow, we made it work and did enjoy our vacation, the pool, sights, and all. The Universal Studios were a great fit for our family. There were more rides and things to do. We had much fun! We played in more of the game rooms and stayed at the poolside more on this trip! The boys never complained about being bored. That was good all by itself! I did spend time with them, bowling sometimes, church, and mostly playing basketball. Melody and I still go to the grocery store or shopping together. I would also, as many times before, sing to her or just be singing songs from the John P. Kee's *Color Blind* album, especially the song "I Know You." Melody would get embarrassed sometimes as I would be receiving many compliments! Wow! We were almost always together doing something. She always tries to stay up most times until I went to bed. Melody always tells me that she just like to be close to me! Truthfully, it was something that I had to get used to, and I did grow not to have too much space from her around the house. Even when she was in a different room. It also counted as being close. Truly I definitely liked space but have gotten used to Melody's style as well. I know I really sleep better as long she touches my lower calf or leg with her foot. I must admit that we did a lot of family things together along with the normal things we did. The one thing the I really enjoyed doing was the family cookout and, I would do all of the grilling and make the deviled eggs! My wife would make the potato salad or coleslaw, bake beans, and corn.

Sometimes, we would even have some collard greens. Now, all I had to do was take care of the family, work, preach, Bible class, and to keep writing music, just in case, I would be able to get going again. Now back at work, it was busier than ever, people coming and going. I remember working with Lt. Col. Steve Apple. His position was moved to the front office, working for the general. The not-so-good part was that I had to take over his duties since I had seniority in the office. We had pretty much a brand-new staff, except for a few of us. I was not trying to leave either! My new job title was now "Chief, Flying Hours, Computers, and Information Management." With this job, I now had job security, and I was tasked to give briefing to the general, but the downsize was. There was not promotion in sight! This was a true sign that it was nearing time to start considering retirement with the twenty years of retirement the I had already accomplished! Yes, I was very marketable with a few more classes that would benefit me in the civilian arena. Shortly after being volunteered for this new position, I had to complete one more enlistment and retirement after that. So on September 10, 2001, I was walking around the Pentagon to do my last enlistment before retirement! Col. Viani would always tell me that I was a blessed man every time his computer problems would work out when I was around. I had him to do the official oath of office ceremony for me in on my last enlistment. We became pretty cool after the e-mail incident back in March when my e-mail account was deactivated for the e-mail that I had sent out to the directorate. Now, my last or retirement date would be on June 30, 2004, I was done and a little disappointed that I was not able to get my well-deserving promotion. One true fact that I have always realized: I had never imagined retirement. I did not have the right Air Force career path. But I know God had it all worked out for me! The truth of the matter was that I have finally let go of that bias promotion system and realize to following my one true calling that was in the church. My promotions became fact—for every promotion that I had deserved in the Air Force military, I received them in the church. But now, I am a pastor and started a church! This ordeal was a fact that I had never seen nor thought that it would be possible for me! I was living it fully! Well, by the end of the day, it was final that my supervisor was Col. Joseph (Joe) Viani. He had taught everyone in our office that *send* does not mean *end*! Then he wanted to do our first offsite to boost office morale.

On September 11, most of the folks in my office and throughout our directorate had met at the office offsite in Gettysburg,

Pennsylvania, with the tour guide. It was about forty people there with their families. My wife Melody was there as well. While I almost did not want to attend this offsite because of everyone's obscene offensive language, I decided to give it another chance that things would be better. Not a chance as we quickly found out upon our arrival. I just had to ignore them folks and press on with Melody. I had even received negative e-mails from some of the same folks that I had to work with. I was good because I knew what I did was the right thing! As we were listening to the tour guide talk about the civil war and attacking the headquarters will weaken the military forces, someone announced a message from their cell phone that the World Trade Center was attacked. Someone else had announced the same thing for the other World Trade Center tower. A short time later, the plane flew into the building we all worked in the Pentagon! As everyone began to call their loved ones, there were no cellular service available. My wife went away from the group to pray for cellular service to call the boys! Then about fifteen minutes later, we were able to talk to Ant to get a message to Big Mike as to where we were to meet. We were so relieved that they were okay. Now we had to get home. Then another plane went down around 10:00 a.m.; the plane was headed to DC to attack again, but that plane flight #93 went down in Shanksville, Pennsylvania, about one hundred miles from where we were at. Wow, that was close! Once we returned back to the group, Col. Viani pulled me to the side. He looked me right in my eyes, man to man, and had asked me to pray with the group. I had agreed! Then, I went to Melody and informed her that we were about to pray for the group and needed her help! Every moment was critical from that point on as we gathered everyone together. I could see the intensity of fear that were on every face! Then I began to pray, "Heavenly Father, look on us right now, in this moment of need..."

Then, my First Lady Melody had joined in with me, and not one soul was praying aloud! Wow, that was a beautiful moment as you could feel the peace of God in the midst of us all! It was at that moment I knew that I was to send that e-mail, and I knew that I was supposed to be on the field trip with my office and my wife. I must say that God knows how to get His glory!

I no longer felt the hatred of me from my coworkers, nor did I hear one curse word from anybody! God is truly good and worthy to be praised! We were very cautious going home as we did not know what to expect, but we really wanted to get home. On the way, before we reached home, I had some church paperwork to drop off to the town clerk's office, so I did! Since the clerk's office was open, I had got my minister's paperwork approved so that I could perform weddings in the State of Virginia. Then we went home and watched the news! My phone never stopped ringing. A lot of people, family, and friends were calling me throughout the day and night to ensure that I was not injured or killed at the Pentagon. One thing that I knew for sure: my mother was so relieved! She just had to hear my voice! I had just known that my mother was on pins and needles! So we continued to watch the news throughout the night and decided to keep the boys home from school on the next day. The phone still was ringing on Wednesday, which was the next day. I had even received a call from Bishop Pope, a voice that I was glad to hear from as well! We did have our church Bible class at 7:30 p.m., that evening, a few people did show up! On Thursday, September 12, my sons went back to school and Melody and I went back to work. I even had Bible study again at the Pentagon, even though I saw that several hallway walls were burnt scorched or charred. I could even smell the burnt smell in the air ventilation system. Then I went by the section that was blocked off. I just had to see for myself. Because the day before, I was in that section on my way to reenlist for more years into the Air Force! I realized that I was one day from death if it had happened a day earlier or on the day of September 9, 2001, if I had not gone on that office field trip to build up team morale.

Yet I was there praying with these same folks! Now, that was truly ironic! No doubt my life was saved on both of those days! I know that that day will forever be in my memories because I was there! The planes were now grounded in all of the United States. Nothing in or out because of 911. I did notice that it took tragedy to bring the American people together! You could see the American flag everywhere, as well as "God bless America!" The Pentagon was still functional, except for the missing section and the 125 lives the was lost on that day. Yet it was business as usual. Surprisingly, people did come to the Bible class. I do remember Brother Ted Agnew attending as he was a real good friend. Ted was one of the guys that if I mentioned something about the Bible. He would challenge me in a very positive way that would promote long discussions between us. He and Sister Pat McNeil (Melody's coworker) were the two trustees that joined our church board to get the church started. God has always place good people around us, even if they came from a Bible study at the Pentagon. We were now at the end of September's last week and even though 911 had happened, my job had changed, and I had to take a budget course call Planning, Programming, Budgeting, Systems (PPBS). This was happening. The course was given by a contracting company called Science Applications International Corporation (SAIC). There was a nice young lady there by the name of Ms. Frankie Washington. She was one of the technical advisors that made sure everything went smoothly. I officially introduced myself and also let her know that I was a pastor and working at the Pentagon. Being more cautious now, by no means did I want her to think the I was coming onto her.

So I kept my conversation innocent, and just before the PPBS class was over, I had invited her to our church. I did pass the course and got my certificate! A week or two had gone by, and I believe that it was on a Wednesday night Bible class. Guess who surprised me and showed up. It was none other than Sister Frankie Washington. Sister Frankie started coming to church on a regular basis and joined our church ministry with her family. We were so glad to have them. Sister Frankie had acted like she had always been there with us, and she really understood our ministry. By this time, my wife's knowledge for what she had known from her job happened. After fifteen years of her employment of working with CBSI, she received a severance package, her 401K plan. Then she was part of a major layoff. Melody no longer had employment! Immediately, she had gone to sign up for her unemployment benefits. We had the church to keep up, our mortgage, and a car payment, with two boys that could really eat! The only thing we could do was to trust God and pray! God is so good as Melody did not need her unemployment benefits. She was marketable enough to obtain a temporary with the Adecco Staffing and Kelly Services (A Robert Half Company) and a few others for $8 per hour, and because of 911, $1 more was added to her pay. It was a drastic pay cut, but with the severance package, we were doing better than we had expected.

But we knew that it was the Lord's doing, even with Sister Frankie joining our church. Melody was working hard and interviewing when possible. It had worked out well for her and us, between working with the various temp agencies and a little unemployment here and there. Melody did stay gainfully employed. We kept praying. The church kept going, and our family never missed a bill to be paid or a meal at our table. Sister Frankie had always said, "Praise God!" Then I started to say it as well, even for now—"Praise God!" We were drawing close to Sister Frankie from our talks after the church services. It was this one particular day that while Melody and I were at her house visiting, and she had a son and newborn baby girl Rebekah. We also had a chance to do some babysitting for Sister Frankie's baby. We also made plans to take her son Lamar horseback riding in October with us and our two sons since Ant and Lamar was about the same age. Anyway, we were sitting in the living room as Sister Frankie was sharing her experiences with church and on how she was there alone. As her husband Roy was in the Army stationed somewhere in Germany. We wanted to be good pastors to Sister Frankie as she and her family were very good for our ministry. It was within another month or so that I was able to baptize her at the Ida Lee Park, the place where we have performed most of our baptisms.

Before the end of the year, she was saved, teaching Sunday school and eventually became our first church secretary. Soon after, I started calling Sister Frankie my daughter since we were connecting like family! The church was growing, and I was getting better playing the keyboard for the church services. The thing was that even though we did not have a drummer, I was preaching and teaching. My wife led the praise and worship, and overall, we were having real church! Then Sister Freda Gerard had joined us and come to find out that she had crossed paths with Brother Frank Paige, growing up in the same neighborhood. My son Ant was bringing in people all the time, even his classmates. I remember that he had three sisters that came in and joined the church. He had always found ways to invite people to church. To say the least, our church was growing! I was getting to know the people, and there was something about Sister Frankie that stood out. My wife and I had met with her because she had wanted to talk to us about this uneasiness and concern for the trust of pastors in particular. What she had revealed to us was unheard of, at least for me, since I was a very brand-new pastor and my wife as a new first lady. I felt that if I was to be successful as a pastor, my wife had to be in the know! Anyway, this sister said that she had gone in an administrative capacity to her pastor's house in a different state and the pastor had begun to undress and chase her around the house. She had wanted nothing to do with that and had left his house in a hurry! My wife and I had felt bad for Sister Frankie and had hoped that she would find Godly trust at our church and in our ministry that she could be a part of! It was right then, and it was a defining moment for me. I had got it! I had told that Sister Frankie in front of my wife and God that her story made me to determine, at that moment, the type of pastor that I wanted to become in my future ministry. That sister and her story affected me in such a way that I knew right then that I wanted to be a faithful, honest pastor, and not use the church to get with women!

Overall, out of all my brothers and sisters, we knew to get married and not just sleep around, which was the Christian thing to do, and that was my mother's way, but most of us would eventually become divorced or remarried. (The first time, while I was married, I knew that later on in life that I would remarry too!) Somehow, it feels more like a curse. The potential was there, but the opportunities were not. In my brothers' and sisters' lives, the decision of our parents may have affected our lives, but only few of us moved on and/ or made some different types choices. Or made the choice to move ahead. Anyone can blame the past, their past in particular—we all, or anybody, can choose to have a future. Do we or were we supposed to add God and church to our lives and everything would be all right? I do not think so! My family or anyone must choose for oneself! Now, I am blaming God for my success to know love and how to love. It works, it truly works! Love happened through my pains, struggles, and pursuit of true love and not lust love or sex love, and the one-night stands was just that—nothing! Believe it or not, my life's experiences have taught me that there was a difference!

I am still in a blissful state of mine that my past afforded me this future. If it is okay to blame God, then I can give God credit too. God is love! Overall, I have done a lot of accomplishments pluses and minuses and not too much to show for it, except for the faithful members at church. From now to the end, I truly believe that I have this chance in my life to know and share a *love* like Melody's. I believe she (Melody) is definitely with me as we are both serving the Lord! My Melody, my love, my heart, and my song! You saved my life!

MICHAEL GILCREAST

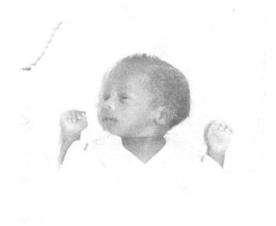

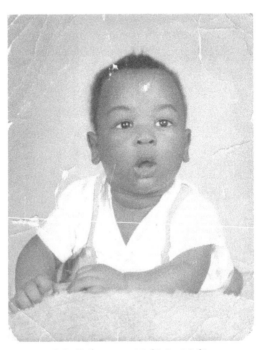

My Baby pics 1962 & 1963

Spare of the moment photo at BX with redskin cheerleaders

NCO and clubing Attire

Air Force Reserve Recruiter

Awards with Gen Bradley

Awards with Gen Bradley

Melody Modeling

Ms Sparks Presented Pentagon going away

Melody Modelling

Hains Point date with Melody

Dec 1993 christmas with sons

My Proposal

My Proposal

Pentagon going away presented to me by Gen Alan Bunger

Honeymoon in Hawaii

Our Wedding

Our Wedding

Our Wedding

Space and Helicopter

Space and Helicopter

SIU graduation

Hollywood CA with Friends and Celebr

Hollywood CA with Friends and Celebr

Hollywood CA with Friends and Celebr

Hollywood CA with Friends and Celebr

Hollywood CA with Friends and Celebr

Hollywood CA with Friends and Celebr

Hollywood CA with Friends and Celebr

After custody family portrait

My Minister Graduation Ceremony with family

Paris My Family Vacation

Judge Greg Mathias

For Additional Resources or to Schedule the Author for
Speaking Engagements, contact:

BMG Enterprises
Michael Gilcreast, Author
(703) 662-3311
info@bmgilcreast.com
www.bmgilcreast.com
or
Higher Hope Apostolic Church
Bishop Michael Gilcreast, Senior Pastor
(703) 662-3311
info@be-blessed.org
www.be-blessed.org

About the Author

Bishop Michael Gilcreast was born in Akron, Ohio, but now resides in the Washington DC metropolitan area since 1994. With many challenges in his life and still, he was driven to write this book while working in a dual or triple occupation—currently working full-time at the Pentagon since 1992 in Washington DC; pastor of Higher Hope Apostolic Church in Charles Town, West Virginia, full-time; and with the remaining time, he sells real estate and life insurance. Not to mention, he is a husband to Melody Gilcreast with two sons (Michael Jones and Michael Gilcreast II) and two grandsons (Darrius Gilcreast and Amahn Gilcreast). It has been many of nights that he was discouraged a lot of times because of his past failures, but he was able to refocus the negative energy and turn the late nights and early morning hours into positive productive energy. He kept telling himself, "What does not kill you will make you stronger!" He just could not quit, especially since he never finished his one desired career path—to become an OB/GYN or emergency room doctor, which was his only childhood dream. He just loved chemistry and math, having intriguing fascinations with science and the human body!

Furthermore, he could not move forward in this book effort without acknowledging the one person that helped him get there. He never knew what the future had in store for him. He kept going because of his faith in God and his adorable wife, Melody, both of which were the best support system that he could have ever known. Melody saw his potential, even when he did not even see it himself. Well, he was able to retire from the Air Force with over half of his military career being stationed at the Pentagon. He then completed his associate degree from the Community College of the Air Force in 1995, and two years later, he completed his bachelor's degree from the Southern Illinois University at Carbondale, Illinois. While not knowing, he was still on the path of becoming a pastor from the minister's training courses. Shockingly, he became the valedictorian from taking courses through the Pentecostal Assemblies of the World, the church organization that he was a member of. Currently, he has been pastoring a church congregation for over twenty years and purchased their first church building in 2014 so he can continue to assist people in building their lives.

While working through the COVID-19 pandemic, he stayed positive and allowed this worldwide shutdown to work as a catalyst for him to write this book, which he started in 2009. He enjoys travelling stateside and international, not to mention his last international trip was as a member with the Apostolic Faith Fellowship International (AFFI) to Israel in December 2019.

Out of all of the times that he could have given up, he did not quit!

Bishop Gilcreast always said these three quotes:

"The truth will always stand by itself!"
"Faith connected to the power of words will
bring forth the reality of God!"
"Be blessed and be a blessing!"

CPSIA information can be obtained
at www.ICGtesting.com
Printed in the USA
JSHW041405240222
23227JS00002B/2

9 781638 746621